Designing an IAM Framework with Oracle Identity and Access Management Suite

Jeff Scheidel

New York   Chicago   San Francisco
Lisbon   London   Madrid   Mexico City   Milan
New Delhi   San Juan   Seoul   Singapore   Sydney   Toronto

The McGraw·Hill Companies

Cataloging-in-Publication Data is on file with the Library of Congress

McGraw-Hill books are available at special quantity discounts to use as premiums and sales promotions, or for use in corporate training programs. To contact a representative, please e-mail us at bulksales@mcgraw-hill.com.

Designing an IAM Framework with Oracle Identity and Access Management Suite

1 2 3 4 5 6 7 8 9 0   WFR WFR   1 0 9 8 7 6 5 4 3 2 1 0

ISBN   978-0-07-174137-8
MHID   0-07-174137-2

Sponsoring Editor
Lisa McClain

Editorial Supervisor
Jody McKenzie

Project Manager
Deepti Narwat Agarwal,
Glyph International

Acquisitions Coordinator
Meghan Riley

Copy Editor
Margaret Berson

Technical Editors
Gary Bodiford
Darren Calman
Rhon Daguro
Steve Wolford

Proofreader
Bev Weiler

Indexer
Kevin Broccoli

Production Supervisor
George Anderson

Composition
Glyph International

Illustration
Glyph International

Art Director, Cover
Jeff Weeks

Cover Designer
Pattie Lee

For Mom and Dad, who provisioned me

About the Author

Jeff Scheidel received a B.A. in Computer Science in 1984, and spent the next decade developing business solutions for both startups and large corporations. Starting in 1993, he built teams of solution architects and sales engineers for a series of successful startups and, from 1997, began concentrating on security and identity, architecting solutions for dozens of Fortune companies. Besides authoring whitepapers, documentation, and articles for Computerworld and other outlets, Jeff has also evaluated technology companies for M&A purposes; lectured on security, compliance, and cloud computing; and published a couple of novels. He lives in the Chicago area with his wife, two children, a room full of guitars, and a dachshund.

About the Technical Editors

Gary Bodiford has been involved in sales and consulting across the spectrum of Security Technology Software and Services for over 15 years. His professional career includes tenure with noteworthy security organizations such as Network General, Network Associates, Netegrity, Computer Associates, and Oracle. His primary specialization over the last decade has been on Identity Management, RBAC, and GRC. His experience includes working with many of the Fortune 500 companies across the midwestern and southwestern United States. Currently, he resides in Plano, Texas, with his family.

Darren Calman is currently Director of Product Management for Identity Management and Security products at Oracle. He is responsible for outbound product management and go-to-market strategy for the Identity and Access Management suite of products. Darren was previously Vice President of Business Development for Phaos Technology, which was acquired by Oracle in 2004.

Rhon Daguro has been working in the Identity and Access Management space since 1998 and has custom-built IAM solutions for several companies prior to implementing world-class IAM solutions with Oracle. He's taken a focus on fine-grained authorization and entitlements and has contributed to the XACML standard, which governs interoperability between the vendors. Outside of work, he has a passion for developing natural user interfaces with touch screens and how they apply to everyday life.

Steve Wolford is Director of Business Development at Oracle Corporation where he is responsible for the go-to-market strategy across Oracle's line of Security solutions in North America. He arrived at Oracle from their acquisition of the role management vendor Bridgestream, where he ran Product Management. At prior startups in Silicon Valley over the past 12 years, he has held key leadership positions in Product Management, Consulting, and Engineering. A native of Atlanta, Georgia, he holds a B.A. in History from Brown University, and currently resides in San Francisco.

Contents at a Glance

PART IV
Pre- and Post-Implementation Advice

Contents

PART I
Defining the Value of and the Need for IAM

PART II
Preparing the Enterprise for IAM

PART III
The Oracle Identity and Access Solution

Acknowledgments

I'd like to thank a number of people for their content and guidance for this project:

- Ed Jackowiak, the best closer in the business, with whom I've traveled, worked, and succeeded, and whom we named the dog after. No kidding.
- Amit Jasuja and Rohit Gupta, for their brilliant technical insight.
- Karl Miller, identity expert, and always the smartest man in the room.
- Gary Bodiford, a great intellect and proofreader.
- Rhon Daguro, a genius who could probably build a nuclear reactor out of toilet paper rolls and duct tape, and who provided me his insights on several subjects.
- Sheila Cepero and Darren Calman, for helping me launch.
- Lisa McLain and Meghan Riley of McGraw-Hill, who patiently guided me along.
- My lovely daughter Margaret for her invaluable help with the illustrations, and my beautiful family in general, whose patience and care made this so much easier.

Introduction

The Meaning of Identity

To be or not to be, that is the question.

—Hamlet, trying to decide if he should create a Twitter account

Excuse me, but who are you, exactly?

You are a father or mother, a son or daughter, husband or wife, a significant other, a rock climber, a kite-flyer, a bicycle enthusiast, a marathon runner, a collector of old movies, a secret novelist, a boxing fan. You are the center of your universe. On the picture collage from the company picnic, which is taped to the wall just inside the cafeteria, you are represented by color photos of you with your colleagues, eating potato chips and tossing a Frisbee.

But to your company… you are a collection of *bytes*. In the recesses of your employer's servers, you are represented in binary.

From Patrick McGoohan's surreal TV show *The Prisoner*, we get the famous line, "I am not a number, I am a free man." Well, forget it. You are a whole *bunch* of numbers, all of them ones and zeros. There's likely a central cluster of ones and zeros that established a foundation for you when you landed the job. Or when you initiated the bank account, or the phone service, or the request to get your refrigerator repaired, or whatever else you did to plant your flag saying, "I exist." And you branched out from there.

Here's your life cycle as ones and zeros:

The first thing you get is a profile. Name, address, phone, e-mail, hat size, all the attributes that say *who you are*. Your profile is the launchpad from which you are propelled into the maze of databases and applications that determine *what you can have, what you can do*, and *what is being done to you*. One day, when you change jobs, get your phone service, or finally have a working fridge, this data transmogrifies into *who you were, what you did*, and *what was done to you*.

The process that determines who and what you are is called Identity Management. It touches *everything*. It drives how you're viewed, how you get in, what you see once you're in, and how you're treated. For the rest of our time together, let's refer to Identity Management as IdM.

Your identity is also the basis for how the system measures your suitability to interact with it. These measurements are founded on policies that match up users with resources. For example, in order to talk to a particular application, the policies may examine:

- Your attributes
- Your group memberships
- Your certifications
- Your current location
- Your online behavior, past and present

Once they've dissected you, the policies match up who you are, and what you have, against what the resources require. If you meet the security requirements of that application, then in you go. Otherwise, take a hike.

The whole idea of having a policy layer is to avoid the situation where coders are putting security directly into applications. Even when your off-the-shelf apps enforce security, that security is still specific to that app. By externalizing security, and layering it between users and interface (and again between interface and backend apps or data), you're taking the burden off developers who write business code for a living, and placing it on the shoulders of the experts who manage security for a living. You're also allowing for a central view of security, instead of pushing it to all the individual corners of the enterprise.

The broader subject of creating identities and then matching those identities with policies in order to govern access to resources is called Identity and Access Management (IAM), which is what we're going to talk about in detail. We'll review this from the perspective of the upper management types who are ultimately responsible for user data, the administrators who must secure that data as well as provide a robust user experience, and the end users who need both access and protection.

Assembling the Pieces

The primary term for years was just plain Identity Management (IdM). This used to mean directory services, and that's before the term "directory services" was invented. In other words, IdM merely consisted of capturing users in a database or LDAP for purposes of allowing users to log in. Once access management matured beyond just certificates and access control lists, it took over the mantle of IdM. The term IAM came in to being slowly as enterprises began to realize that authentication wasn't nearly sufficient, especially in multifaceted environments where not all users were created equal and some people got more access than others.

In the current day, identity management is being subsumed by Identity Access Management (IAM) because, unless you're only generating mailing lists, it serves no purpose whatsoever to store identities unless you're planning on using them to drive access and audits.

If you're in charge of your organization's identity and/or security (because identity is just one, although very vital, aspect of overall security), then you know there is far more to IAM than simply handling logins. Corporate and regulatory requirements dictate that you support strong policies to determine who gets in, how they get in, what they get access to once they're in, how they're reported on, and how they get out. This is a two-way street. Your users need to access your resources, you need them to do so, and everybody needs this done securely.

It's not enough to simply install software and hardware. You need to plan. There can be a lot of moving parts, depending on the depth to which you implement IAM. It can be done in stages, but even the individual stages must be deployed with careful thought so that you can plug in additional pieces or deploy more resources later, as you need or can afford them, and integrate with emerging technologies that you don't even know exist yet. While it's helpful to deploy parts that can work stand-alone, without dependencies, it's *ideal* to have pieces that work together in complementary fashion. After all, one task leads to the next:

- Registration feeds identity.
- Identity allows authentication and provisioning.
- Provisioning feeds authorization.
- All of them support compliance and reporting.

I have to know who you are (and *what* you are) to determine what you get. Then I make sure that's *all* you get. Then I report on what you got.

While it's possible to assemble the plumbing later to string together your disparate pieces, it's a far better proposition to plan their interoperability in advance. Sure, there's always some industry-standard protocol that will facilitate communications between components later, assuming those components support that protocol, but one-size-fits-all standards can also mean *slow* performance (which we'll discuss in the very last chapter).

Framework. I'm going to repeat this term, over and over. Identity and access shouldn't be bolt-ons to your already burdened IT assets. They should be the foundation upon which those assets rest. When you inherit new resources and/or users, they should be able to ride on the identity train you've already set in motion. They represent a policy-based framework that ought to be woven into your infrastructure, providing a guidepost of consistency and security based on established corporate and security standards. So when you launch a new app, don't reinvent the security wheel just for that app. Teach it how to talk to your framework, which then does all the work. It identifies your users, enables your users, governs your users' access, and reports on your users' activities.

For that matter, when you inherit new users, because you've bought another company, signed up another corporate customer, or created a new department, you identify those new users, assign them a place in your enterprise, and allow them to participate in the policies you already have in place.

Framework also encourages best practices. As an organization, you and your colleagues determine how best to get users on board and enable them. By creating policies that reflect the most efficient and secure approach to creating and provisioning user accounts, you provide a lighted path by saying, "This is the way we do things, and we do it this way for very good reasons."

Framework also provides *agility*. Since you are *not* reinventing the security wheel with each new resource or user group, you can react more quickly, for example, to application launches, mergers, and other large events. Even if you are bringing into your enterprise another organization's applications that already have their own security apparatus, you can more easily migrate those applications to your policies. Any new applications can be more quickly deployed because you have a prebuilt security framework in front of them; just add water.

Glossary

One of the biggest speed bumps to agreeing on services and solutions is the failure to connect with other parties on common terms. I have seen, even up to the point of delivery, where a project was suddenly imperiled because after months of discussions and investigation, the deployment team still didn't share common ground with the organization on some of the specific needs. We'll discuss this garbled communication in depth later with regard to negotiating with software manufacturers and integrators. But to level-set right now, let's define a few IAM-related terms. We'll be describing all these items in horrifying detail as we progress, as well as how they apply to the overall process.

NOTE
They're not in alphabetic order here, because they don't work in alphabetic order.

Authoritative Source   This is *the* place to go for absolute truth about an entity, such as a user. If I want to know his employment or membership status, account balance, access rights, or anything else in particular, I go to the authoritative source. It could be a database, a directory, the HR system, a meta-directory that periodically assembles related data from disparate sources, or even a virtual source that aggregates data on demand from multiple physical sources. Regardless, it's one-stop-shopping for a user's state of being, and all other components should take their cue from this central authority.

Privilege   A privilege (or entitlement) is the most granular thing you can do on a system or within an app. Click a button, execute a method, access a file or folder. In any given app, you probably need dozens, if not hundreds, of privileges in order to accomplish anything meaningful.

Role   This term is used so loosely that it can mean a variety of things. In general, it is defined as a collection of privileges. But roles can be designed in so many ways that it's important to determine what you need out of the concept of roles. There are business/enterprise roles that more or less equate to job titles or positions; a business role contains multiple resource-level roles, which function at the level of an application or resource; and application roles themselves, which are often supported by commercial off-the-shelf software (COTS) products. Think of it this way: A business role is what you do for a living. You need an application role for each application to tell you what your privileges are for that app. Most often, your business or enterprise role maps to your multiple application roles. Roles can (and should) play a vital role in both user enablement and user access control. The application of roles to security is called Role-Based Access Control, or RBAC.

Provisioning   The process of enabling a user. A request is made on behalf of a user by a manager, an automated process, or the user himself. That request is routed to various approvers and/or other automated processes for enabling the user's access to various applications. Provisioning has two essential components, workflow and connectors. Connectors are those mechanisms (usually a library, web service, or API) that communicate with target applications or databases. Workflow is …

Workflow A configurable engine that automates a series of tasks in order to achieve a unified result. Ouch! Too complicated. In essence, it is a piece of software that walks through all the steps required to fulfill a request. For example, a user asks to receive access to a target application. Workflow picks up the request, looks up all the approvals that request needs, and notifies all the approvers to either approve or deny their piece of the request. It should also perform escalations (that is, remind approvers to do their jobs, and find backup approvers when somebody's on vacation) and automatically take action when no approver is needed (for example, everybody is put into a directory group with no approval necessary).

Approvals You receive an e-mail telling you that you need to decide if a user who has requested access to a resource you own can have that access. That's one example of an approval. It could also mean a request to change the definition of a role or resource. Ultimately, approvals get you your roles, your resources, and ultimately the things that actually allow you to do the work: your privileges.

Least Privilege This is actually a state of being. At any given point in time, a user should have only those privileges that he's supposed to have, nothing more and nothing less. In other words, the least number of privileges necessary.

Exceptions An exception occurs when a user has privileges that he's not technically entitled to, for reasons that *ought to be* officially approved and documented. Sometimes they're granted for emergencies, or because you're using a contractor to do something a full-timer normally does. An exception should have a finite lifespan, otherwise it should be made part of a rule.

Segregation of Duties (SoD) This is a policy that determines which privileges or roles are incompatible with others for business reasons. SoD is meant to prevent conflicts of interest or other abuses. If I work at a mortgage company, I can't approve my own mortgage.

Out-of-Band Access Out-of-band access is neither a proper privilege nor a legitimate exception. It's access that the user received by going around the business rules. He made a phone call, or fat-fingered his own privileges. This is usually a no-no. It must be discovered quickly and fixed, as well as documented and reported on.

Impersonation Allowing user-1 to stand in for user-2 in order to fulfill user-2's tasks while he or she's away. There are different approaches to this, such as actually allowing somebody to sign in as somebody else (very bad), simply handing over a user's rights to another person (not as bad, but almost), or temporarily assigning certain rights to a qualified and approved substitute, with those rights set to expire at a set time (just fine). We'll talk about how to accomplish the goals of impersonation without actually *performing* impersonation.

Context In the old days, if you logged in to an application, you mostly got what everybody else got in terms of access. But an intelligent IAM framework can drill down into the details and make decisions in situations where not all users are created equally. I am a customer of your company, but only for one particular division, and therefore I can only look up your inventory relative to that division. Or I am a customer of your airline, and because I am a gold or platinum member, I get better seat assignments when I book a trip online. I have an auditor position at your company, but I can only audit transactions at a particular location, while someone else with the same title can only audit transactions at his location. These extra qualifications that add nuance to how a role is used are called context. This context may also determine who approves my requests. If my context is specific to a location or division, then my requests must be approved by administrators within that same context.

Certification/Attestation   A periodic event, usually scheduled, in which one or more approvers must review a list of users who currently have access to a target system. During this review, approvers decide which users keep that access, and which users lose that access. It's a process required by several compliance standards. Certification can also apply to approval of privileges within a role, or privileges relevant to an application.

Reconciliation   An automated process that periodically compares the access that users should have (according to corporate policies) with the access they actually do have. In the event of a conflict, reconciliation may either notify the appropriate parties, take action to put the access back to what it should be, or both.

Use Cases   You'll get sick of this one. These are detailed, step-by-step examples of how a system should be used, including preconditions, actions taken, and expected results. Use cases should reflect real-world examples of how business processes work, and they are employed when testing the system of note. For example, I create a new user, request access for that user, fire off the provisioning workflow, and I should expect to see the approvals performed and the user enabled. Use cases also serve to smooth out disparate terminology. For example, at an insurance company a few years back, simply by walking through the first use case, I learned that what I called a business role, the customer called an enterprise role. And what I called a salesperson, they called a lobby weasel. After that, no confusion.

Finding the Proper Perspective

If you're in charge of building an IAM framework, and you happen to bring in vendors or partners or consultants or anybody else, remember that you're the boss, especially if you control the budget. So whenever you find a particular term that was different from theirs, such as "business role" versus "enterprise role," tell them that from now on, they're going to call it what *you* call it. Later on, we'll be discussing how your IAM system should reflect the business, and not the other way around. Start fresh by making sure everybody uses your terminology. You're the customer. And even if you're simply having internal discussions, it still helps to agree on common terms that you will be using over and over.

To build the most reliable and case-specific identity framework, you have to think like both Us and Them.

If you're in charge, you're Us. The team in charge. The identity management team. Us. If you're a user, a customer, a supplier, a *somebody* in the system, you're a *Them*. The other guys, the ones who get acted upon.

So it's *Us and Them*. A song by Pink Floyd. And it's the way you need to think. You have to think like both *Us* and *Them*. How do you want to be treated, and how do you want to treat others? Identity and Access Management is almost a contract between both sides of the firewall: Keep the users happy, provide them access, and they're more productive, they stay longer, they buy more stuff, they complain less, they tell their friends, they're nicer to *you* because you're nicer to *them*.

Understanding who and what your users are will force you to empathize. That's not to say that you have to be Santa Claus. If *least privilege* means that a user should only have what he should have, then it also means management should enforce that least-privilege scenario.

Various analysts point to the fragmentation of the IdM market, with market share distributed among various vendors resulting from the many functions contained within the general heading of IAM. These include

- Authentication and single sign-on
- Privilege authorization
- Role management
- Federation
- User provisioning
- Business intelligence, compliance, reporting, and analytics

A common negative view is that these functions are not necessarily integrated across the many "solutions" on the market. Some vendors do integrate several of these functions, and Oracle provides all of these, in a comprehensive, open, and integrated fashion.

I'm virtually certain you will see some things in here that have been discussed by other people in other venues. I'm also certain you will find some things in here that nobody ever brings up, because they're awkward, and yet extremely relevant. As my wife always complains, I am

- **A pessimist** If it can go wrong, it will. While I will be speaking in terms of an ideal IAM system, it's not easy to build or maintain one. Even in the best scenarios, things get out of sync, things get lost, people abuse or cheat the system, and some aspect or another of your infrastructure will eventually overload and break, so you might as well plan for that. If you think in terms of worst-case scenarios, you'll have a strategy and a framework in place to provide the appropriate response when they occur.

- **Redundant** Sometimes I obsess about certain subjects, especially when I see them done incorrectly all the time. My youngest child rarely remembers to feed her fish, so it's the first thing I remind her of each day after "good morning." Likewise, I see the same mistakes made over and over with regard to identity and access, so I tend to repeat myself. The other reason for this is overlapping subjects. Compliance relates to segregation of duties relates to RBAC relates to provisioning relates to attestation relates to compliance and—you get the picture.

- **A list-maker** In this book you will encounter a lot of bullet points. This way it's easier to pick out the possible lists of requirements or considerations you will need to assemble later for your own IAM project.

- **A pragmatist** We'll talk a lot about theory, but a lot more about reality. Software doesn't always do what you think it's going to do, and people *rarely* do. And what you do is often limited by what you're *allowed* to do or what you can *afford* to do.

SEMIDISCLAIMER
*I have been through the process of envisioning IAM frameworks
with many organizations as a software vendor, implementer, project
manager, recommender, and end user. There are many dozens more
to whom I've pitched IAM and who for various reasons didn't bite.
Throughout my years on the vendor side, while I have aided sales,
I have steadfastly remained on the trusted-advisor, engineering side
of the fence. I have never actually functioned as a salesperson. If I die
and go to hell, I want it to be for better reasons than that. I've heard
it said that every salesperson should have a circus geek for an older
brother, so he or she will have somebody to look up to.*

So now let's take a look at what identity and access mean, how the industry views them, and their value to both the end user and the enterprise. We'll discuss whether or not you need an IAM framework, and how to recognize that need. Then we'll dive into how you get *there* from *here*, designing, building, and/or shopping for the IAM solution that best fits your needs, and creating that framework.

I'll also be covering, from a best-practices perspective, how to create that framework using the Oracle Identity and Access Management Suite of products, discussing them as both stand-alone point solutions and as components of a comprehensive, integrated solution, although the information provided here will be useful no matter which components you deploy.

We'll review all the good stuff you get from IAM, and all the bad stuff you can run into if you don't figure out what you need in advance, plan accordingly, ask all the right questions, make all the right choices, and say your prayers at night.

PART
I

Defining the Value of and
the Need for IAM

CHAPTER
1

Who's Where, and Why Do You Care?

Only the man who crosses the river at night knows the value of the light of day.
—Chinese proverb

 or the majority of organizations, identity has no value unto itself. It is kept for the sake of driving business functions that ultimately benefit the identifiers as well as the identified. But without it, those business functions put you at great risk. Any useful tool in the wrong hands can do untold damage. Therefore you are obligated to validate the owner of those hands.

The Value of Identity to User and Enterprise

In the old, old days, your data was kept in one flat table, and the system generated an identification number for you. Anywhere else you showed up in the system, you were represented by that number.

In the just-plain-old days, you were stuffed into a directory and given a user ID, which then represented you in all those apps.

In the present day, you're still in a directory, but on top of that, within that directory you're a member of myriad groups. You're also in five other directories, with multiple IDs, all of which may or may not be aware that they share you, because at the time your accounts were created, those stores all had their own naming conventions. You may very well be

- John.**Q.**Smith@MegaBigCorp.com
- JSmith
- Smith.J
- JohnS
- JS1234

Your identity, split up into pieces, across multiple data stores, may need to be brought together in total or in part when needed.

As Mr. Enterprise, I don't need you, my user, all in one place. Maybe I have no desire to break the ID requirements of all those legacy systems. Or perhaps, for the sake of security or privacy, I don't want you all in one place, and you don't want to be in one place either. This way, if any one part is compromised, it's not your entire identity spilling out. But for the company's purposes, it may be handy to virtualize your identity on occasion, and bring together every bit of you from the various places you exist. We'll cover the value of virtual directories later, under "Design."

 NOTE
Here, "virtual" means virtual views aggregating distributed data from multiple data sources, not VMWare or its brethren.

The process by which you enter, move about, and are ultimately ejected from the system is called Identity Management. It is the framework for your lifecycle within the enterprise. It governs your birth, life, and death as a system entity.

- You're hired, promoted, transferred, and fired.

- You become a customer, register your credit card, order stuff, order more stuff, request service on the inadequate item you bought, send nasty-grams about the service, send e-mail requesting that they refund your purchase and never call you again.

- You start an investment account, then you transfer in cash, send requests to your broker, check your portfolio once a week, watch your holdings go down the toilet, and transfer your cash out when the firm is bought and your broker moves to another place.

- You continue to get statements, because the managers of the different funds within your portfolio (or, rather, their systems) don't all know simultaneously that you've split; the ones that *do* know continue to beg you to come back.

Don't laugh at those last two bullet points. I listened to a broker in an airport bar describe these very scenarios in awful detail.

NOTE
Sometimes there is no definitive end to your relationship with a company, although inactivity alone (which we'll discuss later) may affect your standing, even without any intervention. It's not that you are necessarily a nonentity to your old employer; it's that your status has changed. They may have to account for you for years after you've left, for legal or auditing reasons.

An Identity and Access Management (IAM) framework manages these different slices of your profile, including your memberships, groups and organizations, roles, resources, resource-level roles, risk, history, status, and so on. If there was originally no rhyme or reason to your profile being sliced and diced, probably because of legacy memberships, the framework can bring them together. You might remain split into atoms, or you may eventually be assembled into a working molecule, even if it's only a virtual molecule.

Framework. This word implies design. You know, the way the Great Turtle made us all with perfect parts, and your appendix is simply a self-defense mechanism you haven't figured out how to use yet.

Wait, what do you mean? My appendix is useless. Hmm. So is half your identity data, by the way. We'll get to that later.

IAM touches everything. It establishes you in the enterprise. It drives your access and single sign-on. It makes you available for audit. It protects your privacy. It personalizes your applications. It remembers your favorites. It keeps you safely among those applications to which you are entitled. It safeguards you from phishing. It reduces risk. It ensures compliance. It does all this, and more—but only if you build it correctly to begin with, based on sound corporate security policies and your own specific use cases.

General Benefits of IAM

Identity and Access Management has great value above and beyond simply letting you log in to a site. It entails a two-way street of intangible benefits:

- Security for you, since it protects your data; security for the enterprise, since it keeps out bad guys.

- Compliance for you, by insisting that your data be secured; compliance for the enterprise, by logging the data it needs for auditors.

- Self-service, which makes your life easier when you forget your password or change your phone number, and takes the cost and burden off the guys in the back room.

- Productivity, since it helps you get a running start as a user.

- Delegated administration. Local administrators, line-of-business operators, departmental bosses, and other sectional chiefs don't want to have to make a phone call every time they add a resource or a user, transfer a user, or fire a user. And IT help desks don't want to get those phone calls either. By delegating the responsibilities to manage local users and resources, IT empowers these people, making them more productive and just plain engendering better feelings. It's also a better practice, since local admins are much less likely to make mistakes within their own domains.

The Value of Identity to the Enterprise

Believe it or not, it's not all about you. Any organization with which you interact (employer, bank) certainly wants you to have a happy user experience. But that's actually incidental to IAM. Why does the enterprise want to control identity and access? It may seem obvious: security. But it's more than that. It's managing what ought to be an ordered process. Security isn't just "you get in or you don't" and "here's a report of who got in and when." It's ongoing management and monitoring of what's going on with the user population. It's analysis of user behavior and mitigation of the risk, which is the combination of lots of resources and lots of users. It's providing access based on user profile, group memberships, and context.

Here it is in a nutshell: The value to the organization is that users only get access to what they're supposed to have access to. That is, assuming you've got the right pieces in place and have configured them with the right policies. It's called *least privilege*. The default should always be that you only get that which you need and which has been approved. Nothing else.

What else does the organization itself get out of this?

Self-Service, Part I

Help desk staff spend the majority of their time handling two types of issues, passwords and provisioning. They're constantly unlocking user accounts, and enabling (or disabling) those same accounts. By allowing users to reset their own passwords, unlock their own accounts, request resources, and track the status of their requests, management frees up those overworked help desk folks to concentrate on more enterprise-facing issues. Don't forget, the servers themselves are needy too.

A simple password tool can handle simple resets, if you're talking about Windows or Active Directory accounts. But if you want to tie it to an entire single sign-on mechanism, across all applications and databases, and also integrate with provisioning, account resets, requests and approvals, and all that good stuff, then you're looking at something with more muscle than a tool that only requires you to download and click setup.exe.

Depending on which study you read, 60 to 90 percent of all help desk calls are for password resets. It's a lot of person-hours on the part of the help desk folks, who would much rather be handling more critical issues. Let's be honest about it, most help desk staff hate most of their users. It can be an unhappy environment for everybody. Self-service can help smooth that over.

Privacy, Part I

For the people who hold your confidential data (only as needed, of course), the issue is liability. Lawsuits, government penalties, and dented stock prices can all result from a single, well-publicized breach. The most conservative study I've seen on the subject says stock price drops an average of 2 percent with a known breach.

You never hear about one individual whose credit card data is stolen. You hear about hundreds of thousands of credit card holders in a single event. One organization in the Midwestern United States had an ugly breach of credit card info, and in addition to the pain and embarrassment, they put out a hefty figure to pay for two years of credit monitoring for all those affected.

In parallel with ongoing stories about stolen privacy data, you hear about cloud computing. Sure, a lot of that is just marketing. After all, GMail is considered a cloud service. But at the same time everyone is crying about identity theft and privacy concerns, more and more data services are being offered out there in space, outside your own firewall. It's like somebody standing in front of a school yelling that all the kids are overweight, and at the same time offering them bags of potato chips. It's a frightening IT world, and we just keep making it scarier. IAM should be there to reassure us that we're safe, even as it leverages the data we provide to help us get the access we need. Users worry about the privacy of their data, while the data-holders worry about *consequences*.

Productivity, Part I

At my last cubicle job before I started flying all over the map (somewhere around 1990), I had duties that took me to the server room to pick up reams of reports on a daily basis. I couldn't physically enter the room, and always had to wait at the service window, unless I could weasel my way in. This was because my boss was more concerned about status quo and rocking the boat than about getting me an electronic entry badge that I was entitled to so that I could do my job. I was reduced to begging for entry. More than once, while working late, and with nobody in the server room, I literally climbed through the service window. Only when I got in trouble for breaking the window did the whole story come out, and I got my badge.

Loss of productivity means a dent in the bottom line. When you hire a new person and spend weeks training them and enabling them, they're eating up salary and putting little to nothing back into the organization. But if you get a new employee up and running more quickly, your Return on Investment (ROI) on that individual is phenomenal.

So many companies that actually have workflow products (engines that automate the steps needed to provision users) never take the time to deploy them in such a way as to take away all the manual labor that goes into the provisioning process. Automation is one of the single most underutilized functions in IAM.

Managing the Masses

You think of you as *you*. But face it, we're not all that unique. We all share characteristics with others that make it possible for us to be, for lack of a better term, lumped together.

The folks who create the policies that filter our access like to slice and dice us by *group membership*. They can't possibly create policies based on every specific user. I remember, way back when I was actually coding access rights for individuals, my screen was black and my characters were green and buying a two-foot-square 10MB board for my company's PR1ME-2250 cost five grand. But now it's all done by abstraction.

Sure, access control lists (ACLs) have long managed rights by group. But they tend to be very system-specific.

Access management can be largely described as associating groups of *people* with groups of *things*. It's a far, far easier thing to assign access this way:

```
Group                            |    Resource
---------------------------------|-------------------------------
dc=foobar, dc=com, ou=admins     |    http://www.foobar.com/admins/*
```

than to assign access this way:

```
Group                            |    Resource
---------------------------------|-------------------------------
cn=Skelton Knaggs, ou=admins,    |    http://www.foobar.com/admins/*
dc=foobar,dc=com                 |
```

and then replicate that for everybody else in the group. You think of your group memberships as making it easier for you to get your access; the enterprise thinks of it as making it easier to perform the task of giving you that access.

In essence, *authorization* is deciding which groups of people can access which groups of resources. That's as broad as saying that the purpose of your car is to get you places. It's more complex than that, which we'll expound upon when we discuss the solution.

Another way to manage in abstract is through the use of *roles*. A role is a collection of privileges, logically grouped so that the person who has that role, presumably for sound business reasons, has just the right set of privileges to fulfill the obligations of his job title. The abstraction part comes in the sharing of roles. Too many organizations have more roles than users, which is completely backwards. The further down the organization chart you travel, the more you see shared roles. You've only got one CEO and one president, but you've got multiple VPs, and even more mid-managers, and even more accountants and data entry staff.

When we discuss Role-Based Access Control (RBAC) in detail, we'll drill down into the different kinds of roles, the content of roles, the rules associated with who gets a role, and how roles play very nicely with user enablement, otherwise known as *provisioning*, to make it easier to manage access rights for large numbers of users.

Of course, sometimes it's not as simple as "You're in this group, so you get this stuff." This is why the provisioning gods created exceptions, as well as context. Of course, exceptions should be kept to a minimum, or eventually made into the rule. Context allows you to add qualifications to the rules, such as, "We share a role, but you can only use it in your business unit, and I can only use it in mine." Without context, this would mean two distinct roles, which is how roles proliferate.

So, managing access for *groups of users* is far more efficient for the organization than managing access for *individual* users. You don't like being just a number? Well, if the company numbers its groups, then you're just a number inside *another* number. Get used to it.

The Value of Identity to the End User

Okay, some of it *is* about you. A lot of IAM is about making you feel loved. A user who has ready access to his assigned resources and who can take care of his own needs will always be happier. If customers are happy, they'll keep coming back. If employees are more productive, well, they're more productive.

My wife's a camera fan, and always avoided digital devices. But when she discovered that she could take endless numbers of digital pictures and not worry about how much film she used, she fell in love with the things. Delete or edit the photos you don't like, then upload them to a web site, order prints online, and pick them up when the site says they're ready. But the first site we ever used for this purpose was buggy, difficult to navigate and use, and ultimately we dropped it in favor of a different site. Likewise, I changed online brokers years ago because logging in took almost two minutes. Lost business was the result of bad user experiences.

How does IAM facilitate a happier you? Easy. It drives

- **Single sign-on (SSO)**   Log in once, and get to everything you need.
- **Personalization**   You log in, and you can easily see
  - Your history
  - Your account balance
  - Your favorites
  - The last ten things you were working on
  - The last ten things you bought
  - The last ten things you looked up
  - Related items that are recommended to you
  - Items in the same category as other things you've purchased
  - The customizations you've made to your screen
  - Bulletins specific to your group or department
  - Alerts, reminders, and to-do's
- **Communications and collaboration**   Once you're in, you can chat with, e-mail, or otherwise interact with other authorized users.
- **Security**   You know you're in the right place, and your data is safe.

As an identity expert, you need to consider the value of the user experience. More than once, I've heard security officers laugh off SSO. They don't think that the time lost typing in another password amounts to much. And maybe at some places it doesn't. In theory, it truly is more secure to make users type in multiple passwords for multiple apps. But if you're running enough apps, and they all have their own password policies, it could add up. Without SSO, you will have people locked out of accounts. The compromise here is a term called Reduced Sign-On, in which a password may get you some aggregated access, but not all.

You'll also have people who write their passwords on a Post-It or stick them in a Notepad file named passwords.txt. Guaranteed.

True Story

At one of my employers, we ran literally hundreds of apps for customers and employees, and on any given day, I might use a dozen or more apps, making SSO invaluable. Every 60 days, the password monkey would force me to change my password. But because of a recurring glitch in password sync, I often had to revert to an old password, sometimes two or three passwords back. So I had to keep track of old passwords (problem #1), and sometimes trying out three or four passwords meant that logging in could take three or four times longer (problem #2).

Password policies for end users serve two purposes (three, if you consider "making little old ladies forget how to log in" a purpose). First, it's security. You're saving people from themselves when they craft passwords that are too easy for others to guess. You don't want bad guys getting into your customers' accounts, right? Second, it provides the *appearance* of security. By enforcing expiration or complexity policies on passwords, you're telling the world, "Look, we care about safeguarding our user base." As we'll see later when discussing compliance, it's not just about security, it's also about the evidence of security.

Now, if we're talking about IAM for employers, it's a slightly different story. It's kind of nice to think that your company wants you to be happy. But come on, it's capitalism. If you're happy, that's an intangible benefit. In this case, it's all about productivity.

Exceptions

As we previously discussed, groups are good. But what about the stuff you have that's unique to you? What if you're treated oh-so-slightly differently because you're the only notary public in your department, or you're certified in some application that nobody else is in order to approve documents?

You may share resources or even roles with others in the organization (and in fact roles *should* be shared), but your context may be different. For example, you're a Data Entry Clerk in the manufacturing division, and someone else is also a Data Entry Clerk, but in accounting. Same role, but with access to different cost-center data.

Also consider the if-then-else situations in granting access. For example, only full-time HR employees with senior status can review salary data, except for fully authorized auditors who are approved by the CFO.

Self-Service, Part II

You could argue that self-service is more of a benefit to the organization than the individual, because you're getting paid whether you're working or you're sitting on hold with the help desk, waiting to get your password reset. But when you've got tasks to finish, and the boss is breathing down your neck, you'd much rather be doing your job than bugging the help desk guys to get you unstuck.

If you have the ability to manage certain aspects of your own identity, you're empowered, so you feel better about yourself, you're more autonomous and more productive. At the same time, the enterprise is also happy that you're more productive, and they're assured that you can only operate within the boundaries they set for you. More about that one later.

Privacy, Part II

Let's touch again on protecting your data. It's about *privacy*, yet another two-way value. You don't want your most confidential information being available to anybody who's not fully authorized. Even people who might need to reference your social security number should only care about the last four digits 99 percent of the time. Your banking info, your family's healthcare data, anything and everything that is (or should be) sacred to you needs to be under lock and key, accessible only when absolutely necessary, and only to personnel who are properly authorized. Evil people with bad intentions can use that information in so many ways. They want to open credit card accounts, take out mortgages, acquire loans, or get free healthcare, all under your name.

A robust IAM framework ensures that only the right people, including you, have access to your information assets. Your employer, your credit card company, your doctor, and a host of other parties possess chunks of your most precious and potentially dangerous secrets. IAM is their guard dog.

Productivity, Part II

Let's face it, people *want* to be productive. They want to earn their paycheck, and they feel more job-secure when they're contributing. If they've got access to the resources they need, they can do their jobs more quickly, more efficiently, and with more focus. Especially in a bad economy, they want to provide the most value. They don't want to bug their managers or help desk about the stuff they can't get to, any more than the managers or help desk want to hear from them. IAM ensures that the right users can get at the right stuff at the right time, with the right level of access.

IAM also aids productivity by helping personalize content. Amazon remembers you, checks out what you've previously bought, and recommends other items that might interest you, based on your history. This is why my wife and kids have so many books about teenage vampires.

Getting What You Need from IAM

In the next few chapters, we're going to look at the various components of Identity and Access Management. We'll get into deep specifics regarding how users come into the system, how they're enabled, how they authenticate and are authorized, and how security and compliance are handled.

In describing each of these facets of IAM, I will be discussing what is *possible*. There is no set standard as far as what is *recommended*. Not all commercially available software can perform all the functions I will cover. But because I'm dealing with realities, anything I cover *is* commercially available in one form or another, and certainly from Oracle. Naturally, anything you can buy, you can also build, but you might not want to. Sure, you could reinvent the skateboard, but not the automobile. In some areas, I will even cover how viable or necessary a particular technology even is. Just because you *can* do something, doesn't mean you should, or should have to.

For more than a year, I've been trying to get a particular vendor to add a small piece of functionality to their product to make it easier to use. They keep delaying it, in order to ultimately provide something incredible. I keep telling them, I don't need a nuclear reactor next year, just a car battery tomorrow. They insist on the nuclear reactor. So instead of getting what I need now, I'll get something I don't really need, later. When you're putting together your own IAM system, get what you need, when you need it.

CHAPTER
2

Determining Your Need
for an IAM Framework

Necessity is the mother of invention.
　　　　—George Farquhar

 f you're reading this nonsense, you may have only a sneaking suspicion that a robust Identity Access Management (IAM) system is what your organization needs. But let's look into that. Everybody needs IAM, whether in part or in whole. How do you recognize when IAM, or at least more capacity than you've already got, is an absolute necessity? After all, it's not something to be entered into lightly, considering the costs, labor, and time (with labor and time equaling more costs).

Investigating Your Internal Necessities

Given the maturity of the space, there are actually two ways to consider the question of whether identity management is a necessity. First of all, you may find it hard to believe that there are still a lot of organizations out there who don't have a true identity/access system, unless you're one of them. Everybody's got pieces of it, but few organizations have an end-to-end, fully integrated identification and user enablement platform covering all their assets.

Not to say that you need such a beast, at least not all at once. You may have the requirement to secure only your most critical assets immediately, with an eye toward covering the rest at a later date, as time and budget allow. Regardless, putting the basics in place will allow you the agility to ramp up in the future, without having to reinvent what you've already done. Why build security around a couple of apps, completely app-specific and custom, and then repeat that process for the next piece of software you deploy? Wouldn't it make more sense to arrange a framework as a launching pad for those resources you don't yet suspect you need?

Putting up such a platform is a no-brainer, if you've got certain assets online, with users approaching them from various starting lines, especially the cloud of the Internet. But even if it's all inside, with only employees for users, you still need IAM.

I spend a huge amount of my time discussing with my clients whether to complement or outright replace their existing identity infrastructure. And there are a lot of reasons for doing that.

Starting from Scratch

As I said, everybody's got some identity components or other. You may have been getting along on LDAP or HR alone. You must be doing some kind of basic authentication, and if you have something as simple as Active Directory (AD), you've got domain security policies that may be sufficient on a very small scale, if not exactly cross-platform or robust enough to cover the authorization needs for all the different kinds of applications you run. For provisioning, you might be using a help desk app to track requests that are manually fulfilled. So when is it time to graduate to the big-time?

Time for Compliance

Here's another one I'll repeat over and over. Compliance does not equal reporting. In fact, reporting is the absolute end of the compliance food chain. It tells you what happened, but in fact real compliance now should translate into nice, clean reports later.

Audit, security, corporate mandate. Any system can be made "compliant" if it can limit who gets access to what, and it can cough up sufficient data to create the necessary reports. But how readily does it support policies that not only dictate least privilege (you *only* get what you need and nothing more), but also *ensure* least privilege by enforcing policies after the fact? Can it react to out-of-band access? Can your system help you conduct reviews of who has what, and help you disable users when they have access that is inappropriate to their job title?

Can your system generate audit-friendly reporting without SQL joins that look like the world's ugliest if-then-else clause? Can it provide instant troubleshooting data? Remember, if your system makes it difficult to kick out useful reports, your life will be that much harder when auditors demand report formats and content that you never thought of before.

Application firewalls are all the rage at a company when there's been a breach. But compliance has been the number one thing that gets me in the door to discuss upgrading an organization's IAM architecture. After the introduction of Sarbanes-Oxley (SOX), I thought regulatory compliance might have run its course in terms of that first big wave of spending and design, except that I forgot the most basic human principle governing our behavior (after procreation and beer): procrastination. Many outfits simply did what they needed to do, and nothing more. But once some of the provisions kicked in with a big bite, where penalties could actually be incurred, it got more serious all over again.

Whether or not you're in the healthcare business, in the United States you worry about the Health Insurance Portability and Accountability Act (HIPAA). If you're publicly traded, you practically have a tattoo that says "Sarbanes-Oxley." Even if you're not bound by regulations like SOX, you deal with other companies that are, and so you still have to abide by it. In Chapters 4 and 12, we'll look at the many international regulations a little more in depth, including their provisions, and how they help drive IAM requirements around the globe.

All-Manual Processes

Enablement is by e-mail, second and third e-mails, final "no kidding" e-mails, fat-fingering names into databases and AD groups, and setting domain policies one set of pages at a time. You're manually tracking down users with out-of-band access and manually remediating them back into their least-privilege status, *assuming* you can track down these errant privileges and *assuming* you're in the minority of organizations that actually take action on this situation.

It's time to automate. It's time to create policies that automatically determine who can have access to what and when. You need to be able to punch information for a new employee into the HR system, have it calculate their roles and privileges, then push out all the requests to the approving managers who receive auto-notifications asking, "Is this person good enough to use your app?" And if the approvers don't reply within a reasonable amount of time, the system needs to automatically escalate. "Aha! There's the bottleneck! It's Benson, in accounts payable! Send out the winged monkeys!"

You'll never completely eliminate the need for your assistant to run down the hall and say, "You need to take care of this," but you can drastically reduce the things that fall off the table, don't get taken care of, don't get followed up on, or just plain can't be found because they're not recorded anywhere. As we'll cover in detail later, automated processes drive progress, keep everybody on track, make sure nobody and nothing slips through the cracks, and capture everything in a log. It's like Post-It Notes with teeth and a stopwatch.

I visit a lot of universities. They seem to have more decentralized apps in place, with users defined multiple times in multiple apps and directories, all held together by manual processes, than my commercial customers. And yet they have a more transient user population than anybody. This means that they are forever behind in change management.

Hard-Coded Security

When there are new requirements, a new application launched, a change in policies or security mandates, your coders have to open up the jar files and start hacking away. Java geniuses who know nothing of the core business are making their best attempts to create the filters that hopefully let the right people in and keep the wrong people out. There is no consistency to the security, since it's custom-built for each resource. Nothing can be duplicated across the platforms. There may be no single source of authority regarding who is who and what they can have access to. When the auditors ask to review the policies, they shake their heads at the patchwork you've stitched together.

On top of the provincial nature of these disparate policies, there is the additional drain of coding time that is devoted to silo security instead of business logic. The burden of identity and security is spread around to everybody's unqualified shoulders, instead of being placed in the laps of a centralized, qualified, security-minded authority who can provide security to all parties.

Expansion of the Business

You're big enough that you can't get away with those manual processes. The volume has gotten too, uh, voluminous. You're looking at using more IT resources just to keep up with the existing ones, instead of managing the process. You've got twice as many help desk staff members as you did a year ago. You don't bother tracking overprovisioned users or orphaned privileges or rogue accounts because that would be a luxury. When new user groups are brought in, because of partnerships, a new bank branch, or an acquisition, you are receiving CDs with flat files, having someone use Notepad or vi to verify the content and schema, and writing code to import the names and addresses into your system. And likely you're running this process multiple times, because the first five times you do it, the app server is throwing out all sorts of messages on the exceptions that don't fit the format.

One IAM project I worked on was initiated because a large multinational retailer wanted to launch a portal for its dealer locations. They needed to build in strong authentication as well as single sign-on and granular access control for their chosen portal platform. So it wasn't existing infrastructure driving it, but a whole new piece of business. They didn't even want to talk about IAM for their current users, only the new, external ones.

Expansion or Sudden Popularity of a Resource

You put up a new site, and everybody suddenly says, wow! And they jump all over it. I helped put in place a subsite where corporate users could download desktop software that the customer had leased. Nobody at the organization could have predicted how in-demand this set of pages became almost overnight. The sudden surge in downloads crashed the thing twice toward the end of the first week.

Another recent culprit is Sharepoint. Having quickly grown from a little collaboration tool into the *portal du jour*, it's great for quickly slapping sites together, sharing content, and growing beyond the ability of the site creators to track and control who gets into what. The admins of individual subsites end up creating their own access policies (if they even bother), instead of allowing for enterprise policies. Sharepoint also doesn't manage granular protection of privileges. By using group policies, you can enforce the notion that not all users are created equal. But this fails to take into account that even within a directory or a single page, not all *content* is created equal. If all of us can hit the same piece of HTML, does that mean all of us can take whatever's linked there? Hmmm, maybe not a great idea.

A little later we'll discuss the problems (and solutions) related to the rampant and unregulated use of Sharepoint, as well as Active Directory.

Replacing or Augmenting IAM

Why would somebody *replace* an existing Identity Management (IdM) infrastructure? For lots of reasons. The bulk of the IAM business I've done the last handful of years has been replacements, in part or in total. Many clients have decided that what they had either wasn't working or wasn't working *enough*. In a lot of cases, they've been told by their bosses, their users, or their auditors that there were enough deficiencies to mandate an upgrade or a massive change. In some cases, my customers already have something in place, in total or in part, but it's not getting the job done. They may even want to maintain some of what they've got, to preserve the investment or because what little they have is doing what it's asked to do. And there's nothing wrong with that, but on occasion I tell customers in that situation, if you're going to add a bunch more functionality with additional tools, you might as well replace the little widget you've already got. If you're using a little homegrown workflow to create help desk tickets, you might as well replace it with a full-blown workflow engine when you put in a real provisioning package. Just because you're getting around with a unicycle doesn't mean you strap it on to your new car so you can avoid buying a fourth tire.

So when do you look at boosting, or even replacing, what you have?

Persistent All-Manual Processes

Way back when, before it was scrapped, *Omni* magazine used to run a series of cartoons designed to poke fun at the evolution of technology. One of them sticks in my head, decades later. It featured the usual caveman pondering how best to move a huge rock. For this purpose, he invents the wheel, then attaches two of them to a cart. Then he puts the rock in the cart, and finally lifts the cart, boulder and all, and carries it away.

This is exactly how systems treat you when you don't make them do what you need, instead of you doing what *the system* needs. The promised automation turned out to be far less performant than was advertised. After a time, you may find yourself feeding the beast that's supposed to be feeding *you*. You're punching in required data that never really comes back out in useful form, or you're running batch processes just to keep data in sync, something that doesn't really make your job easier and takes up more time than before you installed this lousy package. Or you're creating ASCII files to move from one system to another, forever exporting and importing either by sneakernet or cron job before you even get down to processing the new records, instead of telling your system to use connectors and workflow to migrate data from source to target and automatically processing it into its proper place.

I cannot *believe* the person-hours some organizations put into their identity requirements because their systems aren't up to speed. Something as simple as putting users into Active Directory. Manually generating reports. Manually performing certifications (which we'll cover in great detail later). Manually generating notifications to approvers, admins, group owners, and end users. This is what workflow is supposed to be for. And remember, the more things you do manually, the more mistakes creep into the data. A couple of companies back, my last name was spelled differently between HR, health plan, and 401K, causing considerable reconciliation troubles.

Software is supposed to provide intelligent automation. If you've bought or built a package for identity and/or access management, then it should automate identity and access. All the time I see situations where workflow is so weak that administrators end up processing requests so that they end up in queues, which then must be manually released, which is pointless. Instead of automating work, inefficient systems can actually *generate* work.

Too Much Customization

When you've patched and coded and monkey-wrenched enough changes to whatever you've bought or built, the maintenance can get out of hand. We've all heard the stories about lost or undocumented source code, or code that wouldn't readily migrate to the company's new choice of app server. Migration in fact is a huge issue. Highly customized environments are huge hurdles to upgrading to the next release of anything, because those customizations don't carry forward automatically.

"It works, but the guy who wrote it is long gone, and we don't have the source code any longer." That's like saying, the plane's flying great, but the landing gear has fallen off. So we're fine, as long as we stay in the air.

I did some mergers and acquisition (M&A) investigation on a company that built connectors for linking applications to legacy identity stores. The company founder was also its original coder, and he'd written everything in Assembler. If you know anything about Assembler, you know that it's one step up from coding in ones and zeros. Virtually none of his code was documented. It was a worst "bus accident" scenario: If this guy had been hit by a bus, his product would be instantly frozen in time, forever.

At some point, you want a system that's standards-based, GUI-driven, fully documented, with a published API that's extensible by any reasonable professional services provider.

Insufficient Business Support

Remember, the system is supposed to support the business, not the other way around. It should replace or augment human processes in progressing your core business value (shipping, manufacturing, financials, whatever it is your company is known for), generate reports, provide analysis, and enforce compliance. If it's not doing this, can you get away with bolting on the extras you need to pull this off, or is it time to start swapping out pieces, if not start out completely fresh?

Patchwork Systems

If your system is a combination of multiple vendors and/or homegrown components, you face chronic finger-pointing.

"It's not our app server, it's their lousy directory that's so slow."

"It's their custom code that's making our product throw exceptions."

"Your network's latency is causing our sessions to time out."

"Your mother dresses you funny."

I recall a particular episode in which an integrator bid on a job for which they weren't exactly qualified, and in performing bulk loading into the customer's new software, they jacked up the log levels on the app server to the point where every new record caused two dozen messages to pop up. This led to an episode that in hindsight was quite hilarious, but which at the time was not.

Everybody got blamed: the software, the app server, the integrator, and the customer for hiring a cheap partner.

Shortening your list of providers, even if you don't get it down to a single provider, streamlines problem resolution, and also simplifies expansion. You may still hear excuses, but there will be fewer bodies for the excuse-makers to hide behind. You want one throat to choke, or one toll-free number to call.

Purely Business Reasons

Years ago I was in the app security and testing business. Our product was competitive, but in some respects not the best one on the market. The big gorilla in our space had better resources, but one of the worst possible reputations. Fifty percent of our wins came from better execution, and the rest of them resulted from our prospects simply not wanting to do business with the other guys. There are players like that in the identity business as well.

With an enterprise decision, you're not just buying a product; you're buying a relationship. It's how you're treated before and after the sale. It's how you're supported. How you're involved in the evolution of the product. How confident you are in the direction of that company and its products. The number of other customers with whom you can share best practices.

How much input do you have, as a valued customer, in future releases? Does your vendor have a customer advisory board? Do they take feedback seriously? Are bug fixes incorporated into future releases, or are you forever patching? Do you have a forum in which to share your experiences, good and bad, including workarounds, with fellow customers of your vendor?

In other words, if you're not feeling the love, it might be time to take your love elsewhere.

Nonintegrated Systems

In the past year, I've had discussions with companies who already have "provisioning" in place. But their solutions only provision to two things: Active Directory and their help desk app. So the apps that enable users through AD are covered, and the rest get provisioned this way: The bare-bones workflow opens a help desk ticket, the app owners get e-mail notifications, and they fat-finger the new users into whatever database is required. This is one step above using carrier pigeons.

Help desk tickets should be the last resort for those apps that absolutely require manual intervention. You should expect true connectivity, through either out-of-the-box connectors or connection wizards or APIs that help you build real communication between provisioning logic and target systems. Otherwise you're stuck with only one useful result, Day One enablement. Change management is not supported (what happens when Harry in accounting transfers?), user disablement is a jumbled mess (fire drill! Harry just got fired and needs to get flushed from all the systems), and there is no automated reconciliation to guarantee that users have least privilege based on established policies.

Let me restate that last point again. Connectivity allows for automated processes that keep an eye on who's got what. If your provisioning is based on too many manual steps, you cannot— *cannot*—enforce policies through the system on an automated, scheduled basis. And actionable certification/attestation (that is, the ability for access reviews to automatically correct user privileges) is impossible. You will be generating hard copy and zipping it around to all the managers' desks, then manually correlating the results based on highlighter and best guess.

Vendor No Longer in Business

There's a software company out there with a product line that's well-known in the industry. That product is a cash cow for them, and has bankrolled their entry into a whole bunch of other markets, where they've failed miserably. They bought into the identity market, and badly. I've visited various customers of theirs over the years who were quite happy with their highly customized, Frankenstein-monster IAM installations. These contraptions worked fine, as long as you didn't touch them. If you asked, "Can we make it do *this* next?" the answer was always No. Those organizations who had the political will, and some discretionary cash, eventually migrated. I visited a financial institution with this patchwork of a solution that saw no reason to dump it, as long as it was supported. About a year after I visited, their vendor dropped the product. Ouch. Within a week of the quiet announcement that this vendor was getting out of the identity market, we received calls from three of their customers.

Inadequate Workflow Capabilities

I've heard this one plenty of times. I've seen so many kludgy workflow setups, based on "this was all we needed at the time." People were relying on Lotus Notes, or just their help desk app. But then their processes or user requirements expanded to where the old workflow simply wasn't adequate.

Here's a good one. A customer told me they didn't like their workflow engine because it didn't integrate with much, couldn't generate parallel requests, and had a tendency to freeze up. It even had a hard-coded limitation on numbers of steps. But it had one customization they liked and which they'd built themselves: It could take multiple notifications to the same approver and bundle them into one e-mail. If you had three approvals to perform, you'd get one notification email instead of three. So I asked, "You have such a high volume of approvals that this saves you bandwidth or e-mail storage space?" The answer was no, it just saved people from getting additional e-mails. So they stuck with the crummy workflow because somebody thought this minor enhancement with limited benefits was worth all the other things it couldn't do.

"My car doesn't start if it's below freezing. But the eight-track player is killer."

Mergers and Acquisitions (M&A)

It's common for companies that are acquired to keep their own systems, at least for a while. And sometimes forever. One of my customers is not so much a functioning manufacturer as they are a holding company for hundreds of smaller manufacturers. All their individual holdings maintain their own systems for HR, provisioning, and so on. But there has to be a lot of trust there. More typically, somebody is migrating to somebody else's identity platform. And if two or more smaller organizations turn into one big organization, the sum total of their identity platforms may be insufficient to handle the new family. This is especially true if they're running on different operating systems, with different data stores and app servers. A new identity framework can serve as the glue, preserving existing investment in IT assets while simultaneously unifying the reporting functions and other processes already in place.

A little later, we'll talk in-depth about *framework*. That is to say, laying the foundation for identity and access management, so that, when you are handed additional user groups and/or IT resources to manage, you can plug them into an existing infrastructure, with existing policies, providing instant support and consistency.

Obsolete Systems

When you've taken an IT job and inherited any kind of system, you'll rarely say, "Whoopee, I can't wait to take this thing for a ride." Usually it's more along the lines of, "Oh heck, it can't do *that*?"

But even when you've personally implemented the thing, there's always this consideration: *things change*. Things get bigger, more complex; they behave in ways you hadn't anticipated, system limitations breed mountainous customizations, business requirements become more stringent, Sarbanes and Oxley invent Sarbanes-Oxley, throughput increases, bottlenecks develop, you buy another company, another company buys *you*, or you add a technology that's so easy to use that people go crazy with it and create more pages and groups than you can shake a stick at (Sharepoint, Active Directory). The system that you used to own now owns you.

Throughput Expansion

You've gotten bigger. Or your transaction level has gotten bigger. Your old Windows-based, script-based IdM system can't handle the load, can't do single sign-on to non-Windows platforms, can't scale.

If you're running a lot of redundant servers, and all of them need to run the same configuration, do you have to change them all individually? Think web server plug-ins, filters that intercept and mitigate resource requests. They perform that mitigation based on policies stored in a central server, which is also redundant. Can you push configuration changes out to all of them at the same time? If not, then you're spending a lot of hours doing it manually. You've got situations where some servers are out of sync for a period of time, and you risk not making the changes uniformly.

Does your system even support linear scaling? Can you add servers to increase throughput?

User Expansion

You're growing. You've bought. You've *been* bought. You're now allowing in external users. Oh, and you don't treat external users the same way as internal; they're not kept in the same directory, and they authenticate (of course) from outside the firewall. You're allowing self-registration for customers or partners. You now need gated security for levels of external users. You need delegated administration so customers or partners can add their own individual users, but under your rules.

Excessive Cost

The idea that the system "has gotten too expensive" made sense a couple of years back, but not any more. It's taken on a life of its own, to the point where it's become like cold fusion: It takes in more energy than it puts out. There are a lot of possible reasons for this.

- You're outsourcing too many processes and stores.
- You're relying on too many consultants.
- Authentication is based on expensive, difficult-to-replace hard tokens.
- Despite all the software and hardware, you're still performing too many manual tasks.
- You spend too much time converting data dumps because your system doesn't communicate via standard protocols.

- Audits mean dropping everything, pulling people off regular duties, and becoming an audit monkey for a month.
- Your vendor, who hasn't upgraded the product in ages, is concentrating on new customers and has upped your maintenance costs.
- You've added it all up and decided to bring more of it in-house (instead of outsourcing), or at least build a more efficient system.

Augmentation of Existing Systems

Just because your system is old and not completely functional doesn't mean you're going to get rid of it (although we will discuss later the ins and outs of maintaining legacy components). But maybe it doesn't have enough firepower to get you everything you need. You might be ready to take the next step from a promising start. Or maybe your pieces have gotten away from you (proliferation of LDAP groups or Sharepoint sites, acquisitions, a flood of new users or customers, a failed audit). Perhaps you're now adding roles to your entitlements system.

A Bad First Choice

Later on, we'll discuss this one in detail, but occasionally companies pick software for reasons other than what they think is a best fit. Somebody knew somebody; a vendor flew everybody out to the coast for meetings and golf (and yes, this still happens); somebody in the organization decided on a product early on and geared the whole process toward that vendor to the detriment of proper diligence. Now that you're getting around to doing it the right way (presumably), put everything on the table, and involve all the right parties. If you goofed before, don't goof the second time. And if you weren't around when they picked the first package, you can be a big hero.

As with bad plumbing or unwanted visits from relatives, the longer you wait, the worse your problems will get. More people will end up with privileges they shouldn't have. LDAP groups will proliferate. Security and compliance mandates will be harder to match up with access policies. More silo applications will be launched without benefit of corporate security governance. And the uglier your next audit will be.

Whatever your reason for considering a (new) IAM framework, take the *time* to learn from your mistakes, your homework, and your peers. You belong to some user groups, right? Some mailing lists? You network a little, hopefully? Ask around. See what other people have done, and maybe have done wrong. Or done right. It's just the start. There's a lot of investigation to do.

Making the Business Case, Round One

If you're at the point where you firmly believe you need to bolster your identity and security capabilities, and you don't have the petty cash sitting around to do it yourself, you obviously need the support of the higher-ups. Not only that, but any significant changes you feel you need to make for the sake of augmenting security may have far-reaching effects, and therefore it's not something to enter lightly. In other words, you'll need cover.

In the lifecycle of designing and building an IAM framework, you'll have at least two, if not dozens, of walkthroughs with management. The first one is to get permission, or a sanity check, for even investigating. No matter what your needs, if management says, "Have fun looking, but we're paying for absolutely nothing," then you're somewhat wasting your time. At that point, keeping a running tab of your trials and tribulations might be worth it for trying again next year, or waiting for either a change in management or an action-demanding security breach.

The nice thing about getting management to buy off on investigation is that you get away with spending the cycles, as well as eating up the time of those around you.

At the very least, get permission to start exploring what you need. If there have been any high-profile breaches or issues, it's definitely an easier sell. Nothing gets the ball rolling faster, or frees up more budget, than a break-in or poor audit results.

A few years back, a large food manufacturer spent over ten million dollars, and took literally hundreds of people off their regular duties, to get compliant early on with Sarbanes-Oxley, among other smaller requirements. They bit the bullet, built and bought what they needed to, then were able to go into maintenance mode, with a *framework* in place that allowed them to respond to future regulatory needs. They anticipated the flood, sacrificed, and essentially got it over with, instead of facing death by paper cuts. The majority of organizations, however, have done nothing of the sort, building compliance in pieces, and only as absolutely needed, based on audits or breaches.

Part of making that initial case is to highlight your risks. What are your critical assets, how are users granted access to those assets, what kinds of controls are in place to secure that access, and what kinds of reports are available to validate actual access events?

During your internal investigation, spell out (at least some of) the risks, and identify at least one stakeholder with reasonable expectations. If the process down the road doesn't go as smoothly as desired—and it won't—it's nice to have a buffer.

Speak with partners, customers, suppliers, vendors, contractors, and anyone else who might interact with your resources. They also matter. More efficient processes and better security may grease the tracks for increased traffic and business. They certainly paint you as a more forward-thinking organization.

It's not just your current needs you need to consider. Think about the future. During investigation, find out what your department managers are envisioning for down the road. Factor in room for growth, agility for responding to new requests, and handling the unknown. Once again, consider the value of a *framework*. If you have one of those in place, you're already ahead of the game in terms of providing a place to deploy and secure a new resource you haven't even thought of or heard of yet. New security mandates, new compliance requirements, new protocols or standards can all be integrated into your *framework*. (See, I *told* you I was redundant.)

If possible, cozy up to your board, and let them know you're investigating, if they're not already aware. Not only do you make it look as if you care about what they're thinking (whether you do or not), but you may also be establishing contacts to leverage at a later date. You're telling them, here's our task, we're looking to improve our processes, our efficiency, our security, and ultimately our bottom line. When possible, point out the ways in which you will make use of your existing investments in IT. After all, you're not going to be throwing out every server, database, and piece of custom code, and you certainly won't be dumping your business apps. In fact, you're going to be complementing a lot of your existing technology.

It certainly helps to find like-minded bodies to help petition for an IAM system. But it will feel like herding cats, trying to get all the parties lined up in order to build momentum for planning, funding, and building an IAM framework. As with any funding request, there must be an obvious, quantifiable need that you can demonstrate to management. Line up your horror stories, breaches, auditor comments, and use cases.

Outline your proposed solution in general; never state a problem without a solution. Now, this doesn't mean at this early stage that you're going to outline the entire architecture of hardware and software you think you might need. Getting the green light to discuss IAM internally is completely different from discussing with anybody externally, and you *will be* doing that at some point. This will be a high-level schematic.

- Hey boss, we need delegated administration, we're all bogged down with remote requests.
- Hey boss, we need integrated segregation of duties (SoD), the auditors are shredding us.
- Hey boss, it's taking us weeks to provision all those people from the service group we bought on board.
- Hey boss, we have no idea how many AD groups we have or how they're used, and the auditors are shredding us again.
- Hey boss, we need behavioral analysis as part of the access management, there are too many varied hacking attempts.
- Hey boss, it takes us over a month to completely disable a terminated user, and the auditors are going crazy.
- Hey boss, we've been hacked!

At one IAM organization, I taught a class five years in a row to the sales engineers, on *how to sell our junk*. Besides showing them how to use a whiteboard without leaving a mess, how to perform discovery with a client, how to begin with the end in mind, and all that other sales nonsense, I had one particularly important lesson for them that I now give to you about trying to state your case.

You're not selling features and functions to upper management. It's all about *business value*. Myriad business benefits have to be realized from IAM:

- Cost savings
- Productivity
- Ease of use
- Efficiency
- Security
- Compliance
- Simplification
- Automation
- Integration
- Consistency
- Self-service

The fact that there are features and functions is incidental, as they just come bundled with the business value. These features are only the means to the end, the tactical supports to the strategic goal.

Depending on the makeup of your organization, it may be too soon to talk about funding right now. You haven't finished making the case yet, and before that, you have to find the ammunition.

But if you successfully make the case to go exploring, then two things are certain. First, you've already decided you need to do this for the sake of the organization. Second, management is at least willing to listen. Now you've got to build the second business case. You *will* be back in front of the bosses, probably in a few months, with a more detailed plan, and this will have dollar amounts attached. Of course, to come up with the amounts, you have to first come up with the product, which consists of software, processes, and labor. And to come up with that, you have to plan.

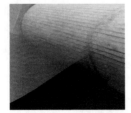

PART II

Preparing the Enterprise for IAM

CHAPTER
3

Planning an IAM Project

A fine invention is nothing more than a fine deviation from, or enlargement on a fine model.
—Edward Bulwer-Lytton

ou don't go on vacation, change apartments, buy a house, go to Grandma's for Christmas, or do anything else in life, without a plan. Why are we doing this, what are we doing exactly, what do we need to bring with us, what are we going to accomplish, and when do we get home?

You may or may not be planning an IAM project in anticipation of a second pass at management for approval. This depends entirely on the organization. If you've had enough ongoing issues, and management is already on board with the idea of IAM, you might already be empowered to put a working plan together. But I know what it's like to help a customer do a first pass with management, followed by a plan, followed by a second pass at management in order to validate not only the need for, and business value of, an IAM framework, but also the ability to deliver a solution. In other words, before they give you the green light, they want to make sure you're not going to crash, so they want to see that plan. We'll cover in Chapter 5 the ins and outs of putting together a more business-based presentation to management, in order to make a stronger business case, which will in turn secure budget and resources.

Resources, Both Digital and Human

Certainly putting together an IAM framework is a considerable investment in time, money, and manpower, and requires a plan. How do you go about such a daunting task? From start to finish, in very basic summary (which you'll break out in detail when you make your business case to management), let's outline what you need to put together.

The Processes

This is all about process to begin with, so start there. You must secure and augment the business. You must secure assets (the resources that actually run your business), enable users, get those users in and out of your system safely, and ultimately report on all activity. You must define those processes, including the setting, the actors, the actions, the reactions, and the end results. And of course, you want to *automate* as many of these processes as possible. Keep thinking *automation*. And by the way, when you get to the point of looking at buying or building, that's when you expand those process plans into use cases that reflect specific real-world situations.

- **Creating accounts**   You can't enable users until you give them a place to live. How will they come into the system? Bulk load? HR event? Self-registration? Will an administrator key them in? It will likely be all of the above, depending on the type of user, and you will have multiple types. Define the processes first. We'll get to the actual landing in a moment.

- **Provisioning**   How will users get access to their resources? Automatic grants based on attributes or roles? Direct assignment by managers? Resource request by self or manager? A combination of these? What approvals will be needed for requests? And what information must be communicated to the target systems so that they recognize the new users when they come calling?

- **Change management** When a user is promoted, demoted, transferred, or terminated, what needs to happen? Remember, termination is simply another state. A darn important one, but it's a change, just like a transfer, except that the terminated user tends to lose a lot more access than a transferred user.

- **Authentication and authorization** What information must a user provide in order to access resources, and what is the process for that authorization? This *must* be automated, obviously. They are two different processes, but they must happen one after the other. I log in according to requirements (password, token, pin), and then the system must authorize me right away so I can get to the good stuff. As part of that, what information must be communicated to the target system, and by what method, so that a properly authorized user can gain entry?

All these processes we just discussed will generate a lot of logging. What data is captured, *how* is that data captured, where does it go, how is it recalled, and in what form?

Everything from here on is only meant to feed those processes. This is all about getting users in and out of the business resources in a secure manner. Define those processes, and the pieces should start to make themselves obvious—you would hope. What's next?

The Requirements

You say you need to be able to get to the store, buy a lot of groceries, and get it all home. That's your process. The first requirement is transportation. So start thinking about your options.

- To fulfill the process requirements, there are supporting definitions to create. These are the objects (and yes, a user is an object) to be defined which will be players in those processes. What does a user profile look like? How about group structures? Role definitions? How will these work together? Will groups serve as roles, or vice versa? Will roles or groups be assigned via user attributes? Before you can assign privileges to a user, you must define what a user looks like, and what he needs to have in his pocket before he can receive those privileges.

- Figure out the extras you need, those gaps you need to fill, in addition to what you already have. What's not working? What's not there? What are the deltas between current and desired functionality? What is on everybody's wish list? Automation? The ability to remediate? The ability to quickly terminate? Providing access to external users? This is not to say that everything you want, or even everything you think you need, will result from this process. But there are needs, and there are *critical* needs. Focus on the immediate needs of the various parties, and how those needs might intersect, as well as how the solutions to those intersecting needs might complement each other. And while you're at it, find out what your auditors can do for you. They can be a font of information on your deltas. "During the last audit, you failed to provide these reports."

- Don't forget the things you haven't even thought of yet: new audit/compliance requirements, new resources, new user groups, new technologies, and anything else that will require agility and openness on your part down the road.

The Pieces

Now that you've figured out that you need transportation to get to and from the store, you extrapolate that requirement to mean that you need a car. So now you think in terms of the pieces you need to satisfy the requirements for your processes.

- You *will* modify your perceptions of the technologies you need as you progress and investigate what's available to buy and/or build. But you should have some notion of at the least the technical functionalities you'll need to have in place to make this work. Don't even think right away about building versus buying, but simply about actual functions.

- Inventory what you already have. What data stores are in place, and how is the data used? Which applications are operating; how are they secured and provisioned; what communications do they have with other apps; what are their data stores? What are your existing resources, and how can they help you? These can be human as well as digital assets, of course. Do you have a workflow engine? How about help desk software and personnel? You've already inventoried processes. Now determine how many of them are manual. Remember, automation.

- Build a list of what else you need—what in your identity and security infrastructure isn't working, and what the deltas are. What are your auditing requirements? What was needed for the last audit? What will the auditors want this time around?

The People

To help gather this information, to validate the requirements, to help build the case, and to provide the resources, you will need to inventory the people available to you, or at least the people you'd like to have available. There's no guarantee that when you identify a stakeholder, you will get that person on your side.

- Get management on board with the notion of providing a framework. Show them what you've put together. Make sure the people with the wallets will even let you think about possibly spending some of their money to upgrade. If the answer is no, you might still want to spend some free cycles assembling elements for a business case that might get a better hearing when the business environment improves or, heaven forbid, you suffer a breach. If the answer is "maybe" or "yes," then go ahead.

- Identify stakeholders and champions. Figure out who's on your side. You will need them. I repeat: You will need them. Sell them on the value. Remember, you may not get everybody on your side all at once, so occasionally it helps to get one or more stakeholders to help you get even more of them on board with the plan. One big suggestion: When you're trying to entice somebody to integrate their resources with the framework, be careful not to insult what they already have. Unless their homegrown, silo-based security has caused a breach, you can't beat it up. Simply sell the value of participating in the overall security umbrella. If you call their baby ugly, they in turn will set very high expectations for you.

■ Form committees to set standards and requirements. If the company will let you outline all the needs yourself, based on your cursory investigations, you will still want input. You won't think of everything yourself. And even if you could, somebody will invent something else. If the scoping and building are limited to a small group, then that group is liable. This is the opportunity for people to make their voices heard. Get a comprehensive view from the crowd, and also (sad to say) limit your liability. In other words, more voices will lend obvious weight to your arguments.

The Resources

These aren't solely your digital resources. It includes the human capital you need to get this project off the ground.

■ Explore buy vs. build compared to buy-and-build. Some stuff you'll code yourself. A lot of it you probably won't. Start searching, and match up your desires with what's available. And always remember, internal staff will often want to do it themselves, for job security reasons, and they will almost always *underestimate* the time it will take. You will be involving them, for a variety of reasons that we'll cover later, but you should remain in charge.

■ Decide on whether to get help. Whether you buy or build, or buy *and* build, can you scope, acquire, build, manage, and deploy on your own? Or will you want outside experts? Perhaps you've already got relationships with consultants who can help. Remember, these people are the opposite of your internal staff; they will almost always *overestimate* the time it will take.

■ Determine the levels of time and investment. How many resources will this take? You will surely be pulling people off their regular duties, and they will be drafting additional equipment. It will cost money and time, which is actually money *twice*. Don't discount the amount of effort you and your staff will be devoting to it. It's not just the software and consultants; it's you. Your time is valuable. A very basic deployment plan will help.

■ Engage vendors and integrators. Start dragging in the other organizations who may be providing software and/or labor. Vet them thoroughly, their capabilities, resources, expertise, estimates, references. We'll be going over this, believe me.

The Design

You can't just pick up the pieces you need. You must fit them together, so that collectively they serve your process requirements.

■ Knowing the software and hardware and labor requirements allows you to compose a more detailed design: what's prebuilt, what needs to be built, what's kept, what's tossed, and who's providing what.

■ Make the business case to management for funding. Once you've got it all tallied up, you go to the bosses and say, here's what it will take.

■ Design review. Let everybody beat it up. And this they will do. Wear your thick skin to the meetings. Sure, it's the same people who helped you come up with the requirements. Doesn't matter. Things change.

- Determine internal resource requirements. Now that you've vetted the outside folks, return to the inside folks. You will need to recalibrate your internal resource requirements after engaging vendors and consultants.

- Implementation plan. What happens in what order over how long? What are the timetables? How do you set milestones and deliverables? Who is responsible for what pieces? In what stages or phases will the deliverables arrive? You will not be doing everything in parallel, and even if you plan to do this in steps, which you should, all the things that go wrong in the first step will delay the second step. Just expect it.

- Final design. Everybody's had their second and third say. Roll it all into the plan.

The Roll-Out

It's not enough to figure out what you need in terms of process and pieces and then create a design. You need to know in practical terms how you will implement.

- **Acquire and/or build**　Start matching up software, processes, and use cases. This phase includes construction, unit testing, and enforcing timetables and deliverables.

- **Phased deployment and testing**　Actual rollout of pieces to departments. More in-depth testing.

- **Training and hand-offs**　These go hand in hand with the previous step. Train the admins on how to manage the new pieces and processes. Train the end users on what to expect.

Remembering the Goal

You won't be doing this alone, right? You're going to solicit a lot of input, as well as feedback to your *own* input. It's easy to get distracted once you've engaged all the special interests within the company, because while you might have a purpose in mind, the herd may take you in different directions. Remember to lead, and to periodically remind people of the goal(s) of your project:

- The final IAM system must serve the entire organization.

- It will take more work up front, but ultimately will save on labor.

- It must *reflect* and *augment* the business. If your company generates its profits by making widgets, it should help you make those widgets. If you sell insurance, it should help you sell insurance. IAM's not widget software? You're right. But it should allow the line-of-business people to concentrate on the widget business by taking identity and access management off their shoulders. IAM should model the organization and its job titles. It should let people in and keep people out, as dictated by business requirements. It's all about the business you're in. This is just a helpmate. It has no reason to exist except to help the business. The variations should only come when you see the opportunity to *improve* your processes. This should be apparent early and often; otherwise, why are you doing this insane thing?

- Any suggestions made by your committees should be to improve processes or make up for shortcomings in the way you do things now. Don't allow the little wish lists to take you off target.

Periodically review your high-level goals, and use them as a barometer of any recommendations or requests. Do the recommendations help the business? Do they reflect the business? Do they get you closer to helping the entire organization? Do they meet integration, reporting, and audit standards? Do they fall within the domain of what you set out to do, or are they part of some provincial need that somebody tried to tack on so they could ride your coattails? Nothing attracts followers like a project with a budget. Don't be somebody else's meal ticket. Stick to the plan.

Getting Ready to Break Things

When I was in the process of publishing my first book, I was reminded by my editor more than once, with a phrase that made my wife cringe, "Don't be afraid to give up your babies." In other words, you fall in love with something you've created—a paragraph, a phrase, a piece of software, a piece of ugly furniture you kept from a long-ago yard sale—and you don't want to give it up, even when it doesn't fit any more. But if it's in the way, if it's part of the problem, or if it simply isn't part of the solution, consider it a candidate for setting aside.

Your manual processes are working? Wonderful. But they're manual. E-mails from the boss get the approvers to move on requests? Great, as long as he remembers to send them, and he's not on vacation.

That's not to say everything's got to go. Let's say you're provisioning to customer relationship management (CRM) via some help desk app, like Remedy or Magic (which usually means opening a ticket to push requests that are ultimately fulfilled manually). If it's working, maybe you don't want to mess with it, at least for now. So when you put in your new provisioning system, perhaps you can make that help desk app one of the target systems which proxies for CRM. You may or may not change how you provision to CRM later.

Or you might say, why have the help desk app serve as a middleman? If it's going to slow up provisioning to CRM, why not put the CRM package on the framework? Remember, that's the point, to build a framework that your apps simply hitch a ride on.

One point you may wish to make to any potential vendors or partners is your desire to preserve as much of your existing investment as possible:

- Don't spend money where you don't need to.
- Don't make the transition any more difficult than it needs to be.
- If it ain't broke, don't fix it (although it might need tuning).
- If changing something will drastically interrupt service, we'll attack it later, or just differently.
- It might not be the best, but it functions for now, as long as it doesn't get in the way.
- It won't get in the way of the new stuff that we absolutely do need to build.

Whenever you take on a big project, you should expect to hear from management, why do you want that? And this is a good question. Sometimes you're so used to doing things a certain way out of necessity, you might come to find you don't need to do that any more because the new system will bring you improved processes. Here's an example.

At a huge financial services customer, one of the requirements was to perform data imports from a weirdly formatted file. Yeah, we could do that, but it was a pain, and early on we were smart enough to ask, *why do you want this*? And the reason was that their old request system required incremental data dumps from the old HR system to keep users in sync with entitlements, and that was simply the way they'd been doing it.

We said, that's dandy, but guess what? We have a connector for your HR system; we can query the data directly and bypass the whole dump–massage–upload process. On top of that, once we have the users and the entitlements in hand, we manage the synchronization and periodically reconcile users with entitlements, ensuring least privilege. So sure, we can do that upload thing, but you won't need it any more.

I spent literally years pitching, strategizing, implementing, and helping to support a multimillion-dollar IAM project at a global manufacturer. My company was forced, for political reasons, to partner with an integrator who had impressed the client. The integrator brought in a particular brand of a barely known third-party authentication tool to complement our own framework. And it worked great with one browser, but not with another. When the tool was finally modified sufficiently to work with the second browser, it broke the first.

The origin of this situation was the fact that the integrator had some kind of sweetheart reseller deal with this other tool's provider. So the wrong tool was picked for the wrong reason. This caused all sorts of problems and finger-pointing until the integrator was finally pushed off the project. One of the first things we did when they left was replace that authentication tool. Nobody complained, because there had never been an internal champion for it.

Pick the right tools and the right people for the right reasons. Don't start compromising or you will lose your way. Sure, there are always political considerations, but if you don't focus on the ultimate goal, and remind your self of that goal regularly, you may end up off course.

Determining Specific Requirements

Zen and the Art of Motorcycle Maintenance is a tough read. When you get to the end, you'll say it was worth it, but getting there isn't easy. But I took away some great lessons on writing and creating from that book. One of the most useful of those lessons (and the timing was perfect as it was just as I was transitioning from typewriters to electronic keyboards) was *not* to try to make something perfect the first time through.

Years ago, there was a cereal commercial where a guy sits on the deck of his cabin preparing to write his Great Novel. So, he sticks the paper in his Olivetti and starts typing, Chapter One. But it doesn't work that way.

In *Zen*, the author teaches you to *make a mess and then clean it up*. Before you rearrange your hall closet, you pull literally everything out of it, figure out what's staying and what's going, and only then do you put things back. Otherwise, if you only take half of your stuff out, you shift things around and it's worse than before. You have to shake things up.

So when planning your IAM project, put everything on the table. You may not actually destroy everything and rebuild from scratch, but put it out there. Make an inventory of your wants and needs, the stuff that works and the stuff that doesn't, the stuff you've never had but really need, the stuff other people (like your auditors) keep telling you that you need, and the stuff you don't absolutely need but would like to have.

It's only a wish list, right? So make a mess, and throw the kitchen sink in. A lot of wishes will never make the final cut, but nothing is set in stone to begin with.

The Essentials of IAM

Let's make a mess by tossing around the IAM functions (and these are not necessarily IT functions) you need to consider:

- **Source of truth or authority on user identity and privileges**   Where and how are you storing everybody and everything? Everybody knows they need a user store. But you also need to inventory your IT assets and their attributes. Will this data be kept in a single store, or distributed? If it's distributed, how will you aggregate it when you need to (and you *will* need to)?

- **Roles and their relationships to access**   How do you want to define and use roles? Remember, you should end up with fewer roles than people.

- **Registration, by user, by manager, by import**   How will new users be introduced to the system? For that matter, how will you get existing users into your new infrastructure?

- **Self-service**   What functions will you allow users to do for themselves, and how will you expose those functions?

- **Requests and approvals**   Who can make requests and how? Can users make request on their own behalf? Can managers request access for their employees? How do you want to notify managers that they need to take actions to enable users under their control?

- **Provisioning, re-provisioning, de-provisioning**   What will your policies look like? Remember, you want to automate as much provisioning as possible. It's more sustainable, and reduces your manual processes. You need to get users on board; you need to manage change when they, their roles, their attributes, their groups, or their place in the organization is modified. You need to get them *out* as quickly as possible. And you need all of this audited, logged, and recorded. Who did what and when? Who requested it, who approved it, who actually executed it?

- **Integration between security apps and business apps**   IAM enables users for the business now, and governs access to it later.

- **Authentication methods (what will make you feel secure?)**   What credentials, PINs, tokens, security questions, biometrics, or charm-and-good-looks will make a user acceptable?

- **Authorization/access management**   What sort of mechanism or policies do you want in place to match up assets and authenticated users? Where will the information that you need in order to determine if somebody is eligible to access a requested resource reside?

- **Coarse-grained vs. fine-grained enforcement**   How deep in the weeds are you willing or required to go in enforcing access ("this group can access these pages" versus "individuals with this value in this attribute can view this account")?

- **Compliance and how it's built into the system**   How will your framework enforce regulations *before* bad things happen?

- **Reporting and audit support**   How easy will it be to get comprehensible information out of the activity later? Do you merely need to report on what happened, or do you need to review types of activity, spot trends or reassess policies, risks, and privileges?

- **A good end-user experience**   Happy users hassle you a lot less. They speak well of the organization. They back you up when you change policies. They don't e-mail your bosses demanding your head. They cut you slack during outages or upgrades.

- **Business partner requirements**   Even if your company doesn't face certain regulatory requirements, your partners may, and therefore you can inherit those requirements. In addition, if you ultimately want your systems to interact with those of your partners, there's a whole other layer of integration, perhaps even authentication and authorization, that we'll talk about later.

- **Industry-specific needs**   Does your particular market labor under specific provisions? There are casual compliance guidelines (meaning suggestions) and strict laws (meaning absolute requirements) that target particular industries. These include insurance companies, manufacturers, drug companies, healthcare providers, higher education, and so on. We will discuss these in more detail throughout various upcoming chapters.

Governance by Committee

This is also known as "Death by Committee," because too many decision makers without common ground can bring a needed process to a halt. Everyone has an opinion, and you will hear each and every one of them. But while painful, and occasionally tedious, it is also necessary. You may absolutely know what you want and what the organization needs. You may be the smartest person in any room, the moral authority on the subject. Everybody else in the company might look to you and say, "We're all idiots, please lead us to the promised land." And still you will form at least one committee to beat up any and all suggestions that arise, and to lend weight to the results.

None of us is as smart as all of us (although all of us are slower than any one of us). It takes a village. We're all in this together. Whatever clichés you want to employ, they all apply. You need multiple eyeballs on everything. It might all be the same actual group (although chances of that aren't great), but you will need to fulfill multiple functions, which likely means multiple groups of helpers.

Still, remember this important point: Every quest requires a leader. If you're that leader, then lead. Don't let the chair or emotional leader of any particular committee sidetrack you or the project. Be in charge. But at the same time, take advantage of both the wisdom that may come from the unwashed masses, and the cover provided by the forest of bodies.

It helps to delegate a little. Assign tasks. Give responsibility. Even if you don't mean it, sell it. People will perform better for you, and certainly behave more nicely, if they feel empowered.

NOTE
It's not just about software. As you're engaging the various groups, it's about their business processes. With regard to their place in the widget-making business, what goals do they need to achieve? What responsibilities do they have? What tasks must they complete? The software's just there to serve the goals. Think "process" at all times.

Committee rule often has bad connotations, as it conjures up images of some important matter getting bogged down in endless discussions and paralysis-by-analysis. But when you're talking about something this potentially large and *strategic*, you absolutely must sanity-check the big issues.

A Preposterously True Story

Here is how not to plan an IAM project. Just before the new millennium, a large manufacturer wanted to build, deploy, and secure an international supply chain portal. The customer's project manager chose his vendors for directory, database, routers, servers, portal, and access management (my company) based strictly on demonstrations. His design methodology consisted of gathering all the vendor reps in one room at the same time for half a day and having them cook him up an architecture.

Naturally, none of the vendors saw a problem with this approach, since they were all fairly guaranteed to get a purchase order. In this room full of happy people, I was the troublemaker, asking about a project plan, an integration map, a list of deliverables. The project manager replied that the salespeople in the room were going to provide him with that blueprint for success during this half-day meeting.

It gets worse. I made the mistake of asking what his timeline actually was. He said he wanted to go live in two months. "Let me get this straight," I said, "You're going to purchase, take delivery of, install, build out, and integrate all the software and hardware, populate the directory, install the database, set up the routers in front of the servers, build your portal, set up the auth schemes, and go live in 60 days?"

The rep from their integration partner spoke up at this point and insisted, "We know it's aggressive, but we think it's workable."

By now, I'm already unpopular with the other vendors, and since we're all going to get sued anyway if we go along with this insanity, I figured, what the heck. "If you had all this stuff already installed today," I explained, "you would spend the next two months just testing. Aggressive is not the word."

Apparently because we were the only ones speaking the truth, my partner and I became the trusted advisors, and in fact got the first actual purchase order. We went live against some existing applications, while some of the other vendors were dropped. When the original manager who brought us in was moved off the project (no surprise), I ended up with a very good relationship with his successor, who called me regularly for years even about unrelated technology. The integrator was also replaced.

This is an absurd (although true) example, of course. Nobody should commit budget and energy to a bag of air. You are responsible for your own destiny. Vendors want to sell software; consultants want to generate billable hours. That said, everybody should want you to be successful, because if you fail, you're a lousy reference.

But it's your project, so lead the way. You may engage third parties to help (and in fact you likely will, for some portions), but you're on the hook. You have to tell people what you want (as well as what you'd like to have, and remember that these aren't necessarily the same things), and in order to do this, you need a plan.

If *you* are the advisor, tell people the ugly truth. And if they're going off a cliff, don't go with them. When that project fails, your name is attached. Better to know the tough stuff up front and avoid going down a ridiculous path than take a chance that has, well, little chance.

Engage Stakeholders

Involve the actual line of business owners. If you're in charge of implementing security, chances are you're not a stakeholder, a line-of-business owner, someone with something to gain through an IAM framework, or someone with something to lose by sticking with business as usual. So you'll need to pull in those people to see where they may feel security is lacking. As you compile their wants, be sure to provide two important elements:

1. **Guidance.** Let the stakeholders understand that you're building a framework, not their own personal security system. They will be part of a larger picture. Tell them you will attempt, as time and logic and budget allow, to incorporate their needs into those of the entire organization. Without the guidance of this wish list, you will die from scope creep. Be prepared if, once you start building a list, interested parties try going over your head to force you to add their pet functions to the list. Part of this guidance ought to be anticipating what kinds of wishes you're going to get from the populace, so that you can have a notion of how you're going to accommodate them (if possible) in advance. Nothing sets people at ease, and keeps them off your back, better than proactively demonstrating that you're on the case and already aware of what they need.

2. **Proper expectations.** Tell them early and often that they won't get everything they want. You will need to prioritize the bigger picture, so tell them to prioritize their *smaller* picture.

Which Committees to Assemble

Bear in mind that a lot of these committee structures will come in useful again when it's time to actually deploy a solution. They will be helping to oversee, test, validate, and ultimately govern what comes out of a deployment.

So here are the different group initiatives or committees you may want to consider.

Executives and/or Stakeholders

Depending on how big your organization is, this might be the same group. These are the same folks who presumably signed off on the work, the costs, the budget, the requirements, the staffing, and so on. Make sure they stay on board with you, mentally, physically, and financially. If you're very, very lucky, you'll only have these kinds of committee meetings to update them on your wonderful progress. If there are any hiccups, these are your opportunities to remind the bosses that nothing is guaranteed in life and you're on top of it in any event.

Resource Governance

Who will represent the various IT assets that will be folded into the new IAM system? Somebody must own or speak for those assets. There will be integration requirements, perhaps some customization, and certainly the need to determine how those assets will communicate with the new IAM pieces. It's also a good time to ask what these resource owners will require later in terms of access review (for example, attestation).

Role Governance and Segregation of Duties (SoD)

I lump these together because, while duties are often segregated at a very granular level within individual applications, the goal of SoD is to not concentrate incompatible privileges in the hands of one individual.

Role definitions play a huge part in provisioning. They serve as the bridge between the business and the technical aspects of user enablement. The business says, "You're an accounts receivables clerk," and that translates into "You get a data entry slot in Peachtree, reporting rights in Oracle Financials, this set of menus in Siebel, and this set of reports in the CRM package."

What goes into a role from the top to the bottom has to be agreed upon, in a management sense, from the top to the bottom. HR and/or upper management decides what jobs need to exist just to run the place, middle management decides what actual job functions go into each position, and IT helps map the IT assets to those job functions.

If and when you perform role discovery on existing user-privilege data (something we'll discuss in functional detail in Chapter 9), what you end up with are resource-level roles, or application/resource level roles. These are the contents of a business or enterprise role. To reiterate, a job title or position is the equivalent of a business role. It gives you access to all the resource-level roles you need in order to do your job. Each resource-level role contains all the little privileges needed to execute that role.

If you're enforcing privilege-level SoD, there's a chance that nobody on your committee will have the information they need to create those policies. If you produce or purchase a library of these, and they exist for a number of off-the-shelf packages, then you're pretty well set. Recreating those kinds of libraries is not a fun business. Sometimes they come as part of an enforcement package, but otherwise you can typically provide them as source data for your provisioning or access control software.

If you're going to enforce SoD at a higher level, all the better for you. It's far easier. But be aware, as much as this idea is beloved, and is even supported by the National Institute of Standards and Technology (NIST) standard for RBAC, it won't necessarily get you through an audit. Find out what your auditors will insist on.

If your IAM software supports it, it's a great thing to associate roles with branches or individual nodes of the organization. Not only does this help with automatic role grants and approvals, but it also lets you take two possible approaches on higher-level SoD. If you have a position down one branch, it prevents you from having one in another branch. And whatever software you run, it had better support role grant policies. Within these policies, you should be able to specify inclusion and exclusion rules. To have a role, you should be in a particular group or branch or line of business. Or perhaps to have a role you must specifically *not* be in a particular group or branch or line of business. So these policies that I keep harping about should help you create prerequisites and also walls of functional segregation.

Audit/Compliance Requirements

Your financial department is probably a good place to start when recruiting for this group. Compliance really starts with the money. But it certainly doesn't end there. You may have industry-specific regulations that must be addressed via IT security. Insurance, healthcare, higher education, and a host of other arenas of special interest have their own requirements.

Audit support too often gets put off until you're scrambling during that first post-IAM audit. You can't get the reports out of it that you need. Or those reports are all custom. Don't let the vendor or partner slide by with a wink and "Oh yeah, we can squirt that out later." Ask to see examples. One of the first? Attestation. But remember, with a proper provisioning tool, attestation isn't just a report; it's a process with a report that comes out at the end. It shouldn't *be* just a report.

Of course, your outside auditors, just to show they're doing their job, *will* ask for custom reports, so make sure your report writer is up to the task. There's nothing sneaky or illegal about going to your auditors, asking what they'll want to see, and just plain telling them that you're putting a new IAM framework in place.

Roll-Out Plan

This committee will actually have two functions. First, planning a phased rollout and sanity-checking it with the rest of the crew. They need to devise a reasonable plan. The other function is devising a communication plan that will keep the organization in the loop as the rollout is taking place.

Let's start with communications. There will be hiccups and surprises. There will also be a lot of good stuff. By keeping the corporate populace informed, you will insulate yourself to some degree when the inevitable mistakes do occur. You're also providing named personnel who can field questions. Set up an internal blog, an e-mail list, a landing page, or all of the above so that everybody knows what's going on, what will happen and when. Let them know the proper channels to use when they have questions: call this number, click this link, e-mail this contact.

Okay, so there's the communication of what you're doing. Now, you must do it. While it might be fairly simple to place the entire organization under a basic authentication bubble, it might take a bit more to get everybody integrated with the single sign-on umbrella. You have to teach SSO how to provide the necessary attributes (quite often header variables) to each application following the initial authentication. But even then, SSO is one of those low-hanging fruits.

A *huge* part of rollout planning is deciding which resources get brought on board and in what order. You may decide on some combination of resources that

- Are most critical to the business
- Are SOX-based
- Have already been breached
- Are owned by key stakeholders or budget masters
- Have the most users
- Process the most daily transactions
- Are customer-facing
- Are managed by staff who have the cycles to help

Cut-Over

Yes, yes, you're rolling out in phases. But for each individual component, there's a single nanosecond in history when you move from no-framework/old-framework to new-framework. You throw the switch and *bang*, you're now authenticating against the new web server plug-ins and new directory and so on. For new applications being launched, you have the opportunity to beat them up in a test environment. Yes, you can do this with the existing resources as well, but now you're talking about people in production suddenly being thrust into a new scheme.

For the last large cut-over I worked on, we kept a couple of dozen willing volunteers behind on a Friday evening, performed the necessary actions to move from one platform to the other, then had people sit down, log in, and go through several use cases using recoverable production scenarios. Recoverable, in case something completely unexpected occurred. This was not the same as unit testing or load testing. These were real people. This was more nerve-wracking than the load testing with a hundred times that number of virtual bodies, because these volunteers could point out our mistakes, real-time, and in what had now become the live, production system. There was one small glitch, quickly remedied, but all the hundreds of hours of prep paid off.

In a global operation, it's obviously a different story. But if you have segregated environments, or a scheduled blackout, it's possible to do this. There is *never* a good time for a shutdown, even a well-publicized, scheduled shutdown. Someone will always complain. No way to avoid it. With luck and preparation, it should be very brief.

Here's why a committee is a good thing here: planning the actual cut-over day. Consider this. There's Day One, and there's everything after. This is the Day One Committee. The really ugly stuff, as in loss of service, broken links, people who suddenly can't authenticate, people who panic because they haven't listened to all the information you've been broadcasting all along, all that stuff happens on that first day. Once you get past that day, it gets better. Even when things go smoothly, and with enough planning they will, things will also be *different*, and all the individual users who didn't take advantage of your rollout blog or emails will be in the dark. Nobody listens to the flight attendant when she's explaining how to escape in the event of a water landing, right? Nobody pays attention to the first five e-mails warning you to change your password before it expires, right? Same deal here. The Cut-Over Crew will remind people as the fateful day approaches that it is indeed coming, and they will be there to hold the hands of all the idiots who ignored them.

An Iterative Process

This approach requires multiple passes. As you have your meetings and get your committee feedback, you will revise your plan and your ideas. You will reprioritize multiple times. You won't get this right the first time through.

No matter how much you plan, something will go wrong. It's inescapable. But the more you plan, the less will go wrong. And the more you communicate, the less people have a right to complain. Communication is also a two-way street. You put out information, and you get opinions in return, and some of them may be quite valuable. You don't know what you don't know.

If basic name and password are not sufficient for all lines of business, then you will not get instant agreement on a common authentication scheme. And IT professionals who are used to doing everything based on LDAP often feel that group memberships are sufficient arbiters of authorization; others depend on attributes, organizational placement, and relationships, while more sophisticated approaches employ roles. The point is that consensus is an elusive goal, requiring the revisiting and negotiating of the ultimate solutions.

In Chapter 5, we'll discuss in greater detail how to make the ultimate business case to management, that is, explaining the value of IAM to the enterprise. Once again, having at least the semblance of a plan will provide the appearance, and the structure, of organized thought. If you get the go-ahead, then this planning, your committees, your lists of must-haves and wants, will form the basis for your actual deployment plan. It would be nice if you could just get to where you're going. But you need a map, and gas money.

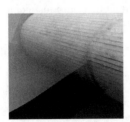

CHAPTER
4

Compliance
Considerations

It is a very easy thing to devise good laws; the difficulty is to make them effective.
                                        —Bolingbroke, trying to interpret Sarbanes-Oxley

ne of the big complaints about the book *Moby Dick* is that, right smack in the middle of it, the author digresses with a chapter on whaling. He interrupts the story about a kid named Ishmael to explain to you what this whaling thing is all about.

So here is the whaling chapter. Many, many IAM projects are now being launched *because* of regulatory compliance requirements. At the very least, your IAM project will have to contend with at least some aspects of compliance, so we're going to digress on the subject. Compliance requires that companies put IAM in place, so it generates the demand for IAM controls. And because compliance *should be* baked into your framework, it also generates design considerations. So for these two reasons, let's do a brain-dump on many of the possible regulations that have been enacted just to make your life more difficult—I mean, to guide your organization into becoming more secure. That's what I meant to say.

Face it, while there are many aspects to compliance that are very necessary to protect both the consumer and the enterprise, and compliance has driven countless companies to create or improve the processes that should have been in place already, there are still parts to compliance that you address simply because you have no choice. Even if they don't benefit you directly, there's a compelling reason. Auditors will beat you about the head and shoulders if you don't meet the prescribed provisions, because that's their job, and because they do not make their money or enhance their reputations by telling you how wonderfully you do everything.

The following sections focus for the most part on those compliance laws that pertain to elements you would find in a security framework. There are compliance requirements governing business processes that are regulated from the boardroom, and have little to no relevance to IAM (for example, Basel II). I am mostly bypassing these and concentrating on those laws which can be encoded into your policies for identity and access management.

What Compliance Typically Includes

In the interest of being redundant, let me restate: Compliance does not mean reporting. Logging and reporting activity is a part of compliance, but for the sake of security and liability, you want to prevent bad activity more than you want to discover it after the fact.

While the United States has often been seen as being at the forefront of both technology and regulation, it hasn't always led the way. Germany blazed the trail for requiring digital signatures, for example, and Asia Pacific (APAC) has been out front in terms of risk assessment.

Laws have been enacted for consumer protection, political considerations, or occasionally both (for example, Gramm-Leach-Bliley). Various scandals and breaches have certainly driven passage of provisions (Sarbanes-Oxley, Massachusetts 201). And even if you aren't necessarily in a particular industry (finance, telecommunications, medical) or state of being (private versus public), you may still be subject to the laws that govern those industries or states because you do business with others who are.

Your auditors will be more than happy to tell you what your requirements are. Your CFO should certainly be able to help there. Your business partners and customers will tell you without reservations what *they* need out of you.

Compliance Components

If I were to summarize the mandates of all the many international compliance laws, the list would be something like this:

- Protecting private data
- Transparency
- Change management
- Risk management
- Controls on access and policies
- Monitoring and reporting
- Audits
- Conflicts
- Oversight
- Disclosures
- Responsibility

Some of these apply to actual IT touchpoints, while others apply to business processes. Of course, IT can support, frame, and even drive those processes. But to do that, compliance needs to be in your system's DNA.

What Compliance Should Include

Compliance should be part of your design because it *should not be a bolt-on*. Compliance needs to be woven into the very fabric of your IAM framework. Compliance isn't just reporting after the fact. Compliance is directly related to policies and processes that should be part of all your thinking and doing in the context of IAM. Compliance–policies–process: It's a three-headed dog. As a package, they do this for you in regards to who gets what, who does what, who sees what:

- Determine what should happen.
- Ensure that this is what happens.
- Figure out what just happened.

You determine what should happen by employing policy-driven user creation and provisioning. I give you an account, and then I give you only the access you should have.

You ensure this condition by employing resource-centric authentication and policy-based authorization. You have to provide sufficient credentials for the resource you're trying to reach, and your profile must match the appropriate policies for said resource, in order to gain access day to day. To ensure that these policies are followed, reconciliation automatically reviews (on a schedule) who has access to what, and remediates any situation where a user is out of policy.

Attestation compels managers to manually review these accesses as well. We'll be talking about these last two processes in just a moment.

Finally, you figure out what happened with reporting and analytics.

Too many people think of compliance as reporting. This is completely wrong. *Wrong*. The reporting part is only there to make sure that you've been compliant all along. If you've had a material breach, all the reports are going to do for you at that point is verify that yes, you are truly in trouble, and this is going to cost you.

There's stuff you do because you want to, and stuff you do because you must. Happily, the twain sometimes do meet. And this is how policies are born.

Face it, if you're the reporting organization, a lot of security rules you follow, especially the regulatory stuff, aren't to protect you from anybody. They're to protect everybody from *you*. Accountability, transparency, privacy, data protection. That said, they're still good things. But boy, do they create a lot of work.

Remember "Pirates of the Caribbean" when it's said that the Pirate Code isn't really a law so much as a set of guidelines? Well, for a few years, compliance initiatives were the same, really just strong suggestions. But then the more serious provisions started kicking in, like time-release cold capsules, and companies started facing real fines. Some companies find that the cost of fixing their compliance flaws outweighs the penalties, so they just keep paying those penalties.

One of the things I keep hearing from universities is that they don't fear the malicious breach so much as the stupid mistake. I've heard some awful stories from big schools as far as very sensitive data that was exposed because of data extracts, downloads, and the innocuous (if incredibly dumb) posting of data on a school portal.

Most companies are well-aware of their SoD situation, and many retain their SoD violations simply because it's easier business-wise to let people do double-duty, even if their duties conflict; they need certain people in certain slots to keep doing their thing.

Auditors will tell you that you'd better be strictly enforcing SoD, and severely limiting exceptions. Companies will tell you that as long as they fully document their exceptions, they keep getting away with them. "Look, we know this would be wrong as a regular practice, but it was only for a week, and see, we specifically recorded who approved it and when and for how long."

But let's double back a minute. The rules are there to protect everybody from *you*? Well, sort of. But compliance is also your great excuse for strengthening your controls. Many organizations take their cues for tightening up their processes from compliance mandates. And if you want or need IAM in place, compliance is your biggest stick to wave at management.

Let's look at some of the general aspects of compliance, the kinds of things regulatory provisions require (at least as far as they apply to IAM), before we look at the compliance laws themselves.

Controls

The impetus for the day-to-day aspects of compliance revolves around access, that is, who can look at, review, enter, report on, or delete what. This equates to authentication (logging in, proving your identity to the system) and authorization (once you're in, what it is you can actually do). Sounds simple enough, except that before somebody can authenticate and be authorized, they first must be registered in the company directory, have all pertinent account information established, request the access, and be approved (likely by multiple approvers).

This requires a full-blown provisioning process for granting appropriate access, automating approvals, handling changes to profiles that would affect access, de-provisioning upon transfer or termination, and an authentication/authorization model that enforces access policies.

By the way, the one single thing that almost all compliance laws around the world have in common is access control. That is, they decide who gets access to what. If this is in place, a lot of the other requirements fall into line.

Privacy

The original tagline for Spider-Man is "With great power comes great responsibility." When it comes to storing identities, the tagline is, "With lots of data comes lots of liability."

Whatever information you handle, you must secure. It used to be that everybody wanted every piece of data they could get their hands on. And for telemarketers, that's still the case. But one of the gentle pushes for federation these days is the notion that being an identity-handler is fine, but being an identity-keeper can be a land mine. If you keep names and numbers in your database, you'd better make sure they only come out when absolutely necessary. Social security numbers, account numbers, contact info, dependents, phone numbers, hat size—they all need to be sealed up tight.

Attestation and Reconciliation

It's either called attestation, certification, or recertification, depending on the phases of the moon. They all mean the same thing. Let's go with attestation for now. It describes the process by which you periodically review who has access to a particular resource. Point to a resource, produce the list of everybody who can currently access that resource, and decide if they still can. If a user is deemed no longer worthy to access that resource, his access is revoked. If it's a critical application, defined as processing critical data, indispensable to the business, or related to compliance processes, it is reviewed every three to six months. Everything else is reviewed perhaps once a year.

Attestation is most often a manual process. An IT guy produces the lists, sneaker-nets them to all the approvers, who then mark up those lists and hand them back in, and finally the IT guy fat-fingers any scribbled-up changes. For example, every name highlighted in red loses their access for the designated resource. Anybody highlighted in yellow is somebody whom the approver can't vouch for, so that user must be rerouted to another approver.

Ouch. It's all dependent on a slow, error-prone process. If the IT guy misses somebody, that user may end up keeping access they are supposed to lose. I worked with a public utilities company for whom a single resource could take two weeks to complete attestation. Once the auditors had established the fact that attestation was now a completely necessary, ongoing requirement, the process absorbed a full-time person who then became the de facto attestation body. Overnight they lost a headcount to this requirement.

Reconciliation is the automated version of attestation. It ensures proper access, but strictly according to policies and without eyeballs. A lot of systems don't have this capability, but it's a great way to ensure that your policies are adhered to. In theory, reconciliation is an automated process that reviews policies on a scheduled basis and puts back anything that's out of place. For example, as part of your sales management job, you get access to the forecasting system to review your region's pipeline. But you want to get an occasional look at the pipelines for the other regions, to see how you stack up, so you fat-finger your way into the membership of the other LDAP groups that give you this ability. Reconciliation would come along at noon, see that you've got something you're not supposed to have, send a notification to your boss, and pull your id out of those other groups.

In Chapter 12, I will discuss the absolute best possible method for automating attestation, reducing the process from days or weeks to hours, and guaranteeing that no user falls through the cracks.

Segregation of Duties (SoD)

SoD in essence says that certain duties defined within your organization are incompatible with other ones, so you either get one set or the other, but you can't have both; otherwise, you have a conflict of interest. You cannot request a payment that you yourself will approve. I once advised a mortgage company where their worst-case scenario had been an officer who'd approved his own multimillion-dollar loan.

Even better are *enforceable formulae*. You can't have Privilege A if you already have Privilege B, that's easy. What about a combination, where you can't have A if you already have B and C? Even better.

Everyone assumes you're going to enforce SoD at one level, deep in the weeds. If one job function excludes another job function, what about the individual buttons and widgets on the screen that are associated with those functions? Which individual application privileges are incompatible with which others? This is often what auditors want to see. Enforcing at the level the auditors often want is a lot of work. It's like scrubbing a floor with a toothbrush. If you are allowed to enforce SoD at a job or group level, not only is it easier, but when you actually provision users at that level, the jobs or groups include or exclude the privileges as part of the package. If you can't have the job, that means you won't be granted all the privileges (and the accompanying conflict) that go with it.

A little later, under compliance solutions, we'll discuss the ways to enforce SoD at those different levels, along with the ins and outs of the different methods.

Audit Support

Anybody who's ever worked in IT and has had to support an audit knows what it's like to be the Gunga Din of reporting. "Here, son, I need a printout of all purchases of this inventory item from the first of the year through the first of June, sorted by vendor, and within vendor sorted by quantity. Oh, and get me a sandwich."

I've worked with various systems supporting certain crucial pieces of functionality that can be a giant ROI at audit time.

- Event scheduling
- Enterprise reporting
- Read-only interfaces
- Virtualization or data vault
- Forensics
- Analytics

These items not only help tactically during the actual, physical presence of auditors, but they also aid you strategically in preparing for audits, as well as creating an environment in which audits shouldn't scare the pants off you. Let's walk through all of the functionalities I just listed and what they do to help you be audit-friendly, or at least not audit-phobic.

Event Scheduling

By events, I'm talking about those processes that you can schedule to keep your system in top shape from an auditing perspective. Scheduling in and of itself may not have tons of value, if you're already on top of which events need to take place on a regular basis. But who can truly track and manage all those events without a little help? Besides that, scheduling implies, and even enforces, a little discipline.

Look, it's the end of the month, or it's been six months, or it's been a year already. You're getting nagged. Here's your notification, your reminder, you need to perform attestation. Better yet, attestation is performing itself; you simply have to perform the accept-reject cycle it's prompting you for.

Attestation is the perfect example of an event to throw on a scheduler. Critical apps, SOX-based apps, the resources that contain your most precious assets—they get attested to more regularly, on a tighter schedule. The rest? Maybe once a year. Define them, define their scope, the user groups and resource groups involved, wind them up, schedule their frequency, and they should show up like clockwork. By maintaining these strict schedules, you are uber-prepared at audit time.

Look, Mr. Auditor, here's the record of our certifications.

Reconciliation is even more schedule-ready, since it's an automated procedure (again, assuming your solution supports this). It might run as often as every night. Automated processes, of course, must be scheduled based on more than criticality. If they are CPU hogs, or memory-intensive, you need to measure how much impact they have on other processes.

Sure, you can go back and run reports for any particular point in time (although snapshot-style reports that tell you the exact condition or circumstance for any point in time are something that not every system supports). But reporting is something that should be run on a regular basis to prove that you are tracking user activity and process data. In other words, the data in the reporting is valuable, obviously, but the reporting has value unto itself. "Look, Mom, I'm doing my job!"

Enterprise Reporting

You may think that this is a terribly obvious thing to include. But the term "enterprise reporting" is tossed around so casually that it's come to mean "real good reporting." Let's put a solid definition on this one.

Enterprise reporting means being able to bring together data from across the organization into a single, logical view, to create a useful, business-oriented presentation of that data. This means cross-platform, cross-department, and self-explanatory.

The people who acquire the sheet metal are in a completely different department, using completely different applications, from the people who subsequently turn that sheet metal into ductwork. But when looking at the big manufacturing resource planning picture of when orders in the pipeline can be fulfilled, you need to look at materials as well as manufacturing. Profits are calculated on revenue over expenses. And so on.

This may also require ETL capabilities, meaning *Extract, Transform, and Load*. This means dragging data from whatever source in whatever format, reformatting it to a form that is digestible by your report writer, and sticking into a database accessible by that report writer.

In order to aggregate this disparate data, you may further need a data warehouse to bring that data together for easy, timely reporting.

On top of this functionality, let's add a few layers of usability:

- Report wizards for users who are allergic to things like database schema
- Reports generated on schedule or on demand
- Report templates (*canned* report skeletons that can be modified as needed)
- The ability to specify a target format (PDF, Word, Excel, CSV, and so on)
- Target delivery method (SMTP, FTP, or just plain dump it in a folder)

Forensics

It's incredibly handy to specify a date range and pull up transactions, changes, or requests that took place within that range. But forensics is just a hair different. Specify a timeframe, then examine the entire picture of a change that took place. For example, pick a person's status for a given day, following a given request, and look at

- What the user's privileges were before the change
- What the change was, who made it, and who approved it
- What the user's privileges were after the change

Forensics is about re-creating events, where the circumstances and players came from, and how they evolved. Forensics in the IT world is often associated with deducing the origins of an attack. But now we're talking about IAM. Forensics means trying to determine how one or more users received access to a critical resource.

Analytics

Reporting? Good. Forensics? Great. Analytics? Fantastic.

A couple of years ago, Gartner conducted a survey regarding how different organizations defined the term *analytics* and found it was all over the map. In the same way that years ago all the portal vendors seemed to migrate toward the terms "app server" and "content server" as the portal market soured, plenty of reporting tools and business intelligence (BI) companies have started abusing the term "analytics."

Analytics does not mean Online Analytical Processing (OLAP). It's definitely not just reporting. Here is the correct opinion on what analytics *should* mean.

It's analysis of an action or request, the circumstances and context around that action/request, and the (possible) prompting of a reaction. You could say that any access policy that allows or disallows a resource request is performing mini-analytics, but in fact true analytics goes deeper than that.

Insurance companies have long used analytics to determine risk. For example, an applicant's credit score can actually be used to determine their likelihood of filing an auto claim. Retailers target marketing campaigns and mass snail- or e-mail customers most likely to buy whatever it is they're selling. Obviously this is most useful in hard mails, since those involve far more material cost. So analytics are used to not only generate new revenue, but simultaneously spend more efficiently.

Now with those examples, you could argue that analytics has more business than compliance value. And in many ways it does. But analytics can drive examination of compliance issues, such as the discovery of fraud detection rates, risk analysis, or SoD violations.

Let's examine a couple of examples. First, here's a normal business transaction. It involves illegal activity, but hey, that *is* something businesses deal with every minute of the day.

- Thief tries using stolen credit card at gas pump.
- Thief enters incorrect zip code when prompted.
- Transaction is refused.

Since we're talking about IAM, here's another:

- User requests a role with certain privileges.
- User already has another role with conflicting privileges.
- Role request is flagged for either denial or granting of an exception.

Depending on how, where, and when SoD is enforced, it could also go like this:

- User requests roles with conflicting privileges.
- User receives both roles.
- When user tries to actually exercise one of those roles, actual action is flagged and prevented.

Just to quickly digress… the better way to handle that last situation is to stop the role request before it's granted. The user knows up front he can't have both roles, and can ask for an exception, if it's warranted, before a business situation comes up that requires immediate attention. Because if I'm that user, I say, don't give it to me now if you're going to tell me I can't use it later.

Healthcare agencies in the United States employ analytics against their Medicare payments to prepare for, or proactively appeal, Recovery Audit Contractor (RAC) audits. When a medical claim is filed, it is *coded* for viability. In healthcare, incorrect coding can lead to improperly denied claims, and insurance companies are often accused of doing just that, because a claim denial is a cost savings. Analytics can also identify not only coding outliers (cases that fall outside the statistical norm for costs), but also the factors that led to the anomalous coding in the first place. With healthcare reform so much in the news as of 2009 and 2010, this subject will only increase in scope and attention.

Data Retrieval

This has nothing to do with additional tools or add-ons to an IAM system. I'm talking about functionality that should be an intrinsic part of an IAM system, namely the ability to always say, "I can get there from here," no matter where you start.

I'm always astounded when I hear about systems whose data designs don't allow you to pull open definitions of objects. You should be able to navigate anywhere *from* anywhere. For example, you should be able to conjure up, without customization:

- All roles for a user
- All privileges for a user

- All privileges within a role
- All roles in which a particular privilege is used
- All users who possess a particular role
- All groups for a user
- All users for a group

We're way past the point where canned reports get the job done. I don't want to have to generate a report for every possible anomaly. Let me have a quick look by clicking a few buttons.

What helps in this endeavor is a well-planned schema. It doesn't matter how good your engine is, if the desired analysis or report requires writing SQL joins that look like spaghetti. You should not need to cross-correlate multiple screens or reports in order to find the results you want. Bad schemas translate to *can't get there from here*. Good schemas let you navigate from any point to any other point.

In Oracle Identity Manager or Oracle Identity Analytics, for example, everything is a container, and everything is content.

- A business role contains resource roles.
- A resource role contains privileges.
- A resource role contains the business roles that include it.
- An entitlement contains the resource roles that include it.
- A business role contains users.
- A users contains his multiple business roles.
- An entitlement contains the users who have that privilege because of their roles, and so on.

Given this cat's cradle of how everybody's related to everybody else, directly or indirectly, I should always be able to *get there from here*. So if I want to know who could possibly have the ability to access a certain folder via the folder entitlement, I can walk back up the tree from entitlement to resource role to business role to users.

In an ideal situation, you shouldn't even think in terms of reporting. You should think in terms of *on-demand tactical data delivery*. To monitor my resources, to satisfy the auditors, to analyze my users' behavior and evolve my policies accordingly, I should be able to get instant analysis. Again, this should not be an additional tool, but rather functionality that is baked in.

Now that we've had an overview of the kinds of tools that enforce or support compliance, let's look at the compliance laws themselves.

Regulatory Compliance Laws

There have always been rules in place to govern how companies do business. I'm big on capitalism; it's how I paid for my house. But unchecked capitalists have the ability to do a lot of damage, and that's why government has long provided oversight. Naturally, for as long as there have been rules, there have been people skirting those rules. For example, in the United States, it's long been the rule that your auditor can't also do consulting work for you because of the seemingly obvious conflict of interest. And yet I saw all sorts of examples of this very behavior (pre-Enron) with the explanation, "It's okay as long as their board signs a waiver."

We've covered some of the aspects of compliance as they apply to IAM. These laws are far broader than that, but there are whole books just about compliance laws themselves.

What makes it tough is knowing the context of the laws. What applies in one country probably won't apply exactly the same way in another. And within the United States, it's even confusing when crossing state borders. An international standard might be a standard, sure, but that doesn't make it an international law.

In general, far too many compliance laws are far too vague. That kind of wiggle room has led to numerous lawsuits in numerous countries, primarily filed by companies claiming that they've been improperly sanctioned. Sarbanes-Oxley (aka SOX) is a good example. Ambiguity has also led some authorities to rewrite or augment their original laws, for the sake of both the government and the governed. In India, their 2000 law governing information technology was originally far too vague on "certifying authorities," "reasonable security measures," and other provisions, leading to controversy and major revisions. Tom Marchok, a very smart gentleman who's been in the identity and security business a long time, once told me, "Saying that you're SOX-compliant is like saying you can make good barbecue. There's no precise definition for either."

By contrast, in the United States, PCI compliance is fairly specific, or at least most of the provisions are. The Philippines enacted a law regulating the use of "access devices," and the folks who wrote it were smart enough to take the time to actually define what they meant by "access device" and "use." This reduces the fuzziness in the enforcement. Definitions, in fact, are one of the weak spots in the compliance business. The word "firewall," for example, is used loosely and badly by several of these laws.

Organizations must detect and prevent security failures by monitoring user IDs, passwords, and access. A big component of it is *de-provisioning*, which we've discussed, and will discuss further yet. Also watch for a mention of confidential data when we discuss penetration testing.

Let's do a world tour of compliance regulations. If it were completely, utterly comprehensive, this whaling chapter would stretch on for another book. But we can examine the structure and scope of the bigger regulations, and try to take away their commonalities. By understanding the general intent of these laws, we can create identity and security frameworks that provide protection not only from the threats these laws are meant to thwart, but also from the penalties these laws can inflict.

Also bear in mind the idea of *flexibility*. Sure, you can build a framework that supports compliance (to the best of your ability to define compliance), but you don't know what's coming down the road. Make sure that your framework allows you to migrate as regulations are created, revised, or suddenly morph from friendly suggestion to strict law.

The United States

The United States appears to have far more compliance laws than any ten other countries put together. That's not even taking into account the collection of state laws, which vary in their mandates. In some states, you can't publish somebody's Social Security number or credit card number. In other states, this is only a violation if published alongside the bearer's name. We'll concentrate on the more well-known and industry-specific laws, the ones touching the most organizations as well as individuals.

Infrastructure, Healthcare, and the Public Good

The North American Electric Reliability Corporation (NERC) is an organization of North American electric grid operators, tasked with ensuring the reliability of U.S., Canadian, and Mexican power systems. NERC devised a set of standards for cyber security known as Critical Infrastructure Protection (CIP). These standards can almost be used as a blueprint for anyone, in any industry, for assembling the information needed to construct an IAM framework, as well as physical security of internal systems.

What is the very first requirement of NERC CIP? Identify critical assets. Make that inventory. Know what you've got. I don't know how many customer meetings I've attended where the various parties within the organization were learning about each other's applications and databases for the first time. When performing a formal security audit, the first task is defining a security perimeter and identifying all the resources that sit behind it.

Next, wrap those assets with security management, policies, process, procedures, classification of incidents, reporting, and data security itself. This is all about workflow, roles, access policies, and enterprise reporting. CIP-004 involves personnel and training, including risk assessment.

Once again, we find *ambiguity*. CIP-003 calls for "minimum security management controls." Who's to say what "minimum" is? Better yet, for the sake of security and liability, how about "maximum"?

CIP includes risk assessments. These are combinations of a possible action, who's requesting, what are they requesting, how are they requesting, and when are they requesting. Put it all together, and give it a score. What do you allow, what do you deny, and when do you say, "I'll allow it, but only after you give me your PIN"?

CIP also requires security patch management, monitoring (see what's happening), logging (tell me what already happened), and incident response planning (what do we do when things happen).

Here's another important definition in CIP. It's called Supervisory Control and Data Acquisition (SCADA). In essence, the systems that monitor and control the grid. In theory, a hacker seizing control of SCADA can control the power grid. For this reason, SCADA is considered a "key vulnerability," and it's recommended by many experts that SCADA systems never be web-enabled. But guess what? That's happening anyway. I see utilities walking through that recommendation as if it were paper tape. So the answer is to secure the thing to death. NERC audits are among the most stringent of any kind, because a failure in the system can mean power outages and downright disaster.

The International Traffic in Arms Regulations (ITAR) require validation of any export of arms. But here's the kicker; these regulations also govern the export of *technical data* relevant to arms exports to any foreign national, even on U.S. soil. For this reason, organizations concerned with ITAR try to protect this data at the DBMS level as well as the front door. It doesn't matter if you've got access management on your portal if you're sending off data dumps.

The Fair and Accurate Credit Transactions Act of 2003 (aka FACT Act or FACTA) was passed by the U.S. Congress in 2003 as an amendment to the Fair Credit Reporting Act, allowing citizens to request a free credit report once a year from each of the three major credit-reporting companies (Equifax, Experian, and TransUnion). To this end, the three parties put up annualcreditreport.com to provide the appropriate access. FACTA also allows for citizens to place alerts on their credit histories to prevent identity theft. FACTA further calls for fraud alerts, the truncation of credit and debit card numbers, and the dreaded "red flag" rules that are the most concern to small businesses, since provisions that were (possibly) meant to cover large institutions were so broadly written as to cover just about any business at all. The terms "creditor," "financial institution," and "covered account" left too much wiggle room for interpretation. In addition, some consumer groups complained that FACTA overrode existing, stricter laws. Good intentions do not a good law make.

Congress passed the Communications Assistance for Law Enforcement Act (CALEA) in October 1994 to require telecomm manufacturers and carriers to configure their equipment to support surveillance activities. Since then, ISPs and VOIP providers have been defined as being included. Congratulations, you're part of Big Brother. Any organizations providing Internet access, including schools, are in the mix.

The Family Educational Rights & Privacy Act (FERPA) is designed to protect the private data of students. While parents and guardians usually manage their children's data, once a kid reaches college, he's old enough to make his own calls. If a parent (or anybody else, for that matter) wants to see the medical, educational, or other confidential data kept by a university on a student's behalf, the student must give the okay. You might say, "Hey, I'm the dad, I'll look at whatever I want, because I'm paying for all this expensive schooling." But I've spoken to all sorts of administrators in the higher education arena with stories of divorced parents who try to weasel confidential data from schools. In some cases, sadly enough, it was for the purposes of somehow getting back at an estranged spouse through the child. FERPA's been around for decades, although it has been amended, and is strictly enforced.

The Health Insurance Portability and Accountability Act (HIPAA) is a set of standards for protecting electronic health data. Even if you're not in the healthcare business, you need to worry about HIPAA. If you *are* in the healthcare business, you live and breathe HIPAA. By the way, there's also a version of this that covers dependents, the Children's Online Privacy Protection Act (COPPA), which covers every single aspect of online security you can think of.

HIPAA's Privacy Rule establishes standards for the use and disclosure of patient data as well as informing those patients of their privacy rights and ability to control use of their data. Nobody likes regulations, naturally. My doctor hates the idea that, without express written consent, he's not allowed to leave what could be vital information resulting from tests on a patient's voicemail, because an unauthorized individual might hear it. But it's all or nothing. Sure, you don't care who gets and passes on the message, "You need to come to the emergency room right now." But maybe you don't want your wife to be the first one to hear, "Mr. Knaggs, you need to come in for a penicillin shot for that thing you picked up during that business trip to Vegas."

A division of the Department of Health and Human Services is on the hook for enforcing these standards and investigating complaints. This includes imposing penalties when privacy rules are violated. An offending party may (or may not) get some slack if they were unaware of a failure to comply, but if the party *should have been aware*, then ignorance is no defense. If you own the data, you're responsible for safeguarding it. If there is no "willful neglect," and the failure is corrected within 30 days of notification, or if the Department of Justice has already prosecuted, then you're in the clear. It is this kind of loophole that makes HIPAA look much kinder than NERC. However, if you're keeping an eye out, you should be avoiding that 30-day time bomb and preventing a breach in the first place, right?

Knowingly obtaining or misusing health data can cost you $50,000 and a year in prison. "False pretenses" and the intent to use the data for profit can ratchet those penalties up to $250,000 and ten years. Luckily, the cap on penalties for a calendar year is only $1.5 million. Drop in the bucket.

Fine-grained access control is a good value-add in supporting HIPAA. Just because another doctor is checking out your case doesn't mean he should get to see everything about you. Nobody who's not properly authorized should be able to review your medical data.

You can always spot the security wannabe in a meeting when he misspells HIPAA, most commonly as HIPPA.

True Story

While visiting my then-company's HQ back in the late nineties, I stumbled into a jovial conversation between company officers who were laughing about which staff members were on Prozac.

In addition to HIPAA, there are of course Medicare and Medicaid requirements, and as every party in the healthcare field begins adopting the use of Electronic Health Records (EHR), there will be additional requirements. In theory it simplifies communication for purposes of making sure patients get the right care, don't get conflicting prescriptions, are properly referred to other physicians, and are properly billed. Medicare payments could be streamlined as well. Okay, there's the big money, right? And with big money go big requirements, including access control. EHR is a bit hairy in that the standards are fresh off the press. As of July 2009, the Healthcare Information Technology Standards Panel has approved EHR standards that are aligned with the healthcare IT portions of the federal stimulus package. The standards include schema, interoperability standards, and information exchange. Whenever information is aggregated and exchanged, again you have the need to control who sees what.

California SB 1386 requires that organizations notify California residents if their personal data is compromised. And of course the ideal here is to disallow that compromise in the first place.

Effective January 1, 2010, Massachusetts 201 CMR 17 mandates the protection of SSN, driver's license, and credit/debit card numbers. Like Sarbanes-Oxley, this one came along as the result of a massive data breach involving TJX, which cost a lot of people a lot of money and resulted in many tens of millions in penalties. This kind of data loss feeds identity theft, which in turn feeds legislation.

Financial Controls

A few years back, all I ever heard was "HIPAA." Now, all I ever hear is "SOX." The Sarbanes-Oxley Act of 2002 (aka Sarbox or SOX) is designed to protect investors and citizens from corporate fraud. It came about as a reaction to a number of accounting scandals, and the billions in lost investments, resulting from nefarious activities at companies such as Tyco, Adelphia, Peregrine Systems, and of course Worldcom and Enron. It does not apply to privately held firms, although plenty of those still end up abiding by its requirements because they do business with public firms. I've talked with many non-U.S. firms that deal with it for the same reason. Under SOX, financial institutions must store certain data "not less than five years." Some analysts say that this storage requirement is why your IT departments care. Yeah, well, because of that and the whole rest of the thing.

Just to provide a taste of the seeming enormity of it, Sarbanes-Oxley entails a lot of oversight:

- Auditing, quality control, inspections
- Investigations and disciplinary procedures

- The use of accounting firms
- Board oversight
- How to engage audit partners
- Reporting and corporate responsibility (no more "I'm not the guy who signed the financial statements, don't send me to jail!")
- Conflicts of interest
- Ethics and disclosures
- Authorizations

The most important sections, or "titles," of SOX with regard to compliance are 302, 401, 404, 409, and 802, because they deal with financial statements and disclosures. Why do we care? Because of the need to control access, enforce policies, and provide data to support audits. So while SOX is not explicitly an IT-related set of provisions, IAM is perfectly suited to ensure system controls that support a portion of the intent of SOX. Section 404a mandates "adequate internal controls" on financial reporting. But remember what we said about ambiguity? "Adequate" is in the eye of the beholder.

Authorization is part of those controls, and naturally you can't be authorized until you've been properly authenticated. Access to specific financial data must be controlled. In addition, there must be periodic review of who has access to what. You may recall our description of attestation and reconciliation.

If you're in the insurance industry, you contend with the Model Audit Rule (MAR). As of January 2010, insurers in the United States may be subject to MAR rules, depending on adoption by individual states. MAR is similar to Sarbanes-Oxley, in that it protects investors, provides stability in the securities markets, and enforces transparency and fraud prevention. Insurers must have formal audit committees to meet with external auditors. But unlike with SOX, MAR is not limited to publicly traded companies. It also requires annual, audited financial reporting.

The Gramm-Leach-Bliley Act of 1999 (GLB) includes requirements for privacy, data safeguards, responsibilities, and customer rights. Of course, many experts say that GLB contributed directly to the great financial collapse of 2008 by allowing financial institutions to consolidate different offerings, such as banking, securities, and insurance, thereby creating the environment for the subprime mortgage mess. The idea was to let all these different types of businesses compete with each other and perhaps bring about better consumer prices. But as the airplane was invented and immediately turned into an instrument of war, GLB was invented and immediately turned into a path to large-scale conflicts of interest.

One more little thing about GLB as well as other privacy laws: While they mandate that companies must protect your data, they don't necessarily give you any kind of jurisdiction over the data that these companies hold on your behalf, and certainly don't guarantee that they can't sell your name for cross-marketing purposes. Privacy doesn't automatically entail not sharing with anybody. The devil is in the details.

PCI

Let's highlight this one a bit more than some others. PCI is just a wee bit different than most of the regulations out there in that it's far more focused on IT. Specifically, the Payment Card Industry (PCI) Data Security Standard (DSS) requires safeguards on payment account data. The PCI DSS has requirements that are both strategic as well as tactical. Not all of its provisions are necessarily pertinent to IAM, but many are. We will repeat these later, with proposed solutions to each, in Chapter 12.

- Install and maintain a firewall configuration to protect cardholder data.
- Do not use vendor-supplied defaults for system passwords and other security parameters.
- Protect stored cardholder data.
- Encrypt transmission of cardholder data across open, public networks.
- Restrict access to cardholder data by business need-to-know.
- Assign a unique ID to each person with computer access.
- Restrict physical access to cardholder data.
- Track and monitor all access to network resources and cardholder data.
- Regularly test security systems and processes.
- Maintain a policy that addresses information security for employees and contractors.

Just a side bar: PCI auditors recognize that e-mail is always a potential leak, and therefore they always make a strong case for solutions that keep an eye on e-mail traffic and the patterns of information (for example, Social Security numbers) that are included in messages.

As you can see, these provisions lend themselves to the disposition of and access to data. It is very IT-focused, with the emphasis on access and controls. Authentication and authorization are clearly spelled out. These all scream out for an IAM framework.

Greater North America

Mexico has laws that specifically target personal data protection. The Federal Freedom of Information Act (FOIA), similar to the U.S. version, was amended to protect personal data aggregated by the federal government, and includes the right of individuals to examine and correct that data. What is classified as personal data is a lengthy list, but it is a list nonetheless, removing any fuzziness. The law is based in part on the European Directive, which we'll come to shortly.

Like many other countries, Mexico has amended its various telecommunications laws to cover Internet traffic, including the privacy of transactions concluded online. Mexico also has its own version of HIPAA, with insurance and medical records protected by various articles of the General Health Act.

Very similar to the Australian and New Zealand standard for risk, Canada has produced CAN/ CSA-Q850-1997, a guideline for risk management. They also have a Federal Privacy Act, a law on Personal Information in the Private Sector, and the Canadian Security Intelligence Act, all of which mandate access controls and operational monitors. Their Telecommunications Act has morphed, as in other countries, to cover Internet security, even though that was not its original intent.

Latin America

When I visited Brazil in 2005, I was surprised to find that the majority of the population did their banking online, whether from available kiosks or their own homes or devices. As one might expect, Brazil leads the way in South America in the depth and breadth of laws governing electronic commerce. Brazil is a leading, and yet still emerging, economy, largely based on agriculture, but also in banking and other financial services. The country has continued making vast improvements in its telecommunications infrastructure to support Internet access. One of the few hurdles the last several years has been the fact that a relatively small portion of the population held credit cards, the primary vehicle for Internet spending.

Brazil is also a good example of how quickly the changing world is overtaking the developing one. In 2003, there were 11 phones for every 100 Brazilians. But by that time, mobile phones were already overtaking landlines. eCommerce sales doubled from 2004 to 2006. The number of Internet users increased from 20 to 25 million from 2004 to 2005, with the number of Internet consumers also climbing 40 percent in that same period. Brazilians spend the most time online, followed by the Japanese.

More consumers mean more transactions, which mean more sensitive data changing hands, and in this case, it's a flood. Brazil's Financial Institutions Secrecy Law states that "financial institutions will preserve secrecy in their active and passive operations and services." Sounds great, except for the loopholes, such as the data exchanged between financial institutions themselves, or data reported to the Federal Revenue and Customs Secretariat. In 2001, ISPs were required to maintain information such as name, address, IP, and other data about users, which seemingly creates a conflict as well as a target. At the same time, Brazil mandates strict privacy regulations. It's a legislative attempt to cope with the sudden surge of concerns resulting from the sudden surge in technology. Certainly it's a good step, although it's a shame that so much regulation is reactive, rather than proactive.

In July 2008, Brazil enacted a Digital Crimes Bill that instantly caused problems by requiring total identification of an individual before they could be allowed to take any action on the Internet. This was quickly revamped, but the law did stipulate various cybercrimes regarding obtaining, misusing, destroying, or falsifying someone's online data. It also specifically outlaws web site attacks, phishing, online discrimination, and the biggie, "non-authorized access." As with so many of these kinds of laws, the term "non-authorized access" is a little fuzzy. In fact, a lot of terms in that law were not as specific as they could have been. But the way I look at it, if you're not in my LDAP, you are unauthorized.

Argentina, Paraguay, and Venezuela all have laws specifically targeting the protection of personal data. In 2004, Ecuador passed the Transparency and Access to Information Law, similar to laws in Guatemala and elsewhere. All public institutions and other groups receiving federal money must publish regulations, plans, staff salaries, services, contracts, budgets, and other such data, and specifically establish web sites for this purpose. Naturally, threatening someone's funding is always a good way to get their attention.

Asia-Pacific

As a general comment, reading through the various provisions, segregation of duties doesn't seem to be a big emphasis in Asia-Pacific (APAC).

In China, besides the security requirements baked into Article 37 of the constitution, there are also the more comprehensive mandates in the regulations that translate essentially as the Protection and Management of Computer Information, Network, and Internet Security. They mandate access controls, auditing, monitoring, reporting, managing electronic records, and risk management. China has long tracked communications in and out of the country; therefore, they also specify records management for telecomm as well.

Hong Kong, although back in China's hands for years, still enjoys particular treatment for the territory. The Basic Law of the Hong Kong Special Administrative Region Article 29 ostensibly protects citizens from improper entry to their homes and premises, but is also interpreted to cover access control of electronic assets. In addition, because of its long-standing position as an international financial hub, Hong Kong mandates its Data Protection Principles, with provisions for access and change management, auditing, and risk. Hong Kong also has laws regarding privacy data and telecomm records retention.

Taiwan also has access control baked into its constitution, in addition to a pair of 1995 laws mandating access control and operational monitoring. For that matter, they still enforce the 1934 Telegraph and Telephone Act, now interpreted as governing access to information. The June 1999 Communication Protection and Surveillance Act piles on even more controls, and then the Telecommunications Surveillance Act Article 315 is more comprehensive yet with regard to monitoring, reporting, audit, and records management.

Japanese laws concentrate on protection of data, with the 2003 Japan Personal Information Protection Act, the horrendously named 1988 Act for the Protection of Computer-Processed Personal Data Held by Administrative Organs, a second law augmenting the "organs" law, and a set of guidelines for the protection of computer-processed personal data in the private sector. Japanese spend more time online than anyone except Brazilians, although I've got to imagine American teenagers rank way up there.

The Japanese also have put special emphasis on risk management, and in fact hosted the first meeting of an international symposium on risk in October 1998, to develop risk management terminology and international standards. This was all part of an initiative on corporate government and best practices, before Enron had exploded. Publicly traded Japanese companies and their subsidiaries are bound by the Financial Instruments and Exchange Law (known informally as JSOX), legislation spawned by the Japanese Financial Services Agency, which has provisions similar to select parts of Sarbanes-Oxley with regard to risk management.

In the Philippines, the Access Devices Regulation Act of 1998 regulates the issuance and use of access devices. A "device" could be a credit card, plate, account number, code, PIN, or other service, device, or piece of equipment that can be used to obtain money, transfer funds, goods, services, or anything else of value. The great thing about a law like this is its attempt to *define* what it purports to regulate. "Device" is often interpreted as a piece of technology, but in this case, it's any "thing" that you might use or misuse to obtain value. Maybe it's the rare case where the spirit of the law outweighs the letter of the law.

In addition, the country also passed in 2000 the Electronic Commerce Act, governing operational management and records retention. They are mandating that you get ready for your next audit. This is a good thing.

Singapore has a host of laws regarding electronic data: the E-Commerce Code for the Protection of Personal Information and Communications of Consumers of Internet Commerce, the Computer Misuse Act, the Electronic Transactions Act, the National Computer Board (Amendment) Act, the Private Sector Model Data Protection Code, and the Guidelines Regulating the Scanning of Computers by ISPs. All of them mandate access controls.

South Korea, I believe, has the right idea. Just about every one of their regulatory laws includes requirements for access control. There are two different laws regarding both the protection and disclosure of information managed by public agencies, starting in 1994. The following year, they implemented the Act Relating to Use and Protection of Credit Information. In July 2001, three large credit card companies were fined under this law, having disclosed to insurance companies their customers' data, such as salary, account numbers, credit transaction records, and personal data (name, address, phone), without consent. Cross-marketing seems to serve only the corporations, and provides plenty of leaks for identity theft data. Other laws regarding secrecy and telecommunications data are also on the books. In general, South Korea has taken a well-rounded approach to user data protection.

Besides protections interpreted from their constitution, Thailand enforces its own Data Protection Law, Electronic Transactions Law, Electronic Data Interchange Law, and Electronic Signature Law. Their very forward-thinking government in 1987 formed the National Information Technology Committee (NITC) to oversee policy on the development and use of info-tech. This resulted in nationwide networks for school and universities, for both education and research; a government info network; and a project for promoting software development within Thailand itself. Much of their emphasis for electronic commerce has been concentrated on smart cards and private keys (PKI), again as the result of policy. They even have a standard for EDI. The point of the Electronic Transactions Law is to allow electronic documents to be used as evidence in court proceedings and to allow the use of electronic signatures as legally binding, equal to handwritten signatures for e-commerce transactions. Naturally, this translates directly to the preservation of electronic docs.

Malaysia has on the books the Communications and Multimedia Act, mandating access control and records management; the Personal Data Protection Act; and two laws from 1997, the Digital Signature Act and the Computer Crime Act. Both require strong access control as well as preserving digital records for computer forensics.

India, a hotbed of technology and cyber-development, saw the Information Technology Act put in place by the Parliament in 2000—pre-Enron, so good for them. (This is not to say that everyone has followed the direction of the United States on the policing and securing of technology, although the sheer weight of the Enron disaster definitely reverberated around the globe and gave rise to various international laws beyond American borders.) The Info Tech Act has been amended multiple times since then to reflect changes in technology and policy. It has a very controversial history, with many claiming it has resulted in unnecessary prosecutions. Besides recognizing the validity of electronic transactions and digital signatures, it also defines crimes within electronic commerce, and specifies punishments. Its earliest incarnation was said to hinder eCommerce within the country, and stifle development and innovation. It was, perhaps, too strict about acceptable means of authentication, for example. Another provision with its heart in the right place, but its head maybe too loose, specified the need for organizations that maintain sensitive data to enforce reasonable security measures to protect that data. Good idea, right? Closely guard my user ID or credit card numbers. But the definition of "reasonable" was never put in place. Thus, the reason for repeated surgery on the law.

In Australia, the Victorian Electronic Records Strategy (VERS) mandates the capturing of government-related docs, files, and records, making them available in standard formats, and tracking their status. The goal is long-term preservation of documents.

The Privacy Act of 1988 got an update in 2001 for the Internet era. While some countries, like the United States, make the presumption that pre-Internet telecommunications laws just sort of reverse-grandfather in Internet companies and technology, Australia did not make that leap, and specifically acted on updating their legislation.

Let me highlight AS/NZS 4360, a common law between Australia and New Zealand regarding risk. It is in fact a standard for an entire methodology for assessing risks and vulnerabilities, as well as the context for risk, preventive measures, and contingencies. Because of continuous monitoring and review, it is an iterative process. It is considered so well thought-out that it was adopted by the British National Health Service as the basis for its clinical and corporate governance. The 4360 standard was hatched by the insurance industry, but was configured to be generic enough to apply across industries. Originally it was intended for submission to ISO (the International Organization for Standardization), but at the time (1996), no appropriate ISO group existed to address risk. The proposed guidelines were largely championed by the Japanese, helping this standard migrate to other countries.

Europe, the Middle East, and Africa (EMEA)

The European Union seems to have been all over this subject, although beneath the surface, the desire to promote commerce also seems to have created inherent weaknesses.

The "Eighth Directive" on corporate governance covers all major aspects of info security: access, change, continuity, privacy, operations, data preservation, audit, risk, and SoD. A number of other EU directives cover access control, which is where it all starts, right? Then they branch into more access control, electronic surveillance (which gets a little off our mark), data transfers, and electronic documents. What they're really trying to get a handle on is the movement of goods, services, and the accompanying transactional data that govern that movement. One of the reasons they need that handle on the movement of assets is because they so heavily encourage that movement, sometimes perhaps at the expense of security.

The EU Data Protection Directive is meant to provide for trust, confidence, transparency, governance, and accountability. Sounds like SOX compliance, doesn't it? But in May 2009, an analysis of the Directive called for "establishing consensus over the interpretation of several key concepts," including the need to define the term "privacy." There's that pesky ambiguity thing again. One possibly alarming thing to come up was the idea that they could debate "under what circumstances can personal privacy become secondary to the needs of society" (Review of EU Data Protection Directive: Summary, May 2009, Prepared for the Information Commissioner's Office, United Kingdom). Seems to me that an individual's right to privacy should just about always be sacrosanct. Now, you'd think that the "needs of society" sounds like an excuse for intelligence-gathering (which is not always a bad thing). But in the case of the EU, it's also relevant to the promotion of commerce.

The Directive does, however, spell out the need for standards, if not consistent standards themselves. It also specifies the importance of a framework; that is, a set of standards from which to build data and privacy protection. Risk assessment, transparency, and accountability are also included. Again, sounds like SOX, right?

A few years ago, the Europe-based Consumers International conducted a study in which they determined that self-regulated American web sites did a better job protecting private data than European government-regulated sites. Quite an astounding thing, considering that self-regulated polluters usually cause more smog. But that led to some examination of how Europeans allowed data flow (for the sake of fostering cross-border business) at the expense of security, while at the same time some European groups advised the United States on not completely bottlenecking information necessary to commerce. But hey, that's why somebody invented federation, which we'll talk about in more detail in a little while.

Many European countries have laws specific to the protection of individuals' data: Belgium, Bulgaria, Finland, France, Germany, Greece, Hungary, Iceland, Ireland, Italy, Lithuania, Netherlands, Norway, Poland, Slovakia, Slovenia, Spain, Sweden, Turkey, and the United Kingdom.

Any European nations whose laws aren't specific to protecting privacy-related data can interpret their other statutes as covering the same. But ambiguity is never a good thing.

All that said, the countries on the Continent aren't all on the same page. In the summer of 2009, Germany chose to adopt stricter codes on the maintenance of mailing lists for marketing purposes. This move was seen as infringing on the European Data Protection Directive, which tries to balance privacy with the free movement of goods and services, a concept the EU was originally formed to promote. Remember "open borders?" This directive also helps illustrate the differences between the European and American approaches to privacy. The United States prefers a *sectoral* combination of laws and industry regulation to enforce privacy concerns, while Europe leans toward more umbrella-like legislation, given its greater sensitivity to the use of personal data.

Neither Sweden nor Switzerland has many data protection laws on the books, but the ones they do have are quite comprehensive, covering access on the front end to preservation and protection on the back end. Slovenia has no less than three laws that definitively address privacy.

Perhaps following the early lead of Germany, several Euro nations have laws regarding digital signatures, meaning "here's what's acceptable, and by the way, it *is* acceptable." Allowing electronic signatures empowers business, but specifying what constitutes a signature is always necessary. Leave no wiggle room.

I like this one: Slovakia's Act on Protection of Personal Data in Information Systems. Oracle's approach is to encrypt data where it's sitting, when it's in transit, and wherever it's in backup. Slovakia likewise covers the notion that privacy data shouldn't be secured just when it's moving around or changing hands; it should also be securely locked up on a daily basis.

Like the APAC laws, the European laws in general don't say much about Segregation of Duties. These kinds of things can get you in trouble. You run on multiple servers, or with mirrored systems, to avoid a single point of failure. If you allow any one individual to have too many keys, he can get into too many rooms. This has caused some memorable trading crimes (for example, in Hong Kong), resulting in gargantuan losses.

Check out Ireland or Lithuania. They both have a version of a Freedom of Information (FOI) law, but also laws protecting the data of individuals. Usually, FOI at a federal level, in any country, means having to make a request, rather than just surfing to what you need (as in Ecuador, or the United States). But when you open one gate, you need to secure another. A server containing one type of information that is networked to another server that houses another type of information must be walled off. Access to how your taxes are spent shouldn't get you access to other individual taxpayers' data.

Several European countries put up new telecommunications laws in the 90s, ostensibly to protect data flying around online. But that's when a lot of connectivity was still based on landlines. Now there are dedicated trunks, satellite, iPhones, you name it. While the laws need to be kept up to snuff with changes in technology, even more changes in technology must keep up with the huge increase in unauthorized access attempts.

Let me make one more point on the EU (although it may not be limited to them). Some EU countries have regulations regarding *data jurisdiction*; that is, they have policies on where your data may reside. You may need to find out if there are any data elements, such as those related to privacy, that you are not allowed to host on a cloud vendor.

The Takeaways

So what is the summation of these many international laws? Control access. Provide transparency. Enact controls. *Protect private data.* This is all about identity and access management, at both a high level and at a very granular level. And remember, reporting is all good stuff, until it shows that you haven't been doing the rest of it. Reporting only verifies what has already transpired. Compliance needs to be baked in, needs to be an integral part of day-to-day activities and processes. If compliance is being regularly and *consistently* enforced, then reporting will serve to verify this enforcement, and will be a mere formality, rather than being considered to be the process itself, which is the most common mistake.

Compliance is not a tool or set of functions. It is a process and a mindset that are supported by those tools and functions. And before you implement those tools and functions, you need to seriously consider which compliance laws apply to your organization, which ones will apply later, and which ones apply to the other parties with whom you do business. We're all connected now, and if it's important to our partners, it's important to us, or will be very shortly.

CHAPTER
5

Making the Business Case

The first duty of a wise advocate is to convince his opponents that he understands their arguments, and sympathizes with their just feelings.

—Samuel Taylor Coleridge

 y this time, your investigation is done. You've uncovered the current requirements of the organization, along with what the various departments think they might need down the road as well. You've found the trends, the issues, the problems, the concerns. You have a good idea of how compliance impacts, and will continue to impact, your policies and procedures.

Earlier, I said that you have to think like Us and Them. That is, "Us" are the people in charge who put the processes in place. "Them" are the users who will be affected by your decisions. Well, now turn that around. "Them" is now pointing the other direction up the food chain, at the management layer, whom you will ask for money and resources to implement an IAM framework. You must state your case, which is also *their* case, since it's for everybody's good within the company. But they won't necessarily think like that. If they're doing their thing and making money, why rock the boat? You must make that case, one more time, and now you need to think like "Them." What are their hot buttons? What will get them on your side?

A very smart ex-boss of mine named Ralph used to repeat the mantra, "it's not what you do, it's how you do it," and he used to practice that in order to serve as an example to his employees. Once in a while you have to deliver bad news, but there's a proper way to do it. For example, a salesman will tell you it's not a bad thing that a proposed discount goes away after the end of the quarter; it's a good thing that you can take advantage of that discount if you act sooner rather than later.

Round Two in Front of Management

So here's your chance to do it the right way. Management has heard some of this from you already. Now you need to revisit that information, only this time you're armed with the data from your investigations. *How you present that data* will make all the difference.

You don't buy your spouse a birthday present and then toss it at him or her. You wrap it up nicely. Well, let's start wrapping.

Sell the Business Value

People at the top of the food chain don't always understand bits and bytes. Frame everything you say in terms of the value to the organization. You won't say, "We need connectors that support SMTP and RACF." You will say, "We need automated e-mail notifications, and we need to pull our mainframe into the framework." Everything should be stated in terms of cost savings, operational efficiency, security, and so on. Identity management is not a value unto itself (unless IdM itself is your business); it must serve the larger goals of the company.

Look Organized

Avoid the classic salesman mistake they call "show up and throw up." You'll get around to all the pieces, eventually. But do them in the right order. Build the case from the bottom up. State the issues, the problems, the concerns, and then the solutions. Don't forget the problems that you haven't yet encountered, but that you anticipate will bite you in the behind in the coming months or years. Prioritize (we'll discuss that more in a minute). Put your issues in categories, maybe constituencies: administrators, end users, employees, partners, customers, or departments, geographic locations, lines of business, areas of concern. And once you've got it all organized, rehearse. No kidding. Put in the time to actually know your material. Don't read your slides; know your stuff. A script is a good thing, but treat it like a set of suggestions to remind you to say what you already know. "We need IAM, and here are the reasons why."

Believe in Your Message

This will sound like an oxymoron, but *be passionate, yet not emotional*. Sound as if you care, because surely you do. But sound rational. I watched a guy in Detroit once get so agitated trying to convince his own management of the need for a particular piece of software, that after the meeting, the managers were questioning the man's self-control, and wondered if he should be in charge of the effort. I've also seen presentations that were delivered in so mundane and bloodless a manner that management was far from inspired to provide budget.

Prioritize

You may or may not get budget for everything you need, but you can just about guarantee you won't get budget for everything you *want*. Pick your big dogs and put them at the front of your list. It also makes perfect sense to prioritize in the order you will implement, since most often the pieces will build on each other. For example, you might state that first comes the user directory, then authentication, then authorization, then SSO, and so on. These will help you provide those deliverables.

Another aspect to consider is which incremental pieces will be most disruptive. If you can put off the uglier stuff until later, it's not a bad idea. Remember, if you're upgrading, it's likely more natural. Single sign-on is a basic function. But moving to an RBAC-based system from standard groups is far more transformational, and therefore a potential cultural leap that requires a greater learning curve.

Compile Real Evidence

It's not enough to say, "Hey boss, IAM will make everything better." You need to make an actual business case. In a minute we'll talk about Return on Investment (ROI). When aggregating the data, shoot for real dollars. When putting together the "soft ROI" that represents the more intangible benefits (for example, user experience), gather as much anecdotal evidence as possible. Interview end users, system admins, customers, your auditors, and whoever else may be affected directly or indirectly by your current system limitations. If possible, when you put together that compelling presentation, have some of those folks you've interviewed come to present their personal stories. I've been told for the better part of two decades that my use of real stories, containing real customers with real issues (with all the names changed for obvious reasons), is my best ammunition when stating the value of a security solution.

Anticipate Objections

Someone might argue, "Well, you wanted one of these, so naturally you rationalized it so you can get it paid for." But the counter-argument to that is, "No, we already knew we needed it, but what we've done is *quantify* it with empirical data. It's not just needs any more. It's *documented* needs. Let me show you the documentation."

Take the position of the devil's advocate, and take the time to figure out what somebody will throw back at you. "We can't spend this money because we haven't had a breach. Nobody's complaining to *us* about how long it takes to log in. We're not currently subject to Sarbanes-Oxley. Manual provisioning has been working so far."

An executive sponsor will help you prebuild those defenses, by providing you insight as to the concerns that upper management will have, besides the obvious one, costs. In fact, that's the big one, right? "This thing will cost too much." So what's the obvious defense? "Let me tell you the cost of doing nothing." And this will point directly toward the consequences of a security breach, or the costs of failing an audit, or the dollars wasted in manually driven processes.

Getting Help with Your Pitch

You can get a lot from people when they think there's a payoff up the road. You may or may not have an idea of what you need, but chances are you at least have a notion. So invite in some smart folks. Get some freebies. Start with the big ones, the large consulting firms, many of whom double as auditors.

NOTE
If a consulting company is your auditor already, they may be able to advise you on what you need to fix, but there's a 99% percent chance they can't actually help you implement anything. There have always been rules about auditors not being able to consult for their auditing clients, and there were always paths around those restrictions. Since Enron and other scandals, that is no longer the case, except for grandfathered projects.

Auditors or other partners may be able to put you in contact with officers from other companies (most likely companies that don't compete with you) who have been through this before. Their experiences may very well help you put together your business case.

Analysts can provide you not only validation for your concerns, but also the value proposition for a solution. If you can't afford to bring in an actual analyst (which isn't necessarily cheap), you can usually purchase corroborating data, and in fact you can find a lot of it online. The analysts themselves pay people big bucks to examine the trends, the risks, the consequences, and the solutions, and they make this data available to their customers, naturally for a price. Don't just grab, for example, Gartner's magic quadrant info for provisioning or access management for the latest calendar year; get hold of one of the whitepapers. Also check Forrester, Burton, and so on. An analyst will also, for a price, give you a checkup. If you go this route, of course, be ready to write a check, and don't ask them to tell you what you want to hear—ask them for their honest opinion.

Request Budget

Going to the people in charge for budget is a big game, a gamble. You could

- **Ask for the whole thing at once.** It's bigger than any individual piece. But if you don't get the whole thing through now, you may never get any of it. It might be harder for management to back out of it when it's all or nothing and you're halfway through.

- **Ask for it in phases.** Makes it more digestible to upper management. It shows more planning, more discipline. It could be easier to get the first phase or two approved and funded. Of course, it's always possible that you'll get what you need for Phase One, and then management may decide that's all you need for now, effectively killing Phase Two and beyond. If you've been through the prioritization process already, you can easily translate that into what pieces you need now to build for the future.

Software vendors like a particular word: champion. It's their "in" guy at a customer, somebody who likes their story and will help them sell the product internally. Well, when you're trying to pitch the notion of IAM to your bosses or stakeholders, find yourself at least one champion. You need help to sell the concept, to build the case, to support your existing case, and eventually to petition for budget. This might be somebody you can later encourage to support you by making their favorite critical apps candidates for the first round of strong authentication or single sign-on.

NOTE
If you end up shopping for software later (rather than building it yourself) and you find a product you like, you may end up becoming the champion for that vendor. In other words, you'll be used heavily and regularly by that vendor. But is that necessarily a bad thing? That salesperson will do everything in his power to make you look good and get you all the material you need, not just to sell that product up the chain, but just to sell the concept up the chain. It's all part of the game, but use it to your advantage when the time comes.

Here's an extremely common occurrence: A customer-facing or revenue-generating project will more often than not take precedence over an identity project, despite the clear value of security and identity. It truly helps to highlight the risks of not having identity management and access control.

Return on Investment (ROI)

If you're begging for money, then you have to justify it. This means demonstrating to management what they're getting for their investment, which means clearly stating ROI. Software vendors and consultants are repositories for documents, spreadsheets, slide decks, and whitepapers describing the incredible Return on Investment for an IAM system. There's "soft ROI," which is "it's wonderful, it'll provide a better user experience, it'll give us more control and security." Then there's "hard ROI," which is an actual dollar amount. They will tell you how much you'll save with IAM in place.

Hard ROI

Let's take a look at those areas where you can attach actual costs. In every operation, you have the opportunity to quantify the ROI in deploying an IAM framework.

■ **Replacing hard tokens**   If you're using RSA or some other token setup, that carries a particular per-user cost. These setups are secure, no doubt. They can be integrated as just another authentication scheme by common authorization and SSO engines. They're also no fun to roll out or upgrade; they're expensive, and they break. Some people swear by them, since it involves your bodily presence to authenticate. Sure, so does logging in, but in this case, you're providing a physical representation of yourself to authenticate. The main thing is, they're not cheap. If you can authenticate without them, it's an obvious ROI.

■ **Self-service**   This old chestnut gets beaten to death, but it still holds true. It will save you not only dollars that you're spending on help desk hours, but also a metric ton of aggravation for both your help desk and your users if those users can maintain their own profiles, reset their own passwords, and unlock their own accounts.

■ **Provisioning**   This includes the entire life cycle of enabling, modifying, and disabling users. Managing a user's privileges not only eats up administrative time, but it can also easily cut into a user's productivity. On the front end, you're paying somebody a salary for sitting around waiting for access. In the back room, lack of automation translates directly into manual processes. As of this writing, I've just returned from a scoping engagement in which an institution of higher learning admitted they have more than twice as many service desk personnel as they'd need if they could automate access grants. So a good provisioning system has definite staffing and productivity ROI.

■ **Audit support**   There's no arguing with the benefits of good reporting. And good reporting is built on good log data. Supporting an audit with a weak system takes a lot of labor. Audits can eat up plenty of a staff's time, as they compile custom reports at the request of auditors. And let's take one step back and talk about provisioning one more time. The more manual processes you have in place, the more mistakes you'll see, guaranteed. Automated processes give you the consistency and the logging you won't get with fat fingers doing all the work. The more mistakes that are uncovered, the more the auditors will *attempt* to uncover. Don't give them any more ammunition than they're bound to find anyway.

■ **Putting developers back to work on business apps rather than security**   By providing that IAM framework, you're taking the security burden off the guys who should be doing other things, and who probably aren't qualified to manage security in the first place. It's a common question for a developer: How much time are you spending on security code and policy creation?

Soft ROI

So after you've tackled the hard ROI, go after the soft ROI. Sure, it might not exactly have dollars attached, but it can cause more noise among the rank and file, affecting end-users' and administrators' day-to-day activities, thereby allowing you to gather more anecdotal evidence of the need for IAM than the hard stuff. Soft ROI manifests itself in a variety of obvious ways:

- **Superior end-user experience** Self-service is a big piece of this. Not only does this lend itself to hard ROI in terms of staffing and productivity, but it also makes for much happier end users who can handle their own password, account lockout, and resource request issues. These same capabilities also make your help desk people happier, since nothing sucks the life out of you more than handling the same old password reset for eight hours a day.

- **Faster time to market** By taking away the need to re-create security for every app on its own, you are making it far easier and quicker to launch apps. Security is already taken into account by the framework.

- **Competitive advantage** Not only will you have more cash to invest in business-building activities to overtake your rivals, you can say, "Look, you happy customers, we've got the tightest security in the market, and our anti-phishing capabilities always let you know you've come to the correct web site to do your banking or shopping."

- **Protection of your good name** I cannot overstate the damage to your reputation if you are hacked. I also cannot overstate the value of a good end-user experience for a non-captive audience. An employee will put up with a certain amount of interface hassle. I've never heard of somebody quitting a company because he didn't like the GUI tool they built the corporate portal with. But if paying customers make enough use of your online tools, and dread logging in, they'll vote with their fingers and their mice. A few years back, during a time of market volatility, my broker got tired of my bi-daily phone calls and suggested I could more easily get my questions answered on their web site. I pointed out to her that they had the world's slowest authentication scheme, and an awful-to-navigate site with dreadful menus, meaning that from the time I clicked Submit on my password to the time I got my data, it could take me several minutes. If I were someone more liable to manage my own account online rather than through a broker, I most certainly would have dumped them.

- **Protection against even worse consequences** Fail an audit, lose customer data, suffer a material breach, and it will cost you big money. You will face penalties, lawsuits, lost business, and possibly paying extra costs such as credit monitoring for customers whose account info you've lost.

- **Overall satisfaction within the organization** When you take into account operational efficiencies, end-user experience, cost savings, reputation, and other advantages, it all adds up to a happier organization with the appearance and feeling of being in charge of its own destiny. Every single company, without exception, has at least one system in place that everybody complains about. It's like that drunken uncle who comes to all the weddings and funerals, and you're stuck with him, and there's nothing you can do to avoid the usual embarrassments. But robust security and identity is not only a vital corporate function; it also indicates that you've got a handle on the single most important thing you can provide, outside of the actual product or service with which you make your profits. Where I work, provisioning is like good housekeeping. It's so smooth that we don't even think about it. If I request access to something, I get it within a reasonable period. If I didn't have that, I'd be screaming. But I do have that, so I don't even notice how efficient it is. This allows me the convenience of complaining about a whole bunch of other things.

Preserving Your Existing Investment

This is neither hard nor soft ROI, but rather getting more mileage out of what you already own. Naturally you currently have in place at least some pieces of an identity foundation. You may want to stay with your user directory, individual workflow engines, or account creation scripts. Not all of it is going away, and in fact when selecting vendors and/or technologies, part of what you will ask is, "How much can we keep?"

Maintaining current components as part of the new framework has multiple values. First, it's less labor. If you have connectors to legacy apps, discrete workflow processes, scripts that create accounts on legacy platforms, and if you can connect them to a larger framework without losing efficiency, then you are calling on those pieces, rather than having to build them from scratch (although you'll still have to configure your new workflow to use them). Second, those may represent pieces you don't have to buy (connectors, directory).

Therefore you've got a better message for management: "Look, boss, our new security platform is friendly with our old one, which translates to continuity and cost savings."

Asking for Help, One More Time

Again, think about getting backup. This is especially useful if you think you've found the right technologies and/or partners to assemble your project, or if you're tight with your auditors. Your auditor may render aid just to keep on your good side. And any outside company who *isn't* your auditor won't make a dime off you unless you get your internal approval. So make them work for it. Have them help you put together a business plan that includes ROI, business case, and so on. I've been asked by literally dozens of customers to provide ROI for them to push up their own food chain.

When you're trying to get budget and resources from your own management, you are doing what software and hardware vendors do all the time: sell. In this case, you're not trying to make a profit; you're trying to improve the quality of life at your organization, as well as positively impact the bottom line. The problem, of course, is that in the short term you will be *negatively* impacting the bottom line, so the trick is to get management to perceive the long-term, bigger-picture benefits.

Oracle has an excellent program called Insight, in which they visit customers for a three-to-five day conversation. They interview all the pertinent staff, in large and/or small groups, and ask questions that the customer perhaps never thought of asking themselves. It helps when they bring in a team that is familiar with the particular vertical the customer is in, such as insurance, banking, healthcare, higher education, and so on. At the end of the process, they regurgitate to the customer what they heard, to make sure they have an accurate reading, then present recommendations—and no, they don't all involve installing software. I've participated in a number of these, and I see the definite benefit to some organizations of having external validation of issues that customers already know they have. In addition, the Insight team can help IT staff make that business case for improving processes, and realizing that return on investment. In most cases, IT staff builds solutions for a living; they don't make presentations for a living, so a little professional help can, well, help.

Later, we'll discuss how to vet software vendors and consultants.

Finalizing the Request

Naturally, at the end of the business case process, do what salespeople have always done: ask for next steps. What else do the managers need to hear? Is there a heartbeat? Did what you say resonate? Do they understand your issues? Do they understand how your IT issues impact their business issues? Do they *see the value to the business*? That's the $64,000 question.

As we already discussed, they may approve some portion of a proposed solution. Make the most of that. If you don't get everything, then think back on *it's not what you do but how you do it*. So think of it as an opportunity. Deliver what is approved, and that's your best chance of getting approval for the next batch of wishes off the list. Failure to deliver that first batch will pretty much kill any future initiatives. So if you ask for it and get it, then make sure you can do it.

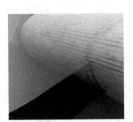

CHAPTER
6

Achieving Pitfalls:
Common Mistakes in IAM

We learn wisdom from failure much more than from success.

—*S. Smiles*

hy a chapter on how to fail completely? It's for the same reason that my neighbor makes his kids watch those TV shows where teenagers videotape themselves suffering hideous injuries while trying to skateboard down a set of stairs. If you know the possible disasters, you will work diligently to avoid them. "Does it look like that hurts? Yes, it does. So don't do that."

Whenever you take on a large project or responsibility, you have the opportunity to shine, to really show what you can do. It could be your finest hour. It could also be an opportunity for abject disaster. There, now wasn't that a happy thought?

Mistakes Both Large and Small

There are several common mistakes people make when embarking upon an IAM project. Some could apply to almost any sizable endeavor, but some are more specific to the subject matter at hand. Mistakes can be strategic, meaning that you have failed to master the big picture, or that you have the right idea about what you want but have failed to plan adequately for how to get there. Mistakes can also be tactical, in which you fail to handle the many details that, although individually small, can aggregate into a large problem because of their impact on delivery.

Boiling the Ocean

"Boiling the ocean" is otherwise known as "eating the whole horse," or "biting off more than you can chew," or "inviting everyone in your wife's family." When you attempt to do everything at once, you will accomplish very little. In 2000, I was invited into a large food company in Texas with many sub-brand companies. They wanted web access management, portal security, and single sign-on, and they wanted to cover all their holdings. I recommended starting out with just one or two, even some cross-domain SSO between them, to prove out the model and then expand. But no, they insisted on charging forward with all their directories, portals, and subsidiary sites at once. Then they failed to convince or force all their departmental IT chiefs to get on board with a central solution. As a result, all these many years later they have coverage in silos, as different children acquired their own solutions.

The implementations that I've seen that took the longest, or the ones that took far too long to show the simplest results, were the ones that tried to do too much. Yes, you sold everybody on the value. Yes, you told everybody they'd be in on the results. But you can't satisfy everybody in the short term. Pick the critical apps and/or the critical user groups to bring the new IAM framework on board. At one transportation company, they had over 1200 apps. For the first phase, we scoped out authentication, authorization, and cross-domain single sign-on for seven of those apps. Seven out of more than a thousand. We picked the low-hanging fruit, to prove that we could have success, to learn a few lessons, and therefore to convince management that our direction was sound.

When you're first trying to sell the idea of IAM internally, you might propose including in this low-hanging fruit a resource belonging to a key stakeholder or champion. Get them on board, keep them on board, impress them, cement their loyalty. If somebody has clout and influence, get their app on basic authentication and SSO. Maybe password reset. From an implementation perspective, *those* resources are low-hanging fruit.

As you bring resources and people on board in stages, you will learn from your mistakes, and perfect your methodology. You'll know how to set expectations and deal with the unexpected as you progress. No matter how much you plan, you still won't know what you don't know, until you've been through a couple of rounds, and then you know it. The other benefit is, as you progress and can show results a department or an app at a time, the stakeholders will start coming to you and asking when they can get on the train as well.

I was contacted by a state government body a couple of years back about installing password reset. They were in Year Two of the five-year rollout of a large IdM vendor's total solution, and they didn't expect to have password reset, one of the simplest aspects of IdM, up and running for another year, and needed an interim solution. So much for those little deliverables that let you know you're making progress.

An East Coast bank called me in a year after that. They were in Year Four of a two-year rollout from that same large IdM vendor. No, you didn't read that wrong. They wanted to see if RBAC could bridge the gap between corporate requirements and provisioning, *while* they awaited a possible custom solution from their vendor and SI, who were already two years behind.

Think of implementation as an iterative process. With your first phase, you will design, then plan how you will achieve that design, then deploy, with transparency and communication as you make your way. How progress is communicated (and perceived) is almost as important as how it is executed. You will also make mistakes, and you will develop best practices. Once you understand what works and what doesn't, the next iteration will go more smoothly (although never perfectly). And this is the basis for deploying IAM one bite at a time.

Failure to Communicate

Sorry to repeat myself, as I just talked about this. In some instances, because you're going into production, you may very well be performing an intrusive procedure. Make sure that any party whose processes you're going to affect is well aware in advance. If there are any obstacles, make sure they're communicated and not hidden. And as you achieve even the smallest victories, document those as well. Once you've got something that is worth sharing, share it. "Look, we have cross-domain SSO between Chicago and Tokyo." If you're using an integration partner, get clear, comprehensible progress reports. Don't let people hide things on you—which leads to …

Trust, But Verify

If you have others performing the implementation, smile when they tell you how well it's going, then ask to see it. There should always be a plan, with deliverables. Make sure those deliverables are showing up at the prescribed intervals. Dates will always slip, but they shouldn't fall off a cliff. Reasonable delays shouldn't turn into huge ones.

At a customer in Canada, an entire year went by with the internal sponsor happily accepting the glowing progress reports from the integrator. And after that year, they literally could not authenticate to the new portal. Couldn't even log in, after a whole year. They were building a huge IT contraption and hadn't tested the most basic possible function, putting in a name and password, as one of those early deliverables. Needless to say, this ended badly.

No Corporate Sponsorship

Without buy-in from management, you will get nowhere. This isn't free. This isn't easy. You will absolutely need a mandate to get cooperation. You will need requirements from the end users and stakeholders, you will need data, you will need them to participate in what you build. Unless you're related to everybody by marriage *and* they owe you money, you won't get them to budge without some prodding from above.

Many times I've been called in by IT management to help them scope out solutions to their provisioning and security issues, only to have them tell me they can't get funding. It's a sad fact, but quite often IT does not control its own budget.

Lack of a Governance Committee

You may actually need more than one of these, which we've discussed. But besides the decisions you need at the departmental level, you will want an oversight group or groups to decide on standards, platforms, policies, role definitions, and those components that will drive security, compliance, and strategy across all user and resource groups. It's not going to be just you and/or a chosen implementation partner.

For almost 20 years I've been working at a weekly bingo game for a charitable organization I belong to. We have a whole crew. I've worked the desk and the floor and the back room, but the one job I refuse to do any longer is actually call the numbers. No matter how you call, half the room will say you're calling too slow, and the other half will say you're going too fast. You absolutely cannot win. So once you've launched your IAM project, people will complain that your role definitions will be too narrow or broad, your SoD policies are too loose or too restrictive, your identity attributes are too dangerously centralized or too needlessly distributed.

Any decisions not based on groupthink will later be subject to shredding. And if there turn out to be weaknesses or *perceived* weaknesses, somebody will ask, "Who's the dummy who came up with all this?" By subjecting decisions to committee, you not only get more eyeballs on the process before it's set in stone (which gives more people a chance to recommend and help vet pieces of the puzzle), it also allows you to (and I hate to say this one) spread the blame. It's going to happen at some point that somebody won't like something you've devised. Be ready for it. But again, if enough educated people have reviewed the process, there should be much less blame to assign.

Scope Creep

Everyone knows this problem: You begin with one set of requirements, and end up with another. Occasionally there are acceptable reasons for this, such as keeping an important stakeholder happy. But if this becomes the rule rather than the exception, it will greatly impact your timelines, and perhaps even your basic requirements. You should begin with a solid idea of which users and which resources will be included in your initial rollout, and stick to that. This is where a governance committee will be invaluable. Any requested additions to the plan should be vetted by the appropriate group and not simply allowed to slip in.

Single sign-on might be an easy one. "Please allow my application to be reached through the common credentials." But fine-grained authorization? No, not yet.

Being Nailed to Legacy Systems

You will have those who say that their current platform is more than adequate. The devil you know is better than the one you don't. Or even if there's agreement that you need to upgrade your identity system, there may not be sufficient will to migrate certain functions or storage off those legacy systems, handicapping you from the start. One of the items your governance committee can tackle early on is how much of your current structure you will maintain, and to what extent it will integrate with the new picture.

A lot of the time, customers want export abilities for reporting. But if the new platform has full reporting, is this a concern any longer? Well, you never know. Sure, a decent reporting tool should give you the ability to "report" data into a CSV file, so you can load it into any other reporting or analytics tool you're already using, but if the reporting engine can produce preformatted reports as well as on-demand reports, why support out-of-band tools?

At one client, the CSO had learned how to use a weak off-the-shelf tool for creating his own reports, and he wasn't giving it up. It was his toy. One of the use cases for the proposed new IdM system was creating a delimited file so that this one guy could load raw data into his tool and create his own cute little reports. But hey, when somebody is a major influencer, you'll get the product to generate him a chocolate chip cookie, if it'll help.

A common holdover is the use of help desk apps for provisioning. It's fine to keep that app for tracking tickets (although the framework should be able to track requests all by itself). But the way help desk apps actually perform provisioning, if you can call it that, is routing tickets to administrators who subsequently use a keyboard to create new user accounts. That's not provisioning; that's just notifications. Your IAM framework should be *automatically* creating those accounts.

At some point you need to get everybody on board with the new framework. It's simpler, more functional, and infinitely easier to support.

Overselling

One thing you learn from working for vendors for years is how to set expectations. If you do what you say you're going to do, and maybe even a little extra, then you keep your credibility. If what you're proposing isn't good enough to pique someone's interest, then you weren't up to the task in the first place. But if you oversell, and subsequently under-deliver, your credibility is completely shot. So I try to follow the advice of my very brilliant former boss Ralph: under-commit and over-deliver. Offer enough to get your foot in the door, and then finish strongly.

But whatever you do, sell what you *can* deliver. Be practical. If you promise the moon and only show up with a moon rock, your credibility, and that of the project, takes a hit.

Failing to Meet Deliverables

Remember that low-hanging fruit. Hit those early deliverables. Completely secure that one critical app. Deploy password reset. Or configure SSO across a selection of apps. Automate provisioning to e-mail and LDAP. Create workflow definitions and demonstrate how they generate notifications for approval—something that indicates progress, an initial return on investment, and credibility. Perception is reality.

Meet the timelines to the best of your ability. The early ones are perhaps the most important. They're confidence-builders. Even if subsequent deliverables run late, your early wins show that you're capable of meeting deadlines, and perhaps there were extenuating circumstances. Because guess what—there *will* be. But if you don't hit those early requirements, you're behind schedule the rest of the way, and confidence wavers. And if approval for the next set of initiatives depends on succeeding with the first set, you may have killed the rest of the wish list.

An IAM project is measured in feet and inches. You can almost see physical progress in terms of users, apps, functions, workflow definitions, and approvals.

Presuming Everybody's on Board

I've been married for two decades. I'm past the point of having to sell myself to my wife. She's stuck with me at this point. And yet I keep selling. Why? Besides being the right thing to do, it makes everything run more smoothly, especially if I have to account for mistakes. Here's why I did this, and why it makes sense. The Oreo you found in the couch cushions? It was there for a logical reason, and everyone in the family benefits from it. And by the way, I cleaned the kitchen sink for you.

Even if you get that corporate sponsorship, don't stop selling the idea of IAM as a value-add to the entire organization. You need cooperation from the different branches of the organization. They need to know, and eventually need to see, what's in it for them. And even when you do deliver a piece of functionality, beware of the situation where you think it's a wonderful thing, and someone else says, "Oh, is that all it does?" Don't assume everyone sees the same value in all the components as they come online. When this situation does arise, remind your users that each deliverable is only a building block in a larger framework. Remind them to be patient, and that more is on the way. Keep selling.

Failing to Plan for Integration

One of the hairiest parts of the rollout will be getting your new IAM pieces to talk to your user stores, applications, and legacy systems. Make no assumptions. Integration should be tested early on in the process, for both function and bandwidth, so that when you put production connectors in place, it's a formality.

Here's something so basic that it's hard to believe it ever comes up, and yet it does. As of this writing, I just dealt with this issue this morning, no kidding. And the issue is *versions*.

"Will it run on Weblogic? Yeah? Good, we're all done."

Wrong. What version of Weblogic? And on which platform?

I've seen version issues get uncovered during *deployment*. I've listened on con calls as vendors explained to the customer, after deployment had already begun, that the actual version the customer needed wouldn't be certified for another few months. And here's the customer, having already paid for the stuff and brought an integrator in the door. Ouch, that hurts.

Investing Before Analyzing

As much emphasis as I've placed on stating the business case and striving to get your must-haves funded, it's amazing how quickly something can get done when somebody knows somebody else, and how much money can be thrown into ill-considered ventures.

I knew a CEO who ignored acquisitions he should have made (and later, when it was too late, finally attempted) in favor of an acquisition he absolutely should *not* have made, because somebody managed to convince him that the bad technology he bought was the best possible fit, and the result was $100 million wasted. I witnessed another acquisition that was made for political purposes, because both company boards shared board members (and wanted one company to bail out the other), with the result being a shareholder lawsuit and an unnatural merging of both product lines that the market utterly rejected.

And at a large insurance customer of mine, I was brought in to discuss a proxy server architecture as well as integration with a technology they'd just bought: a desktop-based, thick-client, web SSO tool. Not for enterprise SSO to thick-client apps (where it's still a necessity), but web SSO.

I mentioned to the VP in charge, "Oh, so you're now in the desktop support business." He asked me what I meant by that. I explained to him what fun he'd have rolling out and eventually upgrading thousands of desktops for the sake of something that other vendors were doing strictly via browser and web server. Before our meeting got under way, he cornered the guy who'd made the purchasing decision, and despite having spent over a million on this thing, they never deployed it.

At multiple customers over the years, I've been told, "We'd like to replace the identity tools we've bought, but after all this investment in software and services, the company doesn't want to start over." And so they kept moving ahead with deficient solutions. I've also had customers just plain admit, if they had to go back to management and ask for new software, people would get fired for picking the old software.

Failure to Invest the Internal Resources

As of this writing, I am working on replacing two different vendors' products with my own. In both cases, we're upgrading the customers' functionality. Also in both cases, we're providing functionality that they could have possessed with their current vendors, had they only taken the time to deploy them. For example, connectors. "Yeah, we could automate that account creation, but we just send a notification to the administrator, and he runs a script."

With my customers, I insist on that effort. Your vendors and partners can do great things for you, if you let them, and help them help you. Identify those people you need internally, and give them the tools and the time to provide support to the project.

You're going to be making an investment. Get the most impact for your money. I hired a young engineer in Texas who on one occasion picked me up at the airport in his brand new Firebird. He drove in the right lane, about ten miles slower than everybody else. A couple of days later, when he was driving me back to the airport, I had to remind him that I had a flight to catch, and that he was allowed to do the speed limit, at the very least. I told him, "You could have bought a used station wagon and saved the cash."

One of the trickiest things in an IAM project is integration. Your new framework has to connect with other systems, to get data, to provision, and to provide access. That means you absolutely need cooperation from the owners of those other systems. They will provide the information necessary to build the integration, and they will help you test that integration. You also need *domain experts*. These will be not just techies, but line-of-business people, those who know not only how the business works, but how it *should* work.

Make the best use of what you've got, in labor and software. If you're going to put in the initial investment of time and hassle, go the extra mile. Do a good job, and make the most of your investment. Your organization is depending on you. Also remember that your vendors and helpers and advisors and stakeholders *want* you to succeed, because they're attaching their name to your project, and they have knowledge you will need. Take advantage of that.

Forgetting the Goal

As the project takes shape and gains momentum, you will have doubters and others who won't get on board. That's a shame. But you will also have people who will jump on board with both boots, and who want everything they can get out of it. Remember to hold the reins tight to guide the process. This isn't an excuse to be Santa Claus. If your goal is to provide an IAM framework to benefit the entire organization (in phases, of course), don't let it get sidetracked into security or SSO only for somebody's pet applications.

Remember what we discussed about scope creep, and the need for strict governance to ensure that you stay on track. I've seen particular parties appropriate a project for their own narrow goals and sidetrack the bigger picture, simply because they were able to exert undue influence. Avoid this by sticking to your plan. This is your organization's chance to improve life for everybody. Keep your eye on that objective.

PART
III

The Oracle Identity and Access Solution

CHAPTER
7

Designing an Oracle
IAM Framework

If I had six hours to chop down a tree, I'd spend five hours sharpening the ax.

—Abraham Lincoln

n identity and access management framework does not consist of software that you install and start running. It is a set of processes for which you happen to use software and hardware as support. An IAM platform doesn't run the business; it augments the security, enablement, and compliance of your business processes and systems. The more these components work together (integrate), the more efficient and accurate the results will be. There are many fringe benefits as well, as we've been discussing. Compliance used to be one of these fringe benefits, but it has migrated to being an actual primary driver.

I've been in the identity and access management arena for many years. I've watched this area of the market grow and evolve. I've worked at or with or against all the players, big and small, at one time or another. I've seen them complement, work with, defeat, or absorb each other. I've seen how they've stolen each other's ideas, even intellectual property, and driven each other to improve; and I've seen how all this churning has helped the market pass through the gauntlet to the point where there are some powerful solutions available to any organization that needs to secure, process, and empower the identities associated with its users.

In the next few chapters, I will discuss what is currently the most thorough, well-received, comprehensive solution available on the market today for identity and access management, the Oracle Identity and Security Suite. What this includes is the framework for identifying, enabling, and controlling resource access for enterprise users. In 2009, Gartner named Oracle *the* leader in its magic quadrant for user provisioning for the second consecutive year, based on the IAM suite. The other major analysts also pronounce Oracle the leader in provisioning as well as access management. This is based on two factors: vision, and the ability to execute. Anybody can be a member of the standards groups and hype their roadmap, but they must be able to deliver.

I remember one particular security "guru" who used to walk around the Bay Area (San Francisco) trade shows with an entourage, literally dragging interested parties from booth to booth demanding demonstrations, which he would summarily tear apart. When a colleague of mine looked at going to work for the guy, I pointed out, "His company has never made a lot of money, and for all his intellectual capacity, his products just aren't that amazing." A short time later, the guru sold his company for peanuts. It's a cliché, but you must be able to talk the talk and walk the walk. Oracle has put the time, money, engineering, and planning into delivering a comprehensive solution for identity, security, and compliance that is in use in some of the largest identity deployments in the world.

The Latest and Greatest

As of Oracle Identity and Security Suite 11*g*, there are a number of improvements in both usability and performance. Other companies have also acquired technology to build out their stacks, and ultimately they end up with a menu of tools that all look and act differently. Across the entire stack of Oracle's identity and access products, there is a consistent look and feel, from installation to daily use to back end reporting. The interface is based on Oracle's Application Development Framework (ADF), for an improved user experience. Instead of disparate scripts, there is a single installer, in which the user selects the modules to be installed. A consistent workflow engine runs throughout the suite, and Oracle's BI Publisher provides enterprise reporting for all the modules.

Oracle also provides consistent Identity Shared Services no matter which modules are deployed, meaning that users are maintained centrally. Legacy user management in Oracle Access Manager, for example, is now consolidated in Oracle Identity Manager. These uniform services will also provide identity functionality across the Oracle business application stack. PeopleSoft, Siebel, and E-Business Suite will come with run-time identity functionality for managing their users. These apps also benefit from LDAP-based users and roles, with Oracle Virtual Directory abstracting the details for single sign-on and LDAP itself.

As of February 2010, Oracle finalized its acquisition of Sun Microsystems, and began integrating certain of Sun's identity management components into the Oracle suite, for enhanced functionality, analytics, and connectivity. Many organizations use the term "best of breed" in describing their tools, but with Oracle this is truly the case. As they have acquired and built out functionality, Oracle has created a best-in-class hybrid offering, and with the Sun acquisition, has continued refining its security suite, keeping the best of breed, so that the final framework provides optimum capabilities. We will be discussing where the individual components fit into the larger framework picture, and how they function seamlessly together. As the Oracle suite continues to evolve to include the best of its existing functionality, the additions from Oracle product management, and the inclusion of the best of the Sun identity suite, the look and feel (including the menus, tabs, and locations of options) may also evolve. This is to make sure that you don't get too comfortable knowing where everything is.

The combination of products in the Oracle suite is not meant to simply deliver features and functions. Those are simply the tools it uses to do its actual job, which is to model the business requirements, structure, and processes that drive identity and access throughout the enterprise. These processes enable an organization to securely execute its core business functions knowing that its digital resources are available to the right people, and *only* the right people.

I will revisit many of the subjects we've already covered, but with an eye toward specifically solving the problems associated with those subjects. You may recall that in the Introduction, I didn't list the important terms in alphabetic order, because you don't encounter them in alphabetic order. Likewise, I will not cover the design strictly one product at a time, because you don't deploy the products in their entirety one at a time. You deploy them one piece of *required functionality* at a time. In some cases, you make use of one aspect of a component early on, then another aspect later. The products themselves operate in a similar fashion, in that they are organized either hierarchically or by way of most-used functionality. And we still need to take into consideration the other, non-Oracle components that you will need to employ in your final design.

I will walk through the building blocks of an IAM framework, and how to construct that framework, the way you would need to do it from the bottom up, in the proper order. In other words, we'll talk about design first, focusing on the necessary building blocks, followed by a discussion of how the products' features support that design, and deliver the functionality required to drive those all-important identity and access processes.

We'll also discuss integration, meaning connecting the pieces that need to speak to your business apps and databases, as well as to each other. Different functions require their own repositories and schema, and therefore have their own communication requirements.

Whether you're buying or building, don't become a slave to your new system. It's surprising how quickly I've seen people begin subjugating themselves to new technology. "It requires us to feed it data, run batch processes, do all sorts of things that don't directly aid the business and which we never had to do before." I can't stress this enough, so I'll immediately repeat it. Your IAM framework should not *create* work. It should *facilitate your existing work*. It should complement the business, not become a whole new business unto itself.

Of course, that's after it's in place. Up front, it'll be a LOT of work. Don't let anybody tell you this will be easy. But if you do it right, don't let anybody tell you it wasn't worth it.

The Purpose of the Framework

Like tuning a slide deck for a presentation, rehearsing your answers for an interview, or lining up your arguments when asking for budget, it's all about preparation. If you go into an identity management project without laying down the rules and requirements, you'll end up like the majority of those who already have IdM in place and wish they'd done it differently.

Okay, now you need to stop thinking like a mere user, and more like the mysterious guy in the back room who decides how to *process* the mere users. There's a lot on your plate. You've got to bring a lot of individuals into your system, convert them into bytes, put them in their proper places, give them their toys, and keep them happy. You have to make them *think that you care*.

Identity and access management isn't an application. It's not even a *collection* of applications. It's participants, policies and, above all, a set of processes, supported by a framework.

Back to this word *framework*. Why not *system* or *application* or (my wife's favorite word) *thingy*?

Because it's a platform, a skeleton on which you will build your methodologies, which are merely supported by the software you put in place as the joints. Remember, software serves the maker, not the other way around, unless you're helping prop up one of those social networking sites that you think actually cares what you had for lunch.

It's literally a frame for holding the picture, the skeleton that holds up the body of your enterprise. Instead of constructing and reconstructing the necessary provisioning, authentication, and authorization with every new app that you build, buy, or host, you are providing a framework on which to position your resources. Think of it as a service, a platform, an identity party that your apps get to attend.

It's a win-win. The creators of new apps don't have to build security directly into their code. You are providing identity services *for* them. At the same time, you are charting the course that they must follow, in terms of security, compliance, and corporate policies. You don't want all those code monkeys creating their own security policies anyway. By owning the identity aspects of the enterprise, you are

- Making application developers more productive and focused by relieving them of the burden of security
- Putting security people in charge of security
- Maintaining standards
- Providing consistency
- Providing a landing for mergers and acquisitions
- Allowing management to centrally model changes and reorganizations to accommodate smoother transitions
- Providing a single source of truth for *who's who* and *who gets what*

It's the exact same kind of mutual benefit you will see later when we discuss delegated administration.

IAM can't do everything. It can, and should, enforce those things that are within its domain. Identities are leveraged for the data they provide for the purposes of processing or providing access, thereby securing the business apps that truly are the bread and butter of your business. Face it; enterprises that don't sell IAM for a living rarely make money from their IAM implementations.

When possible, IAM should not be intrusive, but rather complementary. This is another reason to consider it as, and design it as, a framework.

Rex Thexton, a managing director for PricewaterhouseCoopers who has spent years advising clients on building IAM platforms, suggests several "critical elements for success":

- "Design with the end in mind. Initial phases may be simplified for time-to-market purposes, but it is critical to gain an understanding of the overall vision and strategy to ensure you don't need to re-architect the solution in later phases."

- "Take a pragmatic approach to implementation. Don't try and boil the ocean. Focus on a few high-value targets and systems for the initial phases."

- "If you are going to be making event-driven provisioning decisions from an authoritative source (e.g., PeopleSoft), it is important to do a data quality audit to ensure that the data provided from the authoritative source is populated and accurate in order to insure success."

- "Engage the business early. Walk them through the technology and user interface early on so they can visualize the end game. I have seen when the business is only engaged via documentation through the requirements and development phases. There are often changes required late in the game in order to get the business sign-off."

- "Leveraging access policies and groups within OIM [Oracle Identity Manager] is a powerful way to implement role-based provisioning."

The Oracle Identity Suite

Just as we defined important terms that we have regularly referred to (and will continue to), let's summarize the components of the Oracle identity and security stack to which we will refer in building an IAM framework. Again, we will visit individual functions of these components as we plan their use. For example, each of them provides reporting capabilities, but you don't kick out any usage reports until you've used them, and that doesn't come until you've deployed multiple components.

The individual components of the suite can all function on their own, but provide great additional value when integrated. Let me give you a high-level example of what I mean. Oracle Identity Manager (OIM) is the cornerstone, in that it establishes users at the time of account creation. Once established, those users can receive business roles and privileges through Oracle Identity Analytics (OIA), and authenticate and be authorized via Oracle Access Manager (OAM), which can invoke the Oracle Adaptive Access Manager (OAAM) for strong authentication and fraud prevention. Those same users can be matched up with granular entitlement policies through Oracle Entitlements Server (OES), and checked for Segregation of Duties violations with OIA or Oracle Access Controls Governor (OAACG). All activities, by users and admins, can be audited and reported on by BI Publisher. In other words, all aspects of identifying, registering, enabling, and securing a user are covered by the integration of the point solutions that make up the larger framework.

It sounds like a lot of pieces, but with a consistent interface, workflow, and reporting structure, the suite will function (and from a user's perspective, *appear* to function) as a single, integrated entity. In this chapter, we will summarize the components, then dive into basic design requirements, recalling the functionality of these components as needed, by requirements rather than by product. As I stated a few pages ago, you don't implement a solution by *product*; you implement by *need*. In subsequent chapters, we will look at more granular functionality and how it serves that design.

There is no one way to design an IAM framework. Everyone's requirements, and ability to fulfill them, are different. You may have the perfect picture of a framework in your head, but an imperfect budget or set of internal resources. Hopefully we will cover a sufficient number of options to suit your purposes and capacity.

Within that framework, you are defining integrated pieces. At the highest level, you are defining:

- The organization
- The users within that organization
- The roles that run the organization
- The resources supporting the organization
- The processes (based on security, compliance, and best practices) that associate the users with the organizations and the roles in order to govern access to the resources and enforce compliance
- The business intelligence requirements for compliance reporting

But these are not *simply* higher-level definitions. Within the Oracle suite, each category provides enough granularity to support the most atomic needs of the business. Organizations drill down from the line of business to individual users. Resources drill down from application deployments to specific instances down to granular privileges. Roles drill down from job titles to functional roles to privileges. And so on. Let's examine the definitions, and how they ultimately work together to build the framework, before we get into the more granular specifics of products, along with their features and functions (which, remember, are only there to support the framework which in turn supports your business). For the rest of this chapter we will paint the big picture of the tasks ahead, the large design considerations, and then in the following chapters we will paint the smaller, more detailed pictures that make up the bigger picture.

Defining Your Organization, Top to Bottom

Modeling the organization is the very essence of creating a framework. While some corporate assets may be used by everyone (for example, e-mail), a large number of them will be departmental, just like your users. "I work in Accounts Payable, and here are the applications we use there." Therefore, preparing an organizational structure for users and resources to reside in ensures that the right people are aligned with the right resources, for security, compliance, approvals, reporting, and just plain business sense.

This can be done within Oracle Identity Manager by creating organizations as simple containers, with suborganizations and parents, in a virtual hierarchy. Resources can be associated with an organization, so that users added to the organization may inherit access to those resources. This keeps use of those resources in the family, as it were.

Within OIM, you can also add the layer of groups that may exist within organizations. Groups have traditionally been a more primitive version of roles, although within OIM they are evolving into more robust structures representing roles. For a group, you can manage its members, subgroups, administrators, and even group-level access policies. Members can be managed manually, of course, but the better option, which we will describe later, is the use of provisioning workflow to assign users to groups and organizations.

Now consider these approaches (which are not mutually exclusive):

- A resource is associated with an organization. A user is added to the organization, and gains access to the resource.

- A role is associated with one or more resources. Get the role, access all its resources. An extra wrinkle is a grant policy that automatically (pending approvals, of course) gives the role to a user who is placed in an organization

There is no right or wrong way to do this, necessarily. You may associate a resource with an organization, or associate a resource with a role, which is in turn associated with the organization. The method you choose may depend on who actually controls the resources, or what your corporate policy is. Auditors certainly tend toward role-based access, since so many regulatory compliance rules mandate roles.

Does using the role-based approach entail an extra layer? Perhaps. But role-based access control (RBAC) allows you more granular access within an organization. Not everybody in a line of business is created equal, right? There are managers, admins, submanagers, workers, and so on. RBAC is more about provisioning than access to begin with, although the first ultimately leads to the second. We will cover RBAC in more detail in a little while, as well as the differences between groups and roles.

Oracle Identity Analytics can be employed to discern, define, and further refine business structures or hierarchies. OIA can also be used for assigning users to one or more business structures. Roles and resources can subsequently be assigned to users based on organizational affiliations.

Defining Your Resources

Once you have your organization laid out, it's time to define the resources that your organization makes use of. We did it in this order because you associate resources with the groups, organizations, branches, lines of business, or other units that own them, so those typically come first. Resources may be databases, applications, folders, files, or anything that a user must be provisioned to within the enterprise. Ultimately, these are what it's all about: the digital assets that your users need access to, and which you must secure.

This is more than just a list of resources. Within OIM, you are also defining how they are managed, and by whom. There are also connectivity considerations. If you are creating a user account in a data source, or appropriating a user from an existing account, you need to specify how that exchange takes place. Therefore, for each resource, you define additional attributes and governing processes:

- Administrators and managers
- Groups (who can access this resource)
- Resource type
- Scheduled tasks

Preparing Resources for the Job of Provisioning

It's not enough to simply define a list of resources. They must themselves be defined in such a way that makes them usable for their job, which is to allow users to access them. You divide them into types that help determine how they're used. You define processes that help govern them. And you define how they are connected to the enterprise so they can be used as sources and/or provisioned to as targets.

Resource types determine what subparameters must be defined that indicate how that resource is provisioned later. If the resource is something physical (that can't be sent by e-mail or used through a browser), such as a desk, a phone, or a building access card, then it will likely be provisioned via e-mail notification to an administrator. But if it's a database, there will be additional connection information required, such as service account, IP address, lookup and reconciliation procedures. If it's Active Directory or LDAP, there will also be connectivity and account parameters. With Active Directory as a resource, you will also want to specify if you have installed AD synchronization, which ensures that users and passwords are synchronized between OIM and AD.

Connectivity must also be specified if the resource is a mail server. In fact, mail servers are among the most commonly defined resources, since you will not only be provisioning users to e-mail accounts; you will also be sending notifications to approvers and administrators to perform provisioning and other identity tasks.

Another common resource is *HR Feed*. In a truly automated, compliant identity system, users will not be manually entered into Oracle Identity Manager, but rather a system of record such as a human resources application (for example, PeopleSoft). Once entered into the HR system, a user must be migrated to OIM for provisioning. In the event OIM (or another connected data store) is used instead of the HR apps for creating an account, all necessary targets must be made whole. In other words, wherever a user is created, he must be made known to all the stores that need to know about him. This can be done at the storage level by use of Oracle Internet Directory (OID) or Oracle Virtual Directory (OVD), or directly through OIM via a scheduled task. We will discuss in more detail the use of HR feeds for account creation in the next chapter.

Scheduled tasks are processes that run on a timetable and frequency you specify, to handle common housekeeping chores. A common use for a scheduled task is to reconcile users between stores. A scheduled task that ensures that user accounts are properly synchronized between sources is typically called *reconciliation*. Once users are created in the system of record (such as Human Resources), reconciliation runs on a scheduled basis to bring those users into OIM to begin the provisioning process, matching up those users to their designated resources. Later, we will discuss the provisioning process itself in great detail.

Other common scheduled tasks reconcile passwords as well, such as when a user password is changed on one system but not centrally. This may be due to forgotten password reset, password policies that are not in sync, or a simple desire to change the password.

Two more notes on resources. First, you may also configure the ID formats for your respective resources, meaning that the way a user is represented in one resource may not be the same as the next. You may be *John.Smith* in one application, *JSmith@MegaBigCorp.BIZ* at another, and so on. Within OIM, you can configure how a user is instantiated in each target. Second, you will eventually subdivide your resources. For example, while a resource may be an Oracle database, you will not provision all-or-nothing rights to that database. You will later define in your provisioning processes specific database user rights, admins, basic users, granular permissions, and so on.

Making Resources Available for Provisioning

Oracle Identity Manager has a number of out-of-the box (OOTB) components for connecting to resources for the purpose of provisioning and reconciliation. These include databases, LDAP, Active Directory, various user stores (including mainframe), and a very large number of off-the-shelf applications (for example, PeopleSoft, Siebel and, for higher education, Banner). When a target resource has sufficient market demand (or when a customer demands it), new connectors are born. For those situations where an off-the-shelf connector is not available, OIM provides the Adapter Factory (inside the Design Console) for rapid integration with a legacy or custom application. The Adapter Factory comes with a GUI for building connectivity, without the need to code or script. Once created, a connector is maintained in the library for future use and, when needed, modification.

Source(s) of Truth and Authority

One of the cornerstones of your IAM framework will be a definitive, authoritative source of identity. While there are some organizations who don't actually have one of these, I highly recommend it, because in those instances where it doesn't exist, there *will* be considerable confusion at some point or other as to where the absolute values lie in terms of someone's attributes, access rights, duties, titles, or varying credentials across platforms. In other words, I have seen some of my customers simply continue to spread user info across multiple sources, not for any business reason but simply because that's how it is now, and they haven't devised a method for aggregating the information in order to provide a practical, single source of "who is he and what does he have."

Some organizations will say, "This LDAP is our authoritative source for identity. This relational database is our authoritative source for permissions. This other directory is our authoritative source for this particular application. Customer contact info is in the CRM system." That is to say, they have no authoritative source. It's like having multiple bosses.

Where this may be acceptable, if only because of security or business reasons, is when you have multiple authoritative sources for multiple populations. I've seen in many instances, for example, a source for employees and another for non-employees. And companies who host applications and/or data for their customers are often required to segregate those customers by database, file system, or even hardware, which is understandable.

It may be fairly difficult, if not impossible, to construct a single authoritative source to replace existing multiple ones. Why?

- If it's even possible to do so, it can take an organization many months to construct a schema flexible enough to support all identity and application purposes. One of the reasons that Service Provisioning Markup Language (SPML) hasn't taken off as a standard is the lack of an agreed-upon user schema.

- Politics: Will the owners of those various data sources allow you to copy *all* their data? Will they agree on a common set of security rules?

- Corporate policies may require the separation of data relevant to different groups (employees, customers, partners, and so on).

But within a single population, it is highly useful to have that authoritative source for the sake of performance. It can enable single sign-on and reduce the number of queries it takes to authorize a user for resource requests. If provisioning and/or authorization are based on group memberships or attributes, virtualization can also greatly simplify assigning and authorizing users for resources. If you have constructed a model of your organization, you can represent that in your authoritative source. Oracle Identity Manager allows you to define groups and organizations, but these are more containers than actual structures, so while they're certainly useful, the ability to populate users within a structure allows for context and inheritance.

If you plan on launching additional applications (and who doesn't?), you can greatly expedite the process by providing that source of truth, and avoiding the use of yet another proprietary identity store.

True Story

In 2009 I visited a university with quite a number of user groups: applicants, students, student workers, grad students, alumni, teachers, faculty, staff, emeriti (with special privileges), retirees, board members, boosters, summer camp attendees, high school kids kicking the tires, and a few others. It was an insane bunch of groups with differing needs to keep track of. But the university did all of this using just two types of directories. They had avoided directory creep. There weren't a whole lot of pockets of LDAP, AD, MySQL, Access, RDBMS, and so on. By keeping their directory structures fairly simple, they set themselves up for success later on when they decided to investigate putting a framework on top of all this. When we went in to give them a checkup and recommend various technologies to help, we were able to honestly tell their executive staff what a smart bunch of IT folks they had.

You may already have a directory that you love. If it provides all the capabilities for supporting provisioning, authentication, authorization, and compliance, then constructing a new source of truth may very well be unnecessary. But there might still be at least one good reason for front-ending that directory with a meta-directory or virtual directory (such as Oracle's OID or OVD): extending the schema. You might want to

- Bind Active Directory credentials to a real LDAP or application that expects this
- Add virtual groups or attributes
- Protect certain attributes from those outlets that don't require them
- Extend the schema's abilities to serve a greater purpose
- Merge the schema/data from different user groups

What Goes into Those Authoritative Sources?

A user is more than a set of attributes such as name, address, and e-mail. It is an entity with attributes that relate it to the things it owns, to the things that own it, and to the enterprise. If you start with the user, you can work your way up and down. Better yet, if you've started with the organization, you can now put users into it. Before, I said that resources were what this is all about. Well, kind of. Without users to use them, those resources are just shelfware.

With or without an organizational structure, you can still create organizations and groups. But without a structure, these may be simply containers. Within a structural hierarchy, a user may inherit memberships and therefore resources and access, as well as other attributes. So if you've assembled an organizational structure, you instantiate it within the authoritative source. If your Human Resources app supports it, you may be doing it there. Otherwise, LDAP is a great place. There are a few popular ones, such as Sun (now the Oracle Directory Server Enterprise Edition [ODSEE]), Novell eDirectory, and the sort-of LDAP known as Active Directory. We'll talk about two more in a moment.

Users themselves must be defined. I'm not talking about actual human beings, but rather the delivery mechanism, the user objects. You have a structure for the organization, but what about the people? What does the baseline for a user look like? It must be constructed in such a way that it contains, or at least refers to or inherits from, all the attributes that a user will need in order to be provisioned, authenticated, authorized, and reported on. These attributes provide the *framework* for how the user interacts with the identity system and ultimately the business applications and other resources that make up the enterprise system.

Anyone reading this nonsense likely already knows the definition of the word *schema*, but let's just take a quick look at it anyway. A schema is the structure of a database or directory, describing the tables or objects, the attributes in those tables or objects, and their relationships. There exist many generic and very useful schema for supporting user objects that lend themselves to provisioning and access. Some have been developed for specific verticals. For example, eduPerson and eduOrg are LDAP schemas designed for use in institutions of higher education. Universities are definitely subject to more convoluted requirements, given the many concurrent positions a user may inhabit. Depending on the institution, these may be perceived as more fundamental than functional roles.

In a commercial environment, there are fundamental user types such as employee, customer, contractor, vendor, supplier, and so on. Within these higher-level groups functional roles will exist, such as data entry clerk, manager, auditor, claims adjuster, administrator, and so on. In an educational environment, the more fundamental user types are applicant, student, alumnus, faculty, administrator, staff member, adjunct, retiree, board member, booster, emeritus, and so forth. A graduate pursuing a second degree while also serving as an assistant *and* working in the book store might wear four hats. This begs the question of how to handle all the possibilities.

Here's a terrible way to do it: Create roles for all the possible combinations (student-employee, student-alumnus, and so on). I never would have thought to do this, until I visited a university that did just this. Just about any approach would work better, although I would recommend multiple role assignments, and the use of organizational mappings to provide context (in this branch I am only a student; in the next branch, I am an alumnus). As we'll discuss a little later under the topic of RBAC, most users already have multiple roles in any enterprise, even if they have a single job title, and this example is simply a bit more taxing. Regardless, design a schema that accommodates complex needs, and can be extended if and when requirements change. A user's attributes, whether explicit or inherited, will be utilized later for authorization decisions.

One last consideration when designing a user object: self-service. There may be certain attributes you will let a user maintain for himself. In fact, for the sake of both users and help desk personnel, this is a very good thing. Password resets, account unlocking, security questions should all come under the heading of self-service. Empowering the users is a win-win for the organization and its members.

Oracle Directory Services: OID, OVD, and ODSEE

For years, the construction of an authoritative source in an environment where multiple stores already exist has been a challenge, often necessitating redundancy and messy transformation and synchronization. Run the cron job, gather the far-flung data, scrub and transform that data, then stuff it into that single source, because it was either that approach or, at run time, having to execute multiple time-consuming queries to complete a transaction. This is a worst-case scenario for authentication and/or authorization, when a user is sitting there watching the hourglass on their screen, waiting to be told whether or not they can gain access. Oracle, to better service these use cases, provides Oracle Directory Services (ODS), which is composed of the following components:

- Oracle Internet Directory (OID) synchronizes and stores distributed data. It is a meta-directory built on the Oracle database, with massive performance capabilities, having been benchmarked with two billion entries, and which is used in some of the largest LDAP deployments in the world. Its purpose is to serve as the only general-purpose directory needed in any organization. By aggregating data from disparate sources, as well as extending those sources, it also helps preserve and add value to an existing investment in data stores. OID can be used by Oracle Internet Federation for creating Security Assertion Markup Language (SAML) assertions, by Oracle Identity Manager as an identity repository, and by the Oracle Web Services Manager to propagate authentication and authorization of service calls.

- Oracle Virtual Directory (OVD) aggregates and transforms data without the need to synchronize or store. It performs real-time queries from multiple sources and presents results in an LDAP interface.

- Oracle Directory Server Enterprise Edition (ODSEE), formerly the Sun Directory Server, has an embedded database and robust Independent Software Vendor (ISV) support. It is well positioned to service heterogeneous application environments, with more granular connectors than many other competing offerings, and also for lighter-weight deployments. As of this writing, it is being integrated with the Directory Integration Platform (OID's synchronization engine) and the Oracle Directory Services Manager (described conveniently in the very next bullet point).

- Oracle Directory Services Manager (ODSM) is a console for centrally managing both directories. ODSM also integrates with Oracle Enterprise Manager (OEM) for centrally monitoring OVD, OID, and other components, and integrating with BI Publisher, Oracle's enterprise reporting tool. We will discuss OEM in greater detail in the last chapter.

While you may yet have silo directories of user stores for discrete purposes, using ODS to create a centralized corporate directory, to serve as the source of truth for identity, authentication, and authorization, gives you greater control over what it means for users and groups to participate in your business processes. Those disparate data stores may still provide those discrete functions and enable localized identity, but can now also provide the building blocks for a foundational corporate identity structure and the centralized identity and security policies that govern the entire enterprise.

The ability to centralize storage with ODS is far more than simply retrieving data. The actual presentation is all-important; that is what makes this option a truly authoritative source, in that you are providing a view of enterprise data in a way that best serves the general needs. Those disparate data sources as they currently exist serve their own legacy purposes. The silo-oriented data they hold can be transformed, extended, and presented for enterprise purposes.

Let's recall that we're designing a foundation for the IAM framework. If a legacy app currently performs its own user authentication based on its proprietary data, this isn't serving an overall purpose. However, by centralizing and transforming this data (along with a central context or schema), you are supporting all the benefits of an IAM framework:

- Providing a central spot for data management, Part One. This is in keeping with the best practice of empowering security personnel to manage the data used for security decisions (while still supporting delegated administration).

- Providing a central spot for data management, Part Two. It's common to create multiple instances of a directory in order to provide a variety of schema for multiple applications (for example, Active Directory Lightweight Directory Services [LDS]). ODS eliminates the need for this situation for providing different contexts.

- Exposing only those data elements that are necessary. Earlier we discussed "least privilege" as a means of ensuring that users have the access they need, and nothing else. When aggregating data from disparate sources, you are exposing the data that users or authentication/authorization services need, and nothing else.

- Supports extending a user profile, and the possible use of attributes that aren't currently used or haven't even been created yet, as authentication, authorization, and compliance policies evolve. If new requirements appear, a central directory simplifies the necessary modifications.

- Extending the use of one or more directories without having to extend those directories themselves. Let me give you an excellent example that can be extrapolated for many uses. Oracle provides a tool called Enterprise User Security (EUS, which we'll discuss a little later) for centrally creating and enabling privileged database users. Through EUS, you can modify the directory schema to create centralized, enterprise database roles that aggregate the roles found in individual databases. In many instances, you may not wish to extend the schema of the existing directory (especially if it's Active Directory, because then you're stuck with those changes). If you front that directory with OID, you can make the necessary changes to the OID schema, leaving the back-end store untouched. This preserves the current state as well as the investment of the current directory while extending its use. In fact, you may model other changes in OID to make use of values or attributes across multiple stores in order to achieve a result that is only possible by combining the data from disparate data sources.

Also consider that by virtue of synchronization, you can match up disparate data sources that are not in agreement. A couple of pages back I mentioned a university where they had kept their directory structure simple. Two weeks after I visited them, I visited another institution with the exact opposite situation. They had every conceivable type of database and directory, few of them linked in any meaningful way, although several smaller "directories," actually just relational databases, had been initially constructed from extracts of a larger database. Lack of synchronization meant that a student in the larger database (ostensibly the source of authority) who had been deactivated still appeared alive and well in any one of the smaller databases. An audit of all their databases would have revealed a large number of departed users who still had access in a number of departmental apps. By synchronizing these kinds of contradicting user stories, you can truly provide a source of truth from existing directories, even when they don't line up.

Oracle Virtual Directory (OVD) provides similar benefits as OID, but without actual storage or data copying, presenting an LDAP interface on data aggregated from multiple sources. It retrieves data in real time and transiently, assembling the results only when queried, so there is no synchronization. Here I am talking about only a virtual representation of one or more data sources. These sources may be LDAP, relational databases, Active Directory, and even web services. Once again, you are assembling a system of truth from across your stores.

Because it's not actual storage, but essentially a query engine, you can create multiple queries and therefore multiple views, which must be authenticated to. As just a side note, not only is OVD a foundational component of a secure framework, it is secure in and of itself. Views are created to be limited in scope, to provide application-specific snapshots of identity data, and the views themselves may be configured to require qualified, authenticated distinguished name (DN) and IP address for use. OVD supports split-profile views, meaning the ability to join identity data from multiple sources.

A client may connect to OVD through LDAP (most common), HTTP (common, but not as much), or DSML (don't hear much about this one yet). Remember that a client may be a browser, an LDAP query tool, or an application. What matters is that the client must authenticate to a desired view. Out of the box, OVD connects to back-end sources via LDAP and JDBC. OVD also supports a Java API for creating custom adapters to Java Message Service (JMS) or web services. It also comes with prebuilt features for publishing identity to Siebel and PeopleSoft.

Oracle Virtual Directory has several benefits and applications beyond simply fronting for back-end stores:

- Aggregating data (for our purposes, a user's attributes) from multiple sources for a coordinated view
- Transforming the data as needed for identity purposes
- Improving the speed of real-time snapshot reporting
- Migrating users from one system or group to another
- Safeguarding all other source attributes, and obscuring the original sources, acting as a sort of data firewall

Let's just dwell on that last point a moment. The owner of a data source that is being referenced by an OVD view still retains ownership of that data, and can turn off the source at any time. That owner is also assured that the copy of the data that is being used by the OVD-enabled partner is working with the most recent and therefore presumably most relevant data.

Picture this: a summary view of a customer's current status, pulling from multiple tables or databases, as shown in the following illustration.

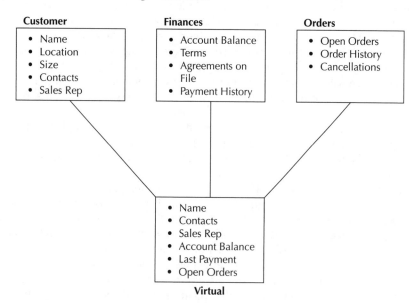

We have information about a customer spread across multiple data sources, and we need to expose some, but not all, of that information for accounting, reporting, or auditing purposes. So we select only certain data elements, present them in a single view, and obfuscate the actual sources. This is what the virtual directory does.

Any sensitive or proprietary information is left behind. OVD can even decide, based on security context or through integration with the security restrictions of a source, if the querying client is authorized for a view. OVD also supports a variety of authentication schemes, and can protect from malicious attacks by denying malformed queries, and by configuring limits on the number of connections and operations.

The various stores may also represent completely different user groups, such as employees, customers, partners, vendors, suppliers, and so on. If you can find common denominators, then it may still make sense to keep them under a common directory structure, at least further up the tree, while at the same time maintaining some degree of separation. An application with the requirement of only admitting users from the base *ou=users* might cause you to place groups from different stores under the same node, and inheriting that same organizational unit, while at the same time branching into separate sub-orgs for the sake of separating them for access control to other apps. For example, *ou=users* might get employees and contractors into the dev environment, while *ou=users, ou=contractors* might get only consultants into the time-reporting app. But moving down the tree from the same root allows you to share commonality between users. Why reinvent the wheel for each group when they share elements?

Chances are that your data stores were not designed with security or compliance in mind. Why should they be? They were meant to hold data, and nothing else. But now you've got to sweat security and compliance. If your schema aren't suitable to the task, this is where a meta- or virtual schema come in awfully handy. You can design a meta- or virtual schema as the perfect authoritative source for identity, without impacting the structure of your current data stores.

Populate Your Authoritative Source(s)

Most likely, even if you're only beginning to design a proper IAM framework, you've already got one or more (and it's likely more) user stores, whether database or directory. And chances are that, for at least the time being, you will continue to support those same user stores, and will incorporate them into your new framework, perhaps through synchronization or virtualization, which can compensate for any weaknesses they may have as enterprise identity-supporting components. We will actually discuss in Chapter 14 a detailed approach to legacy components, including existing user directories. In the meantime, let's very briefly discuss the design considerations for populating your user directories in an efficient and compliant fashion going forward. Even if you keep your existing stores, there is a good chance that with a new IAM framework, your method for instantiating users will change. In the next chapter, we will discuss the actual mechanics of creating user accounts, but right now let's discuss some of the design considerations.

Ideally, you will be using an HR application for creating new employee entries. Non-employees may very well be coming in through other means, and are being kept in a directory different from that for your employees. Let's start with that HR app. If you have a directory, let's assume that the creation of a new user account also creates a directory entry. Does it also initiate provisioning, which in turn fills in the values that will later drive authentication and authorization? This is where a feed from HR or that originating system can seamlessly move users from that initial Submit button to placement in all authoritative sources for identity and access management. A commonly used resource within Oracle Identity Manager is an HR Feed. OIM can reconcile from your chosen HR application on a scheduled basis, to kick off the provisioning process and help synchronize new users across the enterprise.

If you are building that directory of truth from scratch, there are various options (which we will discuss in the very next chapter) for migrating users to it from elsewhere. Even if you are bulk-loading numbers of users, you should have a strategy, for the sake of performance and indexing. You can't just do a giant data dump; you must bring those bulk users into the directory in such a way that instantly makes them secure, and indexed for tracking and provisioning. I've seen projects where users were moved in large numbers from one database to another, and with little verification, leading to inaccuracies and redundancy. The indexing of new users may (or may not) take place in tandem with the loading (something we'll also discuss in the next chapter), but at the very least, it should follow shortly thereafter. This not only validates the load, but it also makes those user profiles instantly useful.

You may empower users to create their own accounts. In the last handful of years, I have visited exactly one organization that allowed users to self-register with little to no validation. "You want an account on our server? Here, create a username, password, and preferences, and you're on." When I expressed my incredulity at this, the project manager admitted it was completely against his wishes, but the business was driving it. At the very least, you need to enforce some small approval workflow, or request some kind of identifying data that can be verified in an automated fashion, even if it's through a third party.

Assigning users to groups provides a structure for reporting and review. Even service accounts should have owners so that they are not orphaned and unregulated. To further administer users, you must also establish password policies, specifying acceptable password formats (minimum and maximum length, use of numbers or special characters) and expiration periods. Password policies may also be enforced locally.

Oracle Identity Manager itself can be used for user creation, via the user management interface, but this is not its true calling. It is meant to manage users and their resources as they come into the enterprise through applications that drive the business. Chapter 8 is devoted to the creation of user accounts through several types of common business processes.

Service Accounts

You may read on some websites that *service accounts* are provisioned just like any other user. This is only partially correct. Service accounts aren't used directly by users, but rather by processes, such as web services, or by other services that do work on a user's behalf. When you use OIM, for example, it is talking to the source and target systems using the context of a service account. It logs into a back-end database, for example, and stays logged in for as long as the service is running, with enough rights to create, retrieve, modify, and delete users and groups. If you navigate to a page that subsequently kicks off a web service to perform a task for you, it is doing so using its own account, and at that point, you're just an argument in a call.

These accounts more often than not have greater privileges than the average enterprise user, and therefore the access that makes them so valuable is also dangerous in the wrong hands. Naturally, they can be created through whatever means you are using to create other accounts, naturally. Administrators may request their creation, so that they are approved like any other account, which is a generally good idea (although you'll need *at least* one in advance just to run the necessary provisioning process). These accounts should be resource-specific, since they will perform very specific functions. But for the sake of the very precise tracking required, they should be visible to OIM so that they may be audited and attested to. People tend to forget about them because there are no humans attached, so at the very least, they should be part of your attestation process, which we'll discuss near the very end of this chapter, and again under Compliance Support in Chapter 12.

Enabling Your Population: Roles, Privileges, and Access

Let me toss a notion out there to which there is no right or wrong answer. Which comes first, role definitions or access policies? Do you define the roles to which users are assigned, and which subsequently point them to the right access policies? Or do you create access policies that are assigned to groups, which themselves are subsequently associated with roles?

Here's that painful answer again. *It depends*. Will you be doing role management, proper RBAC in which you associate business roles with resources? It's highly recommended, because:

- Compliance laws often love roles, as do auditors, because they like knowing that users have access rights for sound business reasons.
- RBAC is more business-friendly than standard provisioning.
- LDAP or identity groups are typically more static than roles, providing less granularity looking south and less business association looking north.

Groups are sufficient in fairly flat, non-distributed environments with few variations. But in a varied environment, you will end up with the problem of group proliferation, with a different group for every job code, department, location, and so on, as shown in the following illustration:

Using true RBAC, you can create a base model for a role, with attributes for assigning context. In this instance, I can have a single role for consistency, maintenance, compliance, and a million other reasons. When it is assigned, I add the context, as shown in the following illustration:

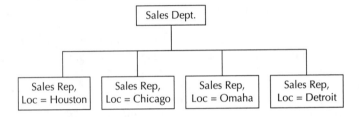

That said, role definitions themselves take time and labor (more on that in a minute), and supporting roles as part of provisioning takes a bit more construction as well. So *it depends* on what you have to first show in terms of results, and what overhead you're willing to build to support RBAC. If provisioning is primary, access policies should come first, while you are in the process of defining roles. You may not get all the granularity and context you need for the most precise assignments, but you can provision the big things by either direct resource grants, approvals of self-requests, or group/organization-based policies. You can associate roles with policies at a later date. By the way, when associating specific roles with specific resources, we're talking about resource-level roles, not the kind of business role that is more closely associated with a job title, although those business roles ultimately drive the resource roles (just wait one more paragraph). And remember, nothing is completely carved in stone. You can always modify policies as makes sense, and as such modifications are approved. Access policies in OIM are assigned to administrators or owners, who decide how and when a policy is maintained. One more point: the people who construct access policies are very close to the people who know what goes into a resource role.

NOTE
Because the final stages of provisioning and approvals involve specific resources, it's common to associate OIM groups with resource roles.

If compliance is the biggest driver, then role definitions should definitely be going on at least in tandem with policy definition, if not first. And now that we've partially answered that first set of questions, let's throw out another. Which comes first, IT-level roles that specify a user's privileges within a given application or resource, or the business roles that define a user's place in the hierarchy and contain the multiple resource roles he needs to do his job? Chicken versus egg. This question is actually much easier to answer. They typically *do* get performed in parallel, but by different parties. So while in the previous paragraph I said that access policies and resource roles may be created by the same parties, business roles and resource roles are *not*. Business roles are defined from the top down by business analysts, people who know which positions they need to fill in order to do the business of the organization. These business roles must be mapped to the resource roles that are specific to the resources needed by the organization, and which are discovered and/or built from the bottom up.

So while the business people extract the business functions from the organizational chart, the IT/access folks extract the IT roles from the resources. Later, the two parties must work jointly to map one set of findings to the other, with the result being business-friendly provisioning. Assign a user to a business role, and that role maps to the IT resource roles the user needs to do his job. As part of the design of a business role, you map it to the organization that we designed earlier. Where does that business function belong in the organizational chart? Is that role related to one or more regulatory compliance mandates? What is the policy for automatically granting a business role? Who are the business-level approvers for that role (and I don't mean people, but approver roles)? These approvers are of course different from the more granular approvers who sign off on the individual resources provided by the business role grant.

Role grants require business-level attributes. You need to decide during design which business or organizational attributes allow or deny a role for a user.

- I must belong to a specific business unit to qualify for a specific role.

- If I belong to a particular group, I am specifically excluded from having a particular role.

- If I have a particular role, I am excluded from having another specified role, because of Segregation of Duties requirements.

We will look at specific configurations for role policies in Chapter 9.

Remember that compliance dictates that users should have roles (and therefore access rights) for sound business reasons. But of course, there are exceptions. When possible, consider building those exceptions into your policies or rules. Admin rights to application-1 may only be granted to a user in location-1 with senior certification and, at a minimum a manager's title, *or* to any direct report to the COO. Naturally, exceptions by their very nature are not always anticipated. You may have heard the IT term *firefighter,* as in "We've had a breach, and I'm assigning firefighters to do the forensics." This is when (temporary) exception grants are made to allow database or server exams of log files. When possible, you should assign expirations to these grants, so that temporary duties don't become permanent simply because nobody remembers to clean them up. It helps to periodically review exceptions to decide if an exception should be revoked as a violation, accepted as an acceptable (and ongoing) exception, or rolled into the policy so that it becomes part of the rule rather than a permanent exception.

Whether or not you are employing RBAC, ultimately it is your provisioning tool's access policies that perform the actual user enablement. OIM provides a designer tool for associating users with groups, attributes, and just plain *logic* in deciding who gets access to what. Here are some best practices to consider when designing access policies:

- Resource owners are probably your best source of information as to the approval steps for granting access to a particular resource.

- Always remember least privilege: Who absolutely needs access to this resource?

- Always remember segregation of duties: How do you define conflicts via rules in OIM and/or integration with OAACG and/or role grant rules?

- Do you need to put an expiration period on a grant?

- What are the compliance requirements? Do they have relevance for approvals, least privilege, notifications, or certifications for the requesting party?

By this point, we're presuming we've designed a user repository and resource definitions. Now for the purposes of provisioning, we are designing *workflow definitions*. These are the procedures that actually enable users. Provisioning essentially consists of two components, workflow and connectors. The true decision making is performed within the workflow. Workflow definitions do not have to be overly complex, and most of the time, they won't be. OIM's visual workflow tool allows you to graphically design provisioning sequences, including automated tasks, approvals, and dependencies.

Workflow definitions are more than just ordered steps, however. You are also designing around the possibilities. Most workflows include approvers who sign off on (or deny) resource requests. But what if an approver is not available? How long does the process wait before sending a notification? Before escalating? What are those escalation procedures? Who are the backup approvers? Who is ultimately notified to take over the process when it completely breaks down because of human error? These factors must all go into the design to ensure timely and accurate provisioning. It sounds complex, but remember that a lot of these procedures are repeatable.

Let's step back into RBAC again. Oracle Identity Analytics (OIA) supports the building of business roles associated with the organizational hierarchy, and which map to resource-level IT roles and entitlements. These roles themselves have grant policies for including or specifically excluding users, by way of attributes, memberships, existing roles, and so on. Once a role has been granted via policy, OIM provisions the resources associated with the role. Virtually the same considerations in designing access policies also apply to role grants. Least privilege, SoD, and compliance all come into play, except now you may be creating these policies one layer up, taking into consideration memberships in business units or existing business roles.

Mapping granular privileges into resource-level roles can be time-consuming. Many organizations do it manually, creating spreadsheets based on interviewing every user and manager in the place to find out what they do, and two weeks after these spreadsheets are filled out, they're obsolete, at least in any typically dynamic organization. To expedite this process *and* keep the data current, Oracle Identity Analytics can process user and entitlement data. To provide these benefits, OIA does the following:

- Analyze existing user-privilege data from directories and apps such as AD, RACF, PeopleSoft, and so on

- Suggest clean-up of over-provisioned and under-provisioned users

- Identify underused or unused privileges, and orphaned privileges

- Discover inherent roles within the privileges

- Associate resources and entitlements with the business hierarchy
- Discover default policy rules for the discovered roles
- Apply Segregation of Duties policies
- Create lists of users to be de-provisioned, and candidates for provisioning
- Provide these roles and rules for use in provisioning

The essential methodology for role discovery (expressed here in over-simplified form) is the aggregation of the most commonly partnered IT privileges. When a set of privileges is assigned on a regular basis, those privileges form an implicit role. Privileges without partners are considered "orphaned," meaning that they may be one-offs or exceptions, or perhaps privileges that should be given extra scrutiny, since privileges in theory should only be granted as part of an overall business role for sound business reasons.

Remember that this discovery process results in the creation of IT roles and rules, which must still be mapped to the business roles as defined by business analysts or managers. There is no magical, completely automated process to role creation. It is an interactive and iterative process, requiring regular reviews and updates to ensure accuracy and compliance.

IT gurus have been using the term *Role-Based Access Control* (RBAC) for years, but usually have no idea what they're talking about. The word *role* has a hazy definition, with many variants that not everyone agrees on. What matters is how *you* need roles to work for your environment. Later, when we cover Requests for Proposal (RFPs), those pesky collections of questions you give to vendors, we'll go over again the notion of how to communicate your exact needs. But for now let's get a grasp of this term *roles*, so that once again you can talk apples and apples to vendors and partners and even your own stakeholders.

The National Institute of Standards and Technology (NIST) has a proposed standard for RBAC. Their core notion of roles is just fine, although stated slightly out of order, which I will now correct. Permissions are assigned to roles, then users are assigned to roles, and therefore users get the permissions by virtue of having the roles. They also state another useful notion that so many, many organizations have gotten wrong over the years. A user can have many roles, which has always been the problem, but *a role can have many users*.

What do I mean by that? Well, the thing so many companies have gotten wrong is: they have 10,000 users and 30,000 roles. If I can do five different things as part of my job, then I have five roles. If the guy sitting next to me also has five different roles, then between us we have ten different roles. Ouch! I've actually heard of even worse examples, where organizations had literally millions of roles, with the excuse being, "Everybody is unique." As a product manager at Oracle puts it, "When everybody is unique, *nobody* is unique."

Let's say I'm appearing in a Shakespeare play. Let's go with *Titus Andronicus*, because it's extremely violent and bloody, much like the software market. If I'm appearing as Titus in one theater, and there's another production of the same play down the street, I'm not Titus-1 while the other guy is Titus-2. We're both reading from the same script. We're both Titus. We've both been assigned that same role. What's different is our *context*, since we're in different theaters, and besides that, I'm tall, swarthy, handsome, and articulate, and the other guy's kind of ugly. But we both have the same essential role, speak the same lines, and end up in the same horrid way.

So instead of 30,000 roles for 10,000 people, it should be 10,000 roles for 30,000 people. But wait, there's more! It should probably be more like 100 roles for 10,000 people, a vast order of magnitude less. Don't turn a slight variation into an excuse for a whole new role. If the plastics division has a Quality Control Officer, and so does the metals division, then you have one role, with the context being the division. The grant of that role may still require different approvers; remember not to confuse the role with the granting of that role. But the baseline definition of the role will be consistent, yet flexible. Using context as a qualifier on a role keeps the number of roles from exploding.

So back to NIST for a moment. They state another useful aspect to roles, hierarchical RBAC, wherein roles within a hierarchy may inherit permissions. If, during your role definitions (which we'll also address momentarily), you devise a role hierarchy, you make inheritance and prerequisites much more practical. At one of my banking customers, they had a base role for all tellers, called (boringly enough) Teller. From there you might become a junior teller, senior teller, or one of four other possible types of teller. The base teller role provided the basics of being able to log in to a register. After that, it was a matter of the size and types of transactions you could process.

Consider a cashier at a register at a store, who can pretty much check out any product, except liquor. In most places in the United States, a cashier must be 21 years old to do so. Cashier is the role; age is the context that provides a variation on that role.

When the Tail Wags the Dog

There is a strange, emerging approach to role definitions that is being championed by various software vendors who are making the case that because they have a hammer, every problem is a nail. This approach is *continual mining and redefinition*. What it consists of is hooking up connectors to target systems and pulling any new entitlements a user has into that user's roles. Not only does this assume that the access a person has is the access he *should* have, but it also bloats the roles and breaks the entire governance model. The correct idea behind defining roles and using them for provisioning is for a user to be assigned a role, whether directly or automatically, and then have that role tell the target systems what privileges the user should have, rather than the other way around.

If a user is granted out-of-band access, that new privilege shouldn't then become part of the policy without a review. So rather than simply mining on a never-ending basis, think more in terms of *certification*. When new privileges are discovered, it is useful to certify their place in the ongoing framework, and adopt them into your roles in a logical manner, rather than simply pull them in. We will discuss role certification in more detail in Chapter 12, when we cover compliance support.

Here's a philosophical question that lends itself directly to your access and role policies: Do you automatically grant your users all the things they're eligible for, or do you wait until requests are made? There are pluses and minuses to both approaches. You can associate resources with OIM groups, and/or create dynamic roles within OIA, to perform automatic grants based on attributes or group memberships reconciled from an HR feed; this enables your user population more quickly and reduces the possible request bottlenecks later. This especially makes sense for a resource that you know will be heavily used, and is the best possible use case for dynamic roles.

But consider the application that a thousand people are allowed to use, but maybe only a hundred ever will. Will usage reporting be more complicated later? Will you be eating up licenses that you might want to direct toward other users later? Let's just digress on that example for a minute.

I buy a collaboration tool for my thousand users and, being cheap and short-sighted, I license only a thousand seats. I automatically provision my users to it. Now I buy another company, and I want them to be able to collaborate as well. I have three alternatives. I can expire users who haven't logged into the thing in more than, say, two months, which would include everybody who's *never* logged in to it. This would free up seats. Or I can buy more seats. OR I can get into my time-travel machine and return to the moment before I provisioned everybody, and change the policy to make provisioning to the collaboration tool a request-only proposition.

I might still expire inactive users after a certain period of time. But this way I've got some buffer on the number of seats. Also consider, if I was prepared to automatically provision all eligible users to begin with, the approval process likely isn't too strict, so bottlenecks may not be such an issue. Requests also give you another metric, besides just pure number of transactions, as to how viable that tool is within the organization. If nobody signs up, then perhaps you've wasted your money.

The point I'm *not* trying to make is that you do "either or." Some resources you most likely want to grant access to automatically, such as e-mail and any application that you know is absolutely crucial to a particular job title. But if there's any ambiguity, or the possibility that a resource will not be used by default, then you may consider not including that resource in a dynamic role. Just like users, not all resources are created equal.

Authenticating and Authorizing Your Population

Once you've defined your user population and your resources, and executed the policies that match up the two, you have built the foundation for the daily routine. Everything we've done up to now has been setting the stage for what will come. In other words, the more *static* work has been performed. This is not to say that you won't maintain, modify, and evolve your resources, users, and policies. But they won't be nearly as *dynamic* as what is next, and this is the day-to-day interaction of users with resources.

Now that they're identified and provisioned, your users will be logging in and requesting resources every minute. The act of identifying oneself to the framework is *authentication*. You are presenting credentials of one form or another. Once it's validated your identity, the framework can access more detailed information about your profile, such as any attributes or group memberships that mitigate which resources you can access. This is *authorization*.

I've heard this question more than once at various presentations and seminars: "If only the right users are provisioned to the applications, why is authorization so important? Users can't get to those resources anyway, if they haven't been provisioned to them." Here are the multiple answers to that one.

First, *things change*. There may be just the one factor giving you day-one rights to an application. But there are often multiple factors considered at authorization to allow or deny access. Therefore authorization is an important tripwire. Second, if you begin allowing federated access, you haven't performed the provisioning on those users in the first place, and so authorization and the trust between you and your federation partner are all you have. Third, authorization can be configured (assuming your solution, like Oracle's, supports it) to consider real-time factors. Okay, so you're in Human Resources, and can therefore access employee data. But if you try accessing salaries from outside the trusted firewall, on a weekend, from a Blackberry, or from a banned country, the policies may look at all those factors and deny you access. Fourth, authorization engines typically track your activity, for the sake of security and auditing, and for analyzing usage and pointing to necessary changes in policies.

For the framework to intercept and mitigate requests, it needs to sit someplace where it can do so. Oracle Access Manager (OAM) provides the necessary components to create policies, intercept requests, and match the two up for deciding whether or not a request is valid.

- OAM Policy Manager is the administrative interface for creating authentication and authorization policies, matching up groups of users with groups of resources.
- OAM WebPass is a web server plug-in for validating identity.
- OAM WebGate is a web server plug-in for validating resource requests, and so serves as a Policy Enforcement Point (PEP).
- OAM AccessGate is a client for handling web and non-web requests.

When a user hits an OAM-protected web server, the request is intercepted, and the user is redirected for authentication, based on the authentication needs for the given resource. Once identified, the user is subjected to the appropriate access policy. For example, if you're in the accounting group, I'll let you into the accounting page you requested. I might also reject you, because you're in the wrong group, and redirect you to a nice page telling you you're out of luck. OAM will also create a session ticket for single sign-on. This is the incredibly oversimplified explanation, of course, and there are many possible variations on this configuration to handle complex login and access needs.

The key here is how you design the policies for *authentication* and *authorization*. In other words, how do you want users to log in, and how do you determine, once a user *is* logged in, what resources he can access? Authentication and authorization are placed together here because more often than not, the same solution that performs one also handles the other, as does OAM. This is not true 100 percent of the time, but it is true a majority of the time (we will discuss the two main variations shortly). Much of this has to do with the fact that the information that users provide during authentication is used to locate the information needed for authorization. You provide the system with initial credentials, which it must validate against a directory to let you in, and now that it has access to your directory entry, it can access your group memberships, attributes, and keys to other data it may need to decide what you can access. After all, it's not, "Welcome to the portal, take anything you want." Not all users are created equally. Customers, contractors, suppliers, and employees all have different needs and different rights. And even within a group, you subdivide. Employees can be regular users, admins, HR, auditors, and so on.

Before you put the solution in place, you must determine what your requirements are. Let's start with authentication. What credentials will you require of your users? It's not enough to say, give me your name and password. You have different kinds of users, and different kinds of resources. And you will not only be authenticating directly to resources; you will also be coming in via SSO. This means you will be constructing tickets or cookies that convince the various applications that the user coming in is fully authorized. Username not enough? Then you might make network address a requirement as well, so that if I sniff out your ticket and try to use it as my own to retrieve your mail, the extra attribute requirement trips me up.

Within your user base, you will be segmenting between standard, privileged, non-employee, administrative, and other user groups for both authentication and authorization. Or at least you *should*. These segmentations will manifest themselves as either different authorization requirements, or the use of different directories to validate credentials. They will almost certainly dictate the use of different authorization schemes, most often based on groups or group-based attributes. You will also segment again based on behavior, such as whether a resource request originates inside or outside the firewall. You will expect some user groups (for example, customers or partners) to always come in from the outside, whereas with employees you will see both. Some employees will never be allowed to access their resources from the outside. And some resources you will not make accessible from the outside on any occasion, to anyone.

The entirety of an organization's authentication strategy should consider not only this segmentation, but also the matrix of all the possibilities, that is, all possible user groups accessing all possible resources in all possible circumstances. Of course, you can't create a different authentication challenge for all the extrapolations, and therefore you think in terms of policies. For which resources or domains will you only challenge for name and password? And for which ones will you require more?

Let's dispel a couple of myths: Strong authentication doesn't just mean tougher password policies, and multifactor authentication does not automatically mean the use of hard tokens. That doesn't mean you rule them out, but neither should you be limited by them. Hard tokens are just plain expensive to purchase, ship, and maintain. Of course, with that said, Oracle Identity Manager has been used for support of hard tokens, including the use of self-registration to register an actual token and reset pins, and to handle logins to an ACE server.

Authentication options mean

- Something you know (your creds, your security questions, your secret phrase)
- Something you are (a set of attributes, biometric)
- Something you have (token, device, location)

And be sure to add Where and When you are. If a request is originating during off-hours or from an unknown IP, you might factor these in. Do you require additional data? Or do you just plain deny? You could also consider a secondary challenge. "So you're the head of HR? Great. But you're requesting a page with confidential employee data, and it's Sunday night, and you're definitely not in the building. Let me ask you a few more questions, or request a PIN. And by the way, I'm going to prompt you using a virtual authentication device in case anybody's sniffing traffic from outside the firewall." Simply enough, what kind of challenge will you put up, given what you know about the requesting party and the resource?

Once a user is authenticated, now you authorize. "I've validated your identity. And yes, I allow HR admins to access employee data after hours and from home. But you're in the temporary workers group, and therefore you're out of luck." You can further create risk profiles that consider a combination of factors, including user data (profile info, group memberships), behavior (when and from where you're making the request), and environmental data (where you're making the request from). Set that baseline for what is considered acceptable behavior, the what-where-when factors.

There will certainly be times when you reject users, after a bad authentication or when the framework decides not to authorize a known user. For the sake of branding, a good user experience (because even your customers will fat-finger the wrong password on occasion), to remind potential hackers that you're in control, or to provide options to users when they fail a challenge or are otherwise denied access, make sure your policies redirect to a friendly landing page. Don't let the web server throw up a default "oops" page with an error 404. Handle the failed attempts in as friendly fashion as the successes.

OAM allows you to build policies that deploy standard (and custom) authentication methods such as basic, basic over SSL, basic over LDAP, basic with AD, certificates, form-based, and others. These will likely handle the bulk of your authentication needs. But for resources requiring more powerful protection, Oracle Adaptive Access manager (OAAM) provides support for multifactor, strong authentication, behavioral analysis, fraud detection, and the ongoing evolution of risk profiles. OAAM in fact can serve as the strong authentication policy enforcer for OAM, being called by OAM as another authentication scheme in its library. Admins can adjust policies based on user activity. However, you will want to establish a baseline for our initial deployment.

When employing strong or multifactor authentication, you need to think about what your user community will bear. With the use of overlapping methods and virtual authentication devices, you can seal up a set of resources to be airtight. But piling on multiple authentication schemes and challenges can slow down your users. Choose the schemes that best fit the resource requirements without unduly burdening your users.

Federation, you may recall, isn't really about authentication, since it's presumed that a federated user has already been validated. This is about authorization. Oracle, through a combination of OAM and Oracle Identity Federation, has the technology of federation covered, for creating and processing assertions. But it's up to you as to the protocol you will employ for those assertions, and of course the parties with whom you will establish a trusted relationship. The main issue to overcome with federation is not a technical one; it's a business one.

Another significant aspect to authorization is the enforcement of fine-grained entitlements. These are decisions that must be made about requests made against resources that go deeper than mere URLs. If OAM and OAAM match up users to pages, apps, and other tangible assets, Oracle Entitlements Server (OES) supports policies with more complex players. You still have a user and a requested resource, along with a response. But now the resource can be something far more granular, such as a web service call, a method, the part on a page, a button, or a transaction.

Just as context can keep the number of roles inversely proportional to the number of users, so too can context-based OES policies keep the numbers of those policies from exploding. OES supports the building of dynamic policies that take into account variations within a transaction. For example, the response to a request to process a transaction may vary based on the transaction amount. A single policy may be established to handle ranges, rather than line up individual policies to individual amounts. The added benefit is the performance gain you realize from evaluating a single policy rather than multiple policies. Hierarchical policies, allowing for the inheritance of access rights, also improve performance, in that they allow the evaluation process to traverse the tree and reach the appropriate conclusion faster than evaluating flat policies. Given the granular nature of OES decisions, where the responses may constitute only a part of an overall transaction, proper policy design for the purposes of performance is crucial.

Another design consideration with OES is the actual configuration of the decision points. Besides a policy administrative console, OES also provides Policy Decision Points (PDP) which push policies out, and Policy Enforcement Points (PEP) which are local to the resources (the equivalent of a WebGate), intercepting requests and utilizing policies to either allow or deny access. Oracle recommends, when possible, to place the PEP and PDP together, as this can improve the performance from an average of 700 responses per second to 7000 responses per second.

In general, with any of the authentication and authorization components, you need to consider sizing. Hopefully, provisioning is not something that takes up huge amounts of bandwidth, but users are requesting resources every minute of the day, with large numbers of authentications, and far larger numbers of authorizations, going on possibly 24 hours, depending on your business. Here you need to consider, not the number of users, but the number of *concurrent* users when planning sizing, throughput, or capacity as reflected in the number of policy servers and gates to be utilized.

Governance, Compliance, and Reporting in the Design

Let me bore you one more time with this pronouncement: Compliance is not reporting. Reporting merely tells you that you've been compliant (or not), so that you can provide evidence of good design, and fix the gaps in the bad design. Compliance needs to be built into all your processes, all your procedures, all your solutions, so that you build and launch applications to be used compliantly, provision users in compliant fashion, and require authentication and authorization to follow compliance mandates. And as I also keep repeating, compliance should not be a bolt-on; it's easier to wire the house for burglar alarms before the walls go up than to do it later. Same thing here. If compliance requirements are part of your policy design up front, they'll be much easier to enforce, and much easier to modify later, when your regulatory mandates change, as inevitably they will.

Let's start with resources. Within Oracle Identity Manager, they can be defined as SOX-related, GLB, and so on. If you have additional regulatory requirements, you can customize OIM to help you define resources as such. This can affect which users you provision to a resource, what credentials are needed to access it later, and how you will perform attestation. Roles can likewise be tagged as being relevant to SOX, HIPAA, GLB, Basel II, and so on, with customizations possible as well. As you may guess, this can help determine who may be assigned such a role.

Provisioning policies in general must be designed in consideration of strict access control, which is one of the most basic tenets of any regulatory law. In fact, when it comes to resources that are specifically tagged as regulation-related, role grant policies can be lined up to allow or deny access based on the corresponding tags in the role definitions. Automated policies are one of the most powerful aspects of any compliant system, in that you build your compliance and security requirements directly into the workflow definitions that make up those policies. Within OIM, you construct policies that make use of your authoritative source(s) to ensure that access is granted based on both the resource (which should be defined and tagged with its own requirements for access) and the user (who must meet those requirements). And because compliance typically also requires the use of eyeballs to verify even the results of automated processes, your policies also will likely require approvals, which is what provisioning is all about. A request is approved implicitly by an automated matching of user attributes to resource requirements, or explicitly by a designated human approver. Reconciliation is the automated process for keeping approved users in a state of compliance, but there is also an eyeball-driven version of that, certification.

Certification (also known as attestation or recertification) is the periodic review of which users have access to which resources. The process is meant to ensure that users maintain access to only those resources they are entitled to. We will describe this process in detail in Chapter 12. Certification policies as defined in Oracle Identity Analytics adhere to what I've said previously about compliance: there are things you do for security, and things you do because you're told to. So for applications that have been tagged as compliance-related, you may be certifying more often than once a year. In fact, for Sarbanes-Oxley-related applications, you will be certifying quarterly. Your auditors will provide guidelines on the necessary frequency. When certification is left to your discretion, you should at *least* consider an annual review, and definitely more often for resources with a lot of turnover. Yes, you normally think of *users* as experiencing turnover, but think of the resources whose users are more transient. If you have large, temporary customer bases, users who register for contests, special offers, or time-sensitive resources, and you don't automatically expire those users, then you need to review who is still provisioned to those after a certain period.

Schools are prime candidates for heavy-duty certification, and not just when you think. Yes, at the end of every term there are large numbers of students who leave, along with a certain amount of turnover in faculty and staff, who are also cyclical. However, also consider:

- Students who register, even matriculate, and never showup for class

- Students who drop throughout the year, some immediately, some just before the cut-off for transfers, and many between semesters (some of which are early grads)

- Students who *don't* drop but who sign up for school jobs they end up not working

- Student-workers who are signed up for next year but may or may not return after the summer

What this means is that certification against class material applications (such as Blackboard) should be performed no later than directly following the cut-off, if not also a couple of weeks into the first semester. Then it should be repeated on that same cycle in the second semester, and of course after the school year ends. Universities always seem to be in a hurry to grant access, and slow to rescind it.

Another outstanding reason for certification is to review the assignment of temporary duties, which often become permanent for two parallel reasons: the resource (or grant thereof) is not physically capable of being expired, and nobody ever bothers going back to erase those "temporary" rights. Regular certification helps perform that cleanup. This leads to another point: resources, such as DBA rights on critical databases or any privileged user situation, are also prime candidates for defining certification events.

Let me mention one other Oracle solution that mitigates the risk of unauthorized access based on finer-grained roles at the database level: DataBase Vault. DBV can specifically address provisions of SOX, HIPAA, GLB, PCI, the Japanese Privacy Law, and other global mandates, by restricting access based on database roles. It can also enforce Segregation of Duties requirements at the database level.

On a day-to-day basis, of course, your authentication and authorization policies should enforce access policies with every single request. Remember strict access control? PCI spells it out as "need to know." This can also be translated as "least privilege." It also specifies that you should not use "vendor-supplied defaults for system passwords and other security parameters."

Oracle Access Manager (OAM) and Oracle Adaptive Access Manager (OAAM) provide simple-to-strong authentication methods, as well as complex authorization policies, for flexible, powerful solutions to the question of "Who are you, and why should I let you in?" But as we keep saying, your solutions are only as strong as the processes they support. We've already discussed the importance of strong authentication policies, but when considering compliance, you need to constantly think in terms of "least privilege." OAAM can also provide the strong authentication that's required by HIPAA.

The Oracle Entitlements Server can also make use of multiple factors, typically beyond the web server, for powerful, real-time authorization decision making. OES policies can be truly granular and compliance-specific, to also include non-browser apps and services. If you have in place strict provisioning rules with OIM, strong role policies in OIA, strong authentication policies with OAM and OAAM, and strict authorization rules with OAM, OAAM, and OES, you have created a multilayer compliance engine that will enforce regulatory mandates across the enterprise, and serve to back each other up. We will examine in detail the building of authentication and authorization policies, including fine-grained authorizations, in Chapters 10 and 11.

Let's add yet one more set of checks. One of the most poorly named products in the stack, the Oracle Application Access Control Governor (OAACG), provides enterprise-wide segregation of duties enforcement. While SoD can be performed at a role and organizational level with OIM and OIA, OAACG performs this function at a very granular level across all applications at run-time. Complex policies can be created in OAACG to enforce SoD across an entire organization, utilizing data decision points from available sources. It has been preconfigured to provide SoD enforcement for Oracle E-Business Suite and PeopleSoft, but can also be used as a repository and SoD decision engine for all other enterprise apps as well. OAACG can be used in a preventive fashion, so that conflicting privileges are not assigned to begin with, or in a detective fashion, so that at run time, conflicting duties are not executed. If integrated with real-time processes, OAACG can detect that a user is attempting to use a privilege that is in conflict with another, existing privilege, and create the proper alerts so that administrators can take corrective action in real time as well. Where the deep thought really comes into this is the construction of those policies. If SoD definitions are not readily available, or if you are applying OAACG to a custom application, then you need to define two types of conflicts: one on one, and combinations. Request-Payment is not compatible with Approve-Payment. Easy enough. But you also need to account for things like this:

(Create-PO *or* Modify-PO) is incompatible with (Authorize-PO)

Bear in mind that conflicts may also span applications. A privilege in one system may be a violation when used in conjunction with a privilege in another system. Finally, you need to design the responses to violations.

And so we come to this question once again: If we can create and enforce SoD policies at various levels, where *should* we enforce them? The comprehensive answer, of course, is at all of the levels. Just as you want both provisioning and access control, enforcing access before and during requests, it is ideal to enforce SoD before conflicts can be assigned and again before they can be executed. This may not always be possible, of course, and therefore the correct answer is, it depends. Ouch, what a lousy answer. But here it's not bad.

A few chapters back I briefly mentioned International Traffic in Arms Regulations (ITAR), which governs the export of sensitive technical data from the United States. It may be enforced by access control or (better yet) at the database level. Whenever I am asked about ITAR and where it should be enforced, the answer is, *it depends...* on who will own responsibility for it. And so there is our answer on SoD. I have seen it enforced proactively and in real time, but only rarely in both places. So when designing your SoD solution, the answer is, who will define it? Who owns the requirement? Is it sufficient to do it at the role level? Roles contain the privileges that come along for the ride, but many security experts don't feel entirely comfortable leaving SoD there, at least in its entirety. Whether through simple provisioning policies or more complex policies in OAACG, it seems more logical, if you are only performing SoD in one place, to do it in the provisioning process, preventing conflicting assignments. Why allow a user to have a resource now if you're just going to deny its use later? But as we've already said, *things change*, and if for some reason a user slips through the cracks, or is denied an access point at provisioning time only to pick up a group membership later that gets him that conflicting access, the detective version is the final safety net. Again, a combination of preventive and detective is ideal, but obviously not easy to implement, and requires possibly redundant human functions. With the use of OAACG, you can create one set of policies that can be evaluated in front and in the back, but you must create an entry point. OAACG has been integrated with OIM, and can also be integrated with run-time processes.

Regardless of the Oracle solution in play, and regardless of whether the actor in a transaction is an end user or administrator, all activity is captured, audited, and ultimately analyzed. Compliance often means forensics—going back and examining what was done, how it was done and, when possible, why it was done. Accountability is one of the huge keys that resulted from, for example, the collapse of Enron. This means accountability at a very high level, all the way down to who added a resource to a role. Some analysis may be done in real time, such as with OAAM or OAACG. Intelligent reporting is available for analysis after the fact.

So finally we come to reporting, and for this purpose Oracle provides BI Publisher, an enterprise reporting tool. And once again, when it comes to compliance, there are things you do because you want to, and things you do because you're told to. BI Publisher supports both. For regular reporting, meaning the kind you generate on a weekly or monthly basis, you can schedule reports in BIP that are created from the desired data sources, sorted and branded for your needs, delivered in the required format (Word, Excel, PDF, text, CSV, and so on), at the appointed time, and via the desired transport (SMTP, target folder, and so on). But you can also generate reports on demand, and in fact easily create them through the wizard. BIP comes with a large number of preformatted templates, based on the most commonly requested report formats. When they come close but are not exact, these templates can also be modified, and you can generate new ones as well for regular reuse.

Before we conclude the discussion of design, let's make one more point about compliance. In the Oracle suite, everything—meaning all objects, which include users, groups, roles, hierarchies, resources, authentication and authorization policies, access policies, and anything else you can define—all these objects are assigned owners. You must be authorized to create, maintain, activate, and deactivate objects. When any of these objects is created or modified, the name of the person who did the deed is captured.

We will cover, in much more specific detail, how to build compliance into your Oracle IAM framework, including the use of OAACG and BI Publisher, in Chapter 12.

Centralized and Delegated Administration

Across the entire Oracle identity and access management suite, you can centrally define objects, processes, and policies. You can also have the ability to support Delegated Administration.

Remember what I said about self-service? It's a win-win. Users are empowered to control aspects of their own identity and access; they don't have to hunt down the right guy on the phone for every little thing, so they get what they need quicker. The organization is happier because they're not wasting money on servicing every lost password or account lockout, and users are more productive while doing their jobs than when begging for reset passwords. Delegated administration is the exact same kind of win-win. It is the process by which pockets of the organization are empowered to run their own little piece of the universe. They can maintain their own domains, policies, users, user groups, approvals, resources, and so on. They're happy, for example, because they don't have to call the super-admin every time they need to add or change a user or policy. The super-admin is happy because, hey, he didn't receive that same call or have to do any work.

Depending on the Oracle components you use, there are various ways to enforce the boundaries that naturally occur with delegated admin. If I let you run shipping and receiving, you shouldn't be able to affect anything over in purchasing. I might do this through the use of roles. You're the S&R Manager, so you can manage S&R. I could limit what users you own by way of the directory itself, makeing you the domain administrator. This is not to say that you would need to know how to operate an LDAP interface, if I've got provisioning in place to simply make use of the directory while providing you a GUI.

Often, people ask in RFPs about management *portlets*. What they're usually asking about is the ability to insert administrative functions into a business application. The last such demo I worked with was based on a car dealership. Salesmen who logged in got some basic personalization and the ability to modify their own profile data. But the individual dealer chiefs could create groups and users, and the super-user could create all new dealerships. All these functions were available from within the dealer app itself, which also featured cars, prices, sales, discounts, and an oily sheen. When deciding to allow delegated admin functions to be performed locally, you should also decide *how* to provide that functionality.

Also recall that not all LOB owners are created equal. They might know how to run a car dealership, but that doesn't mean they know what an LDAP group is. You might create the groups they need, and let them populate those groups, but if you give them the ability to create groups themselves, what do you want to bet that dealership will end up with more groups than users?

In the end, delegated admin is a mutual benefit: super-admins are happy because the local admins can't get outside the sandbox, and local admins are happy because they've got a sandbox to play in. But part of your design is designating those delegates, choosing who will be the local admins, and deciding what functionality you will give them. You may allow them to manage their own users, but not create them, since that is in the hands of Human Resources. You may only wish them to be able to maintain those user attributes that govern access.

As of 11g, Oracle Identity Management includes more fine-grained delegated admin policies, which provide, as one example, the ability for managers to manage users who report to them, based on attributes rather than static organizations. This gives you that extended ability to deal with dotted line relationships, not just solid lines. The hierarchy indicates who my actual boss is, while attributes may indicate the group leader for a project to which I've been assigned.

Designing a delegated admin environment also entails creating the administrative groups for those local admins, and designing views of the interfaces that provide (and properly limit) the functions they are now empowered to use. For example, in OIM you can create administrative groups, and assign to them limited menu sets. In fact, only super-admins should have access to the full breadth of the OIM menu.

Using the GUI framework provided by the Oracle suite, you can customize views of all the products to provide limited (and locally branded) views for delegated admins. The fully published APIs that come documented with the suite can be used for creating custom interfaces and even web services to provide identity and access functions throughout the enterprise; although, for the sake of pure labor costs, it is advisable to investigate the ease of using administrative functions for customizing the UI layer.

The business aspect to all of this is that those delegates must be willing and able to perform the task. Most local admins will welcome the duty, since they are empowered, but you will find some who will be more than happy to make those phone calls, send those e-mails, or open those help desk tickets and let someone else perform the labor. Management may decide to help by pushing those tasks out to the lines of business, which is where it truly belongs anyway. After all, it is a framework, not just a central console.

Security in the Development Process

One of the great benefits of an IAM framework is its strategic placement between users and resources. Not only is it providing authentication, authorization, and so on, but it is also doing so without the need to completely customize for coarse-grained security. Even in the case of fine-grained entitlements, you may in many cases be able to intervene at the application server level, rather than in the code itself. However, in some cases it may be desirable to provide security functions within the context of the development environment.

Oracle Platform Security Services (OPSS) allow developers to extend the identity framework to their new code. Exposed as an API and integrated with JDeveloper (through wizards) to support the inclusion of security functions (authentication, authorization, logging/auditing, encryption), OPSS gives developers the ability to secure their applications during the design phase, while saving them the effort of building the details of those functions by abstracting these identity functions via generic API calls. OPSS represents security as a service in Oracle Identity Management, and it is the security foundation for Oracle Fusion Middleware, of which identity management is a major component.

The End Process: Termination

I have segregated this as a separate section because of its significance, not only to the security of the enterprise, but also to pure compliance. Don't think of provisioning as simply giving access to users. It is the process that controls what a user gains and loses, meaning the access they get on their first day, the changes to their access during their extended lifecycle within the organization, and the loss of access when they leave. In other words, provisioning handles all deltas in access, for good or bad.

I will repeat this here, and again a little later: It's not enough to simply prevent a user from authenticating when he or she leaves the organization. Most especially in a heterogeneous environment, you are enabling your users across multiple, disparate resources, adding to your risk with every stop. Bearing in mind security, compliance, and standard audit requirements, here are the steps you need to take when a user account is terminated:

- Set the appropriate attributes in the system of truth or authority
- Disable the user across all resources
- Send notifications to the appropriate parties
- Retain all necessary records
- Log all activity to these ends and verify all termination steps

You may have heard this term: hire-to-fire. When planning onboarding, always think of it as only part of a life cycle. Users come in, they change, they leave. Many organizations consider termination a more important function than onboarding, and in fact on many occasions when invited in to discuss identity, de-provisioning is the primary business driver.

Let's repeat the same nonsense one more time. In theory, and in fact in decent practice, the same policies that perform user enablement are the same policies that handle change, and are the same policies that make you go away. But there are some additional steps to take when planning for de-provisioning.

It used to be that when your time was up at your company, it was easy. They deleted you. Your record, as in singular, was purged. It hasn't been that simple for a long time. Once you leave your company, you're still there, at least in spirit. You are a mark on the wall, an entry in the audit logs, a body to be accounted for even after you have gone.

True Story

At the last company where I lived in a cubicle (that is, before airports became my second home), our primary business was maintaining customer mass mailing lists. For one particular customer, they were regularly given a subset list of addressees who had died. The notion that somebody on the big list might one day pass on, or even ask to be removed, had not occurred to the original designer, and since they were using an off-the-shelf database product, they had no ability to change the schema to include a status field, such as a Boolean ("Active-Y/N").

So some rocket scientist there decided to mark the records by appending the word "deceased" to the last names. The mailing program was modified to check for that particular string and, if found, the record was skipped. You can see this coming, of course. The list was appropriated for some cross-marketing, to be printed by a different app, but that new app had not been appropriately coded. The result (which also didn't say much for Quality Control) was that more than a few widows received mailers addressed something like this:

```
Mr. John Q. PublicDeceased
```

The auto industry used to (secretly) call it "planned obsolescence." At some point, stuff goes away, so you might as well plan for it. But in a post-Enron world, nothing gets deleted. You keep *everything*, because you never know. The rule of thumb is, they have to keep you around on the system for six months before wiping you out—but that never happens any more either. Storage is cheap. Six months? Try forever.

To keep things clean, you might get moved to a group specifically designated for "former users." This way any sweep of active users is nice and neat. The simplest way to indicate that a user is terminated? Attribute. A Boolean. Active or inactive. Some definitive indicator in the system of truth. And regardless of the system of truth, as already discussed, you're everywhere. You might be quite dead in the HR system, but you might look quite lively in the CRM package, procurement, engineering, e-mail, and so on.

Killing the network password isn't enough. It's *not enough*. I have heard this one many, many times: If you can't get in the front door, what's the difference if you have the key to the washroom? The answer is: Because of all the back doors. In July 2009, the Forum of Incident Response and Security Teams (FIRST) issued a press release about insider threats, focusing on disgruntled ex-employees, and stating that an organization is not necessarily safe once an employee is gone and outside the firewall, since former insiders often know where the back doors are, representing a significant threat.

At one manufacturer in the far north, my team was called in specifically because of the slow pace of the termination process. They described to us how it took them up to five weeks to completely provision a new user, but up to *seven weeks* to completely disable a terminated user and verify that disablement across all target systems. The first step to disabling a user was taking away his portal password and killing his e-mail account. Their horror story? An angry ex-employee who dialed back in from home to a 3270 green screen application. A non-browser, caveman interface. The damage he did wasn't financial so much as very embarrassing, but the potential was there for something far worse.

At another client in the Southwest, we came in after they'd failed a security audit. Specifically, they had far too many terminated employees with current access rights. Again, there were no working portal creds, but there existed the potential for backdoor access. So every six months, the client had to cough up a list of all users who'd left the company in the interim, voluntarily or otherwise, and the auditor would then proceed to check the system for access rights still possessed by any of those ex-users. The results got better and better, but it was pretty ragged for a time.

Cleanup and the Creation of Artifacts

As we've discussed, no one deletes departed users as a common practice (except, as I've witnessed, in higher education). Instead, these users are deactivated and de-provisioned. For the sake of cleaner and faster searches of live users, it's common to migrate these users to a directory group specifically for terminated users. This also supports what is called a negative policy model, in which particular values specifically negate entry (as opposed to a positive model that requires particular values for entry).

This is the point at which the source of truth for membership is properly set, including the specific elements, flags, attributes, values, or memberships that indicate state of being. Having the ability to explicitly designate a terminated status is part of the philosophy known as "hire-to-fire." You know that one day, any given individual will no longer be associated with the organization, and therefore you plan for it, in terms of both definition and process.

Besides entries in the audit logs, the process of de-provisioning does not inherently generate a large number of bytes. However, terminated users may still leave in their wake a wealth of already generated material. In the movie "Rocky," the hero loses his locker at the gym. They take his gear, put it in a bag, and hang it up in an area for the walking dead. *This* is what you do with a terminated user's stuff.

De-provisioning-process artifacts, if you wish to call them that, consist of any assets a user leaves behind. At a customer in Houston, their procedure was to tar up all files, home directory, and e-mail contents. The advantage here is making it easier to conjure up those docs and data in the event of an audit or any other requirements for recreating activity.

True Story

A couple of years ago, my wife and I had numerous problems with a financial institution, because our account manager was someone who could charitably be called incompetent. One of the many issues we had was having to send him the same documents multiple times, because he kept losing them. How you lose attachments to email, we could not figure out. The company finally gave us another contact, and fired the man after they admitted to us he had fouled up not only our account but several others. Everything all better now? No. We had to send the same documents yet *again*, because after they terminated him, they could not access his e-mail or other files. Their process design did not allow for any other staff members to recover and reassign that material. They literally could not tell what he'd been doing in the last several months of his employment.

At various universities I've dealt with, they document their policy regarding the retention of documents, and stick to that. One chancellor told me that their policy was to keep a user's e-mails, for example, for 30 days, after which they wiped them out. If someone showed up with a subpoena a day later, they were out of luck. Now that some of the initial shock of "emergency" regulation has worn off, more organizations are now specifying policies on how long they will retain records. In most publicly traded companies, at least, this means years.

Naturally, if you don't have the material to turn over to auditors or legal authorities, then that's the end. But if you are subject to regulatory mandates that require you to retain those kinds of documents, you need to bake that into the de-provisioning process. This means one of two options in your OIM workflow definition.

1. An e-mail notification to an admin who will perform the steps necessary to stash the files

2. Initiating a script (or more likely a series of scripts) to zip up, store, or otherwise archive the material

Deciding When Design Is Completed

We keep beating up the term "use cases" for many useful reasons. Use cases help figure out your initial requirements, they help you test vendors' software capabilities later, and they help you test your deployment even later than that. But in between, they serve another useful function: They help you come to agreement as to when design is complete. This by itself serves two purposes. The first is to ensure that you are providing the benefits of the framework to the admins and users you are serving. The second is to cover yourself. It's like a wedding, when the minister asks if there's anybody in the congregation who has any objections to the marriage. If they don't speak up now, they have no recourse later. Get your lines of business to sign off on the final design, so that when you deliver what was asked, they can't accuse you of holding out. If they think of something they want *after* they've signed off, they'll be relying on luck, your generosity, or budget going into Phase Two.

Therefore, under Framework Design, come to agreement with stakeholders, department heads and, resource owners as to what "complete" means; in a phased deployment, you will be satisfying requirements for groups of users (for example, provisioning, SSO) and groups of resources (how to successfully provision to an app, and how to adequately secure that app with both authentication and authorization policies). Make it clear to the different stakeholders that when the time comes, you will want them to *sign off on completion of a deliverable*. So agree in advance on the rubric, which should be the satisfaction of their own provincial *use cases*.

While my new house was going up, the builder told me, it's easier to wire the burglar alarms before the drywall goes up, than later when everything is sealed. Nothing should necessarily be written in stone, but it's better to decide ahead of time, since it's easier to *build* it the right way than to *rebuild* it. Besides, changing any one configuration or policy may have ripple effects. This is why it's called design. It is your blueprint. Soon, you will be building.

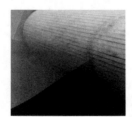

CHAPTER
8

User Account Creation

And Adam gave names to all cattle, and to the fowl of the air, and to every beast of the field.

—Genesis 2:20

With some components of the framework in place, you can begin building on it even before fully deploying. Now that we have resources and a directory designed, we can begin assembling the users from their current hiding places, or bringing them into the enterprise brand new, and in either case establishing identifying attributes for determining access. There are various methods for doing so, and you may in fact use any combination of them. If you have built a new authoritative source, you are likely to populate it in bulk to begin with, and then go into maintenance mode using regular synchronization. If Oracle Virtual Directory becomes your authoritative source, there is not much maintenance beyond any schema changes you may find necessary later.

If you already have a user directory in place, you will still likely need to provide additional attributes or groups to govern the access you will be granting those users, meaning that you will perhaps be overlaying an extended schema. This is a common use of Oracle Directory Services: assimilating and augmenting an existing schema.

Let's walk through possible options for creating user accounts in preparation for provisioning, authentication, and authorization:

- Bulk loading
- One-time reconciliation
- Identity management interface
- Human Resources integration
- Customer service
- Self-registration

It's a good possibility that you will be employing bulk loading or full reconciliation to start, using the IdM interface for maintenance, HR integration for incremental reconciliation, and self-registration as well. These are not mutually exclusive. Regardless of the methodology employed, you must construct rules around how that method is to be used, to ensure that you achieve the desired result, which is a source of user truth that can safely and compliantly feed the entire IAM process. I've seen large uploads go badly because certain data elements were not formatted properly, indexing was not complete, or referential integrity was destroyed because not all the necessary elements were present during processing. One word you hear from experts when they talk about populating the source of truth is: make sure the data is "clean," and that word is itself ambiguous.

Bulk Loading

You came to the company with a whole bunch of other people. Your company was bought by another company. Or your broker, like mine, was sold by its parent company to a bigger broker. Or your bank, like mine, was bought by another bank, and then *that* bank was bought by a third bank. The acquired party provided the acquiring party with giant dumps of employee and customer data. Sure, you're still on your old bank's system, but the new parent wants to immediately present you with promotional offers, as well as pleas to stick with them through the occasionally bumpy transition.

It could be as simple as moving users from one database or directory to another, or else growing or collapsing domains. Regardless, it's not something you do haphazardly, although this does not have to be complicated. The Oracle suite has a number of tools and utilities for bulk loading of user data. Since the most common user directory within Oracle's customer base is the Oracle Internet Directory, let's start with that. OID is not just an LDAP interface. It *is* a directory server in the traditional sense. It also consists of an underlying Oracle database, which allows it to manage far more objects than a traditional LDAP server. Naturally, it serves as a DIT (Directory Information Tree), and provides synchronization with source data, as well as a catalog engine for indexing. It also includes Oracle Directory Services Management (ODSM) for centrally maintaining the directory itself. This management interface, by the way, can also be used for maintaining Oracle Virtual Directory (OVD) and Oracle Directory Server Enterprise Edition (ODSEE, the former Sun LDAP). And finally, OID provides the `bulkload` command-line tool, for pushing large numbers of records into the directory server.

The `bulkload` command-line tool (which uses the Oracle SQL Loader) requires input files to be in LDIF format, which has been defined by the Internet Engineering Task Force (IETF). Information specific to the format is available at their web site. In summary, there are "sub-formats" for adding and deleting entries, as well as for modifying schema. Sequencing of entries is important in that parent entries should precede child entries; that is, build the house and then let the kids move in. Any object classes or attributes relative to an entry must exist in the target schema or be added as part of the load before the entries themselves can be loaded.

The `bulkload` tool operates in three phases:

- Check, in which it validates all records in the LDIF file for schema and duplicates. Any errors are reported, and must be corrected before the process can complete.

- Generate, in which the input data is converted into a format that is acceptable to the SQL Loader.

- Load, in which the converted data is loaded into the directory server.

There are two modes for bulk loading, incremental and just plain bulk. Incremental allows you to append data to existing directory entries. While not as fast as bulk loading mode, it is still faster than other methods. Incremental is meant for small data loads. What makes directories perform so well for lookups is the heavy indexing. It's the same reason you don't use them for transactional data, because with every new entry, all pertinent indices must be updated. Because incremental loading uses SQL inserts, it automatically updates established indices, and therefore this process can impact performance.

Bulk loading mode is meant for just that, bulk, that is, large numbers of entries. For this reason, existing indices are dropped, and indexing itself is not used during the load. Think of it this way. If, for each entry, you need to index ten fields, then with each insert, you would load a record, update ten indices, then repeat. The performance would not be optimal. Instead, bulk loading shoves the data in, and then goes back and updates the indices after the fact.

As I indicated early in this section, mergers and acquisitions often prompt this kind of bulk assimilation of users, so that the identities of multiple organizations can become participants in a single identity framework. Mergers are also common reasons for using the next method, reconciliation.

One-Time Reconciliation

For the sake of assimilating users from a source in order to launch the new framework, Oracle Identity Manager can perform a one-time reconciliation with legacy systems as a form of user discovery. This brings those user accounts into the OIM directory. Once this process is completed, OIM becomes the system of truth for identity.

This one-time reconciliation is considered a *full* reconciliation. In other words, it brings over all accounts so that you have a foundation for your identity system. Subsequent reconciliations will be *incremental* events, meaning you will retrieve only new, modified, and deleted accounts. Yes, that sounds wrong, bringing over deleted accounts. What you are doing is reconciling the fact that a deleted user will no longer participate in your IAM framework. However, in the era of compliance, you will rarely delete users, at least not for a long time after they're gone. You will deactivate and de-provision them. In the meantime, in that window between deactivation and deletion, chances are you will be reporting on them, which is a lot easier when there's a shell to work with.

Identity Management System

Oracle Identity Manager has a full interface for creating, provisioning, and managing users. It can also be used for assigning them to groups and organizations, unlocking accounts, and resetting passwords. For the sake of customer service, limited views can be created for this purpose as well. If a user already exists in the HR or authoritative source, but does not exist in OIM for the sake of access-related identity, the OIM interface is well-suited, since *HR identity* is not necessarily the same as the *OIM identity* if you are not synchronizing in real time.

In some organizations, OIM is in fact used as the HR system. However, this is not what it was designed for. Robust human resource apps, such as PeopleSoft, track more than identities. For example, they can track applicants for jobs, including the entire life cycle of contact, resume, interviews, and status, all the way through to hiring and the necessary transitions. PeopleSoft and its brethren also interface with payroll, can determine based on where you live how you are taxed, track if you've been sent the appropriate tax documents, and everything else related to an employee life cycle beyond the access management that OIM is designed for.

That said, you *can* customize OIM to track these items via workflow, and the schema and landing pages can also be modified to handle additional attributes, but you may consider whether it's worth it to reinvent the wheel.

HR Event

After bulk loading, after the original population of your authoritative source, the *ideal* methodology for maintaining your user directory is a proper human resources channel, automated by incremental reconciliation. It is the way most organizations do it, and should in fact be a funnel, if not *the* source of truth. If nothing else, it should be the starting point that ultimately feeds the source of truth. The human resources manager, hiring manager, or other designated body fat-fingers you into PeopleSoft, Siebel, or another package per the prescribed procedure, and this is where the entire process of identifying and provisioning begins.

I see in many enterprises that the human resources application is *not* the source of truth, but simply the mechanism for populating it. The HR directory provides status, drives benefits and salary, and manages reviews and other organizational needs, but is often not the source for enterprise identity and access. If a user's life cycle indeed starts with HR, then the information must be extracted and turned into the driver for IAM.

Within the design phase, you specified the process for provisioning. There is a starting point, then the initiation of the workflows that place a new user in all the appropriate targets, including the approvals and connectors necessary to enable the user across the resources that are appropriate for his role and/or job title. But the initiating resource, the HR feed, serves as the beginning for the other resources. As we discussed in Chapter 7 when we covered design, resources are more than members of a list of applications or databases. Their definitions include the mechanism and frequency for communication, the adapters that manage the interactions, and the specifics of how they are extracted from and updated.

The most common methodology for using HR as the starting point is defining an *HR Feed* for OIM to reconcile with. As we discussed in the previous chapter, you can define scheduled tasks that run as needed to perform a variety of functions, and one of the most common is reconciliation with a human resources package or database. This reconciliation may be incremental, extracting only the changes since the previous reconciliation (the recommended method), or a full reconciliation for the sake of a completely clean copy of all data (*not* recommended). There are connectors available in OIM for a number of packages, including PeopleSoft and SAP. Additional adapters can be created through the OIM adapter factory for custom packages. Incremental changes for existing users may consist of mapping data columns to directory attributes, but in the case of a new user account, you may be updating more than one target, all of which may need to be aware of each other.

You may create different tasks or processes to reconcile for different specific purposes that may be scheduled or on demand. For example, a normal task is to take a new user, read his department, and assign him to the standard workflow. An alternate task is to take a new user, read his department, and assign him to a workflow specific to that department.

Customer Service

You're the newest client of your bank, phone company, or Internet provider. Their friendly service folks keyboard in your name and assign you a user id. Or perhaps, as at my bank (which uses my company's software), you already have an identity, but you're not yet enabled for online service, so you visit the web site, click to register, and provide account information that must be verified before you can be fully enabled. In other words, you're data, not really a user. Administrators can create views within OIM allowing customer service personnel to manage users in a customer-focused directory. Another option would be synchronizing a customer service database with OID, or via a scheduled task in OIM. This process would be virtually identical to synchronization with the HR system.

You might also create a customer-service-oriented interface to OIM, with a limited or specialized menu of functions (create or manage users, create and track requests).

Self-Registration

Self-registration is more than simply filling out a form and jumping in the pool. A user must identify himself sufficiently to gain the trust of the host, providing information that should be validated by a process and/or human approvers. There are micro and macro considerations. Let's start with the user experience first.

Within Oracle Identity Manager, you must first decide whether to allow self-registration at all. Some organizations do not permit users to request an account to begin with, and even after they have been established, may not allow them to request their own resources. This is obviously a corporate decision.

User profile pages come with default fields, some of which you may allow a user to edit, and some you may not. For example, an existing user may request membership in a group, which they may or may not be granted, but cannot explicitly place themselves in that group. The profile page should be configured to display all required and optional fields, with emphasis on those values that reviewers (whether human or process) need in order to decide whether to approve the registration. Approvers also have pages, and they must review all required values. So while this sounds like common sense, let's say it anyway: Make sure that any fields required on the self-registration page also appear on the approver pages.

You can also build custom forms that submit requests to the identity service behind OIM. Submitting a registration request should subsequently kick off an approval workflow, so that the required parties can review the request and rule accordingly. Since a registration is the first step in identity, it may be wise to make this workflow an all-or-nothing proposition; if any step is refused, then the entire request chain is null. Consider the following.

Because I'm a customer in good standing, I decided to stop going into the lobby at my bank, and visited my bank's web site to register as an online user. I provided enough identifying data to create that online account. I received a message saying that approval would take up to twenty-four hours. It was in fact two hours, and was likely an automated process, which generated an e-mail notification of the approval. I was then able to view my accounts, and request the ability to actually move money around. That second request prompted a call from a customer service representative asking if I was happy with the experience (but probably really checking up on me and verifying that it was me by virtue of the phone number on file). It also sent me a final e-mail. But that's workflow in action, with approvals and notifications. I received e-mails telling me I was approved, and a customer service rep was notified to call me. Above all, nothing was instantaneous (in other words, approvals had to take place), although it was timely and efficient.

When creating that first account, you may be assigned a default password provided to you by e-mail, which seems like a security hole, but is quite common because you have to authenticate with your e-mail first to get to the default password. If you are enabled to log directly in to OIM, you will be prompted the first time in to change that password. You will also be asked to choose and answer security questions. OIM comes with default questions, but administrators can configure others.

Universal Requirements

No matter how your initial user account is created, Oracle Identity Manager can mandate security measures and consistency with current policies as well as legacy requirements. User names can be reserved so that they cannot be reused, even if their original owners are gone. This is a relatively good practice, to avoid auditing confusion and for the sake of convenience in the event a previous employee returns. A manufacturing customer of mine, the largest employer in its home city, keeps user names reserved indefinitely because of employees who have come and gone multiple times.

OIM can generate user names compliant with corporate policy, including the ability to increment similar user names, as when your company employs multiple John Smiths. OIM also supports localized notification templates based on a user's configured, preferred language.

OIM can randomly generate passwords compliant with the policies of the target systems, and can configure these passwords for one-time use, requiring users to change those passwords the first time in. This may also be set up as a requirement of the database or directory you authenticate against, and enforced by Oracle Access Manager. New users are subject to approvals, attestation, password policies, and other security requirements.

Users can be created with a start date (when they can log in and manage their own OIM account), end date (when that account is disabled), provisioning date (when their target accounts are to be created), and de-provisioning date (when those target accounts are to be killed off). Let's revisit those all briefly. You know when the account was first instantiated. You know when it is to be *completely* disabled. You know when that account should be enabled to interact with business accounts, when it should be disconnected from the business. There are several use cases in which you might pull a user out of the business apps, but not wipe him out entirely, such as a scheduled departure in which the user is still receiving some type of benefits, mail, or other communications.

While it's possible to continue using disparate password policies across multiple directories, it is definitely not advisable. Why should you have umpteen expirations, password formats, and interfaces to visit? As someone who accesses literally hundreds of possible applications using only two passwords (with reduced sign-on, rather than completely single sign-on), I can attest to the improved user experience and efficiency. Best practices dictate a centralized password policy, with format, expiration, and enforcement across all (or most) apps. The Oracle Identity Manager Design Console allows you to specify a password policy regarding what a password should contain and how long it lives before expiring, as shown in the following illustration.

It's a sad fact that, if you don't enforce policies on the makeup of a password, a large number of people will (guaranteed) use "123456." This is not an exaggeration. Every incremental step-up in a password format, such as requiring a mix of upper- and lowercase, or the inclusion of numbers or special characters, weeds out another layer of amateur hackers.

Another important last stage of setup is security questions. *Please read this short section carefully.* It's actually very important. These are the questions that can verify that you are who you say you are when you're locked out or have forgotten your password (we'll cover that later), so you can re-enable yourself without having to call and wait for the help desk. Security questions are a vital part of self-service as well as security. Remember, you're protecting yourself as well as the organization when you set up your security questions, so don't take them lightly. They can actually present more of a system vulnerability than your password itself.

During the 2008 American election season, Vice-Presidential candidate Sarah Palin's Yahoo account was hacked by somebody who simply clicked the forgotten password link on her login page to bring up her security questions, the answers to which were all easily found on a Google search (a hazard for someone with a high profile). This is an example of having to protect people from themselves.

> **True Story**
>
> During one client visit, my hosts were describing their brand-new customer portal, which had been quickly slapped together. During the meeting, one of the IT staff tried a random name for an account, just a first name, and discovered that it was being used. He wasn't going to try guessing the password, so he clicked on "forgot my password" and tried out the user-invented security question: favorite color. He failed on "red" but hit on "blue," and he was in.

In general, it's a bad idea to let people create their own questions. Give them a choice of company-invented questions. Provide at least a couple of dozen, from which they must choose five or six. When it's time to use them, present three at random, so it's not the same three every time. A hacker should never be told which of the security questions he got wrong, and if it's not the same three every time, it gets a lot tougher to get the right combo.

And while the system can't determine if your answers are accurate, it can employ logic to ensure the answers aren't easy to guess by virtue of being too vanilla, all the same, or just lazy shortcuts. Otherwise you get something like this:

Q: What year did you buy your first car? **Red**

Q: What's your spouse's mother's maiden name? **Red**

Q: What is the air speed velocity of an unladen swallow? **Red**

Q: What's your favorite color? **Color**

Because of its pedigree in handling this process, Oracle Adaptive Access Manager is now integrated with the overall suite to support logic behind even the answers to security questions, including preventing those answers from being part of the user's name, or part of the question itself.

If you have configured role and/or access policies to dynamically grant roles and rights, then the next steps may be handled without any additional intervention, meaning the initiation of workflow to provision the new account, at least for those default roles such as Employee, Contractor, Benefits Holder, Hourly Worker, and so on. Additional grants may rely on requests by the hiring manager or the new user himself. But at least the foundation has been built by creation of that initial account. Once you're known, you must then be given the keys to the resources that you were hired to manipulate in the first place. So we'll discuss that next.

CHAPTER
9

Provisioning: Now That I'm In, What Can I Have?

And so he handled the sword... and fiercely pulled it out of the stone... and said, "Sir, lo here is the sword of the stone, wherefore I must be king of this land."

—Arthur Pendragon, requesting a new role in Le Morte D'Arthur

 number of years ago, when provisioning was all the rage, suddenly every tiny little company that could stuff you into a single LDAP called themselves a provisioning company. "We provision users to LDAP." Well, a coffee table with a small TV on it is not an entertainment center, and creating a single LDAP object is not provisioning; it's data entry.

Another poor man's version of provisioning, still being sold by some vendors, entails mapping a list of resources to a multi-valued attribute within a user's profile. When an admin checks a box next to a resource, it adds that resource to that attribute. This approach assumes that when the time comes, a given application will come to that user's profile and find out if the user is allowed access. There are some apps that can do this, and then there's the other 99 percent of the world.

And here's one more, and it probably sounds familiar. It's *called* provisioning, but it's really just a lot of calls to the help desk, followed by the opening, tracking, and closing of a lot of tickets. When I hear of this, it's often accompanied by "we use Lotus for workflow." Okay, so you've automated notifications, but the actual enablement is still all manual, with no real escalations, no fallbacks, no user tracking, no parallel processing, and certainly no enforced timetables. A user gets his resources when everybody's done screwing around.

In simplest form, provisioning can be summarized as two functions, workflow and connectors. But driving a complex, real-world organization requires true enterprise provisioning, which means intelligent, decision-making user enablement across multiple resources, based on roles and rules (which in turn are based on security and compliance policies), rather than simply creating an inventory of resources at the user level. To support these requirements, full-blown provisioning must include:

- Role-based access control
- Request management and tracking
- Policy-based workflow and approvals
- Partial to full automation
- Full compliance

This is where the framework comes in. Ideally, you can launch a new app with the confidence that only authorized users can access it; launch new users with the confidence that they will receive the right resources (and *only* the right resources) to do their jobs; and that the policies which secure both resource and user will keep you in compliance with regulatory and corporate mandates. This is the true enterprise provisioning you can construct with the Oracle suite.

Let me tell you how *not* to provision:

■ Using only a meta-directory. There are solutions out there that rely on this as their primary engine. Meta-directories, such as Oracle Internet Directory (which provides the foundation for some of the largest web sites in the world), are powerful things. They *support* provisioning. But they shouldn't *be* provisioning. The way this approach (sort of) works is this: You change the centralized user entry in the meta-directory by updating the attributes that map to rights in back-end applications, and when the meta-directory synchronizes to those back-end databases, the user has the right flags for access. Wow, that sounds simple. So what's the problem? No intelligence to drive events such as approvals or notifications, or take into account any dependencies. Limited ability to roll back approvals A and B when C gets rejected. No parallel processing. There are other limitations, but hopefully you get the idea.

■ Giving the job to your help desk or individual admins. I visit far too many customers where provisioning is a strictly manual process. A help desk app is not a provisioning tool. It's meant to track tickets. There may be manual stops in a provisioning process where a help desk ticket or notification may be used to prod someone to take a manual step. But you need to have policy-driven workflow, with request creation and tracking, notifications, escalations, and fallbacks, to ensure timely user enablement and change management.

■ Using the workflow in your collaboration tool. If all you're doing is notifications, then you don't have provisioning; what you've done is semi-automate a still very manual process.

Oracle Provisioning

Oracle Identity Manager (OIM) is a powerful identity management system that administers users and their access to target resources. It provides a policy-driven, secure, and compliant system for managing the entire life cycle of both users and resources, for the purpose of matching them up.

To this end, OIM is configured to define user profiles within the context of an authoritative source, that is, a single source of truth for a user's identity and attributes. OIM also defines enterprise resources (databases, applications, folders, and so on), including the source systems from which OIM draws data and the target systems to which it must provide data, including the user-privilege data necessary to enable users to access those target systems. To fully support enterprise provisioning, OIM also provides:

■ Administrative profile management

■ User self-service, including profile and password management, password reset, and security question configuration

■ Request management—the ability to request and track resource access

■ Delegated administration—configuring localized admins to manage their own resources and users

■ Policy management—determining how users gain access to resources

■ Workflow management—configuring the steps in the approval process following a request, the means of communication with approvers, and automated steps not requiring human intervention

- Reconciliation—automated propagation of user creation, modification, and termination.

- Attestation—allowing admins to review and remediate user access

- Rogue/orphan account management—reconciling and remediating accounts that have been created out-of-band or that have no valid user associated.

- Deployment management, for moving an OIM instance from one server to another, incrementally and securely

- Operational and historic reporting—how the system is configured, and how it has been operating

These functions are available via the Oracle Identity Manager administrative menu, which is shown in the following illustration.

In addition to the functions in the administrative interface, OIM provides a Design Console for configuring identity system settings, including the definitions that show up as selections in the administrative interface. It manages processes (for example, reconciliation), password policies, forms and attributes, lookups, rules, and adapters, all of which we will cover in more detail as we proceed. In essence, the Design Console is used for defining those pieces that will be used by day-to-day identity managers. For example, the forms, rules, and adapters will be used in registering, processing, and provisioning users. In most places in this chapter (and others)

where we talk about something being configurable, the configuration is performed in the Design Console, as shown in the following illustration.

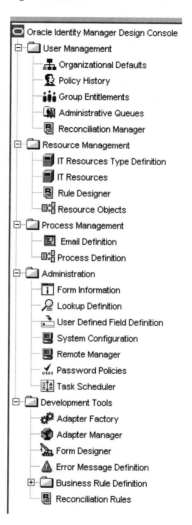

Oracle Identity Manager operates in multiple tiers. The presentation layer is an intuitive, user-friendly interface for managing users, resources, and the policies that bring them together. At least two instances of OIM are deployed on a J2EE app server in a secured zone, where it manages requests, workflow tasks, and scheduled processes. OIM maintains its own repository for policies and audit data, usually behind a second firewall. In some deployments, a separate instance of OIM is maintained just to run those scheduled tasks. The following illustration shows these relationships.

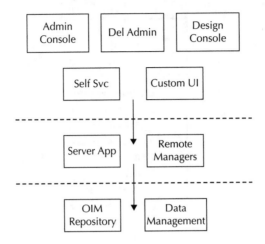

A couple of notes on the presentation layer:

■ The interface can be secured for authentication and single sign-on using the Oracle Access Manager. In other words, the framework can be used to secure itself. We'll be discussing OAM in detail in Chapter 10.

■ OIM has been localized into a number of languages: English, Japanese, Chinese (simplified and traditional), French, German, Danish, Italian, Spanish, Portuguese, and Korean.

■ OIM has also been internationalized by way of the separation of code from text, labels, prompts, images, and so on; and management of times, dates, currency, and other responses relative to the appropriate character set.

Organizations and Groups

The way in which you define your organization will depend on how (or whether) you wish to apply roles; how you intend to maintain your organizational structure; and how you intend to manage change in the organization and its effects on access rights.

Organization does not imply the overall enterprise, but rather nodes within it. To this end, when creating or maintaining an organization within OIM, you are specifying an organization's own place within the larger structure, including its corresponding department and branch, as well as its parent. In fact, an organization may very well *be* a department or branch, or even its own company, if you are operating a multientity corporation. Think of this as a more textual version of an organizational chart.

Groups are for collecting users who share functions, access rights, permissions, or roles. These groups can operate completely separate from the organizations, be a subset of an organization, or span organizations. They can be used for administrative purposes, such as limiting the menus and views of their members within OIM itself. Groups can also be assigned resources, so that members inherit access. Rules can be set governing membership or, simply enough, users can just be assigned to groups. Just as an organization can be a parent, groups can have subgroups. The following illustration shows the Group Details screen.

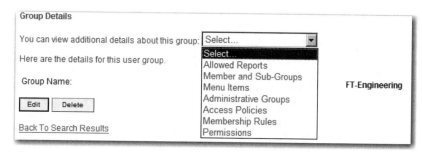

In addition, Oracle Identity Analytics allows you to discover and build a business hierarchy, for use in associating roles and entitlements with portions of the organization. A user derives these entitlements from his place in this group. This role can only be executed as part of an organizational membership. And so on.

While groups can be used for obvious provisioning purposes, they do have some limits in this regard. Also under RBAC, we'll discuss the relative merits of using groups versus business roles. Since groups have more purposes than just the inheritance of resources, groups and roles are not mutually exclusive.

Defined Resources and Connectors

For the purposes of integrating with the most common source and target resources, Oracle Identity Manager supports a large number of connectors. These communicate with commercial apps and directories, in order to create, maintain, and provision user accounts. Each connector makes use of the most appropriate technology relative to the given resource. In some cases, the technology is proprietary, but in many cases it is standards-based. What constitutes appropriate is of course relative, but usually takes into account performance, maintainability, and on occasion the cooperation of the vendor of the resource.

In some cases, there are multiple connectors for a resource. This makes sense when the processes supported by the resource itself require different kinds of communications or protocols. For example, some resources require a connector for reconciliation (the processing of new or modified users) and another connector for processing password changes. The following is a high-level list of connector categories.

- BMC user and ticket management
- Mainframe (ACF2, RACF, Top Secret)
- OS/400
- Lotus Notes
- Active Directory user management and password sync
- Exchange, Windows, and Unix
- Database
- Novell eDir and Groupwise

- PeopleSoft, JD Edwards, Siebel, E-Business Suite, SAP, Oracle Warehouse Manager
- RSA Cleartrust & Authentication Manager
- Oracle and Sun directories

There are actually two database connectors, one for managing actual database users such as DBAs, and one for database tables when managing users who are represented as database records. Also remember that when it comes to directories, there's Active Directory, and everybody else. Active Directory doesn't hash passwords like anyone else, and it doesn't behave exactly like an LDAP V3-compliant directory (although this can be accomplished by putting ODS in front of it).

In addition, Oracle has acquired through Sun a number of other connectors, including more specific platform, packaged application, database, and directory connectors. As time passes, Oracle will be finalizing a strategy for providing a standard connector protocol to bring all Oracle and Sun customers under the same connector framework for better support.

To accomplish simple connections to source systems, such as through data feeds, you can make use of the Generic Technology Connector, in which you can specify the format of an incoming data feed, and map the values in that feed to target attributes, as shown in the following illustration. The interface easily walks you through the process. The result is a reusable connector that provides trusted source reconciliation using flat files, and without the need for custom coding.

When more complex decision making is required for customized connection needs, OIM provides an Adapter Factory for the creation of communications with proprietary resources, meaning those for which OIM does not have a connector already built. These adapters determine how a user is provisioned to those resources. For many applications, a user must be placed in the app-specific database. In the case of many off-the-shelf apps, this is not possible, for reasons of referential integrity (when the app says, "just give me the data, and I'll handle everything the right way"). In those cases, the adapter may present a packet or call to the application, which then uses its own business logic to fully instantiate the new user in its directory. The Adapter Factory has a graphical interface that allows you to create adapters in most cases without scripting or coding. What it does under the covers is generate Java classes for you. This avoids the use of messy, proprietary C code. Many of the standard connectors were developed using the Adapter Factory, making them far easier to extend and maintain.

When I have performed *insights* (detailed drill-downs of current resources and roadmaps for customers), a common concern I run into is, "We already run a number of scripts to create accounts in AD, Unix, and so on. Do those all get tossed?" The answer is, not necessarily, or at least not right away. An important piece of advice we've already discussed when building an IAM framework is, don't boil the ocean. When individual resources are provisioned by way of custom code or scripts, and these can't be quickly or easily duplicated, they can be preserved and integrated into the OIM provisioning process. The trick is to create an adapter to pass to the code or script the information it needs in order to do its job. Especially at universities, I've seen large numbers of scripts and cron jobs that are not part of any framework at all, but of course you eventually want to bring those into the fold, and OIM provides the framework to do just that.

In fact, at more than one university, I've seen them reinvent the wheel with every new resource, creating custom feeds, flat files, and their own versions of EDI, with all the intellectual property in somebody's head. If nothing else, using the Adapter Factory provides you with self-documenting views, which is more documentation that many of these custom links will ever see.

One standard that's actually gained traction the last several years is Service Provisioning Markup Language (SPML), developed by the Organization for the Advancement of Structured Information Standards (OASIS) for exchanging resource, user, and provisioning data between organizations. Like federation, the use of SPML assumes trust and cooperation. SPML is a protocol for making provisioning requests. When Oracle Identity Manager is installed, the process generates a batch file that, when run, deploys the OIM SPML Web Service. This service can interpret incoming SPML requests and turn them into provisioning tasks.

Another benefit to proper provisioning policies is governance of some of your resources. For example, if the creation of LDAP groups is limited to those that are used and provisioned via workflow, then you will avoid the extreme explosion of groups, *especially* Active Directory groups, which tend to multiply like rabbits. If you've got no handle on your AD groups, then guess what? You'll have far more of them by this time next year. With regard to compliance, we'll discuss Active Directory and its tendency toward proliferation (along with both preventive and detective solutions) a bit more in Chapter 12.

User Profiles

Your user repository may or may not be what you authenticate against, but it *is* where you store your primary user information. Once again, it may not even be your actual source data store, but it will be where you aggregate sufficient information for making determinations on provisioning, and will likely serve as your white pages, that is, where you go to search for users and their essential attributes. It should provide or at least point to the mapping of a user to his multiple instances, if they even exist. Recall that you may have an authoritative source for identity, and another authoritative source for authorizations.

Administrators can maintain user profiles, including a user's attributes, groups, and resources. You may or may not allow users to maintain their own profiles, or at least a subset of their attributes. It's common to allow end users to have access to their own profiles, but not edit, or even view, certain of their own attributes. The following illustration shows a default user profile. This is configurable.

Please remember that these user accounts within the IAM framework do not represent the friendly face of the user within the company. These are the user profiles that are used for provisioning and access management. We've already discussed account creation (in Chapter 8) and the fact that user accounts may be created from bulk loads, or already exist in a directory that you will point OIM to. This accounts for existing users. Going forward, however, you will want a procedure for acquiring and provisioning new users, as well as changing (and terminating) existing users.

By setting up reconciliation tasks within OIM, you can retrieve, on a schedule, any changes in the originating system—the authoritative source for user existence (such as a directory or human resources)—so that you can look for new and/or modified users or groups. Reconciliation looks for deltas in the authoritative source and propagates those changes as needed across target systems. A user created in PeopleSoft, for example, may be processed by OIM, with her identity created in the IAM framework, and her access granted to the necessary applications. New groups are likewise retrieved, along with any changes in memberships to existing groups.

To help with this account creation process, OIM supports a number of connectors specific to the most common people-moving applications, as well as the most common directories. For example:

- BMC Remedy
- Active Directory
- Windows
- JD Edwards
- Oracle eBusiness
- PeopleSoft
- Siebel
- SAP

Bear in mind that these are only some of the connectors supported by OIM, but they are the most common ones when we're talking about grabbing users from HR-type systems. While OIM can be used for managing user profiles and group memberships, it may very well be corporate policy to maintain that data from the HR system. In this case, a scheduled reconciliation task can go out and find new users and create provisioning and access accounts for them in the OIM repository.

While it's advisable to maintain a super-user view of OIM with all menu items enabled, you could choose to provide limited views for delegated admins to prevent the creation or modification of user accounts/profiles within OIM, in order to ensure that these objects are maintained via the designated HR application. Now, HR is not likely the source of provisioning truth, but it can provide the ammunition for the automated provisioning processes to run later, by assigning attributes or group memberships that a provisioning task will feed on in order to make provisioning decisions. We'll talk about that shortly.

Now that we've covered orgs, groups, resources, and users, let me state this. You can always, quite easily, investigate who contains what, or is contained by what: users in a group, groups or resources for a user, groups in an organization, and so on.

Legacy IDs

OIM supports the linking of legacy application IDs, that is, target resource username formats that don't match up. You're John.Smith on the first app, Jsmith on the next, and JohnS on the third. Now, by linking I mean the ability to provision a user to those various targets using their desired formats. It is possible to create a task that periodically discovers and maps those user IDs, so that for purposes of centralized provisioning and single sign-on support, those IDs are associated with the central user profile. However, this assumes some commonality between those identities, such as a user number or account number. Without that, you may be out of luck. Many times over the years I've been asked by customers who've allowed the creation of unlinked user accounts across multiple targets, "Can you map these IDs?" I will instantly ask them, "Well, can *you*?" And if their answer is no, then my answer is no as well.

But wait… there are a few options for solving this problem, although not all are out of the box:

- New in OIM 11*g*, there is an administrative interface for the ad-hoc mapping of disparate user IDs to a single identity. Since it's manual and admin-based, it would be used on a case-by-case basis.

- A custom self-registration scheme can be built to allow users to provide their credentials (including username) to their multiple resources, thereby mapping themselves.

- Oracle integration partners have also devised account claiming interfaces, integrated with OIM, for the purposes of also allowing users to perform their own mapping.

A while back, I proposed just such a custom self-registration scheme at a customer, using Oracle Access Manager, allowing their users to map their own disparate IDs. I also proposed that the customer send out multiple bulletins, alerting their users that with the first authentication under the new scheme, they would be prompted to self-register their multiple apps. By providing the bulletin, they'd know they weren't being phished.

Let's digress on one subject, delegated administration. Imagine you've got a customer or line of business to whom you've granted the ability to manage their own users. Delegated admin makes it easier for those entities to create separate users, and therefore avoid the temptation to simply let multiple users log in as a generic user, often called a shared account, in order to accomplish the business of the group. Shared accounts obscure who actually used a resource, and therefore you've got the risk of "Nobody can tell I did this," and "the log file tells you nothing useful."

Since we're discussing users, let's jump ahead and talk about what a user can do for himself. For one thing, a user can

- Register his own security questions/answers
- Reset his own passwords
- Request access to resources
- Track his requests
- Maintain his own attributes (or at least those he's allowed to)

Workflow Definitions

So now it's time to match up your user and resource definitions. Workflow is where you define the policies that do this. Workflow specifies the steps (tasks) and the stops (connections) that need to be executed in order to fulfill the requirements of a policy. I've heard it said that workflows must be flexible to reflect real-world use cases. This is *wrong*. It is the *design* of workflows that must be flexible, to allow admins to build in the possible avenues or exceptions. ("This transaction can be completed by anyone with the proper certification *or* by anyone with a C-level title.") But once they're defined, workflows must be fairly rigid, to enforce least privilege.

Where do you get the raw material to build workflows? We already discussed this. It's really two avenues. One is your *use cases*. At some point you had to devise the steps that had to take place in order for a user to get from Point A to Point B, including those all-important approvers. You came up with scenarios for users to be created, enabled, changed, and ultimately terminated. Perhaps you didn't come up with one for every single scenario, just enough to evaluate and purchase a supporting solution. Fine, so now you must design more.

But the other avenue is your *committees*. These workflows must fulfill an agreed-upon set of steps and approvals. At many customers, I've seen *virtual* workflows, that is, semi-documented or undocumented processes that were followed with some regularity, but they just happened to be all manual, often involving lots of e-mails, voicemails, and help desk tickets. With workflow, you're committing these processes to the firm hands of the *framework*, which provides a more rigid mechanism involving an actual workflow engine that will not only fulfill policy, but *enforce* policy. The help desk should now be mostly pulled out of this process.

Let's revisit two concepts, with one feeding the other. First, "least privilege" states that at any given time, a user should have only the access rights to which they are entitled, and nothing else. Out-of-band access entails any rights a user has to which he is *not* entitled, in violation of least privilege.

When you are determining your sizing requirements for OIM, meaning the number of servers or degree of redundancy, you should consider:

- User population, including the number of transactions you expect to perform on a daily basis. Just as with any other load consideration, it's not so much the number of users as the number of *concurrent* users that matters.
- Number of resources to be provisioned with the average request.
- External calls or services to be leveraged in the average workflow.
- Layers of dynamic rules to be evaluated for enablement.

Exceptions can be built into the workflow definitions, but only of course if those exceptions can be predicted. For example, if you know a particular function is going to be made available on a semi-regular basis to a user other than one with the normal qualifications, you can bake that in. Let me give you two examples from personal experience:

- A banking customer has a pool of server specialists who are granted, at least once every two months, temporary access to a set of Unix servers for purposes of conducting forensic exams. Access to these servers is typically granted only to developers. Because this temporary access is granted to a set of users whose attributes are already known, the workflow definition contains branches for both sets of approvals.

- I can think of several examples involving auditors who, once or twice a year (depending on the set of resources), are granted rights to analyze sensitive data that is by default available only to employees.

Otherwise, exceptions are usually out of the norm, unanticipated, and not necessarily granted to users with typical qualifications for the given resource.

In OIM 11*g*, you have enhanced support for bulk requests involving multiple resources for multiple parties, and the ability to handle sub-requests in the batch. These enhancements allow administrators to spawn mass requests, then make granular decisions in approving them in pieces rather than in an all-or-nothing batch. This is a great benefit when enabling numbers of users simultaneously for projects or M&A situations.

Workflow Designer

Presumably you've already been using some kind of request and approval process, even if it's been mostly manual, perhaps based on a help desk or other ticketing app. How automated will it be going forward? What will workflow look like? In any more-than-basic approval workflow, you may have stops that take place in serial, and others in parallel.

"If Jack approves this request, then Fred and Mary can both have a look, even at the same time. If it gets past the two of them, then it moves to John." And so on.

If you have not automated your approvals before, it is now going to be a formal process. Things don't just get thrown over the wall by e-mail or sneakernet. You specifically configure the positions required to approve a request, and the order in which they are invoked.

What will notifications look like? Just about every workflow engine in the world can talk SMTP. The actual content of a notification e-mail is somewhat trivial, although I've seen a whole hour go by in a meeting at an HMO where they debated exactly what a notification e-mail would look like. Should it contain a direct link to the approval page? Sure, why not? But don't let it automatically log you in, since that would be a big security no-no.

Remember, you're not deciding what the automated requirements are for resource eligibility. A request should only be spawned if someone is eligible, unless it's a manual request. You are deciding, for each resource:

- What individual approvals are necessary for final approval
- What order they occur in; some may occur in parallel
- Which steps can be automated, which are manual (for example, once you're past step 3, you are automatically stuffed into the LDAP, but help desk staff must specifically enter you into the CRM package)
- Who the designated backups are when an approver is unavailable
- What the timeouts for escalation are (kick it to designated backups after what period of time)

- How notifications are delivered (provisioning interface, e-mail)
- What notification looks like
- Who the ultimate process owner is when there is a bottleneck that cannot be handled by escalation (and this is going to happen, guaranteed)
- What should happen when a request, or a piece of a request, is rejected or canceled

A workflow definition specifies where and how a workflow starts, all the steps that need to be completed, the possible directions it might take (depending on events or decisions along the way), and the possible endings. Yes, that is a plural, since there is no guarantee that a request that spawns a workflow will be completely fulfilled, or fulfilled quite the way it is intended. Pieces may be rejected, approvers may not be available, the request could be canceled, or other events may take place to affect the outcome.

In design, we discussed envisioning the requirements for provisioning a resource, that is, a user's qualifications, how the request is spawned, what approvals are required, which tasks are manual and which are automated. In workflow design, you define the actual process that must execute to fulfill those requirements.

The OIM workflow design tool allows you to create a visual definition of a workflow sequence, including the tasks (both automated and manual), approvals, relationships, and dependencies. It's available from a drop-down menu on the Resource Detail page, under Resource Workflows. The Workflow Visualizer (shown in the following illustration) is a drag-and-drop tool, allowing you to drag elements into the flow and place them as needed. You can double-click on a task component to expand and modify it.

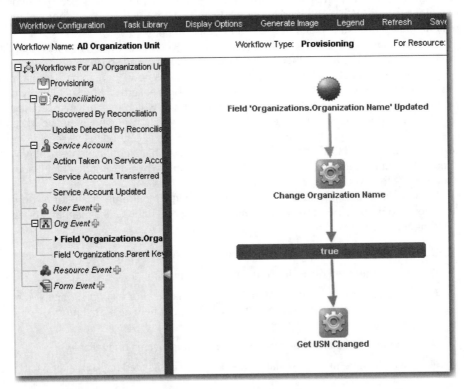

It's advisable to name your workflow definitions something meaningful, for example:

- New Accounts Reconciled
- Customer Access Approved
- Employee Transfer

We've all done flowcharts at one time or other. This is the same idea, except that now you are defining the flow of subevents for an overall provisioning event. You can add Markers, elements that are simply descriptive or that reference a task in a different node. Let me tell you when these can be especially useful. It's certainly possible to create a workflow definition of great complexity, especially if you are provisioning multiple resources using multiple approvers and multiple branches (and you may branch one way or another, depending on the action taken by an approver). Instead of making a crowded mess of your workflow view, you can reference another branch, which might be pictured separately. Think of it as a family reunion, where you can't possibly get everybody into the picture, so you get pictures of different branches of the family and put them in an album.

You can create branches, with Response SubTrees, representing the possible actions that may take place depending on actions taken at the critical joints, just like any other flowchart you're familiar with. In other words, if the approver takes a certain action, branch one way, else branch another.

There are two types of tasks within a flow, manual and automated. A manual task requires a user action, such as a manual creation of an account, or the physical sending of a resource like a phone or laptop. An automated task requires no user action, but does require plugging in an adapter to take an action instead. This could be the automated creation or modification of a resource account.

You specify Response Nodes that indicate the result of a task: Completed, Rejected, or Canceled. These trigger what happens after a particular result. For example, if you define a flow as all-or-nothing, that the user must either receive all or none of the resources in a request, then the result of a rejection or cancellation may be the rollback of everything he *did* receive up to that point. A well-rounded workflow design takes into account all the possibilities, since there's no guarantee that all the steps will be approved, completed, or even attended to in a reasonable timeframe. Therefore, these possibilities should be handled by the appropriate tasks:

- A Response-Generated Task is initiated when a triggering task is successfully completed.
- A Dependency Task is defined as being dependent upon the completion of another task. These are useful for layers of approval or verification.
- A Recovery Task is initiated after a rejection.
- An Undo Task is initiated after a cancellation.

Workflow can include dependencies to ensure that before being provisioned, a user has:

- Agreed to specific terms
- Read certain documents
- Been certified as eligible

These types of dependencies, of course, depend on having an established rubric, that is, somebody checked a box on a form.

The vectors, or arrowed lines, connecting tasks and responses are called Links. The relationship between the connected items is indicated by the color of the link. Once you have linked a pair of nodes, if you subsequently move one of the nodes, the link faithfully follows it. It's often a good idea to move things around a little anyway, since by default the tool likes to space the nodes out a bit.

Workflow Events

You can make use of a number of event tabs associated with the workflow definition. The tab describes the tasks for the given event. These events are often not the kind associated with a request, but rather with an event not specific to the user but which ultimately affects him (or *them*, since a group event affects all its members).

- Provisioning
- Reconciliation
- Service account
- User event
- Org event
- Resource event
- Form event
- Attestation

Think of reconciliation as really another type of provisioning task. Based on the result of a reconciliation decision, a user may lose access to the given resource. Provisioning as an overall process, remember, isn't just the granting of access, but any change at all to access, whether it's getting it, losing it, or having it changed (for example, I'm still an Accounting Clerk, but now I'm in Manufacturing instead of Shipping/Receiving).

A user event reflects a change in the user's record, such as updating an attribute. If legacy applications have their own naming conventions that don't match the new corporate standard, as in *firstname.lastname*, you may be updating the user's wallet of app IDs. Likewise, a resource event is one that responds to changes in the state of a resource, such as its status (active vs. inactive).

The purpose of these event tabs is to specify what should happen if one of these events take place. Therefore you can establish adapters that perform tasks in response to these events. What you're trying to do here is cover all the possibilities.

A customer of mine in the Southwest had a workflow policy specifying that nothing got provisioned until after midnight. No requests could go through until after the calendar day had rolled over because, in theory, some admin might review the bucket of pending requests and make a change before allowing processing. I never saw them actually use that option, but it was there.

Workflow Separation

Oracle Identity Manager provides for breaking up workflows functionally and administratively, which allows you to distribute the management of the components of an overall workflow, as well as isolate the effects of change on only those components that need changing, without impacting other components. That was a mouthful, so let's break it down.

First, workflows can be (and should be) broken up into subprocesses. A single group membership may include access to multiple resources, each of which may require multiple approvals or tasks. The HR approval segment may be routed for email, benefits, and single sign-on approvals, while another segment may pertain to business application approvals, and so on. These multiple segments can be represented within the workflow designed as separate chains, which can be subsequently linked, as shown in the following illustration. Individual nodes in a workflow outline can be linked to sub-workflows in which dependent tasks are performed. This makes it far easier to delegate the management of these segments (and also avoids the improbability of trying to show an entire, complex workflow in the Workflow Designer interface at one time).

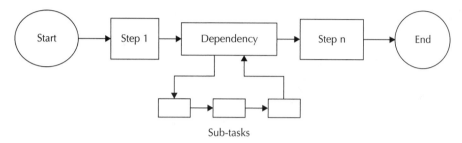

Sub-tasks

Second, OIM allows you to separate approval workflow from provisioning workflow. This has multiple benefits.

- Changes made to the business process, such as the reordering of steps, do not impact the technical process.

- The business requirements of an approval are necessarily separate from the granular actions needed to actually communicate with an endpoint resource.

- You can take advantage of external processes or workflows, and make them part of the new framework.

Notifications

Approvers and admins who must be notified of alerts or, more commonly, requests to make approval decisions on resource requests, can receive these notifications in a number of ways. More and more often, I see workflow steps kicking off cell phone text messages, whereas in the old days they might get a message on their pager.

But the more standard approach is to send e-mail. If an admin logs into Oracle Identity Manager and checks under his pending tasks, he will see pending approvals. When you are configuring the format for a notification e-mail to an approver, it's not a bad idea to include a link to the page where they will perform this duty. It *is* a bad idea to have that link automatically authenticate that approver to that page (and I keep bringing this up because I have customers who do this). You want to require the approver to authenticate to OIM.

You can dynamically assign a task to a user based on lookup. For example, you might look up a user's manager in order to route an approval request from that user. Escalations can be initiated when the approver fails to fulfill the requested task (approve or deny) within a specified period. A secondary approver may receive a notification if a failsafe threshold is eventually reached.

Manual Provisioning

No matter how powerful mid-range computers get, there will always be a place for mainframes in large organizations. Likewise, no matter what automation you put in place, there will always be a place for manual provisioning. Some positions will be enabled through direct grants, or by requests entered by either the end user or his manager. And there will always be a need for exceptions.

Within the OIM interface, an administrator can assign to an authorized user a new group membership, organization membership, or resource. This is certainly preferable to a help desk staff member actually cracking open Active Directory or an application-centric user store and creating or modifying an entry. Using the OIM interface not only provides the admin with a menu of choices, it also centralizes the function, maintains a central log, and ensures that all the appropriate tasks are fulfilled. If manual provisioning is done case by case, outside the framework, then you've lost that safety net of compliance-driven policy. Not all is lost, since the other safety net is *reconciliation*, which runs on a scheduled basis to make sure that users only have the access they're supposed to have (thereby enforcing least privilege).

If you are deploying full RBAC, you can direct-grant by using static roles, which don't operate strictly on role policies for automation. We'll be discussing static, as well as dynamic, roles in a few pages.

In previous incarnations, OIM approval and provisioning workflows were both tied to resources. In 11*g*, the request model is disconnected from resources, and based on templates specific to the user or (more likely) his role or memberships. This means the user (or the manager requesting on the user's behalf) can only see the roles, resources, or entitlements applicable to the user.

While automated provisioning is the ideal, there are at least a couple of very good use cases for manual provisioning (other than the fact that creating policies can take a lot of time and labor). First, emergencies. You need to grant someone immediate access to a resource because the usual person handling that resource is out of pocket. Or you need someone to perform forensics. Someone's been terminated without warning and another body must be plugged in to handle day-to-day functions until a replacement is found. And here's one more we'll talk about more in our chapter on compliance. Due to unforeseen circumstances, and in order to avoid an interruption of service, a user is granted access rights to which he is not normally entitled because of Segregation of Duties rules, so that he can provide essential services. Auditors will tell you this is a big no-no, and it normally is, but it happens all the time. The important thing is that by using OIM for this purpose, the entire event is fully documented and logged, and later you may review out of band or exceptional grants to determine whether to revoke them, document them as ongoing exceptions, or make those part of the user's permanent role.

If SoD rules have been configured within Oracle Identity Analytics, any resource request with OIM that violates these rules will trigger an error message and/or alerts requiring management intervention, including approval, remediation, or outright denial. This is accomplished when the OIM resource request queries OIA to check for any violations.

Impersonation and Proxy Users

There's a common method of providing somebody rights. It's often more method than function, because not all systems support it, and in some cases for a very good reason. I'm including this here, since it's usually accomplished manually, as there's no good way to automate a rule for it. This method is technically called modeling, but is commonly called "Make Bob Like Tom." In other words, "Bob needs access rights. We don't know exactly what all he should get, but he'll be doing the same job as Tom, so just give him what Tom has."

Sounds simple, right? But since this method is essentially based on ignorance—that is, we don't know what the correct permissions inventory is, so we'll just make a copy of another user and drop it on the new guy—it's a highly inexact method. What if it's been a long time since Tom was enabled, and nobody knows for sure what exact rights Tom has these days? What if he's picked up extra rights in the last couple of years? That means Bob picks those up as well, and the auditors shall surely shred you.

Here's the only situation I believe makes this almost workable, and that is the application of *context*. I might very well give Bob access to the resources that Tom has, or maybe the same role, but everything must be based on Bob's context. Now, this could be location, department, seniority, or any combination of them. But let's say Bob and Tom are both in sales, except they sell different product lines, and Tom's a manager while Bob's a salesperson. These resources might be

- CRM
- Forecasting
- Commissions
- Quotes

So what context brings to the table is this: Tom sees all customers, forecasts, quotes, and commissions for his salespeople, while Bob sees only his own customers, forecast, quotes, and commissions. When they look up pricing, they can see it only for their respective product lines.

A situation where you *would* want one user to have another user's rights is when that second user must perform some or all of the duties of the first user. Someone goes on vacation, or is overwhelmed keeping up with tasks, or you just plain plan on redundancy. One thing you definitely don't want to allow is for one user to log in as another user, because then you lose the context of that user's identity for auditing purposes. Consider various ways to mitigate the risk behind this requirement:

- As already mentioned, context. I might have your title, but can only exercise similar access within my own line of business.

- Temporality—I get your job duties while you're on vacation, but only for two weeks, after which those rights expire. If you decide to stay at the resort an extra week, I'll need to get renewed, which is a better inconvenience than me keeping those rights indefinitely.

- Attestation—Make sure that any anomalous access grants get reviewed periodically.

In addition to other manual steps, Oracle Identity Manager provides for *proxy users* who can execute other users' functions. Within self-service account management, a user can specify a proxy user for a specified date range. Within that range, the proxy user is automatically assigned any tasks that would normally be assigned to the original user. It's also possible to configure which users are eligible to be proxies. In other words, proxy users should be drawn from a pool of qualified individuals.

Automated Provisioning

Naturally, doing anything at all in an IAM framework, whether it's provisioning, granting real-time access, or auditing, usually means matching up groups of users with groups of resources. Performing these actions or even just creating the definitions in terms of groups is far more maintainable.

In the design chapter, we discussed associating resources with groups, so that membership in a group automatically leads to a user attaining those resources. Likewise, role policies allow for the automated assignment of roles for those users whose attributes align with the policies. Initial roles and their associated privileges can be automatically assigned once the user has been reconciled from the authoritative source into Oracle Identity Manager. We will discuss role policies in just a couple of pages.

Access Policies

In Oracle Identity Manager, access policies define the relationships between groups of users and resources. A user placed into a group can inherit the resources associated with that group. A group may be associated with a location, a department, line of business, and so on. Multiple resources may be associated with that group, with each resource having its own adapter for determining how a user is to be presented or provisioned to that resource. Each resource may have its own approval requirements as well. The OIM Access Policy wizard walks you through all the steps to create an access policy for provisioning users and groups to a resource, as shown in the following illustration.

Access Policy Information Provided		Change
Access Policy Name	locHouston	
Access Policy Description	Located in Houston	
With Approval	No	
Retrofit Access Policy	Yes	
Priority	16	

Resources to be provisioned by this access policy				Change
Resource Name	Revoke if no longer applies	Resource Form	Process Forms	
Building Access Card	✓		Building Access Card Edit	
AD User	✓		AD User Details Edit	
Database Access Oracle User RO	✗		Database Access Provisioning form for Oracle User Provide Information	

Note the Priority field in this illustration. This specifies a priority level for the policy, and must be unique for each policy you create. The lower the number, the higher the priority. The purpose of this value is to avoid the conflicts (such as SoD) that can occur when a user is subject to multiple access policies.

Pre-Provisioning

You may make the decision on this on a case-by-case basis, but here's the choice: do you pre-provision all eligible users for a resource, or wait until they make a request or absolutely need to be in? If a thousand people are eligible for access to an app, but only a hundred will actually use it, do you grant them all access in advance? It would sure make it cleaner if you *don't*. If you are required to buy user licenses for that resource, you have another incentive to wait for requests. On the other hand, if you're talking big numbers, no user license limitations, and the possibility of plenty of usage later, it might be better to get all the approvals out of the way. There is no right or wrong on this one; simply, deal with it now, or deal with it later. Or in some cases, you never end up dealing with it, because some people will never end up accessing that app.

Bear in mind, if you set up policies that automatically grant privileges based on automatically granted dynamic roles, then it's a moot point.

Reconciliation

The word "reconciliation" is used in multiple contexts within Oracle Identity Manager, but the term has essentially the same meaning in each. It means in a broader sense the act of reconciling changes between a source and a target, in which OIM may play either part. A little later, when looking at compliance processes, we'll discuss using reconciliation for ensuring that users only have access rights in agreement with policy, *after* initial provisioning. And under RBAC, we'll discuss how reconciliation retrieves role assignments for provisioning. Right now, let's talk about reconciliation to *initiate* provisioning.

As we stated while discussing account creation, identity management is not the same as human resources. You're not hiring, offering letters, processing payroll, generating tax forms, and the like through IdM. The purpose of our framework is provisioning and access. Therefore it's common for a user to be born in a human resources package, such as JDE, PeopleSoft, Siebel, SAP, and so on. A *reconciliation* process runs, on schedule (perhaps every hour, or twice a day, or as frequently as makes sense for your organization), discovers the new users in that HR package or other point of origin, and creates endpoint accounts for them. It may also discover modified users, those who have been promoted, demoted, transferred, or terminated. Regardless of their status, these users represent *change*. The access policies you have created match up user attributes and memberships with resources and then initiate the proper workflows to begin the provisioning, re-provisioning, or de-provisioning tasks. The beauty of this approach is *automation*. By automating your provisioning tasks, you are benefiting in several ways from the power of the framework:

- Taking the manual guesswork out of provisioning
- Enforcing organizational policies that have been encoded in your workflows
- Enforcing the compliance policies that are (hopefully) inherent in those policies
- Taking the burden off your service desk personnel
- Greatly expediting the enablement of users who will be productive more quickly than if they were waiting on manual processes

This is not to say that approvals are out of the picture. I'm only saying that the initiation of the provisioning process gets kicked off, and in fact any automatic assignments that have no dependencies can be provisioned instantly. But any steps that still require approval will of course need to be eyeballed, as usual.

You will never create a provisioning structure that is either manual or automatic. Every organization has the need for both. I have customers who started out with the notion of creating an ideal system in which all access grants would be automated based on job codes or other attributes, assigned through HR and bubbling to the provisioning system. But in every single instance, they ended up with at least some roles or even direct resource grants that were manual, because of exceptions that were difficult to codify through policies, or emergency situations they had not thought of during design and didn't have time to create an exception policy for.

When reconciling users from their point of origin into OIM, you can perform the process *fully* or *incrementally*. By default, reconciliation is *full* the first time you run it against a system, allowing OIM to build a baseline of user accounts. Subsequently, reconciliation is *incremental*, including only those user accounts that have been added, modified or, in those rare instances, deleted. I say rare because, in the age of compliance, you rarely delete users; you deactivate them.

For the sake of completing a reconciliation cycle within a certain window (for example, between midnight and the start of the next working day), you may configure reconciliation to run as *batched*, meaning with a specified number of records. In this way, the process can be broken into a reasonable batch size. It may require an initial couple of runs to determine if this is even a need.

As stated elsewhere, you might put a separate instance of OIM on a different server altogether for the sole purpose of running scheduled tasks such as reconciliation, to isolate the load and limit the impact on day-to-day tasks.

With 11*g*, Oracle has greatly improved the performance model for reconciliation, optimizing it for bulk processing of events, which can include reconciling users, user target accounts, entitlements, and role memberships. Again, the point here is to ensure that only current users are in the system, and that those users have only the access proper to their needs and the needs of the organization. The model also provides retry support for out-of-sequence events that can cause race conditions, that is, the run-time engine delivers the necessary data to the queue only when the workflow is in an idle state awaiting that data.

Role-Based Provisioning

Role-based access control (RBAC) is an increasingly important part of provisioning. A *role* is a business-related collection of entitlements or privileges. Get the role, inherit the entitlements. Most users are granted at least two roles. The first would provide the basics, such as portal logon, e-mail, access to benefits, and other resources that would apply to all users within an organization, from data entry clerk to CEO. Subsequent role grants would provide access to business functions that are relative to a user's place in the hierarchy.

RBAC provides benefits in security, compliance, and administration:

- RBAC relates access to business functions.

- A role presents an easy-to-manage abstract that contains the details of the associated entitlements.

- Roles allow for drill-down on the entitlements a user has by virtue of role membership.

- Roles make it easier to provide and to take away entitlements in logical groups.

Oracle Identity Analytics allows you to define the roles that run the business, along with the business hierarchy in which they operate. Roles should be, when possible (and in fact most of the time), tied to those business units that own and can maintain them, and where a user may execute the associated duties. If I'm a Quality Control Officer for a manufacturing organization, my role should not be maintained by accounting, and I should have no entitlements within the accounting resources through my role membership.

The roles that are engineered and maintained within OIA are provisioned through the integration with Oracle Identity Manager. Roles can be configured with policies that determine automatic membership based on user attributes. Policies can be built in OIA using a point-and-click interface, matching up required values with a user's attributes in order to determine role eligibility. These policies can be expressed using basic if-then-else logic, such as in the following GUI example:

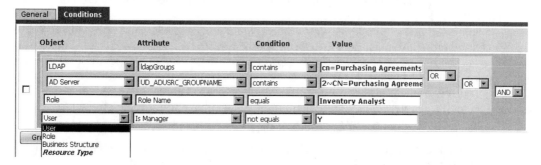

The interface itself here is of interest because it means using a simple GUI, rather than XML or proprietary scripting in order to codify the logic of the policies. I may be automatically eligible for a role based on those attributes that specify any combination of the following:

- My location
- My certifications
- Whether I am an employee or a contractor
- My job code or title
- My place in the organization
- Any other relevant attributes that are exposed

Such policies are the *ideal* situation in RBAC. Why? Automation. I create a user account in HR, that user is reconciled to OIM, which uses the roles and rules in OIA to calculate and grant that user's initial roles. Additional roles and entitlements may be requested later, but the user's Day One access is handled automatically. The granting of roles via a rules engine has huge benefits for the organization:

- The initiation of request workflows simply by entering the new user in HR
- Greatly reduced reliance on the inaccuracies and bottlenecks of the help desk
- The consistency of rules that are rigid enough for compliance, but dynamic enough to fit business needs

A quick digression on the automatic granting of roles: Hypothetically (although I've seen this in practice), you allow the system to grant a role, containing multiple entitlements, to a user on Day One. Later, during access certification (which we'll discuss in great detail under Legacy Considerations), you take away one of those entitlements. You haven't changed the rules, or my attributes, that gave me the entitlements in the first place. My role gives me five target systems, and you've just taken away one of them. It's possible that during the next reconciliation, I'll get that target system right back again, because according to the rules I can have it. If this indicates a condition that will be semi-permanent, you may wish to modify the role definition, meaning the entitlements it contains, during the next role certification (which we'll discuss again in Chapter 12).

Having just discussed the relative merits of manual and automated provisioning in the previous section, let me just say that roles-based provisioning can also be either. You may define some roles as dynamic, with policies allowing them to be automatically granted, while others must be manually granted.

Some end-user applications—lots of them, including PeopleSoft and SAP— already have a notion of roles. Admins specific to those apps know how to assign those roles. But how many users of those apps work only in those apps? Where they are implemented, these systems are a huge part of the enterprise, but they're not the only game in town.

This means that a user whose profile entitles them to PeopleSoft or SAP access will have a specified role to execute within them, but they also have roles in the other enterprise apps. An application may have any one of many methods for accepting rights for a user.

- It already supports its own roles, so at provisioning time, simply tell it which role the new user gets from that list.

- It relies on groups from a directory, so grant the new user the appropriate memberships in LDAP.

- It maintains its own access repository, so create a record in that database for the new user, with the appropriate entitlements spelled out.

- It accepts at login time a list of entitlements the user can exercise for the session, so when you sign that user in to that app with SSO, the application retrieves the multivalued attribute with those entitlements, or grabs that data from wherever it is, and injects them as header variables.

Roles have the ability to provide for any of these scenarios; they simply have to be asked. Roles have a business context, an application context, and a granular privilege context. But because you start with the assignment of a role, a business function that is far easier to comprehend than application privileges, you are putting a business-friendly face on the otherwise cumbersome process of provisioning. By assigning that top-level role, I'm allowing the user to ultimately inherit the resource roles, followed by the resource privileges, that map all the way up. Think of RBAC as power steering on your car. You're not really moving the wheels; you're using a powerful mechanism to do it for you. Your hands are one degree removed from the tires. With RBAC, you're not directly granting access rights; you're providing direction, and the mechanism does the real work. Yes, OIM supports the provisioning of individual entitlements, but when you can use the abstract of a role, user rights management is far more efficient.

What's in a Role?

True role definitions, as opposed to simple groups, require more work, but can do more work for you later. This is an industry-standard structure for roles:

Business role → Multiple resource roles → Multiple privileges

You often hear the terms "top-down" and "bottom-up" when describing role design. Here's what that means. Top-down means creating a business or enterprise role, possibly a job title, that relates to multiple downstream resource roles. If your title is sales manager, you can access the forecasting, customer contact, and billing applications. Bottom-up means the aggregation of individual privileges into usable groups, or resource roles. If part of my job is printing invoices, reconciling them with incoming payments, and adjusting customer balances, that group of privileges equates to an accounts receivable clerk role within the accounting package.

A question I'm often asked is, which should be done first, the top-down definitions, or the bottom-up discovery? The answer is, they can be done in parallel. Business analysts and managers decide which job titles or functions they need in place in order to accomplish the business of the organization. But those people don't necessarily (and in fact rarely) understand the IT functions behind those business functions. It's a three-layer cake. A single individual with a particular job title will likely have multiple business functions. This is where the mapping comes in. Preferably, when you assign privileges, you're doing it from the business level rather than the functional level. The top-down mapping gets you from that business level to the functional level, and perhaps beyond.

The Oracle role solution supports the notion of nested roles, in which roles can be embedded in other roles, which not only better model your organization, but which also allow you to map business functions to the many subfunctions they entail. The following illustration describes these relationships. After all, as part of your own job, how many applications and other resources do you have access to?

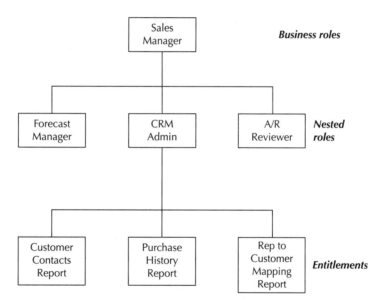

Roles are composed of multiple many-to-many relationships.

- A role contains multiple entitlements (usually).
- An entitlement can be used in multiple roles.
- A role can have multiple users.
- A user can have multiple roles.
- A single business role can provide a user with accounts on multiple systems.

Within Oracle Identity Analytics, you can also classify the responsibilities that exist within a role, meaning that you associate them with business units or organizations. The policy for a role can take these classifications into consideration when auto-assigning roles. For example, membership in a group may automatically entitle a user to a role associated with that group.

Building Roles

Roles can be assembled and refined by way of role mining (which we discuss in greater detail in Chapter 14). This entails the processing and analysis of existing user entitlement data to build roles based on common usage, and is accomplished with the use of Oracle Identity Analytics (OIA).

But there are other ways to create and refine roles through OIA:

- Create a new role from scratch.
- Create a new role using an existing role as a template.
- Create a new role using all the entitlements from a selected Global User.

A role can be associated with a department and/or job code to make it far easier to assign. When something as specific as a job code is available, it certainly makes the job of determining role membership a simpler thing.

OIA also supports a structure known as a Role Hierarchy, meaning a structure in which roles can have child-parent relationships. If a user is assigned a child role, then that user is automatically given a parent role. If membership in the parent role is revoked, then the child role is also automatically revoked. Just as the business hierarchy associates roles with layers of the business, the role hierarchy further supports this by indicating, for example, prerequisites. Only if I qualify for the parent role can I have the child role. At one banking customer, you needed the basic Teller role before you could have a locationally based teller role, and then a Master Teller role, which allowed you to review and correct the transactions of other tellers.

Role Life Cycle

Like a user, a user account, a resource, or the grant of a resource, a role has a life cycle. It is designed, activated, granted, modified, and perhaps retired. Consider a role that is associated with a job function, such as Quality Control or Accounts Payable Data Entry Clerk. The role is defined as containing a certain set of nested roles or entitlements. It is maintained by a specified role owner. It may lose one entitlement and gain another. This action would result in the re-provisioning of all role members the next time OIM reconciliation runs. If the role is decommissioned, then it would be disassociated from all member users.

Another important aspect of the role lifecycle is *versioning*. This capability allows role owners to create multiple versions of a role without impacting the original model of the role. Any change in a role definition automatically generates a new version. As with the original, any subsequent version requires approval before it can be activated. Only one version of a role can be active at any given time, although OIA tracks all versions, and you can revert to a particular version if the need arises. This ability gives you very tight control over the access associated with that role.

OIA supports graphical version comparison, displaying the properties of two roles simultaneously, side by side, to help you troubleshoot and get a new version just right.

Role History

As with users, resources, and just about every other type of object you can define in the identity suite, Oracle Identity Analytics allows you to view the entire history of a role without having to correlate multiple reports. It's all on the screen. For each role, you can view the following:

- Role membership history, including all members, current and past
- Policy history, including all policies added to or removed from the role
- Owner history, with all owners added to or removed from a role
- Attribute history, meaning all modifications made to the attributes associated with a role
- Certification history, listing the details for all certifications performed on a role

Included for all these items is the OIA administrator responsible for the action listed (for example, who changed the membership, who changed the owner, and so forth).

Database Security and Provisioning

Let me quickly make it clear what we're about to cover. Since this book is about identity and access, this section describes securely managing the creation and access rights of database users. Managing who gets what within the database environment itself shouldn't be solely the function of DBAs. For too long, it was just a given that database administrators were simply the safe guys who held the keys to the kingdom. As an old DBA, I know exactly what it's like to be able to discern who got paid what, and to have the ability to enable myself (if I were evil enough to do so) for anything at all, and all of it out of band, behind the scenes and not governed by any business logic whatsoever. It's long been the case that there were database users, and then everybody else.

But this is the wrong approach. The database, while a foundational piece of everything you do, is still just another digital asset in terms of your inventory of what you use to run the business and must protect. By treating the database like its own kingdom, you end up applying inconsistent policies. Second, you are putting too much power, risk, and vulnerabilities in the hands of too few people without review or governance.

What makes database user accounts so critical is that they fall into two very powerful categories: administrators who control one of your most necessary and critical resources, and service accounts that perform tasks on behalf of users and processes. Your web services typically don't log in as the users who make the requests; they log in as a service, a non-human, and yet they still need to be scrutinized and managed.

Not all database users, of course, are DBAs. I have a number of customers who authorize many users to create reports directly out of the database rather than use reporting tools. The relative merits of this practice are debatable, but not within the scope of this book. However, this is a whole other user community to be managed.

Having done talks in front of large groups about database security, I've run into more resistance with this story than anything else. I am telling DBAs that they are essentially untrusted. But this is not necessarily the right way to look at it. Yes, you are protecting the chickens from the roosters, who may not always have the best intentions. But you're also relieving them of the burden of creating and managing these accounts. This is the original purpose of the framework, remember? You are applying consistency and security to the database, just as with the provisioning and access to every other resource in the enterprise.

Oracle provides two solutions for provisioning database user accounts, with some more robust than others, depending on the structure and dependencies you wish to deal with. These are UM4DB (User Management for DataBase) and EUS (Enterprise User Security). They operate in very different ways, however.

UM4DB is a focused version of Oracle Identity Manager just for enterprise databases. It provides full-blown provisioning, with workflow, approvals, and group management. In this case, the resources are limited to Oracle and SQL Server database user accounts. The main purpose of UM4DB is to maintain privileged database user accounts, and provide a robust compliance umbrella for those users, including the ability to audit historical data on those users, audit administrative actions on databases, and detect orphaned database accounts.

Enterprise User Security is a direct-grant interface. EUS can be used to create roles containing specific rights within individual databases, which can then be aggregated into enterprise database roles. These roles can then be associated with LDAP groups, which means that when a user is added to such an LDAP group, he automatically gains the enterprise database role, thereby granting him the necessary rights on the necessary individual database instances. EUS also provides centralized password management and self-service password reset. It is a very hands-on solution, since it does not support workflow, and therefore requires manual maintenance of user accounts.

In order to accomplish the mapping of the global roles created in EUS, you need to store the metadata in somebody's schema. For this purpose, you can make those schema changes in Oracle Internet Directory, and synchronize it with your user directory. You would grant your DBAs the rights to update OID. Obviously this requires the use of the additional directory, which handles the synchronization for you, but yes, it is additional overhead. You can make the required changes in your own directory, such as Active Directory, although I've seen very commonly in my customer base that corporate policy forbids changes to the AD schema. I also have seen a limited number of customers use Active Directory Application Mode (ADAM) for this purpose.

When it is possible to make those schema changes in an existing directory, you can avoid the use of the additional directory and make use of Oracle Virtual Directory. With this configuration, there is no need to maintain a separate directory. However, as stated DBAs don't often have rights to update a corporate directory, such as Active Directory.

A highly recommended design is what Oracle calls the *split configuration*, in which both OVD and OID are used. This requires minimal changes to your existing schema. OVD aggregates the schema mappings from OID and the user-role data from the user store.

For authentication, EUS supports name/password, Kerberos, and X.509 certs (incompatible with OVD). One more note: AD hashes passwords in a way that's incompatible with just about everybody else. For that reason, this solution requires the installation of a password filter on the domain controller in order to store passwords in a hash that is acceptable across other stores. The bottom line is, even with a fairly manual provisioning tool such as EUS, there are still security controls in place.

Reporting and Compliance

Don't be fooled by this section title. Just to remind you, reporting is not compliance; it is simply a small part of it.

Whenever a user or administrator or process performs a task related to provisioning, log data goes into the database. With OIM, this is usually an Oracle database, since it handles data in high volumes, and can report from it simultaneously.

Now since we're talking IdM, we'll forget business transactions for now. Your IdM data might contain your current balance, or that might be a virtual element that's dynamically recalculated with every request. But provisioning doesn't care about that. The transactions we care about are

- Creation and modification of users, resources, and other definitions
- Requests, both successful and failed
- Provisioning and other tasks

Let's summarize this as everything that's been created, deleted, granted, along with who did it, and when. Within Oracle Identity Manager and Oracle Identity Analytics, you have literally dozens of operational reports (all the entity and process definitions) and historical reports (how these entities were used).

To summarize the groups of reports available from OIM:

- Access policies
- Attestations, requests, approvals, task assignments
- Groups, orgs, memberships, admins, history
- Password activity and policies
- Resources and entitlements, activity, admins, access

Beneath the covers, these reports are generated by the Oracle Business Intelligence Publisher, known more commonly as BI Publisher. It comes with the templates for all the reports, all of which can be easily modified for the sake of branding, delivery, format, and so on. It's quite possible that by the time you are reading this, even more report templates will be available, since new ones are being created all the time, available for download to Oracle customers. BI Publisher can also be used to create reusable, custom report templates.

These reports *support* compliance by providing the kinds of summaries that you need for ongoing decision making regarding your policies, and which you also need when the auditors say, "Let's have it."

But compliance is truly built into the overall provisioning structure, or at least it should be. Your policies, workflow, resource definition and connectors, your adapters, your role definitions and policies—all of these should reflect your security and compliance requirements. Role grant policies should be configured to specifically deny conflicting role duties (SoD). You should leverage the business hierarchy and group memberships to enforce the notion of rights that are associated with departments, lines of business, location, or other abstracts. Roles and resources should be configured to contain *only* the most absolutely necessary privileges for the necessary business function.

For investigative purposes, OIM and OIA both allow administrators to readily analyze the entire hierarchy of objects: users for a resource or role, roles or resources for a user, privileges or policies for a resource, and so on. This does not require cross-correlating multiple reports, but simply pulling up the appropriate interface.

We'll talk about this in more detail, including the integration of Oracle compliance controls, and how to apply the Oracle suite to specific compliance processes and mandates (for example, PCI), in Chapter 12.

But now that we've discussed enabling users to access resources, let's move on to how those users actually sign on to and make use of those resources.

CHAPTER
10

Authentication and SSO: Accessing What I've Been Granted

The answer is Man, spake Oedipus. And so the Sphinx threw herself from the mount, and Oedipus entered the city of Thebes.

—An example of authentication in ancient mythology

W e're past the building blocks, the design and assembly of the foundation for the framework. Now we're ready to use the framework on a day-to-day basis, the processes that govern users as they log in and make use of the organization's digital resources. A user is identified, cataloged, placed in the hierarchy, provisioned for access, and is now ready to use those assets. The system knows who you are, but now you have to log in and say, this is me. This means authentication. It may seem simple, because the majority of the time it's just username and password, but there's a lot behind that, and sometimes username and password aren't enough.

We do this every single day of our lives. We authenticate. We need to convince the sites that manage our mail, our money, our utilities, that we are who we say we are. Nobody escapes it. A member of my family is an auto mechanic, probably the smartest mechanic in the world. It's not exactly an IT position. Still, he goes online to look up auto parts. He sends and receives e-mail. He banks online. He pays bills online. To do so, he presents credentials. He authenticates.

Authentication by itself is not enough to get a user to his resources. But it serves as the gateway to authorization. We covered these together in Chapter 7, because conceptually they work together to route a user to his applications; authentication says who you are, so that authorization can align your identity with your resources. However, now we're into the dirty details, and there's enough here to split them out again. We will cover some aspects of authorization in this chapter, because of how it is intertwined with authentication, but we will cover authorization in greatest detail in Chapter 11.

At this point in the evolution of IAM, we are long, long past the point of telling a user, "Give me your creds and in you go." That may look like that's all we're doing, but if we're doing our job correctly, then we've already defined our resources (and their requirements), our users (and their groups and attributes), and our policies (which match up the resources and the users). We've also built the architecture that enforces those policies, giving access to users and securing those resources. So even though you as a user are only entering two pieces of data most of the time, there are a lot of things going on behind the scenes, to keep the daily interaction of users and resources secure and compliant.

Let's look at the architecture, policies, and integrations that make up the seemingly simple, yet all-important process of logging in.

Authentication Architecture

Let's start out with the easy stuff. A user fires up his browser, and clicks a bookmark to start out his day with e-mail, or his most often-used application. He could link to the login page, but why? He heads right for the main menu, because that's where he wants to go. But the system has other ideas. It has a look and determines it doesn't know who this person is yet, and so it says, hang on, I'm going to ask you for some credentials. So he's prompted for name and password and, after those are validated against the official user store, he ultimately ends up where he was going in the first place.

It sounds very simple. So let's look at what all is behind that, and how we build it using Oracle Access Manager. The following illustration shows the very basic architecture behind the example we just used.

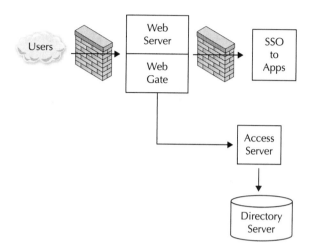

When the user sends a request to the web server, that request is intercepted by what is called in OAM a WebGate. This is a plug-in (for example, NSAPI, ISAPI, or ASAPI filter), which serves as the Policy Enforcement Point (PEP). The WebGate forwards the request to the Access Server, which serves as the Policy Decision Point (PDP), evaluating the request against the access policy for the requested resource. The Access Server not only evaluates the policies, it also performs authentication, authorization, and auditing functions. It determines the appropriate response to the request, and prompts the WebGate to enforce that response. If a user navigates directly to a login form, then he logs in. But in a more common use case, the user navigates directly to his desired resource. If the user has no valid active session, the WebGate detects no session ticket, and the response is a prompt for authentication, which usually means the Access Server tells the WebGate to redirect the user to authenticate, using the method necessary for the resource. Once authenticated, the user is given a cookie for the authenticated domain and, if so authorized, is subsequently redirected to his resource.

In order to do its job, the Access Server must connect to the directory server in order to validate user credentials, and the policy repository in order to retrieve policies. For the sake of performance, policies can also be cached at the WebGate, so the policies don't have to be fetched with every request. Load balancing and failover are built into the Access Server. For non-HTTP gateways (such as WebLogic, Websphere, and Oracle Containers for J2EE [OC4J]), OAM provides an AccessGate, usually in the form of an implementation of the OAM Access API.

WebGates can work behind a reverse proxy. This requires additional setup, such as using ACLs to prevent users from bypassing the proxy by pointing directly at back-end servers, and configuring the Policy Manager to intercept requests to the proxy. But there are advantages to deploying OAM in a reverse proxy architecture:

- Instead of installing a WebGate on every web server, you only need to install on the proxy.
- If you funnel requests through the proxy, there is no need to create custom AccessGates for unsupported web servers or platforms.

You associate a WebGate with an Access Server (so it knows who to go to for its information), or with a cluster of Access Servers. These are commonly clustered for the sake of load balancing and failover.

Now that we've covered the basic architecture, let's examine the pieces you must build, assemble, and/or integrate. But before you think that such language makes it sound complicated, I will say this much: If you have a common HTTP server and LDAP, you can deploy a simple authentication scheme and basic authorization rules in literally a day or two. But of course, your enterprise probably demands some level of design that takes into account different tiers of users and resources, each with their own requirements.

The components and concepts you need to understand in designing an authentication architecture are:

- Authentication schemes
- Session cookies
- Single Sign-On, for single and multiple domains
- Strong authentication
- Fraud prevention

To create a security umbrella within Oracle Access Manager, you define policy domains that specify (and essentially encircle) resources to be protected; rules for authenticating, authorizing, and audit; an expression to evaluate those rules; policies to govern subsets of the domain's resources; and information for delegated administration (who is allowed to modify the policy domain). The following illustration shows the Resources tab, where these options are located. We will discuss the authorization rules in the next chapter.

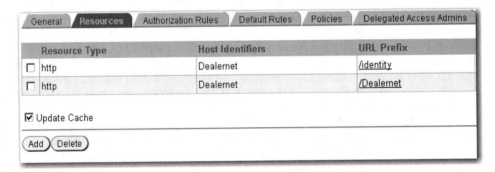

When it comes to authentication and authorization, you need to decide what is the *minimum acceptable threshold*. This definitely needs to go through committee. What credentials are required for each set of resources? What roles, attributes, or memberships are necessary for participation in a set of resources? The reason you want to think in terms of minimums is this: It's possible to get very close to completely locking down your resources, in such a way that they will be nearly impossible for anyone to access them, including your users. Therefore, you must choose the authentication and authorization requirements that best suit your purposes of security, compliance, and usability.

Simple Authentication

There are many options for authenticating. The one you use is dictated by whatever site you're visiting. Nine-hundred ninety-nine times out of a thousand, you're providing a username and password. This is the simplest authentication there is. The system confirms that the name you've provided is there, then compares a hash of the password you entered with the hash in the directory, and if they match, you're in.

Here's a quickie ten-thousand-foot view of hashing. You don't want anybody breaking into your directory entry and stealing your password. So it's stored in an encrypted state. It's been *hashed*. When you enter your password in a login form, that set of bytes you typed in also gets hashed. The hashed versions get compared. If someone breaks into your record, they'll see a lot of gibberish they can't use. If you were to enter your hashed password into a form, the system would try to hash *that* before sending it along, and the doubly hashed password wouldn't pass muster. You'll hear the term *one-way hash*, which means data can be encrypted, but not decrypted, which is why the system must compare the two encrypted versions. You would think that by this time in this market, everybody is already on board with this little issue, but I still get asked all the time, "Does your solution encrypt passwords?"

Oracle Access Manager provides default authentication schemes, and you can create additional ones as needed. You may deploy more than one, across multiple realms of protection. For example, you could use basic authentication for most of your applications, which is most likely, but use something stronger for critical, SOX-based, or human resource-related apps. Even if you use multiple schemes within your enterprise, you can still centrally manage how and when they are employed. This makes it easier for you to swap out one method for another if you decide to make your login requirements more stringent, or if you use different methods for different sets of resources.

- **Basic username and password authentication** validates simple credentials against LDAP, Active Directory, a database, or even Windows. It's the easiest scheme to set up, but provides a login "form" that is completely generic. This might be fine for an internal app, but does not provide an interface to the outside world that is befitting your organization.

- For **X.509 certificate authentication,** the WebGate redirects to another server that is configured to process certs, initiates SSL, authenticates the certificate, then redirects the user back to the original URL.

- **Anonymous authentication** is used for unprotected resources, such as a login, forgotten password, or registration page.

- **Forms-based authentication** provides a branded user experience by specifying a customized page to prompt for credentials, with your background colors, logo, company slogan, and any additional functions you may wish to provide, such as links for forgotten password or new member registration. It's a form of your devising, providing a friendly welcome. Under the covers, it's posting the credentials to the web server, where the WebGate intercepts and validates those credentials.

Third-party or custom-built schemes can also be added to OAM as authentication libraries.

The most common Windows Server authentication scheme is Kerberos. OAM supports Integrated Windows Authentication (IWA) for authentication across directory servers across this environment. Kerberos is by itself an SSO mechanism, albeit a very complex one that is vulnerable to password hacking and doesn't support non-repudiation. An alternative, spawned in Europe as an answer to the vulnerabilities in Kerberos, is Secure European System for

Applications in a Multivendor Environment (SESAME). It has a different cryptographic model and a simpler architecture, but has some of the same weaknesses as Kerberos. Even among my European clients, I haven't heard much from SESAME, although like other standards, it may eventually take hold. Or not.

Defining the Authentication Scheme for a Resource

When defining the requirements for the authentication scheme for a particular resource or set of resources, you are telling OAM how high to set the bar for users. What do they need to prove to the system in order to get in? When determining these schemes across the enterprise, you are straddling the line between what is there now for each application, what the app owners want going forward, and what can reasonably be supported. In theory you could have different authentication schemes (for different resources) sharing the same security level, but it means that when you authenticate to one app via one method, you must satisfy the requirements for the second one when you perform SSO. Recall that you are providing a framework, something that all the app owners can participate in. You may need to sell the authentication schemes that your governance committees are recommending.

When defining an authentication scheme, you need to assign it the attributes it needs to do its job, as shown in the following illustration.

- **Name and description**   This is just to identify the scheme. Try to be clear, not cryptic, with these naming conventions. If you are allowing delegated admins to choose available schemes from your list, you are telling them what they need to know to make that choice. Remember the value of delegated administration: You are giving those admins some power, but you are also keeping them in the box. Here's the list of schemes; you must pick from here, but hey, you get some prebuilt schemes, with easily interpreted names.

- **Security level**   This is an integer-based security designation. Remember how not all resources are created equal? If you authenticate to a given resource with a given security level, and then later navigate to a different resource with the same or lower security level, you're good to go; that is, you don't need to authenticate again in that session for that lower resource. But if you hit a resource with a higher security level, you will be prompted for that higher authentication scheme. So once again, assign your more critical or sensitive applications a stricter authentication scheme.

- **Challenge method and types of credentials**   How are you prompting? And what will you prompt for?

- **Challenge redirect URL**   Should user requests be sent to another URL for processing? If the user is asking for a resource that is on another domain, and their current security level is good enough for that resource, you've got to generate an SSO cookie (which we'll talk about soon). If the user makes a request over HTTP but the authentication must be performed over HTTPS, they will also be redirected.

- **Status**   In other words, is the authentication scheme enabled? You may build and test the scheme, but not launch it until the time is right.

- **Whether the cache on the Access Server should be updated when changes are made to the auth scheme**   In other words, you update the scheme, you change its parameters, and you want those changes immediately reflected.

You can also specify multiple directories in which to search for a user (assuming he has the same username across those directories). This is especially useful if you have a directory specified for failover, *or* you're transitioning users from one directory to another. Once you've completed that transition, you can simply remove the extra directory from the scheme.

Single Sign-On

The Holy Grail in the authentication world is single sign-on, or SSO. Authenticate to one app, then automatically gain access to all the others, thereby saving time and increasing productivity. Within a particular security domain, that may be perfectly acceptable. Part of your design is deciding which apps can share a security level, that is, the necessary credentials are good enough to go around. For those situations where those credentials are *not* good enough, you will employ an authentication scheme with a higher security level, as we just discussed. I have visited (a very small number of) customers over the years who literally do not believe in SSO, since in theory it means that if a hacker compromises one set of credentials, he can access everything.

But in environments with many applications being accessed in a given day, SSO provides efficiency and productivity. In my current situation, I may access up to four dozen apps in a given day, and I only need to worry about VPN and SSO credentials. This is an example of Reduced Sign-On (RSO). I actually use more than one set of creds, but it's still a manageable number. An authentication scheme with a higher security level may only require the same number of credentials as the lower one (or something more complex yet), but they're still different. It's not total SSO, but it's still not four dozen sets of name and password.

One other advantage to SSO is the burden it takes off developers. As with the rest of the IAM framework, the function of SSO is performed in advance of approaching the application, and developers can assume that if someone presents a valid ID, they have already been authenticated. That said, you can configure SSO to provide whatever parameters are necessary to create trust.

Thick-Client SSO

Single sign-on is most often associated with thin-client (browser-based) applications, but it can also be effected with thick-client or client-server apps. For this purpose, Oracle provides Enterprise Single Sign-On (eSSO). In addition to strong authentication and password reset to the desktop, eSSO supports password policies even for legacy apps that do not inherently include them. It allows logon and SSO to any Windows, host-based, Java, or mainframe application, without the need for custom connectors or scripts, using any combination of authentication methods (passwords, biometrics, smart cards, tokens, and so on). Its provisioning gateway allows integration with Oracle Identity Manager, meaning that even thick clients can be made part of the IAM framework. Once again, a great value of the framework itself is the elimination of silos of identity and security. It stands in front of your resources, augmenting or providing from scratch those functions that they don't inherently provide themselves, and which allow them to participate in a larger set of community policies.

eSSO protects passwords and related data in the authoritative directory, in transit, in memory, and in local cache. They are protected wherever they are located, in your directory, in transit from the directory to the client, in client local disk cache, and in client memory, using strong encryption.

Web SSO

For supporting single sign-on in the browser-based world, we return to Oracle Access Manager (OAM). To facilitate web-based SSO, OAM provides an authenticated user with a session ticket, called an ObSSO cookie. This enables that user, for the duration of his session, to access resources with the same or lower security level as the one he started with. Another part of your design is determining how the cookie enables SSO. In order to provide a user with SSO into an application, the cookie must contain the proper HTTP header variables to satisfy the requirements of that app. Of course, for SSO to be successful, the application must be able to use those variables. Also remember there is a 4K limit on headers.

Cookies must be secured between the AccessGate and the user's browser. For this purpose, OAM uses a shared secret function for encrypting the cookies. There are always two keys in use. The newer secret is always the default key to use. If the AccessGate fails to decrypt a cookie, it will use the older secret. The cryptographic key may change periodically, so that if a potential hacker breaks the key, he is still severely limited. Let's hover on this one a moment. There are multiple encryption schemes available, and they are quite stringent. If a hacker intercepted a cookie or sniffed out your traffic, and then threw the cookie at his supercomputer to break it and was actually *able* to do so, by the time he was successful, the key would have changed several times. In other words, the shared secret function is extremely secure. Whenever the cookie is used for authentication, it is checked by the Access Server to ensure that it has not been tampered with. In other words, it's still you.

Remember what I said about getting stakeholders and resource owners to sign off on design decisions? You will need to get agreement on which resources can share the same authentication scheme. It's not like they're polluting each other, but look at it this way: A whole lot of the time, it's going to be username and password based on an accepted corporate directory. When you have a highly distributed environment, it may be different, such as the in case of holding companies, or any situation where you segregate internal from external users by user store. But right now I'm talking about the majority, who will all be happy with that username and password combination (although different groups authenticating via the same method, such as name/password, may still be authenticated against different back end stores). You may have more difficulty getting agreement from those with more sensitive applications. This is where you'll see a divergence, from PIN numbers to hard tokens or certificates. The issue you will have as the provider of the framework is the number of different schemes you will need to support in your library.

Cross-Domain SSO

While SSO across multiple domains is similar to single domain, there are still differences. This is not to be confused with federation. Too often, the word "federation" is used to mean multidomain SSO. And it is, essentially, but the term refers to navigation between domains that communicate via standard and somewhat generic protocols, such as SAML, and without the benefit of running on the same access framework. Because it really lends itself more to authorization, we'll discuss federation in the next chapter. But right now I'm referring to SSO between domains that are all governed and secured by OAM.

With OAM single-domain SSO, each protected resource within a given domain can use the same SSO cookie. When navigating to a different domain, you must receive a cookie that is valid for that domain. Therefore you designate one of your authentication servers as the provider of cookies for all domains. When the request is received for access to that next domain, that designated server generates the proper cookie (assuming the user is eligible for the requested access). Here's what you need to know and/or configure to make that happen:

- You need WebGates installed in each of the desired domains.

- All WebGates must have access to all the authentication schemes.

- All Access Servers must have access to the same policy repository (or at least a copy).

- One authentication server in each domain must be configured as the *primary* authentication server.

- Cross-domain SSO does not work with AccessGates, only WebGates, unless you front for them with a proxy.

Yes, this sounds complicated, but it really isn't. You're using a single infrastructure to move you around multiple domains. Let's summarize what we're doing:

- Everybody has to be able to speak the same language (via the components).

- Somebody has to be designated to give you what you need to move from A to B.

Just as you had to decide which *resources* can share the same authentication scheme and security level, you must decide which *domains* can share those same requirements. When a user requests a resource on a domain other than where he originated, his session ticket and ObSSO cookie are forwarded to the second domain so that the cookie can be set for that domain.

You can also configure the central login server, or designated authentication server, to set the multidomain cookies for all domains at the time of the first authentication.

You can specify how long you want a user's session to last. This could be indefinitely, but you *don't* want a user to be able to log in once and stay logged in for the next year. A more reasonable limit is expressed in hours. By default, it's one hour. It's common to say that my standard session is, let's say, 60 minutes, but if I navigate to a more sensitive application with a higher security level, maybe I'm only good in that domain for 30 minutes. The domains do not have to share the same time limits. Naturally, if you log out and kill your browser and therefore your cookie, your session is dead. You can also configure an authentication scheme to provide a persistent cookie, which can allow a user to stay logged in for a specified period of time rather than just a single session.

If you have configured cross-domain SSO, you may wish to enforce logout across all domains by setting an absolute session timeout. When the WebGate logs a user out, by default it is only removing OAM cookies, although you can customize the process to also remove third-party cookies (for example, application-specific) from the user's browser. Consider this sweeping up after yourself. You may be logged out of a domain, but still in theory have a session open on an app. You should establish a policy dictating session limits and cross-domain limits as well.

Strong Authentication, Historically

The terms "multifactor" and "strong" are often used interchangeably when discussing authentication. But this gets very fuzzy. First, username and password is only considered single-factor, since username is only the identity piece, and password is the mitigating "factor." Meanwhile, multifactor usually means "two factor," because after three prompts it starts getting pretty silly. "Two factor" itself usually means prompting a user to provide something from two of these three categories:

- Something you know, such as your name and password, and possibly an additional PIN
- Something you have, such as a hard token
- Something you are, such as a biometric

To many security people, strong authentication means something very simple, hard tokens. Sure, tokens are strong, since they require you to physically produce them. In fact, I've talked to security admins who think that there *is* no strong auth without a physical token, that is, something you have. But I've also spoken to several security chiefs over the years who aren't thrilled with the cost of acquiring, provisioning, shipping, and maintaining smart cards and USB tokens. The average cost for a single token user is $50 to $100 U.S. per year. Even those admins who use them usually admit they're not ideal.

Besides these obvious costs, physical tokens are no guarantee of safety from man-in-the-middle attacks. They can also be problematic if they're used for keeping digital certificates. So while they might certainly have their place in some organizations, it seems truly limiting to think that the only strong option has to be a little gadget we carry in our pockets.

Very Strong Authentication, Alternatively

A lot of what we've traditionally used for authentication is still valid, but in theory, any bad guy can guess or discover what we know, and steal what we have. It's obviously more difficult for a hacker to be what we are, or be where we're expected to be, but it's also tougher to incorporate that into your policies. Biometric authentication is a good one, but even human fingerprinting requires special hardware; although, of the multiple machines on my own desk, two have the ability to use fingerprints, built right next to the keyboard, and it's pretty easy to set up. Other biometric hardware (retinal, voice) is exceedingly rare, and that's an understatement. So while those technologies may also have a place in the enterprise of the future, for truly sensitive, critical resource protection, requiring an utter identification of all possible factors (including you, your environment, the resource, and your previous interactions with that resource), think in terms of

- A combination of who and what you are
- When and where you are
- What and when and where you *were*
- What you're doing and what you've done
- What *else* you have

Oracle provides its own multifactor, strong authentication option in the Oracle Adaptive Access Manager (OAAM) for identifying users beyond simple name and password. In addition,

OAAM has capabilities for creating an ultrasecure authentication and authorization model, using methodologies more comprehensive than the standard contents of the three-category model. Besides authenticating with hard and soft tokens, digital certificates, and smart cards, it also incorporates fraud detection and prevention, as well as behavioral and risk analysis. OAAM supports the following as part of its authentication and authorization schemes:

■ Virtual authentication devices

■ Device and location ID

■ Historical data

■ User behavior, past and present

■ Knowledge-based authentication

I get asked this fairly often by people unfamiliar with the technology: What if I'm using biometric, such as fingerprint or retinal scan, and I come to work one morning with dirty hands or a black eye? The way these things work is, when you first register your biometric value (that first scan), it turns your print or retina into an image and/or a numeric representation. When you come back for subsequent authentications, it compares the digital value it just calculated from your finger or eyeball to the one you've already got registered, and unlike a password, which must be an exact match, it's just got to come close enough. In other words, there's a tolerance factor. However, I've heard a few stories about people who because of illness or injury could not authenticate biometrically. Retinal scans work by taking a picture of the blood vessels in your eye, and pregnancy, along with other conditions, can affect these vessels and change the outcome of a scan.

The Oracle architecture makes it easier to plug in strong authentication as a complementary technology by simply allowing the configuration of OAAM as an authentication scheme within OAM, to be associated with those resources requiring greater protection. The following illustration shows the options within OAAM for default rules.

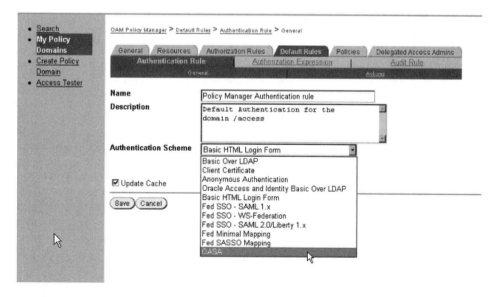

The integration is easy to understand in terms of the authentication flow we discussed earlier with just OAM. There are just a couple of extra steps, as described in the following bullets and illustration:

■ When the user requests a resource through a protected server, the OAM WebGate redirects the user to OAAM's secure login JSP.

■ OAAM serves up a virtual authentication device to prompt for credentials, then forwards those credentials to the OAM Access Server.

■ OAM authenticates the user and sends back a session cookie through OAAM.

■ With the session established, OAM determines user-resource *authorization* (which we will discuss in greater detail in the next chapter).

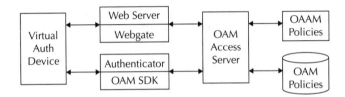

Let's break this out in more detail and examine how to use OAAM to architect an authentication model that makes it almost impossible for a hacker to impersonate the total package of who, what, when, and where you are, as well as what you've got. Remember, all these factors can be used in combination, and as part of a policy that matches up with requested resources. As with OAM, you may be challenged for simple credentials for most resources, but subjected to much stronger authentication for more critical applications. OAAM still makes use of what you have, know, and are, but greatly enhances what those mean.

■ **What you know** For initial authentication, or for step-up authentication from lower to higher security levels, OAAM can leverage third-party sources to prompt a user for additional information (beyond username and password) that only that person could know, for example, car registration or banking data. OAAM could also use an external library to send a one-time-use PIN number to the user's phone. "You want to finish logging in? Check your phone, and give me back what I just texted you."

■ **Device fingerprinting** The definition of "what you have" can be greatly expanded. OAAM can be taught to recognize particular machines, including computers and cellular phones. What device are you coming in on? What is its ID? Has OAAM been configured to like that machine? Have you previously registered it? Is it a *kind* of device from which you're allowed to access the resource you've requested? There may be no logical reason why anybody, even a human resources director, would need to access employee salary data from a Blackberry.

- **Location**   Credit checking should never be performed outside the firewall. Or... you may have logged in as the CFO, but you're trying to examine financial statements from Paris, and you live in São Paulo. There's also the Theory of Improbable User Acceleration: If you logged in from Chicago, then again ten minutes later from London, at least one of those sessions isn't really you, and one or both may be terminated. For that matter, you can configure policies to consider not only geographic location, but connection and routing types. What kinds of activity have been generated from a particular location in the past?

- **Behavior and history**   And this can get involved. Do you normally log in at this time? Is this out of character for you? Is it out of character for the group you belong to? Does anybody ever access sensitive medical privacy data in the off-hours? At your electronics manufacturing firm, a particular user normally downloads 2 or 3 technical specs a day. Today, he's downloaded 20. OAAM detects the anomalous behavior, notifications are sent, and access to the specs is blocked.

- **Combinations**   The VP of development often stays late to review changes to source code. But after hours from a strange IP address? Not allowed.

You may start to see the pattern here. For any given transaction, OAAM can analyze the behavior based on what the user is doing, what the user has done, what other members of the user's group have done before, and what has been done from that location or device. It can consider all factors, and their behavior both present and past. These combinations determine the risk level and help determine what the response will be:

- Generate alerts
- Challenge for stronger authentication
- Block access
- Put the current transaction on hold
- Kill the user's session entirely

As the security administrator, you can create rules, based on corporate policies, regarding what is considered acceptable behavior, to prevent fraud and secure transactions. For example, you decide what is an acceptable number of failed authentications from a user or device;

which devices, IP addresses or countries to block; and which combinations of user, device, and location constitute the highest risk. The following illustration shows some typical rules.

	Rule Name ▲	Type	Status	Description	Notes
☐	Always On - User	User	Active	This rule always gets processed	
☐	DEVICE: Browser header substring	Device	Active	Checks whether the supplied string exists as a substring in the browsers header information.	
☐	DEVICE: Device in list	Device	Active	Check to see if this device is in list.	
☐	DEVICE: Multiple Users	Device	Active	Maximum users using this device for the past x seconds	
☐	DEVICE: Timed not status	Device	Active	Maximum login attempts for all but the given status within the given time period.	
☐	DEVICE: Used count for User	Device	Active	Device used count	
☐	LOCATION: IP Max Users	Location	Active	Maximum number of users using the current ip address within the given time duration.	
☐	LOCATION: IP routing type	Location	Active	Routing type for the IP. It could be fixed/static, anonymizer, AOL, POP, Super POP, Satellite, Cache Proxy, International Proxy, Regional Proxy, Mobile Gateway or Unknown	
☐	LOCATION: In Country group	Location	Active	If the IP is in the given country group.	
☐	LOCATION: In IP group	Location	Active	If the IP is in the IP group.	
☐	USER: Account Status	User	Active	Account status of the user	
☐	USER: Authentication Mode	User	Active	Check user authentication mode.	
☐	USER: Challenge Channel Failure	User	Active	If a user has a failure counter value over a specified value for more than a specific time from specific channel	
☐	USER: Challenge Maximum Failures	User	Active	Check to see if user failed to answer challenge question for specefied number of times.	

Rules can be collected to build a security model. Think of the model as a filter for analyzing and reacting to various interactions. If you wish to monitor for fraud, you will put together a model, consisting of rules, that watches for specific types of actions involving users, locations, and/or devices. The rules may pertain to which locations or countries you wish to block, a maximum number of failed challenges or password attempts, unregistered devices, and so on. The following illustration show some sample model settings.

Model Name ▲	Type	Run Time	Status	Description
Fraud - Alert Only	Security	Post-Authentication	Active	Applied to groups with no
Fraud - Challenge	Security	Post-Authentication	Active	These rules are run for u
Post-Auth Flow Phase 2	Business	Post-Authentication	Active	Post-Auth Model for phase
Post-Auth Flow Phase 3	Business	Post-Authentication	Active	Post-Auth Model for phase
Pre-Auth Flow Phase 2 & 3	Business	Pre-Authentication	Active	Pre-Auth model to identif
System - Demo model	Security	Post-Authentication	Disabled	Delete this model after d
System - Fraud	Security	Post-Authentication	Active	Fraud models with challen
System - Fraud Blocking	Security	Post-Authentication	Active	System fraud rules. Execu
System - Fraud Monitoring	Security	Post-Authentication	Active	Models meant for fraud mo
System CC Challenge	Business	CC Challenge	Active	Customer care challenge m
System Challenge Question	Security	Challenge Question	Active	System block rules for ch
System Forgot Password	Security	Forgot Password	Active	This model contains rules
System preferences	Business	Preferences	Active	Preferences

To help build and maintain risk profiles, OAAM's Adaptive Risk Manager uses specified parameters to identify patterns of behavior, called *buckets*, whose members are the factors or players in transactions (users, locations, devices). Over time, depending on their behavior, a member may be automatically removed from a bucket. For example, a user belonging to a bucket whose members typically log in from a specific location during particular hours may eventually be moved out of that bucket after logging in continually from other locations during different hours.

For example, let's say you originally set up a pattern that includes the employees who work in a particular office. Those employees who authenticate from that office are prompted for name and password. Any time one of those employees authenticates from a different office, they are prompted for an additional PIN. You may also set up a threshold within the pattern that says, if an employee doesn't authenticate from that office within 30 days (or doesn't authenticate from there an acceptable number of times), she is automatically pulled out of that bucket, and her authentication requirements change accordingly, and permanently. The process by which OAAM monitors this activity and modifies the buckets is called *auto-learning*.

The risk score for a particular type of transaction (such as approving a payment) is calculated against the combinations of location, device, and user. As user activity relative to that transaction type strays from the patterns of behavior (for example, different location, different device), the risk elevates, which could prompt an additional challenge, as well as move the user into a different bucket, permanently affecting how she is challenged.

You can also make use of nested models, which serve as a safety net. If the answers resulting from the primary security model are inconclusive, the nested model kicks in. This method of a secondary model serves to reduce false positives and negatives.

OAAM makes use of essential fraud rules as well. Besides the improbable user acceleration I mentioned, there are also consecutive failures for a user or device, lists of restricted devices and IP addresses, and multiple users from the same device.

You will need to design responsibilities around the OAAM dashboard from which to monitor multiple types of current activity:

■ Locations, devices, and users

■ Risk scores and active sessions

■ Statistics on alert types and levels

■ Rules, models, and actions that have been run

■ Performance

The following illustration shows the dashboard in the Oracle Adaptive Risk Manager.

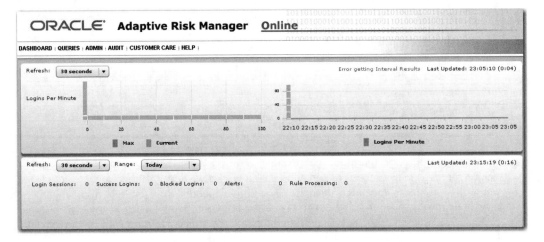

Protecting the User

Be honest—you're building an IAM framework more for the benefit of the organization than for the end user. Some of the benefits to the user are in fact benefits to the enterprise (for example, self-service, auto-provisioning, SSO). But there are things you can do that directly aid your users, and a happy user is more productive, less demanding, and less of a drain on resources. OAAM lets you provide your users with greater peace of mind. If a user has a problem or concern, it becomes yours *anyway*.

Challenge Questions

As I've said elsewhere, you rarely want to let users compose their own challenge questions. These are the questions you require for forgotten password, or step-up authentication. Even the default questions that are out there at e-mail and other free sites practically beg a user to turn a forgotten password scheme into a welcome mat for hackers (as in the Sarah Palin example). A much better solution for a commercial enterprise is a set of prebuilt questions, determined by a committee, for which even the personal ones shouldn't be too easily guessed. OAAM allows you to maintain a library of these kinds of questions. You can also have it make calls to third-party services (bank, auto registration, credit history), although the third-party aspect makes them more expensive and difficult to set up, and adds latency. After all, if that information is more sensitive than "favorite color," you're probably not going to cache it locally.

OAAM challenge questions can be divided into categories (personal, employment, hobbies), and it may be advisable to present users with questions from different categories. You can also apply logic to the answers, so that questions cannot share answers, answers cannot be subsets of the questions themselves (Q: What hospital were you born in? A: Hospital), and so on. Protect users from their own laziness. You can also apply tolerances for common fat-finger mistakes, phonetics, abbreviations, and so forth. It's all a matter of how nice you want to be. Remember Us and Them? You want the user experience to be a good one—just not at the expense of security. The following illustration shows some sample challenge questions.

		ID# ▼	Updated	Status	Question	Category	Registration Validation	Answer Logic Hints
☐	🔧	210	09/26/2007 23:47	Active	What industry was your first job in?	Your Employment	None	None
☐	🔧	209	09/26/2007 23:47	Active	What was the first name of your first boss?	Your Employment	None	None
☐	🔧	208	09/26/2007 23:47	Active	What is the name of the first company you worked for?	Your Employment	None	None
☐	🔧	207	09/26/2007 23:47	Active	What was your first job?	Your Employment	None	None
☐	🔧	206	09/26/2007 23:47	Active	What is the most unusual job you have had?	Your Employment	None	None
☐	🔧	205	09/26/2007 23:47	Active	What year do you plan on retiring?	Your Employment	None	None
☐	🔧	204	09/26/2007 23:47	Active	What was your first yearly salary?	Your Employment	None	None
☐	🔧	203	09/26/2007 23:47	Active	What year did you get your first job?	Your Employment	None	None
☐	🔧	202	09/26/2007 23:47	Active	What was your father's profession when you were born?	Your Birth	None	None

You can allow users to register the first time into OAAM and choose their questions and answers. As an admin, you specify how many questions they need to register, and how many questions they will need to answer when challenged.

Virtual Authentication Devices

Like the lottery, phishing is a tax on naivete. No one is installing anything on your machine; they're simply goading you into doing it yourself. Or perhaps they're luring you to a site where you will be invited to hand them your precious credentials. One of the most well-known hackers ever, Kevin Mitnick, wasn't really a hacker. He relied on social engineering. That's phishing right there, the art of getting you, of your own free will, to click on something incredibly stupid. Yes, the e-mails can be incredibly sophisticated, like the ones that used to come "from" Washington Mutual all the time. But it's fairly simple to verify that a link is taking you to where you think it is.

However, in the interests of better serving its users, an organization can provide a way to let its visitors know that they're in the right place. My own bank uses OAAM for anti-phishing purposes, by prompting for password using a text pad that is illustrated by a familiar image and phrase, both chosen by my wife. We've vacationed in a lot of out-of-the-way places, and one of the silly things she's always complained about is never having seen a moose in the wild. So guess what animal picture is on our keypad?

The text pad is just one of the customizable virtual authentication devices offered by OAAM for entering credentials or PIN numbers. None of them requires the installation of a client. Nothing entered on a virtual device can be deciphered while being entered or while in transit. You can configure registration to allow users to choose their own device, like the ones in the following illustration. They can all be customized, again to assure the user that he is in the right place.

- The Question Pad and Quiz Pad can prompt the user for answers to questions stored in OAAM, in internal databases, or integrated with third-party sources.

- The Key Pad is a virtual alphanumeric keyboard that a user "types" on with the mouse.

- The PinPad and TextPad are used for entering passwords or PINs.

- The Slider (pictured at the bottom of the previous illustration) requires the user to line up alphanumeric characters with graphic characters, providing an extreme of data entry security.

The virtual devices foil cookie hijacks, keystroke loggers, mouse-click captures, and over-the-shoulder and man-in-the-middle attacks. With the mouse, the user can enter passwords, PINs, challenge answers, or other data, which at no time are handled by the browser. The devices can also play back differently with each instance, with location and keys moved around, so as to foil malware that might play back by coordinates.

Think about this one: Perhaps the single most important piece of information to secure in order to ensure everyone's safety is the password or PIN, that first factor that goes with identity. Safeguard that one piece of information, and you've kept out a large portion of the people out there with bad intentions. No one solution handles all situations, which is why you want a framework and defense in depth. But securing passwords is a major value unto itself.

Gated Security

Whether configuring policy domains in OAM, or stronger authentication schemes in OAAM (for use with OAM), you are segmenting your resources according to their respective security requirements, and placing multiple points of protection in front of them. Therefore the term "gated security" is actually used by different groups to mean two different things.

- Users must pass a number of checkpoints, including username, password, and possibly PIN and other strong authentication datapoints, in order to access a desired resource. And beyond credentials, there are also authorization rules.

- Credentials that are good enough for one set of resources may be insufficient for other resources. As we discussed in design and earlier in this chapter, it is advisable to cordon off more sensitive applications and data from those applications that are more commonly accessed.

- Just as resources are in groups, so too are users, starting with internal and external, followed by subsets within each.

Therefore, as part of your design, you are not just creating the gates themselves, but determining where they are placed, which resources are grouped, which users are grouped, which users are associated with which resources, and what policies determine who passes through each gate.

In this chapter, we've been discussing how you make yourself known, that is, successfully walk into the room where the resources are. Next, we will discuss additional functionality in OAM and OAAM, as well as an additional solution, to show how a user can be securely authorized to actually use the stuff in the room.

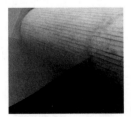

CHAPTER
11

Authorization:
Now That I've Got It,
How Do I Get to It?

Little pig, little pig, let me in.

—The wolf in the story of the *Three Little Pigs*

ou don't really log in to an application in order to be handed the keys. Authentication is just the first step. You have informed the framework as to who you are, which is fine. But now it must take that information and match it against established policies in order to govern what actions you are able to perform after that. This is called *authorization*. The difference between authentication and authorization is subtle. Think of it this way.

- When you authenticate, you're going to the coat room and handing in your claim check.
- The hat check girl gives you your coat and hat, which are your identifying features.
- The valet recognizes you because of the coat, so he authorizes you to get your car back. Back home, the dog recognizes you because of the hat, and authorizes you to enter your home without getting bitten.

Got that? Authentication says to the system, that's John Smith, and here are his attributes and group memberships and roles. Based on those, authorize him to actually use his stuff.

Layers of Authorization

There are multiple levels to authorization. The deeper you go, the more detail you can apply, and the more you can segment policies and users. It's the difference between "Bob and Alice can get in, but Ted and Mary can't" and "Bob and Alice can get into this part of this thing, but Ted can only get half of that, and Mary can see it but can't do anything with it." Sometimes security professionals refer to this as "defense in depth," meaning multiple layers give you more insulation. Both the downside (forensically) and the upside (security) to this is that all it takes is a single "nay" to disallow an action. If your firewall, WebGate, and behavioral filter all say "come on in," but your fine-grained entitlement engine says "no," the result is that you don't get what you want.

Perimeter security is as broad a protection as it gets. Firewalls, VPNs, and network access control are all great for deciding who's in the club. It's the first line of defense, and it can keep out plenty of riff-raff. Sorry, we're not really covering that stuff here.

NOTE
A gentleman in charge of perimeter security at a banking customer informed me that the largest number of attempted IP hacks came from Russia, with Romania close behind. Foreign hackers have little fear, since they're anonymous, often trolling by way of other people's IPs, and they know that unless they cause severe material damage, they're beyond law enforcement. But perimeter security handles the vast majority of these attempts, so I'm not downplaying its importance; it's simply not the subject of this book.

Coarse-grained security gives you protection of that next inside ring, the windows to your applications. Gates or agents on the web servers interact with administrative servers to perform authentication and far more granular authorization than the perimeter. Here you can associate *groups of users* with *groups of resources*. You can even examine individual users if you wish (not recommended), and start pulling apart URIs for even greater granularity. You're also able to discern sufficient detail about a user (as an individual and as a member of a group) to provide personalization. "Welcome back, Joe, here's your customized menu and a list of your last three purchases." Of course, even at this level, it's still considered coarse-grained access control. While it can handle the bulk of your authorization requirements, it is not easily configured to consider the context of the transaction, the environment, the time of day, the method of authentication, and so on.

Context-based access considers all factors, not just *who* is asking for *what*. You're looking at how users got there, from where, and when. It can even look at their historical behavior, to find possible anomalies. It also logs a user's current behavior, lumps it in with past behavior, and continues building a profile for future authorization decisions.

Fine-grained access occurs at the application level. Now beyond even the URI, security is analyzing the specifics of a request, behind the web server. You could still plug in at the web server, but better yet at the application server, or the code itself. Even if you find yourself in the unenviable position of having to embed security within the actual application, you are still externalizing the policies and relieving your programmers of the burden of maintaining actual security code. They're simply providing an opportunity for fine-grained entitlements control to do its job within the app.

Let's stop one more moment on coarse versus fine-grained entitlements. Coarse looks at who you are and the *thing* you've asked for. It can be made to drill down a bit further, but that's not its primary function. Still, it handles the majority of your authorization requirements. Fine-grained and behavioral authorizations make decisions based not just on the who and the what, but also the when, the where, the how, and even combinations of these. You might then say, why wouldn't you always put fine-grained access in place? Because anything that does more work will always *require* more work. The policies for coarse-grained authorization could be as simple as this:

ou=AR,ou=accounting, o=MegaBigCorp **gets** /accounting/receivables/*.*

Everybody in the organizational unit or group gets everything in the folder, based on the broad abstract of the policy. Fine-grained access definitely requires more thinking, more planning, and more maintenance.

I've been asked this question twice in the last year: "If users are only provisioned to those resources they're allowed to have, why do we need authorization? By default, doesn't anybody who approaches an application need to be enabled anyway?"

In theory, the answer is yes. But provisioning is mostly providing the context by which a user enters an app or accesses a resource. There are multiple reasons why you still need both provisioning and authorization:

- You still want that decision-making layer in case provisioning activity lags behind security policies. Provisioning may be decided by group (or attributes), but it is at its core an individual-user activity, while authorization is more often than not a group decision. If policy changes are made that affect an entire group, they may not bubble down to the provisioning/workflow activity immediately, in which case authorization is your safety net.

- In addition, provisioning policies are security- and compliance-minded, certainly, but those are secondary to the business context they truly have. You get access to a resource because you need it for *business* reasons. But you are authenticated and authorized for *security* reasons. These components, provisioning and access, are often governed by different parties, and for a very good reason.

- Provisioning says, here you go, you've got it. It doesn't say, you can have it any day of the week, any hour of the day, or from any IP address anywhere in the world. Authorization manages access based on configurable conditions.

- Just as with provisioning and authentication, you provide authorization in an externalized layer for two primary reasons: to enforce consistency in your security policies, and to take the burden for security off the shoulders of your developers so they can concentrate on the business logic.

- Commercial, off-the-shelf apps in general don't have the ability to enforce fine-grained, rules-based policies.

- Authorization provides the framework for real-time Segregation of Duties (SoD), which can be enforced during execution (and which we will discuss in greater depth in Chapter 12).

Regardless of the solution layer you're looking at, you can simplify the types of authorization rules into two groups, allow and deny. This is true of all the models we will discuss in this chapter. In some solutions, the same rule may specify both possible conditions, while in other solutions, these may be two different rules. The point is that you can create conditions that specifically allow or deny access to a user if he meets the qualifications. You may have heard the terms "positive model" and "negative model." Same idea. If you have a single rule consisting of both conditions, and a user doesn't qualify under either, the result is a deny.

"Allow" rules are easier in that they're inclusive. "Out of a hundred groups, everybody in Group #3 can have access" is far simpler than "I'm going to deny everybody in Group #1, Group #2, Group #4, and so on." Deny rules are useful, however, when you have definite targets to exclude from access, such as internal versus external users. Deny rules that exist under a blanket allow rule are usually termed an "exception-based policy."

Quite often, Active Directory is used for managing local security policy, domain security policy, and domain controller security policies, and it can do this by organization or group. It can manage access to actual computers just fine. But it can't really lock down applications in a meaningful, business-facing fashion without extending the schema and then enabling the apps themselves to take advantages of those extensions. Group memberships themselves don't provide enough granularity or context to differentiate between types of users within the same group or organization. If I have a hundred users in accounting who have access to a set of resources through a Group Policy Object, but I want to provide senior-level access to ten of them, do I configure my access control lists? Do I create a sub-ou just for seniors, spreading out my users and making my structure more complex? And will the accounting chief have any idea how to do this, or will she just ring her IT bell and yell for help? Active Directory is obviously quite ubiquitous as a corporate directory, but should be considered just a component in an overall identity and access framework, not a corporate security mechanism. It also has a tendency toward proliferation of groups, which we'll also discuss in detail later.

Let's look at how the different kinds of authorization policies work, and how they help keep the business secure and compliant.

Coarse-Grained Authorization

In the previous chapter, we discussed how Oracle Access Manager provides the authentication component for your IAM framework. It also provides a high level of authorization for simple association of groups of users with groups of resources. It bases this level of security on *policy domains* that specify the *rules* governing how a given set of resources are to be protected. Remember that policy domains define the resources to protect, the rules and expressions for protecting them, the policies for resource subsets, and delegated administration configuration. Within a policy domain, you associate groups of users with groups of resources, but you can toss in mitigating circumstances such as day of the week, time of day, and user's IP address.

Resources aren't just target applications or files. A resource in this context includes the target, as well as the operations you can execute against it:

- For HTTP resources: GET, POST, PUT, TRACE, HEAD, CONNECT, OPTIONS
- For EJB resources: EXECUTE
- For databases: ADD, DELETE, UPDATE

By using AccessGates, you can also protect other non-HTTP resources. There are prebuilt integrations allowing protection and SSO with JSPs, servlets, SAP, WebLogic, WebSphere, and other endpoints.

Groups can also be expressed in multiple ways, such as role or directory group, which can be a static group, nested group, or dynamic. Quick digression: a dynamic group is normally constructed on the fly by query (such as "everybody with a current balance of more than $5000") and may be supported natively by your user directory.

The same infrastructure that provides authentication services also provides authorization, meaning the WebGates, AccessGates, and Admin Server described in Chapter 10. Once a user is authenticated and identified, his profile, memberships, or other attributes can be matched up with the conditions and the resource being requested to determine if he is allowed, per the policy domain for the resource, to attain access.

Coarse-Grained Protection of Web Services

Oracle Web Services Manager (OWSM) also has the ability to act as a Policy Enforcement Point (PEP) in providing coarse-grained authorization for web services. In other words, OWSM supports high-level authorization rule enforcement, without the need to insert code.

"RESTful" web services are used for managing resources over HTTP, in which the noun, or identifier, for the resource, is generally stated as a URL, URN, or URI. This means that OAM has the ability to protect these resources in a coarse-grained fashion.

True Story

When I was selling one of the earliest access management tools involving web server plug-ins several years ago, a customer asked, "What happens if your plug-in, or the policy server it connects to, goes down?" I asked what he would *like* to have happen. "I'm afraid my users will get locked out. I'd want the thing to get out of the way."

I said, you're exactly correct, they'll be locked out, but no, you don't want it to get out of the way. If your security framework stops functioning, you don't want the users outside getting in with no policies in place to mitigate their actions. Of course, this situation should not occur, which is why some genius way back when invented redundancy.

Authorization Rules

On the previous page we discussed how it's possible to set both allow and deny conditions on a resource. In Oracle Access Manager, a single rule can specify both conditions. The conditions themselves specify which users qualify. Here's who is allowed, here's who is denied. If a user comes calling on the resource, and qualifies for neither condition, then by default she is denied. For the user portion of the rule, you can specify

- The machines from which a user can access the resource
- The acceptable days and hours during which the resource can be accessed
- An LDAP group or filter for which the user must have the proper criteria (good)
- A role the user needs to have (even better)
- A specific user (maybe not so good)

If you're creating rules for specific users, hopefully you're not doing too much of it, since that doesn't really scale, does it?

You can aggregate one or more OAM authorization rules (possibly mitigated by an operator) into an authorization expression. A user may need to meet the conditions of multiple rules within an expression in order to gain access. Remember what I said: It only takes one "no" to deny access. It is the same with rules. Failure to qualify for a single rule means a denial.

A policy domain, with which you associate one or more resources, contains a single authorization expression.

A rule itself does more than just allow or deny. There are many situations in which you may want to provide a *qualified* yes; that is, I let you in, and while I'm at it I'm going to perform a redirect based on your role or group or attributes. Of course, it is often just as simple as, "you asked for it, you're qualified, and here you go." But in a deny situation, you almost always want to take some kind of action. You don't want a generic message, a "page not found," or an "access denied" message. The framework should be a babysitter of sorts, which includes accounting for even the failures. This gives a greater appearance of control, and a better user experience. If I can't have something, tell me why, or send me to a place where I do have access. Therefore, in addition to allow and deny conditions (who qualifies), and timing conditions (when they qualify), and a general description, an authorization rule also contains possible response actions:

- Setting HTTP header variables and/or cookie values, typically to be used by the target resource
- Redirects

The headers can be used for personalization or other purposes. The redirects can be used to send a user to a friendly landing page. In the event of an authorization failure, the user should be directed to a page that says, as nicely as possible, "You don't get in." In these situations, it's advisable to give a user some options. If you can identify that user as someone who should definitely not be there, you might make it a warning page. However, even for a success, it can be very useful. Besides personalization, consider multiple tiers of users (for example,. silver, gold, platinum) all using a common URL, but being sent to their respective landing pages. The framework in this way augments the business logic. Developers simply need to provide the landing spots, while OAM gets the users to the right ones.

Using headers or cookies, you can pass a user's distinguished name (DN) or profile information, along with static text. Remember that when you consider the entirety of variables and cookies, you've got 4K to work with. Also remember that a major function of OAM is single sign-on. Header variables are perfect for passing data that downstream apps need for authentication.

I mentioned operators that mitigate how rules can work together. They're actually very simple: AND and OR. For example, if you wish to limit access to a particular group who can only touch the resource from the office, the expression might look like the following illustration.

Authorization Expression

Rule 1: Allow Human Resources
AND
Rule 2: Allow 193.168.2.10

Modify   Delete   Delete All

It's also possible to create more complex rules, such as the equivalent of

(HR-Group AND Allowable-IP) OR (External-Auditor-Role)

An extremely useful tool within OAM is the Access Tester. With this interface, you can simulate all the necessary conditions to test the authentication and authorization rules for a policy domain without having to actually launch an application or page, essentially acting as your own client. With Access Tester, you specify the URL to hit, the operation to attempt against it (for example, PUT, POST, and so on), the IP address to simulate coming from, the date and time, and the user(s) to simulate. You can optionally choose to see which policy and rule get fired off. You will hear from some people that this is a great tool to use before putting policies into production. Let me qualify that. This is a great tool to use before handing your framework over for regression and load testing that *precede* production, and which we'll discuss in Chapter 15.

Extending the Authorization Model

Oracle Access Manager also provides an authorization API with which you can build custom authorization plug-ins to provide decision making not readily available in OAM. This may include making use of third-party logic or data sources not supported out of the box. Bear in mind, when you're doing so, you must be careful not to overdo it. The more information you can retrieve from the user directory itself, the better. In Chapter 15, I have a lovely story about how an integrator wrote so much custom code using an access tool's API that it added a minute and a half to every login. The more layers you pile on, the more latency you can potentially add as well.

Basing Authorization on Risk, Activity, and Behavior

In the previous chapter, we discussed the use of Oracle Adaptive Access Manager for the creation of patterns or buckets with which to monitor user activities based on resource, point of origin, time, trends, and so on. At the risk of being redundant, the same types of challenges that are used for stepped-up authentication challenges also apply here for authorization. When activity is judged as entailing enhanced risk based on behavior, the result as generated by OAAM can be a denial of access.

Presuming a user has already been authenticated, the framework must now monitor actual activity, not limited to simply the choice of resources but also how those resources are used. Even if potentially risky authentication has been approved (such as a known user authenticating from an unknown IP or device), the flow of activity may flag the user as being at odds with policy, leading to a denial or additional challenge. The risk models and weighted scores that drive authorization within OAAM may evolve over time (and in fact they should). We will cover the evolution of those models in Chapter 13.

Within OAAM, you can define a transaction (which is any process or series of tasks that a user can perform once he's authenticated) as a group of elements, and use that transaction entity as the basis for fraud analysis and authorization. With standard coarse-grained authorization, you may allow a user to post the contents of a page. With OAAM, you might map the contents of that page as a transaction, and decide, based on the values of the elements, that the post cannot take place.

Despite the seeming granularity of this action, this is still to some degree coarse-grained authorization because the elements of the transaction are still mapped to the client, with the decision making all based on values available before they are posted to the application itself. True fine-grained authorization is enforced with the Oracle Entitlements Server.

Fine-Grained Entitlements

A typical web app is a three-tiered model: browser interface, a web server behind the first firewall, and the actual business logic behind a second firewall. Coarse-grained entitlement security makes decisions on access before a request even makes it to the application layer, which is a good thing. Not only does this take the burden of security away from developers, it takes the strain of making security decisions off the app server. But when it comes to making those security decisions, the security mechanism can only decide based on the same elements that the web server itself can see. Once a request disappears behind the DMZ, visibility is gone. In most organizations, this level of security is sufficient, and for the majority of security requirements, it will be sufficient for some time to come (except in the financial industry, where fine-grained access control and web services security were effectively born).

But with increasing regulatory requirements, the trend is to move some aspects of security closer to the resources themselves. To this end, Oracle has increased the number of options it has for securing the database and the users who access it. But before the database, there is an application layer that can also be secured. This is what fine-grained entitlement management is all about. These elements are considered fine-grained because of the components being protected: database objects, business objects (transactions, reports, accounts), user interface components, and server-side transactions.

Oracle Entitlements Server authorizes activity on business objects beyond the reach of the web server. Like coarse-grained authorization, it can take into account conditions such as request origin and temporality, but then can make use of additional elements accessible only to the business logic, then enforce authorization decisions at that logic level. It is also more suited to being embedded with the logic, either in the code itself or, when possible, with the app server, to provide a more easily maintained, externalized layer of security.

An OES security model is similar to that of OAM. It consists of:

- Resource (app component such as page, portlet, bean, submit button, and so on)
- Action (grant, deny, delegate)
- Privilege (user actions that may be executed)
- Subject (role, group, user, system)
- Constraint (user, time/date, groups, attributes)

A policy can cover any application and the components that make up that app. When a request is made to that application, by either a user or process, the policy evaluates the request based on attributes related to the system, transaction, user, role, group, or the resource itself. And as with OAM, a user may be considered as an individual, as a member of a group, or as someone assigned a particular role. In fact, the user could be evaluated as a combination of those factors (for example, allow any user with the role of Claims Adjuster and belonging to the group location-London).

Consider this example. Doctor Howard can look at his patient's records. When Doctor Howard refers certain of his patients to a specialist, Doctor Fine, only the records of those particular patients can be viewed by Doctor Fine, and only the relevant parts of those records. If Doctor Fine is asked by Doctor Howard to examine a patient's broken leg, Doctor Fine doesn't necessarily need to know that the patient was taking Viagra four years ago. If the patient himself can review medical data by way of his health plan's website, he can only view his own records.

Quite often, a fine-grained decision is based on a transaction that is initiated not by a user, but on behalf of a user by a service account. A service call may be initiated based on the requesting user's credentials, or the calling process or service using the user's context simply to validate that user's permissions. Identities may be provided over HTTP/S, JMS, or even IIOP (everybody remember CORBA?), and represented as simple user tokens, Kerberos tickets, X.509 certs, or increasingly as SAML assertions. Although OES does not support SAML 2.0 protocol, it does support SAML 2.0 providers, and can use attributes from a SAML token, which can be retrieved in multiple ways.

Just as the ammunition for making authorization decisions in OES is more fine-grained, so is your ability to define resources. There may be a hierarchy of components within the application (app, servlet, Enterprise JavaBeans [EJB]) as well as for the logical entities of the business logic. A business object could be a purchase order, invoice, financial account, and the like. You can therefore apply a hierarchy of rules to create a baseline for a policy, along with the cascading variations to cover the levels of the hierarchy. Imagine a set of mutual funds managed by an office. Regular funds for the average investor may have a transfer limit, transfer approval requirements, and a number of qualified managers. As the funds get larger and/or more diverse, the transfer limits get larger, the requirements more strict, the number of qualified managers smaller.

Consider the resource tree shown in the following illustration. With a policy written for the highest level in the tree, the children can inherit the policy. Here you can also see a list of all policies associated with any given resource. This allows you to drill down on the granular details of what authorizations are taking place.

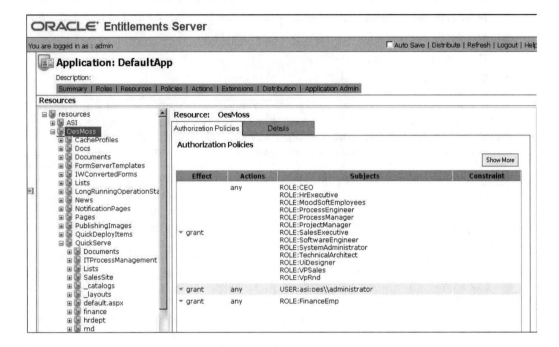

Just as with OAM, the OES admin console contains a simulation tool for testing the policies for an application before that application is even available.

OES also allows for run-time delegation of rights between users, assuming that policy evaluation determines that both parties are permitted. This type of action cannot be easily accomplished except at a fine-grained level.

OES Architecture

In an ideal situation, Oracle Entitlements Server will plug into the supporting architecture for the application in order to intercept, evaluate, and generate responses to requests. A significant portion of the time, this means attaching to the application server. Let's look at this ideal situation, and some not-so-ideal situations. But first, let's examine where OES sits in the infrastructure.

Like other access control structures (such as OAM), Oracle Entitlements Server has a hierarchy of components through which it provides fine-grained protection:

- Policy Administration Point (PAP), or Administration Server, which includes an interface for creating and maintaining resource definitions and policies; it is supported on WebLogic Server, Tomcat, and WebSphere, and provides full delegated administration capabilities.

- Policy Decision Points (PDP), which are distributed components for receiving policies from the Admin Server and evaluating requests against those policies.

■ Policy Enforcement Points (PEP), which are agents that plug into app servers or web servers; the PEP intercepts the request and queries the PDP for a decision on how to enforce policy and which actions to take in response.

Failover allows PDPs to switch over from a down PAP to a secondary.

Together the PDP and PEP are defined as a Security Module. The security modules also serve as the touchpoint for user authentication, single sign-on, and any external attributes that must be evaluated as part of a policy. In OES, it's common practice, and in fact Oracle's preference, that the PEP and PDP be configured side by side for the sake of performance. Web service calls between the two could go out at a rate of 700 per second in a normal configuration, but with an embedded PDP, that can scale to 7000 per second. A more centralized PDP configuration, with multiple PEPs per PDP, can provide a less costly infrastructure, although the latency can be higher.

The PAP pushes policies out at intervals or in real time, as configured, to the PDP. If the communication between the two goes down, the PDP operates off the last known policies until communication is re-established.

To centralize the administration of enterprise-wide policy sets, while still segregating applications by line of business, OES supports the concepts of Applications and Organizations. Each organization might contain multiple applications whose policies must be kept separate.

In the past, application servers made use of Java Authorization Contract for Containers (JACC), in which a third-party security mechanism provides authorization data to the app server for application security. It's largely an all-or-nothing security blanket, without consideration for multiple roles for a user, for example. In fact, the JACC spec doesn't provide much guidance for mapping users to even a single role, and there is nothing to provide context for a particular request.

More common these days is the Security Support Provider Interface (SSPI), although many vendors are denigrating their SSPI support. SSPI also has limitations when it comes to context. OES eliminates the need for both SSPI or JACC by providing far greater functionality and granularity, on top of GUI-driven policy management.

It may not always be possible or desirable to deploy a PEP. This may entail embedding calls to the OES engine for policy evaluation directly into the code. However, even this type of implementation can still provide great benefit to developers, and minimize the amount of labor typically associated with embedded security logic. By simply calling out to OES with the transaction parameters necessary for policy evaluation, developers can avoid having to code the complex logic required for most fine-grained security decisions. Consider the following example:

Authorization Logic

```
If userTitle = "Fund Manager" AND
fundType = "Balanced" AND
xferAmt <= xferLimit THEN
submit fundTransfer
End If
```

OES-Enabled Authorization Logic

```
accessResult = mgr.IsAccessAllowed
(fundTransfer, Username, Submit)
If accessResult.isAllowed = "Accept"
THEN  submit fundTransfer
End If
```

Any required changes in the policy, which could possibly affect multiple code chunks, require only a centralized change through the OES PAP interface. Whether the policy is embedded or not, the interface for maintaining the policy remains the same, as in the following example:

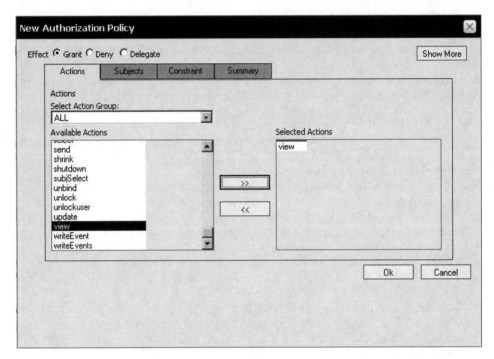

The design you put into fine-grained policies requires a different mindset. You need to consider the business transactions themselves rather than just the interfaces to them. Similar to the way you need business and IT people to come together in order to map business roles to nested roles, fine-grained entitlement protection requires that business and IT people come together to map out the guts of your most critical transactions. Even if you provide fine-grained policies for *some* of your transactions, that doesn't mean you have to cover everything. In fact, it'll be nearly impossible anyway. You'll need to choose which transactions require this kind of security, based on criticality. You will choose two types of transactions: the ones you need to secure, and the ones you want to show the auditors that you've secured. A lot of the time, these will overlap. Sometimes they won't.

Authentication is mostly non-incremental, meaning you will provide *some* kind of authentication to everyone from the very start. Authorization policies might be incremental in that you may apply more stringent requirements as time goes on. Fine-grained protection will most definitely be incremental, at least for legacy applications. But going forward, it is highly advisable that you provide a way for developers to expose a transaction map for applying fine-grained policies at launch.

One last benefit of the Oracle Entitlements Server: It can enforce fine-grained access control on data sets returning from Oracle database queries, by using the Oracle Virtual Private Database (VPD) as a Policy Enforcement Point. A feature of the Oracle database, VPD has the ability to enforce its own policies to apply application context for row- or column-level security, and can also provide the platform for OES to examine result sets.

Sharepoint

Imagine if you had a flying machine. You're a computer geek, right? So what if the propeller on your hat actually worked? You could pop to the store and back in a jiffy. You could defeat traffic. You could fix your roof without risking your neck on a ladder.

Now imagine you lend your propeller hat to your ten-year-old. He could get himself to piano lessons. He could escape bullies. He could get home on time from little Billy's house. And before you know it, he'd be dropping rocks on other kids, ringing doorbells and flying away, and swooping in on little girls to pull their pigtails.

Useful tool, but almost too useful.

So now imagine having a product for creating web sites that's so easy to use that you can create all the pages you ever need, and so can your users, and before you know it, you've got more sites than you've got people. Well, here it is! It's called Sharepoint.

A few years back, the portal market was on life support, and companies that had been marketing their "portal servers" started calling themselves app servers, personalization servers, or anything other than a portal. Now that market's doing well again, and Sharepoint's a big part of that. But its ease of use also lets it get out of hand. The critical mass that Sharepoint has achieved as an all-purpose collaboration and portal tool is just about equal to the mass it has acquired as an out-of-control site generator, to the point where it rivals its creator's LDAP clone, Active Directory, for *ease of use* that's turned into *leap of pages*. Sharepoint allows for the administration of security policies, roles, and groups to migrate into the hands of the line-of-business owners who can too easily create sites and subsites, and out of the reach of security admins.

Fine-grained access control, based on attributes and memberships, can provide the solution to not only who can create web parts but who can see them. Oracle Entitlements Server ships with a Policy Enforcement Point (PEP) specifically built for Microsoft Sharepoint Server 2007, to provide fine-grained Microsoft Office Sharepoint Server (MOSS) protection. A single security module may support multiple MOSS servers.

OES can perform resource discovery on a Sharepoint server, and then import those resources into its inventory. There a policy can be constructed at a point in the resource tree that can be inherited by the child objects, such as web parts inheriting from a parent. Protection can be easily extended to:

- Sites
- Pages
- Web parts
- List items
- Documents
- Microsoft Office Active Server Page Framework (ASPX)

This control can be so granular that you can tag sensitive content, and even "turn off" unauthorized parts, on a page that is otherwise viewable.

Standard MOSS security involves the use of static groups, with one group for every page or site. Inheritance becomes a bad idea, since it's an all-or-nothing access on down the chain. With OES, you can tie fine-grained access control to dynamic groups, and assign access via attributes, roles, or hierarchy. The use of externally administered dynamic groups and attributes for access decisions, instead of just static groups, provides multiple benefits. First, it's a far more flexible approach than just "you're in or you're not," and the decision making itself becomes more dynamic, since it can be predicated on values that may have changed. If your account balance has dropped below a certain level, you're out. If your mileage balance has exceeded the "Average Flyer" level, you're in.

This means you can mitigate access to a subpage level. Web parts, list items, document libraries can all be subdivided by policy. You and I can both visit a page, but I can't touch the admin links. Maybe I can't even *see* them.

By not having to rely on MOSS-specific groups, you are free to make policy decisions based on groups and attributes that may be used across platforms or apps. It's one of the benefits of RBAC in itself: I assign you a role, and that by itself grants you access to *all those resources* to which you need access in order to do your job. The way Sharepoint is deployed in the enterprise, it's rarely the only thing you'll be touching. Remember the framework? Sharepoint is just one of the resources riding on that train, and doesn't have to be its own beast, separate from the rest.

OES not only protects the content, but also the administrative functions. Therefore it is managing who can create pages and publish content, and then who can access it. Remember, Sharepoint's strength in ease of use is also its weakness in allowing runaway sites. So by plugging in an authorization model, you're controlling who can create what, and who can *see* what.

Another reason to plug in an externalized access control mechanism into Sharepoint is compliance. In addition to enforcing SoD policies that Sharepoint itself cannot provide out of the box, the presence of a plug-in that mitigates requests also allows for usage reporting. Otherwise, you might be relegated to Internet Information Server (IIS) logs, which is even worse when you're talking about IIS farms, and having to collate reports from multiple logs. The centralized security provides you with data on both requests and responses, one-stop shopping for reports on all Sharepoint instances.

By employing this model, you are keeping a leash on both uncontrolled growth and uncontrolled access, and allowing Sharepoint to be a useful platform without making it a vulnerable spot in your enterprise, or a compliance nightmare.

Federation

We'll take just a moment to explain federation, since too often it's not fully understood, and is sometimes misinterpreted as simply multidomain SSO. You enter a building, you check in with the security guard, and he checks out your ID, and off to the elevator you go. You've signed in, and that's good enough to get you into certain rooms with certain assets. But now you want to go to another building, owned by another company with whom your organization has an arrangement. Either your security guard gives you a badge that's good enough for the guard at the other building to let you in, or else a piece of paper explaining who you are, and when you show up, the second security guard calls *your* company's security guard to verify your identity, and then off to the elevator you go. You've been federated.

Federation is moving from one domain to another, without having to reauthenticate. Wow, that sounds like cross-domain single sign-on. Why can't I just do that? Because in regular cross-domain SSO, you own both domains, allowing you to implement cookie providers on your web servers. In the case of federation, you start in one of your own domains, but eventually navigate to another domain that you don't own.

What's the business case for that? Usually when you're branching into other apps hosted by sites that provide services for your users.

- Click a link on your company portal that lets you check your outsourced benefits, medical insurance, 401K, and so on.

- Allow your suppliers to check your inventory, to facilitate bidding on upcoming requirements.

- At my employer, I can shop for company-approved peripherals, at company-negotiated prices, get approval for a purchase, pop over to the vendor sites, order the goods, then pop right back and authorize payment.

Before the establishing of standards for federation, and even before it was commonly referred to as federation, there were other ways of accomplishing the same end, although they were somewhat limited. One mechanism that seemed to dry up overnight was *affiliation*. Much like a web server plug-in methodology, affiliation relies on installing an affiliate plug-in or agent on a trusted service provider's web server. By means of encrypted tunneling, the affiliated plug-in communicates with the IdP's identity framework. It wasn't a bad architecture, but had a major hurdle: No matter how much I trust you, I don't want to install your plug-in on my web server. Even if it's nearly impossible, I fear that somebody compromising the IdP's administrative server would have an open door, through the tunnel to the affiliated plug-in, into my web server. This architecture has always been a tough sell because of the need for *trust*.

So federation is all about trust. This is not a technical issue; it's a business one. You must decide that a federation partner can be trusted; that is, if they send you an assertion for a user, you can trust that they have properly authenticated that user. But the difference between affiliation and federation is that both parties are hosting their own platform for dealing with it, not each other's.

Federation between parties requires two things: trust, and speaking the same language. In a federated association, the user authenticates at one site, the Identity Provider (IdP), which is most likely home base. She wishes to visit a second site, the Service Provider (SP), which most likely partners with home base. The IdP provides an assertion, a package of authentication and authorization data, stating that the user is worthy of visiting the SP, and by the way, here's the stuff she should be able to access while she's there. After all, the domain cookie from the home base domain won't suffice.

Let's boil down the simplest use case. The user authenticates at her home domain. She decides to head to the second domain. The IdP generates a ticket for her to be used at the SP. The SP validates the ticket, and provides her with a session cookie for the SP's domain.

The IdP and the SP must have an established trust, to recognize and digest each other's tickets, which are called assertions. They *assert* your worthiness to enter the second domain. The IdP and SP need to share a protocol for these assertions. One of the most common protocols is Security Assertion Markup Language (SAML), which itself is a form of framework, for exchanging security data so that one site or process can interact with another. It is XML-based, and facilitates both authentication and authorization. For example, a user has an identity that is established in a particular domain, and she wishes to do business in another domain. SAML is the basis for her ticket from the first domain to the second. The primary piece of information is the user's *name identifier*, which is often her e-mail address, since it's a unique ID, and clearly states the user's domain of origin.

One of the great benefits of federation is not having to maintain the identities of users coming from a trusted partner site. They maintain the identities for you, and vouch for them when they come for a visit. There is also the liability that can come with storing that identity data.

There are a variety of standards (surprise , surprise) for federation. We have the OASIS and Liberty Alliance groups, which are all about open standards; WS-Security, driven by Microsoft, VeriSign, and IBM, and which is still a standard per se, but perhaps a little more platform-bound; and Shibboleth, which is another academic standard (that is, higher education). All are constantly evolving. In the past year, I sat in the audience of an hour-long, hundred-slide presentation on the differences between SAML 1.0 and 2.0, and it barely scratched the surface. They support different attributes and identifiers. This topic would be a book unto itself—in fact, it's already several—so grab one of those books, find a spot on the beach, and go nuts.

NOTE
Shibboleth is an authentication and authorization infrastructure designed to grant students access to educational resources. While authentication is still a function of the student's home base (that is, school), authorization is provided by the service provider. Access is typically based on user attributes and/or role, without the need for personal data, which protects student privacy. Throughout the process, users and/or their respective institutions may need to provide additional info for authorization. This is actually an elegant model, and barely adopted.

So federation is authentication and assertions. If you're only the service provider, you may only need to *digest* assertions. And by the way, there are lots of different kinds of tokens, including simple identity, certificates, SAML assertions, biometrics, Kerberos, and so on. It really depends on the requirements of the target system. The essence of it is that federation requires running an assertion engine.

Federation is one of those many things that everybody talks about, but not nearly as many people actually deploy. I've done many presentations and RFPs regarding federation, and only a modest percentage deploy it. If you only need cross-domain SSO within your own enterprise, it may be more infrastructure than you need. If you are federating to another site merely for the sake of SSO, and will bring no information home with you, you may consider whether it's worth it to generate assertions simply to save another login.

But in the increasingly cross-functional, cross-pollinating corporate environment we live in, true federation is becoming not only useful, but utterly compelling. Many of the larger manufacturing customers I have, for example, to whom I was invited separately, now do business with one another, embedding and/or selling each other's products and services. They trade information on suppliers, inventories, manufacturing schedules, and customers. This is where federation allows for timely and secure interaction without that unfortunate dinosaur of data exchange, the *flat file*.

Without the trusted security of federation, many organizations are failing to take advantage of Software as a Service (SaaS). Having your users authenticate to an external site is not the same as seamlessly interacting with that site from the familiarity of the home portal. Besides that, it means a proliferation of identities. Federation allows users to make use of partner resources based on their own identity, which is additionally a benefit to the service provider who can not only recognize a trusted partner's user base, but also save themselves the maintenance of another set of user accounts. However, in some cases it may be desirable, for enhanced security, to maintain those identities. The approach you take depends on how much *trust* you have. We'll cover both angles in a bit.

Oracle's Federation Solution

To address the need for federation, not as a point solution but as part of an overall IAM framework, Oracle provides OIF, or Oracle Identity Federation. It is a highly scalable, easily deployable, standards-based federation platform. By integrating with a wide variety of applications, directories, and data stores, OIF preserves existing investments in corporate assets.

A common hurdle in federation is the time required to deploy new partners in the framework. With OIF, partner sites can be brought online and integrated with your processes quickly, making use of any standard federation protocol:

- SAML 1.0, 1.1, and 2.0
- WS-Federation
- Liberty Alliance ID-FF

You still manage identities centrally and securely. As a federation consumer, you can also integrate with external authentication and authorization schemes. OIF publishes a toolkit for integrating with any IAM platform your partners may deploy. It allows you to act as the ID, performing authentication and generating assertions, which can be digitally signed and encrypted. You can also act as the SP, validating and authenticating assertions from trusted partners and authenticating the federated users locally. OIF also supports X.509 certificates for digital signatures and encryption. Through the console, administrators can manage certificate authorities and certificate revocation lists.

Let's go back to the concept of the framework. Oracle Identity Federation is managed via Oracle Enterprise Manager (OEM), which we'll talk about in more detail under postimplementation concepts in Chapter 19. In summary, OEM provides the ability to monitor the performance of the components of a solution, including the non-Oracle components such as directories and application servers. OIF comes bundled with OEM. By providing enterprise-level operational management tools, OIF allows administrators to

- Ensure the health and performance of servers and adapters
- Monitor from a single dashboard the complete architecture of all Oracle and non-Oracle components in the federation platform
- Generate alerts
- Trace transaction activity across components
- Use BI Publisher, Oracle's business intelligence tool, for generating reports on all user and administrative activity

OIF also comes bundled with WebLogic Server, which provides a command line scripting tool for additional customizations.

Oracle is also integrating into OIF the *Fedlet*, a lightweight extension to federation inherited from Sun (although not full-blown federation), which allows a Service Provider (SP) to quickly federate with an Identity Provider (IdP), for providing single sign-on and retrieving attributes from the IdP. Oracle has also inherited STS (Security Token Service), which establishes trust between business partners online, by way of web services. STS supports exchange and validation of security tokens, and is integrated with OAM. It's a form of federation without *real* federation. One of the key hurdles to establishing a federation partnership is a lack of federation capability by one of the parties. If you're not speaking the same language, the exchange of data is a moot point. So having a lightweight option opens the possibilities.

Federation Types

Even in a trusted relationship, there may still be limitations. Certainly you don't share all information, even with trusted partners. You're not trusting them with your life, only with your common transactions.

As stated earlier, federation can be looked at as either authentication or authorization. I chose authorization because the first type of federation, *transient federation*, does not require dual identities. The user is authenticated only in his originating domain, and only his session is communicated to the trusted domain. A large part of the trust is the presumption that the sender is enforcing all necessary access controls, and therefore Oracle Access Manager is often used as the authority for authentication and authorization in conjunction with OIF.

For those partners for whom transient federation is too much risk, there is the more secure, and more complex, solution of *account mapping*. In this configuration, users have identities residing with both partners, which must have some type of commonality, such as a UID. An assertion must contain this accepted identifier and validate it locally before granting access. This architecture provides the SP a greater degree of control. Mapped accounts can also be managed through the OIF console.

Additionally, *account linking* provides the ability to update the target directory in the event account mapping does not readily find a common user this time around, but wants to find them next time.

If a partner doesn't wish to maintain another partner's identities, they can employ *attribute federation,* in which the assertion provides roles, attributes, privileges, or other access control elements that determine not who the user is, but what they can do. Naturally, this requires that the trusted partners agree on what these roles are in advance, and the necessary attributes to assign access during a session.

Database Security

I want to stop briefly on a subject that we'll cover a bit more under compliance, and that is database security. To reiterate an earlier point, databases are often treated separately from other corporate assets. They are often considered part of the infrastructure, with insufficient thought as to how the databases themselves are provisioned and governed. For this reason, Oracle provides a number of solutions. One of these falls at least partially under the heading of authorization, and that is Oracle DataBase Vault (ODV).

DataBase Vault provides the ability to create realms of protection around application data without having to modify application code. Privileged users can be limited to essential functions, and be kept out of application-relevant data. Security realms act as database firewalls, controlling the areas that these privileged users can work in. It can also enforce Segregation of Duties, ensuring that policy of least privilege I keep mentioning. With regard to authorization, ODV can make use of mitigating factors such as authentication method and originating IP address to determine access to trusted realms. Policies can be applied to database commands for more granular control. Data cannot be read, moved, or modified except by authorized users.

As with OIF, DataBase Vault can be managed via Oracle Enterprise Manager. Full reporting is also available, to track administrative and user activity.

Specific integrations have been built and certified for a number of business applications, including Oracle eBusiness Suite, PeopleSoft, SAP, Siebel, and JD Edwards. This means that ODV understands realms of protection that are application-aware, with consideration for separation of duties within those application functions.

In the last few chapters, we've discussed how to identify, onboard, and secure users, then authenticate and authorize them to use corporate assets. Throughout, we've included the means to secure these functions, for safety and compliance. Next, we will discuss additional compliance considerations, including industry-standard requirements. When it comes to regulatory mandates, you can't just worry about yourself; you're required to worry about everybody else as well.

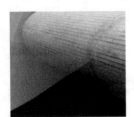

CHAPTER
12

Compliance Support

Laws are like cobwebs, which may catch small flies, but let wasps and hornets break through.
—*Jonathan Swift, explaining the term "too big to fail"*

 said it earlier, and I'll say it again: There are things you do because you want to, and things you do because the auditors tell you to. Sometimes they overlap, which is convenient. But increasingly they *should* overlap, because there are plenty of compliance mandates that probably should have been put in place years ago, and these are forcing organizations to make security decisions that are long overdue.

If you are trolling for budget from management to put IAM in place, one of the best weapons you have is compliance. It's not just your internal security needs any more; it's what keeps the auditors, and therefore the government, much happier with you. So it has twice the value. If you add in the automation and efficiency, the value just keeps coming. Of course, compliance in and of itself has a cost. You are paying to be audited. You are paying for remediation. You are paying salaries for the time spent creating policies and reviewing access. Automation is at least a partial remedy for much of this.

In many countries, even industries or segments that are not subject to certain compliance laws act as if they are, because they must deal with other organizations who are subject to those laws. In the United States, many universities are already planning for the day when they will be subject to SOX compliance, despite not being publicly traded entities.

As we discussed in Chapter 4, many of the compliance regulations have common elements, meaning that the framework elements that you put in place to handle one set of mandates will likely cover at least some portion of another set. Compliance involves the control and segregation of access, data, duties, and privacy. While it might represent a lot of technology to implement, it is quite possible to create enough of a framework to cover almost all possible compliance directives. If you actually manage to do that, then the part that will still kill you is all the reporting requirements.

Let's say it one more time, *reporting is not compliance*. It's a piece of it, but compliance is the security, approvals, monitoring, and other policies that drive all the activity surrounding your business functions.

Let's also recall that many regulations are so vague regarding *how* you should comply that it's largely up to *you* to determine the right solutions. "Secure the data" and "protect privacy" and "permit authorized personnel only" sound specific to those who don't have to implement them, but wide open to those of us who do.

Common Elements of Regulatory Compliance

When it's time to pass an audit, or report to the board that you are in compliance, you will need to know the specific mandates imposed on you by the government, by your own auditors, or by the authorities who govern business in your market, and how you complied with those mandates. But if you address the most common elements of all regulations, you are most of the way there.

At a high level, financial regulations call for

- Accountability
- Transparency

- Preventing conflicts of interest (no, nothing to do with SoD)
- Independent auditing

Little of that is relevant to IT, although you could make the argument that some aspects of the first two could be partially governed by IT, while the second two could be supported by IT. Now let's look at the most common elements that pertain more closely to IT:

- Privacy
- Need-to-know basis
- Access controls
- Auditing and reporting
- Reviews
- Forensics
- Data retention, retrieval, and analysis/analytics

These are exactly the types of requirements that an IAM framework can address at multiple layers, providing compliance throughout the entire process of identifying, enabling, and securing users and resources. There are multiple ways to perform some of these functions. You may apply more than one, depending on whether one department is comfortable with another department being responsible for the security of their common transactions. But you may say, "I can enforce segregation of duties at this level, or this other level," and no matter which way you do it, you may be covered in the event of an audit. As we progress, we'll discuss how to choose the method that is best for your organization.

While many of these requirements are common to multiple regulations, don't presume that because you're compliant with one that you're automatically compliant with another. It's important to get educated opinions from your designated company officers or external auditors as to what your specific requirements are. It's quite possible to be subject to multiple regulations with similar requirements, and to need multiple solutions to cover the same apparent requirement.

Let me restate one particular concept we've discussed more than once: *least privilege*, which states that at any given time a user should have only what he needs to perform his job function, covers by default "need to know" and "access controls." And if you enforce least privilege, your reporting, reviews, and analysis will be much cleaner, and your reviews will create a lot less remediation work when it's time to fix people's access.

We won't cover all the international regulations again. Instead, I will highlight a few that are representative of compliance in general.

Privacy Requirements

I give credit to the Europeans for getting things into law more quickly than almost anybody. And one of the subjects they identified years ago and codified quickly was privacy. Here is a summary of their principles of privacy:

- The reason for gathering data must be specified at the time it is gathered.
- Unnecessary data should not be gathered.
- Data cannot be used for anything other than the stated reason.

- Data should be kept only as long as needed for the stated reason.

- Only individuals necessary to the stated task should have access to the gathered data.

- Personnel responsible for securing the data should not allow it to be leaked.

These principles are found throughout many privacy laws: What are you asking, how will you use it, who will do the using, and what happens to the data when you're done? The least malicious thing that can be done with it is that it might be sold to marketing companies who sell your name all over the place, and you start getting bombarded with calls and e-mails. The worst that could happen is... *who knows*.

Some of these are easy, and some are a bit harder. The first item, stating your reasons, is solely a business consideration. Your framework won't do it for you. After that, they're all business considerations that can be strongly supported by the framework.

Let's start with the collection piece. If you don't ask for it, you don't get it; it's that simple. One of the values of transient federation is that the service provider doesn't need to maintain identities, meaning less infrastructure and a lot less liability. Same thing here. Remember what I said about compliance requirements forcing organizations to rethink security? By mandating privacy, the EU is also indirectly forcing people to avoid undue liability.

Quite often, data is *gathered* or *collected* when individuals are registering for a benefit, a job, access, or some other specified event. This requires a form, with predetermined fields, at least some of which are mandatory. If mandatory fields aren't filled in, then the submission will be negated. Registration forms can be customized, for example, in Oracle Identity Manager, with the fields most often being mapped to user attributes in the user directory. Obviously, if you don't require the fields, then you don't put them on the form, and you don't have to worry about them.

With regard to not using data for other than the stated reason, you might lump that in with "only necessary individuals may see it." The data isn't going to use *itself* for malicious purposes, is it? Allow the right people, and in theory you are allowing the right uses—not completely, which we'll get to, but to a large degree.

It will be necessary to segregate that data from any applications that aren't relevant to the stated purpose. There are multiple ways to accomplish this, but you need to ask a couple of things. Who will own the solution? Who will be responsible? The solution you choose depends on who owns it, who is responsible, and at which layer they will perform enforcement.

- **User responsibility** By use of RBAC, as with a combination of OIA and OIM, you can assign specific access to users who are responsible for using the data. This would be at the application layer, or even at the database layer, depending on how the data is accessed.

- **Access level** Face it, you're going to use some version of provisioning in your enterprise. It's a given. And if you're doing that, you'll also employ access control. Here is where you set domain policies that govern access to those applications or other resources that would give a user a window to the sensitive data. Strong authentication and authorization, as we discussed in terms of Oracle Access Manager and Oracle Adaptive Access Manager, determine who gets in and who doesn't, up to the web and app server layer.

- **Service account level**   Using a tool like UM4DB or EUS, you can create app-specific service accounts. So whether or not you've secured the role of the user who launches the applications using the data, the apps themselves will need to authenticate to databases or web services. Now the onus is off the end user.

- **Application entitlement level**   Beyond even the service account on whose behalf the applications run, you could put a security layer on the app server or embedded in the code to enforce fine-grained entitlements. While a service account might be one of the factors considered in evaluating fine-grained policies, there could also be the context of time period, origination of request, type of request, and any other condition. This is what Oracle Entitlements Server is designed to do.

- **Database level**   Look at the requirement itself. You're protecting the use of the data. So how about protecting at the source? If the data is to be used for specific purposes only, you might segregate that data from the general space. With a tool like DataBase Vault, you can create realms of protection with specific authentication requirements for authorized DBAs *only*. And since we're talking about "stated purpose," you could segregate users by purpose, by employing the SoD options available in DataBase Vault as well.

Depending on the criticality of the data, you might create multiple layers of security. This is in fact highly recommended, to avoid a single point of failure. This is not to say that one of your security services might go down, because by default that means *nobody* gets in. But as we stated way back in the beginning, your framework is only as good as the processes you define. Therefore your security is only as tight as the policies you put in place. Yes, you're perfect just the way you are, but you never know. So providing multiple levels of security is always preferred, but only up to the point of acceptable latency and cost.

In keeping with that notion of multiple levels of security, in May of 2010, Oracle acquired Secerno, which provided database firewall functionality for Oracle and non-Oracle databases. This solution is positioned as a form of data firewall for the network, mitigating the SQL coming in from outside the database. This supplements the operational controls within the database, such as Database Vault, as part of a multi-layered approach to data security. Think about access management for a moment. You may have overlapping policies that evaluate you as the member of multiple groups, or as having various attributes in your profile. One policy says you're okay to enter, another says no. But all it takes is a single NO, and you don't get in. With multiple layers of database security, it's the same result. It's a strategy that is sometimes referred to as "defense in depth." Is any security tool perfect? No. But if a hacker must hurdle a group of obstacles instead of just one, his odds of success are greatly diminished.

Okay, so I said that *in theory* if you enabled only the right people, you were mostly getting the right uses. But what happens when this is not the case? You need to discover those situations where people are looking at or manipulating things that they shouldn't. This may be done at the resource level, in which case you would employ reconciliation or attestation, which we will discuss a little later in this chapter. In other words, review what functions a user has access to that would give him the ability to look at data to which he is not entitled. The other approach is from the data angle. This is a little off the IAM map, so I will only mention this briefly. You need to monitor database activity, diminish the number of casual viewers, and keep an eye on even your privileged users. Oracle Audit Vault can aggregate log data from a number of sources to create a centralized view of who's doing what inside your Oracle, DB2, SQL Server, and Sybase databases. The available reports are shown in the following illustration.

If data should only be kept as long as it's needed, I read that as, when you're done, make sure you delete it. In relation to an IAM framework, I see two possibilities here. First, if you virtualize or synchronize multiple data stores into a single authoritative source, you may segregate that expiring data in a separate store, and wipe the entire thing clean, so that there's no risk to the other data that doesn't go away. Otherwise, you might consider writing a scheduled task, and putting it onto your framework to execute on schedule. This would not be a common scheduled task, such as in Oracle Identity Manager, but this is why we have custom code.

PCI

I want to highlight the United States' *Payment Card Industry* Data Security Standard because it has several provisions, common to other global regulations, that are specifically IT-related. PCI, as it's known, requires safeguards on payment account data. Because it involves privacy data as well as financial information, it is a critical set of regulations. PCI has rules on how to screen employees and how to protect against hackers (sort of), but the industry itself conducts no audits. That's left up to third parties.

The PCI DSS has requirements that are both strategic as well as tactical. Not all of its provisions are necessarily pertinent to IAM, but here are the ones that are (at least in my opinion):

- Install and maintain a firewall configuration to protect cardholder data.
- Do not use vendor-supplied defaults for system passwords and other security parameters.
- Protect stored cardholder data.
- Encrypt transmission of cardholder data across open, public networks.
- Restrict access to cardholder data by business need-to-know.
- Assign a unique ID to each person with computer access.
- Track and monitor all access to network resources and cardholder data.
- Regularly test security systems and processes.
- Maintain a policy that addresses information security for employees and contractors.

Because all of these provisions are very relevant to IT, I will address each of them in the following sections.

Maintaining a Firewall Configuration

To protect cardholder data, naturally the first thing you think of is an actual firewall, which is part of every single corporate network, regardless of whether external access is permitted. However, you can employ data-level security, assuming your database supports this, to filter out access from specific IP addresses, or employ a positive model only allowing access by specific IP addresses. DataBase Vault's security realms are the equivalent of database firewalls, segregating data by strategic use, and accessible only by authorized users via specified authentication requirements.

Avoiding Vendor-Supplied Defaults

Vendor-supplied defaults should not be used for system passwords and other security parameters. Complex password policies as well as configurations that require a user to immediately change passwords after first login will handle this. Oracle Identity Manager can enforce password policies from target sources. However, it's best to centralize password management within OIM to ensure consistency and complexity, including the enforcement of password formats and expirations. Oracle Adaptive Access Manager can not only provide strong authentication, it can also enforce greater security for security questions that are used for forgotten password and step-up authentication.

Protecting Stored Cardholder Data

The requirement to protect stored cardholder data is one of the reasons that a lot of organizations, including universities, are outsourcing the processing of credit card information. Many places prefer to pay a percentage of their revenue from those credit card transactions to a third party who will handle them (of course, if your third party allows data to escape, you're still on the hook). If you can tokenize the information (encapsulate it in a ticket or assertion) at the time of sale or card swipe, such that you're verifying it without storing it, it vastly limits exposure. But if you're hosting that data yourself, then you have plenty of liability, and plenty of options, and you should employ a number of those options.

Because this requirement is so vague, it comes down to something I said several chapters ago: Compliance means what you interpret it to be. This is one of those provisions that you need to interpret. This does *not* mean doing only the bare minimum, since we're talking about extremely sensitive data, the exact kinds of data that hackers most like to get their hands on. But what it *does* mean is that you get to determine how to address the vague requirement.

The hacker who stole tens of millions of credit and debit card numbers from a number of large retailers (and maintained malware servers in the United States, Latvia, Ukraine, and the Netherlands) used simple SQL injection for some of his more successful attacks. A completely effortless hack. Simple input validation would have stopped that. You could also employ an application firewall, the type that also watches for parameter tampering, buffer overload, and so on. Data encryption or data masking (both of them Oracle database security options) could be configured to limit the usability of the data that is returned, depending on what capabilities have been granted the service account. But we're in the middle of an IAM discussion, so let's look at those options.

The presentation layer is not logging into the back-end services on behalf of the guy sitting in front of the screen, if he's even logged in at all. It has its own context, likely a service account of some sort. By properly provisioning and limiting access on those service accounts, as with UM4DB or Enterprise User Security, you can prevent their misuse, although this depends entirely on what rights you need that service account to have.

Fine-grained entitlements in the apps themselves should be examining any request to the data layer (as can be configured with Oracle Entitlements Server), when you're talking about data this critical. At the application level, OES can take into consideration not only the service account itself, but also the context of the request, the resource, the action being attempted, and so on.

SQL injection is most often attempted against end-user interfaces, meaning apps that should return single-user results. There are multiple database security options to evaluate the viability of a request. However, when it comes to web vulnerability hacking such as SQL injection, it's best to catch it higher up the stack, and not make the target system have to deal with it.

Encrypting Transmission of Cardholder Data

Encrypting transmission of cardholder data across open, public networks is not strictly an IAM function, but strong authentication-related virtual devices keep credentials from being transferred in the clear when you're talking about a cardholder logging in and checking her own account. However, what they're really talking about is when individual credit card transactions are being moved from retailer to validator, or when large amounts of credit card data are being moved to another server for processing. The more localized version is a chronic problem that can be solved with localized encryption. The larger version is a case for an encryption scheme that keeps data encoded while at rest (day-to-day storage), in transit, and in backup, such as Oracle Advanced Security Option.

Restricting Access to Cardholder Data

Restricting access to cardholder data by business need-to-know is what least privilege is all about. At any given time, you should only have the access that you're supposed to have. If for any reason that access changes, automated, actionable reconciliation should compare what you have to what you're allowed to have, send out the appropriate notifications, and immediately remediate. OIA and OIM can assign need-to-know roles at provisioning time, OAM and OAAM can enforce the rules at run time, and DataBase Vault can enforce this at the database user level. You could argue that service accounts don't come into play here, since the requirement includes the word "business," but remember this: When a business user logs in to an application, for example to look at data, she's not actually touching the data under her own identity, but rather using the identity of the service account that the web service or application uses to query for her. However, that business user's context is likely used as a parameter, for logging purposes. Fine-grained entitlements could look at that context as one of the conditions they use for determining whether to allow a query or function to be executed.

Assigning a Unique ID to Each User

One of the curses of auditors and forensic experts who have to re-create who did what (when something bad happens) is *shared accounts*. You can't tell exactly who executed a risky or malicious action if everybody in a location is using the same credentials. Therefore, you need to assign a unique ID to each person who has computer access. You hear this one a lot when allowing outside parties such as partners, suppliers, or customers access your system. You can enforce a policy disallowing this, and penalize when you see it, internally. But it's much more difficult when it's being perpetrated by a third party. There are three aspects to policing this: before, during, and after.

Before a shared account might be used, your provisioning process should ensure that all users receive unique IDs, particular to the ID formats for each target system, in the event a global ID does not suffice. Oracle Identity Manager easily handles this function. You can also prompt for two-factor authentication, which has a tendency to make people shy away from sharing their credentials, although you can't bet on it. One more tip: Oracle Adaptive Access Manager can help pinpoint activity indicating that accounts are being shared, such as a user ID that is being used from different IPs, devices, times, locations, and the like.

True Story

In 2005, I spent a couple of days configuring a security solution at a small company in Florida, where they used a timeshare application for EDI. The guy who had established the account with the timeshare provider set up his initial password as the very vulgar nickname he'd given his dog (which I won't repeat here). He could only change the password every 90 days, and so he was obliged to share this nickname with three other people when they unexpectedly started using the app as well.

Tracking and Monitoring All Access

You should track and monitor all access to network resources and cardholder data. This should not just be considered tracking who did what. You also need, for security and forensics, to track who received the *ability* to do what they do, or did. Here you have many options, before, during, and after.

- OIM and OIA reports (or screens, for that matter) will tell you who received access, from whom, and when.

- OAM and OAAM reports will tell you when a user accessed, or attempted to access, a resource. You can also report on all user access attempts, successes, and failures, for a particular resource.

- Audit Vault can tell you who executed which queries on your databases, and can in fact aggregate log data from multiple sources.

Testing Security Systems and Processes Regularly

Security systems and processes should be tested regularly. The word "test" here is a bit broad. Ongoing regression and load testing are always good things. Once you've protected yourself from SQL injection, parameter tampering, and so on, you're probably okay there, provided you haven't launched any new applications. And by the way, load testing doesn't just expose whether or not you can handle user loads. When a system breaks down, it may occasionally cough up sensitive information, so it really is a security consideration as well.

Oracle Enterprise Manager, which we'll discuss in greater detail in Chapter 19, is an enterprise operational management solution for monitoring the health and performance of not only the components of the Oracle IAM suite, such as your identity and access servers, but also the non-Oracle components they interface with, such as the app servers and directories. Each component is given its own home page, if you want to call it that, from which the respective component managers can get a high-level view or a drill-down analysis of all relevant performance metrics and alerts.

Let's extend the definition of "testing" to include regular reviews. A couple of IAM suite functions we discussed under provisioning, and will discuss in greater detail later in this chapter, are

- Attestation, which invites resource managers on a scheduled basis to review those users who have access to a specified resource, and gives those managers the opportunity to modify that access.

- Reconciliation, an automated, scheduled process that corrects any out of band access.

- Review of activity versus configured models in OAAM, for possible modifications to patterns of behavior recognition; in other words, see how people are behaving, and change the filters to catch malicious behavior. Some of this OAAM does entirely on its own, if you tell it to.

Maintaining a Policy on Information Security

A policy that addresses information security for employees and contractors should be maintained. There are two ways to interpret the word "policy," but in this case, one leads to the other. The first use of policy is stating (meaning *publishing*) how you expect everybody to behave. It's the opinion of many security experts that every organization should make it clear to its users, partners, customers, suppliers, vendors, and so on what it considers acceptable behavior, and what the penalties are. PCI non-compliance can cost an offender up to $500,000 U.S. per breach.

As we discussed multiple times in this book, once you've determined your *corporate* policies, you then have a baseline for determining your access policies, which enforce the behavior you've mandated. Now, if one of your published policies states that data should not be put on a laptop or thumb drive that physically leaves a secured area, and you allow database extracts to external devices, there's nothing your framework can do to prevent that extract from walking off. But you can segregate data and other resources by user type, such as employee, contractor, vendor, partner, and so on.

PCI auditors often find common flaws with their clients' procedures that indicate extreme shortcomings in their security frameworks as well as their human practices:

- Lack of consistency in their encryption practices
- Lack of adequate activity logging, which has been attributed to lack of *network* logging, but of course they should also be logging within the apps, the app and web servers, and the databases
- Unnecessary data storage
- Failure to prevent data from moving across non-secure servers
- Failure to scan for vulnerabilities or abnormal behavior
- Thinking that being SOX and HIPAA compliant meant they were PCI-compliant

The ones that stand out immediately are centralized, aggregated logging (as with Audit Vault), monitoring for abnormal behavior (as with OAAM), and failure to prevent data from moving across non-secure servers. With this last one, you might consider something like database-level SoD (as in DataBase Vault) to prevent access rights that might allow insecure data actions, or Advanced Security Option, which encrypts data even in transit.

I have previously mentioned, and will mention in a later chapter, Oracle Enterprise Manager. The configuration pack for this enterprise operations management tool ships with the Center for Internet Security (CIS) benchmark, allowing you to scan your databases for compliance.

Certification: The Ugliest Compliance Process?

Because it is so often a compliance requirement; because it is most often a manual process; because it involves most users and most resources (if not all); and because it must be performed on a regular basis; certification is often thought of as the ugliest repeatable event in compliance.

Also known as *attestation* or *recertification*, certification is most typically a scheduled event in which designated approvers must review lists of users with access to specific resources, and decide which users get to keep that access. Standard applications such as e-mail may or may not be included. Common applications that are used across the population and represent little risk may only be attested to once a year, while more sensitive apps, such as human resources or financial apps, might be attested to semiannually or each quarter.

Certification is a compliance safety net. Good provisioning practices, in theory, guarantee that any user who shows up on a certification report belongs there, since they are properly provisioned to that resource, and reconciliation is designed to automatically keep access rights in line with policies. But there are several reasons a user may show up on the list for a resource when they don't belong:

- The de-provisioning process is lagging behind.

- Reconciliation is not configured or you're in between reconciliation windows.

- There *is* no de-provisioning process, and certification is how the user is disabled.

- The user has been given an exception grant that has not been undone.

- Someone has directly tampered with privileged data in the database or application.

True Story

I have visited a number of organizations who use their manual certification process as their de-provisioning "tool." One of these is a university, where this process may fall off the schedule at the end of a term, and not be performed until the new fall term, meaning a three-month period during which graduates or other non-returning students or student-employees keep access they should have lost in the spring.

It gets a bit worse. In general, universities share the bad habit of over-provisioning incoming students before they've had their first day of class. Some students register but never show up for class and drop out. Student-employees may show up for class but never end up working. And yet these no-shows keep those privileges. At one particular university, it was possible for a registered student who dropped out before the first day of class to keep privileges, including e-mail, for an entire year before getting de-provisioned by manual certification.

There are slight variations on the certification process. Administrators may decide to group resources. They may subdivide the users so that multiple managers are taking different sets. Here's a variation I've seen on rare occasions: instead of certifying by resource, a department manager gets a list of all his employees, and certifies all at once to all their resources. This works if you've got a fairly small number of apps to manage. At my current company, that would never work, since I have access to literally hundreds of applications and folders. The following illustration shows a typical type of report that a certifying manager sees.

Resource	User	Keep	Lose
Billing	Sid Vicious		
	Skelton Knaggs		
	Quincy Wagstaff		

The report indicates the purpose and the process, and it fails to take into account that it isn't always as simple as "you keep it or you lose it," since managers don't always have enough information in front of them to make those decisions for every user.

The reason certification can be so ugly is that, for so many organizations, it is primarily a manual process, and therefore prone to error. The original lists are hard copy, the distribution is by sneakernet, the "modifications" are by pencil and highlighter, and then the final modifications are keyboarded in one at a time. And because it's all manual, there are always mistakes, and some may not be caught until the auditors find them. Let me just give you the steps followed by one of my clients, a public sector organization that takes roughly a week to perform this process for just a single resource:

- IT sends out an e-mail a week in advance to announce that they'll be coming around with the reports.

- IT generates printouts listing all the users for a resource, attempting to sort them by their respective managers, and manually distributes them to those managers.

- Managers mark up the reports:
  - Redline the users who should lose access.
  - Add a notation next to the names of users who actually belong to some other manager.
  - Add question marks next to names of users whom the manager doesn't know and can't certify.

- IT bugs senior managers to bug the regular managers to get the process done in the allotted time.

- IT collects the reports, then fat-fingers in the changes.

- Any users who went to the wrong managers get put on different lists and sent to those managers.

- IT has to hunt down the right managers for any users with question marks.

- The rerouted user changes get entered in a second round.

This is not to say that everybody in the organization is down for a week while this is happening. But some of the IT staff is devoted to little else during that time, and it can definitely be disruptive. No matter what, even if you've got a more efficient process in place, it's going to be *somewhat* disruptive, simply because it has nothing to do with running the business. You don't help yourself make widgets or sell insurance or manufacture rocket parts by performing certification. So the point here is to make the process more efficient, less disruptive, and more accurate. It's all for naught if you do a lousy job and the auditors make you do it all over again, which is something I've seen happen.

Let's make this sound even worse. In some cases, users are certified by their reporting managers, and in other cases by the owners of the resources. Resource owners often don't know all their users. When IT staff can't easily deduce who should receive a group of users, they will simply print out multiple copies of a report, then hand them out to multiple managers, and hope that those managers take the time to pick out the users who apply to them. If a user is not specifically crossed off or highlighted, they may end up keeping access that they shouldn't. And really, those are the exact users whom certification is targeted at, the ones who should *lose* access.

But wait, it can get even worse. At one financial services company I visited, for critical apps, they actually removed all access by default, and a user had to be certified to regain it. Everybody out of the pool, and we'll let you back in one by one, and once we start, we need to finish quickly, or nobody's enabled to transact certain types of business. Can you spell *interruption of service?*

The frequency of this process depends on the criticality of the resource. If it's a "SOX app," meaning its functions come under the scrutiny of auditors for Sarbanes-Oxley purposes, it might get certified every three to six months. Other apps, perhaps only once a year.

Auditors will ask, how often do you certify this app? How is it performed? Show me the certification report for that last event. In other words, show me which users got kicked off, and show me the list of managers who kicked them off. Bad certification reporting can lead directly to a deeper audit of which users have which privileges.

Automated, Simplified Certification

Your IAM framework absolutely, positively, unhesitatingly needs to support this process. For the sake of your security, and for the sake of your audits, it needs to help you with this. Certification can truly be the ugliest thing you do, if it's not *automated*. But if it is automated, it's the difference between chopping down a tree with an ax and using a chainsaw. Of all the compliance requirements there are, the ROI on automation of the certification function alone is stupendous. Let me explain to you the version of this process that the Oracle solution supports, and how it changes the entire outlook on certification. Not only is the configuration of the process far superior to a manual approach, but the certification task from the certifier's perspective is exponentially more accurate and more efficient, taking into account the anomalies that normally generate even more work.

Actionable, resource-level certification has long been available in Oracle Identity Manager (found in the menu as Attestation). But with the addition of Oracle Identity Analytics (OIA), Oracle can now perform certification at various levels, from various perspectives, and at greater granularity.

Certifications are defined as recurring events, running on a schedule. The definition includes:

- What is being certified
- Who is doing the certification
- How often the certification is to be repeated

In summary, a certification process owner configures the scope of the resources to be certified, the players being certified against that resource, the certifiers participating in the event, and the recurrence of the event. For example, we may define the certification of user access for a particular application. So we choose that application from the set of resources tracked in OIA. We then choose which users to certify against that application. We may then configure as certifiers or approvers the application owner, the respective managers of the users chosen, or specific named individuals. Finally we may say, "We will perform this certification for the first time next Monday, and then repeat this certification every six months." Then we launch the event.

Again, the purpose here is regular review to ensure that users have only the access to which they're entitled. Certification tackles this from multiple angles, including who owns the resource, what entitlements the resource provides, which roles contain those entitlements, and which users have those access points.

In terms of access, OIA can certify every user for a resource, or every resource for a user. More often than not, auditors like to see certifications based on resource, that is, "show me that you have reviewed who can access this application."

Just as role management provides a business-friendly face for provisioning, OIA puts a business-friendly face on certification. Instead of a highly manual process, certification becomes a point-and-click exercise for both setup and execution. To begin with, you choose which type of certification event to create:

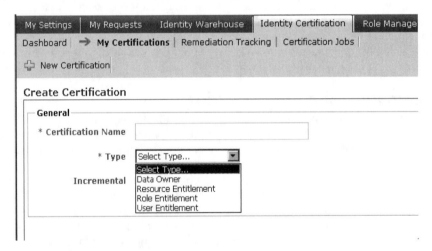

OIA supports four types of certification:

- User entitlement, in which you certify a user's memberships in a role, or their granular entitlements

- Role entitlements, meaning the privileges contained within a role

- Resource entitlements, meaning the entitlements pertaining to an instance of an application

- Data owners, or who has been assigned ownership of a resource

Naturally, this is extrapolated to all users, roles, resources, and owners. It's up to the owner of a particular certification task to determine its scope and granularity. Certifications can be full or incremental, reflecting only those changes to the specified source since the last certification for that source. Role and application certifications are performed on the basis of specified business units, while user access certifications support the choice of selected users, as in the following example:

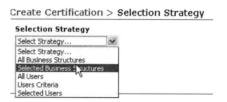

We may then select the players. For a user access certification, we might select users from a particular location, business unit, or other group, as in the following example:

	Attribute	Condition	Value
☐	Department	starts with	IT
☐	Job Codes	contains	NC8000
☐	Manager	=	rjohnson

User Search

Advanced Search

Group   Ungroup

When configuring a user search for an access certification, you can apply additional rules to narrow down the user selection, validating against user attributes. In addition to organizational considerations, you may wish to certify only those users with particular titles, certifications, job codes, and so on.

Choosing certifiers or approvers is more relative to the kind of certification being performed. An application owner, for example, may be the best person to certify which entitlements are contained within his resource. However, while he may work with the application vendor or coders and keep the application server running, he may not be the person in charge of provisioning to his own application, and therefore may not be the best certifier for user access against his own resource. While you may name specific named reviewers, you can also choose to have OIA look up and route certifications to the users' respective managers.

OIA certifications can be performed on demand, but normally they are scheduled events, based on the security and audit requirements for a business unit or resource. The options for scheduling are shown in the following illustration.

It's common for Sarbanes-Oxley (SOX) related resources to be certified on a quarterly basis, for example. The date range specifies the period in which the certification is expected to be completed, as shown in the following illustration. Beyond that, certifiers are notified by e-mail that they are delinquent in their task (based on the thresholds you can set), after which the notifications are escalated to a designated process owner.

The Value of Automated Certification

Once a certification is defined and launched, the configuration and automation truly pay off. Oracle Identity Analytics notifies certifiers of their need to perform the scheduled task within the specified period. If they fail to do so, the task is escalated. Within the certification interface, they are presented with their list of users, resources, or roles automatically, and provided with options for certifying as well as for dealing with the unexpected. If I am to certify a list of users, and am presented with a user who doesn't belong to me, I can mark that user essentially as not mine, so that they are routed to the appropriate certifier. If I was doing this manually, what would happen? I would draw a big red line through that user's name, or circle them, or place a question mark next to them. Instead, I am allowing OIA to properly reroute that user.

Again, what are the two biggest problems with manual certification? First, it's slow because it is manual, which leads to the second problem, it lends itself to inaccuracy. The purely manual certification (done with a marker) is exacerbated by the purely manual remediation (somebody reads off my paper and keyboards in the suggested changes). But if I am presented with an easy interface, such as this:

Certify All	Revoke All	Unknown All	Exception AllowedAll
○	⤺	○	○

I can choose, for example, to revoke the listed access, and have it be automatically deprovisioned. The user I am certifying loses that access. I can automatically remove an entitlement from a role. I can remove an entitlement from a resource. Click those buttons, submit, and have the process execute my choices. Fast, easy, and removes the inaccuracies that come from doing it all by hand.

If you are performing user access certification, you may very well find users with out-of-band access. Such access might be marked as an exception, and reviewed again in the next cycle. Most often, in the real world, users receive additional access for a sound reason, perhaps for emergency, forensic, or "firefighting" purposes, in which case simply removing that access may cause an interruption to the business. However, this kind of access is often meant to be temporary, and is never turned off. Certification is another opportunity to clean it up. In the event of a decision to de-provision a user from an entitlement or role, there are multiple ways to remove that access. OIA can integrate with a ticketing system (such as Remedy or Magic) to notify an administrator to take action, or (a better option) leverage the provisioning system, such as Oracle Identity Manager, to automatically take action.

As with the role mining that can be performed by OIA, data can be processed from flat files. Better yet, OIA can leverage an existing provisioning solution, such as CA, Novell, Sun, and of course Oracle. These tools already connect to source systems, and OIA can take advantage of that connectivity.

With this kind of configuration and interface, the process of certification has been automated and enforced, with the results being acted upon by the framework. The entire process takes far less time, is far more accurate, is self-documenting, and provides reports at the end to provide evidence for audit purposes.

Oracle Identity Analytics also simplifies the management of all certification events. Among other snapshots, the compliance dashboard provides a graphical summary of certifications that are new, in progress, completed, and expired, along with summaries and statistics on targets, sources, users, and accounts currently certified, as in the following example:

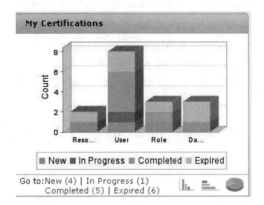

Historic and most recent certification activity is also immediately available to give compliance officers a bird's-eye view of those compliance activities that most immediately affect system access.

Role Governance

So let's review what we just discussed. User attestation involves the periodic review of resource access for users: who has access to a specified resource, and who can keep that access. *Role attestation* is the periodic examination of the privileges provided by a specified role: what privileges are in a role, and which ones should stay there.

OIA can also be used for defining segregation of duties policies, which can subsequently be used for preventive SoD checks in Oracle Identity Manager when roles are requested.

Out of the box, OIA also provides a role dashboard, as well as exception detection and remediation, as discussed in our section on role mining (Chapter 9). Exceptions, the bane of auditors, can be properly routed into auxiliary roles, or ad-hoc requests. In simpler language, if you don't meet the requirements for role membership, you may qualify for an exception role, or a non-automated role request. What this means is that any exceptions become subject to approval, rather than undocumented, out-of-band access.

Compliance is an iterative process, as well as a layered process. If provisioning policies are in place to ensure proper enabling of users to roles, then the role definitions themselves should likewise provide the security of ensuring least privilege by containing only privileges that avoid SoD violations, and which are periodically certified.

Reconciliation of User Accounts

Reconciliation in this context (as opposed to synchronization of new or modified users from HR) is a scheduled, OIM-driven, policy-based task similar to attestation, in that it's a periodic review of who has what and whether they should have it. It is not a standard compliance process that is mandated by auditors. However, it is invaluable in that it keeps you compliant in terms of least privilege. If your provisioning policies are clean *and* you run regular reconciliation, then your attestation processes will also be cleaner, in that you will be rejecting far fewer users.

The significant difference between reconciliation and attestation is that reconciliation does not require human review. It runs invisibly, comparing user privileges in target systems with user access as configured in policy, and flags those users whose privileges are out of sync with what their profiles say they should have. This occurs when users are provisioned to target systems by circumventing standard request practices, for example, somebody with access to the Active Directory admin console giving himself group memberships manually. A target system account providing out-of-band access is commonly referred to as a *rogue account*.

There are three options to handling rogue accounts. Reconciliation can be configured to:

- Notify the user and/or the appropriate manager(s)
- Remove the out-of-band access rights
- Notify *and* remove

Many organizations prefer notifications over automatic remediation, for fear of interrupting service. I've also seen instances where IT staff has specifically granted temporary access to one-off resources for "firefighting" or forensic duties; the issue there being that because these rights were granted for unexpected reasons, it's all manual and those rights never get properly taken away. But where remediation is not the option, administrators can assume they've captured and logged the improper access so that it will be scrutinized, but don't want to take away something that might cause a user to be unable to perform a needed task.

Reconciliation can also look for *orphaned accounts*, that is, target-system accounts that no longer have an active user attached. This means that the user has been deactivated in the authoritative source, but because of a flaw in the de-provisioning process (or lack of a definitive de-provisioning mechanism), she still has an active account in one of the corporate applications. These can be flagged and/or deleted.

You'd like to think that a majority of the time, people end up with out-of-band access for a good reason, such as troubleshooting. If they're in the middle of dealing with a situation and you deactivate them, you may have hurt the organization. So consider these points:

- If an account doesn't have a legitimate user ID associated with it, it's considered an orphan, and should be killed regardless.
- At the very least, you should generate notifications, especially to the user's manager.
- If you *do* deactivate these on a regular basis and get resistance, the way to explain it is this: Access should be granted according to best practices. Users should request it the correct way, and by rolling back out-of-band access, you are enforcing those best practices. It's against policy. And by the way, if it's not, it *needs* to be.

Reconciliation can be a bit of a hog on your system, since it has larger scope than simply processing new or modified users (likely a very small subset of your total user population). To ensure that reconciliation doesn't negatively impact day-to-day operations, you might want to follow a few friendly suggestions when configuring it:

- Perform reconciliation after normal working hours.
- Be aware of any other nightly processes that might compete for CPU.
- Process the data in batches, such as scrutinizing one group or resource at a time.
- Set up a separate Oracle Identity Manager instance just for processing scheduled tasks.

Now, you could argue, "Hey, why do I need attestation if I've got reconciliation?" Reconciliation is automated, it can be configured to fix any anomalies, and it adheres strictly to policy, while human decision makers may not. And there's some merit to this. However, it's good to have human eyeballs on this process. For one thing, auditors often require attestation reporting. Second, not paying attention (as with creating service accounts and forgetting about them for years) is how a lot of systems get away from their creators, users end up with the wrong privileges, and suddenly the system owns you instead you owning *it*.

Segregation of Duties

The purpose of SoD is to prevent fraudulent activities that require two or more functions to be combined for nefarious reasons. Let me reuse my favorite example. If I can request a payment, and then approve a payment, I can drain a lot of funds. There are a number of cases related to municipal governments where local administrators, with little oversight, were able to set up dummy suppliers, request payments to those suppliers, then approve payments, with no checks or balances to prevent it. Just a few examples:

- A person who requisitions a purchase should not be able to approve that same purchase.
- A person who approves purchases should not be able to reconcile financial reports.
- The person requesting access to a system (for himself or another) should not be able to approve that access.

We discussed earlier the notion that if a nefarious action requires more than one person to execute, it actually decreases the likelihood that it will be executed, and increases the chances that it will be discovered if it is executed.

Segregation of duties is an essential part of many regulatory compliance schemes, specifically to provide accountability by guaranteeing more than one set of eyes on critical transactions. Since the Enron case, an American CFO might prepare the financial statements, but the CEO must also sign off. While SoD is implied in some of the more vague requirements under the heading of "access controls," some of the regulations out there (for example the United States' North American Electric Reliability Corporation [NERC] Critical Infrastructure Protection [CIP] regulations for utilities) are more forthright about the need to assign duties that don't come into conflict.

While there is no one universal standard for SoD, meaning a methodology to define rules for separating functions, there are many sets of recommendations out there. A typical approach consists of breaking down consecutive pieces of the business. Breakdown Number One is identifying those areas of the operations where you have the most chance of material loss.

- Any authorization processes (remember what I said about approving your own access?)
- Any group that handles corporate assets, such as data, cash, inventory
- Any group that logs activity and then must generate reports based on that activity
- Financial and reconciliation services
- Anyone who implements operational changes to processes, location or assets, or code

Breakdown Number Two is dividing these areas into every business-critical function with potential to be misused. For example, acquiring inventory means

- Shopping for stuff
- Ordering stuff
- Receiving stuff
- Paying for stuff

Breakdown Number Three is choosing the most sensitive subfunctions and breaking it out into the abusable pieces. The last item from the last list entails:

- Receiving an invoice
- Approving the invoice
- Requesting the payment
- Approving the payment
- Sending the payment
- Reconciling the financial statements with all payments later

The last breakdown is where SoD really happens. What you're ultimately doing is separating the function into interdependent subfunctions, meaning that any subset of functions requires cooperation in order to fully complete the transaction, and assigning those subfunctions to separate groups or roles. Once again, if I can request the payment but not approve it, then without collusion I can't approve a payment to myself.

As we discussed in an earlier chapter, some organizations have a difficult time, with limited staff, fully separating the functions. I have read online about different organizations in that situation where they identified groups of duties and specified that no one user could have a particular subset of them. One example was a set of six duties, and no one person could hold more than any three of them.

How Deep Should SoD Go?

If the "D" in SoD stands for "duties," you now get to decide what you mean by "duty." Is it the job position that gives you that access? Is it the role on the actual resource you use for executing a function? Is it the individual IT entitlement that says you can click the submit button? The position might be too broad, in that an Accounts Payable role might give me those conflicting privileges, and the conflicts need to be locked down at a lower level. Be aware, the more granular you get, the more work you will create.

It can be virtually impossible to design SoD that takes into account every single privilege on a system. You know how many individual privileges there are, for example, in PeopleSoft? Just shy of a hundred thousand. If you were to create policies around all those individually, it would be like scrubbing a ballroom floor with a toothbrush.

But wait. There are two things to help you here. First of all, you can design SoD around those subfunctions that actually make things happen. Look for those chokepoints. Maybe I'm allowed to get to the page where I can approve a payment, but clicking that last button is denied. That might be a lousy example only because I will complain loudly if you let me fill out the form but not submit it. So consider where the entry point is.

Here's another big helper. There are tools out there with those definitions, those catalogs, prebuilt. Often the companies that provide these are founded by former employees of those business app companies. Former SAP guys, for example, have SoD and other complementary tech for SAP. No surprise. These can save you a lot of labor. They can also be quite proprietary, and specific to that app. In other words, the same engine that enforces SoD for SAP won't necessarily help you with Oracle Financials or Siebel, especially if you need to set rules on privileges across apps.

So there's one more thing to consider. When you're talking about conflicting privileges, they may not be in the same resource. Payment requests may be performed in one application, and approvals in another, and you don't want one user to have access to both simultaneously. Roles will more often than not contain privileges across applications. So RBAC design will be vital for SoD, even if you don't prevent violations in advance using roles. In other words, if you enforce SoD elsewhere, but you create roles with inherent privilege conflicts, you may be finding the violations after the fact, and an app-specific SoD monitor will not help you much. A more externalized SoD engine that can handle more than one repository, or which can define violations across platforms, is ideal. The other beauty to an external solution is the ability to enforce SoD across applications.

- Payment requests are submitted by filling out a form and submitting in App A.
- Payment requests are approved by pulling up the list of requests and approving them one at a time in App B.
- If I can click one submit button, I should be prevented from clicking the other.

In order to pass muster with a lot of auditors, SoD must be enforced at a privilege level. What widgets can you click on if you've already got widgets you've been approved for? What actual database tables or fields are accessible to you? The difficulty with doing this is the sheer volume of privileges in any given system, as with PeopleSoft (which is why its designers created their own notion of roles years ago). Here's a difficult situation I've run into more than once: I'm recommending a higher-level SoD because it's actually achievable, but the customer says they can only get away with privilege-level SoD, which is too much work, and the result is that they do *nothing*.

Preventive Versus Detective SoD

There are three times when you might deal with conflicting duties:

1. When they're requested (but before they're actually assigned)
2. During reconciliation, after duties are assigned
3. When a user attempts to use those duties

The first one is preventive. It keeps conflicting duties from being granted. The next two are detective. Number two lets you know there are conflicts out there. The third one keeps them from being used. Which one do you use? It's easy to say, "All of them, of course." But as I said earlier about defense in depth, the more layers you add, the more latency and the more labor you create. Let's pull this apart.

The ideal approach, naturally, is preventive. Tell Oracle Identity Manager not to hand out conflicting privileges in the first place. We'll talk more in detail in a bit about how to do that. In theory, if a user doesn't have a bad combination of duties, they can't do bad things. But here's the hole: *out-of-band access*. If, after provisioning, I pick up additional, illegitimate privileges because my friend the Active Directory admin added me to a group, I may have those privileges until reconciliation or attestation runs. There's the window for committing fraudulent acts. This is where the detective comes in.

Sometimes these conflicts may be legitimate exceptions. There may be a very good reason for this conflict. Was it a temporary firefighting grant? "Quick, we need this breach examined, and Wagstaff is our most able investigator." In such a case, that firefighting privilege should have gone away after a period of time. Remember also the notion of temporal grants, time-sensitive approvals that should automatically disappear. Can you make time bombs out of these?

Let me take a moment to really annoy a bunch of people. In a room full of auditors, you will hear that you cannot assign conflicting duties, period. In a room full of IT admins, you will hear that it's done all the time, and they get away with it provided that the assignments are documented and that there were good reasons.

A useful thing I saw practiced at one of my banking customers was the definition of specific "firefighting" roles that were subject to regular review, their equivalent of attestation. Because of chronic break-in attempts, they were forever enabling network admins to perform forensic duties that gave them access to multiple servers. Because of the potential for abuse, any and all firefighting role assignments were reviewed every month. It's a good practice and, if adhered to strictly, just as good as any software you might put in place. But there's the problem, strict adherence.

Then there is run-time detection, meaning controls that discover an attempt to execute a privilege that is in contact with another privilege possessed by the same user. This is the safety net. You'd like to think that by the time a user gets this far, both provisioning and reconciliation have combined to prevent potentially harmful conflicts. Most of the time, you'd be right. But again, there is that window between receiving out-of-band access and having the access remediated.

Therefore a combination of preventive and detective is the ideal solution. Preventive SoD enforces good business practices and will *prevent* most potential conflicts from being executed, and is also useful for heading off interruptions in service that happen when people think they have the proper access, only to find out at a critical time that they can't use that access. Detective SoD fills in any holes in your provisioning policies and out-of-band access.

Preventive and Detective SoD Options

There is more than one way within the Oracle suite to prevent the assignment of segregated duties. Before you can implement any of them, however, you must first construct your policies regarding which duties are in conflict, as we discussed at the beginning of this section. With some commercial applications, there are libraries available in which these conflicts are already codified, at least to *somebody's* satisfaction. Oracle provides some of these as well, as we'll discuss in a moment.

So perhaps a better option to managing SoD at the weedy level is managing it as an abstract, much as you do with provisioning or access policies. Remember those? Which groups of people can access which groups of resources? A capital idea for SoD. For example, if I have the payment requester role, with all its attendant privileges, I cannot also have the approver role, with all *its* privileges. The Information Systems Audit and Control Association (ISACA) suggests separating conflicting privileges into different positions. So why not extrapolate that very good idea by granting those privileges by those positions?

Roles are best defined as aggregations of application- or resource-level roles, which in turn contain individual privileges. If you're already segregating privileges by role, then when those roles are assigned, the privileges remain separated by default. It still comes down to what level of SoD is acceptable to your auditors.

If you want to use roles for SoD, then the policy is only as strong as your role definitions. This goes back to your RBAC design and governance committee. They must design roles with the privilege compatibilities in mind. However, even then, if you've got fine-grained access control in place, and it specifically looks at the individual privileges at run time (even if they were granted to you via your role memberships), you'll still get kicked out in the event of a conflict. Recall the rule about the chain of access decisions. Out of a hundred steps, if there's a single *no*, then the overall answer is *no*.

Remember the business hierarchy, those different ways to view the organization? You should be able to leverage that here also. Since they may already factor into provisioning, especially RBAC, you can design SoD around it as well.

I worked years ago with a partner firm who had a network of labs in Chicago. The different groups within that same company all despised each other, and would not easily approve of each other's access into their respective labs. So badges were a constant issue. But... it worked. Your badge got you into a certain number of labs, and none other.

You might do this by branch, line of business, whatever. The policy needs to reflect the business—meaning corporate, security, compliance, or audit requirements. SoD is not something imposed on you by the system. It's a process you impose on the business, using the system as your hammer. One more time: It reflects the business.

Want to impress the auditors? Show them your SoD in a way that best shadows how you handle transactions. Who creates, who signs off, who processes, who clears, who audits, and all with those walls between them.

I can't be in the sales group as well as the finance group. Why? Because there's an inherent conflict of interest when it comes to pricing, pricing approvals, discounting, collections, customer ratings, you name it.

I can't be in manufacturing as well as quality control. I mean, why would I ever want to reject the baby stroller that came off my assembly line?

I can't be in insurance as well as mortgages. Why? Because I might sink the world economy. And so on.

Within the Oracle Identity Manager, you can establish policies that prevent bad combinations, or at the very least require special approvals in the event of a possible conflict. Through workflow design, you can create paths that specify additional approvals based on a previous approval in a chain. These are usually referred to as denial policies, that specifically disallow a resource assignment based on rules.

Oracle Identity Analytics, as we covered in detail, supports dynamic role policies that can be both inclusive and exclusive. OIA can examine pre-existing roles, memberships, groups, attributes, organizational affiliations, and any other condition in determining a user's eligibility for an automatically assigned role.

OIA can also be used for creating rules on roles and entitlements to enforce SoD. It can be as simple as building the "Exclusion Roles" list for a role, specifying which other roles are incompatible with the role currently being configured. In very similar fashion, SoD can be specified within OIA at the policy level. For a given policy, exclusion policies can be configured, such that when the given policy is added to a role, the excluded policies cannot be added to that role. These different approaches bring up the question, which method is best? The answer depends on who is responsible for creating Segregation of Duties policies. Is SoD a simple function of creating lists of incompatible duties? Or is SoD a more complex function of security/compliance policy?

In addition, OIA can conduct scheduled scans on user access. Violations can be automatically assigned to specified remediators, who can either remove access or mark it as an exception. OIA can also work with an existing SoD matrix, such as a pre-established, application-specific SoD library or solution.

Now we'll talk about augmenting these identity tools. Let me introduce you to one of the worst acronyms in the Oracle product line, OAACG. This stands for the Oracle Applications Access Controls Governor.

OAACG automates the documentation, remediation, and enforcement of SoD policies within Oracle E-Business Suite and PeopleSoft Enterprise applications. It includes a ready-made library of controls, and can prevent SoD violations in advance instead of reporting violations after the fact. It can be further integrated with other apps, including custom code. While the control libraries for eBiz and PeopleSoft were developed with help from Oracle partners in the auditing and consulting arenas, and tested in customer implementations, the product doesn't stop there. SoD coverage via OAACG can be extended to Siebel, Hyperion, JD Edwards, and other non-Oracle platforms.

Within its various components, OAACG can document and manage SoD policies; support remediation; provide policy change simulation; monitor configuration changes and detect suspicious activities; and enforce real-time policy changes at a granular level.

In your organization, it may not be enough to enforce SoD simply with lists of incompatible privileges. In smaller or more complex organizations, it may be difficult to adequately isolate functions between users. Therefore a more formulaic approach may be necessary. OAACG allows for this. Consider a situation in which, rather than say "these two lists of privileges are quarantined from each other," the organization says that while privileges may be logically grouped, no single user can have the privileges to do all the following:

- Request a payment
- Enter a payment
- Approve a payment
- Issue a payment
- Reconcile invoices and payments

This may require configuring the policy in the context of a formula that supports if-then and and-or clauses. In this example, I could be allowed to request–enter a payment, OR approve–issue payment, OR reconcile. Sophisticated policies also cut down on false positives that prevent legitimate use of privileges and interrupt proper business functions.

Policies can be queried from a provisioning platform to prevent assignment of conflicting privileges, including the provisioning of roles that may contain conflicting privileges. OAACG can be integrated with OIA and/or OIM to examine a possible role or privilege assignment before it is fully approved and provisioned. To some degree, the placement of this integration can mean the difference between this being a business or an IT function. If you use static OIA roles with no policies attached to them, you might use OAACG to watch for the assignment of conflicting roles before these assignments are reconciled to OIM for provisioning. And whether you use static or dynamic roles within OIA, OAACG could be integrated to watch for conflicting IT privileges, meaning that if at a business level an assignment looks good to go, it might still be disallowed at a more granular level. The fun part there is defining privilege-level SoD, if there is no pre-existing library.

How can you straddle between the need for granular protection and the difficulty of defining those conflicts? One answer is determining the highest possible chokepoint. Don't consider the off-limits Submit button as the stopping point; consider the page on which it exists, or web part, or any class of functions that allow for the submission of conflicting transactions.

Database-Level SoD

At a granular realm often forgotten by security admins, Oracle DataBase Vault can enforce SoD policies within your databases themselves. With ODV, it is possible to create rules to wall off command sets, connections, and realms of security that are related to particular functions or even applications. Database roles or realms can be segregated to prevent abuse. ODV establishes three different kinds of responsibility that can be segregated: Account Management, Security Administration, and Database Administration. Different database accounts can be assigned to responsibilities, which themselves can be further divided.

Keeping Things from Getting Away from You

A drunk washes up on a desert island, stumbles over a brass bottle in the sand, and picks it up hoping there's booze in it. Instead, out pops a genie who offers him three wishes. "I need a beer," is his first wish.

Poof, he gets a pint of cold beer. He drains it, and immediately it fills back up again. When the drunk expresses his admiration for this miracle, the genie explains, "It's a magic beer mug. It always fills back up again. Now, what would you like for your other wishes?"

After draining the mug again, the drunk replies, "I want two more, just like this one."

So here's the IdM version of that: Active Directory. Its ubiquitous nature and ease of use let admins create AD groups on the fly. Need a group for access to an application? Bang, here you go. Need a group to represent users who use a particular printer and file share, or for a mailing list? Zip, it's done. Pretty soon, you've got more beer than you can drink.

Can't find the right group for the job? No problem, just create another one. And so the groups proliferate madly. I had one customer who figured they needed fewer than 400 groups. But one day they woke up and had over 80,000. That's an extreme case, but I've heard several versions of this story. When discussing solutions for out-of-control AD groups (or out-of-control Sharepoint sites), I almost always hear the same two words from clients: "That's us."

Another common issue is that the business units who make use of the groups are often not the same people who create the groups. The applications people call the AD admins and ask for a group. Many companies who outsource their operations rely on their partners to also manage the directory groups. These partners sometimes concentrate more on making the customer happy now, rather than later when those groups have to be accounted for. What happens is: at audit time the AD admins are forced to track down the usage of the groups they themselves have created. In some cases, the use of these groups is hard-coded, or mapped through various tables or XML files.

In a relatively small or simple environment, you're reusing the same groups over and over. But in a distributed environment, with a complicated forest, different facilities, lines of business, geographic locations, and with myriad apps and printers and servers and shares, there are too many needs to keep track of manually. Without a functioning directory of your directories, you get a cat's cradle of groups.

Why do you care, as long as everybody gets what they want? Take the example of a public sector customer who would take literally weeks to create a semiannual report telling them who had access to which resources via AD memberships. Audits were brutal. On top of that, trying to then tie those redundant groups to role definitions made those roles equally impervious to audits. I've had multiple customers who pay audit penalties rather than go through what they perceive to be the more expensive route of cleaning up AD.

A simple solution is, naturally, to create a catalog of groups. Make people look up the right one. If there isn't one with the right stuff, *then* you create a new one.

Even better is automated provisioning with the use of roles, which can take advantage of a catalog. The business role definitions include, among other entitlements or nested roles, the proper group memberships, which are associated with the catalog. This goes back to deciding in advance what permissions are proper for a user to do his or her job.

One of the more common targets of OIM policy workflows is Active Directory. If for no other reason, AD may be used as the starting point for e-mail. In fact, because it's so common, basic AD groups often get populated with new users without approval. By locking down AD, and requiring that any new groups to be created must be immediately associated with a provisioning policy, you can cut down on the number of runaway groups, *and* be able to report credibly on how those groups are used. If an AD group is considered a subrole that is part of a larger business role, then within OIA you can instantly tell who is in a particular group, or determine what groups a particular user is in. Within OIM, an AD group that is considered a privilege can likewise be tracked, from either a user or group perspective.

It's far easier to identify a problem with runaway AD groups than it is to clean it up. We'll discuss entitlement data cleansing in Chapter 14.

Audit Support

Anybody who's been in IT long enough knows what it's like to have their life put on hold when auditors come in the door. You might get some warning as to what they want out of you, but there will always be requirements you hadn't anticipated, and which in some cases are designed not to find information, but to test your ability to bark like a dog on command. I've seen comptrollers generate reams of reports that were effectively useless to the audit, simply because somebody on the audit team wanted to gauge how well an organization could react to requests.

An accounting audit is an objective exercise, mostly measuring financial data in quantitative fashion. A compliance audit is a more subjective event (although still quantitative) measuring the effectiveness of your processes, using as its scale the difference between requirements and reality. As we've already discussed, a publicly traded specialty organization could be subject to multiple audits (for example, SOX, privacy, PCI, and so on).

A failed audit can put you on probation, to the point where you are pinged for regular make-up reports for months to prove that you are improving the failed processes that got you in hot water. What helps, of course, is knowing the metrics that your auditors will use. As we said earlier, a lot of regulatory compliance laws provide mandates about installing controls without much clue regarding how to interpret and implement them. Various bodies have come into existence as a result of this vacuum, trying to establish standards for the collective good. For example, Control Objectives for Information and Related Technologies (COBIT) is in itself an internationally recognized framework designed to help IT professionals create policies that reduce the distance between the technology and the requirements. Under COBIT, security pros interpret the application of the controls to the requirements, and the auditors measure how well that interpretation is performed.

Remember this very important point. It is not enough to *be* compliant. You must *prove* you are compliant. If you have the safest operation in the world, but can't quantitatively and qualitatively demonstrate how safe you are, you will fail your audit. Evidence is everything.

Let's consider three ways the Oracle Identity Suite can help you support an audit (which is the polite term for "getting them out the door as quickly and happily as possible") before, during, and after all the audit requests.

Build Your Own Security Audit

To anticipate what auditors might pick on, many organizations conduct their own audits, often bringing in third parties to give them a checkup that doesn't really count. There are various methodologies to this, but let's go with a lowest common denominator that covers the basics of many of them, and discuss how the IAM framework can help you. By giving yourself a checkup, you are not only giving auditors less to beat you up on; you're also preparing yourself to provide the evidence you need to *prove* you are secure.

The first step is to draw a line around those assets that you absolutely need to run the business. This is the perimeter behind which you keep physical and digital resources, such as servers, routers, phones, physical security devices, and of course data and the points from which it can be accessed.

The second step is to consider the ways in which this perimeter can be breached, physically and digitally. If you are building an IAM framework, then you're worrying about being hacked. What resources should you most worry about? Customer data. Employee data. Intellectual property. E-mails and documents. Log data. Anything subject to compliance regulations.

It also helps to recognize the kinds of threats that the various assets are potentially vulnerable to. Physical assets are subject to possible fire, break-in, and so on. Digital assets are also in danger of these, as well as the remote hacker.

An IAM framework is considered an important part of any security perimeter. But it's also a good source of information when building that internal audit. You have already essentially created that asset list, by configuring policies that grant least privilege to your users in order to access your resources. Within Oracle Identity Manager, you must define resources before you can create access policies and workflows. You have defined *how* users are granted access. Within Oracle Access Manager, you have already created a digital perimeter around your digital assets that determine the requirements for reaching them. You may have defined even more granular defenses with Oracle Entitlements Server or Oracle Adaptive Access Manager. The physical assets may or may not have been included in your provisioning workflows (although not likely in your authorization policies).

And better yet, within OIM you have (hopefully) defined the administrators of these assets, who will need to help you catalog every asset and outline every defense. If you've hired the right people, they will also be aware of the possible threats to their piece of the business. Assessment of threats also lends itself to the calculation of risk, which is the weighting of patterns of anomalous behavior (also a strength of OAAM).

Conducting your own mini-security audit is the same as preparing for a debate. Anticipate what your opponent will say, and take his weapons away in advance with your arguments. In the case of a security audit, take a more aggressive stance. Auditors can be looked upon as your friend, since they will tell you where you are deficient. Of course, nobody enjoys a visit from auditors. Better to think of them as an opponent, whom you must cleanly and honestly combat. If you can take away their arguments with a clean bill of health (by auditing yourself and subsequently bolstering your defenses), you will be telling yourself where you are deficient, and you will better address the dangers you face.

Scheduled Reports

By instantiating compliance in the very DNA of your framework through provisioning policies, access and authorization policies, segregation of duties, and both automated and manual reviews of user privileges, you will provide a cleaner picture to your auditors. These policies will most assuredly keep you more secure. However, the trick is to *prove* the effectiveness of your policies for audit purposes. For that, you need reporting.

Regularly scheduled compliance reporting provides several benefits to different strata of the organization:

- It can point out troublesome trends, including anomalous resource usage patterns that indicate the need to modify access policies.

- It shows you where you're doing things right as well, validating your labor and your investments.

- It's an enforcement tool to remind the user population that you're being vigilant.

- It shows to auditors and managers alike that you've been serious about security and compliance, giving you at least that first piece of credibility.

Let me stress that last point. If your parents have been on vacation for a week, leaving you in charge, the first thing they'll do when they come home is try to figure out if you had a wild party while they were gone. If they find so much as a cigarette butt on the front porch, they will instantly be suspicious about who was there during their absence. But the more clean rooms they venture into, the less suspicious they will be. Your archive of regularly scheduled reports shows that you haven't been having a party, that you've been patrolling the fortress, and hopefully provides you some modicum of credibility. I have provided audit support from the perspective of a target (as a DBA and developer) and as a trusted advisor (helping customers pump out activity reports), and it is my experience that the appearance of preparedness definitely makes the ride an easier one.

For enterprise reporting purposes, the Oracle Identity Suite bundles in Business Intelligence Publisher, also known as BI Publisher, which in turn bundles in a wide variety of preformatted reports. It includes a wizard for generating customized reports as well, connecting to the necessary data sources, designing the necessary queries, and providing a tailored, branded format. To help with the requirement for scheduled reporting, BI Publisher allows you to do some pretty nifty things:

- Create those reusable report templates, including the sources, queries, and look
- Schedule them (daily, weekly, monthly)
- Specify output delivery format and method

I get the user termination report once a week, sorted by username, e-mailed in Excel format. You get it once a month, sorted by department and then by last name, and dropped into a folder as a PDF. And so on.

What reports you generate, of course, depend on the metrics you think you need. Just a hint: from a security perspective, one of the more useful reports is an organized dump of all users who've left the organization (voluntarily or otherwise) since the last audit, along with a confirmation that they have no access rights across all resources. A favorite tripwire of security auditors is finding entry points in the context of terminated users.

A general report on security or access domains is of course a useful blueprint. But over a given period, you will want to report on any changes made to policies and the scope of the domains.

Regular reporting on newly provisioned users and what access they received will save you having to generate new reporting later, with the frequency based on volume (if you hire five new people a week, then a monthly report is probably sufficient). Exception grants are also good targets.

Through Oracle Access Manager, you can report on all requests, successful and failed, but that would make for a huge report, even if just for one day. But reports for sensitive resources, or reports from OAAM activity on high-risk resources or activities, would be good choices. Anomalous activity is not only of interest, but if you are using OAAM as a source of reporting on accesses from particular IP addresses or devices, you will be ahead of the game.

Again, the content and format of reports that indicate your compliance depend on what compliance means to you, your industry, and your management. Ultimately, reporting helps you reduce the size of the gaps between where you are and where you're expected to be.

Real-Time Audit Support

An audit usually seems worst when *the auditors are in the building!* Auditors can seem the creepiest when they're nice. But remember that most of the time, they're just doing their job. However, auditors are essentially consultants, and when consultants are tasked with overseeing a third party (and make no mistake, your management might be the customer, but as IT staff, *you* are the third party), they don't earn their money by telling everybody how great everything is. Their job is to sniff out badness. By maintaining the compliance DNA of your framework, you are limiting the badness. And with some excellent GUI options, you can enhance your credibility with investigators. Here's how.

Every module in the suite provides for customized interfaces in two ways. First, for the sake of look and feel, you can easily create a tailored, branded interface. This is especially useful with external users such as paying customers. But the important one here is the ability to create custom views, limiting by role or by group membership a user's ability to navigate the definitions and reports. For example, in OIM you can create an auditors' group and assign certain menu items and read-only access, allowing them to review the data they request (and that you'll allow them to look at). The benefit to you is letting the auditors help themselves, and hopefully take some of the "go fetch that" labor off your shoulders. It also helps build trust and credibility.

I have seen auditors drill down on the contents of a role. They want to know which privileges a role provides, and match those up with the high-level business function. They are validating the entire role definition, from job title to application role to individual atomic entitlement. There are canned reports available to map users to roles, roles to privileges, and so on. But one of the foulest jobs in an audit is generating five different variations on the same report. Better yet is the ability to do this on screen. In OIA, you can always *get there from here*. Think of users, roles, privileges, and resources as objects. You can navigate from any object to any other object. Every object has one-to-many relationships in both directions.

- List roles for a user
- List subroles for a business role
- List entitlements for a role
- In reverse, list the subroles where a privilege is used, and business roles where a subrole is used

Auditors can perform all the analysis they want, with a mouse and keyboard, without the need to correlate multiple hard-copy reports, at least in terms of the definitions you control.

Compliance and the Cloud

When you're researching cloud vendors (that is, if you're planning on outsourcing any of your infrastructure), it's important to validate not only their flexibility, capacity, and uptime, but also their ability to interoperate with your identity and security policies. This includes providing access to data that auditors will need from you. A secure, standards-based pipeline to log data, such as approvals, requests, failures, and successes, will save you the trouble of requesting from your vendor a flat-file dump of that data later. If you are offering services in the cloud, be prepared to provide this information to your users.

To reiterate a point from an earlier chapter, if a cloud vendor suffers a breach, it might be their mistake, but the liability ultimately belongs to their customer.

Forensics

To my daughter, who's hooked on gory cop shows, forensics means dead bodies. But to auditors, it's snapshots in time. They want to be able to re-create a series of events whenever they've spotted an anomaly. In fact, so do you, if you suspect a breach. And it's a series of events rather than a single event, because it usually entails a user who has taken an improper action and triggered at least one response.

Throughout the Oracle IAM suite, you can always trace back activity, and re-create that moment in time, or multiple moments over a period of time.

- When a user was created and how
- Resource requests, approvals, denials, who made them, who rejected them
- Access requests, successes, failures, and which policies came into play
- Attempted accesses from strange IP addresses or devices
- Changes in policies or roles, and the effects they had
- Changes in user profiles or memberships

These data elements are all available by report and by screen. I like to say, when you worry about auditors, you generate reports, and when you worry about a breach, you run for the display.

OAAM is particularly helpful when you are looking for a pattern of behavior, and for generating alerts. But regardless of the tool, you can build in notifications, rejections, and data firewalls that account for the things you know, and watch for the things you perhaps haven't thought of yet. Better to disallow now and allow later, then allow now and regret it later.

One more option here is creating custom reports and enabling them for online viewing (which we'll talk about in a couple of paragraphs).

Post-Visit Audit Requests

No matter what predefined reports and custom views you provide, you will still be creating custom printouts. You cannot avoid it. Even if your operation comes out totally clean, and *it will not*, there will still be requests. I say that it will not, because the auditors' job is to ensure that it does not. If they find nothing wrong, then *their* credibility will be in question. If they have to make something up, they will find something wrong. Users will have out-of-band access, your access policies will be inadequate, or you will have sensitive fields that are not encrypted.

This is when BI Publisher will be even more helpful. Under the context of a BI Publisher developer or administrator role, you can create and edit new reports, as shown in the following illustration.

As with every other object in the entire Oracle suite, for a new report, you start with the properties, and there are plenty:

- **Description** This is how you recognize the object so you can grab it from the folder where the template will reside. Make this as descriptive as possible.
- **Data source** You choose from a list. When you define the data model (which we'll come to in a minute), you can define multiple sources.

There are additional parameters regarding how the report template and data are displayed, how links within the report can be opened, whether it can be viewed online or from the scheduled run only, how the report can interact with Excel, and whether the report content can be cached.

The data model determines how data is derived from external sources. A source can be

- SQL query against any database, including the Oracle BI Server
- HTTP
- Web service
- Data template query using the BI Publisher data engine

- Predefined Oracle BI request
- Oracle BI Discoverer worksheet
- XML file
- OLAP data source

Even in this modern age, too many solutions rely on completely proprietary reporting tools. BI Publisher provides a wide range of options for obtaining and formatting data into usable, intelligent reports.

You also define the parameters to pass to the report, so that it generates based on the context you need at run time.

There are several options for the report layout. In many cases, you or your auditors may wish to mark up a report online, or create yet another variation. For those instances, you can generate a report in a predefined RTF format, or allow BI Publisher to autogenerate RTF. Excel spreadsheets are also available. By creating a stylesheet, you allow for HTML, text, or, when users wish to further generate their own reports or worksheets, XML. For creating EDI transactional data, you can also push out eText.

NOTE
Even if you are providing data to an auditor, when you are providing data in these editable formats, always know how it is to be used. On one occasion I saw a consultant presentation in which their pitch for new auditing business included untouched data from another customer's audit.

Finally, you can generate interactive Flash output. Whether or not you find this useful, it is fairly impressive when you're presenting to board members.

As with the remainder of the Oracle security suite, you can also monitor the activity of your reports themselves, including when they were created, when they were run, and by whom.

There are language options for the BI Publisher interface, allowing you to delegate administration internationally.

Compliance is all about control, of access, of data, of privacy. But you not only have to *be* compliant—you must *show* that compliance.

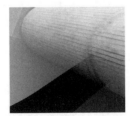

CHAPTER
13

The Time Bomb
Everybody Forgets:
Things Change

He that will not apply new remedies must expect new evils.
—*Sir Francis Bacon, on patch management*

bout the only thing in access management that's relatively easy and quick to put in is password reset. After that, it's serious work. Even if you only implement part of an overall IAM framework, such as access management, you have done significant planning and deployment. So it would be nice to get it working, and then sit back. But you've only begun. Especially in the early weeks, you are monitoring activity just to learn how to monitor. You will deal with the inevitable glut of early calls from users who don't understand new procedures and interfaces, who didn't read the instructions or bulletins (on that informational web site you were supposed to set up), or who were used to how things ran for years and just plain don't get it. Misconfigurations result in users getting insufficient rights, notifications aren't occurring as planned, approvers aren't sure of what they're looking at when requests arrive. It's all fun stuff, while you work out the issues and get past the learning curve.

But even when things are running relatively smoothly, you can't relax, because you work in a dynamic environment. Your IAM framework, you recall, is only there to reflect the needs of your business, which is itself adapting to changes from external forces. Your workforce is moving around, even internally. New requirements, resources, and users will keep you busy creating and modifying policies and connectors.

You've also got recommendations coming in from compliance pressures. A utility customer of mine was audited based on NERC CIP and was found to have two users with access that could not be associated with proper approvals. Two users. This was enough ammunition for their auditors to push them toward some costly and time-consuming policy and software changes. Two users.

There are also constant threats. Cloud computing is as much an avenue for bad behavior as it is for collaborative business. As more and more devices outside the norm of a laptop or desktop come into business use, there are newer and more inventive methods for acquiring sensitive data.

Change comes in various forms and timeframes. Some changes come gradually as the business changes. New resources provide opportunity for new mistakes. Many customers have told me they fear the stupid mistake, such as inadvertent data extracts or the erroneous e-mailing of a sensitive report, as much as the malicious hack. Some changes are laid at your feet with specific timeframes, such as from auditors. And then there are sudden changes that come from breaches and other unpleasant activities. The source, weight, and criticality of a proposed change will dictate how quickly it must be incorporated into your framework's policies. But whatever changes you are thinking of making, you must always measure the effects of those changes *before* you make them.

I once observed the presentation of a pilot system that included dynamic access grants. The sample policies that were designed to dynamically assign roles were (inaccurately) defined in such a way that every single test user account received every single role. Oops. If something like that happens in a production system, you will be in the position of having to either shut down all access while you clean up, or quickly figure out how to redefine those policies and reconcile every user again, back to a correct state, as quickly as possible.

Impact analysis, the process of measuring the effect of a change, should be part of any migration or change plan, so that you aren't having to

- Apologize
- Roll back that change
- Undo the damage from that change
- Explain to the organization why they should trust you with the next change

Whenever there's change, there's opportunity for bad things to happen. Therefore you minimize the risk by managing the change. Some changes are planned, many are part of the plan, and some will catch you by surprise. Part of the value of a framework is the logical application of change. The Oracle IAM suite provides for the constant refinement of policies and structures to accommodate the issue that last week you didn't know existed, and which this week constitutes a threat or panic button. And when changes occur to the players, such as the users or resources, then the policies in place should automatically manage those changes. Let's examine the possible changes you will need to account for in your IAM framework as time goes by.

Impact Analysis

Before we even talk about change, however, let's emphasize that little bell that should go off every time you, your users, your management, or the alerts triggered by the framework say that change is needed. That is, before making any changes to policies, you need to carefully weigh their impact. Between your identity and access management modules, you could conceivably enact erroneous policy or infrastructure changes resulting in

- Improper access, granting privileges to otherwise ineligible users
- Improper authorization, granting entry to otherwise ineligible groups of users
- Improper combinations of grants, leading to segregation of duties violations
- Modified authentication schemes that effectively keep everybody out, including legitimate users

Simple changes, such as adding or deleting access based on group membership, may not need much review. But more complex policies, based on attributes, inheritance, environmental factors, and any combination thereof, should be thoroughly reviewed. Also recall that changes to policies may result in automatic recalculation of existing user privileges, and the initiation of workflows to re-provision those privileges. Changes to the organizational structure could alter the approval chain. Changes in group definitions may grant or remove access based on modified memberships, which would also likely affect attestation.

Because policy structures are based on the specific task (grant privileges, challenge for authentication, make decisions on authorization, move users in and out of behavioral buckets, and so on), the way in which you gauge impact varies from solution to solution. We will cover these structures on an individual basis, shortly. Suffice it to say that outside of the simplest policies, it is advisable to move with caution.

Changes to Users and Policies

Not that we really need to restate this, but the most basic function of your IAM framework is to manage what access your users have to which resources. That access should be based, as much as possible, on policies that take into account users' attributes and memberships. This means that when those attributes or memberships change, those policies should be re-engaged so that access is re-evaluated. Think of it this way: If you change a user, you may trigger policies that must consider her new attributes. If you change the group or role that user is in, you have affected her indirectly, but again in a way that may trigger those same policies. To a group, a user is just a member. To the user, her groups are attribute values.

From the opposite perspective, if you change a policy, you have changed its scope, and will trigger it for those users who are affected by that change.

Several years ago, I received an urgent call from a customer in Detroit who had put a plug-in on his (singular) internal web server to mitigate requests for an internal app and prompt for credentials. He had made an untested change to the policy, the result of which was that nobody could be validated against the LDAP. He had effectively killed access, including to the GUI that allowed him to change the policy back. We were able to fix the problem at the command line, but for a panicky moment he thought he had permanently sealed off his web server, by making a modification whose results he did not anticipate.

Identity Changes

Over a five-year period at a very successful identity management venture, I went from Solutions Engineer to Engineering Manager to Central Region Engineering Director to Director of Field Support. All my wife wanted to know, whenever I got new business cards, was how much more airport time I'd be logging.

When it comes to IAM, this is one of the things that surprisingly enough gets glossed over quite a bit: People don't leave an organization quite the same way they come in. You're hired for one thing, but you end up doing another. Even within the organization I'm currently in, I came in for one function, and migrated through a second before ending up as a third. And when you change, so do your approvals and privileges. There's a common use case (yes, I'm sure you're sick of that term by now), with several variations, called *When Harry Met Sally*. Here's the more robust version:

- Harry is hired and provisioned.
- Harry is transferred and gets a new boss.
- Harry gets promoted and gets yet another boss as well as direct reports.
- Harry can now provision other users.
- Harry hires and provisions Sally.
- Sally transfers to a new boss, marries Harry, and changes her last name.
- Harry gets fired.
- Sally changes her last name back.
- Sally gets promoted and takes Harry's old job.

In reality, this represents multiple use cases, all of which are legitimate tests of how your policies and workflow definitions manage change. A single "change," such as a termination, may trigger multiple workflow segments. Harry must be removed from multiple resources, notifications must be generated, and of course an audit trail is created. In addition, another user may need to be provisioned to critical functions Harry fulfilled.

Too often, a change that does not include termination fails to adequately restate access rights. Let's recall another redundant term: least privilege. One of the biggest failings of provisioning, and much of it because of manual processes, is that it doesn't properly relieve a user of her old permissions when she gets new ones. Not to say that you necessarily lose all old privileges, but you should lose the ones that you should lose.

True Story

A director in the accounting department of a software company was dragged into the financial side of the sales department. After making that move, he was still able to access corporate statements for the viewing pleasure of his new boss, who wanted to know what the CFO had in mind for his part of the business. This story turned out very, very badly.

Oh, and it's not just changes to the user's profile, it's also the objects created on behalf of the user.

True Story

While working for a small company that partnered with a larger company, I was sent overseas for an engagement at a joint customer. Unknown to me, I was labeled a consultant by the larger company, who put me on their e-mail system, as jeff.scheidel@megabigcorp.com. Nobody told me of this mail account, so I never used it, never had a password for it, never accessed it.

Fast forward a year, and I came to work for that larger company, at which time I was informed I could not have as my e-mail address jeff.scheidel@megabigcorp.com, since it was already taken.

ME: "Wait, there can't be another guy with my name here."

THEM: "No, no, that's you. When you were a consultant, we gave you a super-secret e-mail address."

ME: "I didn't know that. Well, can't I just have that address?"

THEM: "No, that was provisioned for a consultant, and you're now an employee. Here's your new account, with your middle initial inserted."

Okay, whatever. One extra letter and a dot, but livable. Except that the old account was left active, and I couldn't access it. Mails sent to it did not bounce, and so people who found it on the company directory and sent mail to it started complaining that I wasn't responding. That old e-mail account became a black hole. I asked for a simple fix: forward those mails to my new address. No forwarding allowed, they said. I asked that they then kill the account. "Can't do that, you're an active employee." Huh?

I received complaints about unanswered e-mails for over a year, during which I lost valuable time, wasted other people's time, looked unresponsive to colleagues, and in two cases I was unable to respond promptly to time-sensitive matters. I finally found a sympathetic e-mail admin who simply broke the rules and deleted the old account manually.

This is a classic case of the need for re-provisioning: responding to change. I morphed from consultant to full-time employee, and the system broke.

I worked an engagement for a financial services client who, in better economic times, onboarded 12,000 new users a year, offloaded 6,000, and in between logged *72,000 changes*. People moved around, changed positions, departments, or geographic locations, were promoted, shifted from consultant to full-time employee, whatever. They specifically invited us in to help manage these transitions.

Lousy scenario #1: "Alice, good luck with the transfer to the home office. I'm taking away all your access today. When you get to your new cubicle, give me a ring, and I'll give you all your *new* access."

There's no rhyme or reason to this, no guarantee that Alice's transition will be handled correctly, and on top of that, Alice won't be ready to hit the ground running on the first day of her new slot.

Lousier scenario #2: "Alice, give me a ring when you get to your new cubicle, and I'll give you your new access."

Wrong. As Alice moves to a new part of the forest, you need to erase her old breadcrumbs. *At any given point in time, you should only have the access you need right there and then.* There needs to be a policy in place that automatically re-provisions Alice into her new and proper access rights while removing her old ones.

But remember the thing about legitimate exceptions? Here's a place for another one. Alice moves on, but her old boss will need help transitioning her duties for the next couple of weeks while she's training a replacement. So you may allow Alice to keep both sets of duties for a finite period, but there must be a cut-off, after which her old rights automatically evaporate, or a scheduled attestation event sweeps them away. Many IAM systems out there can't handle this simple scenario.

Source of Authority on User Changes

Basing changes to users on HR events is an ideal, but is also difficult to pull off in total. Let's review that ideal, the hurdles to it, and the compromise.

IAM should reflect the business, and HR represents the "business side of the business" to IAM. Therefore using HR to drive changes from the top seems to be the best course. IT is supposed to be a tool, the means rather than the ends, especially in non technical organizations. Human Resources is also a good, central authoritative source recognized by the entire enterprise. The bulk of a user's responsibilities should be derived from business-based definitions such as roles, groups, and organizational memberships.

However, it's highly doubtful that a user's profile will support all possible granularity for exceptions, emergencies, or delegated administration. It almost certainly won't cover the minutiae of ever-changing database roles governing tables or columns.

Reporting on IT change events won't be done at an HR level anyway, nor will security audits. Granular access *should* be mapped all the way back to business roles or groups, job titles, job codes, and so on, but OIM and OIA can handle that readily.

Often, granular privileges that aren't derived originally from business-level grants are provided because of unexpected duties that become necessary through changes, anomalous events, *things that come up*. Break-in? Grant privileges to servers and system logs for forensic work. Illness or termination affects the chain of command on a set of resources? Until somebody is officially handed the needed duties, somebody else has to fill in.

When Temporary Changes Become Permanent

But these kinds of events spawn two concerns: staying secure and compliant, and deciding when the anomalous becomes the norm. In other words, you react to unexpected situations by instantiating some kind of change, and once the event you've reacted to is in hand, you need to put things right. This doesn't necessarily mean putting it back the way it was, but whatever the decision, you need to make sure it's in agreement with corporate polices going forward. If you have provided temporary access and were unable or unwilling to put a time bomb on it (making the grant time-sensitive), then you absolutely need a process in place to either change it back or revalidate it. For the latter purpose, OIM provides attestation. As we've already discussed, attestation is meant for periodic access review, typically meaning months apart. However, for special cases those periods may be drastically shrunk.

If you decide that temporary changes need to become permanent, then it's time to turn those changes from exceptions into rules by redefining policy. If those changes translate into SoD violations and notifications, you might be getting alerts popping up from Oracle Identity Manager workflow or Oracle Identity Analytics. "John.Smith is trying to exercise privilege-2 that is in conflict with privilege-1, which he already has." You should *not* be forever hammering that nail back in. There is no consistency to it, and just because you are familiar with the situation and keep approving it, that doesn't mean that the person who replaces you in that function later will understand what's been going on, and your auditors certainly won't understand it. If you can justify it, then you change your policies to reflect the new violation-free policy. If you can't justify it, then you have a problem.

Changes to Roles

Direct resource grants, while not a highly scalable way to provision, at least require human intervention, whereas RBAC involves the aggregation and inclusion of multiple resources in the context of a role that indirectly grants those resources. The individual resources will still be subject to approvals, of course, but my point is that a single business grant results in multiple IT grants. Therefore change to roles cannot be taken lightly (which is why we discussed role governance and role owners to ensure appropriate changes). These changes can be

- Mapping of nested roles to business roles
- Mapping of IT entitlements to resource roles
- Dynamic role policies
- Association of roles with the business hierarchy

It could be as simple as a business analyst or manager adding a newly deployed resource to a role with approvals by the role or resource owner, or something more complex, such as the analysis of existing user-privilege data on a legacy system. You may ask, what is the difference between mapping the privileges on an old app or a new app? And the answer is, it's not just how you would like it to be mapped, but how it has been historically used, with the presumption being that users have *mostly* been granted the privileges they should have.

Regular role certifications (as through Oracle Identity Analytics) serve to keep role entitlements in line with current compliance and functional requirements. You might also consider, rather than adding entitlements to existing roles, spinning off new clusters of entitlements into new resource-level roles, for a very good reason: flexibility. Large, too-inclusive roles are harder to split apart later when you find a conflict between the entitlements within a role (for example, SoD).

But this should only be done after a thorough review, which is what certification is all about. Remember that we're trying to avoid that classic problem of 5,000 users and 50,000 roles. If you've done proper role design to begin your new life within the framework, don't let role creep ruin it now.

Changes to the Organization

Your company may not reorganize on a massive scale on a regular basis—you would certainly hope not—but on a smaller scale, it happens with some degree of frequency. Having been in a position to provide technical support to sales organizations for many years, I've seen this chronic approach: When sales are down, something is wrong, so scramble everything; when sales are up, we need to maximize profits, so scramble everything. No matter what you're doing, you need to do it differently. Another thing I've witnessed over the years is the notion that in order to better safeguard a troubled group or resource, put it under the finance department, where presumably they're more vigilant. When I ran an IT department in the mid-eighties, my department was placed under the controller's in order to safeguard us from a flood of custom code requests. A couple of years later, at another company, IT was placed under finance when it was discovered that my boss was an idiot. In both cases, the result was an increased budget but a much tougher approval process. This is exactly the kind of process you would expect.

When reorganizations happen in a statically defined structure, they can result in some very ugly transitions. Users lose access, group memberships get fouled up, workflows no longer function, approval and reporting structures are broken. In a reorganization, memberships change because, while the users themselves didn't change, the world in which they live *did* change. If you move a group or department, your system should react by re-provisioning, *if* it supports structural change dynamically.

In 1998 I was managing a regional engineering group that fell under an engineering department that supported sales. We weren't officially part of the sales group, but we paralleled them. The following illustration shows the organizational chart.

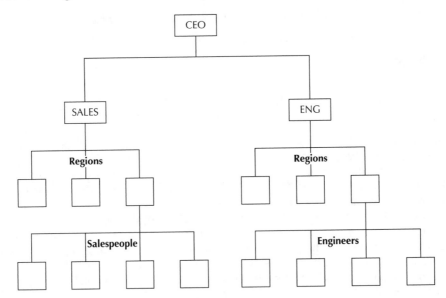

Then somebody decided the sales engineers should come under sales. I moved from reporting to an engineering honcho to reporting to a regional sales manager. Naturally, everybody who worked with me came along for the ride, as shown in the following illustration.

By performing this action, management (unwittingly) affected the entire approval and system reporting structure. Unfortunately for us at the time, most of our provisioning was all manual. Fortunately for us at the time, most of our provisioning was all manual. In other words, the ugly, time-consuming process of manually enabling users saved us from facing the fact that none of our systems could handle a reorganization.

In an ideal situation, as with the Oracle IAM suite, the identity platform allows you to model this structural change (as with organizational management in OIM and OIA), then have all members of the affected nodes re-provisioned automatically. So instead of going to every single member to scramble their access rights, the framework recognizes that all members are affected, and recalculates their access. Approvals are appropriately routed, as are attestation approvals, provided they are defined as routing users to their respective managers.

In this example, approval for expenses would be routed up the chain from the field to the regional sales manager instead of the regional engineering manager. Approvals for travel and resource access, appraisals, and so on, should all be automatically reconfigured for every member of an affected group. This is what *policies* are all about. Those same policies that gave me my access on my first day get recalculated because either the policies or my information was modified. In this case, I was affected, along with my peers and underlings.

If you have created discrete groups within OIM, with no true organizational structure, then modifying the definitions of those groups, or the association of resources with groups, will affect user access only within that group, as opposed to any inherited scope.

NOTE
When designing a corporate directory (white pages), it's advisable not to design it to reflect the organizational structure, so as to protect that directory from organizational changes.

Changes to Resources

It's not just your users who have a life cycle within the organization. Resources likewise have a beginning, a middle, and an end to their existence, the difference being that their middle is usually longer than any one individual. In the mid-80s, I wrote an application for a company that predated even client-server, and it was finally web-enabled years later, with the essential code surviving all those years.

You might apply version control to policies, resources, or roles. And workflow is meant to handle any kind of change, whether it's creation, modification, or termination. But while IAM is not primarily a change tool, the Oracle suite supports an easier migration of both Oracle and non-Oracle components while minimizing the impact on users.

The modular nature of the Oracle suite allows you to swap out back-end pieces while maintaining continuity. Resources (including the configuration for communicating with them) are defined as separate objects within OIM. With authentication chaining in OAM, with a primary and secondary directory, the primary may eventually be migrated out in favor of a more robust and centralized directory. This has been practiced where users were distributed among multiple directories (because of mergers and legacy environments) that were used for both provisioning and authentication/authorization and, as the user accounts were consolidated, the additional directories were eliminated. By moving users from one data source to another, one group or branch at a time, you are also testing this consolidation incrementally. When it comes to access management, these directories don't even have to be the same flavor; they simply have to share credential requirements. Oracle Virtual Directory can also front for these multiple directories, providing a single aggregate view of multiple sources. At cut-off time, you are authenticating against a modified view of the consolidated directory.

Within an OIM workflow, you have a business decision flow that is different from the execution flow. That is to say, a workflow definition that walks a user request through approval (and automated) steps calls out to the logic that actually executes actions on endpoints. This means that you can make changes to the order of those steps without affecting how they are executed. For example, you know that as part of the workflow for granting access to a particular application, Joe needs to be alerted. But how is he alerted? By e-mail? By text message? Does a new item show up on his to-do list in the OIM console, and nothing more?

The notification may not change, but the way in which a user is added to a resource may change. It's not uncommon in deployments with a broad selection of legacy systems, with existing "automation" of account creation, to keep those old scripts in place until such a time as they might be replaced with more current technology. I'm talking about shell scripts, or little C++ programs, or even stored procedures in a database. When you add approval workflow on top of these tasks, so that account creation in a particular system is now part of a larger role-based provisioning strategy, that endpoint "connector" may simply be integrated into your new OIM workflow and eventually swapped out in favor of a non-proprietary, standards-based connector. Or not. It depends on priority. Much as I might recommend that customers migrate to a standard connector, it's hard to argue with "It's working, so why mess with it?"

A change to the resource itself can also ripple back to the security solution. If you have protected the contents of a folder with an access policy on that folder, that protection doesn't follow those contents when you move them, unless you've protected the parent folder and keep them in that tree. Understand the scope of your protection so that your solution can continue to do its job.

Schema Changes

Abstraction is used in many ways within the Oracle suite: to put a friendly face on provisioning with the use of business roles; to enable you to collect related objects (roles, users, grouped resources) for management, security, and provisioning purposes; and to provide access to digital assets while obscuring their true nature or location from any unauthorized user or client. Oracle Virtual Directory also provides abstraction by presenting a secured LDAP view of data sources whose true nature and origin need to be masked. Another benefit of this creation of views is the ability to minimize impact of schema and data changes in remote sources and targets on developers and other clients. Modifications to data dictionaries can wreak havoc on downstream applications whose querying and updating ability is immediately affected by changes to back-end definitions. If your developers are managing integrations through OVD, querying a common virtual schema, then any necessary changes can be made there in the *mapping* between the sources and the LDAP interface so that any changes to back-end schema do not impact their applications.

Validating Policy Changes: Impact Analysis

We've talked about how policies manage change for your users. But what about when the policies themselves change? New compliance regulations, new resources, new management, new acquisitions, new attack types, all translate to new policies. How you provision, how you authorize, how you do everything, will eventually evolve, with some components being more dynamic than others.

When you're making changes to policies, you want to make sure you're doing the right thing, that you will hit what you are aiming for. For simple policies, for example, adding a group membership to the access rule for a resource might sound easy enough. But the policy may require more complex decision making:

- EMPL-Status IS full-time
- Membership IS Accounting-group   AND
- Membership IS NOT Auditing-group   AND
- Title CONTAINS "Manager"

Or

- EMPL-Status IS contractor
- Membership IS Auditing-group

Here you might want to ensure that that your policy execution results in *only* the right people receiving the grant. It gets more complex when you start taking into consideration hierarchical rules, resource trees, organizational structures, or roles. Inheritance may be a tricky thing. And what about dependencies? "Everybody from this organizational unit on down receives everything in this directory tree *except* this one subfolder."

Backing out an improper grant can also be tricky, if you're not sure who all received it. So what's the answer? Impact analysis, what-if scenarios, simulations, whatever you want to call them, give you a crystal ball.

BI Publisher gives you a consistent interface and process for enterprise reporting across the Oracle IAM suite. But because policies are constructed in different ways for different purposes, there are different procedures for conducting impact analysis. Let's check them out one at a time.

What-If: Oracle Access Manager

The OAM Policy Tester lets you simulate a user from a particular IP address accessing a particular resource (and performing a particular operation, for example, PUT, POST, GET, and so on) and viewing the results, including finding out which rules are executed by the simulated access attempt. In this case, it's not as simple as finding out whether the test user is able to access the desired resource. You're looking for the entire response, which could include a redirect or additional challenge.

What-If: Oracle Identity Manager

In the previous chapter I discussed the wonderfully named Oracle Application Access Controls Governor (OAACG), the suite's cross-platform solution for segregation of duties (SoD) violation prevention and detection. It can be readily integrated with OIM to allow the provisioning of entitlements only after an SoD validation process. This allows for a preventive simulation approach to identify and correct possible conflicts in privilege grants, before final provisioning, This does, of course, require additional integration, but is made much easier when the resources are part of the Oracle E-Business Suite or PeopleSoft, and SAP, for which OAACG has predefined libraries.

What-If: Oracle Identity Analytics

In the governance of policies related to how and why users receive access, it's critical to know the impact of changes to any rules that actually decide who gets what. Providing improper access means users with access they shouldn't have, a security and compliance (that is, audit) no-no. Taking away access from someone who *should* have it means an interruption of service.

OIA provides preventive simulation of segregation of duties policies. This is done by creating a policy with potential violations, and instantly viewing those violations before that policy goes into production. This means seeing which users would be in violation. From this list, you can select who might go on an exception list. Think of the advantage here in avoiding interruptions of service. "Here are the people who will need to have these duties. We can keep them off the violation list in advance."

An additional advantage is proactively serving your audit needs. When you put those potential violators on an "exception allowed" list, you associate a date with them in order to determine how long that exception is allowed. In the meantime, every time they "violate" the rule, they won't be put on the "bad" list. When auditors find exceptions, they simply deem them as violations. But when those exceptions are fully documented and properly allowed, with a finite lifespan, they satisfy auditors by staying within established boundaries, and demonstrate process control. Further, by associating an end date with an exception, you prevent that exception from becoming a default rule, and require future review.

OIA also supports what-ifs in regard to role changes. If I modify this policy, who gets this role, and who loses this role? This is where role versioning and rollback come into play. Changes to roles that create unexpected results are caught in the approval process, and may then result in rolling back to an earlier version.

What-If: Oracle Entitlements Server

Oracle Entitlements Server (OES) operates in a granularity that is far deeper than standard sets of policies in any environment. It looks at the same user–resource pairing as access management, but then takes into account additional variables up to and including transactional elements. Who are you, what do you want to do with what resource, what are the hierarchical considerations, what's the amount you wish to transfer, who exactly are you transferring it to, and so on. The variations can be quite complex. Therefore you need to be able to validate, prior to production, these kinds of drill-down policies. OES includes a simulation tool for checking the validity of new or modified policies, regardless of their complexity. The Policy Simulator screen is shown in the following illustration.

This tool allows for what-if scenarios of OES policies. Similar to OAM, in OES you are simulating being a user taking a specified action against a resource. Upon "executing" this action, the tool responds with:

- The user's group memberships.

- The attributes required for evaluating any role or authorization policies relevant to the action. If any attributes have not been assigned values, you can do so at this time.

- The return values of any functions fired off through the role or authorization policies.

- The role policies executed and their resulting role memberships.

- The final authorization results (and policies executed).

If you do not see the desired results, or simply wish to try variations on the scenario, you can modify the listed values and run the simulation again.

Given the potential complexity of fine-grained entitlements policies, it is essential to be able to discern the possible paths that result from changes to those policies. Being that these decisions take place well beyond what the end user sees, by way of the interface you are controlling events in such a way that the results are not immediately interpreted by the user.

What-If: Oracle Adaptive Access Manager

With OAAM, you aren't just creating rules within policies. You have the ability to create entire models, and in fact overlapping models when necessary, to look at all possible aspects of user, group, resource, conditions, and behavior. For that matter, you're looking at the history of not only the user but the groups he belongs to. It's as comprehensive a model as it can be. The advanced risk modeling engine within OAAM enables you to simulate risk rules, and model risk scenarios, to validate the solution's response to various user actions and to proactively model behavior you may not even have seen yet. All this can be done without impact on the production environment.

When you're testing normal types of access policies, it could be as simple as an unauthorized user attempting to access a resource to which she is not entitled. But within OAAM, a user may be entitled to a resource, but only under certain conditions, such as from a trusted IP or registered device. Take that authorized user, and simulate her access attempt from a non-trusted IP, an unregistered device, outside a standard time period, or outside the boundaries of what has been established as standard behavior for her or the group/bucket to which she belongs.

Evolution of Risk Models

We've talked about the risk models and policies in Oracle Adaptive Access Manager. These tools enable security staff to model risk in order to battle fraud. OAAM makes use of various inputs in order to maintain risk scores that help determine the responses to requests. These inputs can be user profile and location, accessing device, workflow, historical data, and even third-party data. User activity and requests can be measured against patterns, or buckets of behavior, that link similar parties. Everyone in an office, for example, or everyone in a particular business unit, may be grouped for analysis. A baseline is established for a group and its behavior, and anomalous behavior is what raises the red flags. By the way, some users of OAAM will use it to monitor behavior and build that baseline for the first several weeks without enforcing any kind of policy. In this way, they discover the behavior patterns of their users to learn what they don't yet know about those users.

Let's revisit a couple of simpler examples. If I authenticate from the office, from within the firewall, from my usual machine, and perform normal duties, I'm fine, and the risk score is low. It's when I begin deviating from the norm that my risk is elevated. I'm asking for data, or volumes of data, that are not standard for me and/or the members of my group. I'm authenticating from a strange IP address or a handheld device. I'm requesting a resource I rarely access, and doing so in off-hours. And so on. The combination of these factors, along with the inputs I use to help with the decision-making, help determine the appropriate response. Not only might my request be denied or deferred, or I might be prompted for additional challenges during my session, but I might be moved to a different bucket, or at least made a candidate for it. "Keep this up, son, and we'll be watching you with a different set of factors." My current activity today becomes historical activity tomorrow, and will be used as part of the decision making the next time I make a request.

The point of establishing that baseline of behavior is that you have to start *somewhere*. Default models are available from Oracle, and can also be loaded from third parties. But from your perspective, your organization is unique, as are your resources and the people who access them. Therefore you will need to refine these models and rules so that they best enforce your security and business policies, generating the alerts, the responses, and the corrected risk assessments. Once again, the IAM framework must reflect the business, even as it evaluates risk, as in the following illustration.

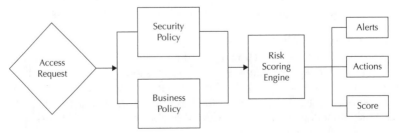

The evolution of adaptive risk is an iterative, cumulative process. The auto-learning capabilities of OAAM allow the framework and its administrators to learn over time. Out-of-band behavior leads to new models and the refinement of existing ones, which ultimately leads to a more accurate, more valuable solution that best reflects your users, your processes, and how the two interact. Between what you learn, and periodic policy updates from Oracle and from third parties, you can keep your framework current with the most recent threat profiles.

Adding Federation

Increasingly, federation is viewed more as an extension of an existing authentication and authorization model than a separate function. This is because *somebody* has to identify a user before that user can be sent out into the cloud for additional services. To this end, Oracle has devised a procedure for integrating Oracle Identity Federation (OIF) with Oracle Access Manager (OAM). OIF can be configured as an identity provider (IdP) or service provider (SP).

If OAM is managing the resources for incoming federated users, it is still doing its essential job, only now it must account for those users coming from elsewhere. You are still protecting your resources with policy domains, as covered in our chapters on authentication and authorization. But now you are providing an authentication scheme of federated SSO, utilizing SAML 1.0, SAML 2.0, Liberty, or WS-Federation. You may also recall how OAM uses security levels to allow SSO between resources that share a level. If your federated SSO authentication scheme is a lower level than your basic authentication scheme, users will be prompted for credentials even if the federated SSO succeeds.

In keeping with the gatekeeper architecture, an OAM WebGate must be installed on every web server through which federated users would access resources.

Accepting Recommendations from Auditors

Remember what I said about consultants and auditors: Their job is to find something wrong. If a single user has the wrong access, your entire process is broken. No matter how tight your operation is, there will be something to report on. If there's a Certified Information Systems Security Professional (CISSP) in the group, he will tell you your light bulbs are the wrong wattage. Sure, there are bound to be legitimate issues, and at least some of the recommendations will be useful. Depending on your national, state, or provincial laws, you may well be subject to legal requirements for remedying your issues in a swift manner. Expect zero tolerance on some issues, and wiggle room on others. There is definitely validity to the statement, "If we found two users with improper access, how many are there we haven't found yet?"

Auditors do this for a living because (presumably) they know what they're doing. Therefore it's also valid to ask them for recommendations. If you don't have your own plan for remediating issues, then following *their* plan has two benefits. First, it's a solution. That simple. The other benefit is, it covers your behind. Also that simple. If you follow the recommendations of the people whose opinions are supposed to carry the most weight, then how can you go wrong?

When you are fixing the problems found by an auditor, you are actually addressing two sets of problems. First is the actual set of cases they've discovered. Users with incorrect access, resources with insufficient protection, privilege assignments with SoD violations, all must be set right. Even if your policies appear to be correct, improper access may have occurred between that window where they were assigned and when reconciliation or attestation were executed. You may not want to wait until reconciliation or attestation is run again. In a typical OIM environment, reconciliation is scheduled to run on a fairly regular basis, but attestation events for a specific resource occur anywhere between a few months and an entire year apart. Therefore you may choose to use the OIM console to manually correct those improper access points.

The second issue to correct is the policies or procedures themselves. How do improper access grants occur? Are they incorporated incorrectly within the definition of a role? Or are they being manually granted and approved? Temporary grants (that end up being semi-permanent) often show up as errors in compliance audits. When these turn chronic, it's likely in particular areas of the business, where 1) it seems necessary to the business, and 2) administrators have the necessary knowledge to grant that access. This may be a good use case for scheduling more regular attestation as a safety net.

In Chapter 4, we discussed the variable nature of global laws. In some countries, what constitutes "control" or "privacy" is spelled out in great detail. In others, it is open to interpretation. In such a case, the solution may also be open to interpretation, as in "here's how we plan on fixing that." And just as you don't deploy everything at once (don't boil the ocean, remember?), you don't make wholesale changes or upgrades at once either, and this includes your fixes. Remember our previous discussion on impact analysis. Make sure your fixes have the desired result.

One more point on audits: I have had multiple customers who have paid penalties, some of them large, in place of implementing solutions. These often relate to cleaning up improper access or runaway directory groups. One powerful reason for tying the creation and use of Active Directory groups directly to role definitions in OIA and access policies in OIM is to prevent the random use of those groups. By mandating that groups can only be generated as part of a larger policy, you are cutting down drastically on the proliferation that causes so many organizations so many compliance headaches.

As long as we're on the subject of audits, let's digress a moment on the kinds of data that auditors care about when they take core samples of data. Oracle Identity Manager takes an audit snapshot each time there's a change in one or more data elements that make up a user profile snapshot. Changes are the result of events, and the events that trigger new snapshots are

- A change to a user's record via an adapter action, admin or user action, reconciliation, and so on
- A change in a user's group memberships
- Provisioning/re-provisioning/de-provisioning of user access
- Changes in status or process of user resources
- Changes to policies that affect the user

Changes to Infrastructure

Years ago there was a TV show episode in which a young woman enters a contest run by a dress shop to design a fancy new dress. The woman sews up something amazing, then adds hundreds of sequins and buttons, creating a masterpiece and winning the contest. She then asks the shop owner how many dresses she wants for resale. "None," the owner replies. "It's a beautiful dress, but it's got so many frills on it, you could never wash it, so who'd buy it?"

This further reminds me of a guy I knew who got his kids a puppy that would one day turn into a giant dog. "You're too lazy for that," I told him. "You won't take care of it, and neither will your kids." Sure enough, the thing turned out to be unruly, was left alone too much, became just about unmanageable, and eventually they had to give the dog away to somebody who could actually handle it.

The moral of the stories? Never build or buy something you can't take care of. Yes, you devised a plan to gather requirements, chose a solution, and deployed, but you also need to decide in advance how to take care of it. In other words, you need a plan for the decidedly unglamorous job of *maintenance*.

This is the stuff behind the scenes, the actual components that make the business solution run. You have app servers, database servers, directories, web services, you name it. You need to monitor their health (which we'll discuss in more detail in Chapter 19). You need to move pieces from development to test to production. And you need to manage upgrades and patches.

Built into the Oracle Identity Manager admin console is the Deployment Manager, which assists in migrating configuration data between instances. It allows you to export and import that data, consisting of those objects or definitions that create the backbone of your provisioning and user management framework. This is ideal when moving from development to test to production, or when replicating a tested environment to another location or instance. Define it, beat up on it, and when the model fits what it is you are trying to accomplish, only then do you make it live.

One side note: when you move your configuration, you might want to bring some test data with you. Creating data in large volumes can be difficult, and if you simply scramble production data, you may lose all useful pointers and continuity. Oracle Data Masking allows you to appropriately and consistently mask sensitive fields within production data, maintaining referential integrity so that you can make use of that data in a test environment without compromising it.

Twenty-Four/Seven Availability

A significant chunk of the Oracle documentation involves the checklists you need to follow when performing upgrades. This includes the individual components, backing up configuration data, and the recovery procedures for when an intended upgrade fails, for whatever reason. In the 24×7 world of web interfaces, web services, remote access and telecommuting, there's often no such thing as total downtime. As an old DBA back in 1987, I remember sending out weekly bulletins informing the users that all services were down between 5 P.M. on Wednesdays and 7 A.M. on Thursdays for backups and general maintenance. But we really can't run web-based services that way. If your business applications can replicate themselves for high availability, your IAM framework should support it as well, with little to no interruption of service.

You have more than one web server, correct? This means if you've got OAM in place, you've got multiple WebGates. They can be upgraded in subsets, as can your admin servers. You might still schedule maintenance time during which you've got partially limited throughput, but you should never be completely down. You should also take into consideration backward compatibility, since there is no solution that exists as a single piece of code, but rather as integrated components which have to take the leap together. For example, you can specifically operate older WebGates with newer admin servers (with the setting of a compatibility flag) during the course of an upgrade. As of OAM 10.1.4.2, Oracle supports the notion of "zero downtime upgrades" that keep you up and running while you put up a new release.

CHAPTER
14

Legacy Considerations

Preserve the old, but know the new.
          —Chinese proverb

et's repeat my same old tired but entirely necessary mantra again: Your IAM framework must reflect the business, not the other way around. It is meant to secure your existing business functions and make them more efficient by taking security and compliance off the shoulders of your business analysts and developers, and centralizing security policies in the hands of those who do security for a living. By putting the framework in place, we're going to provide value-added services to your existing apps, including those that might be considered "legacy" because of their age or technology base. IAM needs to speak the language of older systems and components in order to bring them into the fold. One very important function of the framework is participation: Everybody can now get into the pool. It's how you enforce security and compliance; it's how users and admins can enjoy the benefits of that security and compliance.

Definition of Legacy

First, let's define legacy. When I was considered a client-server "expert," legacy meant one primary thing, the mainframe. In the present tense, it's still funny to me to hear somebody talk about their legacy PowerBuilder apps. I work with kids now who learned XML in college and ask me if I need help crossing the street.

When I first entered the industry in the early 80s, a lot of people were predicting the replacement of the mainframe with the "mini-computer," that is, System/38, RS6000, AS/400, Solaris boxes, and the like. But there are still a lot of mainframes out there, because they're reliable and capable of a large volume of number-crunching. So while COBOL might be clunky, and RPG is indescribably painful, they still have their place. Along with those older systems, we still have RACF, ACF2, Top Secret, and DB2, and I regularly have to discuss how IAM supports those. On a smaller scale, plenty of organizations still host fat-client applications.

My personal definition of legacy is any platform that's too big or necessary to get rid of, but on which you won't be doing any more major development. Uncle Leon's too old to help with the storm windows or the gardening, but he's part of the family, he's not going anywhere, and he still helps with the dishes.

Legacy systems can be more costly as maintenance on discontinued hardware or end-of-life software gets increasingly expensive. It becomes harder to find the right expertise, and you're keeping large boxes or antiquated tools around for applications that ultimately have little future. (Of course, Y2K was such a concern because so many years ago, developers assumed incorrectly that their short-sighted COBOL code would be long gone before they had to worry about four-digit year formats.) To some degree, legacy systems are problematic simply because they're difficult to communicate with, as they were designed before WAN and the web were invented. By connecting them to your IAM framework, you can make those interactions more efficient.

Legacy Business, Legacy Identity

For our discussion, we have to examine both sides of the equation. First, you have legacy *business* apps that must be made secure and compliant. In fact, with regard to the IAM framework, legacy pretty much covers anything that must be hooked up to identity and access systems. Existing applications, databases, directories, and services need to participate in the framework for provisioning, authentication, authorization, single sign-on, and auditing. These resources were the whole reason you started evaluating IAM in the first place.

Second, you undoubtedly have legacy *identity* components. There are user accounts, a source of truth against which they must authenticate, and at the very least some group memberships dictating high-level access policies. If nothing else, you have manual processes for enabling those users to access your business resources. If you are considering a newer, more robust IAM solution, then you likely do not have a central platform for creating, tracking, and auditing the users, resources, and processes that make up identity and access control. Our goal here is to unify the pieces, put them in a larger context, and give you complete control. Ultimately, they should not be pieces, but integrated components.

It's also most likely that the older or more disconnected of your current identity components are going away. When you're talking about smaller components (workflows, services, scripts, databases), participation with the framework can help preserve those investments, even though it may only be temporary, while you migrate them out in favor of more modern technologies. On the other hand, augmentation and extension of older tech with newer tech, for both identity and business apps, may give those components a longer shelf life. We'll examine all these possibilities in the next few pages.

IAM Components to Keep

The common problems with legacy IdM components are that

- They usually are only extensions of manual processes.
- They have no framework around them to make them part of a total solution.
- They have been customized over time to adapt to changing needs.

Manual processes, even when facilitated by some portion of automation, are still manual. When it's used for provisioning, a help desk application is barely better than a legal pad. These processes also are running in silos. You need to make them part of a framework that gives you that control and consistency. Compliance is nearly impossible when you cannot enforce consistent policies across all domains, departments, groups, resources, and users. However, you've put time and money into these components, so the more you can reasonably preserve that investment (meaning don't keep something just to keep it, if it's not doing the job), the better the cost savings. When you are making that pitch to management to acquire budget for an IAM solution, it's always a better story when you can tell them you can keep parts of your existing "solution."

Help Desk

At far too many places, the help desk app *is* the bulk of provisioning, and this isn't what it's meant for. It's meant to track tickets, issues, requests, and problems. But the inputs are e-mails and phone calls, rather than proper workflow, and the outputs are manual reactions to those messages. So while the help desk app might provide support for a manual process, it's still just a crutch. So how, and why, do you involve it in a larger picture?

It may very well be that notification via help desk *is* the last stop in the provisioning or account creation for a particular resource. There will always be some endpoints that require a human being fat-fingering account information (unfortunately), with the notification coming via a help desk ticket. But you can make that ticket initiation, and even its closing, part of the framework's process.

Most help desk systems have at least one or two ways of initiating tickets other than a keyboard. One is e-mail notification. Send an e-mail to the help desk server, with a standard format for the subject, and the application acts accordingly. A good example of an app that allows this is BMC Remedy, perhaps the most common help desk app on the market. In fact, with many help desk apps, you can also modify or close a ticket via e-mail as well. By making e-mail notification part of a workflow definition, you can include the help desk application as a stop in a provisioning workflow, and Oracle Identity Manager has the ability to launch e-mails from workflow.

But for more granular control, when possible you should take advantage of API-level connectivity. Not only is it better performing, it provides more detailed communication. Oracle Identity Manager provides two different connectors for BMC Remedy, one for User Management, and one for Ticket Management.

The OIM connector for user management is designed to create users in Remedy itself. BMC Remedy can be used as a trusted source for identity reconciliation, so that users can be created or modified with input from Remedy. Corresponding OIM user accounts can also be updated, to keep all accounts in sync. In this way, OIM acts as the clearinghouse for user information. Remember that Remedy will only be one of the target systems in the overall framework, even within a single workflow definition. This connector can also be used in provisioning mode, in which data about users in Remedy is used for provisioning resources to those users. Any changes to user profile data can also be synched from OIM to Remedy, whether originating from *another* target system or entered via the OIM console. Reconciliation can be accomplished via a scheduled task (and in fact, it *should* be).

The OIM connector for ticket management is designed to create help desk tickets in Remedy. Through reconciliation (again, in a scheduled task), information on tickets can be retrieved into OIM, but typically involving only those records that were provisioned from OIM in the first place. These are identified by a custom field populated in Remedy through OIM.

These connectors make use of the Remedy API for performance and granular control. Through this architecture, which is shown in the following illustration, Remedy serves as both a target and a source, and can be part of an overall scheme in which Remedy is only one stop, for example in a workflow definition in which multiple sources are consulted and multiple targets are provisioned. Now the help desk is no longer on its own island, but inside the framework. Policies can be constructed to not only automate the tickets, reducing some (if not most) of that manual aspect, but also to include the help desk as an item in an ordered list of provisioning steps.

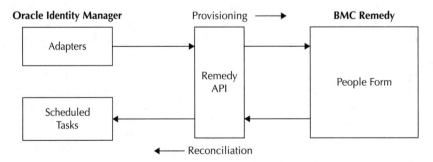

The connector uses the Remedy API to create user accounts in Remedy's People Form during provisioning, and fetch user data from the People Form for reconciliation

Workflow

As we've said before, an advantage of the way OIM separates business logic from execution logic in the workflow engine is the ability to take advantage of existing workflow or other decision-making processes already in place. In other words, OIM workflow operates at two levels, with the ordered steps handing off to the components that actually perform the granular work. At various clients I've seen multiple workflow engines in place, and this separation allows you to preserve those workflows for as long as necessary.

In such a situation think of the OIM workflow as processing the steps necessary for the bigger picture, the multiple resources relevant to a role or group membership, while the silo workflows handle multiple steps required for a single resource. It also has the layer for specifying granular steps necessary for executing provisioning tasks. However, if a discrete workflow has a small number of steps (like *one*), then you should seriously consider claiming it within the larger OIM workflow, where it can at least be tracked, if not configured. Meanwhile, it is possible to frame those older workflow definitions with OIM workflow, which is essentially calling out to them and maintaining state while awaiting a response or completed condition.

Here's a situation where you would not want to do this, however. A customer had built their own workflow with .NET, without any knowledge of how to do such a thing. They only used it for notifications to the help desk, at which time administrators would manually provision. On top of that, their workflow broke on a nightly basis, requiring regular cleanup and manual intervention. When they had me in to help guide them to a better situation, the head developer asked, "How much of our existing workflow can you preserve?" I told him, quite honestly, all of it, but we didn't want to do that. I explained that if we wrapped their workflow with OIM workflow, creating request management at the front end and adding automated provisioning on the back end, the whole framework would still be held hostage to regular breakdowns in the middle. This is called putting lipstick on a pig.

Directories

You already have user stores in place, probably more than one, although likely just one for authentication. But now that you're running a framework, your existing schema may be inadequate for your new provisioning and single sign-on needs. Role definitions, group memberships, personalization attributes, and other elements that were unnecessary before are now indispensable.

Has your new framework created more overhead? Absolutely. But these new elements are facilitators for powerful new functionality. However, you have options for extending your existing user stores.

Directory administrators usually despise schema changes for extending user definitions or creating cross-platform roles—all the more reason to put an abstract in front of the directory. Oracle Internet Directory can not only front for an existing user store, providing a place to make those schema changes and extensions, it can also synchronize changes to and from multiple directories. For example, as we discussed previously, Enterprise User Management can be used for defining global roles, with the necessary metadata being stored in OIM, keeping your back-end store "clean." Your original directory then stores the actual profile data, with OIM providing the extensions. You can make use of those silo stores (despite their lack of necessary extensions) while still gaining the benefit of a centralized directory for identity management.

You can also extend those legacy stores, aggregating identity data from multiple sources and transforming it for application use, without actual data replication, using Oracle Virtual Directory. OVD can serve up non-LDAP data, such as from databases and web services, for use by applications expecting an LDAP interface. A common hurdle to consolidating multiple source directories is the lack of a standard schema (which can be as much a political issue as technical). By putting forth a virtual view (or a choice of views), without the need to copy data, you might give new life to that legacy data.

Authentication Schemes

Basic, basic over SSL, Kerberos, hard token—whatever authentication method you are using, you chose it because it fulfilled your security requirements and it was supported by your infrastructure (which you might have built so that it *would* fulfill your requirements). But just as you can incorporate disparate workflows or user stores into the central framework, you can bring your authentication schemes into the framework as well, with even greater savings and ease of administration.

Silo authentication mechanisms can be retired in favor of a centralized process, which can also support multiple authentication schemes. Now those authentication schemes become simple configurations in a shared service. That same service also provides single sign-on.

Instead of merely synchronizing existing modules, Oracle Access Manager can directly provide authentication services (including supporting, although not generating, Kerberos tickets). And by configuring single sign-on, it can remove the need for supporting multiple authentication servers. If you place OAM in front of your apps, using WebGates and AccessGates at the policy enforcement points, it can intercept requests and enforce a central authentication scheme for resources that share security requirements. OAM may be enforcing authentication from an existing scheme (for example, Active Directory or LDAP), but it can apply that scheme across all similarly secured resources. Once you have configured OAM to provide credentials for those resources, you require only a single authoritative source for authentication.

Single sign-on can also be provided for legacy fat-client applications through Oracle Enterprise Single Sign-On (eSSO).

Scripts, Libraries, and Other Provisioning Bits

IT personnel don't usually write account-creation scripts for laughs, but rather out of necessity. They may even hook these up to workflow engines for scheduled events. As of this writing, I have visited three clients in the last month who rely heavily on cron jobs (not necessarily the best scheduler) to run homegrown scripts for point provisioning. If it's as simple as creating an operating system or LDAP account, you might want to consider using an out-of-the-box connector, which can not only be tracked but also configured via OIM. But if more complex logic is involved, and there are other priorities to focus on, you might consider keeping that script or code, at least for now, and including it in an OIM workflow. This is one of the reasons Oracle separates provisioning and approval workflows, for the ability to manage disparate connections without impacting business requirements.

Existing libraries of identity and access objects do not have to be automatically migrated to the new framework. User profiles, application-specific stores, roles, and segregation of duties lists can all be referenced as needed:

- By OIM for provisioning
- By OAM for authentication and authorization
- By OAAM for policy evaluation
- By OIM, OES, or OAACG for preventive or detective SoD

While SoD definitions and enforcement might be better handled by a solution such as OAACG, it is those definitions themselves that are hardest to create, since they typically require in-depth knowledge of the endpoint application.

IdM Discards

So while preserving homegrown pieces may provide short-term cost savings and limit the disruptions that come with a total replacement, there is also value in retiring certain components, even if they are still effectively functioning. Maintaining these separate pieces, continuing to customize them through separate interfaces, and integrating through different protocols creates a larger window for inaccuracy, inconsistency, and security/compliance issues. The job security they represent seems like a bad trade-off for the lack of centralized control.

Those discrete workflow engines we just discussed might be better off retired, replacing them with a flexible, multistep, enterprise workflow engine such as that built into Oracle Identity Manager, which has the additional advantage of keeping approvals and connections as separate "threads." Naturally, using a consistent interface for managing workflow will ensure a greater level of consistency, providing for delegated administration of this function by resource, and allowing you to build in both serial and parallel processes that include dependencies, escalations, and notifications.

Stand-alone, endpoint provisioning scripts and processes might also be candidates for retirement. Provisioning code that requires cron jobs or manual initiation should either be replaced with standard adapters or at the very least brought into the standard workflow construct. OIM's Adapter Factory provides a graphical interface for rapidly creating integrations with target systems, without the need for coding or scripting, and giving you the option to replace legacy scripts. Yes, we just discussed the notion of, "if it works, just keep it." However, a single point of configuration and management of these connection pieces is a great advantage in continuity.

At the very least, your manual processes should largely disappear. All provisioning tasks should be primarily initiated by HR, resource requests, or other change events, fetched into the framework via reconciliation, then driven through approvals and completion by workflow definitions.

The practice of using your help desk app as a workflow or provisioning engine should also be retired. It's a fine place to track user concerns, and it can certainly interface with OIM for both provisioning and reconciliation, but should *not* be a means unto itself. In a few pages, we'll discuss how to make use of the help desk within the context of the framework.

Let's point directly at a couple of types of "resources" that should be retired as soon as possible:

- Any component or process that "integrates" by creating data dumps that must be manually moved and subsequently imported into another process or database

- Any process or script that must be manually initiated, making a human being that single point of failure

While workflow steps may involve notifying a human to take action (to provision physical assets such as phones, laptops, and tokens), that step itself is further governed (by proper workflow definition) by notifications and escalations. Approvers are notified by e-mail to perform approvals. If they fail to do so in a timely fashion, they can be nagged, again by e-mail or other means, with the next step being escalation to a manager or process owner. Notifications and escalations are automated, with the results automatically audited.

IdM Sources to Mine for Data

Even those existing components you will retire might still provide some data on which you can build your future solution. They contain useful history, audit data, definitions, profiles, and other objects that you can make use of. Before you drive that old car into the swamp, clean out the trunk first. Besides the obvious historic value, this approach can further boost your story with management with regard to preserving your investment. More than once, I've seen where, even in the face of utter necessity, management has balked at additional investment because of their anger over perceived waste in previous expenditures. At a large manufacturer in the Midwestern United States a few years ago, our internal advocate at the customer told me that they needed to replace their existing authorization solution, which performed poorly and was expensive to maintain, but the bosses couldn't justify completely tossing out their $2 million U.S. investment to date. And so they carried on with something that barely worked.

Historic Activity Data

Quite often, audit data is useful for two reporting outlets, the reporting tool specific to the solution that generated it in the first place, and a more generic reporting tool. In other words, it's good for reporting on the silo where it originated. But it doesn't have to be limited to that.

Since user activity is *not* limited to single silo applications, and in fact often moves *across* multiple applications, it's useful to aggregate audit data. Oracle Audit Vault, along with its other functions, can consolidate data from multiple data sources for aggregated reporting, with the ability to secure that data from Oracle, SQL Server, IBM DB2 UDB, and Sybase. Of course, this might be of one-time use against retiring systems, while on an ongoing basis, historic data can also be used by the Oracle Adaptive Access Manager for contrast against current behavior and to make authorization decisions.

Reclaiming User Accounts

When you're moving to an IAM framework, it's imperative to have authoritative sources for your various functions (record of truth on user accounts, authentication, authorization, and so on), which in fact could be the same source, although often they're not. We discussed earlier the use of OID as a meta-directory for synchronizing multiple sources, and Oracle Virtual Directory as a platform for presenting unified views of aggregated data sources.

If you choose to create that centralized source on a directory other than an existing one, Oracle Identity Manager can perform a one-time reconciliation with legacy target systems, for the purpose of importing user accounts from those systems into the chosen OIM user store. Think of this as user discovery. Instead of coding a new account export/import function, or creating your own LDIF or XML dump, you can make use of OIM to perform this task and allow you to concentrate on tasks other than moving ASCII files around. Subsequently, OIM can manage your provisioning for all those accounts and perform scheduled reconciliations as new users come in from a source of truth such as a human resources application.

However, if you have your heart set on creating an LDIF file, you can also use the bulk loading tool that comes with Oracle Directory Services, which we discussed in greater detail in Chapter 8. Either option provides you the opportunity to move your user profile data into an enterprise-class directory.

Role Mining/Discovery/Definition

The concept of role mining or discovery, while still relatively young in the identity market, has already evolved. We won't discuss the short yet bulky history of role discovery, but it involves the processing and refinement of legacy user-privilege data using in a combination of automated and human analysis to create roles for the purpose of automating business-based provisioning.

Let's reduce that to more comprehensible terms. The point of roles is to make provisioning easier. A role is an abstract, a collection of privileges. It's far easier to assign a role to a user, and have the framework expand that role into its many privileges, than it is to assign those privileges one at a time. As discussed in our provisioning chapter, Oracle Identity Analytics can maintain roles as a layer cake: Business roles (very close to a job title) map to subroles (which are specific to resources), which in turn contain the granular privileges. Role discovery provides those initial roles based on your legacy data. This can also be accomplished with Oracle Identity Analytics (OIA).

At the outset of your framework design you will be accumulating data in bulk. Much of the work of mining and refining your roles will be on demand, as you build your foundation. Once you are in maintenance mode, OIA supports incremental discovery tasks, which you would likely run on a schedule. The following illustration shows the Task Scheduler screen.

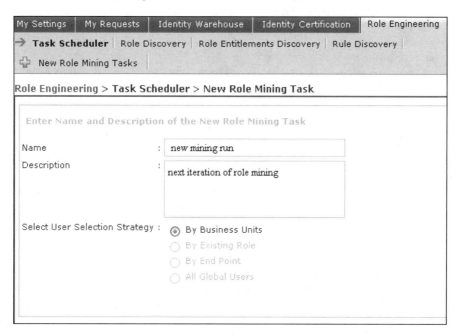

To get to this point of having a viable role, you must assimilate the privileges and users, create business units with which to associate the roles, and then refine the final product. This process is usually called *role mining*, although I prefer the term "discovery" because it sounds friendlier than the image of digging through a mountain of legacy data to uncover the roles that might be hiding there. Discovery also implies uncovering and polishing up the inherent value of your existing data, because

- A whole lot of your legacy data is still very useful.
- A whole lot of it is not.

There is no magic bullet for creating roles. It cannot be done at the push of a button. It is an iterative process of discovery and evolution, involving both technology and human decision making. Let's walk through the process of using Oracle Identity Analytics to define roles for the enterprise to support robust role-based provisioning.

Choosing Your Targets

Think of this as a macrocosm of your overall framework design. Remember the engagement of the stakeholders, the definition of the low-hanging fruit, the prioritization of your resources? This is where you start. Once again, you are not boiling the ocean. You are defining your roles one division, one business unit, one set of resources at a time. Which applications are most sensitive, or most critical? Which attract the most attention from auditors? Which resources see the most user traffic? If you must think politically, then which resources are owned by or are most important to critical stakeholders?

You will see the greatest ROI by defining roles and expediting automated provisioning for those resources that require the most enablement activity. In other words, which application is the hardest to shove a user into?

It is these resources from which you will derive the data in the subsequent steps, as shown in the following illustration.

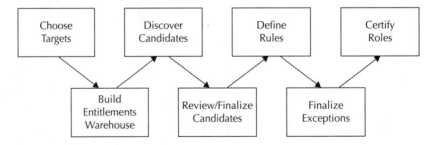

Building the Entitlement Warehouse

This repository is built from two kinds of data: user profile information and entitlements. The user data should contain attributes that pertain to why a user may have access to her particular entitlements.

An optional (but highly recommended) step would be to perform certification against the entitlement data, and here's why. The next step after this is the actual process of role discovery, in which the entitlement data is analyzed to find the roles inherent in the current privilege grants. Since, in just about every single organization in the world, there are users who have privileges they shouldn't have (for reasons we've already discussed), it is highly advisable to cleanse the entitlements before creating roles from them. Users with improper privileges, unused or underused privileges, orphaned privileges, and so on should all be cleaned up. Let's review quickly why users have access they shouldn't have:

- They've cheated, and provisioned themselves.
- They've tampered with target system databases.
- They were given temporary duties that were never taken away.
- They transferred, picked up new access, and never lost the old access.

When creating or scheduling a role-mining task in OIA, you choose the namespace (data source) to mine, and which attributes to mine, as shown in the following illustration. The chosen attributes should be either something useful for reporting or certifying later (such as name,) or something useful for creating rules later (such as job code, location).

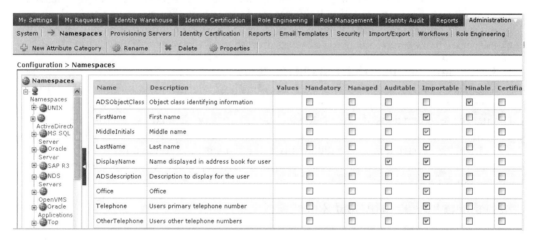

Discovering Candidate Roles

The basic notion of role discovery through Oracle Identity Analytics is this. The process examines which users have which privileges; these privileges are then clustered into candidate roles. If a set of privileges is commonly assigned together, they become a role.

There are three methods for role discovery in OIA:

- **Top-down** By using the HR attributes from the warehouse, OIA builds a context for roles from an organizational perspective.
- **Bottom-up** This method most closely reflects the definition of role discovery stated at the beginning of this section. Commonly clustered entitlements are turned into candidate roles.
- **Hybrid** This method provides the best results for combining the granular entitlement data (who has what) with the top-down perspective (who *should* have what). Ultimately what you want is business-driven provisioning of your IT resources.

Regardless of the method you employ, it requires human review. As I said before, there is no magic algorithm for creating perfect roles. This is why we use the term "candidate." Business and IT analysts need to review the results of the mining process to finalize role definitions.

This review itself is a two-step process. First, you must review the discovered membership for your candidate roles. Users who currently possess roles they should not can be removed. However, users who does not share a common profile with properly provisioned users may be legitimate exceptions, so you should not perform a blanket rejection of those users without (once again) a full review.

The second step is to review role entitlements. The mining process tells you what entitlements are already included in a candidate role. But just because they're in there *now* doesn't mean they should *stay* there. Part of defining the very IAM framework is fixing your broken processes. If everything you were doing up to now was just wonderful, you wouldn't be going through this exercise now.

If you draw data into the role-mining process from multiple resources simultaneously, you will assuredly end up with roles that span applications. From a business perspective, that is exactly what you want. But when managing IT-level roles, you may be better off keeping roles segregated by individual resources. If your job title requires you to have access to five applications, and one of them is retired or deemed at some point to be inappropriate for someone in your role, it is easier to remove that extra resource at a business level than at a lower level.

Reviewing and Finalizing Candidate Roles

Your stakeholders, resource owners, and/or business analysts need to review the information garnered from the mining effort. They must decide on the viability of the discovered candidates, and finalize their definitions. If a role is too inclusive, it may be pared down, perhaps even broken into multiple roles. If a role is underpowered, you may choose to beef it up with additional entitlements.

Once you have finalized entitlements and members for a role, you should then assign each role a formal name, description, and set of owners who will be responsible for maintaining that role going forward.

Defining Role Policies and Rules

Whereas you may manually assign roles to users later, you will best serve the cause of provisioning by defining the rules or policies that govern the automated assignment of those roles. An additional benefit of gathering that HR data into the warehouse is using those attributes to create those rules. OIA can create the initial policy for automatically granting a role by looking at the combination of data available:

- The users who share a role
- The attributes that those users also share

If all the members of a particular role have in common their location, department, manager, certification, and so on, then those attributes make up the default eligibility profile or rule that can be used going forward. When a new user account is created, in which that new user has those particular attributes, Oracle Identity Analytics can make use of that rule to automatically calculate that role membership, which is then provisioned by Oracle Identity Manager.

Reviewing and Finalizing Role Exceptions

As we've already discussed, there will always be users with privileges that are not in line with the roles to which they are legitimately entitled. In other words, these are people who have things they're not supposed to have. This is your first opportunity to review these out-of-band entitlements, but not necessarily eliminate them.

A privilege that exists outside of a role is often called an *orphan*. It cannot be readily partnered up with other entitlements, existing on its own. While it is ideal to encapsulate as many entitlements as possible, it is definitely *not* possible to contain all entitlements within roles. These exceptions should definitely be kept to a minimum—auditors like it when users have access for an identifiable business reason—but there will still be those exceptions.

These exception entitlements may be put into their own roles, although you also want to dramatically limit the number of roles with a single privilege. Regardless, a framework based on the Oracle suite does allow users and administrators to request ad-hoc access, meaning entitlements or IT-level roles outside of a business role. No, this doesn't fit a completely business-driven model, but it does reflect a real-world set of scenarios.

Here's an example, although perhaps a weak one. I visit a number of different offices for my company on a regular basis—another flight, another airport, another local office. When I plug into a local network, I can request access to a local printer. I must literally provision myself to it before I can use it. I may share access to that printer with a local VP, the receptionist, and other regional employees. The only thing we share, besides employment at the same company, is physical proximity to that printer.

Certifying Roles

At the end of the role-definition process is certification. You may recall that user attestation within Oracle Identity Analytics involves periodic review of which users have access to a resource. This version of that process, called *role certification*, involves periodic review of which entitlements are contained within a role. On a scheduled basis, role owners review their respective role definitions to maintain accurate sets of entitlements. The first certification should be performed when discovery is first completed. Once that certification completion puts a final seal of approval on the initial definition of a role, allowing you to confidently launch that role for use in provisioning, that new role also serves as a baseline for future role certification events. After all, things change.

Legacy Business Components

So here we are at the crux of the framework: the ability to communicate with our standing applications, databases, and other resources. They serve as sources for profile and other decision-supporting data, and as targets for account creation and provisioning. Oracle Identity Manager serves as the arbiter of identity and enablement within the framework, and ultimately for the organization, by integrating with your resources. Integration has two aspects:

- Account management, which includes reconciliation of new, modified, or deleted accounts; and provisioning, the creation and enablement of user accounts on target systems

- Reconciliation of trusted sources, in which OIM reconciles identity information with authoritative sources

Provisioning is a downstream process, pushing approved access requests to target apps and databases. Reconciliation, most often a scheduled event, is bidirectional, with OIM claiming modified identity data and updating targets as needed. To facilitate the integrations, OIM supports a large library of connectors for communicating with the most common targets:

- Help desk
- Mainframe identity stores

- Databases
- Unix and Windows platforms
- Various LDAP directories
- Authentication engines
- Common business applications

Altogether, almost three dozen connectors provide coverage for the bulk of Oracle customers' provisioning and reconciliation needs. Connectors are constructed using specific knowledge of the target systems, often using native APIs. This provides maximum performance and security. In addition to a robust library of OIM connectors, Oracle has acquired (via Sun) additional connectors as it continues to evolve its ability to integrate with disparate systems.

A connector is actually an aggregate of components that collectively manage provisioning and reconciliation events:

- A published OIM API set for handling the necessary data for these events.
- A rules-based reconciliation engine for processing the data into action items for execution and completion of an event.
- A management form (known as the Reconciliation Manager) within the OIM Design Console for analyzing the results of rules evaluations, and taking additional actions.
- A Remote Manager for executing actions on the target system. This is an optional piece to be deployed on that target system when it is not capable of facilitating network communication.

In summary, a connector allows you to construct the environment in which Oracle Identity Manager can interact with targets so that OIM can serve as the engine for creating, managing, and provisioning your enterprise resources, and can do so even when those resources are not immediately capable of playing nicely. You may be using a connector to push changes to a designated target or retrieving changes that have been made at that target, or both. For example, you may create an account on a target system via the connector, and you may also retrieve accounts that already exist in that target system.

In addition to the connectors, OIM supports adapters, which invoke the code needed to perform *particular* provisioning tasks on the targets. Adapters often work in conjunction with the published APIs for a target application. In other words, the connector is the pipeline to the target, and the adapter calls through that pipe for specific actions. In order to facilitate the creation of adapters, OIM provides the Adapter Factory, a graphical interface for building and modifying integrations, shown in the following illustration.

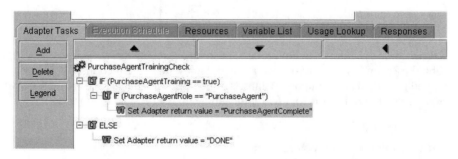

As many connectors were created using the Adapter Factory, you can use the UI to extend the connectors as needed. In addition, OIM provides a Generic Technology Connector for simple integrations that do not require the more complex customizations possible in the Factory.

Here's what you need to know about connectors. They have to match the version of your application/database/target on the appropriate operating system. In some instances, there are multiple connectors for a single target because of specific functional needs (user management and password reconciliation). The most common function of a connector is reconciliation, which can be executed in a number of ways:

- Against targets or trusted (authoritative) sources
- Full or incremental reconciliation
- Batched
- Limited
- Scheduled, on demand, or in real time

In some cases, you are leveraging business functions or logic available in the target system. You might also think of a target as merely a store of accounts. And while some systems provide API-level or other connectivity options, you may also be forced to deal with a true legacy system at a very low level. For example, it's possible to enable an LDAP gateway in a RACF environment, and interact with that system as if it were a regular directory (using Oracle's advanced RACF connector). However, if that gateway has not been configured on that old iron machine, you might revert to integrating via screen-scraping technology (using the "standard" connector). Mining "data" from a 3270 or 5250 green screen interface is the epitome of the word "legacy."

Integrating with your business systems is what this entire endeavor of an IAM framework is all about. Your identity and access solution must reflect, augment, and secure those resources that help you make a living.

CHAPTER
15

Testing Your Framework

But which is the stone that supports the bridge?

—Kublai Khan, looking for the component causing his bottleneck

n earlier chapters, I made the point that compliance is not simply reporting, and that it should be part of the entire identity process rather than something that comes out after all your daily, weekly, or monthly processes have been run. Testing is a similar paradigm. It should be baked into your thinking before, during, and after deployment. Testing should also be used both tactically and strategically, thinking in terms of identity and access. You will want to test granular functions as well as entire use cases, individual actions as well as bulk, single steps and series of steps. These include

- Each piece of functionality as you deploy it, both user-facing and behind the scenes
- Granular transactional data as it moves through each function
- Entire processes to ensure that all steps are successfully completed
- Detached results, such as audit data and federated transactions
- Large simultaneous transactions and data sets, to ensure that the system can handle the load
- XML and other payloads that deliver data between a user interface and remote processes
- Use cases from inside and outside the firewall
- Erroneous or hostile inputs

Let's discuss the types and stages of testing of an IAM environment. Naturally, it's very similar to any other type of deployment, but we'll touch on functions that are specific to identity and access. Some of these methods overlap, for example, incremental regression and load testing.

Incremental Testing

If you wait until the house is filthy to start cleaning, it's a huge task. So do it in pieces. The kitchen you do every day, but then clean a bathroom, the living room, or one of the bedrooms, once a week.

So with your new system, *as it's coming online*, start your incremental testing. Don't wait until the thing is mostly assembled; test the pieces as they are available. Remember what we discussed way at the beginning:

- Registration feeds identity.
- Identity allows authentication and provisioning.
- Provisioning feeds authorization.
- All of them support compliance and reporting.

Therefore it makes sense to test them in order, because if step #1 isn't working, the rest of it is a moot point. Let's try all the stuff that's fundamental. What's the most basic thing you can do, the most fundamental function performed, in a managed access environment? You can log in.

Unless you're doing some kind of complex biometric, like providing a blood sample in order to get access, you should be able to test your first authentication scheme against any old blank page, a "Hello World" piece of HTML. Without authentication, the rest of it doesn't matter; if you can't start the car, it doesn't matter if the stereo or the electric sun roof is functioning.

- Without logging in, navigate to a protected page.
- You're prompted to authenticate (hopefully).
- Log in and then watch the step-up authentication kick in when you request a more sensitive resource.
- Fail a login.
- Lock out an account.
- Forget the password.
- Try out the security questions to get back in without a password.
- Try single sign-on to a secondary application.
- Try cross-domain single sign-on.
- Have a session expire on one domain while maintaining it on another.

Coarse-grained access control is one of the simplest things to try as well. Once again, what this means is correlating groups of users with groups of resources. For example, users in the Receivables group can access the Receivables pages, which may be on a certain domain, kept in a particular directory, or in some other way designated. We're not talking object-level, database-level, web-part-level security. This is the easy-to-maintain stuff.

True Story

An integrator won a contract to implement authentication and authorization at a bank. There were lots and lots of design meetings, lots and lots of billable hours, and plenty of custom coding. Regression testing went very well. Two weeks before launch, they finally began load testing, with one-hundred virtual users. The first test literally killed the server. I was on hand, and offered to sit and log in while a handful of other people did the same thing. After three users, the system became very slow. With five, it was crawling. At seven, we were dead in the water. Over the next two days, they found multiple problems with their custom code, including strange record locking, runaway threads, and huge amounts of memory being cached. They did not end up launching on time.

If, in this case, the integrator screwed up, then so did the customer, by not asking for incremental testing. Status reports may tell you that work is progressing, but not that steps have been completed, or checked for viability. Each piece in the framework should set the stage for the next.

If you're installing just about any off-the-shelf coarse-grained web access tool, you can see almost instant results. Can you log in? Can you set some simple policies that let you in or keep you out? This may not involve the most in-depth policies, but you can at least see the thing function. Pick any LDAP group whatsoever, set the authentication scheme for basic (ask only name and password), and have it allow only that group to access a particular page. It could be a simple HTML page, nothing fancy. It's what is called a "smoke test." This expression has been around a while. Sometimes you hear "smell test." But what it means is, can I turn on this simple machine without it going up in smoke? That doesn't mean it's necessarily doing everything I need it to do, but at least it's passing the most basic possible test.

Within the Oracle Access Manager, there is a built-in tool for testing simple domain policies. This allows you to test a policy before having to launch the entirety of the resources you are protecting. This tool is called, unimaginatively enough, the Access Tester. It is available by bringing up your list of policy domains, selecting the appropriate domain, then clicking the Access Tester button. The Access Tester prompts you for the URL to test, the resource type (most commonly HTTP), the operations to test (for example, GET, PUT, POST, DELETE, and so on), and the originating IP. Then you specify (optionally) a date and time for testing, the user context for the test (specific user(s) or groups), and the results you wish to view (allowed or denied users, and the matching policies or rules). The following illustration shows the Access Tester screen.

In other words, you are specifying all the conditions for the test: who, what, how, when. If you think you have constructed your policy to specifically allow or deny certain users under certain conditions, then you should see that desired result. If the result is other than what you expected, you can easily modify and retest, without redeploying much of anything.

Remember, this is no kind of security test. Rather, this is testing the boat before you put it in the water. It is a functionality test, nothing more. But this kind of test is essential to determine if you are providing the desired result, that which was part of the original design.

Integration Testing

Part of that incremental testing should be verifying the communications with source and target systems. The pipe between the framework and the systems or stores it talks to consists of connectors and configuration data. Before assembling complex use cases with automated provisioning transactions, it's a sound idea to manually create users in OIM and verify their actual creation in the target systems. At times this can be more challenging, depending on the flavor of a target. For example, when preparing to put an RACF connector in place, it's not easy to do a dry run, since most of us don't have a mainframe handy a lot of the time. In fact, when performing proofs of concept involving a mainframe, I always ask the customer for dedicated time from their mainframe staff so we can verify that accounts and groups are being created during the provisioning process.

An enterprise framework will, in fact, need to support cascading connections. Users will originate in the HR system, and through the magic of automated provisioning policies, propagate to other systems. But there is no point to testing the whole thing end to end until the pieces are sound. Create users, retrieve groups, perform modifications.

Regression Testing

This is more than just trying to make sure the darn GUI works. Yes, you're trying to break the interface, but also validate the logic, including testing the integrity of every object on a page. The real basics are things like these:

- Ensuring that links take you to where they should
- Checking hyperlinks of sites and e-mail addresses
- Proper error messages (rather than 404s and the like)
- Input validation (format, length, type)
- No orphaned pages (everybody needs to be linked from someplace)
- Enforcing which fields are mandatory and which are optional

Input validation can head off some of the most basic hacks, such as SQL injection or buffer overload. If you're expecting a date, or only numerics, and only up to a certain length, then enforce that. Of course, if a hacker is going to create his own payload, then you'll have to catch that at the firewall or app server.

Testing also means checking some basic performance metrics. Let's go back to our most fundamental function, logging in. How long does it take a single user to log in? If it's more than a handful of seconds, start asking questions. But many things can affect this. The first thing the vendor will point to is the underlying user store. No matter how fast your tools are, they're only as fast as the slowest component.

If you configure your request engine to pop up only those privileges that the given user is allowed to request, how long does it take that box to populate? Favorites, personalization, messages, and anything else specific to that user... how much time is needed for those items to load?

True Story

There's an old saying: Just because you can doesn't mean you should.

At a global manufacturer, my team partnered with a large integrator to deploy our access management tools. You could extend the product by use of the APIs. But in this case, somebody got overeager. One Friday afternoon I received an anguished call from one of the integrator's project managers saying that the customer was furious because, during load testing, the average login took 90 seconds.

Well, we found the issue. In their zeal to show their value, the integrator had augmented the authentication process via the APIs to evaluate literally dozens of policies with every login. Fifty-seven policies, to be precise. Fifty-seven. Before users could successfully authenticate, the custom policy code checked their memberships, attributes, hat size, and mother's credit rating. Fifty-seven policies.

Besides basic authentication and authorization, you may have instituted fine-grained access policies. If this is the case, then you must have had the need for more complex automated decision making based on more complex parameters. And if this is the case, then these policies must be thoroughly vetted through testing. Since these granular policies are typically based on granular data, and protect more granular elements, setting up test scenarios is more difficult. Fine-grained requirements likely also mean more potential paths, depending on both static and dynamic user and group elements. Reusable, parameter-driven test scripts, rather than hard-coded attributes, will have even more value with fine-grained scenarios.

Remember, we're discussing testing your identity and security, not your business apps. So here are a couple of tips. Instead of logging in, navigate directly to a protected URL. In this example, a tool such as Oracle Access Manager should intercept the request and redirect the user to authenticate, and only then authorize or reject. It should also successfully perform chained authentication: the user is not found in the first directory, so it should find him in the second, or third. And in the case of step-up authorization, navigation from one protected domain to another may require additional credentials.

NOTE
Oracle Functional Testing for Web Applications allows you to easily create test scripts for validating .NET and J2EE apps, as well as web services and unique technologies such as Ajax. You can test web service interfaces using XML and SOAP standards without the need for an end-user interface. When performing regression testing, evaluators often forget about the stuff going on behind the scenes.

Load Testing

There are no good surprises. When you begin load testing, you will *not* find that throughput is better than expected.

When you're buying a directory, you care about the number of users (or at least your vendor does). When you're looking at the applications that process those users, then you care about something different: concurrency. How many of those users will be logging in, making requests, receiving role grants, accessing resources, and so on, at the same time?

The same use cases you developed during your design process, or that you made your vendors show you during your purchasing process (which we'll cover in Chapter 16) can serve as an excellent guide, although now you need to really ratchet them up. You need full-blown, end-to-end, heavy-volume use cases. Also remember that depending on how dynamic your organization is (meaning, how often you hire, fire, transfer, and reorganize your employees), load testing is perhaps less relevant to provisioning than it is to authentication and authorization, two processes that are occurring literally every second of the working day.

Load testing isn't simply creating hordes of virtual sessions, faux users all logging in and hitting the web server all at once. There are a number of parameters to configure in order to simulate real-world scenarios reflecting peak usage:

- Varying connection speeds
- Multithreaded requests
- Think times
- Browser types

You're also talking about authorization. So you're testing successes as well as failures. Proper authorization schemes don't just say "yes/no." We'll be talking later about configuring responses, qualified answers to requests. These entail redirects, and the presentation of response data indicating "You're in, and here's your personal data" or "You're out of luck, and here's the personalized rejection page and the proper registration link." Naturally, these take time to populate and present.

Simulate a real working environment. If you are using an integrator to build out your production environment, you can let them suggest a test bed, but get involved. It might be worth involving a completely different third party for testing as well, and ask them to break the thing.

Load Testing in Increments

It's not realistic to think that you can always successfully make the leap from ten users to a thousand without any hiccups. Concurrent connections, bandwidth, the capacity of the LDAP itself, can all conspire to convince load testing to give you heartburn. And as you load test, you need to keep upping the ante. Create a whole bunch of logins. Now have them make requests. Now have them fail some logins.

There are testing tools out there that can use regression test beds for load testing. I know of a couple in particular that can capture a user's actual keystrokes and clicks for playback of regression tests. These captures can be turned readily into scripts with hard-coded values (for example, I typed in this name and clicked on this specific button). These scripts can then be modified to replace the values with variables, and then the whole thing's thrown into a loop to read additional names and other data from a test dataset and fed into the script. This technology is not new by any means, but it's still quite valid.

Let me point out a couple of Oracle tools that provide some very useful functionality. First, Oracle Load Testing for Web Applications (OLT) can help you test the scalability and performance of your web apps and services. Without having to make use of copious amounts of additional hardware, OLT can simulate thousands of concurrent users performing many different tasks and making various requests. OLT measures the effect of this activity in a collaborative testing environment to help you analyze and diagnose problems, and ultimately tune your environment to handle any issues you find during load testing.

Another, even more unique tool is Data Masking, a feature of the Oracle database. Speaking as someone who creates custom demos all the time, I can personally attest to the hassle of generating sample data. And that's just for demonstration purposes. For load testing, you often need to simulate thousands of unique users in a directory or database. It's very tempting to use production data, but obviously very dangerous as well. With data masking, you can make use of that production data, but scramble any sensitive fields to avoid exposing that sensitive data. During a visit to a major university a few years ago, I was told of an honest but potentially disastrous mistake that caused otherwise secure data to be exposed through its use in a large test bed. Production data extracts containing personal information and being moved to a QA environment were left on an unprotected drive available to students.

I've seen people scramble their own data, but you run into problems when you try to show the transactions that are common to a particular user. If you continually scramble that user's data, then each transaction may appear to be a different user. This results in 10,000 users with 50,000 total transactions appearing to be 50,000 unique users. In other words, referential integrity has been lost. Oracle data masking will, if so configured, consistently mask that data to achieve accurate cumulative results.

Penetration Testing

You build a wonderful toy sailboat, you paint your name on the side, your wife knits you a lovely sail, you glue little sailors on the deck, you put it in the pond, and it sinks just ten feet out, lost forever before you have the chance to correct it. And all you had to do was try it out in the bathtub ahead of time.

Years ago, I helped a customer launch a small new app. It was online at three in the afternoon. By five, we'd logged literally dozens of hacking attempts.

The world is full of bad people. The volume and variety of attacks are ever-increasing. There are teenage script monkeys, lone hackers, teams of interlopers, and extremely organized fraud outfits who are looking for anything from a cheap thrill to a serious haul. Surprisingly enough, some of the same vulnerabilities still exist, years after they've been identified. I wrote an article for Computerworld a few years back listing the most common penetration attacks, and I still hear about those same attacks. I sat in a boardroom in the past year and watched one of the customer's IT staff penetrate their own app with a very simple hack. He did this just to make a point with his bosses in a venue where nobody could ignore him via e-mail.

This is a sampling of the kinds of attacks that you can simulate easily enough with your own fingertips or, better yet, in a large way with some very common tools. We'll just touch on these briefly, since there are entire books just on application vulnerabilities.

- **Parameter tampering**   This is where hackers take advantage of hidden or fixed fields, like URL parameters or hidden values in forms. They capture forms (login pages, password-reset pages, transactionals), hack their own versions, and pass malicious character strings, trying to get the app to cough up confidential information.

- **Cross-site scripting**   A hacker tries to hijack another user's session by embedding an attack script inside a form, which executes when somebody accesses that form. It may be for infecting the user's account with an evil payload, or sending the user's login credentials back to the hacker.

- **SQL injection**   Instead of entering a name or password, the hacker inserts a piece of SQL code, hoping that instead of just doing a search on a particular username, the authentication logic executes the SQL statement. In this day and age, this is a ridiculous hack, yet I just saw a demo of it in 2009 against a public site. If you have authentication code that specifically deflects this kind of attack, try load testing it, because I've also seen how a defense against such an attack can also suck up a lot of CPU. I once brought a customer's test environment to its knees with only ten concurrent SQL attacks. One more note on this hack: when you encounter systems that disallow the use of any special characters at all for username or password (thus defeating strong password policies), this is their lazy attempt to deflect SQL injection by permitting only alphanumerics.

- **Buffer overload**   Years ago, my very young daughter was sitting with me while we looked at a web site geared toward kids. I stepped away for a moment, and when I came back, I found she was parked on the 6 key, had filled up a text field, which had then generated its own carriage return. This caused the site to explode and return a whole series of IP addresses for machines behind the firewall. In other words, a field is expecting a particular data type, and perhaps a specific format and/or length, and you blow it up with lots and lots of wrong characters.

Simple input validation would prevent many of these hacks, by the way. Here is the allowable input format, length, character type, and so on. It really is that simple for the most common hacks.

Key-logging is not something you really try out with penetration testing, but it's something to be aware of. Malware that looks over your shoulder can be mitigated by various means. One of the best is a methodology associated with strong authentication—virtual devices— especially if they require no fat client. I work with one such product that presents any number of virtual keypads, on which you type (with the mouse) your credentials. Whenever one of these keypads is presented, it is scrambled from the last session, meaning that even the position of the characters on the virtual keyboards are "jittered" so that they're not in the same position as last time, thus thwarting any kind of playback based on coordinates.

By blocking any requests that don't conform to allowable formats or characters (if you want a number, only accept a number), you can keep out hostile keyboard characters and stop those attempts before they even hit the app server and eat up precious cycles. Approve or reject input before it hits the app. XML firewalls can also do this job for you, as well as help with Denial of Service (DOS) attacks. Client-side validation is worthless if a hacker can chop up a form before submitting it.

Having specific choke points for data validation also make it easier to keep watch on what's coming in, giving you fewer spots to tighten if you see the need.

One last point of interest on penetration testing. Earlier we discussed compliance requirements for protecting private information such as social security number. Penetration testing tools can actually attempt SQL injection to try to make private info come out, and you can configure them by format. So you can specifically look for phone number and social security number formats. I've seen this happen during penetration testing I've personally conducted. In two cases, by simply setting a regression test to traverse every single link on a site (a process that can take hours), I came across SSNs and other information. Not even an attack, just snooping around.

And one last point on data protection. You can eliminate the risk of any kind of web hack for retrieving private data if you protect that data at its source. For this reason, Oracle provides data masking, which we discussed earlier in this chapter, and data encryption. Masking is irreversible, meaning that once you have created an extract, it is masked at extraction time and cannot be decoded. Encryption, which is part of the Advanced Security Option, allows only authenticated, authorized clients to decrypt data, which otherwise never leaves the database in clear fashion. With these options, it doesn't matter what hack is employed at the application level.

It's ten o'clock; do you know where your private data is, and who it's with?

PART
IV

Pre- and Post-
Implementation Advice

CHAPTER
16

Choosing Software

Between two evils, choose neither; between two goods, choose both.

—Tryon Edwards, explaining best-of-breed shopping

ou've gathered your internal opinions, inventoried your needs, outlined your requirements, presented to management the value of filling in the holes, asked for budget, and now you're ready to seriously determine what's available to craft a solution that is specific to your organization. Up to now, you've examined various tactical, technical aspects of your overall strategy. But at this point, you begin truly looking under the covers at functionality. Yes, there is still a huge strategic need. The tactical bits, taken as a sum, should add up to that strategy.

The strategic perspective is that your solution must serve the overall goal of security and compliance. The tactical perspective is that all of the little parts of your solution need to connect to your directories, applications, and ultimately your users. And whether you buy or build, you will be spending your company's money, in terms of software, salaried hours, and/or both.

Buy vs. Build

Let me immediately discount one-third of this heading. It's likely not strictly a buy-*versus*-build decision. More than likely, it's going to be both. You don't put in place an enterprise solution by clicking the Install button and filling out a configuration page. Whatever solution you assemble, you will need to put in the effort to make it do what you need it to do. The dog might fetch your newspaper for you (or, in the new era, click on CNN.com for you), but you have to teach him how to do it.

You may not be deciding to *buy* your solution or *build* your solution. You may buy major portions, and build other major portions. Regardless, they all need to communicate with each other.

In past years, these types of systems were all homegrown. But especially in the last ten years, identity and access functions have been commercially available in quality form. In the last five years, these solutions have become increasingly flexible and capable of handling our emerging world of universal connectivity, cloud computing, and technologies that are on the horizon but haven't yet been fully realized.

If you choose to build the major pieces such as identity management and access policy enforcement, then face it, you're reinventing the wheel. It's all been done. So you have to make the determination:

- Is building cheaper than buying?
- Will we be able to keep up, in-house, with changing standards and requirements?
- Will we be able to build something open and extensible?
- Can we build something that will scale?
- Going forward, will we have sufficient manpower to maintain what we build?
- As functions are built, who will own them, not only from a maintenance aspect, but from an administrative perspective?

So You've Decided to Build

Remember, you make the decision to build your own IAM solution not just on whether you can actually code and construct and integrate, but on whether you can take total ownership. There's no magic 800 number to call if there's an issue. You're *it*. You are maintaining the database(s) and directory, app server(s), web server filters, logging, reporting, and so on.

A term we often hear when speaking with customers about where the intellectual property lies within an organization is *tribal knowledge*. Internally developed functions are often poorly documented. The advantage of internally owned components is that the people who've developed them are intimate with them, and they can be quickly upgraded or modified without having to get an external quote. The big disadvantage is what I've seen at many companies: When the person who built something leaves, there's nobody left who can step in.

A flock of the major burdens you can create for yourself are the integrations. When providing services for authentication, authorization, and provisioning, you need to acquire data from sources, and push data to targets. You need to interact with workflow, generate notifications via e-mail or messaging, and receive approvals, certifications, and user responses.

As an engineering representative for security vendors, one of the toughest things I've had to make the case for, to both customers and my own product management, is support for integrations. "Will your product run on 64-bit AIX x.x.x with WebSphere x.x and Oracle RAC and blah blah blah?" I've had to convince my companies to build and support various integrations, and I've had to go back to customers and ask them how much of a deal-killer the lack of an integration was.

Here's my overall point on this one: If you build a pipe from one source to another, dependent on versions and platforms, app servers and operating systems, are you willing to maintain parity with upgrades? When I first got my degree in computer science, I learned how to program. Increasingly, the young developers learn how to be plumbers, and hook up Application-1 with Database-2. Even for large companies, building these integrations is far easier than maintaining them, especially when they only have one or two customers for each. Integrations alone take a lot of cycles, so be aware of what you're getting into.

True Story

Several years ago, I pitched access management to a large retailer who wanted to go live within six months. They listened to our presentation, and then said, "That sounds good, but we think we can build that ourselves. It's just a web server plug-in that matches LDAP groups with URLs."

We replied, "Well, there's a lot more to it than that, and just so you know, there are five man-years in this product."

They opted to attempt building it anyway, and less than a year later, they became a customer.

Professional services workers listen to a set of requirements and their instant knee-jerk reaction is, calculate the necessary worker-days, then triple it. When internal developers listen to a set of requirements, their knee-jerk reaction is, "I'll have that done by next week." It's pride; it's concentration on pure coding time without consideration for design and maintenance; it's worrying about job security ("Boss, we can do that ourselves, don't hire any consultants.").

The bottom line is, when you build, you need to consider TCO—the Total Cost of Ownership. After you calculate the worker-hours to design, build, and test, don't forget to add in documentation and ongoing maintenance. The documentation is vital unless you plan on the resources who build it to stay forever.

Open Source

Open source in theory provides a strategic advantage. You're sharing an open resource and can trade ideas, methodologies, and innovation. Open source can be a good idea for a lot of technologies. Its tactical advantages are the standards it can support, and again, the sharing of code. But of course, you still need to adapt shared components to your needs. Open source does not automatically mean *free*. Remember, way back when, how C language was the best thing since sliced bread, since it would be completely transportable; just recompile it and off it goes? Except that it didn't work that way.

Open source means two things to me: roll your own, and unsupported. If you're willing to build your own platform, that's good. You will also take all the calls. Support means a lot of time trolling newsgroups.

This is not to say that support for open source is a bad thing in a software vendor. But in the current day and age, open source should not be the complete foundation for what you run. We're not there yet.

So You've Decided to Buy (or at Least Shop)

The relationship between customer and vendor is often adversarial. There's a natural tendency for anyone spending money to think that unless they keep an eye out at all times, they're getting cheated, not getting what they paid for. And there's a tendency for vendors to think that they're the smart ones and the customers have no clue what they're doing. But this is wrong thinking on everybody's part.

When you're starting to crawl through the list of vendors and their offerings, keep this in mind. You want these people to succeed. By that, I mean you want them to adequately communicate what they do and don't have so that you can make the right decisions. It's all based on having more than adequate data. Therefore, don't think that you have to make vendors jump through hoops. Let me give you an example.

For the last several years, I have represented large, enterprise-style identity access solutions. These aren't simple matters. We're laying down large solutions on top of large infrastructures with large problems. Because on paper or on the web it's hard for customers to tell one vendor's size from another. I know what it's like to compete with teensy solution providers. Because they've often got little-bitty applications that run on laptops and not much else, they can slap a one-size-fits-all demo together in a hurry and turn people's heads. And I've seen these little bitty companies win deals in which their product could not possibly hope to scale across the enterprise. They might function in a small office environment or small manufacturer, but they can't scale in an enterprise with thousands of concurrent users. But because a customer said, "Come tomorrow and show me what you've got," and the smaller place could throw something together quickly, that inordinately affected the decision.

Remember this: If you pull a fire drill, you're testing the vendor's sales team, not their company's ability to deliver a solution. This is going to be an investment in your company's future, so take the time to do it right.

Make sure any product you think you like does what you need. Don't obsess over one or two good things; it has to be the whole picture. If you're looking to mix and match different products from different providers, make sure they'll work together. Patching together multiple products is fairly common. You might get them from the same vendor, or maybe not. One company's authentication tool might be configured to look like just another authentication scheme to another company's access management product, integrated via services, APIs, or other means. However, having an already integrated solution with only one phone number to call for support can also be a big value.

Big vs. Little

Once upon a time I worked with a cute little tool that you could download and install in well under an hour. It was one of those "click on setup.exe and off you go" kinds of tools that had to be installed on everybody's desktop. We had a healthy customer base of smaller shops. If you needed to change your Graphical Identification and Authentication (GINA) in order to deploy it—well, maybe that would work in your smaller situation. But if you had tons of users across a host of geographic locations, it was a completely different story.

If you need provisioning, make sure the darn thing provisions. I reviewed a tool with a fantastic interface for provisioning. It sort of had workflow, but it was all based on e-mail notifications. Strike one. And it didn't so much provision as you could set up line items for all your target systems, and you manually checked off the ones a user could have with no automatic grants. Strike two. Finally, instead of actual provisioning, it took those checkmarks and modified a flag in a multivalued, custom attribute within Active Directory, which it expected the target systems to come and query. Strikes three and four.

That's not provisioning. It's not enablement. It's attribute juggling. If you actually run everything off Active Directory, and your apps will be content coming to AD to find out if a user can get in, dandy. Of course, this is also all or nothing. A simple Boolean: yes-he's-in or no-he-isn't. No access levels, no admin versus worker bees, no account creation on target systems. That's not provisioning.

How to Look

So how do you shop? How do you begin this magical journey? Well, you can start with one of the search engines and pound in the usual terms, although this is misleading. I tried this recently with "identity access management," and this is what popped up:

- A startup with no paying customers yet
- A handful of universities
- Some articles on the subject
- A couple of the major players

If you think you've found a vendor you're interested in, go to their site. Register for their whitepapers. Normally this means giving them an e-mail address. Of course, get ready to be inundated with sales calls. They will be on you like unwanted relatives. But here's what happens. You get nailed by their inside sales people, *maybe* a regional sales person. If you're in the insurance business, you might get an insurance solution specialist. Or medical or manufacturing or whatever matters to you, once they know who you are and what you do for a living. But you use this to your advantage. Once you've got a vendor in your sights, you tell them, "This is what our company does, this is how big we are, these are the things we're interested in. Give me very specific information on that, along with any public references on other customers in the same industry as us, and roughly our size." Then see what they come back with.

If you're up for it, you have them come in to make a pitch. They'll usually bring in a salesperson, as well as an engineer. You always want that engineer there to answer the tough questions. Not to say that a software salesman will deliberately give you bad information. He simply won't know all the answers to the details you need. A friend in the business told me this one: What's the difference between a car salesman and a software salesman? The car salesman *knows* when he's lying.

So attack the engineer with the tough questions. If a salesman is explaining his product to you, and keeps making eye contact with his engineer instead of *you*, that's like reading his mind, which is screaming out, "I think I'm going out on a limb, be ready to step in any second."

Vendor Visits

If you have a vendor in to make a pitch, give them an agenda in advance. It's a no-brainer. Whoever you have in to see you, whether it's a software salesperson or a plumber, tell them why you're bothering. Otherwise you may waste a lot of time. Don't just look like you're kicking the tires. Get down to business. Tell them your issues. "We need strong authentication. We're doubling the business. We're doing too many things manually. We're having a hard time with audits. We have security concerns."

Be specific. If you're afraid of spilling something that might dribble over to your own competitors, make them sign a paper. We'll be talking shortly about non-disclosure agreements. What I'm saying is that you can blow a lot of cycles by saying, "Well, come in for a quick discussion, and if it sounds good, we'll have you in to make a general pitch, and if that goes well, we'll have you in for a detailed discussion, and if that works, then come back with your product manager, and six months from now we'll have an idea of where we're at."

And you'll never, ever get to where you're going.

Get your act together internally. Set your own agenda, your own timelines. Figure out your requirements. Then match them up with the tools you think you need. Put your requirements in front of those tool-makers and ask, quite clearly, "How do you propose to address *this*?"

A pitch, a product demonstration, a proof concept, a paid pilot. Whatever step you're at, make sure it's specific to what you need and/or what you think you *will* need going forward. It's okay to throw some futures in, but don't go crazy on those. You're shopping because you have immediate needs, right now. Focus mostly on those.

One interesting observation from literally hundreds of meetings the last couple of decades-plus… everybody in a vendor pitch has their own agenda. You want the best solution. Some stakeholders may like the status quo and be grumpy no matter what they hear. Some may already have their minds made up on a particular technology and not give the presenters a fair hearing, denying everybody the opportunity to learn everything they should. Internal staff members often look at outside products as endangering their job security. And of course the vendor wants to sell you something.

True Story

I went to a meeting at a potential customer's location in Cincinnati in 2000, bringing along my junior engineer. The staff there *hated* vendors. Their project leader wore a ripped tee shirt and a button with a very offensive phrase. There was no mistaking their opinion of solution providers. I had to explain to my engineer that not all customer meetings were that unfriendly.

Paid advisors are never that blatant. But they can do their own damage, even if they like the product at hand. They feel they need to show value in every meeting so you'll keep them around. Nobody ever thinks they show value by yelling during a meeting, "Wow, this stuff looks great, write them a check today!"

No, they feel they show value by poking holes in everything they see. I did a pitch a few months ago in which the advisor was in charge of responding to the vendors, and asked me questions about the most inane, trivial things. For example, they asked about exactly what kinds of values were set in our access manager's session cookie, in a way that suggested that the content of our cookie was vital to the whole decision. My response was, configure it to hold (and pass along) whatever you need it to. The customer more or less laughed this question off.

If another party starts picking apart the answers to your questions, you might want to ask yourself, "Is that something I really have to worry about?" Pay more attention to those things that are truly important.

What's Truly Important?

Will your solution do the job? You may have a strategy, but you have to think tactically here as well. Features and functions. If you're shopping for IAM, then your chosen technology needs to address some or all of the following:

- Authentication against your chosen directory
- Authorization policies
- Single sign-on
- Federation
- Registration/self-registration
- Provisioning, including approvals and workflow
- Role management
- User life cycle
- Segregation of duties
- Compliance support
- Reporting and analytics
- Customized interfaces
- General extensibility
- Multilanguage support
- Standards-based
- Remote configuration
- 24×365 online, phone, and e-mail support
- End-user and development training

With regard to extensibility, if you buy any off-the-shelf access management tool, chances are very good that unless you're doing the most basic, fundamental, coarse-grained access policies (admins get *this*, all other users get *that*), you *are* going to customize to one degree or other.

Unless you're doing the absolute basics of authentication, you'll want more flexibility than is available in the default configuration. Most IAM products for authentication and authorization provide APIs to let you extend their functionality. Even before you get to coding, you should have the option to add additional filters beyond simple identity. Sure, you want to do basic authentication, but you also want to look up the user's account and perhaps make attribute-or membership-based decisions. At the very least, you're going to customize login forms, and you'll have custom landing pages based on memberships or attributes.

Just to pick at a couple of other things in that previous list…

- **Interfaces**   And I don't just mean screens and skins. I'm talking about all the ways you can interact with the product, whether through a GUI or code. Have your IT people check out the API and the accompanying guide. In a couple of pages, I'm going to talk about the API a little bit more.

- **How's that GUI?**   Is it customizable? Can I brand it? I hate the color; can I change it? Can I modify the menus for different classes of users? I'll let the people in accounting model their own roles, but they don't get to affect the workflows.

- **Is it web-service enabled?**   Or can I at least wrap their API calls?

- **Reporting**   The vendors should be able to supply you with a sample of every canned report. And then you should get a demo of how relatively easy it is to create your own custom reports. Don't be surprised if they say, "We can create a data dump in any format you'd like, so you can employ whatever report generator you like." This means they *don't* have a report generator of their own. Not the end of the world, but features like that reflect on product maturity.

- **Remote configuration**   Do you know where that matters? When you've got plug-ins or agents on remote servers, such as web servers or app servers. Request brokers. If you've got policy data or other configuration data on each of them, can it be pushed out from a central administrative console? If not, then get a rake and chase them out of the building, because their product will be murder to reconfigure on a regular basis.

Get Some Help Shopping

You could also go for help before you go for help. If you really want to know where the intellectual capital is in the space, talk to the people who are out there examining the market. If you have auditors or body shops or consultants you already work with, pick their brains. But whatever they recommend, make sure once again that you're talking apples and apples. If you're a small shop, see what's out there befitting your size. If you're a medium-to-large shop, look for something that can handle your load. So when a consultant tells you about the great tool he's worked with, make sure it's appropriate to your situation.

Also remember that if a consultant already has a working relationship with a vendor, they might push you that way no matter how appropriate the tool might be. However, if a consultant says, "Hey, look at this one," and you do that investigation, and it *does* look good to you, that relationship isn't necessarily a bad thing, because presumably the consultant knows the product well enough to help you deploy better and faster. They're also staking their reputation on their recommendation. If they belong to a large enough group, then they're staking their entire organization's reputation as well. Integrators like to associate themselves with well-performing products, for obvious reasons.

Who else to bother? That's easy. *The analysts.*

Now, there are two primary sources of information from analysts. These are the vendor-specific papers they've written, and the general market analysis they've done.

The vendor papers are written for cash. I come up with a great application in a market covered by my favorite analyst, I give them a couple of bucks, and they give me a whitepaper telling the world that I've invented the best thing since the wheel, and that I will surely be the market leader one day, since I'm obviously the thought leader.

The market analysis is definitely more neutral. Gartner puts out the famous "magic quadrant," which has two axes, one representing vision and the other showing ability to deliver. It's actually four quadrants, but the goal is to reach the upper-right corner of the upper-right quadrant, to show that you excel in both vision and delivery.

Gartner does this for every market they cover. If you indeed manufacture wheels, they don't have a magic quadrant for you, since that was just a metaphor. But for the software business, they have several versions, including identity management, provisioning, and web access. The Burton Group has something very similar. And there are other analysts out there as well. I hate to say it, but before you take an analyst's word, make sure you like the analyst.

The players progress (or digress) in the magic quadrants or reports with acquisitions, new releases, new enterprise customers, and other factors that would presumably reflect in their sales as well, although this is not always the case. Any number of factors can affect how well one does business. A competitor of mine, for example, has an ancillary tool related to regulatory compliance, and it gets great reviews from its field people. We all talk, right? But nobody in their sales force knows it well, so they don't sell it, preferring to just sell the tools they have a comfort level with. Meanwhile, their identity and access management tools, although well-rated by analysts, can barely sell, largely because word of mouth isn't good.

So even after you consult the analysts, you *still* have to do the legwork. References, demos, presentations, perhaps a proof of concept—everything you would do if you found an identity vendor on your own.

Customization

How much of the functionality can you exploit without customization? Remember, you need to know up front how much of that customization will be carried forward a year from now when you upgrade the software itself. Is that customization externalized? When you think of software upgrades, you think of improved GUI, additional functionality, enhanced support for industry standards. But what you don't know is that in 99 percent of these upgrades, the API that the product is built on has been upgraded as well. This can very well affect any customizations made with it.

One question to ask the vendor is, is the API that the product is built with the same one published or exposed for end users to create extensions with, or is there a different one for customers that's a consistent wrapper? There are two ways to look at that question.

1. Yes, it's the same one. Oh good, that means that I have total control over the product, I can make it bark like a dog, because I hold in my hand the same tools that the vendor's developers use. But oh no, when they update the API, does that mean half the function calls I make are no longer valid?

2. No, it's a wrapper. Oh good, that means the custom code I've written is safeguarded from any changes they make to their internal API, because presumably they're protecting me as long as I'm using the public API they expose. But oh no, I'm limited in what I can do in terms of extending the product.

There's no right or wrong answer to this, depending on how the vendor answers questions about upgrades.

Also beware the software vendor whose developers are also their support staff who are also their consulting staff. When they say, "We love you so much, we're sending our developers to work on your project," this translates to, "We're so small, we're sending you whoever's available."

Go with Experience

In the Gartner magic quadrant, they are measuring both vision and ability to deliver. Those vendors who rank well in both categories are usually the ones who've been around a while, and who have the resources to actually provide the values they espouse. Check your barometers on this as well. Larger consultants rarely go to battle with brand new products, unless they're strictly point solutions on a small scale, and again, analysts are betting their reputations on the vendors they study and evaluate. Customer stories are also good indicators, but consider the sizes of those customers. Many small-scale tools have literally thousands of customers, simply because they can be easily downloaded and installed without interaction. These are not enterprise solutions.

True Story

A client of mine made the mistake of being the first-ever customer of another vendor's brand-new directory product, which turned out to be a disaster. One day while gassing up my car, I received a tearful phone call from one of the IT guys crying that he was going to lose his job for helping choose this LDAP product. He didn't lose his job, but his boss sure did. By the way, that directory product turned out to be a great product... two years and two releases later.

Beware of marketing smoke. In the past year I was asked to review the product of a small startup with no customers. In their collateral they used the term "best of breed." This was nonsense. "Best of breed" suggests a product that has been through the wringer, assembled from other market-tested components, has been thoroughly tested by customers, and has survived in improved form.

Go with Commitment to the Space

Example #1: A huge software company with a cash-cow product decided to buy their way into the identity space a few years ago. Nothing wrong with that. Except that they only had a couple of pieces, bought some other pieces that never got much attention, and didn't do enough with the pieces they bought to make them usable. Every deployment was a customization mess. Their largest implementation partner in the space dropped them. They finally dropped the whole line.

Example #2: Not as bad, but... this was an even bigger company. They already had an IdM offering. It's a serviceable product, although flawed. They bought a complementary technology company as well, in the provisioning space. This is where it got ugly. The provisioning tool relied on editing a lot of XML files. Their services people used to joke that the configuration tool of choice was Notepad. Before the acquisition, the smaller company had a terrible engagement where they lost a week allegedly over a single missing bracket in a configuration file. Instead of throwing an XML editor on top of the package they bought, the larger company simply trained their services group on editing the files.

Acquiring technology isn't enough. How do you make the pieces fit? Do they integrate with each other? And even after you've made that happen, can they still run stand-alone?

I came to Oracle via an acquisition. Within the first few weeks, they took my old company's product and integrated it with the Oracle standard Business Process Execution Language (BPEL) workflow engine, and next came standardization of the GUI. They acquired, embraced, and integrated. This is what you should be looking for.

Watch the Strictly Proprietary Stuff

Everybody in the software market, whether it's identity or anything else, has proprietary code. If they didn't, there'd be no point. You don't get rich selling something you didn't invent or don't own. We spoke earlier of open source and its commercial (and therefore support) limitations. But it's the approach, the methodology, that you might want to be more open.

We're talking about access management and identity. This means communicating with one or more source directories or databases. What manner of connectors are they using? And are those connectors extensible? In fact, extensibility should be something you sweat all over this process.

How do they handle segregation of duties? Can they enforce SoD for more than one business app within the same engine? Or are they relying on app-specific SoD rules and connectors? Remember, cross-application SoD is where the world is going.

So while standards-based sounds great, make sure it's the right fit. For years, ODBC was *the* way to go, but for such a long time it was also slower than proprietary connectors. But if something *is* proprietary, you want to know what the migration path is to something more standards-based. Emerging standards sometimes (although not always) become established, and you may eventually acquire or build business apps based on new standards, in which case your provisioning solution will need to communicate with them and your access management solution will need to protect and provide single sign-on to them.

Here's one, though, you must have. Extensibility. What can you do to it that will make it bark like a dog? How can you take what they're giving you and extend it? Even if you don't have a use case for it now, you likely will in the future, when you hit a dead end or bottleneck. And avoid proprietary scripting languages. They're ugly. I've had to try to represent these kinds of tools in the past. "Sure, you can customize the interface. Just use our little script protocol, Custom Rich Attribute Properties."

You're locked in, you can't readily find resources to work with it, and you've done nothing for your resume.

It's not a bad idea to get hold of their SDK guide, and have your own crew give the API the once-over. It's also quite a good idea to ask, is it web-service enabled?

Appliances

One well-known hardware company puts a lot of software on their boxes. Why? Because they make boxes. That's what they do. They don't like to have separate sales groups for software. So they buy the occasional software company, throw their product on the boxes, and dump the sales teams. They don't sell appliances because it's the best way to deploy the software. They do it because they sell appliances.

So again, I'm not necessarily tearing down appliances. But they have to make sense. One company with one foot in the identity space sells an appliance, which means their solution is supposed to be plug-and-play. And yet it often requires more than a year's worth of labor to hook it up to source and target systems, which seems to contradict the value of an appliance in the first place.

Non-Disclosure Agreements

A Non-Disclosure Agreement (NDA) is a document specifying who can't say what about whom. In other words, before we can do business, sign this thing that says you won't disclose any proprietary info you might learn during discussions. Sounds simple? Heck no. These things can be very complicated. Unless you're comfortable with boilerplate legalese, you will dig deep on these. If you don't, your company's lawyers will slap you silly. Here are a few things to know about NDAs.

- In a mutual NDA, both parties agree not to blab secrets. You'd think this would be the default. I don't talk about you, you don't talk about me. But since NDAs typically have to be reviewed by corporate lawyers, it's not uncommon for a company to say, "Send me your NDA and if my lawyers like it (and there's little chance of that) then we might sign it. In the meantime, you *will* sign mine."

- So who's got the muscle in these situations? Well, naturally the customer does. They've got the wallet that the vendor wants to get into. But while the customer has the obvious leverage, they can also put themselves at a technical disadvantage by not coming to agreement. Intellectual property is the lifeblood of software companies, and these companies will often walk away from opportunities if their IP is not secured. You may be canceling out the best software choices for your organization if you're not willing to guarantee Vendor #1 that you won't talk about their roadmap to Vendor #2 who, by the way, is presenting to you tomorrow.

- Because lawyers often get involved in NDAs, there's no guarantee you'll get one turned around in a hurry. This is especially true if you're using outside legal help rather than a company lawyer, since the outside consultants are just like integrators: It's all about billable hours. No kidding, it could take weeks. If you want to do a deep dive in the next month with a vendor or partner regarding their intellectual secrets or roadmap, you'd better get moving *now*. I have seen NDAs consisting of one page, and of dozens of pages.

- Even without an NDA, anyone making use of, or carelessly spreading around, proprietary information is at actionable risk, so whatever a vendor may learn about a customer's business or infrastructure, or whatever a potential customer may learn about a vendor's product or intellectual property, should be respected and kept quiet.

RFPs

Sorry, this section's rather long, but it involves a vitally important step in uncovering the value or potential disaster there may be in choosing a piece of software that will govern your IAM framework. In other words, don't take this step lightly.

There are different versions of this kind of request, and often people swap them around. A *request for information* (RFI) is a list of product or service questions. A *request for proposal* (RFP) requires more detail, such as a vendor's financial statements, their board of directors, pricing, maintenance, roadmap—all the business end as well as the technical. A *request for quote* (RFQ) means, tell me how much it will cost. Let's go with the RFP for now, since there's more guts to it. Besides, you're not just buying software, you're buying the whole company, including the service at the other end of the phone when you need it, and you will need it.

An RFP serves the basic purpose of weeding out the complete undesirables. If the thing is sloppy, misspelled, full of typos, or obviously a masterpiece of cut and paste, then it may be hard to make a decision based on such a jumble. And if, from the technical answers, it's obviously a bad fit, that's simple enough.

However, when reading the responses, you must read between the lines. Occasionally a vendor or integrator will walk away from an opportunity, realizing it's a bad fit. But an awful lot of the time, a vendor or SI will seize on every opportunity, even if they're not really in the same room. Why? For the *money*. And this is when you get answers that you can imagine somebody twisted themselves in knots to compose. The responses are not so much yes or no as they are, "Well, you see, we believe that you should approach it this way, because this is our philosophy or design, and blah blah." We'll talk more in a moment about the *qualified yes*. An RFP digs a little deeper, beyond just the technical answers. It gives you a notion of what it will be like to actually do business with the respondent.

So here's what ought to be in one of these beasts.

First, a cover letter should state your overall intentions. Here's what you need, here's when you need it by. Here's your timeline for coming up with a solution, or at least for getting to the next phase. "If you do well on this RFP, we'll have you in for a presentation after the first of next month." Having a timeline allows respondents to line up all the right resources.

Here's the information that you should provide:

- Description of what your organization does for a living
- Description of your concern, problem, and so on
- Basic architecture of the current infrastructure, including data and applications
- What you want it to look like going forward
- Appropriate diagrams

Here's the information that should be provided about the product:

- Glossary of terms for the tech questions
- Actual tech questions
- Difficulty/ease of deploying
- What types and numbers of resources will they need from *you* in order to deploy

And you'll need to provide information about the processes: Basic use cases for provisioning, approvals, SoD, authentication, and authorization.

Not just "can your product do this" but "how does your product solve this?"

And you'll need this information about the vendor:

- Training
- What services can they provide?
- Who are their deployment partners?
- Roadmap—where is their product line going?
- References—who else in your industry is using their product, and to what extent? More on this later.
- Pricing levels (assume various discounts for numbers of users).

Let's take one step back to the process. There are vendors out there who claim to be what they are not, and whose approach and architecture are far from the norm. The way they may try to solve your issues may be vastly different from everyone else's. If all they have is a hammer, they will say that you have a nail. Every vendor will say "yes" to just about every question on functionality. But you could end up wasting a lot of time with a vendor whose solution is not at all what you want or need.

If you have five clocks in your house, you will always have five different times. Likewise, if you put out an RFP to a services group, or if there's a service aspect to an RFP you issue to vendors, be aware of this unavoidable thing. You will get wildly different quotes on both hours and dollars. Every service group has its own methodology. The bigger groups will inspect every corner of your operation before they actually sit down to do work, so their quotes are often higher. That's the difference between strategic and tactical.

If you absolutely, positively do not wish to consider *futures*, then indicate that up front. In other words, if you're asking for functionality that they're not currently shipping, you can be sure that they'll say, "That's in our next release," and who knows if that's true. If you *are* willing to consider futures, and there's a piece of functionality that is a must-have, make them put their product manager or VP of engineering in front of you to guarantee you that the darn thing's going to be there by the end of the quarter. You will never be more important to them than right before you sign a purchase order. After that, it gets a little dicey. You can ask them to put commitments for delivery on futures in a letter, but you'll rarely get that, because it prevents them from recognizing revenue.

Beware of two kinds of RFP answers:

- **The qualified yes**   If somebody's smart, their answer to nearly every technical question in your RFP is "yes." It may be a *qualified* yes, as in "You need that? Yeah, uh, we can do that." In other words, they don't precisely support integration with your platform of choice, but they have all sorts of widgets that will possibly fake it.

  "PeopleSoft? Sure, we integrate with that. Simply perform a data dump from your HR database, then we'll process it, and let you import the results back into PeopleSoft."

  However… a qualified yes could also be an answer supporting a standard approach, and the way you're currently addressing the issue at hand could be non-standard. Let's say you ask a question along the lines of, "How can you perform this function the way we're doing it now?" It could well be that the way you're doing it now is *stupid*. Check out the first question under the list of RFP questions in Table 16-1 for a good example.

- **Supports**   Heavy use of the word "supports" is a red flag. This means they don't supply whatever you're looking for, but they can supply "supporting" data or functionality. Table 16-1 gives some examples.

Clarity
I've gotten some RFPs that were as clear as mud. I've been asked things like:

- **Can you sync up with an identity matrix?**   Okay, what the heck's an identity matrix? Is this a user store? Why the fancy, non-standard term? I had lunch with a salesman years ago in Troy, Michigan who ordered "clear soda" with lunch, and was unhappy to find he'd gotten club soda. He said he thought he'd be getting Seven-Up. I told him, "Then you should have *ordered* Seven-Up." Be clear.

Answer	Translation
It supports robust reporting.	We capture a lot of data that you can feed into your own report writer.
It supports compliance.	It can execute some Booleans here and there that say "no" once in a while.
It supports provisioning.	It maintains data that your workflow engine is welcome to come and query.

TABLE 16-1. *What Do They Really Mean?*

- **Explain how you identify information**   Okay, this is like saying, how do you fix a computer? Right here is a good example of a question that somebody added to an RFP without another party proofreading it before it went out.

- **How do you protect corporate assets?**   Do you mean, physically, as with a club? Or is this at an operating system level? Or do you mean protecting web-enabled assets via access management?

I've also been asked in RFPs, many times, variations of "Give us your product roadmap for the next three years." That just isn't going to happen. It's software! Even if they did tell you where the product was going over a long period, and three years is forever in this business, it would be baloney. You can usually get a basic direction, and certainly something concrete for the next 12 months. But 36 months? Remember, things change. It's software!

Also, a vendor might refrain from providing a roadmap if a purchase depends on features or functionality in that roadmap, as this could prevent them from recognizing revenue from that purchase until such time as those features are delivered.

Here, you'll laugh at this one, sorry, it's a stupid, trivial thing about issuing RFPs, but something that can save everybody a lot of grief: Don't send them out as Excel spreadsheets. You're asking for a lot of information, and some of it will be cut and pasted, including diagrams and copious amounts of text. Strange things happen when you paste into spreadsheet cells. It not only makes it harder on whoever's filling it out; it's harder for you to read the responses, especially when half the page is taken up by your question, and the answer scrolls down for three pages. Just don't do it. I'd rather cut and paste into Notepad than into Excel, and you'd rather read it that way too. Try Word, or allow respondents to use a separate document for answers, which will be much easier for you to digest. Also, encourage your vendors to use attachments, rather than paste in extremely large chunks. You might also encourage them not to paste in large portions of text from their web site. It shows pure laziness.

I highly recommend against this particular practice: allowing a single vendor to write your RFP *for* you. It's bad for a few reasons.

- You will end up with a document that preordains the *correct* way to deliver functionality. I saw one of these recently in which a low-level vendor with a good but narrowly focused tool had a relationship within the customer. They were given an in, to provide a lot of the questions. The entire document was skewed to make it look as if the way they did things was the way they should be done. All I have is a hammer; therefore all your problems are nails.

- When vendors recognize this, and sometimes it's painfully obvious, they quickly deduce that they are column fodder, and perhaps do not give the RFP their best effort, robbing you of an opportunity to see what's really out there.

- If you have preordained that outcome, and merely go through the motions with the other vendors, and then your project subsequently goes badly, you may have your head handed to you because you have not done proper due diligence.

I have had the morbid pleasure of revisiting customers over the years who chose poorly, and had to have other vendors back in after their original choice failed miserably. You get to look them in the eye and say, "You never gave anybody else a real chance."

You can find RFP templates all over the web. They range from slightly useful to worthless. You might start with one just to get a feel for the format, and you may find some questions you hadn't thought of asking. But tailor the questions to suit your requirements. It's your process, from start to finish, so own it from start to finish.

POCs and Pilots

Proofs of concept and/or pilots should be reserved for only those vendors about whom you're serious. You will likely put in almost as much effort as they will on a Proof of Concept (POC), since you have to provide the lab space, the servers, the sample data, and those things we've talked about so much, your use cases. And this is the relevant term with a POC: use cases. These events are more about process, and solution architecture, than about individual functions, although those functions serve as the pillars for solving the use cases.

Pilots are certainly more complex, in that you're practically asking somebody to build you a system; the vendor considers that a pilot. It's common for vendors to ask for *paid pilots* if they're going to heavily customize a deployment for you. The common response to this request, if you find it acceptable, is to have the cost of that pilot subtracted from the final price if you go with that vendor. It's a fair arrangement for everyone.

The vendor may use a partner for the POC, and throw them the work if they win the business. It's actually not a bad system, since the partner by that time has great familiarity with your requirements.

Sensitive Data

When the time comes for a POC or pilot, you might let the provider bring in their own data. But more than likely you will be providing your own sample data. It could be some junk you made up, or actual production data. Even if you're planning on doing your pilots in a controlled lab environment, you should consider filtering any production data. You should be able to trust anyone who comes in to do business with you, but it's a dangerous world. Besides that, you never know when somebody's going to just plain screw up. A well-known security company panicked its clients when a laptop with sensitive data on thousands of customers was stolen in the San Francisco airport. This stuff happens.

An option available with the Oracle database is Data Masking, which allows you to take production data and irreversibly mask out sensitive fields such as social security numbers. It can also scramble fields, like names. It can even consistently scramble the same data the same way, so that if I want to process the same user multiple times, it will see him multiple times, in scrambled form, maintaining referential integrity. It's a huge time-saver in that it allows you to generate production-quality data without compromising confidential data elements.

A colleague in the business told me of his experience during an engagement, when he received from a customer, for load testing purposes, and in a public e-mail account, a file called *userpasswords.xls*. An Excel spreadsheet with all their user names and passwords. By e-mail.

I know what it's like to be asked if I have any memory sticks on me, any flash drives, any way of siphoning off sensitive data. Customers don't want their information walking out of the lab. And then I had an engagement in the Carolinas where, after we'd signed a pair of NDAs, we had to really push to get the sample data we needed for the POC, maybe a couple of thousand records, placed on a server. Our team was there for several days, and every day I said, where's that data? Finally the sys admin walked in halfway through the week and *handed me a DVD*. Instead of sample records, he had given us several gigabytes of data, including users and privileges. There was nothing on there in terms of privacy, but it was pretty much every user's privileges throughout the entire network.

Prepare an agreement with the vendor to safeguard whatever data you put up. And then don't assume that the internal IT person you designate to deliver that data will follow the rules. The paper everybody signs doesn't actually guarantee that the data won't be dealt with foolishly. It really serves a two-fold purpose: to *remind* them not to be stupid with your data, and to give you all sorts of cause to sue them to death if they *are* stupid with your data.

One miscellaneous thing here… this might also be your segue into testing any bulk loading features, if they are needed.

References: Getting One, Being One

It's never a bad idea to ask to speak with a reference, from both your vendors and your implementation partners. Understand that not every customer will take a call. But if the people you're doing business with have enough of these under their belt, they're bound to have some happy customers, and of that number, it's likely that there will be at least a couple who will willingly speak with you.

Even for very large companies, references are always tough. A lot of companies simply will not speak on the record. They have corporate policies against their employees doing it as well. But those who know how to play the game, and are relatively happy with the products and services they've received, will accept a call on occasion in exchange for other considerations. If you've got a customer who will take calls for you, you will bend over backward to make sure they're happy.

A reference customer may even allow you to visit their site. These are even tougher to come by, since somebody's got to justify taking up a part of the precious business day to essentially lead a tour. If they're a competitor, holy cow, now we're off the charts.

In baseball, the fans assume the fielders will catch every fly ball, but they complain bitterly over the occasional one that gets dropped. And it's like that with references. Whenever you ask anyone in the business for names, a reference is only as good as five minutes ago. I know exactly what it's like to have good reference accounts who, on any given day, want you dead, because today's explosion wipes out, at least for the afternoon, any goodwill from the last 12 months of smooth sailing.

If you end up as a happy customer, being a reference is something to consider. Be candid about the kinds and the numbers of calls you'll take. After that, being a good reference often means unprecedented attention when your system develops the slightest problem. Not a bad trade-off.

Being an engineer, I've rarely had to schmooze customers. That's what salespeople do. But there's been the occasional golf game, and one time in Texas there was a round of Frisbee, and it was probably 110 degrees in the shade. Software is hell.

CPU Pricing vs. Seat-Based Pricing

Vendors sell databases, directories, apps, packages, and yes, identity systems, by the seat. By the user. By the unique ID. Here are a couple of things to keep in mind when doing business, based on what I just said.

From the customer's perspective, CPU pricing allows them to take advantage of processor speed, so if they fine-tune the application to get better performance with less CPU, they could see a lower cost. The challenge is, if they increase an application's functionality, it could require them to purchase more CPU, and over time it could become very expensive. Oracle Identity Manager doesn't require a huge amount of horsepower to provision users, so on the face of it, CPU pricing might be cheaper than per user. But if you purchase per user, you pay a one-time fee for the licenses and no additional cost would be incurred as long as the user count doesn't increase. You could have the most complex application on the planet, requiring thousands of processors, but it wouldn't matter.

On the other hand, vendors may very well adjust their CPU pricing if they know the application isn't hardware-intensive, since they lose out on a recurring revenue stream if the user count doesn't increase. So it's a balancing act on both sides. This is why SOA and app servers are loved by the vendors: They don't charge per user, and as additional apps are deployed, they require additional licenses.

If you have large numbers of users who may or may not come into the system, you might want to ask about pricing the software accordingly. Let me explain. Let's say you're a bank and you allow customers to bank online for free once they open an account. A lot of little old ladies will not do this. And a lot of users may log in once or twice to set their preferences, but once they've got direct deposit configured, they may never log in again. Ever. Do you want to get charged for them? This is a situation where you might ask about server-based pricing, based on expected throughput, rather than seat-based, because out of your million customers, only 50,000 will authenticate on a regular basis. Of course, when you do ask about this, you may be told it's not available. But it never hurts to ask.

If you have a large incidence of turnover, you might also ask, whether it is okay to reuse a license when a user goes away? In other words, I paid for a hundred users, and when one quits, can I plug in his replacement without getting charged for an additional seat? Well, yes and no. Yes, it's just a seat. You paid for a hundred, and only a hundred are using the system. However, as discussed elsewhere in this book, you never really delete anybody. If a terminated user is still in the directory for historical and auditing purposes, then they're still there. If you actually *delete* that user, it's a different story, but fat chance of that happening. Only if you completely offload that user into a different directory not integrated with your identity system is that user considered gone.

Cloud Computing

I still really wonder about cloud computing. In an era when everybody is (justifiably) paranoid about identity theft, phishing, and every other possible online catastrophe, and when so many enterprises can't secure even their own internally hosted enterprise data, we're putting everything out on the curb as services. On the cloud, as they say. Well, if you're one of those folks investigating vendors of cloud-based services, ask all the right questions, then ask them again.

How do they manage privileged user access? This function is even more critical in a cloud environment. Are they standards-based? You won't host *everything*, so you will need to move data and transactions and identities back and forth, securely and with as little proprietary functionality as possible. Do they have other customers? Of *course* they do. So how will they segregate your data from other people's data? Do they support federation? They'd better, because you'll want your users to authenticate locally, then SSO in secure fashion to the cloud host.

When it comes to regulatory compliance, you're responsible for your data. If your cloud vendor allows a breach, it might be their fault, but it's still your liability. Will your cloud vendor be able to ensure that the data you keep for your customers, employees, vendors, partners, and suppliers will be completely secured? A cloud vendor, without proving that its security is airtight, will end up being engaged for only lesser functions. But let's say they're completely safe. How well do they support your audit needs? How responsive are they?

How is data stored? For that matter, where is it stored? Is it stored offshore? Is it stored separately from data they store for their other hosted customers? Would a breach of one of their other customers mean your data is also at risk?

Is your data encrypted? And even if it's encrypted, does that mean just at rest, or as well as when it's in transit or in backup?

In the event of a breach or other misuse of your data, will the cloud vendor fully support forensic analysis?

What about escrow? Make sure that you have a contractual agreement as to the treatment and dispensation of your data if something should happen to your cloud vendor. You presume they're not going to sell it. But you need continuity—that is, no interruption of service—while you either continue doing business with whoever acquires them, or you migrate to another provider. Or you end your paranoia and get the heck out of the cloud while you wait for that market to mature.

Another thing to consider as a best practice: In some regions, as in the European Union, there are restrictions on where you can store certain private data. This may preclude you from hosting certain types of apps or data on a cloud vendor's servers.

It's astounding how many cloud vendors still do not support federation. In other words, they cannot accept an assertion, such as in SAML, from a customer, whose employees or other users must remember a separate name and password just for that vendor. This is one of the purposes Oracle is giving to the Fedlet, which they acquired from Sun as part of that company's old Access Manager. The Fedlet allows a service provider to get on board with a lightweight assertion acceptance.

One Last Thing about Vendors

We discussed this already. Once you have a product you like in your sights, use that vendor. They want to sell you software. You want your IAM project to get rolling. They may pick you (the person, not the company) as their internal champion, to help them. Make it a two-way street. Tell that vendor that you need collateral, ROI data, comparisons, references—whatever it is that helps you get the value across to your management. Make them dance like monkeys. But keep it civil and reasonable, and don't abuse people, because vendors will bend over backwards for people—not just for the money but when they *like* you. A customer I had back in 1990, from when I worked at a place that doesn't even exist any more, still calls me with tech questions. Another one from 1999, and another from 2000, same thing. I get *nothing* from these people, except a thank you. I consider that worth it.

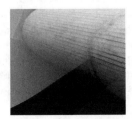

CHAPTER
17

Getting Help with
Your IAM Project

Light is the task where many share the toil.
    —Homer

orget Homer. An identity project worth its bytes will be hard work for *everybody*, which is why spreading out the pain is a great idea.

There's nothing wrong with saying you don't know everything. Or for that matter, you might very well have brilliant people working for you, but simply not enough muscle. Face it, your internal staff doesn't implement IAM on a daily basis. So it's pretty common with IAM projects to shop for help. There are lots of options, not all of them good, but several of them very decent.

I'm not saying you *have to* go to the well for help. But I'd highly recommend it, even if only for guidance. It certainly can't hurt to have a discussion with people who've done this before, to help you get started, get focused, sharpen your approach, point out some do's and don'ts, and so on. I have seen customers call in consultants to point the way, then be so impressed that they decided to keep the consultants on for the entire ride. I've also seen customers get consulting help on clearing the deck and setting direction, then cut them loose and roll their own.

You could pick up some cheap consultants, loners as pure bodies, but then don't expect them to strategize, architect, or work together in harmony.

When I built a new house in the last couple of years, I found a great builder, and I could have been my own general contractor, but I had a regular job to do. I'm on planes too much, and I wouldn't have been around to handle all manner of things that came up. So I used a general contractor to do that for me. Sure, it cost me more money, but my house wasn't built sideways.

Types of External Resources

You know how to run your business. If you don't, then you should be doing something else for a living. So document all your processes, the ones that work and the ones that are handicapped because you don't have a functioning IAM platform. Figure out exactly what you want to have happen, and only *then* do you bring in the outside geniuses to tell you how *they* would get you there.

In my opinion, there are a few ways to go:

- You're running the whole thing, so you only need some bodies. You will make all design and execution decisions. You will point and click and the hired hands will do exactly what you tell them to do.

- You need someone to help you see the path, an outside organization that's done this before. They will advise you on technology, design, compliance issues, communications. But you will actually do the work, while your consultants provide guidance. They may not even hang around to the end. You can go with someone smaller (and therefore more negotiable) or with a larger group. We'll talk about the pros and cons of smaller and bigger in just a bit.

- You need someone else to do the bulk of the work. You don't have the internal resources, and aren't willing to bring any more on, to build out an IAM framework.

You have everyday jobs already, don't you? This outfit may even take over management of the internal resources, the actual employees, whom you put on the project. This can be a very sensitive thing to do. Consultants in this vein may also be hanging around well into post-deployment, to smooth out any wrinkles. It all depends on when and to what extent you are willing to take over all administrative tasks.

■ Use resources from the vendor. No one should know their products better, right? The difference is usually that software vendors are not in the services business per se; they simply have services people to help customers deploy, but they don't manage long-term. If they do, that's not always a great indication as to the maturity of their products. For example, Oracle has a robust consulting organization, meant to help customers deploy solutions as quickly and comprehensively as possible, then turn over intellectual ownership to those customers.

When the Seller and the Builder Are a Package Deal

Sometimes a software vendor walks in with an integrator attached at their hip. Or your trusted advisor/partner has a software vendor whose products they know well. Wow, that sounds like a great deal. But you don't stop asking questions there, obviously.

If you've already got an implementation partner figured out, why have they chosen to partner with that particular vendor? How many joint customers do they already have? Can you talk to any of them? Is it just a financial, reseller-type relationship, or did they actually go with the best technology?

By the way, it's not sinful if the partner has more than one technology choice available to them. But then don't necessarily take their word for what choice they make on your behalf. You still need to vet the software personally.

If you've already got the software picked out, and that vendor has a partner in mind, it's probably a safer deal than the first situation. The vendor will have presumably certified that partner on their software.

In a package deal, you're already talking about a relationship where you'd hope they have good rapport. This is vitally important when there are issues with deployment and support, and there *will* be issues. I'm very familiar with situations where partner resources knew more about the vendor's product than many of the vendor's own staff.

Okay, but just because the partner knows the vendor(s), do they know the relevant product? Maybe they're bidding on something they shouldn't. I've heard it from integrators before: "If we get the business, we'll bring in the right people, or maybe just subcontract right back out to the vendor." This means the customer has just engaged the services of a middleman.

True Story

I sold some access management software to a facility in the frozen north. Our team provided the customer with a list of partners certified on the product. They instead chose another integrator, who we knew did not have the right stuff. "They know your products," the customer explained, "plus they're cheap."

"They know *some* of our products," we countered, "but not the access stuff."

The initial implementation was not good. So the integrator farmed the work out to yet another integrator, and still there were problems. Full deployment was slow, the bills added up, lawyers were involved, and eventually another party altogether had to swoop in and clean up.

The partners that have a viable identity practice can be very deep, and they can draw on various corners of their organizations for whatever they may need. You will often hear of their "offshore development capabilities," which means a couple of things. First off, it implies "cheaper," the value of which can be subjective. It can also mean a development group that is dedicated to just that, pure development, so it is not distracted by sales events.

Small-to-Medium Integrators

When an NFL receiver is slow, they call him a *possession* receiver. When an integrator is small, they call it a *boutique.* But this doesn't necessarily carry bad connotations. Boutique also can mean adaptive, fast-moving, flexible. Also likely cheaper, although you always have to consider total cost of ownership, TCO. If a guy offers to put a new roof on your house in three hours for $500, you'll save a lot of money, but you'll also be buying a lot of garbage cans later to put under the leaks. So it comes down to checking their references, financial viability, number of total resources, and number of resources who know the right technology. A small place might very well count the secretary when you ask about number of resources. What you're looking for is the number of bodies who are actually educated on the relevant technology.

Occasionally you'll see individual boutique consultants popping in and out of a project, because the really good ones on the team will get grabbed to run off to another customer's emergency. You will want continuity.

Smaller means fewer resources. For larger jobs, ones that will make their fiscal year, they may pull in additional bodies. But will those bodies be up to the task in the right timeframe? It's completely normal to ask for resumes of individual contributors.

If you're using the boutique for architecture and not just muscle, you still need to digest their recommendations. If you're only using them for muscle, beware of this: I've seen smaller outfits come in and do exactly, and only, what they're told to do. This means that you'd better know exactly what you want. If you need them to exercise their brain a little bit, you need to spell out what you know and what you don't. But I've had a lot of luck with smaller integrators as well, who know full well that, given their size, their reputation is only as good as their last assignment. They are often fiercely dedicated. They need to be.

True Story

I was contacted about finding a resource to *possibly* take over IAM project management at a transportation company. They'd been through a number of project managers, none of whom had succeeded. One of their software vendors, desperate to keep a trusted advisor role, kept cycling different PMs in and out.

They finally found a guy who owned an IdM practice. He personally came in to do the job. The first clue that this guy had no clue was our discussion about roles and policies. On the first conference call, he started reading the customer's project outline, which was titled "RBAC requirements." Except that he pronounced it "R-Bock," like it was some kind of German beer.

"Ah, you mean R-Back?" I corrected him.

He lasted three weeks. While his employees apparently knew IdM, he himself did not.

Larger Integrators

What's better about bigger integrators? Easy. They're bigger. They have more resources. They probably have more resources trained on any one particular technology than smaller integrators have *total*. They can draw resources from other projects, if need be. They can afford to fix it if they screw it up. They probably have more references.

What's worse about bigger integrators? Easy. They're bigger. They're less flexible. They're also less tactical, because they're looking for strategic relationships, not the more tactical ones that the smaller guys go for. They'll want to analyze your needs for a month before they touch a keyboard.

And if they're churning a lot of junior people in and out, here's what's going on. These guys are cheaper, to you and them. So they get your name on their resume, and then they're farmed out to the next opportunity, only at another 20 bucks an hour. If you've got a contract that says you can't be used as a reference, well, that's lovely, but meaningless. Your name has been used to sell a $70/hour kid as a $90/hour kid at the next one. That is why you ask your integrators for continuity. Make sure you keep the resources they give you, assuming they appear to be doing a good job.

References

Whether you're a software vendor, a consultant, a job-seeker, or a potential nanny, references are golden. Preferably your consultants have referenceable accounts as their own organization, as opposed to individual references for their individual bodies, although occasionally those are nice as well. What matters is that you're comfortable with their ability to bring the right brains and muscles to the table.

Remember our discussion about the Gartner magic quadrant with regard to vision and ability to deliver? You need the same comfort level about your consultants. You need to feel that they understand your requirements, at a functional as well as a tactical level, and also that they can actually deliver on that understanding. It's quality of bodies, and yes, it's also quantity.

If the consultant is in any way tied up with your chosen software vendor or vendors, then the reference may very well come from those vendors. This might sound like a potential conflict of interest, but remember, the vendor desperately wants you to succeed. They want to sell you something else later, and they want (you guessed it) the reference that you might provide them later. So they will (hopefully) not recommend any consulting group that they don't trust to represent them.

Recent references are always the best, and large references naturally carry more weight. The more complex and difficult the deployment they've pulled off, the more ability they obviously have. These types of references also may indicate that the consultants also have background with other technologies relevant to your project.

At Oracle, I have go-to partners with whom I'm personally familiar. Oracle demands that partners be educated, certified, trained on their products. Partners often work closely with product management so they can be on top of any product upgrades that may affect current or near projects.

Transfer of Knowledge

There are three possible approaches when transitioning the end of an IdM project that has been implemented by integrators or partners.

- **They're sticking around**. If you're planning on the partner keeping a steady presence, because you're relying on them to maintain, upgrade, or even run your system, you *still* need somebody in your organization to know what the partner does.

- **They're not sticking around**. If you're planning on the partner disappearing once you've got a handle on things, that means that you need to get a handle on things. Don't wait until the project is winding down. Begin the knowledge transfers early and often. Learn what the processes are.

- **They're sort of sticking around**. If you're planning on having a minimal partner presence after deployment, for whatever reason, then take charge. Otherwise, you will end up with a larger partner presence as time goes by. They will become a crutch. Use them for what you intend to use them for, and don't let their footprint creep up on you.

If consultants don't seem to be in a hurry to transfer their knowledge, it might be that they consider this information job security. Well, too bad, you bought it, and you need to know it, unless you plan on outsourcing this work indefinitely.

If custom code has been developed, it should belong to you. If the consultant has brought in any stubs, extensions, or other customizations of their own, you need to know who owns those as well. Intellectual property developed as part of your project needs to be in your domain. Also make sure you put the upgrades of these customizations on paper.

Keeping the Peace

Before the birth of our second child, we were reminded by relatives to make sure the new baby arrived with a gift for the *first* child, so that nobody would feel ignored during all the attention given to our new addition. We made sure the older one felt loved, involved, and not left out.

This is not to say that your existing employees are babies. But any time there are external resources coming in the door, there is always the risk that those who are already in place will feel threatened or discounted. Not only should you make the effort to ease their minds, assuming you like them, but you should also make sure any consultants who take part in your IAM project also make that effort.

True Story

Several years ago, a high-ranking exec at a partner company had just negotiated a master services agreement with the VPs at a joint customer. In other words, if and when the work comes, here's how we bill you. He was then going into the IT community of that customer, to actually get them to order some services. I explained to him that part of my pitch, when I sold them my software, was that we would help the IT staff master the product, keep them involved, and actually enhance their resumes, which was absolutely true. I further explained to him that the IT staff, while not the ultimate deciders, were extremely influential. They looked upon consultants as a threat to their job security. Therefore I advised him to make friends with them.

Instead, he marched in and told them his outfit would be in charge, he'd be providing all the guidance and architecture, and the IT staff would almost be hired help for his band of consultants. It was no surprise to me when he didn't get the work.

Make sure that you and your staff feel comfortable with any outside deployment personnel. If everybody isn't pulling in the same direction, things will break. Finger-pointing can destroy the chemistry, and delay fixes for any hurdles. In any IAM project, there are many moving parts: the directory and logging database, the plug-ins or proxies that intercept the requests, the authentication and authorization servers, the provisioning system and its connectors, and of course the business applications themselves. If something hitches up, is it the firewall, a third party's certificates, the authentication policies, the LDAP, or sunspots? A good set of relationships between the internal and external parties will help suppress the blame game and get people focused on solving problems rather than self-defense.

NOTE

Here's something that happens on occasion. The customer gets to like the consultant or the vendor's engineer so well that they offer him or her a job. The vendor often lets these things slide, in order to keep the customer relationship, but beware; you can really muck up the chemistry if you steal somebody.

And just to remind you one last time … no matter what kind of help you get, for development, testing, or even project management, it is still YOUR project. Stay in charge, ask for status, ask for deliverables, for results. Later on, any blame for any mistakes will be on you. Of course, you also get the credit.

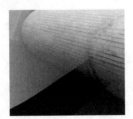

CHAPTER
18

Notes on the Actual
Implementation

"There are no good surprises."

      —Pete, the guy who built my house

he actual deployment period for any project, including an IAM framework, can be an unhappy one for a couple of unavoidable reasons. First, it's a lot of work. Your internal resources are being pulled from their regular duties. There are constant issues and interruptions. And of course, none of this effort is revenue-generating.

Second, there's nothing to show for a while. You are putting effort in, and not seeing any results. Even if you pick those low-hanging fruit, like simple authentication or basic provisioning, it's not instantaneous (although little stuff can be put in place within days). But you have made your plans and, more importantly, your commitments, and therefore you execute.

The point is to stick to that plan, and keep bad surprises to a minimum while you're in the middle of building your IAM framework. Just remember that no matter what you do, you will never keep everybody happy. Things will come up. Bad things will happen. Factor them in and deal with them. Don't try to hide things. And stick to the plan—until you can't.

Keep People in the Loop (Sort Of)

If you tell everybody everything, you will regret it, guaranteed. Yes, that sounds blunt, but it's true. Provide the information to the appropriate parties as necessary, or else you will invite questions and requests that will threaten to derail your timeline. Despite your best efforts at educating the organization as to the plan, there will be those who simply haven't paid much attention, and once they start to comprehend what is being undertaken, they will suddenly *want* to get in on it. I have seen this in multiple projects.

When one of my companies bought another company, we were asked 19 times a day, "What's going to happen with all those people you acquired? And what's the roadmap look like? Which products are you going to keep? Can I get any of their stuff cheap now?" And so on. Many of us could speculate as to how it would all shake out, but we couldn't say for sure, and even if we knew, we weren't allowed to say.

My company put up a web page explaining the latest and greatest, along with all the usual disclaimers. It was terribly handy pointing outsiders to that page and explaining, "I can't tell you, and even if I could, I don't know anything. Go look at the web site."

To keep the mob happy and off your back, or to at least avoid the endless redundant questions during the rollout, provide an internal document or site explaining the rollout, the plan, the effort, the expectations, and maybe, only maybe, some notion of the timeline. As with any large project, you can't guarantee a precise delivery date. And whether or not you're trying to be informative, an information page or wiki, or even simple HTML, will at least make it appear that you're making the effort. Just make sure you've got the project plan well in hand before you do this, of course. Here's why.

Near where I live, there's a vacant lot in a very nice neighborhood with a sign proclaiming that soon they'll be building a shopping plaza. That sign's been there since 1988.

Years ago, a customer of mine put up a single web page about a coming project that became drastically delayed because of dueling budget initiatives. The page itself became a running joke, as the days and weeks dragged on and the project languished. Someone even put up a second page making fun of the first page. Now, if you advertise, and subsequently run into reasonable delays, it's perfectly okay to post the why's and wherefore's, unless the dueling budget requesters decide to kill you.

You don't need to expose every single glitch, otherwise you'll be exposing something every other day. But neither do you expose all your successes. If you have something to show off, especially if it's in keeping with the timeline, that's fine. We've already discussed being able to demonstrate those low-hanging fruit to validate the effort to management. Showing progress is a good thing. If you wish to demonstrate basic authentication and a landing page, perhaps with SSO to at least one application, then by all means, show this to a couple of critical stakeholders. But don't go crazy showing things off, since this might skew expectations. Yes, show progress. But don't look cocky.

Governance

In the movie "Toys," Robin Williams inherits his father's toy factory, and an uncle (played by Michael Gambon of "The Singing Detective" and "Harry Potter") comes in to run the place. Suddenly, the uncle has all sorts of secret projects going on that even the owners aren't allowed to know about.

You think that can't happen to you and your project? If you've got a huge implementation, that doesn't mean you just hand over the keys to the integrator. I've seen this happen. This is how completed items don't get unit-tested. It's how deliverables slip. It's how you suffer scope creep as your own staff starts communicating their requests to the integrators directly without review. It's how the billable hours go through the roof. Because it's so big and complex, and you've got your regular duties to perform, you stop asking questions or keeping up with the governance. Too bad. You asked for the project and the funding, so *pay attention*.

It's not always a matter of not trusting people. It's that *stuff happens*. Did you ever participate in one of those social engineering tests in school, where the teacher lines everybody up, then whispers something into the first kid's ear and says, pass it on? The first kid whispers to the second, the second to the third, and so on. So it starts out as "my dog has fleas" and ends up as "Grandma's made out of cheese." Things get lost in translation over time. You might occasionally need to reset certain strategic or tactical goals. It's almost like the reconciliation process we discussed a while back. When reality begins parting from policy, restate the policy and get everybody back on track.

Occasionally, when a project starts veering off for technical or resource reasons, the goal gets restated so as to match up with the actual results. This is changing the facts to fit the theory.

If you have multiple parties (lines of business, partners, corporate customers) involved with your project, either appoint or make *them* appoint one or more representatives who will serve as the messengers, troubleshooters, and blame-eaters for their respective organizations. They will be the ones with whom you sit down in a room when there's an issue, and there *will be an issue*. Trawling-net meetings, where you pull every single body from every single party into one room, are not necessarily great ways to efficiently troubleshoot problems. Therefore you designate individuals from the stakeholder groups to represent the respective interests.

Set responsibilities. Stay involved. If there's a dispute, do not let the different external parties try to resolve it *without* your direct intervention. It will take five times longer, and will not be properly documented. You need to mitigate any disagreements, and document them (for reasons we'll go over shortly). This also keeps you aware of the dynamics between the parties.

True Story

A very large integrator took over a very large project after a previous integrator had failed. They began to show the customer how a more professional organization did things, including daily design reviews. Whenever a review was called, literally two dozen of the integrator's personnel would leave their keyboards and crowd into a room. Individual projects and solutions were chronically behind because so many workers dropped their duties for an hour or more at a time. Whenever there was the slightest disagreement, the project lead from the integrator would say, "Everybody into the conference room."

As the software vendor's representative, I attended several of these during onsite visits. After the last of three meetings on a particular day, during which several of the attendees spent more time checking messages or e-mail than actually contributing, one of my engineers asked the customer's project manager, "Do you have any idea how much that meeting just cost you?"

After some simple math, she found that this latest short gathering had cost just under $2000 U.S. That afternoon, she issued a memo specifying that from that day forward, only essential personnel would attend the reviews. A year later, another integrator ably took over the project, and with far fewer meetings.

In this case, the customer shouldn't have needed three consecutive integrators. But they handed the keys to somebody else and invested lots of trust but little governance. This is not to say that a third party will take advantage of you every time. I have worked with numerous integrators over the years who made my customers successful, and who very capably deployed my products. Just remember, "Trust, but verify."

Mid-Stream Changes

Part of governance is ensuring that you stick to the plan. But here's where I tell you I was lying. "Stick to the plan" sounds easy. You tell anyone who interrupts you with requests that are not part of the initial deployment that they will simply have to wait. But *stuff happens*.

During a years-long rollout at a global manufacturer, line of business owners who felt left out of the initial rollout kept petitioning for earlier inclusion in the framework. Their users and resources were not scheduled to be integrated for over a year, as systems deemed more critical were first addressed. But influence stemming from long-standing relationships allowed these parties to affect the schedule in their favor. Some of the requests made no sense from a business perspective, but they were put into priority anyway, and then the floodgates opened.

The project managers did the smart thing. With every one of these reprioritized requests, they prepared a document outlining

- How the overall timeline would be affected
- The impact on the other users and resources being bumped from the schedule
- The realignment of internal resources as subject matter experts were juggled around

In fact, their most powerful argument against various reprioritized items was the need to reschedule internal experts. "We expected to pull the PeopleSoft team in October, but now we have to push that to January, and draft the LDAP guys." These movements can have a ripple effect that involve other line of business owners.

The project managers made upper management sign off on all changes, and aid them in communicating changes to those departments who were getting bumped. In several cases, they were able to hold the line, based on the potential impact.

Since we're talking about a framework, in which each piece helps lay the foundation for the next, the other item to consider is, what will a delay of any one component do to the *overall* goal? You can't have cross-domain single sign-on until you have *single* domain single sign-on. You can't have federation until you have authentication. There is no provisioning without an authoritative source.

Compliance is often a big driver for at least some of the functionality within a framework. But it's only in the very last few years that audit requirements have been significant drivers of IAM. Even in the early years of SOX, it wasn't a big consideration. These days, it's common to see organizations putting in at least some aspect of IAM in order to pass their next scheduled audit. That is a powerful argument for staying on schedule.

Phased Deployment

As you had already long surmised, trying to service all users and all resources in the first round is completely impossible. Even if you have a vanilla environment (for example, all you provision to is database tables or LDAP groups), you still likely have lots of these vanilla targets to map out. Therefore you will be rolling out in segments.

As you do this, be sure to record your results. Some things will go smoothly, because of all your intense planning, and all the helpful suggestions you got from your committee members. But there will also be obstacles, unforeseen issues, last-minute requests, unexpected disagreements, and technical problems.

Don't have too many individual projects going at once. Don't let anyone rush you, unless they're willing to learn how to help you expedite the timelines and take responsibility. In some cases, I've seen the need or desire to establish business application connections (for provisioning and/or SSO) prompt local admins to learn the process of creating connectors or adapters so that they could get their own departmental apps online sooner.

And before you move on to the next phase, make sure that the previous one is complete. This means *tested* and signed off on. As we discussed in Chapter 7, it helps to have agreement with individual departments or resource owners as to what "complete" means to them. Getting sign-off serves two purposes. First, you've satisfied the requirements, done the job. Second, you've covered yourself, allowing you to not only report that you've hit another milestone, but that you're okay to move on to the next task in the framework construction timeline.

If audit support is one of your drivers, then obviously this should be out front in the schedule.

Cut-Overs

When the time comes to move a resource from its current state to a protected one, there are several things you can do to lessen the impact. These include having both old and new access methods available for a short period, in case anything strange *does* happen. You can also use the framework to provide both old and new access for a period as well, with the presumption being that once everything looks good, you turn off the old.

For example, a standard OOTB function of Oracle Access Manager is the ability to use secondary user stores for authentication. If you are deploying a new directory as part of your new framework, OAM can attempt to authenticate to the new directory and, failing that for unforeseen reasons, authenticate to additional directories. Fallback authentication methods can be employed as well. Once the kinks are worked out, and those secondary methods are no longer needed, the configuration can be changed to ignore them.

During a cut-over, it's also advisable to monitor the performance of the components as they come online and begin to get hammered with traffic to see if there is a need to make adjustments in the architecture. As we discussed with regard to OAAM, you don't always know *how* users will engage new resources in large numbers. Hopefully load testing has already helped you in validating your system sizing. In the next chapter, we'll discuss the use of Oracle Enterprise Manager for monitoring all the components for a point solution, such as identity, access, and federation.

In Chapter 13, we discussed the Deployment Manager in Oracle Identity Manager. The purpose of this tool is to migrate configuration data between environments, such as between development, test, and production, and in doing so, minimize the most common issues that arise when moving from one server to another. The Deployment Manager governs the migration of the definitions involving:

- Organizations
- Resource, form, field, rule, and email definitions
- Password and access policies
- Lookups, tasks, and error codes
- Adapters

When it's time to cut over from test to production, Deployment Manager is a powerful tool with various functions designed to keep you from making mistakes during migration; but it should be used in accordance with very well documented best practices that are available from Oracle.

Training

Training should start taking place in the weeks prior to the actual launch. And training isn't just teaching people how to use the software. It's comprehending the procedures, the processes, and the options. Make sure everyone understands their responsibilities and their escalation procedures when things break, because they *will*.

If a partner is providing the training on a vendor's product, make sure the vendor signs off on the content. Is the partner certified to provide this training? Or are they simply regurgitating the training that they themselves have previously attended?

Let's poke a small hole in a commonly-used industry term: "train-the-trainer." It's the notion that, instead of training the entire IT department, you train some key people, and they'll spread the wisdom around. And of course they'll remember perfectly what they heard in class, and not miss a beat when they pass it on.

This works *to a degree*. But you will still need access to resources, human or otherwise, who truly know the material. Those trained trainers will have a clear head start, and will no doubt be of great use to the organization. But they will not be perfect resources once their initial training is done. That perfection only comes with time and experience.

Partners are occasionally guilty of misplaced optimism over train-the-trainer as well. And why are they in a hurry to do this? Because they're getting *paid* for it, naturally. Now, this is not to say that integrators are not capable of delivering training on somebody else's product. Oracle has many partners who know its products to an incredibly granular level, for both delivery and training purposes. Just verify that your software vendor signs off on the integrator's ability to deliver that training.

If train-the-trainer is the way you're going to proceed as well, consider performing that training in compartmental fashion. Instead of designating members of your staff to know the whole nine yards, designate target members instead to be subject matter experts (SMEs) on a limited set of features or functions so that they will have greater retention of their lesser scope, at least in the short term. Eventually everybody will absorb more content, but don't let anything fall through the cracks because you made their brains too full right off the bat.

Multiple levels of training will be required. Administrators, end users, and non-employees will all require a transfer of knowledge. If you have an arrangement with customers or partners to manage their own users or policies via delegated administration, then they definitely need to share the burden of knowing how to perform these functions, or else you will be taking a lot of phone calls.

Developers will also require training. They will no longer be building security directly into their apps... *probably*. If you are making use of Oracle Entitlements Server for fine-grained entitlements within your code, then your developers may still be at least setting the table for security. However, what they are doing is simply providing the hooks for the framework to do its job, and OES will still be used for configuring, storing, and evaluating centralized policies. Developers will be opening up the pipe to the policy engine to make authorization decisions and provide responses. In most other cases, security and identity will be handled in the framework as a separate layer. Still, there are best practices for inserting these hooks into the code. Another point to make about Oracle Entitlements Server is that it is not enough to simply know the API. There is an entire design aspect to OES, regarding the definition of resources and rules, that well serves the framework. Therefore don't simply point programmers to the manual and ask them to bang it out.

If you are following the excellent advice of not boiling the ocean, then you will be migrating additional user groups and/or resources into the framework. This means needing to build integrations in a way that is compliant, accurate, and well-performing. In the case of Oracle Identity Manager, this may entail learning the Adapter Factory, which is used for constructing connections to targets or sources for which a connector does not exist.

Rounding Up the Stragglers

During a discovery session at a public sector client, I was astounded at the number of side projects and barely documented applications within the organization. People were given lots of leeway for creating their own databases, web sites, and other assets that were barely or not-at-all secured. We quickly identified these areas as potential security disasters, since so many of these smaller databases were created from data extracts of corporate data. Our first observation was, the auditors will kill you. Our first suggestion was, grab these resource owners and make them get on board the identity platform.

You will be instructing any owners or developers of skunkworks projects on how to join the security framework. You won't want them managing their own access, and they shouldn't want to do it anyway. You are providing authentication (including SSO) and authorization as a service, simultaneously relieving them of the burden and preventing them from creating a security hole. Placing their security needs in the hands of the framework is both a benefit and a responsibility to these folks.

Lastly, training includes teaching users and administrators new procedures:

- **Troubleshooting**   Options are available for diagnosing and fixing problems.

- **Attestation**   Resource owners and managers will need to know what it means when they are called to perform this process, and how to do it.

- **Problem reporting**   Users and administrators will need to know what links, documents, and other resources are available when something breaks or is just plain confusing (because they weren't paying attention to the *first* round of training).

- **Responding to notifications**   A raft of new messages will be showing up on screens and in mailboxes, and they're there for a reason.

- **Self-service**   You can now do a whole bunch of things for yourself, so take advantage.

Make Sure Everybody Plays Nice

Your staff, your vendors, your consultants… they're all your children. And I do mean *children*. If you haven't seen one of these big projects before, you simply will not believe how childish, vindictive, or territorial the parties can become. Vendors want to get paid, but they want a happy, referenceable customer. Integrators want the same thing, although their costs are often not as fixed as the vendor's. Your staff wants a successful deployment, but they also want to maintain control and remind the vendors and the integrators who the customer is, while simultaneously protecting their own jobs. You want all this done as quickly, efficiently, and cheaply as possible. *Everybody* wants to deflect blame when something, inevitably, goes wrong.

Remember the 57 authentication policies? Besides being a cautionary tale of how to abuse a product's API, it's also an example of how the customer raised an issue, and a consultant deflected blame and pointed at the product vendor. The result was a far longer road to resolution, and a damaged relationship between two parties vital to the success of the IAM project.

Sanity-check *everything*. Make sure any deployment partner is telling you what you need to hear, and not just enough to keep you happy so they can keep billing you. If it doesn't sound right, or probable, or *possible*, then it probably isn't.

And at all times, make sure that your staff is involved, and that they *feel* that they are involved. Don't let them think that they're only spectators, especially when there's outside parties tracking mud on the carpet. Your staff will own this thing when it's done. Don't think that adult, professional system administrators can't have their feelings hurt. Assign them duties that give them oversight. It's a good thing to do, and a smart thing. A sense of ownership will give them an incentive to keep a watchful eye.

Control the Communications

You're in charge, right? Even if you put a consultant or other partner in charge of the project, maintain connectivity to all parties. It's common to have one consultant managing other consultants. They are literally managing others who *compete with them*. This means that any feedback you get on those underlings may be colored by opinion or what the managers want you to think or know. "Oh sure, they're doing a good enough job, I guess, but when we get to the next phase, we might consider another party for the coding." Uh-huh. I've seen consultants as well as vendors mess with each other in order to weasel their way more deeply into the customer's affections. So even in situations where you're allowing one group to manage the other groups, stick your head in once in a while and get everybody's opinions on how it's going, and do it in private. They might play nicely in front of you, but behind the scenes, *watch out*.

For each party involved, identify the head person, the one who will *own* an issue or problem. When in doubt, you hit up that person, and say, "Fix this."

If it's one of the auditing/consulting companies, you'll be assigned a "partner," which is an actual term they use. Think in terms of a law firm. When somebody hits a certain level, they're a partner. The ones who will cost you the most, if they are part of the billable team, are the "senior partners." But if you need somebody to jump and get something fixed, have that person's phone number handy, because they likely have the influence to move things around in a hurry, and hopefully they have their lofty position because of their ability to make things happen.

Everybody Protects Everybody Else

While it's a good assumption that everyone involved with an IAM project will keep their lips zipped about anything proprietary they learn, it's always good to have it on paper.

A lot of times you simply don't like to be used as a reference. Bear in mind that when you offer a reference for a vendor or integrator based on two things, a discount up front and a happy outcome on the back end, you will most assuredly receive reference calls. If you have not agreed up front to provide references, then you're done. But that's not to say that your name might not be used for selling purposes. If you absolutely don't want a vendor or integrator to use your name under any circumstances, you need to specify that in the paperwork in advance.

If you thought there was a lot of information floating around during the sales process, that's nothing compared to what's available during implementation. Make sure everybody is comfortable with the protections in place during this phase, including those that keep implementation partners (who would normally be competing against each other) from each other's throats.

Another important tip: If there are any issues, don't blow them out of proportion. There will be multiple parties involved. If any one of them gets heavily flogged for a mistake, they can end up being a scapegoat for everyone else. Fix things and move on.

Educate the Masses

Training is one thing. But understanding the good citizenship that comes with the new framework is another. Think of this as an opportunity to coach your user community not just on software, but on their corporate responsibilities. Make sure they understand not only what you are launching, but what is expected of them. This entails two concepts:

- **Best practices**   This is not to say that everybody has to do things differently just because you've put a new system in place. In fact, the system should adjust to the business, not the other way around, although hopefully you *will* be affecting in a positive way everybody's day-to-day activities through greater automation and transparency. What I am saying is, there may very well be better ways for them to do their jobs. In fact, the framework should just about guarantee that. If you have automated provisioning, for example, not only do you *not* want managers to manually provision as they've been doing forever, but you need them to know that the first time reconciliation runs, those manual provisioning efforts will be erased *anyway*. Managers and users need to take advantage of the new functionality. It's there for a reason.

■ **Required policies** So let's repeat. That manual provisioning should now be forbidden. It's against policy. A lovely landing page, with your stated corporate policy, should pop up the first time everybody logs in under the new framework. At the very least, provide an obvious link to those policies. Have a "lunch and learn." Host a call or web conference. Make sure everybody knows that things are different. And better. And that there are new requirements. As long as you've got the framework, also install the mindset. Part of that good citizenship means things like not creating unregulated data extracts. This is especially important if you don't mask or encrypt your sensitive fields at the database level. Don't share accounts. In other words, an IAM framework can prevent an awful lot of bad things, but a little common sense can help with the rest.

Establish Ownership and Responsibilities

An IAM framework is a powerful and necessary tool. It will provide benefit to management and end users alike. That said, it comes with a price beyond just hardware, software, and salaried hours. It requires care and feeding. Your procedures will be different. This goes without saying (but I just said it anyway). Policies must be maintained.

Across the Oracle identity suite, you have the power of *delegated administration*. You can create those sandboxes in which the administrators can do their jobs. It's a benefit, certainly, in that they are empowered to manage their own resources, users, and policies. But this includes the responsibility to perform that management. Departmental managers should not be calling *you* to create, modify, or delete much of anything. Delegated administration gives them that power, that right, and that responsibility. Make sure they understand this. Training tells them how to do it, but *you* tell them to actually *do* it.

CHAPTER
19

Post-Implementation:
Keeping the Framework
Running

Great works are performed not by strength but by perseverance.

—Samuel Johnson

t last, you're done. It's up, it's functioning. Your IAM framework creates new user accounts, provisions those users, governs their access, and keeps all this activity secure and compliant. There's nothing left to do! Except, you know, the really, really hard stuff.

With the framework operational, expectations will be higher than ever. Those who gave you budget and resources are certainly awaiting results from their investment; auditors are anticipating transparent, comprehensive data; and the employees, customers, and partners who are supposed to see enhanced security, service, and privacy should be *instantly* benefiting from a better user experience.

If evolution is the process by which species adapt to changing circumstances and environment, then consider the evolution of your organization as your identity and access management framework takes root and begins to influence your own environment, hopefully for the better. As your situation progresses, you will need to keep certain processes progressing as well.

Adoption

Remember what I said about how you need to keep selling? Well, if you ever want more budget for another project, or even just a second round for the next phase of the current project, make sure that information about the benefits of what you've done so far gets sent up the chain, although subtly and humbly.

"You mean you want to add *strong* authentication now? Heck, nobody's even using the provisioning tool yet, they're all still fat-fingering people into LDAP."

This means getting people to use the thing. If it's all been planned correctly, and sold internally, then the stakeholders and users should see the benefits of participating. It's meant to make their lives easier. It's likely a mandate. You'd like to think that your kids love you because, well, because they love you, and not just because you're the family wallet. And you'd like your internal customers to use the new IAM system because they love it, not because they must. On the access management side, they really have no choice, since they're getting prompted and policed and audited by the tools no matter what. Ask the web server for a page, pass through the WebGate for authorization. But unless you've got all the provisioning automated, they might still be pounding their own new users into the database and bypassing the requests and approvals. Even if they're following policy, they're not feeding the audit data.

If you need a hammer, remember the big one, compliance. Everyone should be getting enabled, re-enabled, and disabled via the proper protocols, not under the desk or behind the curtain. The second big one is likely security. This by itself serves the purpose of compliance. And then there's automation. This is a cost-savings and time-savings endeavor. There may be other drivers as well. Regardless, you have made the investment for very good reasons, and you need people to use it, for those same very good reasons.

In the meantime, while you're pushing that adoption, remember that there's a difference between implementing and rolling out. But let's revisit it briefly.

Implementing is installing, integrating, launching.

Rolling out is getting your users and administrators on board with the operation. You may or may not have been involving the users in the deployment, but before you throw the switch, it'll be time to get them plugged in, to avoid culture shock, and to make them and the IAM platform as productive as possible, as *quickly* as possible. This is where your education initiatives come in, including training and informational web site or e-mail blasts or whatever means you use to let people know when it's coming, when it's here, and where it's going. As you're implementing, you should be explaining to the community that the project is underway, that the benefits will be a positive thing for all, and there *will* be some differences.

Show Results

As we've already discussed, for the sake of keeping the confidence of stakeholders and/or management, keeping the funding coming, keeping the end-user community focused, and to ensure that everyone stays committed to adoption, it is highly recommended to show early results. These cannot be accidental; as I keep repeating, you should set an advance target, such as simple authentication and authorization, self-service, or provisioning to basics such as e-mail or the corporate LDAP. These early targets should either address the needs of critical stakeholders or the most users possible (or both). Any kind of automation is always something to show off, since manual processes are *de rigueur*, and taking those off the table is not only an obvious benefit; it's just plain *obvious*.

Monitor Those First Transactions

The first cycles are immensely important. Undoubtedly you'll be tuning policies, performance, notifications, and any number of other factors early on. That is not to say that everything will break. But even things that are working will perhaps not work quite the way you expected.

I remember an admin telling me how, shortly after his new identity system was operating, he was surprised by how many automated e-mails he started getting, and he made a couple of adjustments to alert levels and mailing lists.

The purpose of the IAM framework is to support compliance, security, and automation. If things aren't running a whole lot faster and safer, then you might need to do some tweaking.

The reporting engine across the Oracle identity suite is BI Publisher. It preserves and builds on the reports that have always been available through the individual components. These reports consist of both operational and historical data. These reports are not only useful for audit support purposes; they also help in analyzing usage and activity. By examining elements such as requests, approvals, password reset successes and failures, and other activities, you can identify areas where adjustments may need to be made. For example, the most basic of resources, such as access to e-mail, are most often granted automatically upon registration. But I have seen cases where literally every access point was subject to approval, which seems a burdensome bottleneck. Of course, I have also seen the exact opposite (often in higher education), where access to nearly every resource is automatic, while de-provisioning is not, resulting in far too much access for far too many people without benefit of review.

Pass That Audit

Many times I've started solution cycles with customers, from the point of exploration all the way through to choosing software and consulting resources, because of compliance concerns (either a failed audit or upcoming auditing requirements). If you've specifically failed an audit, then it's fairly simple to determine the exact requirements. But if it's a compliance mandate that you haven't faced previously, then you design your approach as best you can and, no kidding, hope that it's enough. Unless you've got internal and/or friendly auditors guiding you at every step, providing a very detailed blueprint, you can never be sure until the time comes that you're going to be judged compliant. In the last few years, audits have gone from fairly predictable events to learning experiences. Such is the nature of our new world.

If auditors are going to personally review your user-privilege data, then there are two ways you can go about making sure users have least privilege. The first is having reconciliation run between Oracle Identity Manager and the target systems. However, this is probably an unlikely short-term solution to your audit needs, for two simple reasons: Early in the project, you probably don't have all source and target systems hooked up to your framework, and even if you did, you probably haven't had time to tighten up all access policies. Either way, within the first few weeks it's highly unlikely that the new framework governs access to all the legacy systems.

The second option, attestation (or certification), is far more likely to succeed for you than reconciliation for that first audit. For one thing, you can generate attestation reports even for resources that are not fully integrated for provisioning (although any resources not integrated will not benefit from *actionable* attestation). Attestation gives you concrete, detailed evidence of a critical and very common compliance process being performed. It's easier for auditors to process this kind of information, since a majority of the time they won't be combing your user-privilege data at a granular level. As we discussed a little earlier, a chunk of compliance is simply the requirement to *demonstrate* that you're compliant, so hard copy always scores you points.

Accountability

Besides basic deliverables, make sure that all parties are sticking to their duties. When you have two or more integrators in play, you will absolutely need to monitor and smooth out communications between them, if you are not overtly controlling all traffic. I have multiple times seen a major integrator in charge of architecture and project management, while another integrator provided most of the heavy lifting. Most of the time they get along, but there's always some degree of jockeying for position.

Quite True and Quite Ridiculous Story

I deployed authentication and authorization on a customer's web site. All's well. Then an integrator was brought in to deploy a firewall. We quickly found that the firewall had a tendency to hand users the wrong session ticket. I log in as me, you log in as you, and some portion of the time, when returning to the server for the next request, I end up with your session. Oops.

You say, time to pressure the firewall vendor to fix their very ugly bug, right? But no. The integrator told the customer that the solution was to have my company's product compensate by intercepting each request, verify the user had the right session ticket, and if not, then look up the right ticket and hand that back to the user.

On a conference call with the customer, integrator, and firewall vendor, I tried to explain the insanity of this: It would require my product to decrypt the firewall's ticket, match it up with a user and, when necessary, invade the firewall's cache. Even if it had been technically feasible, it would have added unacceptable latency.

A pre-existing relationship had led to a preposterous deflection of blame and the incorrect conclusion. Luckily, the integrator's parent company was also a customer of mine in a different state, and when they heard about this crazy situation, they acted immediately. Among other actions taken, the firewall went away.

Monitor, Maintain, Modify

The one constant in life is change. It's not always for the best, but you can't stop it. Once you have your framework up and running, you will have a window during which you will mostly just let it be. And then you will have no choice but to change anyway. On the administrative side, some activities will require more effort and attention than expected, while others will take less.

On the user side, some people will resent new requirements, and some people will use the system in ways you neither want nor expect. You must realize, that's *always* been going on, only now you have better facility to detect and mitigate the situation.

Workflow definitions that route approval requests may be shortened. You may also be adding approval stops as well. Authorization rules sometimes get tweaked to make them more, or less, restrictive.

Once you've got your identity framework in place and working relatively well (after all those initial tweaks), it's time to see if it is actually being used the way you thought it might. You have dashboards and reports (which we've talked about) that allow you to look at the trends and the options:

- The most active users
- The least active users
- The average session length
- How long it takes for a user to be fully provisioned
- Which resources get the most use
- How well are assigned tasks (for example, certification) being executed
- What you can do with that data to make things run even more smoothly

Monitor and Manage the Pieces

Enterprise solutions are never simple, in terms either of their functionality or their architecture. You need to be able to check the temperature of your framework as needed, to ensure it is operating correctly and will continue to do so. Occasional adjustments may be necessary. And even without taking adjustments into consideration, you have distributed components that defy easy management just because of volume and location.

Oracle Enterprise Manager/Grid Control provides a framework (remember that all-important word?) for monitoring and configuring Oracle product components. Like an IAM framework, it provides for additional functionality to be plugged in, in this case in the form of what Oracle calls Management Packs. Packs are available for the range of Oracle products, including identity, federation, and access servers. Management Agents can actually perform discovery on the IAM components to bring them under the management umbrella. Once discovered, these components can all be analyzed individually.

Oracle Enterprise Manager provides a real-time dashboard for monitoring the health of your identity services. It can simulate user access and measure the responsiveness of the components. From a comprehensive console, you can centrally manage your framework, including Oracle and non-Oracle components such as firewalls, app servers, and directories. Enterprise Manager facilitates the discovery of new systems, automates the management of component configurations, and aids in the diagnosis of system faults.

OEM essentially provides a home page for every piece it monitors. If you are monitoring a service with subcomponents, then that service's home page within EM also provides links to the home pages for those components. On the home page for a service, EM displays the following information:

- Server status and performance
- Alerts
- Issue isolation data for diagnosis and resolution
- Resource usage
- Policy violations and their severity
- Links for starting and stopping components
- Server configuration data

By having this kind of data at your fingertips, you can make critical decisions on changes to your framework, including policies, sizing-up, load balancing, and other adjustments that can affect not only performance but security. As of this writing, I watched an engineer, just a week ago, use OEM to hunt down the bottleneck in a reconciliation process during a proof of concept. He diagnosed the problem and determined the solution, by using Enterprise Manager.

OAAM and the Evolution of Policies

Recall that Oracle Adaptive Access Manager provides a dashboard for monitoring possible real-time fraudulent activity. It can help analyze performance, statistics, risk scoring, and devices. You can also use the dashboard to create proactive fraud prevention rules by identifying suspicious activity.

You will have already established a baseline for what is considered acceptable user behavior, but now you will begin analyzing ongoing user activity, including any alerts that may have been generated. This allows you to refine risk profiles. Just to reiterate what has been previously discussed: A risk score is a combination of factors that include not just who you are (or who you purport to be) but also what you are, where you come from, how you act, and when you act.

OAAM is already aggregating historical data on users, which allows it to recognize anomalous behavior and react accordingly by, for example, performing denials or notifications based on activity that is out of the norm. But as an administrator, you help OAAM to do its job by adjusting that baseline.

In Chapter 10, we discussed using Oracle Adaptive Access Manager to create patterns or buckets of behavior (with established memberships) against which OAAM matches user activity, in order to find anomalous behavior. In other words, if members of a bucket aren't acting in a way you expected or care to allow, OAAM can identify those activities and adjust memberships accordingly via auto-learning.

For example, let's say you originally set up a pattern that includes the employees who work out of a particular office. Those employees who authenticate from that office are prompted for name and password. Whenever one of those employees authenticates from a different office, they are prompted for an additional PIN. You may also set up a threshold within the pattern that says, if an employee doesn't authenticate from that office within 30 days, he is automatically pulled out of that bucket, and his authentication requirements change accordingly, and permanently.

It's advisable for administrators to periodically review reports on bucket memberships, usage, and statistics, to determine if there is a need to adjust the requirements. For example, an office that includes a lot of salespeople who spend most of their time traveling might experience a large membership change, in which case the need for a PIN might be coming up more than you'd like.

Because one of the functions of OAAM is fraud prevention, it also provides the ability to open and track agent (fraud) cases. A regular customer service case can be escalated into an agent case (although the reverse is not true). Cases allow investigators to examine user sessions and any pertinent alerts. Sessions can be linked to a case, along with an accompanying importance level. If a suspicious user session automatically creates a case, then that session is automatically linked to that case. Specific data elements can also be linked to a case. Linking sessions and data to cases empowers investigators to focus on only the most relevant information in determining actual fraud.

In customer service cases, there is an option to *unregister* all devices for a user, forcing that user to perform activity from a standard device. Again, things change.

Deploying the Next Phase

You may recall the advice not to boil the ocean, and to deploy in phases. That means deferring some requirements until later. Well, now it's later. You've got that initial deployment online, so it's time to start considering the next phase. You've got more users to bring on board, more roles to construct, more resources to provision, and therefore more workflows to define and more access policies to establish. Make use of your log of what you've learned, what's worked and what hasn't, to refine your procedures for a smoother next phase, which should go faster and with fewer obstacles.

Did you run into issues getting service accounts created? Ports through the firewall? Hardware? Approvers doing their approvals? Do you need someone in management to apply any pressure? Do you need to put in your requests for accounts, ports, hardware, or pressure with more lead time?

Standards Support

Does anybody remember Security Services Markup Language (S2ML)? It morphed into Security Assertion Markup Language (SAML), which people used to laugh at because of the name. I worked at a company whose engineering department had practically invented SAML, and yet one year at a huge industry show in San Francisco, we were the only vendor in our space not demonstrating a product that supported it. It was embarrassing. SAML finally took off in a big way, and it's completely legitimate to ask if a product supports it. In fact, it's a necessity.

Some "standards" are simply trial balloons that are floating around out there, or good ideas that may or may not be validated eventually by the market. That's not to say that ideas necessarily need validation by commercial ventures, but without such support, they don't get far, and they get most of their attention on West Coast university blogs. Eventually some of them build up enough demand to weigh them down and bring them to earth, where they are adopted. And some just keep floating around, or die altogether. I'll bet you've never heard of S-HTTP (not to be confused with HTTPS).

A couple of years back, I was asked point-blank my unvarnished opinion of Service Provisioning Markup Language (SPML). A customer was looking at a couple of other add-ons, and was talking to vendors who didn't support SPML. I pointed out two things. Everybody was talking about SPML, but at the time, hardly anybody supported it; and eventually, whatever products they purchased would surely support it, if the market demand was there. Oracle Identity Manager supports SPML because customers demanded it, and it was an obvious roadmap item anyway. When you install Oracle Identity Manager, it generates a file for running the SPML Web Service, which turns SPML calls into provisioning calls.

However, SPML just isn't being adopted at the rate everyone assumed. Those relatively few vendors who have assimilated it often find themselves customizing their implementations. The standard itself, as of this writing, is too complex and does not perform well. The lack of a standard user schema doesn't help either, and that by itself will be difficult for all parties to agree on.

Client Attribute Request Markup Language (CARML) and Attribute Authority Policy Markup Language (AAPML) are on the way, but they could still be a long way off from full adoption. CARML defines privacy and attribute requirements for an application. It's like WSDL for non-services. AAPML defines when specified data elements (usually identity-related) are made available to applications, and how these elements can be used. I can edit my own home address and phone number, but am I allowed to edit my account number? Will I allow any of my elements to be used by another application for contact or other purposes? The reason someone thought these up is that while identity components have been mapped to use certain identity data, there was no way to describe the purpose of that data, and the rules for using it. Now, you could say that the people who make use of that data in the first place, for provisioning, authentication, authorization, and so on, already know what they need and why they need it. But as the world becomes more interconnected, and cloud computing becomes more the norm (with our data flying all over the place), we might want to package it up in such a way that it says to anybody looking at it, "Here's my data… and here are the rules for using it."

CARML and AAPML are layers of the Identity Governance Framework (IGF), which was created by Oracle to help companies specify how to use, store, and communicate identity information. IGF is now hosted by the Liberty Alliance.

Meanwhile, Extensible Access Control Markup Language (XACML) describes who has access to which resources. Not only is it a useful introduction for a user to a system ("Here's what he can have"), it is also a great way to store policies.

It would be nice to say that one day there will be a unified standard for Web service security, but not in our lifetimes, and that's not for technical reasons.

Why do you care about standards?

- **Federation** Your next big business partner may require that you support what they support.

- **Compatibility** Integration with your next corporate business app may require that you support its favorite protocol for provisioning or synchronization.

- **Quicker integration** My API doesn't like your API? Darn. But hey, we both speak the same standard, so let's communicate that way instead.

Who would have suspected, just a couple of years ago, that social networking functions, mashups, instant messaging, and wikis would become accepted, and even vital, business supports?

I occasionally (as in rarely) hear of Directory Service Markup Language (DSML). This is LDAP translated for HTTP traffic so that you don't need an LDAP client. It enables your browser to deal with LDAP, as well as package up multiple LDAP operations into one request. Does your IAM package need to support DSML? Not immediately, although Oracle Virtual Directory does.

So if all of this sounds so intimidating and complicated, what is the happy thought we take away from this? That's easy. If you deploy your business applications behind an identity and security framework, you have insulated those apps from those changes. Communications from the outside to those business apps can be mitigated by the framework, which intercepts resource requests, and subsequently communicates to those apps only the information that they need to know in order to allow in the user whom the framework has just authenticated and authorized. Here's the session ticket, here's the token, here's the assertion; please let him in, and don't worry about how it was done.

An IAM framework can not only be configured to support particular standards (most often in regard to communications with source and target systems), but it can actually facilitate the rollout of new standards. Here's my main point: Having a separate security layer, in the form of that framework, insulates business apps from having to deal with the baggage of those standards. This means that when new standards or protocols are deployed, the actual linkage is made with IAM, lessening the impact on the business itself.

What Did We Learn From All of This?

The effort to scope, lobby for, design, build, and deploy an IAM framework is more than considerable. It's a lot of very hard work, and requires considerable cooperation and contributions from many parties. The sheer improbability of success makes that success such an achievement.

The information and experiences I've related in this book probably seem like just common sense to many folks. There are likely things in this book you'd long thought of, heard of, suspected, seen done, or at least attempted. But hopefully you've learned a few new things, and if nothing else you've probably found a few things to be afraid of. Fear is a good thing, because it compels you to avoid bad choices, either yours or someone else's.

I always tell my kids, no matter what vocation they pursue in the future, even if it's in liberal arts, it will require (1) using a computer and (2) having good communication skills. Well, no matter what enterprise applications or systems you use or deploy, they will require identity, access, security, and compliance. These are as inescapable as they are necessary. By designing in consideration of these requirements, instead of treating them like an afterthought, you are going beyond providing functionality, and presenting great benefit and value to your organization.

After you've done one (or more) of these IAM projects, your brain will be that much bigger. This is one of the most critical things an organization can do, getting a handle on who's doing what and when, by using technology and standards that continue to evolve, and hopefully you're the one who got them started. Not only can you say you've secured an organization's most private, important, and sensitive data, helped them protect their assets from people with bad intentions, and provided a great service for end users, you've also benefited personally by way of what you've learned. If you've used the Oracle security suite, you will have (at least partially) mastered a solution that the analysts call *the* leader in provisioning and access management. Regardless of your chosen toolset, you've gained a lot of knowledge along the way

Just think of your resumé. It will contain your title, tags, and historical data, including your most recent accomplishment, "Designed and implemented Identity and Access Management at MegaBigCorp." And right above that item will be your name, address, and e-mail. This entire combination will consist of *who* you are, and *what* you are; in other words, your fully qualified identity. It's how someone will contact you when they need to speak with someone who, having lived through the long, difficult, and educational process of building an IAM framework, can now reasonably be called an identity and access management expert.

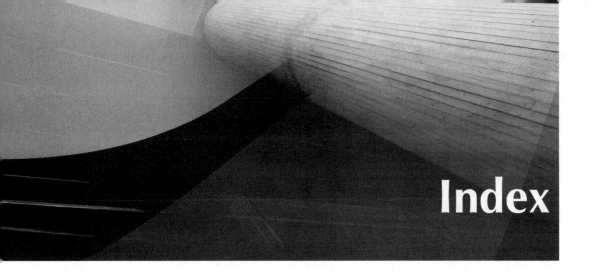

Index

C

S

GET YOUR FREE SUBSCRIPTION
TO *ORACLE MAGAZINE*

Oracle Magazine is essential gear for today's information technology professionals. Stay informed and increase your productivity with every issue of *Oracle Magazine*. Inside each free bimonthly issue you'll get:

- Up-to-date information on Oracle Database, Oracle Application Server, Web development, enterprise grid computing, database technology, and business trends
- Third-party news and announcements
- Technical articles on Oracle and partner products, technologies, and operating environments
- Development and administration tips
- Real-world customer stories

If there are other Oracle users at your location who would like to receive their own subscription to *Oracle Magazine*, please photocopy this form and pass it along.

Three easy ways to subscribe:

① **Web**
Visit our Web site at **oracle.com/oraclemagazine**
You'll find a subscription form there, plus much more

② **Fax**
Complete the questionnaire on the back of this card and fax the questionnaire side only to **+1.847.763.9638**

③ **Mail**
Complete the questionnaire on the back of this card and mail it to **P.O. Box 1263, Skokie, IL 60076-8263**

ORACLE

Want your own FREE subscription?

To receive a free subscription to *Oracle Magazine*, you must fill out the entire card, sign it, and date it (incomplete cards cannot be processed or acknowledged). You can also fax your application to +1.847.763.9638. **Or subscribe at our Web site at oracle.com/oraclemagazine**

O **Yes, please send me a FREE subscription** *Oracle Magazine*.   O No.

O From time to time, Oracle Publishing allows our partners exclusive access to our e-mail addresses for special promotions and announcements. To be included in this program, please check this circle. If you do not wish to be included, you will only receive notices about your subscription via e-mail.

O Oracle Publishing allows sharing of our postal mailing list with selected third parties. If you prefer your mailing address not to be included in this program, please check this circle.

If at any time you would like to be removed from either mailing list, please contact Customer Service at +1.847.763.9635 or send an e-mail to oracle@halldata.com. If you opt in to the sharing of information, Oracle may also provide you with e-mail related to Oracle products, services, and events. If you want to completely unsubscribe from any e-mail communication from Oracle, please send an e-mail to: unsubscribe@oracle-mail.com with the following in the subject line: REMOVE [your e-mail address]. For complete information on Oracle Publishing's privacy practices, please visit oracle.com/html/privacy/html

X

signature (required)   date

name   title

company   e-mail address

street/p.o. box

city/state/zip or postal code   telephone

country   fax

Would you like to receive your free subscription in digital format instead of print if it becomes available? O Yes   O No

YOU MUST ANSWER ALL 10 QUESTIONS BELOW.

① WHAT IS THE PRIMARY BUSINESS ACTIVITY OF YOUR FIRM AT THIS LOCATION? (check one only)

- ☐ 01 Aerospace and Defense Manufacturing
- ☐ 02 Application Service Provider
- ☐ 03 Automotive Manufacturing
- ☐ 04 Chemicals
- ☐ 05 Media and Entertainment
- ☐ 06 Construction/Engineering
- ☐ 07 Consumer Sector/Consumer Packaged Goods
- ☐ 08 Education
- ☐ 09 Financial Services/Insurance
- ☐ 10 Health Care
- ☐ 11 High Technology Manufacturing, OEM
- ☐ 12 Industrial Manufacturing
- ☐ 13 Independent Software Vendor
- ☐ 14 Life Sciences (biotech, pharmaceuticals)
- ☐ 15 Natural Resources
- ☐ 16 Oil and Gas
- ☐ 17 Professional Services
- ☐ 18 Public Sector (government)
- ☐ 19 Research
- ☐ 20 Retail/Wholesale/Distribution
- ☐ 21 Systems Integrator, VAR/VAD
- ☐ 22 Telecommunications
- ☐ 23 Travel and Transportation
- ☐ 24 Utilities (electric, gas, sanitation, water)
- ☐ 98 Other Business and Services _____

② WHICH OF THE FOLLOWING BEST DESCRIBES YOUR PRIMARY JOB FUNCTION? (check one only)

CORPORATE MANAGEMENT/STAFF
- ☐ 01 Executive Management (President, Chair, CEO, CFO, Owner, Partner, Principal)
- ☐ 02 Finance/Administrative Management (VP/Director/ Manager/Controller, Purchasing, Administration)
- ☐ 03 Sales/Marketing Management (VP/Director/Manager)
- ☐ 04 Computer Systems/Operations Management (CIO/VP/Director/Manager MIS/IS/IT, Ops)

IS/IT STAFF
- ☐ 05 Application Development/Programming Management
- ☐ 06 Application Development/Programming Staff
- ☐ 07 Consulting
- ☐ 08 DBA/Systems Administrator
- ☐ 09 Education/Training
- ☐ 10 Technical Support Director/Manager
- ☐ 11 Other Technical Management/Staff
- ☐ 98 Other

③ WHAT IS YOUR CURRENT PRIMARY OPERATING PLATFORM (check all that apply)

- ☐ 01 Digital Equipment Corp UNIX/VAX/VMS
- ☐ 02 HP UNIX
- ☐ 03 IBM AIX
- ☐ 04 IBM UNIX
- ☐ 05 Linux (Red Hat)
- ☐ 06 Linux (SUSE)
- ☐ 07 Linux (Oracle Enterprise)
- ☐ 08 Linux (other)
- ☐ 09 Macintosh
- ☐ 10 MVS
- ☐ 11 Netware
- ☐ 12 Network Computing
- ☐ 13 SCO UNIX
- ☐ 14 Sun Solaris/SunOS
- ☐ 15 Windows
- ☐ 16 Other UNIX
- ☐ 98 Other
- ☐ 99 None of the Above

④ DO YOU EVALUATE, SPECIFY, RECOMMEND, OR AUTHORIZE THE PURCHASE OF ANY OF THE FOLLOWING? (check all that apply)

- ☐ 01 Hardware
- ☐ 02 Business Applications (ERP, CRM, etc.)
- ☐ 03 Application Development Tools
- ☐ 04 Database Products
- ☐ 05 Internet or Intranet Products
- ☐ 06 Other Software
- ☐ 07 Middleware Products
- ☐ 99 None of the Above

⑤ IN YOUR JOB, DO YOU USE OR PLAN TO PURCHASE ANY OF THE FOLLOWING PRODUCTS? (check all that apply)

SOFTWARE
- ☐ 01 CAD/CAE/CAM
- ☐ 02 Collaboration Software
- ☐ 03 Communications
- ☐ 04 Database Management
- ☐ 05 File Management
- ☐ 06 Finance
- ☐ 07 Java
- ☐ 08 Multimedia Authoring
- ☐ 09 Networking
- ☐ 10 Programming
- ☐ 11 Project Management
- ☐ 12 Scientific and Engineering
- ☐ 13 Systems Management
- ☐ 14 Workflow

HARDWARE
- ☐ 15 Macintosh
- ☐ 16 Mainframe
- ☐ 17 Massively Parallel Processing
- ☐ 18 Minicomputer
- ☐ 19 Intel x86(32)
- ☐ 20 Intel x86(64)
- ☐ 21 Network Computer
- ☐ 22 Symmetric Multiprocessing
- ☐ 23 Workstation Services

SERVICES
- ☐ 24 Consulting
- ☐ 25 Education/Training
- ☐ 26 Maintenance
- ☐ 27 Online Database
- ☐ 28 Support
- ☐ 29 Technology-Based Training
- ☐ 30 Other
- ☐ 99 None of the Above

⑥ WHAT IS YOUR COMPANY'S SIZE? (check one only)

- ☐ 01 More than 25,000 Employees
- ☐ 02 10,001 to 25,000 Employees
- ☐ 03 5,001 to 10,000 Employees
- ☐ 04 1,001 to 5,000 Employees
- ☐ 05 101 to 1,000 Employees
- ☐ 06 Fewer than 100 Employees

⑦ DURING THE NEXT 12 MONTHS, HOW MUCH DO YOU ANTICIPATE YOUR ORGANIZATION WILL SPEND ON COMPUTER HARDWARE, SOFTWARE, PERIPHERALS, AND SERVICES FOR YOUR LOCATION? (check one only)

- ☐ 01 Less than $10,000
- ☐ 02 $10,000 to $49,999
- ☐ 03 $50,000 to $99,999
- ☐ 04 $100,000 to $499,999
- ☐ 05 $500,000 to $999,999
- ☐ 06 $1,000,000 and Over

⑧ WHAT IS YOUR COMPANY'S YEARLY SALES REVENUE? (check one only)

- ☐ 01 $500, 000, 000 and above
- ☐ 02 $100, 000, 000 to $500, 000, 000
- ☐ 03 $50, 000, 000 to $100, 000, 000
- ☐ 04 $5, 000, 000 to $50, 000, 000
- ☐ 05 $1, 000, 000 to $5, 000, 000

⑨ WHAT LANGUAGES AND FRAMEWORKS DO YOU USE? (check all that apply)

- ☐ 01 Ajax
- ☐ 02 C
- ☐ 03 C++
- ☐ 04 C#
- ☐ 13 Python
- ☐ 14 Ruby/Rails
- ☐ 15 Spring
- ☐ 16 Struts
- ☐ 05 Hibernate
- ☐ 06 J++/J#
- ☐ 07 Java
- ☐ 08 JSP
- ☐ 09 .NET
- ☐ 10 Perl
- ☐ 11 PHP
- ☐ 12 PL/SQL
- ☐ 17 SQL
- ☐ 18 Visual Basic
- ☐ 98 Other

⑩ WHAT ORACLE PRODUCTS ARE IN USE AT YOUR SITE? (check all that apply)

ORACLE DATABASE
- ☐ 01 Oracle Database 11*g*
- ☐ 02 Oracle Database 10*g*
- ☐ 03 Oracle9*i* Database
- ☐ 04 Oracle Embedded Database (Oracle Lite, Times Ten, Berkeley DB)
- ☐ 05 Other Oracle Database Release

ORACLE FUSION MIDDLEWARE
- ☐ 06 Oracle Application Server
- ☐ 07 Oracle Portal
- ☐ 08 Oracle Enterprise Manager
- ☐ 09 Oracle BPEL Process Manager
- ☐ 10 Oracle Identity Management
- ☐ 11 Oracle SOA Suite
- ☐ 12 Oracle Data Hubs

ORACLE DEVELOPMENT TOOLS
- ☐ 13 Oracle JDeveloper
- ☐ 14 Oracle Forms
- ☐ 15 Oracle Reports
- ☐ 16 Oracle Designer
- ☐ 17 Oracle Discoverer
- ☐ 18 Oracle BI Beans
- ☐ 19 Oracle Warehouse Builder
- ☐ 20 Oracle WebCenter
- ☐ 21 Oracle Application Express

ORACLE APPLICATIONS
- ☐ 22 Oracle E-Business Suite
- ☐ 23 PeopleSoft Enterprise
- ☐ 24 JD Edwards EnterpriseOne
- ☐ 25 JD Edwards World
- ☐ 26 Oracle Fusion
- ☐ 27 Hyperion
- ☐ 28 Siebel CRM

ORACLE SERVICES
- ☐ 28 Oracle E-Business Suite On Demand
- ☐ 29 Oracle Technology On Demand
- ☐ 30 Siebel CRM On Demand
- ☐ 31 Oracle Consulting
- ☐ 32 Oracle Education
- ☐ 33 Oracle Support
- ☐ 98 Other
- ☐ 99 None of the Above

08014/004

Data Science Strategy

by Ulrika Jägare

FOREWORD BY **Lillian Pierson**
CEO of Data-Mania

A Wiley Brand

Data Science Strategy For Dummies®

Published by: **John Wiley & Sons, Inc.**, 111 River Street, Hoboken, NJ 07030-5774, www.wiley.com

Copyright © 2019 by John Wiley & Sons, Inc., Hoboken, New Jersey

Published simultaneously in Canada

For general information on our other products and services, please contact our Customer Care Department within the U.S. at 877-762-2974, outside the U.S. at 317-572-3993, or fax 317-572-4002. For technical support, please visit www.wiley.com/techsupport.

Wiley publishes in a variety of print and electronic formats and by print-on-demand. Some material included with standard print versions of this book may not be included in e-books or in print-on-demand. If this book refers to media such as a CD or DVD that is not included in the version you purchased, you may download this material at http://booksupport.wiley.com. For more information about Wiley products, visit www.wiley.com.

Library of Congress Control Number: 2019942827

ISBN: 978-1-119-56625-0; 978-1-119-56626-7 (ebk); 978-1-119-56627-4 (ebk)

Manufactured in the United States of America

C10010815_060519

Contents at a Glance

Table of Contents

Foreword

We're living in a make-or-break era; the ability to generate business value from enterprise data will either make or break your organization. We didn't get here overnight. For years, experts have been professing how vital it is that business reframe itself to become more data-driven.

Some listened, some did not.

Organizations that took their business by its big data helm (like Netflix, Facebook, and Walmart) set the precedent. You better believe they have extremely robust data strategies in place governing those operations. The ones that did not? This book was written for you.

Sadly, over the last decade, some organizations got caught up in the media buzz. They've spent a huge amount of time and money working to hire data scientists, but haven't seen the ROI they'd expected.

Part of the problem is that it's both expensive and difficult to hire data scientists. In 2018, the median salaries for data scientists in USA ranged between $95,000 and $165,000 (see the 2018 *Burtch Works' Data Science Strategy Report*). Making matters worse, the demand for analytics-savvy workers is twice the supply (see *The Quant Crunch*, prepared for IBM by Burning Glass Technologies). No surprise that it's exceedingly difficult to recruit and retain these type of professionals.

But a bigger part of the problem is just this — contrary to what most advocates will tell you, **just sourcing and hiring a team of "Data Scientists" isn't going to get your organization where it needs to be.** You'll also need to secure a robust set of big data skill sets, technologies, and data resources. More importantly, you'll need a comprehensive big data strategic plan in place, to help you steer your data ship.

It takes a lot more than just implementation folks dealing with all the details of your data initiatives; you also need an expert to manage them. You need someone who can communicate with and manage your data team, can communicate effectively with organizational leaders, can build relationships with business stakeholders, and who can perform exhaustive evaluations of both your business and your data assets in order to form the data strategy your business will need to survive in the digital era. Read this book for details on how to get these elements in place.

All around the world, I've been on the frontlines supporting organizations that know their data's value and are ready to make big changes to start extracting that value. At Data-Mania, we provide results-driven data strategy services to optimize our client's data operations. We are also leading the change by training our client's staff with the data strategy and data science skills they need to succeed. Through our partnerships with LinkedIn and Wiley, over the last five years we've educated about a million technical professionals globally. Across both of these functions and with each project we engage, one message strongly resounds — The people and organizations who are committed to taking necessary actions to transform enterprise data to business value are the ones that will prevail in the digital era.

I want to be the first to congratulate you! Just by picking up this book and making the effort to educate yourself on the problems and solutions related to data strategy, you've already taken the first step. Whether you're a C-suite executive that's looking for guidance on next steps for your organization, or if you're a data professional looking to move forward in your career, *Data Science Strategy For Dummies* will provide you a solid framework around which to proceed.

It's an exciting time to be alive. Never before have businesses had access to such a powerful upper hand. Those of us who recognize this in our business data are the ones who are primed to blaze the trail and build a true legacy with the work we do in our careers. Some of us have been on this path for a while now, while others are new. Welcome aboard!

Lillian Pierson, P.E.

Data Strategist & CEO of Data-Mania

Introduction

A revolutionary change is taking place in society. Everybody, from small local companies to global enterprises, is starting to realize the potential in digitizing their data assets and becoming data driven. Regardless of industry, companies have embarked on a similar journey to explore how to drive new business value by utilizing analytics, machine learning (ML), and artificial intelligence (AI) techniques and introducing data science as a new discipline.

However, although utilizing these new technologies will help companies simplify their operations and drive down costs, nothing is simple about getting the strategic approach right for your data science investment. And, the later you join the ML/AI game, the more important it will be to get the strategy right from the start for your particular area of business. Hiring a couple of data scientists to play around with your data is easy enough to do — if you can find some of the few that are available — but the real heavy lifting comes when you try to understand how to utilize data science to create value throughout your business and put that understanding into an executable data science strategy. If you can do that, you are on the right path for success.

A recent survey by Deloitte of "aggressive adopters" of cognitive technologies found that 76 percent believe that they will "substantially transform" their companies within the next three years by using data and AI. IDC, a global marketing intelligence firm, predicts that by 2021, 75 percent of commercial enterprise apps will use AI, over 90 percent of consumers will interact with customer support bots; and over 50 percent of new industrial robots will leverage AI.

However, at the same time, there remains a very large gap between aspiration and reality. Gartner, yet another research and advisory company, claimed in 2017 that 85 percent of all big data projects fail; not only that, there still seems to be confusion around what the true key success factors are to succeed when it comes to data and AI investments. This book argues that a main key success factor is a great data science strategy.

The target audience for this book is anyone interested in making well-balanced strategic choices in the field of data science, no matter which aspect you're focusing on and at what level — from upper management all the way down to the individual members of a data science team. Strategic choices matter! And, this book is based on actual experiences arising from building this up from scratch in a global enterprise, incorporating learnings from successful choices as well as mistakes and miscalculations along the way.

So far, there seems to be little in-depth research or analysis on the topic of data science and AI strategies and little practical guidance as well. In fact, when researching for this book, I couldn't find another single book on the topic of data science strategy. However, several interesting articles and reports are available, like TDWI's report, "Seven Steps for Executing a Successful Data Science Strategy" (https://tdwi.org/research/2015/01/checklist-seven-steps-successful-data-science-strategy.aspx?tc=page0&m=1) or The Startup's "How To Create A Successful Artificial Intelligence Strategy" https://medium.com/swlh/how-to-create-a-successful-artificial-intelligence-strategy-44705c588e62). However, these articles primarily focus on easily consumable tips and tricks, while bringing up a few aspects of the challenges and considerations needed. There is an obvious lack of in-depth guidance which is not really accessible in an article format.

At the same time, the main reasons companies fail with their data science or AI investment is that either there was no data science strategy in place or the complexity of executing on the strategy wasn't understood. Although this enormous transformation is happening right here, right now, all around us, it seems that few people have grasped how data science will impose a fundamental shift in society — and therefore don't understand how to approach it. This book is based on more than ten years of experience spent driving different levels of strategic and practical transformation assignments in a global enterprise. As such, it will help you understand what is fundamentally important to consider and what you should avoid. (Trust me: There are many pitfalls and areas to get stuck in.) But if you want to be in the forefront with your business, you have neither the time nor the money to make mistakes. You really want a solid, end-to-end data science strategy that works for you at the level you need in order to bring your organization forward. The time is now! This is the book that everyone in data science should read.

About This Book

This book will help guide you through the different areas that need to be considered as part of your data science strategy. This includes managing the complexity in data science and avoiding common data challenges, making strategic choices related to the data itself (including how to capture it, transfer it, compute it, and keep it secure and legally compliant), but also how to build up efficient and successful data science teams.

Furthermore, it includes guidance on strategic infrastructure choices to enable a productive and innovative environment for the data science teams as well as how to acquire and balance data science competence and enable productive ways of working. It also includes how you can turn data into enhanced or new business opportunities, including data-driven business models for new data products and services, while also addressing ethical aspects related to data usage and commercialization.

My goal here is to give you relevant and concrete guidance in those areas that require strategic thinking as well as give some advice on what to include when making choices for both your data and AI investment as well as how best to come up with a useful and applicable data science strategy. Based on my own experience in this field, I'll argue for certain techniques or technology choices or even preferred ways of working, but I won't come down on one side or the other when it comes to any specific products or services. The most I'll do in that regard is point out that certain methods or technology choices are more appropriate for certain types of users rather than others.

Foolish Assumptions

Because this book assumes a basic level of understanding of what data science actually is, don't think of it as an introduction to data science, but rather as a tool for optimizing your analytics and/or ML/AI investment, regardless of whether that investment is for a small company or a global enterprise. It covers everything from practical advice to deep insights into how to define, focus, and make the right strategic choices in data science throughout. So, if you're looking to find a broad understanding of what data science is, which techniques and ML tools come recommended, and how to get started as a data scientist professional, I instead warmly recommend the book *Data Science For Dummies*, by Lillian Pierson (Wiley).

How This Book Is Organized

This book has six main parts. Part 1 outlines the major challenges that companies (small as well as large) face when investing in data science. Whereas Part 2 aims to create an understanding of the strategic choices in data science that you need to make, Part 3 guides you in successfully setting up and shaping your data science teams. In Part 4, you find out about important infrastructure considerations, managing models in development and production and how to relate to open source. In Part 5 you learn all about commercializing your data business and monetizing your data. And, and is the case with all *For Dummies* books, this book ends with The Part of Tens, with some practical tips, including what not to do when building your data science strategy and spelling out why you need to create a data science strategy to begin with.

Icons Used In This Book

I'll occasionally use a few special icons to focus attention on important items. Here's what you'll find:

REMEMBER

This icon with the proverbial string around the finger reminds you about information that's worth recalling.

TIP

Expect to find something useful or helpful by way of suggestions, advice, or observations.

WARNING

The Warning icon is meant to grab your attention so that can you steer clear of potholes, money pits, and other hazards.

TECHNICAL STUFF

This icon may be taken in one of two ways: Techies will zero in on the juicy and significant details that follow; others will happily skip ahead to the next paragraph.

Beyond The Book

This book is designed to help you explore different strategic options for your data science investment. It will guide you in your choices for your business, from data-driven business models to data choices and from team setup to infrastructure choices and a lot more. It will help you navigate the most common challenges and steer you toward the success factors.

However, this book is aimed at covering a very broad range of areas in data science strategy development, and is therefore not able to deep-dive into specific theories or techniques to the level you might be looking for after reading parts of this book.

In addition to what you're reading right now, this product comes with a free access-anywhere Cheat Sheet that offers a number of data-science-related tips, techniques, and resources. To get this Cheat Sheet, visit www.dummies.com and type **data science strategy for dummies cheat sheet** in the Search box.

Where To Go From Here

You can start reading this book anywhere you like. You don't have to read in chapter order, but my suggestion is to start by studying how data science is framed in this book, which is outlined in Chapter 1. In that chapter, you can also learn about the complexity and challenges you will encounter, before diving into subsequent chapters, where I explain how to tackle the challenges most enterprises encounter when strategically investing in data science.

1

Optimizing Your Data Science Investment

Chapter **1**

Framing Data Science Strategy

I n this chapter, I aim to sort out the basics of what data science is all about, but I have to warn you that data science is a term that escapes any single complete definition — which, of course, makes data science difficult to understand and apply in an organization. Many articles and publications use the term quite freely, with the assumption that it's universally understood. Yet, data science — including its methods, goals, and applications — evolves with time and technology and is now far different from what it might have been 25 years ago.

Despite all that, I'm willing to put forward a tentative definition: *Data science* is the study of where data comes from, what it represents, and how it can be turned into a valuable resource in the creation of business strategies. Data science can be said to be a multidisciplinary field that uses scientific methods, processes, algorithms, and systems to extract insights from data in various forms, both structured and unstructured. Mining large amounts of structured and unstructured data to identify patterns and deviations that can help an organization rein in costs, increase efficiencies, recognize new market opportunities, and increase the organization's competitive advantage.

Data science is a concept that can be used to unify statistics, analytics, machine learning, and their related methods and techniques in order to understand and analyze actual phenomena with data. It employs techniques and theories drawn from many fields within the context of mathematics, statistics, information science, and computer science.

Behind that type of definition though, lies the definition of how data science is approached and performed. And because the ambition of this part of the book is to frame data science strategy, I need to first frame this multidisciplinary area of data science and its life cycle more properly.

Establishing the Data Science Narrative

It never hurts to have an image when explaining a complicated process, so do take a look at Figure 1-1, where you can see the main steps or phases in the data science life-cycle. Keep in mind, however, that the model visualized in Figure 1-1 assumes that you've already identified a high-level business problem or business opportunity as a starting point. This early ambition is usually derived from a business perspective, but it needs to be analyzed and framed in detail together with the data science team. This dialogue is vital in terms of understanding which data is available and what is possible to do with that data so you can set the focus of the work going forward. It isn't a good idea to just start capturing any and all data that looks interesting enough to analyze. Therefore, the first stage of the data science life cycle, *capture*, is to frame the data you need by translating the business need into a concrete and well-defined problem or business opportunity.

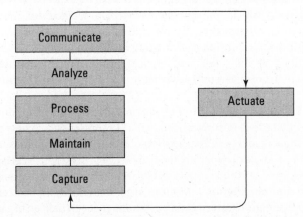

FIGURE 1-1:
The different stages of the data science life cycle.

TIP

The initial business problem and/or opportunity isn't static and will change over time as your data-driven understanding matures. Staying flexible in terms of which data is captured as well as which problem and/or opportunity is most important at any given point in time, is therefore a vital in order to achieve your business objectives.

The model shown in Figure 1-1 aims to represent a view of the different stages of the data science life cycle, from capturing the business and data need through preparing, exploring, and analyzing the data to reaching insights and acting on them.

The output of each full cycle produces new data, which provides the result of the previous cycle. This includes not only new data or results, which you can use to optimize your model, but can also generate new business needs, problems, or even a new understanding of what the business priority should be.

REMEMBER

These stages of the data science life cycle can also be seen as not only steps describing the scope of data science but also layers in an architecture. More on that later; let me start by explaining the different stages.

Capture

There are two different parts of the first stage in the life-cycle, since *capture* refers to both the capture of the business need as well as the extraction and acquisition of data. This stage is vital to the rest of the process. I'll start by explaining what it means to capture the business need.

The starting point for detailing the business need is a high-level business request or business problem expressed by management or similar entities and should include tasks such as

» **Translating ambiguous business requests** into concrete, well-defined problems or opportunities

» **Deep-diving into the context of the requests** to better understand what a potential solution could look like, including which data will be needed

» **Outlining (if possible) strategic business priorities** set by the company that might impact the data science work

Now that I've made clear the importance of capturing and understanding the business requests and initial scoping of data needed, I want to move on to describing aspects of the data capture process itself. It's the main interface to the data source that you need to tap into and includes areas such as

» Managing data ownership and securing legal rights to data capture and usage

» Handling of personal information and securing data privacy through different anonymization techniques

» Using hardware and software for acquiring the data through batch uploads or the real-time streaming of data

>> Determining how frequently data will need to be acquired, because the frequency usually varies between data types and categories

>> Mandating that the preprocessing of data occurs at the point of collection, or even before collection (at the edge of an IoT device, for example). This includes basic processing, like cleaning and aggregating data, but it can also include more advanced activities, such as anonymizing the data to remove sensitive information. (*Anonymizing* refers to removing sensitive information such as a person's name, phone number, address and so on from a data set.)

REMEMBER

In most cases, data must be anonymized before being transferred from the data source. Usually a procedure is also in place to validate data sets in terms of completeness. If the data isn't complete, the collection may need to be repeated several times to achieve the desired data scope. Performing this type of validation early on has a positive impact on both process speed and cost.

>> Managing the data transfer process to the needed storage point (local and/or global). As part of the data transfer, you may have to transform the data — aggregating it to make it smaller, for example. You may need to do this if you're facing limits on the bandwidth capacity of the transfer links you use.

Maintain

Data *maintenance* activities includes both storing and maintaining the data. Note that data is usually processed in many different steps throughout its life cycle.

WARNING

The need to protect data integrity during the life cycle of a data element is especially important during data processing activities. It's easy to accidentally corrupt a dataset through human error when manually processing data, causing the data set to be useless for analysis in the next step. The best way to protect data integrity is to automate as many steps as possible of the data management activities leading up to the point of data analysis.

REMEMBER

Keeping business trust in the data foundation is vital in order for business users to trust and make use of the derived insights.

When it comes to maintaining data, two important aspects are

>> **Data storage:** Think of this as everything associated with what's happening in the data lake. Data storage activities include managing the different retention periods for different types of data, as well as cataloging data properly to ensure that data is easy to access and use.

>> **Data preparation:** In the context of maintaining data, data preparation includes basic processing tasks such as second-level data cleansing, data staging, and data aggregation, all of which usually involve applying a filter directly when the data is put into storage. You don't want to put data with poor quality into your data lake.

REMEMBER

Data retention periods can be different for the same data type, depending on its level of aggregation. For example, raw data might be interesting to save for only a short time because it's usually very large in volume and therefore costly to store. Aggregated data on the other hand, is often smaller in size and cheaper and easier to store and can therefore be saved for longer periods, depending on the targeted use cases.

Process

Processing of data is the main data processing layer focused on preparing data for analysis, and it refers to using more advanced data engineering methodologies, such as

>> **Data classification:** This refers to the process of organizing data into categories for even more effective and efficient use, including activities such as the labeling and tagging of data. A well-planned data classification system makes essential data easy to find and retrieve. This can also be of particular importance for areas such as legal and compliance.

>> **Data modeling:** This helps with the visual representation of data and enforces established business rules regarding data. You would also build data models to enforce policies on how you should correlate different data types in a consistent manner. Data models also ensure consistency in naming conventions, default values, semantics, and security procedures, thus ensuring quality of data.

>> **Data summarization:** Here your aim is to use different ways to summarize data, like using different clustering techniques.

>> **Data mining:** This is the process of analyzing large data sets to identify patterns or deviations as well as to establish relationships in order to enable problems to be solved through data analysis further down the road. Data mining is a sort of data analysis, focused on enhanced understanding of data, also referred to as *data literacy*. Building data literacy in the data science teams is a key component of data science success.

WARNING

With low data literacy, and without truly understanding the data you're preparing, analyzing, and deriving insights from, you run a high risk of failing when it comes to your data science investment.

Analyze

Data *analysis* is the stage where the data comes to life and you're finally able to derive insights from the application of different analytical techniques.

REMEMBER

Insights can be focused on understanding and explaining what has happened, which means that the analysis is descriptive and more reactive in nature. This is also the case with real-time analysis: It's still reactive even when it happens in the here-and-now.

Then there are data analysis methods that aim to explain not only *why* something happened but also *what* happened. These types of data analysis are usually referred to as *diagnostic* analyses.

Both descriptive and diagnostic methods are usually grouped into the area of reporting, or business intelligence (BI).

To be able to predict what will happen, you need to use a different set of analytical techniques and methods. Predictions about the future can be done strategically or in real-time settings. For a real-time prediction you need to develop, train and validate a model before deploying it on real-time data. The model could then search for certain data patterns and conditions that you have trained the model to find, to help you predict a problem before it happens.

Figure 1-2 shows the difference between reporting techniques about what has happened (in black) and analytics techniques about what is likely to happen, using statistical models and predictive models (in white).

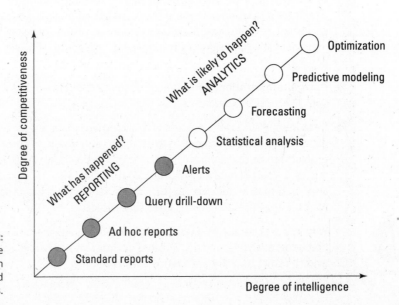

FIGURE 1-2:
The difference between reporting and analytics.

This list gives you examples of the kinds of questions you can ask using different reporting and BI techniques:

>> **Standard reports:** What was the customer churn rate?

>> **Ad hoc reports:** How did the code fix carried out on a certain date impact product performance?

>> **Query drill-down:** Are similar product-quality issues reported in all geographical locations?

>> **Alerts:** Customer churn has increased. What action is recommended?

And this list gives you examples of the kinds questions you can ask using different analytics techniques:

>> **Statistical analysis:** Which factors contribute most to the product quality issues?

>> **Forecasting:** What will bandwidth demand be in 6 months?

>> **Predictive modeling:** Which customer segment is most likely to respond to this marketing campaign?

>> **Optimization.** What is the optimal mix of customer, offering, price, and sales channel?

Analytics can also be separated into two categories: basic analytics and advanced analytics. *Basic* analytics uses rudimentary techniques and statistical methods to derive value from data, usually in a manual manner, whereas in advanced analytics, the objective is to gain deeper insights, make predictions, or generate recommendations by way of an autonomous or semiautonomous examination of data or content using more advanced and sophisticated statistical methods and techniques.

Some examples of the differences are described in this list:

>> **Exploratory data analytics** is a statistical approach to analyzing data sets in order to summarize their main characteristics, often with visual methods. You can choose to use a statistical model or not, but if used, such a model is primarily for visualizing what the data can tell you beyond the formal modeling or hypothesis testing task. This is categorized as basic analytics.

>> **Predictive analytics** is the use of data, statistical algorithms, and machine learning techniques to identify the likelihood of future outcomes based on historical data. This is categorized as advanced analytics.

» **Regression analysis** is a way of mathematically sorting out which variables have an impact. It answers these questions: Which factors matter most? Which can be ignored? How do those factors interact with each other? And, perhaps most importantly, how certain am I about all these factors? This is categorized as advanced analytics.

» **Text mining or text analytics** is the process of exploring and analyzing large amounts of unstructured text aided by software that can identify concepts, patterns, topics, keywords, and other attributes in the data. The overarching goal of text mining is, to turn text into data for analysis via application of natural language processing (NLP) and various analytical methods. Text mining can be done from a more basic perspective as well as from a more advanced perspective, depending on the use case.

Communicate

The *communication* stage of data science is about making sure insights and learnings from the data analysis are understood and communicated by way of different means in order to come to efficient use. It includes areas such as

» **Data reporting:** The process of collecting and submitting data in order to enable an accurate analysis of the facts on the ground. It's a vital part of communication because inaccurate data reporting can lead to vastly uninformed decision-making based on inaccurate evidence.

» **Data visualization:** This can also be seen as *visual communication* because it involves the creation and study of the visual representation of data and insights. To help you communicate the result of the data analysis clearly and efficiently, data visualization uses statistical graphics, plots, information graphics, and other tools. Effective visualization helps users analyze and reason about data and evidence because it makes complex data more accessible, understandable, and usable.

Users may have been assigned particular analytical tasks, such as making comparisons or understanding causality, and the design principle of the graphical visualization (showing comparisons or showing causality, in this example) follows the task. Tables are generally used where users can look up a specific measurement, and charts of various types are used to show patterns or relationships in the data for one or more variables.

Figure 1-3 below exemplifies how data exploration could work using a table format. In this specific case, the data being explored regards cars, and the hypothesis being tested is which car attribute impacts fuel consumption the most. Is it, for example, the car brand, engine size, horse power or perhaps the weight of the car?

As you can see, exploring the data using tables has its limitation, and does not give an immediate overview. It requires you to go through the data in detail to discover relationships and patterns. Compare this with the graph shown in Figure 1-4 below, where the same data is being visualized in a completely different way.

Make	Model	Origin	DriveTrain	Type	Cylinders	Engine Size (L)	Frequency	Fuel Consumtion (L/10 km)	Horsepower	Invoice	Length (IN)	MSRP
Mercedes-B...	E500	Eur...	All	Wa...	8	5	1	1,17605	302	56 47...	190	60 67...
Isuzu	Ascender S	Asia	All	SUV	6	4,2	1	1,3440571429	275	29 97...	208	31 84...
Toyota	Tundra Access Cab V6 SR5	Asia	All	Truck	6	3,4	1	1,517483871	190	23 52...	218	25 93...
Audi	A6 3.0 Quattro 4dr	Eur...	All	Sedan	6	3	1	1,094	220	35 99...	192	39 64...
Volvo	S60 R 4dr	Eur...	All	Sedan	5	2,5	1	1,094	300	35 38...	181	37 56...
Acura	MDX	Asia	All	SUV	6	3,5	1	1,17605	265	33 33...	189	36 94...
Nissan	Titan King Cab XE	Asia	All	Truck	8	5,6	1	1,4700625	305	24 92...	224	26 65...
Toyota	Sequoia SR5	Asia	All	SUV	8	4,7	1	1,517483871	240	31 82...	204	35 69...
Audi	S4 Quattro 4dr	Eur...	All	Sedan	8	4,2	1	1,3835882353	340	43 55...	179	48 04...
Audi	A8 L Quattro 4dr	Eur...	All	Sedan	8	4,2	1	1,1473658537	330	64 74...	204	69 19...
Subaru	Impreza WRX STi 4dr	Asia	All	Sports	4	2,5	1	1,120047619	300	29 13...	174	31 54...
BMW	330i 4dr	Eur...	All	Sedan	6	3	1	0,9600408163	225	34 11...	176	37 24...
Infiniti	FX45	Asia	All	Wa...	8	4,5	1	1,3835882353	315	33 12...	189	36 39...
Toyota	Land Cruiser	Asia	All	SUV	8	4,7	1	1,5680666667	325	47 98...	193	54 76...
Subaru	Forester X	Asia	All	Wa...	4	2,5	1	0,9600408163	165	19 64...	175	21 44...
GMC	Sierra HD 2500	USA	All	Truck	8	6	1	1,517483871	300	25 75...	222	29 32...
Mercedes-B...	C240 4dr	Eur...	All	Sedan	6	2,6	1	1,0691363636	168	31 18...	178	33 48...
Jaguar	X-Type 3.0 4dr	Eur...	All	Sedan	6	3	1	1,094	227	30 99...	184	33 99...
Volvo	S80 2.5T 4dr	Eur...	All	Sedan	5	2,5	1	1,000893617	194	35 68...	190	37 88...
Volvo	XC70	Eur...	All	Wa...	5	2,5	1	1,000893617	208	33 11...	186	35 14...
Audi	A6 2.7 Turbo Quattro 4dr	Eur...	All	Sedan	6	2,7	1	1,094	250	38 84...	192	42 84...
Dodge	Grand Caravan SXT	USA	All	Sedan	6	3,8	1	1,094	215	29 81...	201	32 66...

Figure 1-3 is based on a screenshot generated using SAS® Visual Analytics software. Copyright © 2019 SAS Institute Inc., Cary, NC, USA. SAS and all other SAS Institute Inc. product or service names are registered trademarks or trademarks of SAS Institute Inc. All Rights Reserved. Used with permission.

In Figure 1-4, a visualization in the shape of a linear regression graph has been generated for each car attribute, together with text explaining the strength of each relationship to fuel consumption. (Linear regression involves fitting a straight line to a dataset while trying to minimize the error between the points and the fitted line.) The graph in Figure 1-4 shows a very strong positive relationship between the weight of the car and fuel consumption. By studying the relationship between the other attributes and fuel consumption using the graph generated for each tab, it will be quite easy to find the strongest relationship compared to using the table in Figure 1-3.

However, in data exploration the key is to stay flexible in terms of which exploration methods to use. In this case, it was easier and quicker to find the relationship by using linear regression, but in another case a table might be enough, or none of the just mentioned approaches works. If you have geographical data, for example, the best way to explore it might be by using a geo map, where the data is distributed based on geographical location. But more about that later on.

Actuate

The final stage in the data science life cycle is to *actuate* the insights derived from all previous stages. This stage has not always been seen as part of the data science life cycle, but the more that society moves toward embracing automation, the more the interest in this area grows.

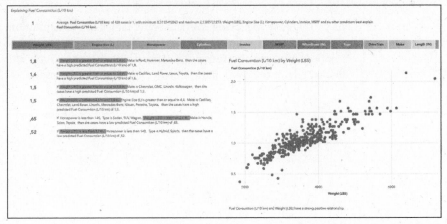

FIGURE 1-4:
Visualizing
your data.

Figure 1-4 is based on a screenshot generated using SAS® Visual Analytics software.
Copyright © 2019 SAS Institute Inc., Cary, NC, USA. SAS and all other SAS Institute Inc.
product or service names are registered trademarks or trademarks of SAS Institute Inc.
All Rights Reserved. Used with permission.

Decision-making for actuation refers to connecting an insight derived from data analysis to trigger a human- or machine-driven decision-making process of identifying and deciding alternatives for the right action based on the values, policies, preferences, or beliefs related to the business or scope of the task.

TECHNICAL STUFF

What actually occurs is that a human or machine compares the insight with a predefined set of policies for what needs to be done when a certain set of criteria is fulfilled. If the criteria are fulfilled, this triggers a decision or an action. The actuation trigger can be directed toward a human (for example, a manager) for further decisions to be made in a larger context, or toward a machine when the insight falls within the scope of the predefined policies for actuation.

REMEMBER

Automation of tasks or decisions increases speed and reduces cost, and if set up properly, also produces continuous and reliable data on the outcome of the implemented action.

The stage where decisions are actuated — by either human hand or a machine — is one of the most important areas of data science. It's fundamental because it will provide data science professionals (also known as *data scientists*) with new data based on the results of the action (resolution or prevention of a problem, for example), which tells the data scientists whether their models and algorithms are performing as expected after deployment or whether they need to be corrected or improved. The follow-up regarding model and algorithm performance also supports the concept of continuous improvement.

PUTTING AUTOMATION IN THE CONTEXT OF DATA SCIENCE

What is actually the relationship between data science and automation? And, can automation accelerate data science production and efficiency? Well, assuming that the technology evolution in society moves more and more toward automation, not only for simple process steps previously performed by humans but also for complex actions identified and decided by intelligent machines powered by machine-learning-developed algorithms, the relationship will be a strong one, and data science production and efficiency will accelerate considerably due to automation.

The decisions will, of course, not really be decided by the machines, but will be based on human-preapproved policies that the machine then acts on. *Machine learning* doesn't mean that the machine can learn unfettered, but rather that it always encounters boundaries for the learning set up by the data scientist — boundaries regulated by established policies. However, within these policy boundaries, the machine can learn to optimize the analysis and execution of tasks assigned to it.

Despite the boundaries imposed on it, automation powered by machines will become more and more important in data science, not only as a means to increase speed (from detection to correction or prevention) but also to lower cost and secure quality and consistency of data management, actuation of insights, and data generation based on the outcome.

When applying data science in your business, remember that data science is transformative. For it to fully empower your business, it isn't a question of just going out and hiring a couple of data scientists (if you can find them) and put them into a traditional software development department and expect miracles. For data science to thrive and generate full value, you need to be prepared to first transform your business into a data-driven organization.

Sorting Out the Concept of a Data-driven Organization

Data is the new black! Or the new oil! Or the new gold! Whatever you compare data to, it's probably true from a conceptual value perspective. As a society, we have now entered a new era of data and intelligent machines. And it isn't a passing trend or something that you can or should avoid. Instead, you should embrace it and ask yourself whether you understand enough about it to leverage it in your business. Be open-minded and curious! Dare to ask yourself whether you truly understand what being data-driven means.

TIP

The concept of being data-driven is a cornerstone that you need to understand in order to correctly carry out any strategic work in data science, and it's addressed in several parts of this book. In this chapter, I try to give you a big-picture view of how to think and reason around the idea of being data-driven.

If you start by putting the ongoing changes happening in society into a wider context, it's a common understanding that we humans are now experiencing a fourth industrial revolution, driven by access to data and advanced technology. It's also referred to as the *digital revolution.* But be aware! Digitizing or digitalizing your business isn't the same as being data-driven.

REMEMBER

Digitization is a widely-used concept that basically refers to transitioning from analog to digital, like the conversion of data to a digital format. In relation to that, digitalization refers to making the digitized information work in your business.

The concept of digitalizing a business is sometimes mixed up with being data-driven. However, it's vital to remember that digitalizing the data isn't just a good thing to do — it's the foundation for enabling a data-driven enterprise. Without digitalization, you simply cannot become data-driven.

Approaching data-driven

In a data-driven organization, the starting point is data. It's truly the foundation of everything. But what does that actually mean? Well, being data-driven means that you need to be ready to take data seriously. And what does *that* mean? Well, in practice, it means that data is the starting point and you use data to analyze and understand what type of business you should be doing. You must take the outcome of the analysis seriously enough to be prepared to change your business models accordingly. You must be ready to trust and use the data to drive your business forward. It should be your main concern in the company. You need to become "data-obsessed."

TIP

Before I explain what it means to be data obsessed, consider how you're doing things today in your company. Is it somewhat data-driven? Or perhaps not at all? Where is the starting point in different business areas?

Figure 1-5 shows a model (with examples) for comparing a more traditional approach to a data-driven approach related to approaching different business aspects.

Business Question	Traditional business (starting point)	Data-driven business (starting point)
• What business shall we do?	Enhance current portfolio Build on what we have!	What is the data telling us? Data is the starting point for everything!
• Base for business decisions?	Experience based decisions What we know, is what we trust!	Data-driven insights/predictions We trust and use the insights for decisions!
• How to get things started?	Ownership and structure A defined setup is the way to get started!	Enablement (data, teams, infrastructure) Focus is to enable teams to find new solutions!
• Focus during execution?	Tools an system interaction It is about efficient tools and systems!	Data, models and algorithms Efficient data utilization, regardless of tools!
• How to track progress?	Reports Standard reports gives us what we need!	Data and measurements Study patterns and deviations in data and measurements!
• Increasing productivity?	Improve processes and tools We know how to be more efficient!	Utilize automation and AI Drive efficiency beyond human capabilities!

FIGURE 1-5: The difference between a traditional business and a data-driven business.

Comparing the approaches in a traditional business versus a data-driven organization is worthwhile. Many companies' leaders actually think that their companies are data-driven just because they collect and analyze data. But it's all about how data drives (or doesn't drive) the business priorities, decisions, and execution that tells you how data-driven your business really is. Understanding what the starting point is will help you define your ground zero and identify which areas need more attention in order to change.

Being data obsessed

So, what does the term *data-obsessed* actually mean? It's really quite simple: It means that you should always assume that the access and usage of data can improve your business – in *all* aspects. Use the following list of questions to determine how data-obsessed your organization actually is:

>> Which data do you need to use as a company, based on your strategic objectives? Do you collect that data already? If not, how do you get it?

>> Do you own all the data you need? If not, how can you secure legal rights to use it for your needs (internal efficiency or business opportunities)?

>> Is the data geographically distributed across countries? If yes, what needs to happen to your infrastructure in order to enable you to use it efficiently?

>> Is the data sensitive? That is, does it contain personal information? If yes, what are the applicable laws and regulations related to the data? (Be sure to note whether those laws and regulations change, depending on which country houses a specific data storage facility.) How do you intend to use sensitive data?

>> Do you need access to the data in real-time to analyze and realize your use cases? If yes, what type of data architecture do you need?

>> What data retention periods do you need to establish for the different types of data used by your organization? What will you use the selected data types for? Are you in control when it comes to expected data volumes and data storage costs per data type?

>> Can you automate most of the data acquisition and data management activities? If yes, what is the best data architectural solution for that?

>> Do you need to account for an exploratory development environment as well as an efficient and highly automated production environment in the same architecture? If yes, how will you realize that?

>> Are employees ready to become data-driven? Have the potential, value, and scope of the change been clearly stated and communicated? If so, are employees ready for that change?

>> Are managers and leaders on board with what it means to become data-driven? Do they fully understand what needs to change fundamentally? If so, are managers and leaders ready to start taking vital decisions based on data?

REMEMBER

The questions I post here don't comprise an exhaustive list, but they cover some of the main areas to address from a data-driven perspective. Notice that these questions don't cover anything related to using machine learning or artificial intelligence techniques. The reason that isn't covered is because, in practice, a company can be data-driven based only on data, analytics, and automation. However, companies that also effectively integrate the use of technologies like machine learning and artificial intelligence have a better foundation for responding to the machine-driven evolution in society.

Sorting Out the Concept of Machine Learning

People often ask me to explain the difference between advanced analytics and machine learning and to say when it is advisable to go for one approach or the other. I always start out by defining machine learning. *Machine learning* (ML) is the scientific study of algorithms and statistical models that computer systems use to progressively improve their performance on a specific task. Machine learning algorithms build a mathematical model based on sample data, known as *training data*, in order to make predictions or decisions without being explicitly programmed to perform the task.

So, here's how advanced analytics and ML have some characteristics in common:

>> Both advanced analytics and machine learning techniques are used for building and executing advanced mathematical and statistical models as well as building optimized models that can be used to predict events before they happen.

>> Both methods use data to develop the models, and both require defined model policies.

>> Automation can be used to run both analytics models and machine learning models after they're put into production.

What about the differences between advanced analytics and machine learning?

>> There is a difference in who the actor is when creating your model. In an advanced analytics model, the actor is human; in a machine learning model, the actor is (obviously) a machine.

>> There is also a difference in the model format. Analytics models are developed and deployed with the human-defined design, whereas ML models are dynamic and change design and approach as they're being trained by the data, optimizing the design along the way. Machine learning models can also be deployed as *dynamic,* which means that they continue to train, learn and optimize the design when exposed to real-life data and its live context.

>> Another difference between analytical models and machine learning models regards the difference in how models are tested using data (for analytics) and trained using data (for machine learning). In analytics data is used to test that the defined outcome is achieved as expected, while in machine learning, the data is used to train the model to optimize its design depending on the nature of the data.

>> Finally, the techniques and tools used to develop advanced analytics models and ML models differ. Machine learning modeling techniques are much more advanced and are built on other principles related to how the machine will learn to optimize the model performance.

Figure 1-6 shows how the different models can be developed, tested, or trained and then deployed. As you can see, analytics models are always developed and tested in a *static* manner, where the human actor decides which statistical methods to use and how to test the model using the defined sample data set in order to reach the optimal model performance. And, regardless of how much data (or which data) you push through an analytical model, it stays the same until the human actor decides to correct or evolve the model.

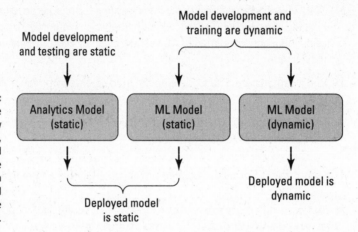

FIGURE 1-6: The difference in how development, training, and deployment are done for an analytical model versus a machine learning model.

TECHNICAL STUFF In ML development, a human actor also decides which technique or method to be used. Training methods in ML differ depending on which technique is used — you can use supervised learning, for example, or unsupervised learning, semi-supervised learning, reinforcement learning, or even deep learning, which is a more complex method. It's even possible to combine two methods, like combining reinforcement learning with deep learning to what is referred to as deep reinforcement learning.

Instead of the static approach used in traditional model testing, with ML models you first train a model using a selected training data set that should represent the target environment where you intend to deploy the ML model. During the training, the model performance is tested to monitor the learning progress as well as measure the model accuracy. Within the scope of the chosen ML method, you then let the algorithm (machine actor) train itself on the training data set to reach the target that has been set. The machine then continues to train the ML model to evolve and find the most optimized model performance as long as you let it. The time will come when the model accuracy cannot be improved on using the training set. At that stage, you have to evaluate whether the model accuracy is good enough for deployment.

TECHNICAL STUFF

If you decide that a sufficient level of training has been reached by the machine actor, you need to decide how to deploy the model in the target environment, — deploy to production, in other words. You have two options at this point. You can decide that the model is sufficiently trained to achieve its purpose and that you can deploy it as a static model — meaning that it will no longer learn and optimize performance based on data, regardless of what changes occur in the target environment. Or, you can decide to deploy the ML model into production as a dynamic model, meaning that it will continue to evolve and optimize its performance driven by the data and behaviors that populate the model in the production environment. This is sometimes also referred to as *online training*.

So, when should you go for what type of model and deployment approach? Well, it depends on many factors. As a guiding rule, you should never use ML if you can get the job done using an analytics approach. Why? For the same reason you don't use a sledgehammer to drive a nail. You might perhaps succeed, but you can just as easily destroy the nail and hurt yourself, causing loss of time and money.

When it comes to a static or dynamic deployment, it depends on the business model and whether the target environment is static (changes happen seldom and are usually minor) or dynamic (changes occur often and on a large scale). If you're developing an algorithm to make online recommendations based on previous user behavior, for example, it's necessary to deploy a dynamic ML model; otherwise, you cannot fulfil your objective.

If, on the other hand, the purpose of the ML model is to let the machine find the optimal way to automate a set of complex tasks that you expect to stay the same over time, it is advisable to deploy the ML model as a static model in its target environment.

WARNING

Be aware that implementing ML models in live environments requires more resources from you. Machine learning training is complex and requires a lot of processing capacity as well as more monitoring of the ML model. You need to make sure that the ML model continues to perform as expected and doesn't degrade or deviate from its objective as part of its live training. Another aspect to consider is the need to ensure that the model can interact with other dynamic ML models in the target environment without disturbing each other's purpose or act in a way that leads to models canceling each other out. (What you're doing here is often referred to as *ensuring model interoperability*.)

Defining and Scoping a Data Science Strategy

To understand the constituent parts of a data science strategy as well the strategy's current and future significance, it's worthwhile to look at some of the major components on a high level. I then address each of these different parts in detail throughout this book. But before that I need to make a short clarification of the difference between a *data science strategy* and a *data strategy*.

On a high-level a data science strategy refers to the strategy you define with regards to the entire data science investment in our company. It includes areas such as overall data science objectives and strategic choices, regulatory strategies, data need, competences and skillsets, data architecture, as well as how to measure the outcome. The data strategy on the other hand, constitutes a subset of the data science strategy, and is focused on outlining the strategic direction directly related to the data. This includes areas such as data scope, data consent, legal, regulatory and ethical considerations, storage collection frequency, data storage retention periods, data management process and principles, and last, but not least; data governance.

Both strategies are needed in order to succeed with your data science investment and should complement each other in order to work. The details of how to define the data strategy is captured in part 2 of this book.

Objectives

If I ask about the objectives of a data science strategy, I'm asking whether there are clear company objectives set and agreed on for any of the investments made in data science. Are the objectives formulated in a way that makes them possible to execute and measure success by? If not, then the objectives need to be reformulated; this is a critically important starting point that must be completed properly in order to succeed down the line.

Data science is a new field that holds amazing opportunities for companies to drive a fundamental transformation, but it is complex and often not fully understood by top management. You should consider whether the executive team's understanding of data science is sufficient to set the right targets or whether they need to be educated and then guided in setting their target.

TIP

Whether you're a manager or an employee in a small or large company, if you want your company to succeed with its data science investment, don't sit and hope that the leadership of your company will understand what needs to be done. If you're knowledgeable in the area, make your voice heard or, if you aren't, don't hesitate to accept help from those who have experience in the field.

If you decide to bring in external experts to assist you in your data science strategizing, be sure to read up on the area yourself first, so that you can judge the relevance of their recommendations for your business — the place where *you* are the expert.

Approach

Taking the right initial approach is a fundamental part of your data science strategy — it will determine whether your company takes the appropriate implementation and transformation approach for the data science investment. For example, is the approach ambitious enough — or is it *too* ambitious, considering time estimates related to available competence? Is there a clear business strategy and expected value that the data science strategy can relate to? Taking the time to think through the approach is sure to pay off because, if you don't know where you're going, you are most unlikely to end up there.

Choices

The term *choices* here refers to the strategic choices necessary to drive the data science transformation forward.

The strategy you create cannot be about doing everything. It's equally important to make strategic choices about what to do as it is to make decisions about what *not* to do.

Decisions can also be distributed differently over time, because the choices can be about starting with a particular business area or set of customers, learning from that experience, and then continuing to include other areas or customers. The same strategy applies to choices of data categories or types to focus on early rather than later on as the company matures and capabilities expand.

Data

Defining a data strategy is a cornerstone of the data science strategy — it includes all aspects related to the data, such as whether or not you understand the various types of data you need to access in order to achieve your business objectives. Is the data available? How will you approach data management and data storage? Have you set priorities on the data? Have you identified and set data quality targets?

Another important aspect of data relates to data governance and security. Data will be one of your most valuable assets going forward; how you treat it is fundamental to your company's success.

Legal

Understanding the legal implications for the data you need in terms of access rights, ownership, and usage models is vital. If you aren't on top of this aspect early on, you might find yourself in a situation where you cannot get hold of the data you need for your business without breaking the law, or, even if you can get hold of the data, you may realize that you cannot use it in the way you need in order to fulfil your business objectives.

REMEMBER

Laws and regulations related to data privacy stretch further than many people think, and they keep changing in order to protect people's data integrity. This is good from a privacy perspective, but doesn't always work well with data innovation. Therefore, as a good investment, you should always stay informed about laws and regulations related to the data needed for your business.

Ethics

Ethics, an area of growing importance, refers to the creation of clear ethical guidelines for how data science is approached in the company. Internally, this term refers to securing a responsible approach to data usage and management when it comes to preserving the data privacy of your customers or other stakeholders. One way of protecting privacy is through anonymizing personal information in the data sets.

Externally, insisting on the ethics of data science is vital when it comes to gaining your customers' trust in how you handle data. When machine learning or artificial intelligence is introduced — especially when automation of decisions and preventive actions are involved — it touches on another ethical perspective: the "explainability" of algorithms. It refers to the idea that it must be possible to explain a decision or action taken by a machine. Machine learning or artificial intelligence cannot become an automated, black box execution by a machine. Humans must stay in control to secure the transparency of AI algorithms and ensure that ethical boundaries are kept.

Competence

Based on the objectives that are set, choices that are made, and approach that is chosen, you must ensure that you put the right competence in place to execute on your targets. Putting together an experienced and competent data science team is easier said than done. Why is that? Well, you really need three main categories of competencies, and the availability of experienced data scientists in the market is now very low, simply because few data scientists have the sufficient experience and because the demand for these types of competencies is very high.

REMEMBER

You can't get by with simply hiring only data scientists. Data engineers with a genuine understanding of the data in focus is fundamental. Without good data management, data scientists cannot perform their algorithmic magic. It's as simple as that.

Finally, you need to secure domain expertise for the targeted area, whether it's a vast business understanding or an exceptional operational understanding. It's absolutely crucial to have the domain experts working closely with the data engineers and the data scientists to achieve productive data science teams in your organization.

Infrastructure

When talking about infrastructure, it's all about understanding what is needed in terms of data architecture and applications in order to enable a productive and innovative environment for your data science teams. It includes considering both a development environment (a workspace where you innovate, develop, train, and test new capabilities) and a production environment (a runtime environment where you deploy and run your solutions).

Infrastructure includes all aspects, from how you'll set up your data collection/ data ingest, anonymization, data storage, data management, and application layer with tools for the analytics and ML/AI development and production environment.

WARNING

It is impossible to identify and set up the perfect environment, especially because the technology evolution in this area is moving very fast. However, a vital part of the infrastructure setup is to avoid getting locked into a situation where you become entirely dependent on a certain infrastructure vendor (hardware, software, or cloud, for example). I don't mean that you should only go for open source products, but I do mean that you have to think carefully which building blocks you're using and then make sure that they're exchangeable in the long run, if needed.

Governance and security

Working actively with data governance and security will make sure you stay in control of data usage at all times. It isn't important only in terms of gaining your customers' trust, but it is in many cases also a necessity for following the law. Keeping track of which data is collected, stored, and used for which use cases is a minimum requirement for most types of data.

WARNING

Overworking the area of governance and security will have an impact on your data science productivity and innovation. A common mistake is to be overprotective with regard to data usage, keeping all data locked in to a degree that nobody can access what they need in order to do their job. Therefore, you should approach the setup of data governance and security with a mindset of openness when it comes to sharing data amongst employees within the organization. Lock the gates to outsiders, but strive for an open-data approach internally, boosting collaboration, reuse, and innovation.

Commercial/business models

As part of your company's data science strategy, you need to consider whether you only want to focus your efforts internally as a means of improving operational efficiency or whether you have ambitions to utilize data science to improve your commercial business models. Improving your business using data science will absolutely expand your possibilities, both in improving current business as well as helping you find new opportunities.

WARNING

Tread carefully when commercializing data. If you haven't transformed internally first by implementing data-driven operations, you'll likely be unable to fully leverage a data science approach externally in the business perspective.

That doesn't mean you need to implement and run data-driven operations throughout the company, but such operations will be needed for the areas connected to the new data-science-based business models and commercial offerings you're aiming to realize.

Measurements

Without measuring your success, how will you ever know whether you have actually achieved your objectives? Or be able to prove that. Still, many companies fail to think of measurements early on.

REMEMBER

Measurements are needed not only from an internal operational efficiency perspective but also to measure whether you have managed to deliver on the promises made to customers. This is important regardless of whether the agreed-on customer targets have been contracted or not. It should always be a priority for you to know how your business is performing against your objectives. The feedback will give you all the information you need to determine where the business stands, what needs to improve, and what has perhaps already been achieved.

Yes, establishing measurements early on is fundamental when it comes to securing continuous learning in your company, but it also shows customers that you care about reaching your targets. However, don't forget to think through the metrics structure you plan to use. It isn't an easy task to identify and define the correct set of metrics from the start. This is also something that needs to be reevaluated over time, based on which measurements actually give you the insights and feedback needed on what is going well — and what isn't going so well.

Chapter **2**

Considering the Inherent Complexity in Data Science

Cities are complex systems, and city policies are typically made in complex environments where many factors covering a whole spectrum of social, environmental, economic, and technological factors must be taken into consideration. However, in recent years, urban complexities have been better managed by evolutions in data science. The ability to perform urban modeling and simulate different future scenarios based on actual data has opened up many new possibilities related to urban planning and investments. These evolutions in data science have enabled government agencies to better understand complex urban issues, anticipate possible scenarios, and make the best policy and investment decisions.

But what does *complexity* really mean and refer to? Well, in my view, society has the general misconception that complexity is always bad. Yes, the simplest solution is often the best one — a truism that has been around ever since the 13th century, when the Franciscan friar William of Ockham came up with the original formulation, now known universally as *Occam's razor*. But in some cases, it's the actual complexity of a matter that makes it interesting for a certain technical solution. This is the case in data science. If the problem at hand is simple and can be solved with a simple solution (using ordinary code, for example). it makes no sense to use machine learning techniques to solve the problem and throw self-learning software at it.

REMEMBER

In fact, if your business is simple and straightforward, and you want to keep it that way and not expand beyond your current business models, you might gain very little value by adding machine learning and artificial intelligence into the mix. However, if you're interested in evolving your business as well as your product or service capabilities beyond what is currently possible, more advanced data science could be a way to make that goal achievable.

WARNING

Nevertheless, the journey will not be simple. Data science is definitely an enabler, and you can use it to start simple and grow from there. But operating with data science at the core of your business requires skilled data scientists and data architects. Data science is a craft that requires skills across several disciplinary fields, including a good architectural understanding. It isn't a competence you acquire simply by taking a course in R or Python; it's much more than that, and you should not underestimate the level of expertise required. More advanced data science where machine learning and artificial intelligence is used is a complex matter that is used to solve complex problems. Therefore, this chapter aims to help you understand the fundamentals of why data science is complex — and also why the potential lies in that same complexity.

Diagnosing Complexity in Data Science

What does it mean when people say that data science is inherently complex? Well, by its very nature, data science — and especially techniques like machine learning and artificial intelligence — are built to solve complex problems that cannot be solved even by the brightest humans. It doesn't mean that the machine will out-play humans on day one, but over time it will — at least as far as we *want* the machines to outperform us, regulated by the policies we use to constrain the machines ability to enhance its learning. At the end of the day, it isn't about how smart machines can become, but rather how smart they can make us humans.

In machine learning algorithms are built to learn how to optimize their realizations first on a training data set in a lab environment and then on real life data later on. Algorithms can be built to learn from many different data sources and parameters, many more than is possible for the human brain to incorporate and process quickly and continuously. Let's face it; as long as they are running on a flexible and scalable architecture, machines need no sleep, no rest, and basically have no limits in terms of capacity when it comes to bringing in more data or other policies and constraints. Humans just can't measure up to that.

REMEMBER

Automating a repetitive task in real-time using many different data sources doesn't necessarily have to be solved by machine learning. Many automation tasks can be carried out using a static statistical model; if the model doesn't need to change and optimize over time, then there's no need for machine learning. It really should only come into play when the problem at hand is dynamically changing and complex. Only then is the machine-learning algorithm needed to manage a complexity that the human brain cannot cope with (in real-time or not), improving the realization fast enough and in as many dimensions as required.

REMEMBER

Since data science serves as the foundation in managing the increasing complexity of our soon fully digitalized and connected society, it's at the core of the solutions needed for our technical evolution going forward. The attractiveness of data science is very much connected to the rapidly growing access to data and higher availability of technologies like machine learning and artificial intelligence. However, managing complexity is often not merely *difficult* to manage with a simple solution — sometimes it's *impossible.*

Given this fact, it's of vital importance to understand that, although data science is the scientific discipline that will be instrumental in bringing our society forward toward a future of more automation, robotics and self-learning software, it has never claimed to be based on simple science. Instead, data science is by nature inherently complex.

Recognizing Complexity as a Potential

If we assume that data science is complex, how can we turn that into a business potential? Well, due to the complex nature of data science, it's going to require skills that are not easily acquired and therefore not something that every company has on hand. Approaching it right, within the right time frame, could therefore be turned into a competitive advantage for your company.

TIP

Because data science is complex, it also means that in order to understand what it's about, you need to invest significant time and money to enhance your understanding of where you need to start, what it means for your business, and which business outcomes you could expect. One key component in getting this right, is to spend time on building a really good and useful Data Science Strategy.

WARNING

Rushing into an investment in data science without a clear objective or understanding of how the business must fundamentally change in order to capture the business value desired could produce the opposite result. There are many ways your investment in data science could go wrong. Some of these problems or pitfalls are more easy to avoid than others. Some are impossible to avoid, but can be managed through increased awareness of how to approach them.

Enrolling in Data Science Pitfalls 101

Part of coming to terms with the complexity of a solution is realizing that — despite our best thoughts and intentions — we are still drawn to simplistic solutions for complex problems. Data science solutions are no exception to this rule. In coming up with a data science strategy, you're bound to encounter many "reasonable" assertions that are in fact far from reasonable and could potentially endanger the success of your data science initiative. (I refer to these "reasonable" assertions as "pitfalls" because if you let them establish themselves, you and your data science initiatives will fall into a pit with no strategy for getting out.) You need to work constantly against the assumption that "the simplest solution is the best one" by stressing again and again that mastering complexity is really the only way you can ensure the success of any data science strategy. Some challenges can be avoided, whereas other challenges are unavoidable and need to be managed.

In order to help you on your endeavors, I'm going to walk you through an overview of some of the common pitfalls you need to avoid (and an explanation on why) in order for your data science strategy to succeed. A lot is won if you can focus your efforts on efficiently managing the challenges you cannot avoid.

Believing that all data is needed

Data voraciousness is a fault common to quite a few companies. They spend a lot of time and money on investing in infrastructure components so they can collect and store all the data available in a certain segment relevant to its business. Data is being acquired without strategically thinking through what is actually needed and when.

WARNING

What happens when you bring in all data? Time and money gets spent on getting the data, sorting it out, and making sure the infrastructure can cope with the huge amount of data being brought in. That means there's nothing left over for investing in the task of making use of the data.

It sometimes even gets to a point where so much effort is spent on managing the data that there is barely any time left over for producing the insights the data was meant to produce. And on top of that, the insights that are derived from the data are often never put into action — the focus is elsewhere, stuck on managing the overload of data coming into the company.

Thinking that investing in a data lake will solve all your problems

Many companies have spent a considerable amount of time and money investing in *data lakes,* believing that by replacing the scattered data repositories (usually spread across various applications and traditional database systems) with a new and common data repository (usually in the cloud), all problems are solved. But you need to be careful so that you don't see the data lake as the silver bullet — that part of your infrastructure that will solve any problem. Please be aware that the data lake should be seen as a temporary storage point for your data, not a permanent one. Remember that it adds value only as long as the data stored in it is used. Of course, a company may have other reasons for storing data — regulations that require storing data for a certain time period, for example. Keep in mind however, that the data lake should primarily be seen as a layer in your infrastructure that should be focused on enabling secure and efficient data usage by the next layer.

WARNING

Avoid thinking of the data lake as a "warehouse" where you throw in all the data you've collected and lock the door for usage only by an unknown individual, for an unknown purpose, later at some unclear point in the future. (It's called a data *lake,* not a data *abyss.*) Think ahead instead; it's of vital importance that you clearly define in your data strategy which data will be stored where, for which purpose, and with which priority. You also need to think about how long you want your retention periods for each different type of data to be, based on what you're aiming to achieve with the data.

Another important aspect to regard strategically involves the costs associated with data storage. If you're collecting huge amounts of data on a regular or real-time basis, which means you anticipate a constant flow of new data coming in that will grow the total data volume over time, you can expect an exponential growth in data storage costs over the short and long term.

TIP

Before data is even put into the data lake, you also need to consider how to structure the data lake so that you'll be able to find data quickly and efficiently. You need to separate between sensitive and non-sensitive data, as well as between data you own versus data that you do not own yourself but have the rights to use. It's also very important to think through the data access rights internally from a data governance perspective. Perhaps not everyone should have access to everything? Just be careful in that regard. Don't overdo it in terms of restricting data access within your company. Locking your data in just to be on the safe side is not a good idea, since it will decrease your data lake utilization efficiency. Restrict only what is absolutely necessary from a legal or company policy perspective with regards to data privacy, restricted customer data, financial data, or other sensitive data.

REMEMBER

Without this basic data lake structure with data categorization, tagging, defined retention periods, access rights and so on, you run the risk of having loads of data at your disposal, but cannot use it efficiently, because it is lost or locked in the lake.

Focusing on AI when analytics is enough

The ambition to stay in tune with the evolution in the industry at any cost, is another typical pitfall that can be found in a growing number of companies. This derives from the fact that companies want to stay in tune with the latest technology evolution in the market but lack a real understanding of what it actually means. When it comes to artificial intelligence (AI), there is a misplaced confidence in what AI is and what it can do, but at the same time there is an underestimation of what analytics can do without adding the complexity of AI.

REMEMBER

Saying that AI is overly hyped doesn't mean that AI cannot be relevant. On the contrary, AI can most probably enhance most businesses in many aspects. However, you should not try to solve a simple problem by using a complex technology like AI if it can, in fact, be solved using analytics.

Analytics helps you explore the data using different techniques, enabling you to find dependencies and correlations as well as build models to forecast or predict a certain outcome or behavior. Analytics falls short when one of these factors exists:

>> The problems are too complex for humans to understand and design an optimized solution for.

>> The data environment where the algorithm needs to run is dynamic and constantly changing.

In these situations, you need something else. An analytics model put into production has a fixed design; its behavior is static and cannot adapt or change, meaning that it will stay the same over time, even if data and conditions change.

Rather than jump immediately on the AI bandwagon, then, take the time to think through which type of environment you're targeting with your solutions and in which context you need these solutions to work. Ask yourself which ones are more static, and thus more likely to stay the same over time in terms of data and behavior, and which are constantly changing. Understanding that to a certain level of detail, will help you to get a better overview of what approach to use for which problem.

Believing in the 1-tool approach

Many companies are of the opinion that a harmonized tool approach offers the most efficient IT environment. And perhaps that is many times the case, especially when you want to drive toward aligned ways of working in the company, harmonizing data input, and so on. But, when it comes to data science, you must consider which parts needs to conform, and which are more efficient if they stay diverse and flexible.

REMEMBER

As a general approach, strive for as much alignment in the basic layers of capture, storage, and management of data. But when you approach the upper layers of analyzing and communicating insights and decisions, you need to allow a much higher level of freedom for data scientists, business analysts, and other interested parties. When approaching data exploration and analysis as well as algorithm development, you need different techniques and tools to be available for your teams.

The same is true when it comes to communicating or utilizing results from the analysis: You need tailored approaches that align best with the information you want to convey. Forcing this to happen in one and the same environment will hinder, rather than boost, innovation and will definitely limit the impact of data science on your overall business. For a data science strategy to succeed, it needs to be integrated into all necessary aspects of your company. And for that you require a variety of tools and applications for different purposes.

TIP

Many companies' leaders tend to view the data science setup from a cost perspective, and often believe that the main cost for the environment is connected to the application layer rather than to the enablement part of the infrastructure — capture, storage, and management of data, in other words. Aligning and optimizing the basic layers correctly in your infrastructure will not only give you cost control of your data science infrastructure investment but also allow the data science teams greater freedom in the layers on top. With this approach, you have a greater chance to enhance your data science productivity overall.

Investing only in certain areas

Leaders of larger companies often tend to think that you can select one or two areas for the data science investment rather than go for a full end-to-end implementation across the company. It's understandable because such an implementation is not only costly but also fundamentally transformative in terms of how tasks are approached and executed. Of course, change on such a massive scale is seen as a major risk from a company-wide perspective.

REMEMBER

To truly benefit from your data science investment, you need to approach it from an end-to-end perspective. As long as you take the time to think through your investment from a long-term perspective, it's not only possible but also advisable to first start small and then grow over time, business area by business area. To achieve that, however, you need a plan to incorporate the business folks in the data science investment. All parts need to transform over time — and that transformation may reach much further than you think. If your company is large, you might even have to consider transforming your relationship with your sub-suppliers and vendors. If your business becomes data- and value-driven in all aspects, can you then really work with a sub-supplier that is cost-driven?

WARNING

When planning to take small steps toward having a company that's fully focused on data science, you cannot count on that approach being the best one from a cost perspective. Instead, it's more likely than not that until data science is implemented as a driving force throughout the company, you will see only minor benefits from a company-wide perspective. Remember that having only parts of the organization become data-driven could even increase your overall cost short term, because it means that you need to maintain two or more types of setups (infrastructure, processes, competences, and so on) in parallel.

Leveraging the infrastructure for reporting rather than exploration

The common problem of being report-focused is typically connected to a situation where top management has the wrong idea about what data science can bring to the company. The situation usually arises because some company leaders believe that the main purpose of data science is to produce a set of answers to certain predefined questions raised by management. Answering these specific questions should therefore be the main driver for the implementation of data science and should thus result in a report back to management.

WARNING

You might be asking yourself what's wrong with trying to fulfill requests coming from Corporate — is not the starting point of all analysis a set of business questions you want answers to? Well, in a sense, that is correct. However, it's equally important to be mindful that the questions you're asking might not be the right ones to ask. Why? Simply because that predetermined set of questions is based on your current understanding of your business, market, and customer base. If your company is mainly experience-based rather than data-driven, the questions might be correct — or not. You simply do not know if you're approaching a certain problem or opportunity from the wrong angle.

TIP

Approach your data science investment as an opportunity for your company to be based on data, insights, and facts that will help guide you correctly in a data centric society. Like in the company Husqvarna that is dealing with outdoor power products, they have now started to enable connectivity for their chain saws. The company is doing this in order to collect data on how they are used, or not used, when cutting trees, to be able to understand more about their own business. Simply exploring the data for patterns or anomalies that might point to new (and perhaps unexpected) questions worth asking, is a good way to start.

Underestimating the need for skilled data scientists

Becoming a data scientist is an acquired competence; it can be learned, in other words, with the help of books and training courses and workshops. Becoming an *experienced* data scientist, however, takes time and requires certain skills that are not as easy to acquire.

It's important to respect the difference between a basic data scientist and an experienced one. It's equally important to realize that the senior ones are difficult to come by, so if you have some in your company, make sure you hold on to them. A senior data scientist in the AI space is someone who has worked in the area between five to ten years, knows several programming languages, but most importantly is very skilled at using various ML/AI techniques when building algorithms. To be seen as senior, it also includes having experience from developing and deploying algorithms based on various use cases and in different types of target environments.

However, the key to creating successful data science teams does not lie in acquiring as many senior data scientists as possible. In fact, it's better to have fewer senior ones and spread them across many teams, which will allow them to function as mentors for more junior data scientists, hence contributing to the overall company data science maturity in a better way.

REMEMBER

Although senior data scientists are expensive to hire, it's worth thinking of them in terms of the contributions you can expect from them. If supported by domain experts, senior data scientists can work across any disciplinary field and, given the right preconditions in terms of data and a capable infrastructure, help you approach basically any problem or opportunity in an efficient and innovative way.

`Navigating the Complexity

Arming yourself with persuasive arguments designed to counter those advocates of the "simple is better" philosophy at your company is a good starting point. Recognizing any and all of the challenges that may arise on your company's journey to becoming fully data-driven is crucial, but just being aware of the challenges doesn't rid you of them automatically. It requires not only a constant awareness of the necessity of not thinking about things the wrong way but also a strategic mindset — and plan — to navigate around these potential problems as they arise.

Taking the time to study up on the different scenarios and the solutions to them is worthwhile. When they occur (and they are certain to occur), you will already have a level of understanding on how to deal with them. Even better, given what you know, you can act proactively to make sure you never end up in one of these less-than-favorable situations for your business.

TIP

Write up your identified risk list and proposed mitigation plan for all scenarios, and add it to the company's data science strategy so that you have an agreed-on view of what to do — and what not to do — when stuff happens.

Chapter **3**

Dealing with Difficult Challenges

This chapter addresses a number of complex challenges that are difficult to avoid and that will require the right set of tactics to manage successfully. More specifically, I'll show you what you need to do to make the right decisions when it comes to acquiring and managing your data efficiently and consistently, setting up your data science environment, managing the legal constraints related to the data and algorithms you need for your business, as well as preparing for rapid evolutions in the area of data science as a whole that is sure to come.

Getting Data from There to Here

When a company decides to embark on a journey to become data driven, the focus is naturally on the data itself, which inevitably leads to a greater awareness of the actual variety of data needed to gain full proactive and data-driven control of their current business. On top of that, companies soon realize that in order to expand beyond what is possible today, the data sets need to become even more varied. At this point, many companies start to realize that the data which is fundamental to becoming truly data driven might actually belong to someone else or is located in another country, with other data regulations. This section explains how to strategically approach such practical challenges as part of your data acquisition.

Handling dependencies on data owned by others

Dealing with proprietary data is an unavoidable yet manageable challenge faced by any company striving toward becoming fully data-driven. Typically, what happens is that you have identified and carefully specified all the data you need in your data strategy and when you then start looking into how to strategically approach capturing the data, you realize that you have a data ownership problem.

REMEMBER

If you use only data generated from your internal IT environment, you have, of course, less of a problem. If that's the case, however, then your company probably isn't truly data-driven in the proper sense. A data-driven business accounts for how its products and/or services are used and how it performs in real-life settings, not merely in the lab environment. And anytime you start using data generated by life in the real world, you run into the data ownership problem.

What kind of data am I talking about? First and foremost, this involves data owned by your customers, but it can also include data owned by your customers' customers, depending on which business you're in. You have to take the time to truly understand the detailed context of the data you need. It can relate to issues of data privacy, but it doesn't have to. It can simply be the case that the data you need in order to better understand your business performance or potential belongs to someone else.

TIP

Don't get discouraged when it comes to ownership issues. Most situations can be solved from a legal perspective if you're willing to address them openly with the data owners, explaining why you need the data and how you will treat the data after it's in your possession. It's all about gaining trust with regard to how, and for what purpose, the data will be used. (It wouldn't hurt to also spell out how your work may, if possible, contribute back to the owners of the data.)

At the end of the day, you need to be absolutely certain that you understand (and are complying with) the legal constraints that apply for each different type of data you intend to use. Your use of the data must also be regulated by way of a contractual setup with the party owning the data, including what rights your company has related to data access, storage, and usage over time.

REMEMBER

Laws and regulations have a habit of changing over time. Lately, the trend is to increase restrictions even further in order to protect an individual's right to their own data. One recent example is the quite restrictive General Data Protection and Regulation (GDPR) enacted by the European Union (EU) that went into effect in May 2018. Given recent news of the misuse of data by entities such as Cambridge Analytica and Facebook, the U.S. and Canada are definitely looking into legislation similar to the EU's GDPR.

Anything that helps to protect an individual's right to privacy is all for the best, but just remember that the way you deal with privacy legislation today will most probably be quite different in the near future. Therefore, you should strategically and proactively think through your infrastructure setup and your data needs to ensure that you account for these types of constraints in your current and evolving data science environment.

Managing data transfer and computation across-country borders

If your company has divisions in a number of different countries or does business (and therefore has many customers) in many countries, one major challenge you might face is how to manage data that needs to cross international borders.

You need to carefully consider a number of different aspects of the data puzzle if your company has an international component. Here's a list of the major concerns:

>> **Legality:** Legal constraints to moving data across borders is a consideration that a company must stay on top of. Laws and regulations differ from country to country, so different solutions may be possible, depending on which country you're doing business in. The restrictions are also different depending on which type of data you're moving out of a country. Data with personal information is usually much more difficult to move than non-sensitive data. Breaking laws related to data transfer can be quite costly and can severely impact the company brand if it is determined that you violated customer trust.

>> **Data transfer approach:** This refers to how you actually execute the data transfer. It's typically quite costly and also differs from country to country. Depending on the volume of data you want transferred, and the data transfer frequency, you can either rent space in existing connectivity infrastructures and data links or — if you cannot get your requirements met regarding aspects such as capacity, security, or exclusivity — invest in your own links.

>> **Possibilities for local computation and storage:** If you can store the data and carry out the analysis in the country where the data has been captured, you might be able to lower the cost and increase the speed of delivery. However, to get this setup to work efficiently, you need to properly think through what your distributed computational architecture will look like. What will be done where? and where will the source data be kept, for example? Will there be a central point of data storage and global analysis, or will there be only distributed setups? How you answer these questions depends a lot on what type of business is being conducted and what the setup looks like in different countries.

Managing Data Consistency Across the Data Science Environment

It might seem like a simple task to ensure data consistency across the different parts of the data science environment, but it's much more difficult than it seems. First off, this area tends to be more complex than it needs to be, eating up more time and resources than originally estimated. The need for consistency includes aspects such as data governance and data formats, but also the labeling of data consistently —using customer IDs across many different sources to enable correlation of different data types related to the same customer, for example.

The challenge is that there is a built-in contradiction in terms infrastructure between enabling usage of special tools to allow data scientists and data engineers to be innovative and productive and at the same time ensuring consistency in the data. This is because specialized tools are optimized to focus on solving certain problems but either don't keep the format consistent or don't interface well with other tools needed in the end-to-end flow. Optimized, specialized machine learning tools are simply not good at playing together with other, similar specialized tools that are addressing comparable or other adjacent problems.

REMEMBER

But is it really that bad? Well, it can lead to real problems, depending on how much freedom is allowed in the architectural implementation and among the teams. Some examples of problems that can stem from a lack of consistency across the AI environment are described in this list:

>> **Ad hoc solutions:** Every case is treated as an isolated problem that needs to be solved *this instant* in order for the team to move forward. The result? No long-term solution and no learning between teams.

>> **Increased cost:** When you have to duplicate tool capabilities in order to manage a lack of consistency or when you have to build capabilities into purchased tools to secure just the basic consistency, those costs add up.

>> **End-to-end not working:** Inconsistencies can occur when the infrastructure is implemented across several cloud vendors, which then makes it difficult or impossible to transfer data and keep data consistent across different virtualized environments.

REMEMBER

Because corporate management cannot enforce, and may not want to enforce, data consistency across the organization as a company policy, they have to use other means to preserve data consistency end-to-end. One way is to ensure that all teams follow proper and relevant guidelines for evaluating and purchasing new tools that incorporate specific directives related to data consistency. Clearly motivating why this is key to a successful data science strategy execution.

WARNING

It's also vital to consider which limits are needed for each individual company, depending on the type of business, their objectives, and so on. Hold the line when it comes to data consistency: Otherwise, you may end up with a cumbersome and costly implementation of data science, one far removed from the productive data science environment you were hoping for.

Securing Explainability in AI

Explainable AI (XAI), also referred to as Transparent AI, involves the ability to explain how an algorithm has reached a particular insight or conclusion that results in a certain decision to take action. Though an important aspect to consider as part of the evolution of AI, it isn't easy to solve technically, especially if the AI is acting in real-time and thus using streaming data that hasn't been stored. To bring this point home, imagine, if you will, that you cannot explain to your customer why the machine made a certain decision — a decision you would not have made based on your own experience. What do you tell the customer then?

REMEMBER

Addressing explainable AI is becoming increasingly important in terms of our human ability to understand more about why and how the AI is performing in a certain way. In other words, what can be understood by studying how the machine is learning by processing these huge amounts of data from many dimensions, looking for certain patterns or deviations? What is it that the machine detects and understands that you missed or interpreted differently or simply were not capable of detecting? Which conclusions can be drawn from that?

WARNING

Ethically, AI explainability will be even more important when data scientists start building more advanced artificial intelligence, where many different algorithms are working together. It will be the key to understanding exactly *what* machines interpret as well as *how* the machine's decision-making process is carried out. Knowing this information is crucial to staying on top of the policy framework needed to set the boundaries for what the machine shall and shall not do, as well as how these policies need to be expanded, or perhaps restricted, going forward.

From a purely existential perspective on one hand and the need for humans to remain in control of the intelligent machines that are being built on the other, you cannot simply view AI as black box. (The *black box* challenge in AI refers to the need to ensure that, when an algorithm takes a decision based on the techniques that have been used to train the algorithm, that decision-making process must be transparent to humans. Algorithm transparency is possible when many of the more basic ML techniques — supervised learning, for example — are being used, but so far nobody has yet found a way to gain transparency when it comes to algorithms based on deep learning techniques. For example, there must be a way to explain why a certain decision was taken when something went wrong. A pertinent example is the self-driving car, where a bunch of algorithms are in play, working together and (hopefully) following policies predefined for how to act in certain circumstances. All works according to plan, but then a totally unknown and unexpected event occurs and the car takes an unexpected action that causes an accident. In such situations, people in general would naturally expect that there would be some way to extract information from the self-driving car on why this specific decision was made — hence, they expect *explainability* in AI.

Apart from the technical, ethical, and existential reasons for ensuring the explainability of AI, there is now also a legal reason. The EU's General Data Protection Regulation (GDPR) has a clause that requests algorithmic interpretability. Right now, these demands aren't too strict, but over time this will likely change dramatically. The GDPR request now requires the ability to explain how the algorithm functions based on the following questions:

>> Which data is used?

>> Which logic is used in the algorithm?

>> What process is used?

>> What is the impact of the decision made by the algorithm?

Dealing with the Difference between Machine Learning and Traditional Software Programming

It is quite well established and commonly agreed in the software industry on what the actual difference is between traditional programming and machine learning. However, when it comes to how this difference should be handled, there's little agreement. Given this division, I want to take the time to explain what to consider when it comes to your implementation approaches as well as how to deal with these differing viewpoints in terms of development aspects as well as the production environment. But first let me start you off by looking at what the argument's all about.

The traditional programming approach, shown in Figure 3-1, has you decide beforehand how to solve a certain problem by using the program being developed. The main target for the software developer is to build the requested functionality.

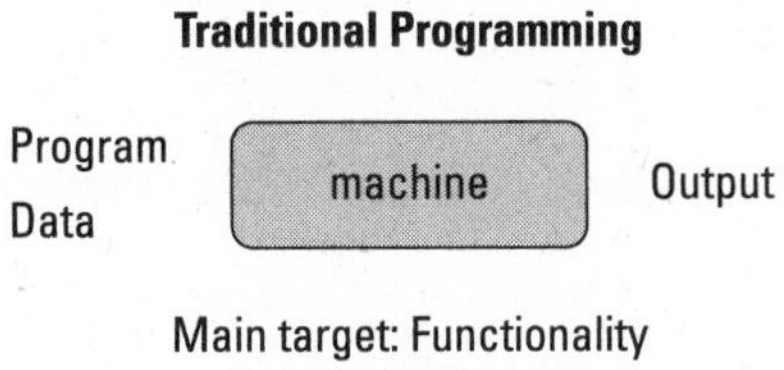

Traditional Programming

FIGURE 3-1: The traditional programming approach.

Program
Data
machine
Output

Main target: Functionality

Based on the data and the program, the machine performs the analysis exactly the way you want, regardless of whether it's the most optimized way to solve the problem. The assumption is that you-the-programmer (rather than the machine) know best how to solve the problem.

On the other hand, when it comes to machine learning development, the starting point is to empower the machine to find the best solution when you set the boundaries of which data to use and which outcome to achieve — and nothing more. (See Figure 3-2.) The assumption is that, given these conditions, the machine will find the most optimized program to solve the problem.

Machine Learning

FIGURE 3-2: A machine learning approach.

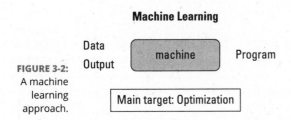

Data
Output
machine
Program

Main target: Optimization

So, what do these distinct approaches mean in terms of your development and production environments? One main aspect to consider is that traditional programming embraces a much stricter process. It's rule-based and follows predefined design principles. The starting point for machine learning development, on the other hand, is much more explorative and open-ended. As you might have guessed, this will have quite a significant impact on how the development environment needs to be set up.

WARNING

Some companies have a tendency to downplay the impact of the development environment setup and which impact it will have on data science productivity. If you start from this vantage point, you may well conclude that you can use the same (or similar) infrastructure setup for both your traditional software development environment and your data science environment. Nothing could be further from the truth — taking such an approach means that you're setting up major barriers toward achieving your goal of useful artificial intelligence/machine learning output.

Traditional programming is much more restrictive when it comes to which programming languages to use and which principles to apply for what task. This, of course, impacts how both the development and production environments need to be set up. Figure 3-3 gives you a graphical representation of how traditional programming happens.

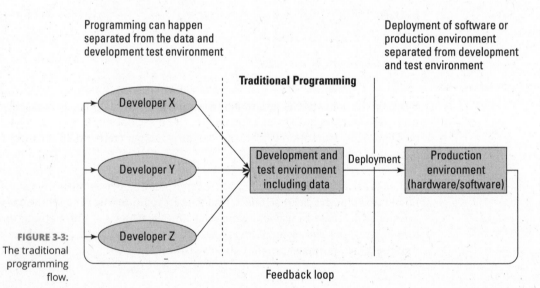

FIGURE 3-3:
The traditional programming flow.

As you can see on the left side of Figure 3-3, traditional software programming can happen separately from both data and the development and test environment. It doesn't have to happen separately, but the fact is that it can be done in isolation — even on a laptop in a coffee shop — and then integrated with other code in the development and test environment. At this point, data can be added to the model in order to achieve the desired output.

Figure 3-3 also shows that the deployment of the software program is done in a separate environment (into a software/hardware product or similar production environment, for example) outside the development and test environment.

Turning once again to a machine learning approach, you need to recognize that the explorative and learning nature of machine learning development requires the setup that's available to your data scientists to be extremely flexible. Efficient data management, easy data access, and a variety of specialized machine learning tools must be easily available. Nobody walks into the process with predefined notions of exactly which machine learning technique to use, because all that needs to be explored and because the most optimized solution may become clear only after the process has started.

REMEMBER

As Figure 3-4 shows, machine learning development cannot happen in isolation and without the data. It all starts and ends with the data in a machine learning development flow because the data itself is what trains the model for an optimized design. For this to work, you obviously have to have a constant data flow, which means that you need a stable data pipeline — preferably, a virtualized one that offers more infrastructure flexibility over time.

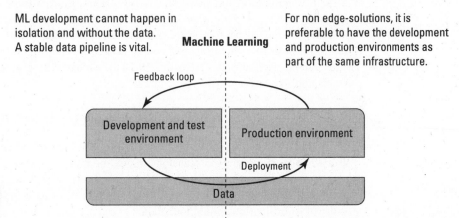

FIGURE 3-4:
A machine learning flow.

TIP

For machine learning virtualized production environments not implemented on the edge (inside IoT devices like a mobile phone, a car, a watch, a fridge, or other types of devices that are connected and where a ML algorithm can run, in other words), try to keep your development and production environment close or as part of the same infrastructure setup. This facilitates machine learning productivity when moving between development and production, with faster and more efficient feedback loops as part of the benefits. You also gain a cost efficiency benefit when you don't need to duplicate the infrastructure, because both are built on the same data pipeline.

Managing the Rapid AI Technology Evolution and Lack of Standardization

AI/ML technologies are constantly evolving and becoming more and more advanced. As computational efficiency increases, such technologies can now adjust to run on a smaller hardware footprint. These advances push analytics, ML, and AI realization also to the edge, meaning that an algorithm has computational support to run inside a device rather than that the device just provides data to the algorithm running remotely in the cloud, for example. That's a good trend, because it will allow society to utilize machine intelligence to a broader extent across system environments and billions of mobile devices and other connected entities. However, one area is not keeping up with all the rapid changes: ML/AI standardization.

The lack of standardization isn't, of course, something that you or a single company can solve, but it's important to be aware of this situation as part of your data science strategy. And of course, at the end of the day, data scientists all have the responsibility to strive toward more standardization in machine learning and artificial intelligence. But just because no official, international standardization exists yet, it doesn't mean that no initiatives exist. The standardizations that are out there are mostly based on something often referred to as *de facto* standardization, derived from influential open source initiatives coordinated through universities like UC–Berkeley (AMP lab and RISE lab) and companies like Google (Google Beam) and AT&T (Acumos).

Another trend that can be detected deals with increased concerns when it comes to access to (and usage of) personal information for nontransparent or even hidden reasons. This has resulted in stricter legislation in different countries, but has also led to more ongoing discussions about the need to increase regulation and impose standardizations related to AI ethics. This positive trend will hopefully continue to push human society to better envision — as a group — what the future of AI utilization should look like.

Of course, this trend has a downside. Because so little standardization is now available to lean on for your data science investment, you need to account for the possibility that you will have to make serious adjustments to your infrastructure when the new standards finally pop up in the near future. The worst-case scenario? You may have to repeat his process several times, or even totally remodel your entire infrastructure.

My advice to you? Continuously follow trends, and be on the lookout for any indication that new laws or regulations or standardization initiatives are coming down the pike — especially open source ones. And be prepared to adjust your data science approach to match the changes that are coming.

Chapter **4**

Managing Change in Data Science

nvesting in data science and a data-driven approach means understanding and dealing with the change that needs to happen. Although the inevitable data science transformation in society may not have fully arrived yet, organizations still need to get ready. The time for standing on the sidelines, waiting to see what other companies are doing, is over. The time to act is now.

Those companies best positioned to manage the needed change driven by data science in the next decade will be the ones that start preparing now. The day has come for companies to invest time in strategically building up an understanding of what is needed and capture the intent in a data science strategy — not just in one area or function, but throughout the company.

Understanding Change Management in Data Science

In a study done by PricewaterhouseCoopers (PwC) and Iron Mountain, 1,800 senior business leaders in North America and Europe at midsize companies and enterprise-level organizations responded to a survey which showed that only a small percentage of the companies actually considered themselves to have effective data management practices.

The study found that although 75 percent of business leaders from companies of all sizes, locations, and sectors feel that they are "making the most of their information assets," in reality, only a minor portion seem to be strategically approaching these major changes in the right way. Overall, as much as 43 percent of company leaders answered that they "obtain little tangible benefit from their information," and 23 percent "derive no benefit whatsoever," according to the study. So, what are companies doing wrong?

One lesson to draw from the survey is that investing in the technology to become data driven is only the beginning. To ensure success, companies must do much more than focus on the tools needed to manage the data. Data science transformation deals with sophisticated and interconnected data, small as well as big data sets, which impacts a whole range of business operations and has implications on people, cultures, organizations, processes, and skill sets in data science. The glue that connects and holds all these elements all together is the people. And the key is to get people motivated. This can be achieved in many ways, but using data to communicate relevant examples and proof points in combination with firm leadership is a good way to start.

REMEMBER

Strong leadership to drive the change includes not only the line management support but is also very much dependent on strong leaders and change drivers who can generate trust that the change will bring results. Without these dedicated change drivers across the company, it does not matter if you have the perfect plan — this type of totally transformative change will not happen, at least not to its full extent.

In data science, the methods and techniques used for everything from knowing how to capture and process data to building models and deriving insights continue to evolve, creating a constant need to manage change. This change is also happening in areas such as regulatory practices, security, and privacy, continually altering the base and framework for how to approach data science. For a data science strategy to succeed, organizations need to understand and accept the fact that the skill sets needed to handle different aspects of data science will continue to change. To manage this continual change, you have to have an open mind and be willing to leverage and explore new technologies and methodologies as they become available.

In practice, this means that individuals need to adopt a data-driven mindset and a commitment to lifelong learning as an extension of their work if they ever hope to manage change. Only when you actively use data to explore new avenues and solve real problems can you justify the data science investment.

TIP

Defining a relevant and applicable process for change management should be a joint organizational effort, approached through brainstorming and idea refinement. Usually, agreeing that change is needed is easier than deciding how change should be approached.

Approaching Change in Data Science

Managing change effectively is a multistep process that requires significant investments of time and money. I can recommend a generic change management approach for you to follow, but you also have to consider some specific characteristics. Figure 4-1 graphically illustrates what has to happen, and the next few sections describe in detail the recommended steps.

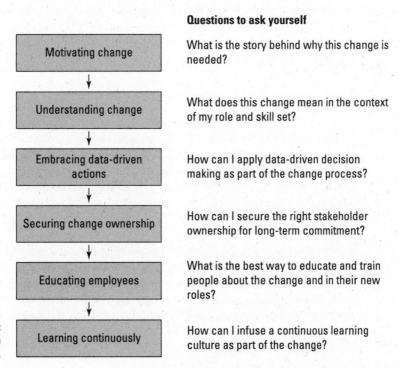

Questions to ask yourself

Motivating change — What is the story behind why this change is needed?

Understanding change — What does this change mean in the context of my role and skill set?

Embracing data-driven actions — How can I apply data-driven decision making as part of the change process?

Securing change ownership — How can I secure the right stakeholder ownership for long-term commitment?

Educating employees — What is the best way to educate and train people about the change and in their new roles?

FIGURE 4-1: Driving change in data science.

Learning continuously — How can I infuse a continuous learning culture as part of the change?

Motivating change

Creating a convincing case for change is a necessary starting point. This compelling story should define what the data science investment will enable for the company and the organization in relation to not only internal policies, processes, and employees but also competitors and customers. By relying on a story-based approach, one which uses relevant business examples as part of your argument, you will be able to help your organizations understand the full impact of the changes coming its way at the very beginning of the process.

REMEMBER

To be able to clearly motivate change, an organization must have a thorough understanding of what each change will mean and where the changes will occur across the spectrum of business and IT operations.

Understanding change

The next step in data-driven readiness is to define the changes in operational terms in a way that employees can relate to. This includes aspects such as explaining the purpose of the change or how upcoming changes might impact structure, processes, skills, and performance goals.

WARNING

Change is never easy. Employees will be exposed to new roles, capabilities, competencies, and ways of working, so the way that companies prepare employees for this fundamental change is critical. First and foremost, you need to focus on educating employees with relevant role-based information and preparing them to be data evangelists in the organization. This personalized approach to making change real and meaningful drives the readiness that is needed for introducing data science successfully.

Embracing data-driven actions

Data science is creating a cultural shift — one that is most evident when it comes to how decisions are made. In data science, decision-making leverages a data-driven approach much more so than approaches relying on experience or gut feeling. It also assumes a culture of collaboration in the organization, because only by working together can people across the organization discover the full value of the insights in a relevant business context that support a permanent change towards data-driven decisions and action.

A reliance on agile methods and DevOps (*development operations*) teams is quickly becoming best practice when managing data science transformations. In an agile approach, an organization empowers its people to work where, when, and how they choose, with maximum flexibility and minimum constraints in order to optimize their performance and deliver best-in-class value and customer service.

A DevOps team approach combines software development (Dev) with information technology operations (Ops). The goal of DevOps is to shorten the development life cycle while delivering frequently in close alignment with business objectives.

These team-related changes also add a layer of complexity for employees, where the traditional walls between organizational teams are displaced to form collaborative teams. Organizations therefore need their leaders to

>> Embrace change willingly

>> Communicate with employees about the changes that are happening

>> Take some time to listen and learn from employees

REMEMBER

In the world of data science, building temporary cross-functional teams like task forces isn't enough to solve complex business problems or build innovative solutions: Organizations must be willing to foster informal groups where individuals are encouraged to seek and uncover hidden opportunities or problems they can address. For leadership, it's equally important to acknowledge the contributions made by such groups in order to empower them and sustain them for the long term.

Securing change ownership

TIP

Without question, the best way to manage the complexity of transformation is to create ownership among the stakeholders who will ultimately deliver on the promise of the new technologies and capabilities.

The idea of appointing traditional change leaders is old-school. Instead, a new innovative model recognizes that business leaders that take on a more operational role as part of the change are the most trusted sources of information and credibility within an organization, and thus should deploy the new technology and own the change as such.

TIP

Create a story that leaders can embrace. One way to do this is by effectively using targeted workshops that demonstrate how the anticipated changes will significantly improve business processes, systems, and practices across different business segments. In these workshops, you can enable early adopters among leadership to work collaboratively with other stakeholders throughout the company.

By using this expanding model for managing data science change, you can touch all the stakeholders you'll need in order to deliver on the promise of data — and also reduce the risk of employees feeling demotivated and alienated by the change.

Educating employees

I recommend blending the necessary education and training programs with elements other than the standard skills training that will (obviously) be needed. Place at the top of your list areas like psychology, gaming, and communication. Adding these elements to the mix helps to focus employee learning and development efforts and enables employees to pick up new competencies and skills beyond the technical aspects of digital or cloud-based data science solutions.

TIP

Consider the idea that it might be necessary to require learning on a broader scale to ensure that the basic principles of data science are understood by a significant subset of your employees. Google, for example, has developed a machine learning course that is mandatory for every technical employee.

Learning continuously

Data science transformation requires a new way of thinking about how change impacts people, cultures, organizations, processes, and more. Don't view the data science program as a small part of the process; rather, you must see it as a part of the entire digital transformation journey for your company.

For example, leaders should maintain ongoing blended learning-and-development programs that engage employees by describing the practical uses of data science so that understanding and familiarity build up among your workforce over time. Ongoing support helps employees embrace the agile culture and creates practitioners who learn in small increments continuously, building knowledge and expertise iteratively.

REMEMBER

Choosing a continuous learning approach incorporates the learning preferences of a multigenerational workforce and is effective where there is significant workforce turnover, regardless of whether it's planned or unplanned. In either approach (traditional or ongoing learning), managing the impact of the change should be seen as the core of a well-planned program, supported by fact-based content and by relevant and timely communication.

Recognizing what to avoid when driving change in data science

Around the globe, a number of businesses have made significant investments in data science, having realized (correctly) its revolutionary potential. Not having done their homework in terms of a proper situational analysis, however, many of these businesses have suffered huge losses rather than the expected benefits.

Failing with the data science investment is particularly common among smaller and medium-size businesses. Why is that? Why are medium- and small-scale businesses unable to derive sufficient value by implementing data science? What obstacles stand in their way?

In an attempt to come up with some answers to these questions, Computer Associates interviewed 1,000 IT managers across companies with more than half a billion dollars in revenue in a range of different industries, from retail to financial services to pharma. Their research findings revealed that the biggest obstacle by far is an insufficient infrastructure. Many times, companies are stuck with their legacy environment due to previous costly investments that "cannot be thrown away." So, rather than creating a new, modern data architecture which puts the focus on the data, companies tend to add applications and system elements to their old environment, making data science inefficient and even more costly.

The second largest obstacle is organizational complexity. This usually becomes a problem when the company management underestimates how transformative data science is. All aspects of the company must change in order to become data-centric, meaning that all managers across the company must understand and use data and new data-driven insights for decision making related to finance, marketing, sales, product and service development, and so on. However, in reality many companies tend to treat data science like a side business by adding new roles and functions to work with data rather than transforming existing functions and roles.

The third most significant obstacle is security and other compliance concerns. This is not surprising, considering the growing awareness of the importance of handling data in a secure and ethically correct manner. New laws and regulations are becoming more and more strict in order to protect people's right to privacy, and as long as there is still very little standardization in data science, requirements will keep on changing.

A general finding in the study was that, based on the type of analytics approach that was chosen, the level of resistance varied. That's worth a closer look, so I walk you through some different types of high-level analytics projects in the following sections. Then you can get a better sense of the major factors underlying the success (or failure) of a data science transformation project.

Descriptive analytics transformation projects

Descriptive analytics projects involve tasks aimed at using data to describe what has happened or how things are right now — why, for example, we have sold x number of products this month of this specific product type. It includes activities such as developing graphs, charts, and dashboards, accompanied by no (or relatively simple) data analysis functions. The focus is on identifying the right set of metrics and presenting information in an effective manner.

REMEMBER

Descriptive analytics solutions generally face lesser resistance challenges in their implementations. The reasons are obvious — the deliverables are easily understood by stakeholders.

However, it is sometimes difficult to justify the business value of descriptive analytics projects. At the end of the day, with the limited analysis happening in descriptive analytics, what is really the value of investing in understanding what happened yesterday when what you *really* want is to be prepared for tomorrow?

Diagnostic analytics transformation projects

The objective of diagnostic analytics projects is to understand the reasons for a particular phenomenon and to conduct a root cause analysis. Diagnostic analytics projects can culminate in the development of statistical models (explanatory models, causal models, and so on) and dashboards. However, the output must include insights and recommendations designed to help stakeholders understand the reasons for what's happening and initiate appropriate actions.

REMEMBER

Organizations are usually receptive for analytical findings and insights based on diagnostic analytics outcomes, but there is a slightly higher resistance when it comes to implementing recommendations. This is mainly due to the fact that business users are aware that some recommendations aren't actionable because they require too many changes or have too many restrictions.

Predictive analytics transformation projects

Predictive analytics projects involve forecasting a certain metric or predicting a certain phenomenon. *Predictive modeling* is the process of applying a statistical model or data mining algorithm on data for the purpose of predicting new or future observations. Predictive models can be used for not just predictions but also simulation purposes. Examples include clinical research, sales prediction, production failure, and weather forecasting.

WARNING

As you might expect, predictive analytics solutions face the highest degree of resistance. Diagnostic and descriptive solutions largely deal with what has already happened, and predictive solutions relate to something that is yet to happen. Thus, business users have reservations about predictive solutions. This skepticism isn't groundless, because the cost of making wrong predictions can be astonishing.

Using Data Science Techniques to Drive Successful Change

For your data science investment to succeed, the data science strategy you adopt should include well-thought-out strategies for managing the fundamental change that data science solutions impose on an organization. One effective and efficient way to tackle these challenges is by using data-driven change management techniques to drive the transformation itself — in other words, drive the change by "practicing what you preach." I'll walk you through some examples of how to do this in practice.

Using digital engagement tools

For companies, there is a new generation of real-time employee opinion tools that are starting to replace old-fashioned employee opinion surveys. These tools can tell you far more than simply what employees are thinking about once a year. In some companies, employees are surveyed weekly using a limited number of questions. The questions and models are constructed in such a way that management can follow fluctuations in important metrics as they happen rather than the usual once or twice a year. These tools have obvious relevance for change management and can help answer questions like these:

» Is a change being equally well received across locations?

» Are certain managers better than others at delivering messages to employees?

Assume that you have a large travel-and-tourism firm that is using one of these tools for real-time employee feedback. One data-driven approach to use in such a situation is to experiment with different change management strategies within selected populations in the company. After a few changes in the organization, you can use the data collected to identify which managers prove to be more effective in leading change than others. After that has been established, you can observe those managers to determine what they're doing differently. You can then share successful techniques with other managers.

This type of real-time feedback offers an opportunity to learn rapidly how communication events or engagement tactics have been received, thus optimizing your actions in days (rather than in weeks, which is typical of traditional approaches). The data can then feed into a predictive model, helping you determine with precision which actions will help accelerate adoption of a new practice, process, or behavior by a given employee group.

TIP

You can find some commercial tools out there — culture IQ polls, for example — that support this kind of data collection. These kinds of polls sample groups of employees daily or weekly via a smartphone app to generate real-time insights in line with whatever scope you have defined. Another tool, Waggl.com (www.waggl. com), has a more advanced functionality, allowing you to have an ongoing conversation with employees about a change effort as well as allowing change managers to tie this dialogue to the progress of initiatives they're undertaking.

REMEMBER

These different types of digital engagement tools can have a vast impact on change programs, but the data stream they create could be even more important. The data that's generated can be used to build predictive models of change. Using and deploying these models on real transformation projects and then sharing your findings helps to ensure a higher success rate with data-driven change initiatives in the future.

Applying social media analytics to identify stakeholder sentiment

Change managers can also look beyond the boundaries of the enterprise for insights about the impact of change programs. Customers, channel partners, suppliers, and investors are all key stakeholders when it comes to change programs. They are also more likely than employees to comment on social media about changes a company is making, thus giving potentially vital insight into how they're responding.

Ernst & Young (now known as EY) is using a tool for social media analytics called SMAART, which can interpret sentiment within consumer and influencer groups. In a project for a pharmaceutical company, EY was able to isolate the specific information sources that drove positive and negative sentiment toward the client's brand. The company is now starting to apply these techniques to understand the external impact of change efforts, and it's a simple leap to extend these techniques within the enterprise. Advances in the linguistic analysis of texts mean that clues about behavior can now be captured from a person's word choices; even the use of articles and pronouns can help reveal how someone feels.

TIP

Applying sentiment analysis tools to data in anonymized company email or the dialogue in tools like Waggl.com can give fresh insight about your organization's change readiness and the reactions of employees to different initiatives. And, the insights gained from analyzing internal communication will be stronger when combined with external social media data.

Capturing reference data in change projects

Have you ever worked in an organization where different change programs or projects were compared to one another in terms of how efficiently they made the change happen? Or one where a standard set of measurements were used across different change initiatives? No? Me, neither. Why is it that organizations often seem obsessed with measuring fractional shifts in operational performance and in capturing data on sales, inventory turns, and manufacturing efficiency, but show no interest in tracking performance from change project to change project, beyond knowing which ones have met their goals?

REMEMBER

Some people may claim that you can't compare change projects within an organization; it would be like comparing apples to oranges. I disagree: Different projects may have unique features, but you'll find more similarities than differences between different types of projects. Capturing information about the team involved, the population engaged in the change, how long it took to implement, what tactics were used, and so on is a good idea. It enables you to build a reference data set for future learning, reuse, and efficiency benchmarking. However, remember that although it may not yield immediate benefit, as the overall data set grows, it will make it easier to build accurate predictive models of organizational change going forward.

Using data to select people for change roles

For quite a long time, companies have been using data-driven methods to select candidates for senior management positions. And today some businesses, such as retailers, are starting to use predictive analytics for hiring frontline staff. Applying these tools when building a change team can both improve project performance significantly and help to build another new data set.

TIP

If every change leader and team member would undergo testing and evaluation before a change project starts, that data could become important variables to include as you search for an underlying model on what leads to successful change projects. This can even be extended to more informal roles like change leaders, allowing organizations to optimize selection based on what they know about successful personalities for these types of roles.

Along these lines, the California start-up LEDR Technologies is pioneering techniques to predict team performance. It integrates data sources and uses them to help teams anticipate the challenges they may face with team dynamics so that the team can prevent them before they occur.

Automating change metrics

Picture a company or an organization that has a personalized dashboard it has developed in partnership with the firm's leadership team — one that reflects the company's priorities, competitive position, and future plans.

These dashboards should also be used to offer insights related to the different transformation investments you've made. Keep in mind that much of the data that can act as interesting change indicators are already available today — they're just not being collected.

REMEMBER

When a company builds a dashboard for identifying recruitment and attrition, it's teaching the executive team to use data to perform people-related decisions. However, it can take quite some time to set it up correctly and iron out the bugs. My suggestion? Don't wait. Start building these type of dashboards as fast as possible now and, where possible, automate them. Why the automation? Change dashboards are vulnerable to version control issues, human error, and internal politics. Automating data management and dashboard generation can make it more transparent and help you keep data integrity.

Getting Started

As organizations collect more data and build more accurate models, change managers will be able to confidently use them to prescribe strategies to enable organizations to meet their goals. They'll be able to answer important questions, such as these:

>> W Which stakeholders are involved? What type of change approach works with groups that share these characteristics?

>> What risks are associated with programs that share these features?

>> What are the techniques that accelerate the delivery of business benefit, and what are their relative costs?

>> What is the cause-and-effect of specific types of investment?

All these questions can be answered with data and will underpin data-driven transformation plans.

REMEMBER

Developing these sorts of metrics isn't quick or easy. They aren't one-off installations, but rather multiyear commitments to capture data, build models, and refine dashboards. Establishing stable and reliable data sets takes time. Data quality is an issue everywhere, and so is the need for a common data language that allows organizations to know that they're measuring what they intend to measure. This has been a problem for data analytics in other fields; there's no reason to think that change management will be any different.

Although it will take time, you'll eventually be able to close the causal loop and make reliable predictions for how an action or initiative in a change program will impact a given metric. This will move investment in change from being an act of faith to being a data-driven decision. Change management will move from a project-based discipline that's struggling to justify adequate investment to one that is advising on business outcomes and how to deliver them. This will lead to a decline in the one metric that is well known across change programs — the failure rate. And, as part of introducing data-driven change management, it should finally be possible to solve the great puzzle of why so many transformation efforts fail.

2

Making Strategic Choices for Your Data

Chapter 5

Understanding the Past, Present, and Future of Data

Business decisions force you to focus, allocate scarce resources, and think hard about exactly how to be unique compared to the competition. It is important to remember that you can't be everything to everyone. Strategically, you should think simplicity over complexity, since a clear and simple strategy is a lot easier to explain and to put into action. But what about making strategic choices for your data? Sure, data can help you understand your strategic options as well as the potential impact of various choices from a business perspective, but how do you utilize data to understand more about data itself?

Well, to make choices, you need to create choices. Real choices for your data cannot be made if you do not know what your options are and what options you are decisively rejecting. When deciding on a viable strategy, too often alternative strategic options are only considered superficially, and you need more to make the right choices. This chapter will therefore focus on sorting out the fundamental elements of data.

Sorting Out the Basics of Data

The terms *data* and *information* are often used interchangeably; there is a difference between them, however. For example, data can be described as raw, unorganized facts that need to be processed — a collection of numbers, symbols, or characters before it has been cleaned and corrected. Raw data needs to be corrected to remove flaws like outliers and data entry errors. Raw data can be generated in many different ways. *Field* data, for example, is raw data that has been collected in an uncontrolled live environment. *Experimental* data has been generated within the context of a scientific investigation by observation and recording. Data can be as simple and seemingly random and useless until it's organized, but once data is processed, organized, structured, or presented in a given context that makes it useful, it's called *information.*

Historically, the concept of data has been most closely associated with scientific research, but now data is being collected, stored, and used by an increasing number of companies, organizations, and institutions. For companies, examples of interesting data can be customer data, product data, sales data, revenue, and profits; for governments, it can include data such as crime rates and unemployment rates.

During the second half of the 1900s, there were several attempts to standardize the categorization and structure of data in order to make sense of its various forms. One well-known model for this is the DIKW (*data, information, knowledge,* and *wisdom*) pyramid, described in the following list; the first version of this model was drafted already in the mid-1950s, but it first appeared in its current state in the mid-1990s, as an attempt to make sense of the growing amounts of data (raw or processed) that were being generated from different computer systems:

» **Data** is raw. It simply exists and has no significance beyond its existence (in and of itself). It can exist in any form, usable or not. Data represents a fact or statement of event without relation to other factors — *it's raining,* for example.

» **Information** is data that has been given a meaning by way of some sort of relationship. This meaning can be useful, but does not have to be. The information relationship can be related to cause-and-effect — *the temperature dropped 15 degrees and then it started raining,* for example.

» **Knowledge** is the collection of information with the purpose to be useful. It represents a pattern that connects discrete elements and generally provides a high level of predictability for what is described or what will happen next: *If the humidity is very high and the temperature drops substantially, the atmosphere is often unlikely to be able to hold the moisture, and so it rains,* for example.

>> **Wisdom** exemplifies more of an understanding of fundamental principles within the knowledge that essentially form the basis of the knowledge being what it is. Wisdom is essentially like a shared understanding that is not questioned; *It rains because it rains,* for example. And this encompasses an understanding of all interactions that happen between raining, evaporation, air currents, temperature gradients, changes, and rain.

The DIKW pyramid offered a new way to categorize data as it passes through different stages in its life cycle and has gained some attention over the years. However, it has also been criticized, and variants have appeared that were designed to improve on the original. One major criticism has been that, although it's easy enough to understand the step from data to information, it's much harder to draw a clear and valid line from information to knowledge and from knowledge to wisdom, making it difficult to apply in practice.

REMEMBER

Conceptual models are *heuristic* devices: They're useful only insofar as they offer a way to learn something new. One model or another may be more appealing to you, but from the perspective of a data science implementation, the most important thing for you to consider is a question like this: Will my company gain value from having the four levels of the DIKW pyramid, or will it just make implementation more difficult and complex? (Personally, I like a pyramid with just two levels: data and insights. That one has worked fine for me so far, and is far easier to explain and garner support for.)

Explaining traditional data versus big data

Traditional data is data in a volume and format that makes it easy to access, work with, and act on. Big data is a different animal, however, defined more by the volume of the data, the variety of the types of data involved, and the velocity at which it's processed. If all three of these characteristics are fulfilled in terms of being too big to handle in an ordinary processing environment, you can assume that you're dealing with big data and not traditional data (now known, after the appearance of big data on the scene, as *small* data).

Furthermore, the term *big data* is used to refer to data sets that are too large or complex to be handled by traditional data processing application software. Big data challenges include tasks such as capturing data, transferring data, storing data, cleaning and preparing data, exploring and analyzing data, searching data, sharing and reusing data, visualizing data, updating data, and managing privacy, data ownership, and governance.

Although big data was originally described by three key concepts — volume, variety, and velocity — two other concepts have lately been added: veracity (data quality, in other words) and value. These additional characteristics have been added to describe two other important aspects of big data that you should consider when estimating the potential benefits of a big-data data set.

What's so important about veracity? If the data set that a certain company wants to explore fulfills the criteria of big data based on volume, variety, and velocity, it could still be useless for the company to invest in if the data quality is poor and cannot be corrected. Poor data quality (the data set is incomplete, corrupt, or biased, for example) directly impacts trust in the data itself, ultimately impacting the perceived value of the overall data set.

Figure 5-1 graphically represents the key concepts, know, as the "five Vs," that define big data.

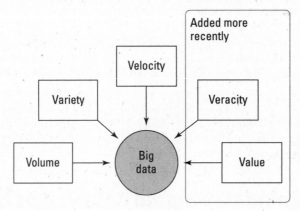

FIGURE 5-1:
Defining big data.

I add my own take on these concepts in the following list:

WARNING

>> **Volume:** Refers to the quantity of generated and stored data. The size of the data determines the value and potential insight, and whether it can be considered big data.

As you begin to unleash the power of big data, you soon discover that the data streams connected to your business will grow exponentially. This sharp increase in data volume can cause your organization significant difficulties if you haven't planned accordingly, because each new data set places considerable strain on your current data storage and computational setup.

>> **Velocity:** Refers to the speed at which the data is generated and processed to meet your organization's business objectives. Big data is often available in real-time. Compared to small data, big data is produced more continually. These two types of velocity are related to big data:

- *Frequency of generation*

- *Frequency of capture*

If you find it difficult to cope with the exponentially increasing volume of data in your company, the fact that the speed will also increase probably sounds like an intimidating detail. However, to take full advantage of big data, you must focus not only on how much information you collect, but also how fast you can use the data to either make business decisions or incorporate and utilize it as part of a service or product offering from your company.

>> **Variety:** Refers to the type and context of the data. Variety helps people who analyze data use the resulting insight effectively. Historically, the data was in a well-structured format at the point of collection. Now, as the use of big data becomes standard practice, it's unstructured data that is fast becoming the norm in the corporate world.

If you're looking to expand your use of big data, you' have to become accustomed to the lack of structured data. But with the right analytical setup, these new varieties of data can increase your business growth, enabling the exploration of new opportunities in what was previously unknown territory.

>> **Veracity:** Refers to the level of noise in the data. The quality of captured data can vary greatly, affecting the accuracy of the analysis. Yes, big data provides your business with the chance to accumulate information from places you never thought possible, but if the data isn't accurate or timely, it doesn't matter what you decide to do with it.

>> **Value:** Refers to the business value gained from big data.

So there you have it — the five Vs of big data: volume, velocity, variety, veracity, and value. Not all of these characteristics of big data are equal in importance, however. Four of them (volume, velocity, variety, and veracity) can be seen as enablers. To achieve the fifth V (value) requires an understanding of what the organization is trying to accomplish. That's why I emphasize the need to be perfectly clear about your overall strategic business objectives before you can leverage volume, velocity, variety, and veracity to achieve value in big data.

Knowing the value of data

The statement "Data is the new oil" is one that lots of people make, but what does it mean? In some ways, the analogy *does* fit: It's easy to draw parallels because of the way information (data) is used to drive much of the transformative technology available today via artificial intelligence, machine learning, automation, and advanced analytics — much like oil drives the global industrial economy.

So, as a marketing approach and a high-level description, the expression does its job, but if you take it as an indication of how to strategically address the value of data, it might lead to investments that cannot be turned into value. For example, storing data has no guaranteed future value, like oil has. Storing even more data has even less value because it becomes even more difficult to find it so that you can put it to use. The value in data lies not in saving it up or storing it — it lies in putting it to use, over and over again. That's when the value in data is realized.

If you start by looking at the core of the analogy, you can see that it refers to the value aspects of data as an enabler of a fundamental transformation of society — just like oil has proven to be throughout history. From that perspective, it definitely showcases the similarities between oil and data. Another similarity is that, although inherently valuable, data needs processing — just as oil needs refining — before its true value can be unlocked.

However, data also has many other aspects that cause the analogy to fall apart when examined more closely. To see what I mean, check out some of the differences I see between these two enablers of transformation:

>> **Availability:** Though oil is a finite resource, data is an endless and constantly increasing resource. This means that treating data like oil (hoarding it and storing it in silos, for example) has little benefit and reduces its usefulness. Nevertheless, because of the misconception that data is similar to oil (scarce), this is often exactly what is done with the data, driving investments and behavior in the wrong direction.

>> **Reusability:** Data becomes more useful the more it's used, which is the exact opposite of what happens with oil. When oil is used to generate energy like heat or light, or when oil is permanently converted into another form such as plastic, the oil is gone and cannot be reused. Therefore, treating data like oil — using it once and then assuming that its usefulness has been exhausted and disposing of it — is definitely a mistake.

>> **Capture:** Everyone knows that as the world's oil reserves decline, extracting it becomes increasingly difficult and expensive. With data, on the other hand, it's becoming increasingly available as the digitalization of society increases.

>> **Variety:** Data also has far more variety than oil. The raw oil that's drilled from the ground is processed in a variety of ways into many different products, of course, but in its raw state, it's all the same. Data in its raw format can represent words, pictures, sounds, ideas, facts, measurements, statistics, or any other characteristic that can be processed by computers.

REMEMBER

The fact nevertheless remains that the quantities of data available today comprise an entirely new commodity, though the rules for capturing, storing, treating, and using data are still being written. Let me stress, however, that data, like oil, is a vital source of power and that the companies that utilize the available data in the most optimized way (thereby controlling the market) are establishing themselves as the leaders of the world economy, just as the oil barons did a hundred years ago.

Exploring Current Trends in Data

Big data was definitely *the thing* just a couple of years ago, but now there's much more of a buzz around the idea of *data value* — more specifically, how analysis can turn data into value. The next few sections look at some of the trends related to utilizing data to capture new value.

Data monetization

Monetizing data refers to how companies can utilize their domain expertise to turn the data they own or have access to into real, tangible business value or new business opportunities. Data *monetization* can refer to the act of generating measurable economic benefits from available data sources by way of analytics, or, less commonly, it may refer to the act of monetizing data services. In the case of analytics, typically these benefits appear as revenue or cost savings, but they may also include market share or corporate market value gains.

REMEMBER

One could argue that data monetization for increased company revenue or cost savings is simply the result of being a data-driven organization. Though that argument isn't totally wrong, company leaders are taking an increasing interest in the market to explore how data monetization can drive the innovation of entirely new business models in various different business segments.

One good example of how this process can work is when telecom operators sell data on the positions of rapidly forming clusters of users (picture the conclusion of a sporting event or a concert by the latest YouTube sensation) to taxi companies. This allows taxi cars to be available proactively in the right area when a taxi will most likely be needed. This is a completely new type of business model and customer base for a traditional telecom operator, opening up new types of business and revenues based on available data.

Responsible AI

Responsible AI systems are characterized by transparency, accountability, and fairness, where users have full visibility into which data is being used and how. It also assumes that companies are communicating the possible consequences of using the data. That includes both potential positive and negative impact.

Responsible AI is also about generating customer and stakeholder trust based on following communicated policies and principles over time, including the ability to maintain control over the AI system environment itself.

Strategically designing your company's data science infrastructure and solutions with responsible AI in mind is not only wise, but could also turn out to be a real business differentiator going forward. Just look at how the opposite approach, taken by Facebook and Cambridge Analytica, turned into a scandal which ended by putting Cambridge Analytica out of business. You might remember that Cambridge Analytica gained access to the private and personal information of more than 50 million Facebook users in the US and then offered tools that could then use that data to identify the personalities of American voters and influence their behavior. Facebook, rather than being hacked, was a willing participant in allowing their users' data to be used for other purposes without explicit user consent.

THE ROLE OF OPEN SOURCE IN DATA SCIENCE

Open source data architectures are no longer analogous to research projects forever running in lab environments for trials and experimentation. Now considered mainstream in IT environments, these architectures are widely deployed in live production in several industries. In fact, it has become so common that if you're building a modern data architecture, chances are you're using an open source stack. Some companies have even found that using open source architectures provides the only cost-effective path to getting something done.

The tipping point is more or less here, which means that the time is now to decide how to strategically react to the opportunities associated with open source. It's past the point where making small incremental changes or playing it safe with traditional proprietary infrastructures was sufficient. Now, if you continue to play it safe or stick with baby steps, you will leave your company at risk of being left behind while competitors move ahead. It's also important to remember that deciding on utilization of open source software is not incremental; rather, it necessitates a full-bore disruptive architectural approach.

The data included details on users' identities, friend networks, and "likes." The idea was to map personality traits based on what people had liked on Facebook, and then use that information to target audiences with digital ads. Facebook has also been accused of spreading Russian propaganda and fake news which, together with the Cambridge Analytica incident, has severely impacted the Facebook brand the last couple of years. This type of severe privacy invasion has not only opened many people's eyes in terms of the usage of their data but also impacted the company brands.

Cloud-based data architectures

More and more companies are moving away from on-premise-based data infrastructure investments toward virtualized and cloud-based data architectures. The driving force behind this move is that traditional data environments are feeling the pressure of increasing data volumes and are unable to scale up and down to meet constantly changing demands. On-premise infrastructure simply lacks the flexibility to dynamically optimize and address the challenges of new digital business requirements.

TIP

Re-architecting these traditional, on-premise data environments for greater access and scalability provides data platform architectures that seamlessly integrate data and applications from various sources. Using cloud-based compute and storage capacity enables a flexible layer of artificial intelligence and machine learning tools to be added as a top layer in the architecture so that you can accelerate the value that can be obtained from large amounts of data.

Computation and intelligence in the edge

Edge computing describes a computing architecture in which data processing is done closer to where the data is created— Internet of Things (IoT) devices like connected luggage, drones, and connected vehicles like cars and bicycles, for example. There is a difference between pushing computation to the edge (edge compute) and pushing analytics or machine learning to the edge (edge analytics or machine learning edge). Edge compute can be executed as a separate task in the edge, allowing data to be preprocessed in a distributed manner before it's collected and transferred to a central or semi-centralized environment where analytics methods or machine learning/artificial intelligence technologies are applied to achieve insights. Just remember that running analytics and machine learning on the edge requires some form of edge compute to also be in place to allow the insight and action to happen directly at the edge.

The reason behind the trend to execute more in the edge mainly depends on factors such as connectivity limitations, low-latency use cases where millisecond response times are needed to perform an immediate analysis and make a decision (in the case of self-driving cars, for example). A final reason for executing more in the edge is bandwidth constraints on transferring data to a central point for analysis. Strategically, computing in the edge is an important aspect to consider from an infrastructure-design perspective, particularly for companies with significant IoT elements.

REMEMBER

When it comes to infrastructure design, it's also worth considering how the edge compute and intelligence solutions will work with the centralized (usually cloud-based) architecture. Many view cloud and edge as competing approaches, but cloud is a style of computing where elastically scalable technology capabilities are delivered as a service, offering a supporting environment for the edge part of the infrastructure. Not everything, however, can be solved in the edge; many use cases and needs are system- or network-wide and therefore need a higher-level aggregation in order to perform the analysis. Just performing the analysis in the edge might not give enough context to make the right decision. Those types of computational challenges and insights are best solved in a cloud-based, centralized model, as illustrated in Figure 5-2.

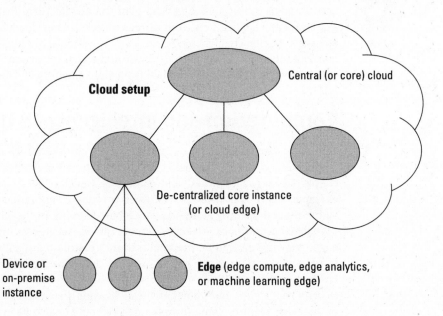

FIGURE 5-2:
A model for cloud/edge computing.

As you can see, the cloud setup can be done in a decentralized manner as well, and these decentralized instances are referred to as *cloud-edge*. For a larger setup on a regional or global scale, the decentralized model can be used to support edge implementations at the IoT device level in a certain country or to support a telecom operator in its efforts to include all connected devices in the network. This is useful for keeping the response time low and not moving raw data over country borders.

Digital twins

A *digital twin* refers to a digital representation of a real-world entity or system — a digital view of a city's telecommunications network built up from real data, for example. Digital twins in the context of IoT projects is a promising area that is now leading the interest in digital twins. It's most likely an area that will grow significantly over the next three to five years. Well-designed digital twins are assets that have the potential to significantly improve enterprise control and decision-making going forward.

Digital twins integrate artificial intelligence, machine learning, and analytics with data to create living digital simulation models that update and change as their physical counterparts change. A digital twin continuously learns and updates itself from multiple sources to represent its near real-time status, working condition, or position. (See Figure 5-3 for an overview of this process.)

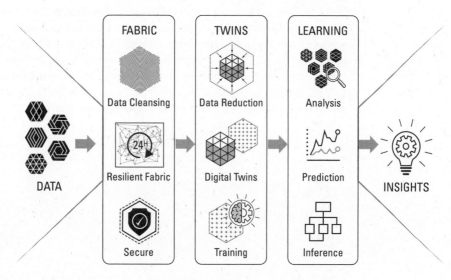

FIGURE 5-3:
How digital twins produce insights.

Digital twins are linked to their real-world counterparts and are used to understand the state of the system, respond to changes, improve operations, and add value. Digital twins start out as simple digital views of the real system and then evolve over time, improving their ability to collect and visualize the right data, apply the right analytics and rules, and respond in ways that further your organization's business objectives. But you can also use a digital twin to run predictive models or simulations which can be used to find certain patterns in the data building up the digital twin that might lead to problems. Those insights can then be used to prevent a problem proactively.

Adding automated abilities to make decisions based on the digital-twin concept of predefined and preapproved policies would be a great capability to add to any operational perspective — managing an IoT system such as a smart city, for example.

Blockchain

The blockchain concept has evolved from a digital currency infrastructure into a platform for digital transactions. A *blockchain* is a growing list of records (blocks) that are linked using cryptography. Each block contains a cryptographic hash of the previous block, a timestamp, and transaction data. By design, a blockchain is resistant to modification of the data. It's an open and public ledger that can record transactions between two parties efficiently and in a verifiable and permanent way. A blockchain is also a decentralized and distributed digital ledger that is used to record transactions across many computers so that any involved record cannot be altered retroactively without the alteration of all subsequent blocks. The blockchain technologies offer a significant step away from the current centralized, transaction-based mechanisms and can work as a foundation for new digital business models for both established enterprises and start-ups. Figure 5-4 shows how to use blockchain to carry out a blockchain transaction.

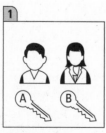 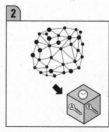 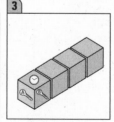 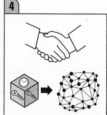

FIGURE 5-4: Creating a blockchain transaction.

When 2 parties initiate a transaction, blockchain assigns an encryption

Blockchain verifies the transaction and creates a block

The new block is appended to the blockchain

The blockchain transaction is now complete and the ledger is updated

WARNING

Although the hype surrounding blockchains was originally focused on the financial services industry, blockchains have many potential areas of usage, including government, healthcare, manufacturing, identity verification, and supply chain. Although blockchain holds long-term promise and will undoubtedly create disruption, its promise has yet to be proven in reality: Many of the associated technologies are too immature to use in a production environment and will remain so for the next two to three years.

Conversational platforms

Conversational AI is a form of artificial intelligence that allows people to communicate with applications, websites, and devices in everyday, humanlike natural language via voice, text, touch, or gesture input. For users, it allows fast interaction using their own words and terminology. For enterprises, it offers a way to build a closer connection with customers via personalized interaction and to receive a huge amount of vital business information in return. Figure 5-5 shows the interaction between a human and a bot.

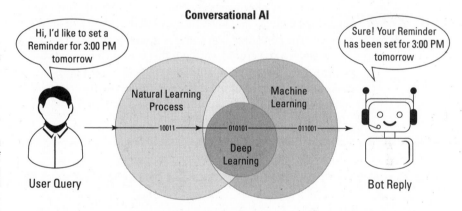

FIGURE 5-5: An example of how to use a conversational platform.

This type of platform will most likely drive the next paradigm shift in how humans interact with the digital world. The responsibility for translating intent shifts from humans to machines. The platform takes a question or command from the user and then responds by executing some function, presenting some content, or asking for additional input. Over the next few years, conversational interfaces will become a primary design goal for user interaction and will be delivered in dedicated hardware, core OS features, platforms, and applications.

Check out the following list for some potential areas where one could benefit from applying conversational platforms by way of bots:

>> **Informational:** Chatbots that aid in research, informational requests, and status requests of different types

>> **Productivity:** Bots that can connect customers to commerce, support, advisory, or consultative services

>> **B2E (business-to-employee):** Bots that enable employees to access data, applications, resources, and activities

>> **Internet of Things (IoT):** Bots that enable conversational interfaces for various device interactions, like drones, appliances, vehicles, and displays

Using these different types of conversational platforms, you can expect increased bot productivity (because they can concentrate on the most valuable interactions), a 24/7 automated workforce, increased customer loyalty and satisfaction, new insights into customer interactions, and reduced operational expenses.

TECHNICAL
STUFF

Conversational platforms have now reached a tipping point in terms of understanding language and basic user intent, but they still aren't good enough to fully take off. The challenge that conversational platforms face is that users must communicate in a structured way, and this is often a frustrating experience in real life. A primary differentiator among conversational platforms is the robustness of their models and the application programming interfaces (APIs) and event models used to access, attract, and orchestrate third-party services to deliver complex outcomes.

Elaborating on Some Future Scenarios

Although the explosion of new use cases (those specific situations in which data science could potentially be used) and applications in data science is happening all around us, there are still scenarios yet to come. In this section, I describe some potential future scenarios in the data science space, including challenges and motivations.

Standardization for data science productivity

Standardization generally ensures the smooth operation of processes and builds credibility over time. Best practices ensure efficiency and reduce redundancy. Today, the amount of data generated in the world is increasing by the second.

As this data is collected and stored, it's critical to standardize and normalize it for optimal usage. Otherwise, it can get very noisy.

One of the biggest challenges in building an optimized data management solution is the lack of standardization when collecting data from all over the Internet — or even just across different parts of a large, global company. Standardization is vital when trying to avoid redundancy and increase accuracy in matching data types. As necessary as it is, it's still a difficult problem to solve. Lack of standardization proves to be a hindrance to many business systems. All data needs to be converted to a predefined format, which requires domain expertise as well as agreement (both internally and externally) on data definitions and structure needs to be reached.

So, are there any reasons why standardization in the ML/AI space is particularly important? I'm glad you asked. The following list gives you some of the reasons why it's particularly needed:

>> **Model interoperability:** Interoperability standards are important for not only a global community in general but also any single company implementing machine learning and artificial intelligence. The reason is that in order to scale company development of algorithms, interoperability between models in production is needed to ensure not only that the models can work together, but that they can also maximize the model performance in a multi-model environment.

>> **Process standardization:** An emphasis on process control also brings into question which standardizations are needed regarding safety, performance, latency, reliability, bias, and even privacy. By standardizing the best practices of developing, for example, complex techniques like deep learning, not only can more teams accelerate their development but more innovative solutions can also be developed independently and be plugged in to accelerate a much larger process.

>> **Human-Machine compatibility:** Here, compatibility refers to standardizing the interaction between human and machine — when the human uses certain words or phrases, the machine uses a standardized set of responses or actions, for example. Many errors can occur because of different objectives and methods for the interactions. For mission-critical systems, imagine a machine-managed air traffic control tower; it could be a disaster if the interaction isn't standardized between systems or at least cumbersome to have to learn all different versions of how to achieve an objective in collaboration with the machine, depending on which implementation is in use and where.

>> **Ethics:** The challenges of AI standardization cover many levels of concern, but this one is vital — any form of AI standardization should include methods for how to best drive AI for the maximum benefit of humanity. It would be a total failure if standardization would lead to more advanced autonomous weaponry or more enhanced methods to predict and manipulate human behavior.

From data monetization scenarios to a data economy

Huge advances in technology have led to an explosion in the rate at which new data is being created. The data economy is delivering what businesses and governments across the world want: Create high-quality jobs, generate economic growth, and enable organizations across all sectors to expand successfully and serve their customers.

But with the growth of data, are company leaders realizing its true potential? As the data economy emerges, changes in customer expectations and technological advancements will transform supply chains into complex ecosystems. Production strategies will shift, and collaboration across organizations and ecosystems will create a more open flow of information and ideas. Companies will need to reinvent themselves by defining their desired roles in the data economy by way of an evaluation of their engagement in these ecosystems. This will allow organizations to assess whether new business units, joint ventures, and acquisitions will be required.

An explosion of human/machine hybrid systems

Hybrid human/machine systems combine machine and human intelligence to overcome the shortcomings of existing AI systems. The need for human involvement to overcome the mistakes and limitations of AI systems is already acknowledged in critical domains such as medicine and driving. (A driver of a semiautonomous car is expected to continuously watch over the decisions of the machine and correct it when needed to prevent accidents, for example.) However, successfully integrating human and machine intelligence has its challenges. Human intelligence is a valuable resource associated with higher costs and constraints like an 8-hour workday for example. The quality and availability of human input may also vary depending on other factors, including the condition of the human, like illness or fatigue.

One way to overcome the challenges of hybrid human/machine systems is to change the way machines access human intelligence. For that to happen, AI systems would need to be equipped with reasoning capabilities that can make effective decisions about how it should access that human intelligence. Here, recent advances in human computation may provide some clues about how AI systems could accomplish this. Crowdsourcing platforms provide easy access to human intelligence on demand in a scalable and adaptable way. Simply defined, crowdsourcing happens when a company or an institution outsources a function once performed by a limited number of employees to an undefined (and generally large) network of people in the form of an open call.

This approach can take the form of peer-production (when the job is performed collaboratively), but is also often undertaken by single individuals. For AI systems in which a user isn't in the loop to provide help, the human help needed by the system may be provided by the crowd. For many research efforts, including the ones presented here, crowdsourcing platforms function as test beds for data collection and experimentation related to the challenges of accessing and working with human intelligence.

Quantum computing will solve the unsolvable problems

If you spend more than five minutes on the Internet, watching the news, and otherwise staying current with the world, you have heard the excitement surrounding recent advances in the development of quantum computer systems.

This is not an exaggeration — it really will change everything. Quantum computers have the potential to blow right through obstacles that limit the power of classical computers, solving problems in seconds that would take a classical computer the entire life of the Universe just to attempt to solve — encryption and research on new advanced medicine, for example. When chemists research new medicines, much of their work is testing hundreds of possible variables in a chemical formula in order to find the desired characteristics needed to treat a variety of illnesses. This process of experimentation and discovery often leads to a development time of more than 10 years before a new drug is brought to market — often at a cost of billions of dollars. Computation today is done on computers that have to combine and recombine elements to test the results.

Needless to say, the race is now on to make quantum computers into practical everyday tools for business, industry, and science in order to gain a competitive advantage. Quantum computing is here to stay, it is growing, and if it doesn't solve all of the world's problems, it could potentially solve quite a few

TECHNICAL STUFF

Quantum computers are qualitatively different from standard computers in how they compute data. On the one hand, you have your standard binary digital electronic computer, where the data needs to be encoded into *binary digits* (bits), each of which is always in one of two definite states (0 or 1). Quantum computation uses *quantum bits* (*qubits*), which can be in *superpositions* of states — that is to say, just like Schrödinger's cat could be both alive and dead, a qubit can be both 0 and 1.

Chapter **6**

Knowing Your Data

Approaching your data strategy in the right way is fundamental for you to secure a stable foundation for the rest of your data science investment. And it's not just about securing the integrity in the data; you also need to make sure that the data types you choose for your business objectives are the right ones and are selected for the right reasons. For that to happen, you need to understand the data you're targeting. To gain that understanding, you have to successfully work four main steps: Select data, describe data, explore data, and assess data quality.

Selecting Your Data

Data selection is the process of determining the appropriate data type and source — as well as the suitable methods — to collect data. Data selection precedes the actual task of data collection.

REMEMBER

The main objective of data selection is to determine the appropriate data type, source, and method(s) necessary to provide you with the answers you need to questions you've posed. The selection is often connected to a certain area — finance, sales, product, or consumer, for example — and is mostly driven by the type of analysis you intend to use, as well as by your ability to access the necessary data sources.

WARNING

Integrity issues can arise when the decisions to select appropriate data to collect are based primarily on cost and convenience considerations rather than on the ability of data to effectively answer the questions posed. Certainly, cost and convenience are valid factors in the decision-making process. However, you have to assess to what degree these factors might impact the integrity of the analysis.

In this first part of the data selection process (see Figure 6-1), consider your answers to these questions:

>> What questions are you trying to answer?

>> What is the scope of the analysis?

>> Within the field you're aiming to analyze, what type of data is the industry generally targeting?

>> What data format is needed to answer your business questions: quantitative, qualitative, or both?

Figure 6-2 captures the main areas of concern related to data collection.

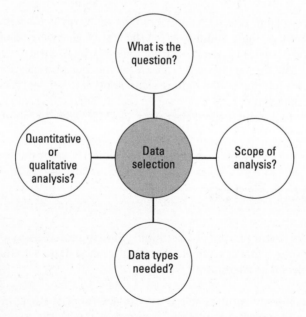

FIGURE 6-1:
Aspects to consider when selecting data.

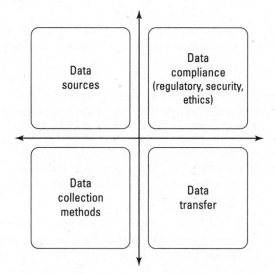

FIGURE 6-2:
Data collection
areas to address.

As part of the data collection process, consider your answers to these questions:

>> Where are the data sources you need to tap into? Do they exist, or do you need to create new data (using a survey, for example)? If the data exists, do you already have it in your company, or do you need to acquire it?

>> Are there any legal, ethical, or security restrictions related to the data you need, like data privacy, data ownership, or data retention periods?

>> How do you need to collect the data? Are frequent batch uploads sufficient, or do you need to stream live data? Will your infrastructure be able to manage different ways of acquiring the data?

>> Is there a need to move data across country borders? Are there legal restrictions related to the specific data you're targeting? If such restrictions exist, how will they be dealt with?

Describing Data

Describing data refers to the task of examining and documenting the collected data so that elements such as data format, quantity of data, and metadata can be noted and recorded. A *metadata* element is data type used to describe other data in order to increase the usefulness of the original data. Creating and maintaining metadata is a vital part of your data science environment.

Keep in mind that you'll encounter a number of different types of metadata when setting up a data science environment. I briefly describe the different kinds in this list:

>> **Descriptive:** Used to describe the main characteristics of a data element for the purposes of discovery and identification. It can include elements such as title, abstract, author, and keywords.

>> **Structural:** Deals with metadata about groups of data and indicates how multiple objects are put together — how pages are ordered to form chapters, for example. It describes data categories, versions, relationships, and other characteristics of digital materials.

>> **Administrative:** Provides information to help manage a data element, such as when and how it was created, file type and other technical information, as well as who can access it.

>> **Reference:** Describes the contents and quality of statistical data.

>> **Statistical:** Describes processes that collect, process, or produce data statistics (also referred to as *process* data).

Describing your data is a strategically important task in order to evaluate whether the collected data satisfies your identified business requirements — and it includes several distinct steps. This list gives you an overview of what activities need to take place:

>> Analyze the data volume and try to estimate the level of complexity.

>> Describe the different tables needed and their relationships to one another.

REMEMBER

Data tables help you keep information organized. If you're collecting data from an experiment or scientific research, saving it in a data table will make it easier to look up later. Data tables can also help you make graphs and other charts based on your information.

>> Check the availability of attributes, which helps to describe the context of each data type — the geographical location it was collected from, for example, or the date it was collected.

>> Determine whether there are different types of attributes needed. Types could include the following:

● *Nominal*: ID numbers, eye color, zip codes

● *Ordinal:* Rankings (taste of potato chips on a scale from 1-10, for example), grades, height in categories (tall, medium, short)

● *Interval:* Calendar dates, temperatures in Celsius or Fahrenheit

● *Ratio*: Exact temperature in Kelvin, length, time, counts.

Consider how you intend to use the data to determine which attributes will be required.

» Describe the value range of the selected attributes (if applicable). Remember that the same attribute can be mapped to different attribute values. (Height can be measured in feet or meters, for example.)

» Analyze potential attribute correlations, such as gender and height or date and temperature.

» Understand the meaning of each attribute, and describe the value in business terms.

» For each attribute, compute basic statistics (distribution, average, maximum, minimum, standard deviation, variance, mode, and skewness, for example) and relate the results to their meaning in business terms.

» Decide attribute relevance related to the specific business objective by involving domain experts.

» Determine whether the meaning of each attribute is used consistently.

» Decide whether it's necessary to balance the data, if the data distribution is distorted.

» Analyze and document key relationships in the data.

REMEMBER

Without the data properties attached to your data, the value and usefulness of your data will be significantly reduced. The documentation of data properties is a cornerstone for further analysis of the data and must be kept relevant as part of your data management activities as long as you intend to use the data in any way.

Exploring Data

A vital step in getting to know your data better is to explore it. *Data exploration* is an approach similar to an initial data analysis, where a data analyst uses visual exploration to understand what is in a dataset as well as the characteristics of the data. These characteristics can include size or amount of data, completeness of the data, correctness of the data, or possible relationships or insights that may be hidden in the data, for example. Visual data exploration is the activity of searching and finding out more about the data using various statistical models visualized through graphical representation of the data — heat maps, geo maps, box plots and word clouds, for example. Just by looking at the same data set, using various graphical representations, it is possible to detect data correlations and dependencies, as well as new insights in the data.

Data exploration is usually conducted using a combination of these types of methods:

>> **Automated:** Can include data profiling or data visualization to give the analyst an initial view of the data as well as an understanding of key characteristics.

>> **Manual:** Often follows an automated action by manually drilling down or filtering the data to identify anomalies or patterns identified automatically. Data exploration usually also require manual scripting and queries into the data (using languages such as Python or R, for example) or using Excel (for smaller data sets) or similar tools to view the raw data.

REMEMBER

The actual data mining task is the semiautomatic or automatic analysis of large quantities of data to extract previously unknown and/or interesting patterns, such as groups of data records (cluster analysis), unusual records (anomaly detection), and dependencies (association rule mining, sequential pattern mining).

Figures 6-3, 6-4, 6-5, and 6-6 show different ways of exploring data. Figure 6-3 starts things off by looking at school grades in Sweden. The bar graph to the left displays the classical medium value per region; in that view, Stockholm is shown to be performing best. But the medium value in the bar graph cannot be trusted. Why? A closer look at the Stockholm region in the box-plot shows that there are problems in that area. There's a very big spread of the grades — actually, the largest spread in Sweden is in Stockholm — and when you study this in more detail you can see that there is a very large difference between the schools. This is referred to as segregation. If you compare these numbers with the Norrbotten region, you will see a much smaller spread of grades, which indicates a higher overall performance.

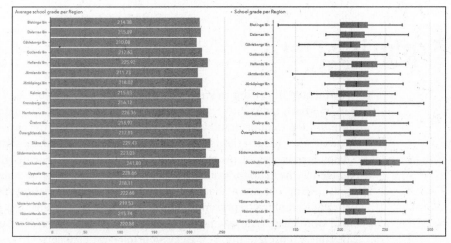

FIGURE 6-3:
Data exploration on school grades in Swedish regions using a box-plot.

Figure 6-3 is based on a screenshot generated using SAS® Visual Analytics software. Copyright © 2019 SAS Institute Inc., Cary, NC, USA. SAS and all other SAS Institute Inc. product or service names are registered trademarks or trademarks of SAS Institute Inc. All Rights Reserved. Used with permission.

In Figure 6-4, you can see an example where a scatterplot is used to understand whether or not the educational level of parents actually impacts school grades. And, as you can read from the graph, there is definitely a strong correlation indicated by the distribution of values grouped along a diagonal 45-degree line from the left hand lower corner to the upper right corner.

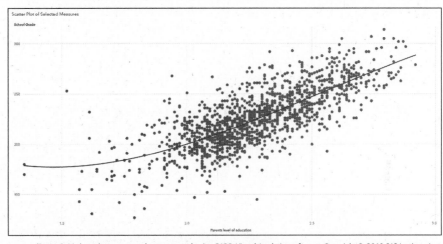

FIGURE 6-4: A scatter-plot exploring dependencies in the data.

Figure 6-5 uses data to show how visitors to a website are moving between different parts of the website. With the data, it is possible to determine where most people tend to start browsing (search engines, referral, direct links and other), and where they tend to move from their point of entry. Gaining a better understanding of these type of patterns can be helpful in terms of understanding the user experience and if there is a pattern to where they tend to "drop-out" and leave the website.

Figure 6-6 shows another way of exploring data using a *heat map* — a graphical representation of data that uses a system of color-coding to represent different values. This example is analyzing manufacturing yield data for various products to find dependencies or correlation between a certain product and the city where it's manufactured. Manufacturing yield refers to the quality of the product from a perspective of how often a product needs to be replaced (level of yield). In the heat map in Figure 6-6, you can see that the coloring reaches from lighter (which is bad) to darker (which is good). By using a heat map, you can quickly get an overview of the situation and see which cities are having manufacturing problems for certain products, based on their yield rates.

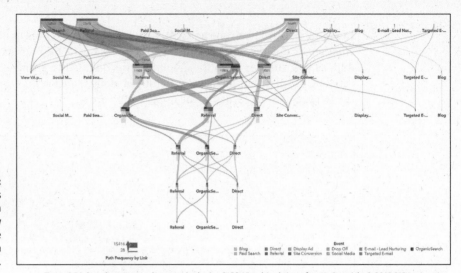

FIGURE 6-5:
A path analysis chart using data to show how users enter, move and leave a specific website.

Figure 6-5 is based on a screenshot generated using SAS® Visual Analytics software. Copyright © 2019 SAS Institute Inc., Cary, NC, USA. SAS and all other SAS Institute Inc. product or service names are registered trademarks or trademarks of SAS Institute Inc. All Rights Reserved. Used with permission.

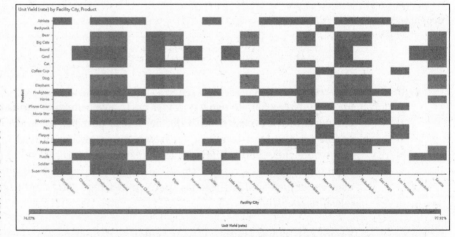

FIGURE 6-6:
A heat map analyzing potential correlation between product manufacturing yield and product manufacturing city.

Figure 6-6 is based on a screenshot generated using SAS® Visual Analytics software. Copyright © 2019 SAS Institute Inc., Cary, NC, USA. SAS and all other SAS Institute Inc. product or service names are registered trademarks or trademarks of SAS Institute Inc. All Rights Reserved. Used with permission.

REMEMBER

All these exploration tasks are aimed at creating a clearer view of the data so you can get to know your data better, all in hopes of gaining some first insights based on your exploration that you might want to analyze further. This is a key first step the analyst and is just as important as defining basic metadata (statistics, struc-ture, relationships) for the data set that can then be used in further analysis.

Assessing Data Quality

Another fundamental part of data understanding involves gaining a detailed view of the quality of the data as soon as possible. Many businesses consider data quality and its impact too late — well past the time when it could have had a significant effect on the project's success. By integrating data quality with operational applications, organizations can reconcile disparate data, remove inaccuracies, standardize on common metrics, and create a strategic, trustworthy, and valuable data asset that enhances decision making. Also, if an initial analysis suggests that the data quality is insufficient, steps can be taken to make improvements. One way to refine the data is by removing unusable parts; another way is to correct poorly formatted parts.

TIP

Start by asking yourself questions such as these: Is the data complete? Does it cover all required cases? Is it correct, or does it contain errors? If there are errors, how common are they? Does the data have missing values? If so, how are they represented, where do they occur, and how common are they?

A more structured list of data quality checkpoints includes steps such as these:

» Check data coverage (whether all possible values are represented, for example).

» Verifying that the meaning of attributes and available values fit together. For example, if you are analyzing data on geographical location for retail stores, is the value captured in latitude and longitude, rather than the name of the regional area it is placed in?

» Identifying missing attributes and blank fields.

» Classifying the meaning of missing or wrong data, and double-check attributes with different values but similar meanings.

» Checking for inconsistencies in the spelling and formatting of values (situations where the same value sometimes starts with a lowercase letter and sometimes with an uppercase letter, for example). Without consistent naming conventions and numerical format, data correlation and analysis will not be possible cross data sets.

» Reviewing deviations and deciding if any of them qualify as mere noise (outliers) or indicate an interesting phenomenon (pattern).

» Check whether there is noise and inconsistencies between data sources.

REMEMBER

If you detect data quality problems as part of the quality check, you need to define and document the possible solutions. Focus on attributes that seem to go against common sense; visualization plots, histograms, and other ways of visualizing and exploring data are great ways to reveal possible data inconsistencies. It may also be necessary to exclude low-quality or useless data entirely in order to perform the needed analysis.

Figure 6-7 shows table formatted to show an overview of a data set. Tables like these are a good way to get a first overview of your data from a quality perspective because it uses descriptive statistics to quickly detect extreme values in terms of things like minimum values, maximum values, median, medium, and standard deviation. The table also allows us to analyze the key values to make sure that they are 100% unique and do not include any duplicated or missing values. If you are studying data related to your customers, for example, you want to make sure that a customer does not occur twice due to a spelling error — or is missing from the list altogether!

Column	Unique	Primary Key ...	Null	Bia...	Pattern Count	Mean	Median	Minimum	Maximum	Standa...
Age	0,09 % (43)	No				39,29	39,00	19,00	61,00	5,59
City	0,09 % (42)	No			16			Auckland	Valencia	
Continent	0,01 % (5)	No			4			Africa	South Ame...	
Country	0,06 % (29)	No			10			Argentina	Venezuela	
Customer	100,00 % (45	Yes			3			ARBUENO...	ZAJOHAN...	
CustomerDistance	100,00 % (45	Yes				5,56	5,74	0,04	10,00	2,34
CustomerInDays	4,54 % (2073)	No				156,66	20,00	0,00	3 647,00	396,05
CustomerLat	100,00 % (45	Yes				25,60	40,52	-37,92	60,07	32,85
CustomerLon	100,00 % (45	Yes				7,20	2,15	-77,14	174,85	55,35
FirstOrderAmount	97,10 % (44	No				199,74	161,82	4,73	1 874,32	159,25
FirstOrderCostOfSales	100,00 % (45	Yes				165,85	140,92	4,20	1 566,99	126,92
FirstOrderCostOfSalesPerc	100,00 % (45	Yes				0,85	0,91	0,57	0,99	0,11
FirstOrderCustomerSatisfac	100,00 % (45	Yes				0,51	0,45	0,18	1,00	0,20
FirstOrderDeliveryTime	0,05 % (25)	No				4,30	3,00	1,00	25,00	3,38
FirstOrderDiscount	0,68 % (312)	No				14,02	6,00	0,00	767,00	27,64
FirstOrderDiscountPerc	57,8...	No				0,07	0,04	0,00	0,88	0,09
FirstOrderExp	3,74 % (1707)	No				0,41	0,37	0,01	1,00	0,20
FirstOrderListAmount	3,93 % (1794)	No				213,76	173,58	5,61	1 905,72	167,17
FirstOrderProductQuality	100,00 % (45	Yes				0,77	0,78	0,56	0,92	0,06
FirstOrderProfit	0,94 % (430)	No				-0,83	-10,00	-234,00	270,00	41,67

FIGURE 6-7:
Profiling the data to get an overview of the data quality.

Figure 6-7 is based on a screenshot generated using SAS® Visual Analytics software. Copyright © 2019 SAS Institute Inc., Cary, NC, USA. SAS and all other SAS Institute Inc. product or service names are registered trademarks or trademarks of SAS Institute Inc. All Rights Reserved. Used with permission.

Figure 6-8 shows a graphical visualization of the same data, but this graph focuses on just one column; country. By looking at the data from a country perspective, you can validate the data distribution in another way, and possibly detect inconsistencies or missing values that were difficult to detect from the overview. In this specific example, the tool actually has a functionality called *Pattern* which indicates when data values are deviating from the norm.

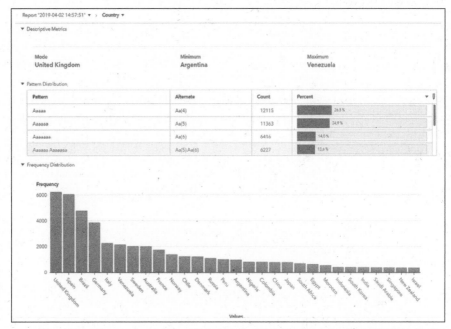

FIGURE 6-8:
Data profiling and validation from a country perspective.

Ask any thriving organization the secret to success and you'll get many answers: a solid data strategy, or calculated risks in combination with careful budgeting. They're all good business practices which come from the same place: a solid foundation of high-quality data. When you have accurate, up-to-date data driving your business, you're not just breaking even — you're breaking records. A data quality assessment process is essential to ensure reliable analytical outcomes. This process depends on human supervision-driven approaches since it is impossible to determine a defect based only on data.

Improving Data Quality

So, what do you do, practically speaking, if you realize that your data quality is really bad? My recommendation is to use the four-step approach outlined below to get started on highlighting the gaps and defining a road map to implement needed improvements in data quality.

1. **Scope:** Define the data quality problem and describe the business issue related to the quality problem. Specify data details and business processes, products and/or services impacted by the data quality issues.

2. **Explore:** Conduct interviews with key stakeholders on data quality needs and expectations, as well as data quality problems. Review data quality processes and tool support (if any) across business functions and identify needed resources for the quality improvement activity.

3. **Analyze:** Assess current practices against industry best practices for data quality and align it with the findings from the exploration phase.

4. **Recommend:** Develop a road map for improving the data quality process and define how the technical architecture for the data quality process must look like, incorporating your findings of what is not working today and what is essential from a business perspective.

Chapter **7**

Considering the Ethical Aspects of Data Science

According to Gartner's CIO Agenda Survey from 2018, 85% of AI projects through 2020 will deliver erroneous outcomes due to bias in data, algorithms, or development teams. This is serious figure that must be addressed. Think about it: if more and more companies and organizations are becoming data and AI-driven as well as automating their operations based on artificial intelligence technologies that cannot be trusted, that means there's trouble on the horizon is — not only for the evolution of AI, but for society as a whole.

In this context, addressing the ethical aspects of artificial intelligence is fundamental and will be my focus in this chapter. But I also want to make clear that you shouldn't start thinking about ethics only when you get around to implementing your data science strategy. An ethical perspective is, in fact, *hugely* important to consider from the start — that is to say, from the moment you start designing your business models, architecture, infrastructure, and ways of working and building up the teams themselves. This chapter explains the basics you need to consider from a strategic as well as practical perspective.

Explaining AI Ethics

So, what does AI ethics actually refer to and which areas are important to address to generate trust around your data and algorithms? Well, there are many aspects to this concept, but there are five cornerstones to rely on;

» **Unbiased data, teams, and algorithms**. This refers to the importance of managing inherent biases that can arise from the development team composition if there isn't a good representation of gender, race, and sex. Data and training methods must be clearly identified and addressed through the AI design. Gaining insights and potentially making decisions based on a model that is in some way biased (a tendency toward gender inequality or racist attitudes, for example) isn't something you want to happen.

» **Algorithm performance**. The outcomes from AI decisions shall be aligned with stakeholder expectations that the algorithm performs at a desired level of precision and consistency and doesn't deviate from the model objective. When models are subsequently deployed in their target environment in a dynamic manner and continue to train and optimize model performance, the model will adjust to the potential new data patterns and preferences and might start deviating from the original goal. Setting sufficient policies to keep the model training on target is therefore vital.

» **Resilient infrastructure**. Make sure that the data used by the AI system components and the algorithm itself are secured from unauthorized access, corruption, and/ or adversarial attack.

» **Usage transparency and user consent**. A user must be clearly notified when interacting with an AI and must be offered an opportunity to select a level of interaction or reject that interaction completely. It also refers to the importance of obtaining user consent for data captured and used. The introduction of the General Data Protection Regulation (GDPR) in the EU has prompted discussions in the US calling for similar measures, meaning that the awareness of the stakes involved in personal information as well as the need to protect that information are slowly improving. (For more on the GDPR, refer to Chapter 3.) So, even if the data is collected in an unbiased manner and models are built in an unbiased setup, you could still end up with both ethically challenging situations (or even breaking the law) if you're using personal data without the right permissions.

» **Explainable models**. This refers to the need for AI's training methods and decisions criteria to be easily understood, documented, and readily available for human assessment and validation. It refers to situations where care has been taken to ensure that an algorithm, as part of an intelligent machine, produces actions that can be trusted and easily understood by humans.

The opposite of AI explainability is when the algorithm is treated as a black box, where even the designer of the algorithm cannot explain why the AI arrived at a specific insight or decision.

TECHNICAL STUFF

An additional ethical consideration, which is more technical in nature, relates to the reproducibility of results outside of the lab environment. AI is still immature, and most research-and-development is exploratory by nature. There is still little standardization in place for machine learning/artificial intelligence. De facto rules for AI development are emerging, but slowly and they are still very much community driven. Therefore, you must ensure that any results from an algorithm are actually *reproducible*— meaning you get the same results in the real, target environment as you would not only in the lab environment but also between different target environments (between different operators within the telecommunications sector, for example.)

Addressing trustworthy artificial intelligence

If the data you need access to in order to realize your business objectives can be considered ethically incorrect, how do you manage that? It's easy enough to say that applications should not collect data about race, gender, disabilities, or other protected classes. But the fact is that if you do not gather that type of data, you'll have trouble testing whether your applications are in fact fair to minorities.

REMEMBER

Machine learning algorithms that learn from data will become only as good as the data they're running on. Unfortunately, many algorithms have proven to be quite good at figuring out their own proxies for race and other classes, in ways that run counter to what many would consider proper human ethical thinking. Your application would not be the first system that could turn out to be unfair, despite the best intentions of its developers. But, to be clear, at the end of the day your company will be held responsible for the performance of its algorithms, and (hopefully) bias-related legislation in the future will be stricter than it is today. If a company isn't following laws and regulations or ethical boundaries, the financial cost could be significant — and perhaps even worse, people could lose trust in the company altogether. That could have serious consequences, ranging from customers abandoning the brand to employees losing their jobs to folks going to jail.

To avoid these types of scenarios, you need to put ethical principles into practice, and for that to happen, employees must be allowed and encouraged to be ethical in their daily work. They should be able to have conversations about what ethics actually means in the context of the business objectives and what costs to the company can be weathered in their name. They must also be able to at least discuss what would happen if a solution cannot be implemented in an ethically correct manner. Would such a realization be enough to terminate it?

Data scientists in general find it important to share best practices and scientific papers at conferences, writing blog posts, and developing open source technologies and algorithms. However, problems such as how to obtain informed consent aren't discussed quite as often. It's not as if the problems aren't recognized or understood; they're merely seen as less worthy of discussion. Rather than let such a mindset persist, companies should actively encourage (rather than just allow) more discussions about fairness, the proper use of data, and the harm that can be done by the inappropriate use of data.

WARNING

Recent scandals involving computer security breaches have shown the consequences of sticking your head in the sand: Many companies that never took the time to implement good security practices and safeguards are now paying for that neglect with damages to their reputations and their finances. It is important to exercise the same due diligence now accorded security matters when thinking about issues like fairness, accountability, and unintended consequences of your data use. It will never be possible to predict all unintended consequences of such usage and, yes, the ability to foresee the future is limited. But plenty of unintended consequences could easily have been foreseen. (Facebook's Year in Review feature, which seemed to go out of its way in to remind Facebook users of deaths in the family and other painful events, is a prime example.)

REMEMBER

Mark Zuckerberg's famous motto, "Move fast and break things," is unacceptable if it hasn't been thought through in terms of what is likely to break. Company leaders should insist that they be allowed to ponder such aspects — and stop the production line whenever something goes wrong. This idea dates back to Toyota's Andon manufacturing method: Any assembly line worker can stop the line if they see something going wrong. The line doesn't restart until the problem is fixed. Workers don't have to fear consequences from management for stopping the line; they are trusted, and are expected to behave responsibly.

What would it mean if you could do this with product features or AI/ML algorithms? If anyone at Facebook could have said, "Wait, we're getting complaints about Year in Review" and pulled it out of production, Facebook would now be in a much better position from an ethical perspective. Of course, it's a big, complicated company, with a big, complicated product. But so is Toyota, and it worked there.

The issue lurking behind all these concerns is, of course, corporate culture. Corporate environments can be hostile to anything other than short-term profitability. However, in a time when public distrust and disenchantment are running at an all-time high, ethics is turning into a good corporate investment. Upper-level management is only starting to see this, and changes to corporate culture won't happen quickly, but it's clear that users want to deal with companies that treat them and their data responsibly, not just as potential profit or as engagements to be maximized.

TIP

The companies that will succeed with AI ethics are the ones that create space for ethics within their organizations. This means allowing data scientists, data engineers, software developers, and other data professionals, to "do ethics" in practical terms. It isn't a question of hiring trained ethicists and assigning them to their teams; it's about living ethical values every single day, not just talking about them. That's what it means to "do good data science."

Introducing Ethics by Design

What's the best way to approach implementing AI ethics by design? Might there be a checklist available to use? Now that you mention it, there is one, and you'll find it in the United Kingdom. The government there has launched a data ethics framework, featuring the data ethics workbook. As part of the initiative, they have isolated seven distinct principles around AI ethics. The workbook they came up with is built up around a number of open-ended questions designed to probe your compliance with these principles. Admittedly, it's a lot of questions — 46, to be exact, which is rather too many for a data scientist to continuously keep track of and incorporate efficiently into a daily routine. For such questions to be truly useful then, they need to be embedded not only in the development ways of working but also as part of the data science infrastructure and systems support.

REMEMBER

It isn't merely a question of making it possible as a practical matter to follow ethical principles in daily work and to prove how the company is ethically compliant — the company must also stand behind these ambitions and embrace them as part of its code of conduct. However, when a company talks about adding AI ethics to its code of conduct, the value doesn't come from the pledge itself, but rather emerges from the process people undergo in developing it. People who work with data are now starting to have discussions on a broad scale that would never have taken place just a decade ago. But discussions alone won't get the hard work done. It is vital to not just *talk* about how to use data ethically but also to *use* data ethically. Principles must be put into practice!

Here's a shorter list of questions to consider as you and your data science teams work together to gain a common and general understanding of what is needed to address AI ethical concerns:

» **Hacking:** To what extent is an intended AI technology vulnerable to hacking, and thus potentially vulnerable to being abused?

» **Training data:** Have you tested your training data to ensure that it is fair and representative?

» **Bias:** Does your data contain possible sources of bias?

» **Team composition:** Does the team composition reflect a diversity of opinions and backgrounds?

» **Consent:** Do you need user consent to collect and use the data? Do you have a mechanism for gathering consent from users? Have you explained clearly what users are consenting to?

» **Compensation:** Do you offer reimbursement if people are harmed by the results of your AI technology?

» **Emergency brake:** Can you shut down this software in production if it's behaving badly?

» **Transparency and Fairness:** Do the data and AI algorithms used comply with corporate values for technology such as moral behavior, respect, fairness and transparency? Have you tested for fairness with respect to different user groups?

» **Error rates:** Have you tested for different error rates among diverse user groups?

» **Model performance:** Do you monitor model performance to ensure that your software remains fair over time? Can it be trusted to perform as intended, not just during the initial training or modelling but also throughout its ongoing "learning" and evolution?

» **Security**: Do you have a plan to protect and secure user data?

» **Accountability**: Is there a clear line of accountability to an individual and clarity on how the AI operates, the data that it uses, and the decision framework that is applied?

» **Design:** Did the AI design consider local and macro social impact, including its impact on the financial, physical, and mental well-being of humans and our natural environment?

Chapter **8**

Becoming Data-driven

nless a company invests big money in becoming data-driven in today's business climate, it will eventually perish. Companies that don't believe that their data is an asset (and therefore should be managed accordingly) will end up in a lot of trouble within the next five years. This chapter explains why it's necessary for your company to become data driven and offers some advice on what steps your company needs to take in order to become data-driven.

Understanding Why Data-Driven Is a Must

Companies and organizations across many business areas have begun their journey to capture, create, and use data in ways that are fundamentally changing how people work and live. And, as you're probably already aware, the starting point for any data-driven organization is simply the realization that data is at the core of everything it does. It is truly the foundation of everything, and organizations across the business spectrum are now becoming aware of the transformative power of data, analytics, and AI.

Companies are also starting to understand the real challenges that lie ahead. For many, it's tough enough to catalog and categorize all the data available; identifying and adding rules for processing and using the data in order to translate the data into tangible value seems an almost insurmountable task. But, although it's difficult, it isn't impossible, and several companies are now starting to address this challenge more strategically *and* more practically. "Nice to know," you might say, "but where do we start?"

TIP

Rather than start by hiring an external data person (as this person is commonly known), my advice to you, based on my experience in the field, is to invest some time and effort in finding a key person in your organization who is willing to lead your data-driven initiative. This person should be someone who can see the bigger picture and help create a data strategy based on thorough insights into how the company functions as well as its future business objectives. That key person should also have the people skills and communication skills to transform an entire organization — with sufficient support, of course — and should be willing (and patient enough) to be on the frontline to move the company from a simple data integrator all the way to a market innovator.

REMEMBER

When businesses today claim to recognize that data has a value, their contentions aren't necessarily correct in terms of the true value of the data. It's easy enough to understand that transactional data can be used for reporting or data analytics, which can then lead to better decision-making. But even though the perceived value of data has increased over the past two decades, many companies still lag behind when it comes to efficiently capturing, sharing, and managing data. This is mainly because their systems and processes reflect an outdated belief that data is simply the byproduct of some other activity — rather than the key to their business success. To move beyond such an approach and actually enter the 21st century, such organizations need to invest significantly more time and effort into creating a data strategy.

That's all well and good, but what does it actually mean when I say that a company needs to create a data strategy? First and foremost, developing a data strategy means making sure that all data resources are positioned in such a way that they can be used, shared, and moved easily and efficiently. In other words, having a data strategy ensures that data is managed and used as an asset and not simply as a byproduct of another application. By establishing common methods, practices, and processes to manage, manipulate, and share data across the company in a repeatable manner, a data strategy ensures that the goals and objectives to use data effectively and efficiently are aligned in a conscious and strategic manner.

Unfortunately, just as many companies still use data as a byproduct rather than as the core value of their businesses, many don't resolve their data problems by creating and following through on their own data strategies, but rather hire data analysts tasked with the chore of "finding things in the data." The result is that instead of having someone onboard with the clear business objective of turning data into insights, you give a bunch of data analysts access to a database and have them run queries that any basic analytics tool could provide in seconds instead. What's the point of that?

WARNING

Without a data strategy, it doesn't matter whether the people you hire are called data analysts or data scientists or data engineers or machine learning/artificial intelligence engineers. If you're hiring people with fancy titles just because everybody else in the market seems to be doing it, it isn't a sign that you have suddenly understood the value of a data strategy. Without clearly defined objectives that you've committed to carrying out in a strategic way, all the hires you make will be worse than window dressing because you'll be investing time and money and receiving little in return. Essentially, you're spending an enormous amount of money to attract and retain data analysts (or scientists or engineers) who spend most of their days extracting, cleaning, and modeling data without knowing a) which problems to focus on and b) how one could create a new business opportunity that generates revenues or profit for the company.

Transitioning to a Data-Driven Model

Becoming data-driven is both an organizational ambition and an absolute necessity. It involves cultural aspects as well as technology aspects. It's about using data to take direct action, in addition to building relationships and trust around the data. But it's also about how you look at the data, and how you come to use it as part of your day-to-day business. Technologically savvy management teams understand that attempting to "boil the ocean" when adopting a data-centric strategy is a foolish thing to do. Some have already learned this the hard way, by undertaking less-than-successful "big-bang" transformation projects. Given the scope and complexity of the dynamic nature of the digital world, companies are starting to understand that change will continue to accelerate, even as they achieve or progress beyond the target state.

REMEMBER

Management must set visionary goals for data-centricity, but they also need to allow for change during implementation — and even perhaps for changes to the vision itself. Given these realities, it's imperative that management approach both data management and analytics and machine learning/artificial intelligence initiatives from a continuous improvement perspective, driving progress toward goals while following a roadmap that is adjusted as business and organizational needs evolve.

Becoming data-driven is a new way to approach your business, and it's understandable that many companies get lost in all their data and ambitions. On top of that, everything is moving very fast in terms of the constantly evolving techniques used in the areas of data science, artificial intelligence, and virtualized infrastructures. (And don't even get me started on the new and expanded policies in regulatory, security, and ethical practices.)

When you introduce a data-driven approach to your organization, it isn't enough to have clear objectives on what needs to be achieved — you also need a way to measure your achievements toward those objectives. On top of tracking progress, you must be able to measure and prove the value and impact that data science and machine learning have on your business.

Securing management buy-in and assigning a chief data officer (CDO)

The most important decision that company management has to make is to make someone fully responsible for data. Doing so sends the right message across the organization not only internally but also externally, toward the market and its customers. You want everyone to know that you're taking seriously the task of becoming data-driven and that it is what will drive the company forward into the future. (For more on the role of the CDO as well as advice on how to establish the function in your organization, see Chapter 12.)

A large part of the CDO's responsibility should be the company-wide management and use of data as an organizational and strategic asset. This means working together with every single department to design a common way to acquire, store, manage, share, and use data. As important as that is, it's even more important to ensure that the culture adopts a data-driven way of thinking so that the decision-making process is informed by discussions enabled by sharing and reuse of data, models, and insights. At the end of the day, it's all about making use of the data in real decisions across the company and as part of its portfolio of products and/or services.

Top management sponsorship and approval is of course essential for the success of any data strategy, but management must take on more than just a stewardship or enforcement function. Leadership must also "walk the talk," embracing fact-based decision-making, pushing for more and better data, and recognizing achievement when efforts succeed.

Management must also provide a clear vision, prioritize analytical applications, understand return on investment, allocate appropriate resources, manage talent, ensure cross-functional coordination, and remove some of the barriers that will inevitably pop up during implementation. Finally, management must insist on compliance with legal and regulatory requirements on the data in scope.

Identifying the key business value aligned with the business maturity

The starting point for any data analysis should be an understanding of the most significant business opportunities and/or problems for your company. Given that starting point, you can then focus your analysis on identifying and describing how a data-driven approach can contribute and provide value in that perspective. In either case, the whole point of a data-driven approach is to provide value where there was none before.

WARNING

Never get caught up in the potential of a particular technology; always stay focused on its application. Rather than asking, "What can this new technology do for us?" you should ask, "What problems do I need to solve?" The situation has intensified due to the rapid technology evolution, creating a skills shortage in most companies. Of course, there's room for some experimentation with regard to what the new technologies can enable, but only as long as you stay focused on the primary goal, which is driving the business forward. Successfully harnessing data, analytics, and machine learning/artificial intelligence ensures that you'll be able to accelerate the benefits of adopting a data-driven approach, which will in turn increase the drive for further deployment.

All companies go through different stages in a *business life cycle* — that progression of a business through various phases over time, most commonly divided into the five stages of launch, growth, shake-out, maturity, and decline. However, it's worth noticing that in large, global companies, different business areas within the same company may be in different stages of a business life cycle at any given time. This happens, for example, when a new business segment or area is added to a setup with a more traditional set of business areas — a new segment addressing digital business for example. This mix of new and more traditional business areas in a large enterprise can be difficult to handle when it comes to aligning business objectives or carrying out a business transformation plan.

In either case, however, it is important to align the business objectives with the business maturity, since the success of implementing a data-driven approach is very much dependent on the readiness of the company. A recently established company in its launch or growth phase might already be based on a fully digitalized business model and half way towards becoming data-driven already. Setting business objectives for such a company should be ambitious and implementation should be pretty straight forward, given that other conditions are favorable such as access to data, rights to data, infrastructure setup and management approach. For a company in the maturity phase or perhaps even entering into the decline phase, setting balanced and achievable objectives for a fundamental change will be trickier.

Given this problematic mix of old and new, a company's approach when transforming itself into a data-driven organization either needs to be aligned with the organization's primary needs for the overall company or for the needs of a certain targeted area. It is possible to transform different business areas at different speeds and different ambitions and even at different times. However, depending on the integration and dependencies between different business areas, that could cause problems related to data and infrastructure dependencies, as well as portfolio offerings and customer communication. An important priority of the assigned CDO should therefore be to determine which approach to take so that it's possible to align it with the overall data science strategy.

The following list shows a few examples of the approaches that could be adopted when becoming data-driven:

- » **The data integrator:** The company should focus its data-driven implementation primarily on a modern, integrated, internal data infrastructure designed to bring onboard new and more data that it can use to achieve business objectives related to the different ways it could monetize its data across the business.

- » **The business optimizer:** A company committed to optimizing its current business should focus primarily on exploiting the currently available data in order to make internal and customer-centric business processes as effective and efficient as possible.

- » **The market disruptor/innovator:** For a company that has the ambition to become a market innovator, the focus should be on augmenting human capabilities using machine learning and artificial intelligence techniques. That will lay the foundation for the company to become a digital market disruptor.

Developing a Data Strategy

After your company's objectives have become clearer, your CDO, as part of an overall data science strategy, needs to create a business-driven data strategy fleshed out with a significant level of detail. In addition, that person needs to define the scope of the desired data-driven culture and mindset for your company and move to drive that culture forward. In this section, I spell out what a CDO needs to keep in mind in order to accomplish these tasks, as well as an example of a data strategy scope.

Caring for your data

One key aspect in any data strategy involves caring for your data as if it were your lifeblood — because it is. You need to address data quality and integration issues as key factors of your data strategy, and you need to align your data governance programs with your organizational goals, making sure you define all strategies, policies, processes, and standards in support of those goals.

REMEMBER

Organizations should assess their current state and develop plans to achieve an appropriate level of maturity in terms of data governance over a specific period. It's important to recognize that data governance is never complete; by necessity, it evolves, just as corporate needs and goals, technology, and legal and regulatory aspects do.

Governance programs can range from establishing company-level, business-driven data and information programs for data integrators, to establishing customized, segment-based programs for the business optimizers and market disruptors/innovators. However, even the best strategy can falter if the business culture isn't willing to change. Data integrators flourish in an evidence-based operational environment where data and research is used to establish a data-driven culture, whereas business optimizers and market disruptors/innovators need to adopt a "fail-fast" agile software development culture in order to increase speed-to-market and innovation.

Democratizing the data

As important as it is to understand the value of the data your company has access to, it's equally important to make sure that the data is easily available to those who need to work with it. That's what *democratizing* your data really means. Given its importance, you should strive to make sure that this democratization occurs throughout your organization. The fact of the matter is, everyone in your company makes business decisions every single day, and those decisions need to be grounded in a thorough understanding of all available data. We know that data-driven decisions are better decisions, so why wouldn't you choose to provide people with access to the data they need in order to make better decisions?

WARNING

Although most people can understand the need for data democratization, it isn't at all uncommon for a company's data strategy to instead focus on locking up the data — just to be on the safe side. Nothing, however, could be more devastating for the value realization of the data for your business than adopting a bunker mentality about data. The way to start generating internal and external value on your data is to use it, not lock it up. Even adopting a radical approach of a totally open data environment internally is better than being too restrictive in terms of how data is made available and shared in the company.

Driving data standardization

A third key component in any data strategy is to standardize to scale quickly and efficiently. Data standardization is an important component for success — one that should not be underestimated. A company cannot hope to achieve goals that assume a 360-degree view of all customers underpinned by the correct data without a common set of data definitions and structures across the company and the customers.

TM Forum, a nonprofit industry association for service providers and their suppliers in the telecommunications industry, developed something they call the Information Framework (SID) in concert with professionals from the communications and information industries working collaboratively to provide a universal information and data model. (The SID part of the name comes from *Shared Information Data* model.) The benefits of this common model come from its ability to significantly support increased standardization around data in the telecommunications space and include aspects such as;

>> Faster time to market for new products and services

>> Cheaper data and systems integration

>> Less data management time

>> Reduced cost and support when implementing multiple technologies

REMEMBER

Organizations have long recognized the need to seek standardization in their transactional data structures, but they need to realize the importance of seeking standardization in their analytical data structures as well. Traditional analytics and business intelligence setups continue to use data warehouses and data marts as their primary data repositories, and yes, they are still highly valuable to data-driven organizations, but enabling dynamic big data analytics and machine learning/artificial intelligence solutions requires a different structure in order to be effective.

Structuring the data strategy

The act of creating a data strategy is a chance to generate data conversations, educate executives, and identify exciting new data-enabled opportunities for the organization. In fact, the process of creating a data strategy may generate political support, changes in culture and mindset, and new business objectives and priorities that are even more valuable than the data strategy itself. But what should the data strategy actually include? The list below gives you an idea.

- » Data centric vision and business objectives including user scenarios

- » Strategic data principles, including treating data as an asset

- » Guidelines for data security, data rights, and ethical considerations

- » Data management principles, including data governance and data quality

- » Data infrastructure principles regarding data architecture, data acquisition, data storage, and data processing

- » Data scope, including priorities over time

WARNING

Don't mix-up the data strategy with the data science strategy. The main difference is that the data strategy is focused on the strategic direction and principles for the data and is a subset of the data science strategy. The data science strategy includes the data strategy, but also aspects such as organization, people, culture and mindset, data science competence and roles, managing change, measurements, and business commercial implications on the company portfolio.

Establishing a Data-Driven Culture and Mindset

An obvious but vital step in becoming data-driven is to take the time to get the employees onboard in terms of what this fundamental change really means in their day-to-day business activities. It will take some time and effort to get there, but not only is it worth the time invested, it's also the main prerequisite for change to happen and to last over time.

TIP

In the early stages of introducing a data-driven mindset, focus on explaining what's happening with the help of examples close to what is already being done. Start with concrete examples of what the changes will actually mean in their daily setup. For example, if the current ways of working in a company are strongly *reactive* — meaning that a process starts with a customer complaint — what would the new starting point be? How would a data-driven and proactive approach impact current workflows, practically speaking, when the flow starts instead with predictive analysis of the data and the ambition to prevent complaints?

On a day-to-day basis as part of ordinary decision-making, leaders must actively encourage employees to a) establish the habit of asking for the data input they need and b) make use of the data at their disposal. A practical and clear request by management to actually use the available data will ripple through the organization and will have a much greater impact than you might think. It's truly an important step to establish data-first thinking in the company. Furthermore, this effort could be underscored in even stronger terms by establishing a system of rewards for those employees who promote and drive the culture around using data as the primary input for the decision-making.

Recently, word has been going around that "analytics are getting easier," and in some respects, this is true. Some quite capable off-the-shelf analytics tools are available, and certain new self-service analytical applications have removed some of the complexity, making data analytics available to more people with different types of roles — and hence supporting a data-driven culture.

However, although analytics may be getting easier, data management is becoming harder. This is mainly because of the growing variety of sources and structures and the ever-increasing velocity at which it is generated. Therefore, it's vital to consider having the right talents and skills supporting data engineering aspects, as well as data science as a whole, and it's also important to keep in mind that this state of affairs will remain so for the foreseeable future.

Chapter **9**

Evolving from Data-driven to Machine-driven

To be driven by data and to be driven by a machine are not the same things. You can call them *related* states in data science, if you want, but they definitely exist at different stages of maturity. Being *data-driven* above all else refers to the idea that any progress in an activity is bound by data rather than by intuition or personal experience. Being *machine driven,* on the other hand, refers not to the boundaries of an activity, but rather to how that activity is carried out — more specifically, that it is an activity connected, automated, and controlled by a machine and its implementation of a certain model or algorithm. Machine driven is the final stage of industrializing and automating data science from end to end, driven by the designed intelligence of the machine.

Today, few companies and organizations are at a stage where they can be said to be fully data-driven or, definitely, fully machine-driven. However, several companies are now starting to explore how to make parts of their businesses machine-driven as a first step toward full transformation at a later stage. This approach is not only possible but also advisable for early experimentation on the potential efforts, benefits, and impact.

When you're starting to experiment with consolidating parts of your business into a more machine-driven approach, you need to be aware of four major steps — all with interdependencies, but with each and every one of them requiring the same starting point: digitizing the data.

Figure 9-1 drives that point home — always digitize the data first. Without that step, none of the other steps can be taken. However, after you've digitized the data and made it available, you can try any of the following steps in any order (although I do recommend following the prescribed sequence in Figure 9-1 for both a full, companywide scope and selected parts of the business). Figure 9-1 gives you the roadmap, and the rest of this chapter describes in detail the steps along the way.

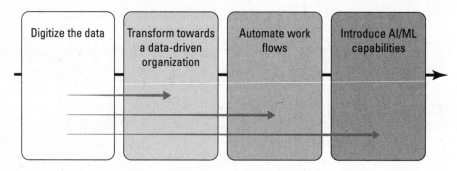

FIGURE 9-1:
On the road to a machine driven approach.

Digitizing the Data

When you digitize data, you're transforming data assets into digital, machine-readable content. Simply spoken, without digitalizing the data in your business, you can't take the next step toward becoming machine driven.

TECHNICAL STUFF

Digitization of data (sometimes also referred to as *digitalization* which I discuss in Chapter 1 in relation to a data-driven organization) is the process of converting information into a digital (computer-readable) format. The output is a digital representation of an object, an image, a sound, a document, or a signal (usually, an analog signal), and it includes the change of analog source material into a numerical format. The result is the digitized data in the form of binary numbers, which facilitate computer processing and other machine led operations.

Digitizing data is of crucial importance to data processing, storage, and transmission because it allows information of all kinds and in all formats to be carried with the same efficiency. Digitized data, unlike analog data (which typically loses quality each time it's copied or transmitted), can (in theory) be circulated an indefinite number of times with absolutely no degradation in quality.

So, which assets am I referring to that need to be digitized? How about *everything*? That means everything from the company's customer data, internal routines, and processes and workflows to employee information, product information, and other types of information. Digitizing all this data opens up the possibility of using the available data as input for data analysis driving internal efficiency improvements and new business opportunities as part of a data-driven approach.

Applying a Data-driven Approach

After the data is transformed into a digital and machine readable format, you can start taking steps toward making your business data-driven from end to end.

REMEMBER

As described in Chapter 8, introducing a data-driven approach is not a minor tweak to current operations; for it to be successful, you need to carry out a fundamental transformation of your organization from end to end, starting with top management buy-in. After the decision has been made to carry out this transformation and it is generally understood what it will mean in terms of not only the expected business benefits but also the required efforts, the first step is to create a solid and well-thought-out data science strategy. This strategy will help you plan and execute all needed activities in order to meet your overall business objectives. If the long term objective includes becoming machine driven, then automation, machine learning, and artificial intelligence aspects need to already be included in the data science strategy at this stage.

When a data science strategy has been defined and agreed on, the hard work to transform the company to a data-driven one then begins in earnest, including aspects such as enabling and using data, establishing a data-driven mindset and culture across the company, and making sure that data is requested and used in decisions and measurements across the entire business.

TIP

To prepare the organization for not only an enhanced data understanding but also a necessary change in mindset and culture, spend some time investigating and experimenting with different machine driven solutions for selected areas. Doing so helps prepare the organization for what is coming and also helps exemplify what it means in terms of competence needed, impact on current ways of working, architecture and infrastructure impact — and also benefits gained. Yes, the starting point for a data-driven organization is that it all starts and ends with data, but for data driven to deliver value, remember that it needs to be understood and implemented in the real context of the company.

Automating Workflows

The step to automate either a part of or all of your processes or workflows can be taken directly after you have digitized your content; it doesn't require that you first turn your business into a data-driven one, even if it's advisable in order to achieve your long term objective of becoming machine driven.

Automating workflows is the first concrete step in transferring control from humans to machines. Remember that, by automating workflows, humans are still deciding on the approach and the steps that the machine needs to take; you're just moving the responsibility of executing the steps to the machine. This method (also called *process automation*) involves using computer technology and software engineering to help systems and processes work better. (The prime examples here are helping plants and factories operate more efficiently, more safely, and at a lower cost in industries as diverse as paper, mining, and cement.)

REMEMBER

Process automation can also be applied at the business level, where it's then referred to as business process automation (BPA). When applied here, it refers to the technology enabled automation of complex business processes. BPA can be used for streamlining many aspects of a business, including enhancing cost efficiencies, achieving digital transformation, increasing service quality, and improving service delivery. A full implementation of BPA usually includes activities such as enabling data, integrating applications, restructuring employees, and applying software applications (machines) to automate the tasks throughout the organization. Robotic process automation (RPA) is an emerging field within BPA, which is taking the next step toward becoming machine driven and can (in more advanced versions) add artificial intelligence capabilities to the machine scope.

Introducing AI/ML capabilities

When you introduce artificial intelligence / machine learning capabilities to your company, you take a significant step toward becoming machine driven. This step includes focusing on what the business objective is and letting go of some human control of when or how certain tasks should be done.

TECHNICAL
STUFF

Adding intelligence capabilities to the machine means that models and algorithms are designed to use the data to find and achieve the best possible way to execute the defined objective. Practically speaking, you must set up and industrialize an infrastructure in the company that is both data- and machine-oriented. There must be room for exploratory development environments for data scientists to identify new opportunities and create new models, but you must also provide a stable production environment to enable the algorithms to run as part of the operational reality of the company. At the end of the day, being machine driven is all about letting the algorithms run and then find and execute the best way to solve or predict and prevent a problem.

THE ROLE OF HUMANS IN AI

Even though being machine driven is all about the machines, don't forget about the human involvement outside of algorithm development. Your main objective here is not to create the smartest machines in the world, but rather to use intelligent machines to augment the human capabilities of your organization so that you can achieve more. Therefore, although the role that humans play in a machine driven business may be different, they're still quite important. The role includes tasks you'd expect, such as monitoring model and algorithm performance to make sure the machine is doing what it needs to do with an expected level of quality, but it also includes directly interacting with the machine.

The point here is that early machine-led activities are usually focused on serving new insights and recommending actions, not on running fully closed-loop automation where decisions are both taken and acted on entirely by the machine. As the technology matures within an organization, however, more and more of these closed-loop, machine driven scenarios will start to come alive across different businesses, especially where you can limit the algorithm scope and complexity. Examples of these types of machine led activities include closed systems designed for particular outcomes in industries such as mining, manufacturing, and smaller IoT systems.

Another important aspect from the human perspective is the level of competence needed and the diverse skill sets required to not only implement a machine driven approach but also design the data science strategy to account for all necessary aspects and dimensions. Unfortunately, the access to experienced data science expertise in the area of full end-to-end machine driven business automation is limited, to say the least, especially when it comes to more complex AI techniques in the cognitive reasoning space.

However, when it comes to the availability of data scientists in a general sense, it is increasing slowly. The interest in various universities across the world is growing, and so is the availability of data science university programs and other types of data science educational programs.

However, because few up-and-running, end-to-end machine driven businesses are in play today, it's even more important to explore the area of machine driven business in small and manageable steps. This will allow competence to slowly grow and spread in the company over time — and allow curiosity to lead the change instead of imposing it from the top down. Enforcing data science in a company without fully understanding either the impact of the efforts needed or the benefits to be expected is not a good way to get started.

3

Building a Successful Data Science Organization

Chapter **10**

Building Successful Data Science Teams

ata scientist has become the most attractive role in today's competitive job market. Entry level salaries can range into six figures, and roughly 700,000 job openings are projected by 2020. What's driving this demand? Simple — business value. The job of the data scientist is to extract insights hidden inside mountains of data — insights that can then be used to achieve diverse business goals, ranging from fraud detection to facial recognition. Acknowledging this diversity at the core of data science is the key to building efficient data science teams, which must be composed of individuals with highly specialized and complementary skill sets in order to be successful. But before you can embark on the journey to get the perfect data science team in place, you need to make sure you have the right leadership in place.

Starting with the Data Science Team Leader

When hiring a data science team leader, keep in mind that you're not hiring a data scientist — you're hiring a *leader* in data science. There's a difference. First, remember that the leadership skills are more important than the expert skills in data science. That doesn't mean that the manager can't be a former data scientist, but it does mean that the person needs to be ready to take on a leadership role.

WARNING

If you appoint a leader who doesn't understand the basic area of data science and how it differs from ordinary software development, building an efficient and successful data science team will be slow going, in both the short term and long term.

Remember that leadership is a skill in and of itself. Just because someone has proven to be a successful team contributor in the past doesn't mean that he has the skills necessary to retain and develop great talent while delivering valuable insights, products, and outcomes to your customers and back to the organization. Great data scientists have loads of career options and won't tolerate bad managers for long. If you want to retain great data scientists, a good starting point is to commit to having great managers.

REMEMBER

If the leader is a former software development manager, it is fundamental to understand that being a leader in data science is different. A minimum requirement in that situation is that the manager of the data science team knows that he or she is not knowledgeable enough in data science and thus needs to keep an open mind and wants to learn more. That situation also benefits from having experienced data scientists on the team that can support the leader in the beginning.

Adopting different leadership approaches

Understanding how to lead data science teams compared to pure software development teams is fundamental for becoming a successful leader in this domain. In this section, I present a list of areas and aspects pinpointing the main differences between pure software development teams and data science teams — differences that must be taken into account as part of leading these teams:

>> **Team working methods:** In data science, the methodology differs from what you'd find in traditional software development. Data science requires much longer development cycles to get to a result and validate that result, because of its dependency on acquiring and preparing the data to a sufficient level of quality before any type of analysis can be done. Because data science is also still in an early phase of its evolution, it's still in a state of flux. That means techniques and methodologies are constantly evolving, which calls for a high degree of experimentation in the approach.

>> **Technology and techniques used:** In data science, you need to use technologies not often used in software development (statistics, machine learning, and artificial intelligence, for example) in order to create dynamic, self-learning algorithms and dynamic implementation environments. Areas such as

robotics are also becoming more and more important in the area of data science. These technologies require other techniques, programming languages, and tool sets on top of what is used in traditional software engineering, depending on the data science strategy and focus. More ambitious and complex machine learning/artificial intelligence modeling and solutions require even more advanced tool sets.

>> **Competencies required:** Data science is its own area of competency, with its own roles and tool sets. A former software developer can become a good data scientist, but it requires a different skill set —one related to the statistical models, with more advanced math competencies, for example. There are also other important roles to consider, such as data architect, data engineer, domain expertise, and automation engineer.

>> **Infrastructure needed:** When dealing with data science, the infrastructure focus is also different because everything is centered around the data. It's all about having a capable infrastructure that can support efficient data capture, anonymization, transfer, legal compliance, data security and governance, ethical considerations, storage, and processing before you even start working on analysis and model development. As you can imagine, the number and variety of data science needs place high demands on the infrastructure capacity and its capability to enable the analysis and exploration of huge data sets while maintaining data quality and integrity.

As a comparison, a pure software development infrastructure generally more self-contained with fewer external dependencies. It has also less need for scalability in terms of compute power and storage. Another aspect is that the software development area is also much more mature from a software ecosystem perspective, which means that it's far more streamlined and standardized than data science, which is still in an experimental and exploratory mode.

>> **Other important considerations:** In data science, the ethical-, privacy-, and security-related aspects of data usage and model performance are of the utmost importance when it comes to understanding and managing a data science team. If due diligence isn't carried out and any ethical or regulatory requirements were to be violated, all data science activities would have to come to a screeching halt. In addition to the costs of downtime, you could also be facing huge fines associated with the breaking of such laws and regulations. As a leader, it's therefore vital to make sure company policies around such matters are built into strategies, guidelines, systems, and control mechanisms during the entire life cycle of the data as well as the models.

Approaching data science leadership

A fundamental aspect of becoming a great data science leader is to think through how to generate trust, authenticity, and loyalty within the team and toward the leader. This may well be true for all team/leader relationships, but it's nevertheless especially true for data science, where companies are still very much confused about its role in the organization. This means that the data science leader is responsible for protecting team members from unreasonable requests and for explaining the team's role to the rest of the organization. Your team needs to trust that you will "have their back."

WARNING

Having your employees' backs doesn't mean blindly defending them at all costs. It *does* mean making sure that they know you value their contributions. The best way to do that is to make sure your team members have interesting projects to work on and that they aren't overburdened by projects with vague requirements, strange use cases, or unrealistic timelines, accompanied by insufficient data and an inadequate data science environment.

To build trust over time, the data science leader/manager should invest in openness and honesty. Data scientists are competent people who are trained to analyze and handle information. Be transparent during the entire data science process, including recruiting, onboarding, ensuring daily operations, and discussing the team's performance and focus — as well as the overall company strategy. Being sincere and open in all aspects can be painful, but is vital for team success.

TIP

Make feedback consistent and bidirectional. Great data scientists excel at spotting whether you mean what you say. If you ask for feedback but do not intend to act on the feedback, you will soon discover that your best employees may want to leave.

WARNING

Valuable employees seldom leave a company because they're unhappy with the company itself. They leave because of poor leadership.

Finding the right data science leader or manager

So, how do you approach finding the right data science manager to build a successful team? One approach is to use the same test for the manager candidates as you do with data scientists. It should include the same challenges, but you should expect different outcomes or results from the test.

TIP

Know what a good result looks like. Thoroughly think through the actual level of proficiency you require from the data science leader. For instance, if you're hiring a manager for a machine learning team, let the manager solve a specific data science task — one that deals with image similarity, for example. A good outcome of that exercise is for the manager to be able to explain the different techniques needed to solve the task, starting with deep learning and moving on to other machine-learning strategies. The idea here is to gauge the breadth of the candidate's knowledge, even if you're not asking them to produce actual models or code a solution.

TIP

I also recommend implementing a two-tiered leadership for data science teams, where one person will be the line manager demonstrating an understanding of the overall business objectives and accepting the responsibility for the team's success, while another person will be the data science expert who reports to the overall line manager. This type of setup creates a dynamic environment that combines a deep technical data science leadership with a good business orientation.

The two levels of leadership will not always agree, but that is the purpose of the setup. The business-oriented manager will challenge the technology manager, and the technology manager will challenge cooperate decisions. It is of the uttermost importance that these two leaders are able to cooperate closely and openly with each other, with a great amount of trust. This needs to be tested as early as possible in the hiring process.

Defining the Prerequisites for a Successful Team

You can often come up with quite specific technical requirements for each role within the data science organization, but there needs to be a common understanding of what is required for a data science *team* to be successful. While technical skill sets are vital for a successful data science team, there is a far more critical set of success factors for a data science team that you need to be aware of. The next few sections walk you through them.

Developing a team structure

How the data science team is structured is vital to the effectiveness and efficiency of the team. The importance of close cooperation between data engineers and data scientists shouldn't be underestimated. Usually, these two different roles are not on the same team, which means it's even more crucial to secure an efficient cross-team collaborative environment. Such a collaborative environment should be able to handle all analytical processes end-to-end across different systems and organizations, and ensure that productivity is not lost along the way.

REMEMBER

As you might have guessed, maintaining these lines of communication is never an easy task. You should nevertheless strive to minimize the inevitable hand-offs between data engineers and data scientists, in the process creating a seamless workflow from data capture to the deployment of models into production. It also drives efficiency if data engineers and data scientists are able to share insights with the business users from the same data system environment.

Establishing an infrastructure

The data science infrastructure needs to be highly scalable — that is, it should enable the data scientist to focus on analyzing data and building models, not struggle with acquiring data or computing data. Implementing a secure-but-enabling infrastructure is the key to success with all your artificial intelligence investments — including the investments you've made in building a successful data science team.

REMEMBER

When approaching artificial intelligence infrastructure work, many companies tend to forget to define a clear data science strategy that is agreed upon across the company before getting started. Remember that a poorly-thought-out infrastructure strategy will inevitably increase complexity and cost in development and operations (DevOps). If you aren't following an infrastructure plan, approaching it in a more build-as-you-go fashion, the complexity can be more difficult to handle in terms of setting up and maintaining the infrastructure over time, managing upgrades and fixes, scaling the infrastructure with growing data volumes as well as in providing high-performance infrastructure for large teams of data scientists, sometimes spread out over a large geographical area.

WARNING

When it comes to increasing data processing efficiency, distributed computing is often presented as the best solution to ensure performance at scale. But be aware that the complexity of managing distributed computing, from cloud-edge to edge on device or component level, requires special skills, which can be difficult to get hold of.

Ensuring data availability

Enabling access to the data that's needed may seem like an obvious task to prioritize, but you might be amazed at how often this is a major concern for data scientists. Sometimes access issues are caused by external factors that are more difficult to manage, such as new legal constraints on data usage, but many times the issues arise because the company has no common and agreed-on strategy for enabling access at a consistent level.

WARNING

It might seem a simple task to ensure that the data is available for data scientists to use in performing their analyses and building their models — much simpler, for example, than chasing data and mending broken data environments. The task is actually far from a simple one. In fact, unreliable data availability is a common source of frustration among data scientists, making them leave for other companies that are better at meeting the data needs. This is really an unnecessary risk to put on your company, so make sure you don't end up in that situation. If you manage to get hold of one of the few senior data scientists who are available on the market, do whatever is needed to retain that person!

TIP

One way to minimize the risk is to lower your ambitions and start with data that is already available to you. You can then work in parallel to ensure that you have all the necessary rights to the data, that the data is secure and governed correctly, and that you have the means to collect and prepare the data for the data scientists.

Insisting on interesting projects

One important aspect to take into account when trying to ensure the success of a data science team is to offer your data scientists interesting challenges and difficult problems to solve. If your problems are too simple, senior data scientists will become bored. If the problems are impossible to solve because of lack of data or a malfunctioning environment, the data scientists might stay a bit longer and try to fix it, but eventually they will leave if they aren't supported.

REMEMBER

Data scientists have the most sought after competence in the market right now. They know their value, and so should you. They won't waste their value on a company that cannot offer the right opportunities for them to be part of a successful data science team, working on interesting and challenging projects. So, if you're after the experts, you must be ready to have interesting ideas and complex problems to offer them.

Promoting continuous learning

Because data science is an area under constant change, data scientists want to (and should) stay updated on new techniques, methods, and trends appearing in the market. There must be opportunities available to all roles in data science to continue to learn as part of their job.

One way to enable continuous learning is to let data science team members participate in different technical data science conferences or open source projects or venues. Formal training doesn't necessarily keep up with the pace that's needed, and data science is still very much driven from an open source perspective, with regard to technology as well as methodology.

Encouraging research studies

Data science team members should also be allowed to spend time on research, including writing white papers and participating in white paper reading sessions based on work done by colleagues. Because the data science area is evolving *fast*, it's crucial to stay in tune with new methods, research, and technology developments as well as contribute to standardization discussions and open source initiatives.

Building the Team

When building a team of data scientists, you should always focus the scope and purpose around questions that reflect your company's strategic business objectives. This focus could mean, for example, attracting new customers, automating processes, or introducing new, innovative data products in the portfolio.

You want to be able to get your stakeholders and decision-makers on board with your data science ambitions as early as possible and be able to argue for the return on investment (ROI). You should, for example, consider these questions:

>> What will drive an optimal outcome, and what are the incentives?

>> How will the data science team work with stakeholders?

>> How are investments in infrastructure approached with regard to priority, approval process, funding, and management?

>> How will costs be allocated?

>> How will business, legal, IT, and data teams operate without creating unacceptable risk?

An effective communication strategy, clearly defined priorities, and the ability to manage expectations are vital, regardless of which approach you decide to take for structuring and developing your data science capabilities.

Developing smart hiring processes

Many professionals are trying to break into the "sexiest profession of the 21st century," so, as a data science manager, you're sure to get lots of applications, and you'll have to be selective. Take advantage of that and be picky in the right way. Make sure you care about your hiring process.

WARNING

One common area where companies fail is in the trade-off between the short- and long-term perspectives. For instance, it's easy to start thinking that you are late to the data science game and therefore there isn't enough time to recruit all the people you need. That approach is a huge mistake. If you believe that there isn't enough time to find the right talent and to scrutinize your interview and onboarding processes, you probably don't have the time to manage a new employee, either. Creating a great hiring process pays off in the long term.

So, what does a great hiring process look like? For one thing, it doesn't focus only on technical skills. Social skills, like empathy and communication, are undervalued in data science and the disciplines from which data scientists usually emerge, but they're critical for a team. Make this a part of your hiring process.

TIP

Rather than focus on whether you can get along with a candidate, ask yourself whether there is a lens through which this person sees the world that expands the team's knowledge and value. That dimension should be valued as highly as you value other attributes, such as technical ability and domain expertise. This is why it's important to prioritize diversity. That includes diversity of academic discipline and professional experience but also of lived experience and perspective.

When it comes to diversity, a few areas stand out as especially important in data science. First, you should not be focusing on hiring senior people. Not only are they expensive and difficult to get hold of, but less experienced employees tend to not be so influenced by history and can therefore more easily ask questions about why things are done in a certain way. The questions asked are more free of the usual assumptions that more experienced professionals at some point stop being aware of having. It isn't difficult to become obsessed with a particular way of doing things and to forget to question whether a favored approach is still the best solution to a new task.

REMEMBER

Data scientists come from a variety of academic backgrounds, including computer science, math, physics, statistics, and many others. What matters most is having a creative mind coupled with first-rate critical thinking skills.

Another important consideration is to hire individuals whose strengths complement one another, rather than build a team whose members all excel in the same area. Having a person who always sees the big picture, someone who can articulate stories with data, and a visualization wizard working together can collaborate to produce outcomes that none could do independently. It's all about taking advantage of these complementary skills to the greatest extent possible in order to create great solutions that nobody had thought of before.

TIP

One way to make sure that the team actually works as a team and collaborates is to ask team members to regularly read each other's code and check each other's models. It's a great way to foster team collaboration centered around technical discussions. Making sure your team engages in these types of planned collaborative activities helps ensure that you get the most out of this sort of team diversity.

Finally, it's important to build a team that reflects the people whose data you're analyzing: For example, if you're analyzing social media data from an application used only by women, the data science team cannot only consist of men. This is the only way to ensure that you have a resilient team that will ask better questions and have a wider perspective from which to ask these questions. This way, each individual's blind spots are covered by another team member's past experiences and skill set.

Letting your teams evolve organically

When you start building your data science teams, you should begin by having small, versatile teams, where each team encourages team members to "wear many hats" and do lots of different kinds of data science. As the teams mature and prove their value in different ways, roles will become more defined and some activities will likely move to other teams. An example of that is that once data science is more established and understood in the company, activities related to infrastructure, operations, security, and so on are usually handled separately, enabling the data science teams to be more specialized.

And yet, I'd warn against specializing teams too soon. Team specialization works only when team responsibilities are clearly defined and efficient ways of working have been put in place to balance the lack of speed and additional costs associated with multiple teams working together. Because accomplished data scientists are hard to find, let the teams organically evolve into more specialization. (My mantra is "Specialization will come; no need to rush it.") And don't forget to pair up experienced data scientists with less experienced ones. It's usually easy to find smart and driven data scientists who (with a little dedicated coaching) are eager to learn more. This includes learning how to appropriately frame a problem, manage a small project, develop and train a model, integrate with APIs, and put a project into production. And, if you eventually manage to acquire a couple of accomplished data scientists, you already have the structure in place to integrate them into these learning teams to make sure you can get the most out of their vast experience.

Connecting the Team to the Business Purpose

Data scientists are generally purpose driven, so to get the most benefit from their time, they need to have a clear understanding of the task at hand and believe in the business objective behind the projects they're assigned to. There must also be room for prioritizing the ideas coming from the data science team itself. Anchoring your team's work in the context of the data science strategy and the overall business objectives are among the most important jobs a leader of a data science team has to accomplish. Unfortunately, it isn't always an easy job to do.

A data science project often starts with a question from someone outside the team. Often, however, the question that the person asks isn't exactly what the data science team feels should be investigated. Therefore, managing a data science team usually involves a lot of discussion and fine-tuning of questions from stakeholders to better understand the information they actually want and how it will be used.

TIP

Don't let questions or requests become projects for your team until you know exactly what the stakeholder wants to understand and how it will be used. Having clear objectives for the data related questions that come your way is one of the most important things you can provide for your team.

At the same time, stakeholders won't always be able to answer the questions from the data science team, even if they want to. They might not know the full context or long-term objective of the question they're asking, what a finished data science product would look like, or even how they would apply it. To overcome this hurdle, try some of the activities described in this list:

>> **Understand business value**. Ensure that product managers understand the business value of data science. They need to understand it in terms of how it drives business innovation and value and be ready to prioritize it even when they might not understand all aspects of it.

>> **Participate in strategy meetings.** Make sure members of the data science team are regularly invited to product and strategy meetings. This way, they can be part of the creative process rather than merely responding to requests. (It also doesn't hurt to ask a lot of questions.) Integrating data scientists into the business dialogue also contributes to an increased company understanding of the data science approach to business opportunities.

» **Collaborate across organizational borders.** Clearly, data science teams aren't the only ones seeking collaboration with business stakeholders, but it is nevertheless the case that they should be given priority when decisions are made concerning who collaborates with which teams across business divisions. It significantly increases motivation for the data scientists when they know not only that they are contributing to something that they understand but also that their contribution is valued and prioritized by the organization as a whole.

» **Prove the value.** Data science teams need to be able to prove their value. If the team comes up with a new idea, the organization and the data science manager must challenge the team with questions such as "How can we prove that this is contributing to our business?" and "How do we know that this is the best solution?"

Chapter **11**

Approaching a Data Science Organizational Setup

The power of the data revolution remains strong, and companies of various sizes are actively building and expanding their data science teams in a variety of ways. Companies realize that they must be able to use data to improve decision-making and operational efficiency, but they also see that they must have the capacity to create new products and processes based on data-driven insights. In order to do so, companies must embed at the corporate level the necessary organizational and cultural changes it will take to succeed.

The organizational structure needed for the data science team varies based on the size of the company, the number of different business functions there are, the geographical distribution, the company culture, and other similar aspects. However, there are some common factors to consider when integrating data scientists into a larger data-driven organization. This chapter takes a look at these factors.

Finding the Right Organizational Design

To figure out the best team setup for the data science function from an organizational perspective, consider these five main tasks:

>> **Decide where in the organization you want to place the data science function, and then figure out the optimal setup.** For example, do you want a centralized model or a decentralized one?

>> **Align the organizational design with its business functions.** As part of that process, you define and implement an efficient governance structure based on openness and transparency toward the business, and you have to build in decision-making structures that allow for the business to impact which problems and opportunities the data science teams should prioritize.

>> **Ensure that the organizational setup fits with your overall business strategy, including partnership setups.** The structure should also enable data science teams to easily connect to needed data science ecosystems related to data, tools, and models.

REMEMBER

In data science, being part of the ecosystem is essential. The evolution is moving too fast and is too complex and costly to address all by yourself. Moving fast requires companies to share as well as reuse components and capabilities as part of a data science ecosystem. This involves an organizational approach that allows participating in — and contributing to — open source communities and other open frameworks.

>> **Identify which roles you need on the team and how many team members for each role.** Consider how many of the roles can be filled via internal recruitment. This stage includes identifying the needed level of training for the team and ensuring that the company executives engage in the training.

>> **Scale the team over the long term.** Consider how that will be approached and what the timelines are. Will external recruitment be part of the scale-up, or will it be based on growing organically, for example. Also consider standardizing processes and governance structures *before* major scale-up in order to better manage growth.

That's the big picture — the bare outline of what needs to happen. The next few sections fill in the details.

Designing the data science function

Time for a closer look at how to approach the first of the main tasks to consider: Determine the setup of the data science function in your organization. The setup options range from a centralized model to a highly distributed model.

A centralized model is sometimes called a *shared model* or a *center of excellence*, where all the data scientists are working together in the same organizational unit. This model encourages collaboration and cohesiveness of the data science team, allowing team members to bounce ideas off each other and get quick help for questions with the data science work. This setup also allows for on-the-job-training for less experienced data scientists.

In large companies, where the business units are financially strong and independent or where the business units conduct different types of business, there's a tendency to instead choose a distributed or decentralized model. In the distributed model, the business units (BUs) themselves hire their own set of data scientists. This allows data scientists to work closely and more continuously with managers, engineers, and stakeholders. In this setup, data scientists have the opportunity to gain valuable domain expertise as well as insights into the real problems that their colleagues face every day. This setup tends to better empower data science teams, but you also run the risk of duplicating some of the work the teams are doing, because coordination and collaboration across teams in different business units tend to be less pronounced.

WARNING

When small data science teams or even single data scientists are embedded into different business units, it can have the side effect of leaving data scientists overly isolated. If data scientists lack data science peers to discuss and elaborate with, the productivity goes down and motivation drops. There is also a tendency to question isolated data scientists more, since data science is not generally understood in traditional software organizations. The best way to mitigate this is to avoid spreading data scientists too thin in the organization.

The *hybrid* organizational model, consisting of one central unit with one or several data science teams combined with multiple specialized teams embedded in business units across several projects, is starting to emerge as the best proven strategy for many companies. From a data scientist's perspective, the main benefit of this model is the ability to work closer to the real business functions, which can mean gaining more knowledge about how things work in practice. Since the hybrid model adopts aspects of both a centralized and decentralized approach, it balances the benefits and drawbacks of those models. In the hybrid model, the central unit serves as a hub to promote sharing and reuse of best practices and propagates those to each of the distributed data science teams.

Another, less commonly used way of setting up a hybrid model is to have all data scientists assigned to specific business units but report into a common centralized data science unit.

Figure 11-1 shows a graphical illustration of the three different ways to set up your data science function in the company. Which one you should decide to go for depends on aspects such as the maturity of your company, but it is also depends on your data science objective and availability of various data science competencies. If you are setting up a data science function which is more focused on analytics than machine learning and artificial intelligence, for example, the access to required competence is much less of a problem than in the machine learning space. When you can count on having access to all the competence you need, you can design the organization as needed, directly from start. The best model can then be chosen depending on the company size, line of business, and ambition around analytics, rather than being limited by a lack of required data science competence.

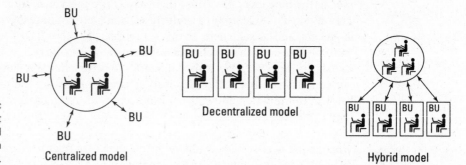

FIGURE 11-1:
The different organizational models for data science teams.

Centralized model

Decentralized model

Hybrid model

REMEMBER

In the machine learning and artificial intelligence space, where the availability of data scientists is scarce and the general understanding of how ML/AI techniques shall be utilized in the company is much less understood, the situation is different. You might come to the conclusion that a decentralized model is what you want, but you realize that with so few data scientists available to recruit, you will spread yourself too thin in the company and not be able to achieve your objectives using that approach. Therefore, starting with a centralized model which offers an adequate number of data science teams working together to make a difference might be the only way to get started. However, over time a centralized model might transform into a hybrid model, as your pool of data scientists grows organically, but also through recruitment. Also, once the area of machine learning becomes more of a commodity in the industry, data scientists can become an integral part of any development unit, and there is no longer any need for the centralized unit keeping it all together.

Evaluating the benefits of a center of excellence for data science

Going for the centralized model for your data science function as your preference or as a necessary starting point really means setting up a central unit in the company, also known as a data science *center of excellence* (CoE). Although there are different opinions about the effectiveness and efficiency of CoE's in the industry, there are still several proven benefits of using a centralized approach when building up a data science function in the company, as listed below.

>> **Speed:** A data science CoE is essential to accelerate the data-driven approach across the business at scale. It reduces implementation times drastically and therefore the time-to-market span needed to deploy new data-driven products and services.

>> **Reuse:** A CoE facilitates sharing best practices and methodologies across different teams in the organization.

>> **Evolution:** A CoE makes it easier to allocate time for the team to stay updated on market trends and the technology evolution in data science.

>> **Skill sets:** The CoE equips the business with the needed set of data science skills when it is needed.

>> **Terminology:** A centralized function helps ensure that the entire organization uses a common terminology and "speaks the same language" by developing a common set of standards while deploying data science methods and techniques.

>> **Culture:** A CoE can serve as the driver for cultural change to become a data-obsessed and action-driven organization when it comes to using data science techniques.

It isn't necessary to set up the centralized CoE function strictly according to the centralized model. You can use a light version of the hybrid model and still gain the benefits of a central CoE. Having a 80–20 weighted setup might still work with the data science resource availability — meaning that you have 80% of the COE centrally located and 20% embedded in the business units and then you can let it grow over time towards a 50–50 or even 20–80 approach.

Identifying success factors for a data science center of excellence

If you want to ensure that your CoE delivers real business value to your company, you have to make sure that it succeeds in achieving these three distinct goals:

>> **The CoE needs to be seen as an enabler of business value:** In other words, the CoE should be recognized as capable of enabling a deep cultural change around leveraging automation, analytics, machine learning, and artificial intelligence. That should include having the ability to attract the best talent possible and be generally viewed as a driver of value.

>> **The CoE needs to be seen as an autonomous entity yet fully supported by management.** The CoE has to function as an independent unit that owns the tools, standards, and methodologies in data science. It cannot be up to anyone in the organization to suboptimize infrastructures and tool sets for specific product or service benefits in various areas rather than for the overall company value. The CoE should also continuously engage supportive senior leadership to further embed data science into the organization as part of its day-to-day business.

>> **The CoE needs to be impact-oriented.** The unit should prioritize work on use cases aligned with strategic priorities and utilize a value-driven use case roadmap with a quantifiable impact.

Making sure that your CoE achieves all three goals significantly increases the chance of establishing an efficient and successful data science center-of-excellence function.

Applying a Common Data Science Function

You have several important decisions to make when approaching the establishment of a data science function common across the company. For larger enterprises, geographical location is usually one of the major decisions to address. And, if you start with the important aspect of where the common data science function should be placed, it might seem that co-locating it with the company headquarters could be a good idea. However, because this is a strategically important decision, make sure that it's based on actual data as well as on well-thought-out selection criteria. Let's look into this a bit further.

Selecting a location

In a traditional center of excellence focused on analytics rather than machine intelligence, the actual location usually isn't an important factor. And yet, since a common data science function usually requires not only niche skills, which are difficult to acquire, but also talent availability for future potential as well as industry ecosystem presence to secure alignment and influence on market standards as they are evolving, placing the data science function at the same location as the headquarters might not make the most sense. However, this of course depends on how well the headquarters fulfills the chosen location selection criteria.

You also have to consider other aspects related to location. The following list describes the four main selection criteria for location, listed in a more structured way, including an estimation of their importance in the overall decision:

>> **Talent:** Refers to the availability of a new and existing talent pool in actual figures at or near the location in question. This criterion is vital — let it carry about half the total weight of the decision. It includes aspects such as tech-related graduates, the existing talent pool in needed roles and competence areas, and the quality of education in the area.

>> **Ecosystem:** Refers to a set of factors that allows for smoother running of data science teams, thanks to qualitative characteristics of locations, such as capacity to retain and attract talent, availability of data scientists and other key competencies, availability of the latest technologies, capacity for innovation, number of start-ups, and potential for venture capital funding. This important criterion should carry about a third of the total weight of the decision.

>> **Infrastructure:** This is all about the practical realization of the data science environment, including good connectivity, data links, the availability of the data itself, and the digital channels you can utilize. (I'd weight it around 10 percent.) It's about making sure that the infrastructure is making the data science environment easy to operate and use for employees as well, including aspects like real estate availability, attractive business and living environments, and airports and other transportation facilities supporting good location accessibility.

>> **Cost:** This refers to cost indications for mainly three areas — labour and real estate costs, as well as salary inflation. However, this criterion is much less important than availability of the right talent and competence and therefore carries only around 10 percent of the weight of the decision.

REMEMBER

Even if you're planning for a centralized setup for your data science function, you can still distribute that function to several geographical locations. Doing so may even be advisable, especially if it means accessing more and better talent as well as improving the ability to start tapping into existing data science ecosystems. (The fact of the matter is, there's little chance of fulfilling all the criteria in a single location, so you might be forced to branch out anyway.)

Approaching ways of working

After you agree on the location(s) of your data science function, it's time to start thinking of ways to make the data science function work for you. Important aspects to consider are, of course, how to make sure the new function is both effective (doing the right things) and efficient (doing things right), as well as keeping the rest of the organization feeling that it's proving its value.

REMEMBER

If set up correctly, the new data science function will play an important role in your organization by bringing together the different business units and finding clear and agreed-on responsibilities related to the IT function.

Figure 11-2 explains how some of the interactions between the business units and the common data science function could look like.

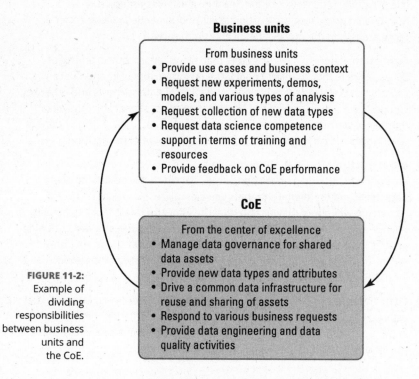

Business units

From business units
- Provide use cases and business context
- Request new experiments, demos, models, and various types of analysis
- Request collection of new data types
- Request data science competence support in terms of training and resources
- Provide feedback on CoE performance

CoE

From the center of excellence
- Manage data governance for shared data assets
- Provide new data types and attributes
- Drive a common data infrastructure for reuse and sharing of assets
- Respond to various business requests
- Provide data engineering and data quality activities

FIGURE 11-2:
Example of dividing responsibilities between business units and the CoE.

Figure 11-2 exemplifies how the interaction can work, but keep in mind that you have many aspects to consider when dividing up roles and responsibilities. Don't be too strict when it comes to what's being done by which unit. If senior data scientists are embedded in the business units and are capable of driving certain strategic areas, let them. Empower people to take charge and make a difference using data science. (This is the long-term goal, anyway.) Just make sure that these distributed groups don't become too isolated and disconnected from the common data science function. (One way to ensure the necessary degree of integration is to insist that such groups share models and insights through the common team, including following agreed-on company standards and principles.)

TIP

Encourage employees to enhance their skills in data science by attending recommended training programs and exploring data and use cases in various areas. As the pool of data science employees grows, working together to carry out the data science function should naturally lead to different teams and groups of people finding ways to network and share insights and learnings across business segments.

REMEMBER

Though it's important to make sure that the IT function has a role to play in the new data-driven organization being built, keep in mind that there is always a balance when it comes to involving the internal IT functions. It varies, of course, from company to company, but my personal experience is that the IT function usually wants to do more than it's capable of, often leading to situations where the IT function makes promises they can never deliver on — not because they don't want to, but because they are driven mainly by cost and they lack the business context needed to understand priorities and make the necessary strategic decisions.

Given this reality, clearly separate the tasks that IT is responsible for in the area of data science and the ones the data science team is responsible for. Perhaps you'll have IT focus on the storage infrastructure or certain aspects of data management. Or perhaps you'll want them to focus on operating the data governance model from a system perspective. Yet no matter how you divide up responsibilities, make clear to IT that taking care of their responsibilities in a data science context is not merely a minor IT issue, but rather a crucial part of the overall business operations in the company.

TIP

IT departments tend to be better at operating solutions than at defining and developing them. So, whatever area you make IT responsible for, do not allocate to them the overall responsibility for data science. They simply lack the business competence and data science competence to manage it successfully.

Managing expectations

Another important aspect to consider is to clearly communicate the common data science function's purpose. Everyone needs to understand that the idea is not to have all the data science work be done in that common function. Far from it. For a company to become data driven and focus on data science throughout, it is vital that this is everyone's business in the company.

So, what is the role of this common data science function? First and foremost, it is to secure cooperation across the company, facilitate the sharing of data and algorithms, support the organization with highly skilled data scientists, and provide other relevant competencies to achieve company objectives. All this needs to happen regardless of whether or not the activities are driven from a centralized function or if competence is injected into the business units to enable and accelerate desired results.

You want to make sure that the organization does not perceive this new common data science function as "responsible" for making data science happen in the company. That is not a desirable situation, since it puts the employees in a state of mind where it is no longer a company ambition or everyone's responsibility to make data science happen. The perception then becomes that it is the common data science function's role to make it happen.

Therefore, to clearly state the role of the common data science function is very important. It is a supporting organization, designed to enable the company to succeed with the data science investment. For some companies, this function is of more importance when starting up than in the longer perspective, once data science is more known and the competence is more spread. But for other companies, the common data science function becomes the hub of the data-driven approach, vital for the survival of data science in the company even from a long-term perspective.

Selecting an execution approach

After you've made all the strategic decisions in terms of where the common data science function will be located and everyone agrees on how the new data science function will operate in relation to the rest of the organization, it's time to get started. But where do you start? In my mind, you have only two logical ways to go about it: the big bang approach or the use-case-driven, scale-up approach. The next couple of sections describe exactly what's involved in the two approaches and list their benefits and drawbacks.

The big-bang approach

One way that you can establish the new common data science function is by using the big bang approach, where you directly define and implement the long-term vision and target organization with the desired head count and the full-blown data science infrastructure all at once. This includes the full data scope, data architecture, data governance framework, competence programs and other aspects, supported by a clear rollout plan that's consistent with the company's strategic priorities.

The benefits of this approach are that it communicates a strong company commitment to data science, both internally toward employees and externally toward the market, customers, vendors, and even competitors. This approach is likely to generate motivation and interest among employees, where they feel empowered and inspired to pursue new opportunities in the area. It's also likely that the investment actually happens, because company management would lose too much credibility if they chose not to honor a clearly communicated commitment.

WARNING

Potential drawbacks of the big bang approach revolve around the idea that the data science organizational setup might be perceived as being forced onto the organization from the top down, without trying it out first or anchoring it in the organization. It's also a huge investment to make up front, before any value-added of the data science investment has been proven. On top of that, the big bang approach makes it difficult for the new common data science function to find time to prove its value and gain support from the business functions when it's stuck on defining a data science strategy, hiring the necessary data science specialists, building up a solid infrastructure, securing data, and identifying and prioritizing first cases of interest.

The use-case-driven scale-up approach

If the big bang approach doesn't fit your company's needs, perhaps you can introduce the new common data science function by using the use-case-driven, scale-up approach. This more cautious approach starts with a detailed design of the strategic steps to take, in which order, and focused on the type of value. This approach enables you to strategically select cases that will prove the value both internally (for the employees, securing commitment and empowerment) and externally (generating external commitment by proving how real value can be achieved using data science in areas that had previously proven to be intractable).

The benefits from the use case-driven approach stem from the fact that the upfront investment is much less and you also get to prove the use value of a data science function on a case-by-case basis *before* scaling up for the next step. You can pick and choose between short-term benefits or high-value use cases. Finally, you gain room to breathe by setting a slower pace, which means that you have time to anchor the setup and approach among employees, which means that they can become more involved in defining requirements and strategic priorities. You can also stop at a less-advanced level of the setup without wasting time or money, if that turns out to be better for the company.

WARNING

In the use-case-driven approach, you run the risk of never proving the worth of a data science function sufficiently enough to stakeholders to actually get the common data science function you need. You get stuck in proving case after case and never gain the final approval, which means that the company never gains the benefits of scale, where a unit can drive a common data science strategy that promotes the sharing and reuse of data, models and insights across the company.

Chapter **12**

Positioning the Role of the Chief Data Officer (CDO)

Assuming that there is strategic agreement on setting up a common data science function in your company, who will then be the strategic spokesperson for all data science efforts? Who will ensure that data science is understood and included on corporate leadership's agenda? It's more than giving a boardroom presentation now and then in order to make sure that the top brass has an idea of what's going on; it's about making sure that data science becomes a vital part of the everyday agenda. Here is where the CDO role becomes extremely important.

The *chief data officer (CDO)* is the corporate officer responsible for overseeing a range of data related functions to ensure that your organization gets the most benefit from what could be its most valuable asset — its data. The position's scope includes enterprise-wide governance and the utilization of data and information as an asset, including all aspects related to data architecture, data management and governance, data utilization, and data commercialization realized through the data science function or functions, regardless of whether it's through a centralized, decentralized, or hybrid setup.

However, the actual placement of the CDO in the corporate structure is not a given, and many examples exist. Although the significance of the role is rising with increased understanding of the value of data, it's still rarely the case that the CDO reports directly to the chief executive officer (CEO). Usually, the CDO is linked to the functions of the CIO (chief information officer), CTO (chief technology officer), or even CSO (chief strategy officer) or CMO (chief marketing officer).

Scoping the Role of the Chief Data Officer (CDO)

To describe the scope of a CDO, you first need to determine how the position relates to that of a chief analytics officer (CAO). Although the CDO and the CAO are two distinct roles, these two positions are customarily held by the same person or else only one role, the CDO role, is used, but when these roles are combined into one, it is sometimes also referred to as a CDAO role. However, in situations where these two roles are separate and held by two different functions, the main difference can be summarized by the title itself: data versus analytics. The main difference in the area of responsibility is captured in Figure 12-1.

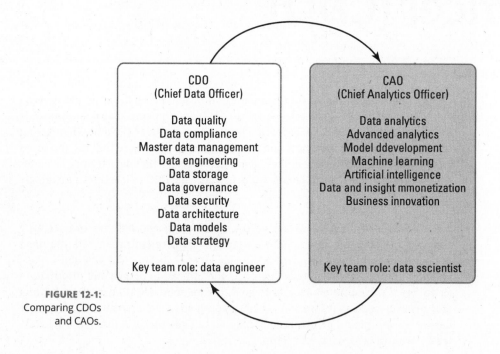

FIGURE 12-1:
Comparing CDOs
and CAOs.

If the CDO is about data enablement, the CAO role is about how you drive insights from that data — in other words, how you make the data actionable. The CAO is much more likely to have a data science background, and the CDO, a data engineering one.

Let me clarify that both the CDO and CAO positions are essentially carve-outs from the traditional CIO job in the IT domain. In the case of the CDO role, the CIO may well have welcomed eliminating some of these responsibilities. However, when it comes to the portion of the CIO role that is about IT cost for new data assets, the CIO can be deeply challenged by the new realities of big data. Both the CDO and CAO would need to argue for initially storing huge amounts of data, even if its value isn't immediately evident. These aspects pose a significant but important change in mindset for the CIO role, one that probably would not have been recognized the same way without the introduction of the CDO and CAO roles.

REMEMBER

When it comes down to the practical implementation of this role, it's all about securing an efficient end-to-end setup and execution of the overall data science strategy across the company. Which solution can function as the most optimized setup for your company will depend on your line of business and how you're organized. Just remember to keep these two roles working closely together, including the teams that are attached to the roles. Separation between data engineering teams and data science teams is not advisable, especially since there is a need for a strong common foundation based on these two parts in data science. The teams may have a different focus, but they need to work closely together in an iterative way to achieve the speed, flexibility, and results expected by the business stakeholders.

In cases where the CDO role is the only role in a company — where CDO and CAO responsibilities have been merged, in other words — the mandate of the CDO role is usually described in terms of Figure 12-2. The area referring to the business mandate refers mainly to driving areas such as:

>> Establishing a company-wide data science strategy

>> Ensuring the adoption of a dominant data culture within the company

>> Building trust and legitimizing the usage of data.

>> Driving data usage for competitive advantage

>> Enabling data-driven business opportunities

>> Ensuring that principles for legal, security, and ethical compliance are upheld

When it comes to the technology mandate, the following aspects are usually included:

» Establishing a data architecture

» Securing efficient data governance

» Building an infrastructure that enables explorative and experimental data science

» Promoting the continuous evolution of data science methods and techniques

» Designing principles for legal, security, and ethical aspects

» Securing efficient data and model life-cycle management

Business
– Aspects that aim to generate data science understanding, trust and compliance

Technology
– Activities that aim to secure a solid foundation for practically addressing opportunities and challenges

FIGURE 12-2:
The mandate of the CDO role, when it includes CAO responsibilities.

Data foundation services	Data democratization services	Data enrichment Services

Notice that, in Figure 12–2, I highlight three distinct services a merged CDO/CAO must manage. This list gives a sense of what each service entails:

» **Data foundation services** includes areas such as managing data provenance and data stewardship, data architecture definition, data standards, and data governance as well as risk management and various types of compliance.

» **Data democratization services** refers to areas such as establishing a data-driven organizational culture through the business validation of data initiatives, making non-sensitive data available to all employees (data democratization) as well as proper evaluation of available data.

» **Data enrichment services** includes areas such as deriving and creating value from data through applying various analytical and machine based methods and techniques, exploring and experimenting with data as well as ensuring a smart and efficient data lake/data pipeline setup supporting a value realization of the data science investment.

Explaining Why a Chief Data Officer Is Needed

In addition to exploring revenue opportunities, developing acquisition strategies, and formulating customer data policies, the chief data officer is charged with explaining the strategic value of data and its important role as a business asset and revenue driver to executives, employees, and customers. Chief data officers are successful when they establish authority, secure budget and resources, and monetize their organization's information assets.

REMEMBER

The role of the CDO is relatively new and evolving quickly, but one convenient way of looking at this role is to regard this person as the main defender and chief steward of an organization's data assets. Organizations have a growing stake in aggregating data and using it to make better decisions. As such, the CDO is tasked with using data to automate business processes, better understand customers, develop better relationships with partners, and, ultimately, sell more products and services faster.

A number of recent analyses of market trends claim that by 2020, 50 percent of leading organizations will have CDOs with similar levels of strategy influence and authority as CIOs. CDOs can establish a leadership role by aligning their priorities with those of their organizations. To a great extent, the role is about change management. CDOs first need to define the role and manage expectations by considering the resources made available to them.

WARNING

Despite the recent buzz around the concept of CDOs, in practice it has proven to be difficult for them to secure anything other than moderate budgets and limited resources when reporting into existing business units, like IT. Moreover, with usually only a handful of personnel, the CDO group must operate virtually by tagging onto, and inserting themselves into, existing projects and initiatives throughout the organization. This, of course, isn't an optimal setup when it comes to proving the value of the CDO function.

TIP

For the CDO function to truly pay off, you need to break up the silos and optimize the company structures around the data. It's all about splitting up the scope of responsibility for your IT department so that you can separate out the data assets from the technology assets and let the CDO take ownership of the data and information part, as well as the full data science cycle when there is no CAO role appointed.

Establishing the CDO Role

The main task of a chief data officer is to transform the company culture to one that embraces an insight- and data-driven approach. The value of this should not be underestimated. Establishing a data-first mentality pushes managers at all levels to treat data as an asset. When managers start asking for data in new ways and view data science competence as a core skill set, they will drive a new focus and priority across all levels of the company. Changing a company's cultural mindset is no easy task — it takes more than just a few workshops and a series of earnest directives from above to get the job done. The idea that one must treat data as an asset needs to be firmly anchored in the upper management layer — hence the importance of the CDO role.

Let this list of common CDO mandates across various industries serve as an inspiration for what can fit in your company. A CDO can

>> Establish a data-driven culture with effective data governance. As part of that project, it is also vital to gain trust the trust of the various business units so that a company-wide sense of data ownership can be established. The idea here is to *foster,* not hinder, the efficient use of data.

>> Drive data stewardship by implementing useful data management principles and standards according to an agreed-on data strategy. It is also important to industrialize efficient data-quality management, since ensuring data quality throughout the data life-cycle requires substantial system support.

>> Influence decision-making throughout the company, supported by quality data that allows for analytics and insights that can be trusted.

>> Influence return on investment (ROI) through data enrichment and an improved understanding of customer needs. The idea here is to assist the business in delivering superior customer experiences by using data in all applicable ways.

>> Encourage continuous data-driven innovation through experimentation and exploration of data, including making sure that the data infrastructure enables this to be done effectively and efficiently.

As in most roles, you always face a set of challenges impacting the level of success that can be achieved. Just by being aware of these challenges, you'll be better able to avoid them or at least have strategies in place to deal with them if, or when, they arise. The following list summarizes some of the most common challenges related to the CDO role:

>> **Assigning business meaning to data:** A CDO must make sure that data is prioritized, processed, and analyzed in the right business context in order to generate valuable and actionable insights. One aspect of this could be the timing of the *insight generation:* If the time it takes to generate the insight is too slow from a business usefulness perspective, the insight, rather than steering the business, would merely confirm what just happened.

>> **Establishing and improving data governance:** The area of data governance is crucial for keeping data integrity during the life cycle of the data. It's not just about managing access rights to the data, but very much about managing data quality and trustworthiness. As soon as manual tasks are part of data processing activities, you run the risk of introducing errors or bias into the data sets, making analysis and insights derived from the data less reliable. Automation-driven data processing is therefore a vital part of improving data governance.

>> **Promoting a culture of data sharing:** In practice, it is the common data science function that will drive the data science activities across the company as it promotes data sharing from day to day. However, it's also significant to have a strong spokesperson in management who enforces an understanding and acceptance of data sharing. The main focus should be to establish that you won't be able to derive value from data unless the data is used and shared. Locking in data by limiting access and usage is the wrong way to go — an open data policy within the company should be the starting point. With that in place, you can then limit access on sensitive data and still ensure that such limitations are well motivated and cannot be solved by using anonymization or other means.

>> **Building new revenue streams, enriching and leveraging data-as-a-service:** A person in the CDO role also promotes and supports innovation related to data monetization. This is an inspiring task, but not always an easy one. Driving new business solutions that require data-driven business models and potentially completely new delivery models might inspire a lot of fear and resistance in the company and with management in general. Remember that new data monetization ideas might challenge existing business models and be seen as a threat rather than as new and promising business potential. "Be mindful and move slowly" is a good approach. Using examples from other companies or other lines of business can also prove effective in gaining trust and support from management for new data monetization ideas.

>> **Delivering Know Your Customer (KYC) in a real and tangible fashion:** Utilizing data in such a way that it can enable data-driven sales is a proactive and efficient way to strengthen customer relationships and prove how knowledgeable the company is. However, there should be a balance here in how data is obtained and used: The last thing you want is for your customers to feel intruded on. You want the company to be perceived as proactive and

forward-leaning with an innovative drive that is looking out for its customers, not as a company that invades its customers' private sphere, using their data to turn it into an advantage in negotiations. The CDO must master that balance and find a way to strategically toe that line — a line that can be quite different, depending on your business objectives and line of business.

>> **Fixing legacy data infrastructure issues while investing in the future of data science:** This challenge is tricky to handle. You can't just switch from old legacy infrastructures (often focused on data transactions and reporting) to the new, often cloud based infrastructures focused on handling data enablement and monetization in completely new and different ways. There has to be a transition period, and during that period you have to deal with maintaining the legacy infrastructure, even when it's costly and feels like an unnecessary burden. At the same time, management is expecting fast and tangible results, based on the major investments needed. But be aware that the longer you have the two infrastructures working in parallel, the harder it is to truly get people to change their mindset and behavior toward the new data-driven approach realized through the new infrastructure investments. Neither will you see any real savings, because you need to cost-manage both the legacy environments and the new environments. Even if it proves difficult, try to drive this swap with an ambitious timeline, keeping in mind that there's no going back.

The Future of the CDO Role

The appointment of chief data officers in large organizations has ramped up in recent years as companies realize the importance of data as a fundamental business asset, with nine out of ten enterprises expected to fill this role by 2020.

Businesses are increasingly placing the chief data officer (CDO) at the hub of their operations, with a responsibility linked to all functions, as the dependence on information and data-driven decision-making increases. At the same time, the CDO role is becoming broader and less technical. In many firms, smarter analytics tools are rendering moot some of the complex data science formerly required. Only a few years ago, a CDO would typically have been expected to have a highly technical background, but now the role is emerging from various parts of the business.

TIP

CDOs now need to know far more about business contexts, strategies, and risks than what was required just a decade ago. The data in focus today isn't just "customer data" — it's everything in a business, and that's why the role is changing. The ability to act on real-time data is central to business strategies, which is why elevating the role of chief data officer as an all-encompassing responsibility is such a big deal. At the senior level, the CDO needs to be someone who understands the business, is able to equip teams with the right infrastructure and tool set, and knows how to make data accessibility both efficient and simple.

WARNING

So the role of the CDO is obviously evolving, in terms of both its placement in the organizational hierarchy and its increasing scope and mandate. As the CDO role matures, it seems to be following a certain path, especially in those companies that established the role early on. You can see a high-level view of these steps on the way to maturity in Figure 12-3.

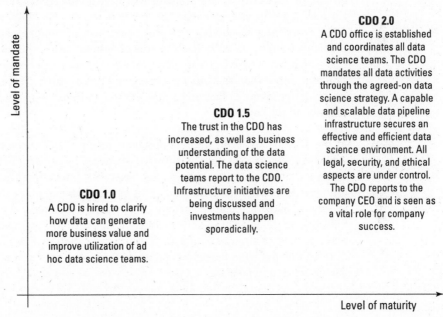

CDO 2.0
A CDO office is established and coordinates all data science teams. The CDO mandates all data activities through the agreed-on data science strategy. A capable and scalable data pipeline infrastructure secures an effective and efficient data science environment. All legal, security, and ethical aspects are under control. The CDO reports to the company CEO and is seen as a vital role for company success.

CDO 1.5
The trust in the CDO has increased, as well as business understanding of the data potential. The data science teams report to the CDO. Infrastructure initiatives are being discussed and investments happen sporadically.

CDO 1.0
A CDO is hired to clarify how data can generate more business value and improve utilization of ad hoc data science teams.

Level of mandate

Level of maturity

FIGURE 12-3: The evolution of the CDO role.

When you're talking about a CDO 1.0 company context (refer to Figure 12-3), you probably start out by testing some initial initiatives, which usually means hiring data scientists sporadically across the company. After you determine that the piecemeal approach isn't generating much value, you usually establish a few data science teams as supporting roles around the data scientists. Then, finally, a CDO is hired to try to bring some order to the chaos, making sure that the data science teams are utilized efficiently. The person in the CDO role usually reports to a C-level executive in the company management team or one management level below.

In the CDO 1.5 context, some recognition and trust is starting to happen around the role as such, and common investments are being made. There is nevertheless still a lack of company-wide strategic alignment, and a lot of ad hoc activities continue to pop up. However, some alignment between different data science teams is usually ongoing, and management is starting to express its expectations when it comes to results. At this maturity level, the CDO isn't yet part of the company management team.

Finally, in the CDO 2.0 maturity level, the company truly recognizes the importance of the CDO role for company success. Usually, a CDO office is established, the CDO reports directly to the CEO, and all activities and investments are driven from an agreed-on and approved data science strategy. Data science organization setup is agreed on and coordinated throughout the company by way of the CDO office, which also ensures standards, principles, and infrastructure alignment.

So, where can CDOs turn for assistance to drive up the recognition and maturity of the role? Many problems for the CDO relate to proving the stability of the function when everything is evolving *fast*. When members of company management have problems keeping up with how the area of data science continuously transforms, it is seen as an area to be treated differently — more like a start-up or an innovation unit rather than as a business function like any other. This sidelining, which is a major problem, is hindering the CDO role in becoming a vital and integrated function in the company.

WARNING

At the day-to-day level, the real problems facing the CDO come from having to wade through the vast number of services offered by the data industry: transformation agencies, cloud services, data cleaners, and algorithm designers, for example. How can a CDO find the right services among all of this? In this case, success is hard to judge, especially in a role that has yet to be well defined by industry, whereas failure can be pretty obvious. If your company is front page news because of a major data breach or privacy violation, it's a bad day to be the CDO. To find out what makes a good day — well, that requires more companies to dare to trust, and invest in, a CDO.

Chapter **13**

Acquiring Resources and Competencies

Nearly every company now has the ability to collect data, and the amount of data is growing larger and larger. This has led to a higher demand for employees with specialized skills who can effectively organize and analyze this data to glean business insights. Unfortunately, not only does the demand for data scientists surpass the available supply, many of the aspiring data scientists in the market don't have the skillset or experience needed for available positions.

WARNING

The specialized, complex nature of data science work poses a significant problem for hiring. In fact, there's still genuine confusion in the job market about what the term *data scientist* actually means. There are often specific technical requirements that different roles within the data science organization demand, but there needs to be a common understanding of what is required for a data science team to be successful.

Identifying the Roles in a Data Science Team

In the past couple of years, an avalanche of different data science roles has overwhelmed the market, and for someone who has little or no experience in the field, it's hard to get a general understanding of how these roles differ and which core skills are actually required. The fact is that these different roles are often given different titles, but tend to refer to the same or similar jobs — admittedly, sometimes with overlapping responsibilities. This crazy-quilt of job titles and job responsibilities is yet another area in data science that is in need of more standardization.

Before attempting some hard-and-fast role definitions, then, let me start by sketching out the different task sets you'd typically find on a data science team. (See Figure 13-1.) The idea here is to scope the high-level competence areas that need to be covered on a data science team, regardless of who actually carries out which task. The three main areas are mathematics/statistics, computer science, and business domain knowledge.

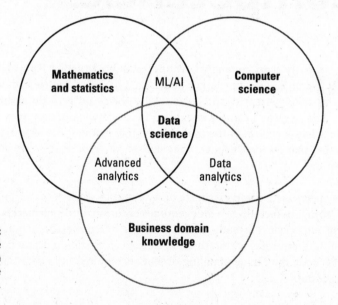

FIGURE 13-1:
Competence
areas needed on
a data science
team.

Figure 13-1 shows the easy part because there's general agreement on which competencies are required for a successful and efficient data science team — though you still need to define the roles and areas of responsibility for each team member. The definitions in this section aim to give you a general understanding of the most important roles you'll need on your data science team. Just remember that variants may apply, depending on your own specific setup and strategic focus.

Data scientist

In general terms, a *data scientist* produces mathematical models for the purposes of prediction. And, because the development and interpretation of mathematical models requires deep technical knowledge, most data scientists have graduate level training in computer science, mathematics, or statistics. Data scientists also need strong programming skills in order to effectively leverage the range of available software tools. Aside from being technically savvy, data scientists need critical thinking skills, based on common sense as well as on a thorough understanding of a company's business objectives in order to produce high quality models.

REMEMBER

Sometimes, a role referred to as *data analyst* is set apart from the data scientist role. In such cases, the data analyst role is like the Sherlock Holmes of the data science team in that they focus on collecting and interpreting data as well as analyzing patterns and trends in the data which they draw conclusions from in a business context. The data analyst must master languages like R, Python, SQL, and C, and, just like the data scientist, the skills and talents that are needed for this role are diverse and span the entire spectrum of tasks in the data science process. And, to top it all off, a data analyst must demonstrate a healthy I-can-figure-it-out attitude. It's really up to you to decide whether you want to have all your company's data scientists take up the tasks associated with a data analyst or if you want to set up a data analyst as a separate role.

Within the role of the data scientist, you'll find another, more traditional role hidden away: the statistician. In historical terms, the statistician was the leader when it came to data and the insights it could provide. Although often forgotten or replaced by fancier-sounding job titles, the statistician role represents what the data science field stands for: getting useful insights from data. With their strong background in statistical theories and methodologies, and a logically oriented mindset, statisticians harvest the data and turn it into information and knowledge. They can handle all sorts of data. What's more, thanks to the quantitative background, modern statisticians are often able to quickly master new technologies and use these to boost their intellectual capacities. A statistician brings to the table the magic of mathematics with insights that have the ability to radically transform businesses.

Data engineer

The role of the *data engineer* is fundamental for data science. Without data, there cannot be any data science, and the job of data scientists is a) quite impossible if the requisite data isn't available and b) definitely daunting if the data is available but only on an inconsistent basis. The problem of inconsistency is frequently faced by data scientists, who often complain that too much of their time is spent on data acquisition and cleaning. That's where the data engineer comes in: This person's role is to create consistent and easily accessible data pipelines for consumption by data scientists. In other words, data engineers are responsible for the mechanics of data ingestion, processing, and storage, all of which should be invisible to the data scientists.

If you're dealing with small data sets, data engineering essentially consists of entering some numbers into a spreadsheet. When you operate at a more impressive scale, data engineering becomes a sophisticated discipline in its own right. Someone on your team will need to take responsibility for dealing with the tricky engineering aspects of delivering data that the rest of your staff can work with.

REMEMBER

Data engineers don't need to know anything about machine learning (ML) or statistics to be successful. They don't even need to be inside the core data science team, but could be part of a larger, separate data engineering team that supplies data to all data science teams. Based on my experience, however, you should never place your data engineers and data scientists too far apart from one other organizationally. If these roles are separated into different organizations, with potentially different priorities, this could heavily impact the data science team productivity. Data science methods are quite experimental and iterative in nature, which means that it must be possible to continuously modify data sets as the analysis and algorithm development progress. For that to happen, data scientists need to be able to rely on a prompt response from the data engineers if trouble arises. Without that rapid response, you run the risk of slowing down a data science team's productivity.

Machine learning engineer

Data scientists build mathematical models, and data engineers make data available to data scientists as the "raw material" from which mathematical models are derived. To complete the picture, these models must first be deployed (put into operation, in other words), and, second, they must be able to act on the insights gained from data analysis in order to produce business value. This task is the purview of the *machine learning engineer*.

The machine learning engineer role is a software engineering role, with the difference that the ML engineer has considerable expertise in data science. This expertise is required because ML engineers bridge the gap between the data scientists and the broader software engineering organization. With ML engineers dedicated to model deployment, the data scientists are free to continually develop and refine their models.

REMEMBER

Variants are always a possibility when setting up a data science team. For example, the ML engineer deployment responsibilities are often also handled by the data scientist role. Depending on the importance of the operational environment for your specific business, it can make more or less sense to separate this role from the data scientist responsibilities. It is, again, up to you to implement this responsibility within the team.

Data architect

A *data architecture* is a set of rules, policies, standards and models that govern and define the type of data collected and how it is used, stored, managed and integrated within an organization and its data systems. The person charged with designing, creating, deploying, and managing an organization's data architecture is called a *data architect,* and they definitely need to be accounted for on the data science team. (For more details on data architecture, see Chapter 14.)

Data architects define how the data will be stored, consumed, protected, integrated, and managed by different data entities and IT systems, as well as any applications using or processing that data in some way. A data architect usually isn't a permanent member of a single data science team, but rather serves several data science teams, working closely with each team to ensure efficiency and high productivity.

Business analyst

The *business analyst* often comes from a different background when compared to the rest of the team. Though often less technically oriented, business analysts make up for it with their deep knowledge of the different business processes running through the company — operational processes (the sales process), management processes (the budget process) and supporting processes (the hiring process). The business analyst masters the skill of linking data insights to actionable business insights and can use storytelling techniques to spread the message across the entire organization. This person often acts as the intermediary between the "business guys" and the "techies."

Software engineer

The main role of a *software engineer* on a data science team is to secure more structure in the data science work so that it becomes more applied and less experimental in nature. The software engineer has an important role in terms of collaborating with the data scientists, data architects, and business analysts to ensure alignment between the business objectives and the actual solution. You could say that a software engineer is responsible for bringing a software engineering culture into the data science process. That is a massive undertaking, and it involves tasks such as automating the data science team infrastructure, ensuring continuous integration and version control, automating testing, and developing APIs to help integrate data products into various applications.

Domain expert

It takes a lot of conversations to make data science work. Data scientists can't do it on their own. Success in data science requires a multiskilled project team with data scientists and domain experts working closely together. The *domain expert* brings the technical understanding of her area of expertise, sometimes combined with a thorough business understanding of that area as well. It usually includes familiarity with the basics of data analysis, which means that domain experts can support many roles on the data science team. However, the domain expert usually isn't a permanent member of a data science team; more often than not, that person is brought in for specific tasks, like validating data or providing analysis or insight from an expert perspective. Sometimes the domain expert is allocated for longer periods to a certain team, depending on the task and focus. Sometimes one or several domain experts are assigned to support multiple teams at the same time.

Seeing What Makes a Great Data Scientist

There's a lot of promise connected with the data scientist role. The problem is not only that the perfect data scientist doesn't exist, but also that the few truly skilled ones are too few and too difficult to get hold of in the current marketplace. So, what should you be doing instead of searching for the perfect data scientist?

TIP

The focus should be on finding someone with the ability to solve the specific problems your company is focusing on — or, to be even more specific, what your own data science team is focusing on. It's not about hiring the perfect data scientist and hoping that they're going to do all the things that you need done, now and in the future. Instead, it's better to hire someone with the specific skills needed to meet the clearly defined organizational objectives you know of today.

For instance, think about whether your need is more related to ad hoc data analysis or product development. Companies that have a greater need for ad hoc data insights should look for data scientists with a flexible and experimental approach and an ability to communicate well with the business side of the organization. On the other hand, if product development is more important in relation to the problems you're trying to solve, you should look for strong software engineering skills, with a firm base in the engineering process in combination with their analytical skills.

If you're hoping to find a handy checklist of all the critical skills that you should be looking for when hiring a data scientist, you'll be sorely disappointed. The fact is, not even a basic description of important traits the role should possess is agreed on across the industry. There are many opinions and ideas about it, but again the lack of standardization is troublesome.

So, what makes coming up with a simple checklist of the needed tool sets, competencies, and technical skills required so difficult? For one, the area is still evolving fast, and tools and techniques that were important to master last year might be less important this year. Therefore, staying in tune with the evolution of the field and continually learning new methods, tools, and techniques is the key in this space. Another reason it's difficult to specify a concrete checklist of skills is because the critical skill sets needed are actually outside the data science area — they qualify more as soft skills, like interpersonal communication and projecting the right attitude. Just look at the data scientist Venn diagram of skills, traits, and attitude needed, shown in Figure 13-2. The variety of skill sets and mindset traits that a perfect data scientist must master is almost ridiculous.

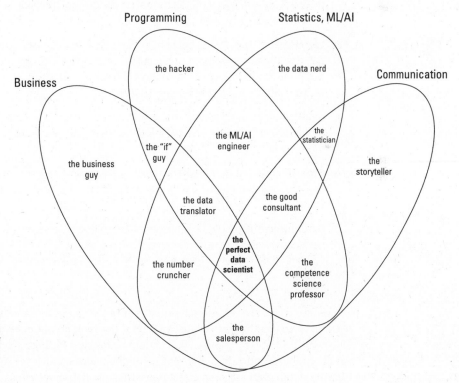

FIGURE 13-2:
A data scientist Venn diagram of skills, traits, and attitude needed.

So, bearing in mind that specifying competencies needed for a data scientist is more a question of attitude and mindset in combination with a certain skill set, I have still compiled this list:

>> **Business understanding:** Having the ability to translate a problem from business language into a hypothesis is important and refers to how a data scientist should be able to understand what the business person describes, and then be able to translate that into technical terms and present a potential solution in that context.

>> **Impactful versus interesting:** Data scientists must be able to resist the temptation to always prioritize the interesting problems when there might be problems that are more important to solve because of the major business impact such solutions would have.

>> **Curiosity:** Having an intellectual curiosity and the ability to detail a problem into a clear set of hypotheses that can be tested is a major plus.

>> **Attention to detail:** As a data scientist, pay attention to details from a technical perspective. A model cannot be nearly right. Building an advanced technical algorithm takes time and dedication to detail.

>> **Easy learner:** The data scientist must have an ability to learn quickly, because the rapidly changing nature of the data science space includes technologies and methodologies but also new tools and open-source models that are made available and become ready to build on.

>> **Agile mindset:** Stay flexible and agile in terms of what is possible, how problems are approached, how solutions are investigated, and how problems are solved.

>> **Experimentation mindset:** The data scientist must not fear to fail or try assumptions that might be wrong in order to find the most successful way forward.

>> **Communication:** A data scientist must be able to tell a story and describe the problem in focus or the opportunity that he's aiming for, as well as describe how great the models are once they are finished and what they actually enable.

Of course, there are additional skills of interest, such as in statistics, machine learning, and programming, but remember that you do not need one person to fit all categories here. First of all, you should be looking for data scientists who possess the most important skills that meet your needs. However, in the search for that top notch data scientist, remember that the list above could also be used for hiring a complementary team of data scientists which together possess the skills and mindset needed.

After your team of data scientists is in place, encourage their professional development and lifelong learning. Many data scientists have an academic mindset and a willingness to experiment, but in the pursuit of a perfect solution, they sometimes get lost among all the data and the problems they're trying to solve. Therefore, it's important that they stay connected with the team, though you should allow enough independence so that they can continue to publish white papers, contribute to open source, or pursue other meaningful activities in their field.

Structuring a Data Science Team

When building a data science team with the right type of skill sets, it's all about finding that optimized set of team members. What are the key drivers for different types of roles, and how should you combine them into one team?

Let's be honest: There's no formula you can apply that will solve this equation for you. It's a little more complicated than that. How the team structure needs to look and be balanced is very much related to what your objectives are, what your processes look like, how the intended target environment is defined, and so on. However, you can always start with a simple standard setup based on the role descriptions in the previous section and work from there. You can see this simplified setup in Figure 13-3.

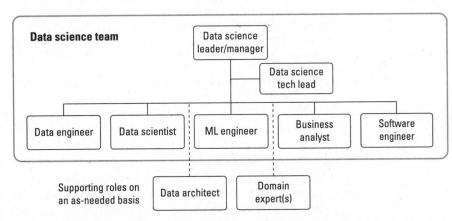

FIGURE 13-3:
A typical data science team structure.

When balancing needed resources per role in the data science team, you need to consider aspects such as the ones described in this list:

>> **Data scope and complexity:** What is the scope of your data science challenge? Are you targeting internal business efficiency gains, or are you going for a commercial data business? The scope of the data needed and the

complexity of the data acquisition involved will, for example, impact the need for data architectural support and experienced data engineers.

» **Data product or service type:** If you're going for a commercial data product, are you aiming for something sold off-the-shelf or are you aiming to build an operational model from a data service perspective? How do you aim to deliver your data product or service? Depending on the offering type as well as the delivery model, it's certain to impact the number of software engineers you will need for the end-to-end solution development and delivery platform creation.

» **Level of machine learning/artificial intelligence techniques used:** How complex are your use cases and the targeted solution? Is there a need for a highly technical solution with a lot of self-learning algorithms, or is a simpler model sufficient? The level of complexity involved will drive the need for different data scientist skill sets, ranging from analytics to advanced analytics and from machine learning to artificial intelligence competence.

» **Data science environment setup (development and production):** What will the data science infrastructure look like? Is it cloud based or on-premise based? Is it globally distributed, or is there a single local instance? Or do you have a global setup with a centralized instance and cloud-edge instances in different countries, or even edge instances on device level? The infrastructure setup can vary a lot between companies, depending on the size of company, if it's local or global, the line of business it is focused on, whether the data is owned or you need rights to use it, and so on. However, from a resource balancing aspect, you will soon realize that the data science environment setup impacts the number of data science teams you will be needing and also which competences you need more of — as well as where in the world the teams need to be placed.

» **Data science organizational model:** This refers to the organizational setup you have decided on in terms of having a centralized team, a decentralized team, or a hybrid. (See Chapter 11 for more on these models.) The resource balancing depends on which role a centralized function will have in your company. For example, if you have a common centralized data science function, does that mean all data scientists should work there, serving the whole company? Or does it mean that the centralized function works only on common parts, which is relevant across different business units, meaning that the rest of the organization is allowed to acquire and build their own data science competence? Those are important questions to be clear about in order to better understand your data science resource balancing parameters.

Hiring and evaluating the data science talent you need

When making hiring decisions in data science, your goal is to have a well-functioning team, not just a set of skilled individuals. Equally important is the need to create a diverse team, where individuals with different backgrounds and different life experiences can work comfortably together. The trick is to start your search by looking for individuals who represent the different disciplines — data scientists, data engineers, and software engineers, for example — but then to always make the final decision based on a candidate's ability to function well within a data science context.

So, how can you tell whether someone will function well in such a context? I always look at three main areas when evaluating whether a candidate has the right skill set and personality traits to succeed (by the way, I always apply these criteria to *all* individuals On the team, not just a select few):

>> Cultural fit

>> Engineering skills

>> Data science competence

In the area of engineering skills, look for competencies in system design, formal coding, and algorithm development. As for data science skills, you should insist on competencies in instance modeling and algorithms, ML framework and tools (like TensorFlow), and data processing.

When it comes to a cultural fit, start out by looking at people who clearly share the values of the company as well as the other team members. From there, move on to evaluating how the candidate works as part of a team and then gauge their personal motivation and drive. However, remember the rule of not hiring people who represent the same background, gender, education, and age. A diverse team secures diverse results and actively works against bias in the data and insights.

TIP

To evaluate the candidates from all these aspects, it's important to have a clear and mutually agreed-on perception of what good looks like. This should be in the form of generic evaluation criteria that everyone who is participating in the hiring process is in agreement about — and you should definitely have it in writing. This seems like an easy thing to do, but it's often hard to do in practice because what "good" looks like is very much a matter of personal opinion. But as hard as it is, defining evaluation criteria is really important to do. All candidates need to be evaluated in as unbiased a fashion as possible against the same criteria.

To get the data on your candidates you need in order to evaluate the different areas, you should use a combination of assignments and tests with interviews. Test results, outcomes, and any insights gained from personal interviews then need to be mapped to what good looks like. For instance, you might do a screening interview, an engineering and system design interview, a data science assignment, followed by a data science fundamentals interview. If the candidate progresses through all these stages, the data science leader then needs to evaluate the cultural fit to make sure that the right *person* (and not merely the right *skill set*) is hired.

You might be wondering why you should be evaluating a data engineer by looking at the same areas and using the same criteria you'd use for a data scientist. I'd argue that it pays to be able to gauge the breadth of a candidate's knowledge, especially in neighboring fields of expertise. Regardless of the findings, it could be useful to know whether a candidate is a skilled data scientist but a pretty bad engineer, even if that individual might never be asked to do any coding. And, when you come right down to it, there really are some important cross-functional skills that are essential for a data science team. For example, it would be best to have a data engineer who is skilled with coding and knows about system design and DevOps, yet knows enough about the fundamentals of data science to know to what extent and in what way their talents can be put to use in a data science context. No, that person doesn't need to have the same level of data science understanding that a machine learning engineer with a background as a mathematician would have, but they need to be at a level where they know how they can contribute.

To cater to these needed cross-functional skill sets, you should map what skills and responsibilities are either less important or more important for the different roles on your team. Yes, a data scientist should take the system design test, but if he scores poorly, it should not be an immediate black mark against him. But then you should require this candidate to score high on his understanding of topics like naive Bayes methods and logistic regression techniques as a counterpoint. Figure 13-4 shows a high level mapping of skill sets to certain roles in order to define what good looks like.

After mapping the relative importance of various skill sets, be sure to map out which areas or skill sets you expect the interviews, assignments, and tests to provide data on in order to make sure that you cover all needed data points for evaluating the candidate properly. Keep in mind that it's really quite hard to build successful teams, and it also costs a pretty penny. Take this work seriously and come well prepared for the interviews. This is also important because the access to experienced competence in data science is scarce, and it's not only you who is evaluating the candidate — the candidate is also evaluating you and your level of competence in the area, as well as the maturity of the company. Being well prepared and having a well-thought-out interview structure is a good starting point.

Area	Skill Set	Data Scientist	Data Engineer
Engineering	System design	Relevant	Important
Engineering	Formal coding	Relevant	Important
Engineering	Code-based problem solving	Important	Important
Engineering	Data architecture and data models	Relevant	Important
Data science	Data processing	Important	Important
Data science	Modeling and algorithms	Important	Relevant
Data science	Analysis and evaluation	Important	Relevant
Data science	Frameworks and tools	Important	Relevant
Culture fit	Company fit	Relevant	Relevant
Culture fit	Personal motivation	Important	Important
Culture fit	Career goals	Relevant	Relevant
Culture fit	Team fit and diversity aspects	Important	Important

FIGURE 13-4:
An example of mapping the importance of skill set to certain roles.

Retaining Competence in Data Science

What can companies do to get the most out of their data science teams and to motivate them to make a more robust contribution to the business? One important part is giving data scientists the time they need to invent. Remember that you're dealing with people who, on one hand, want to push the boundaries and, on the other hand, get bored easily if they're asked to do the same thing over and over again.

REMEMBER

These scientists are scarce talents who want to work on the company's most important functions. If they're asked to spend their time performing repetitive tasks such as data acquisition, data management, and extensive massaging of results forecasting, they often feel underutilized. Tasking data scientists with forward looking projects gives them the opportunity to invent the way the company can benefit from big data.

Also make sure that company management is involved at the right stage of the data projects. Without access to senior management, data science teams may focus on the wrong problems. This should preferably be managed by way of the CDO role, if that role is in place within the company. (For more on the CDO role, see Chapter 12.) In general, it's crucial for data science teams to engage senior management at three stages in any project: early on, to help define the problem the company wants to solve; after the first results start rolling in; and when it comes time for the resulting insights to be implemented or acted on.

If handled correctly, your data scientists can develop a tremendous reputation for knowledge inside the organization. Ensuring that the dialogue between the data science teams and senior management occurs early and often also increases the likelihood that data scientists' suggestions are actually implemented. Again, this is a vital role to play for the CDO.

TIP

When it comes to motivating strategic data science talent to stay in the company, one other strategy is to let data scientists out of the data box. Data scientists are natural learners who are positioned to see all aspects of the business as informed by data, rather than through a traditional software development or marketing lens. Because of this perspective, they can make connections others can't to broader conversations and innovative ideas through their observation of the overall business.

I'd also recommend that you consider cross-training your company's data scientists. Whether or not data scientists have the sexiest job of the 21st century, as *Harvard Business Review* declared, is debatable, but what is not in dispute is that they're hard to identify, hard to recruit, and in short supply. *Cross-training* data scientists means moving people from a data science organization into operations management, digital marketing, or customer relationship management, which are all analytically grounded disciplines and can open up new opportunities for personal and career development, not only for the data scientists but also for the company as a whole when their competence and knowledge are spread out in a more practical manner, driving data-driven thinking and applying statistical models in practice outside traditional domains. Such cross-training can also act as a motivator for more people to want to learn more about data science and pursue a career in that area through formal and on-the-job training.

REMEMBER

When business leaders confuse data reporting for analysis, a company can have trouble addressing problems effectively. By the same token, data scientists need to learn how to address senior management on senior management's terms. Data scientists tend to want to explain everything they've done, describe how hard they've worked, and emphasize what an accomplishment it was. Senior management, on the other hand, has three rules: Be clear, be quick, and be gone.

TIP

Developing the business acumen of data scientists helps them contribute more holistically to conversations within the company, allowing them to initiate analyses and experiments rather than simply react to requests. That is a long-term benefit that costs companies little to implement, but it's a crucial competence over the long term.

Understanding what makes a data scientist leave

Unfortunately, whatever your ambitions are in terms of the new data scientists you're bringing into the company, many data scientists tend to move on, often within their first year. Why is that? To complement the earlier section on what you should do to retain your valuable data science resources, this section aims to pinpoint four main concerns that drive data scientist dissatisfaction. Here's my list:

>> **Expectation doesn't match reality.** Many companies hire data scientists without really understanding what data science is all about. For example, without a suitable infrastructure in place to start getting value out of their data science investment, coupled with the fact that these companies fail to hire senior or experienced data practitioners before hiring juniors, you now have a recipe for a disillusioned and unhappy relationship for both parties. The data scientist likely enters the company with the ambition to write smart machine learning algorithms to generate insights, but soon discovers that they can't do this because their first job is to sort out the data infrastructure and/or create reports on demand. In contrast, many times, the level of data science maturity is so low in the company that all they want is a chart they can present in their board meeting each day. Leaders at such companies then get frustrated because they don't see value being generated quickly enough and all of this of course leads to the data scientist being unhappy in the role and eventually leaving.

>> **Company politics is more important than data science skills.** A data scientist often assumes that knowing lots of machine learning algorithms will make him the most valuable person in the company. However, the data scientist soon discovers that those expectations do not match reality. The truth is, the people in the business with the most influence need to see the worth of any employee they're thinking of entrusting with greater responsibilities, regardless of whether they are data scientists or not. From a data scientist perspective, that means first making yourself available and then working to make yourself irreplaceable. For that to happen, you need to be ready to handle a constant flow of ad hoc work, such as getting numbers from a database to give to the right people at the right time, doing simple projects just so that the right people get the right perception of you, the data scientist,

as someone who is trustworthy, reliable, and innovative. As frustrating as it may sound, putting yourself out there is a necessary part of the job that any data scientist must accept if they hope to get to the point where they can achieve something more interesting and impactful.

>> **The data scientist role isn't understood.** Following on from doing anything to please the right people, those same people with all that power often don't understand what is meant by the term *data scientist.* This means that data scientists are expected to be the analytics experts as well as the go-to reporting folks, and let's not forget the database experts, too. It isn't just nontechnical executives who make too many assumptions about data scientist skills: Other colleagues in technology assume that the data scientist knows everything that is data related. The conventional wisdom states that the data scientist should know her way around Spark, Hadoop, Hive, Pig, SQL, Neo4J, MySQL, Python, R, Scala, TensorFlow, A/B testing, NLP, anything related to machine learning, and anything else you can think of that is related to data. But it doesn't stop there. Because the data scientist supposedly knows all of this and obviously has access to all the data, the expectation is that the data scientist has the answers to all the questions within minutes. Trying to tell everyone what you actually know and have control of can be both difficult and frustrating.

>> **Working on an isolated team limits productivity.** When you see successful commercial data products, you often see expertly designed user interfaces with intelligent capabilities and, most importantly, a useful output, which, at the very least, is perceived by the users to solve a relevant problem. Now, if a data scientist spends his time only learning how to write and execute machine learning algorithms, he can only be a small (although necessary) part of a team that leads to the success of a long effort that ends up producing a valuable data product.

That's one scenario — yes, part of a larger team, but that often means being a small cog in a much larger machine. Still, this is probably preferable to being shunted to the side and asked to work in isolation on something "data science-y." When cut off from those processes that actually create products to sell, data science teams end up struggling to provide value. Despite this, many companies still ask data science teams to come up with their own projects and write code to solve a problem they've defined. In some cases, this can be sufficient. For example, if all that's needed is a static spreadsheet that is produced once a quarter, the team can provide some value. On the other hand, if the goal instead is to optimize how to provide intelligent suggestions in an adjustable website, this will involve many different skills that shouldn't be expected of the vast majority of data scientists. (Only the true data science unicorn can solve this one.) So, if you task an isolated data science team with this project, cut off from all other resources, it's most likely to fail (or take a very long time to solve, because organizing isolated teams to work on collaborative projects in large enterprises isn't easy).

The time-proven wisdom about managing teams bears repeating: Data scientist teams, like others, flourish best when there is effective leadership, a strong mandate from the company executive team, and clear objectives based on a solid and agreed strategy in place. Remember that keeping your valued data scientists in your company requires not only a path for data science teams to take key initiatives in a collaborative and agile manner from design through implementation enabled by a fit-for-purpose data infrastructure, but is also very much about managing expectations. In both directions.

4 Investing in the Right Infrastructure

Chapter **14**

Developing a Data Architecture

Building a data architecture is similar to what happens when a traditional architect designs a home or a building: First create a blueprint that aligns with the short- and long-term objectives of an organization, and then make sure that the blueprint becomes a reality.

A general view is that a data architecture defines a standard set of products and tools that an organization uses to manage data. But it's much more than that. Any truly effective data architecture must take into account the unique cultural and contextual requirements of an organization, like the company size, setup, and line of business as well as potential technical, legal, security, or other constraints. In addition, a data architecture needs to define the processes to capture, transform, and deliver usable data to business users. Most importantly, it identifies the people who will consume that data and their unique business requirements. I cover all of this (and much more) over the course of this chapter.

Defining What Makes Up a Data Architecture

Within the area of information technology, a data architecture consists of models, policies, rules, and standards that govern which data is collected as well as how it's stored, arranged, integrated, and put to use in data systems and in organizations. Data is usually one of several architectural domains that form the pillars of an enterprise architecture or solution architecture for business operations internally or for a commercial data product or service portfolio offering externally.

REMEMBER

A data architecture should set data standards for all the data systems as a vision or a model of the interactions between an organization's various data systems. Data integration, for example, is dependent on data architecture standards and structures used by the various business units and the selected system applications and defines how the data interaction must work. These standards and structures address data in storage and data in motion and include descriptions of data storage solutions, data categories, and data types, including mappings of those data entities to data quality levels, relevant applications, usage or storage locations, and so on.

One key cornerstone in how a data architecture realizes a company's business objectives is how the data architecture describes how data is processed, stored, and utilized in an industrialized setting or system at work. It has to provide criteria for data processing operations to make it possible to design data flows and also control the flow of data in the data science life cycle.

When it comes to defining the overall data architecture, the responsible party here is, of course, the data architect. However, the data architect is also typically the key person charged with making sure that the data architecture blueprint is followed and understood as part of the realization and build-up of the actual data science infrastructure. This could, of course, also include modifications of the data architecture itself, because of the real-life adjustments that need to happen based on potential legal, security, ethical, geographical, cultural, or technical limitations occurring when the data architecture blueprint is put into practice.

Describing traditional architectural approaches

A data architecture includes a complete analysis of the relationships among an organization's functions, available technologies, and data types. When defining a data architecture for your company, you should approach your task with these three perspectives in mind:

>> **Conceptual:** A conceptual data architecture, also sometimes referred to as the *semantic data model*, represents all relevant business entities from a data perspective.

>> **Logical:** A logical data architecture, also called a *system data model*, represents the logic of how the included data entities are related and linked to each other from a data flow perspective.

>> **Physical:** A physical data architecture represents the actual realization of the architecture in its physical environment — in other words, how the actual data architecture is implemented as part of the technology infrastructure.

The data architecture should be defined during the planning phase of the new data infrastructure setup. As part of that process, your data strategy needs to capture — in a manner that is complete, consistent, and understandable — all the major data categories and data types, as well as the sources of data necessary to support the enterprise's strategic ambitions.

REMEMBER

The primary requirement at this early planning stage is to define all relevant data categories and data types in relation to your organization's business needs and objectives, not to specify which tools or applications should be used to deal with them.

Elements of a data architecture

When it comes to data architecture, it's crucial that certain elements already be defined during the design phase. For example, you need to define the administrative structure and related methodologies and processes required for managing the data during the different stages of its life cycle. Not paying enough attention to the importance of administrating both the data and the data architecture could result in chaos, corrupted data, or a serious blow to your data integrity — any of which could seriously impact the value and usefulness of the data for your company.

REMEMBER

A vital part of your data architecture includes a description of the technology choices. Will your architecture be realized through a virtualized and cloud based environment, or through an on-premises solution, for example? Or will the realization include a local, single site and instance, or will it be deployed in a larger, multisite setup? Will it perhaps even be globally distributed? All these questions need to be understood and answered early on, in order for your data architecture to be designed in a way that supports your business objectives.

TIP

Consider the kinds of interfaces your other systems will need to access your data, as well as the kind of infrastructure design necessary for supporting common data operations (emergency procedures, data imports, data backups, and external transfers of data, for example.)

WARNING

Without the guidance of a properly implemented data architecture design, you might have common data operations implemented in wildly different ways, depending on where you are in the organization. Such a crazy quilt approach makes it extremely difficult to understand and control the flow of data within your organization. This sort of fragmentation is highly undesirable, not only due to its potentially increased cost but also due to the data disconnects that it could involve. These sorts of difficulties are not uncommon in rapidly growing enterprises or in enterprises that have a broad product and service portfolio serving different lines of business.

TIP

Properly executed, the data architecture design phase forces an organization to precisely specify and describe both internal and external information flows. These are patterns that the organization may not have previously taken the time to conceptualize and think through properly. It is therefore possible at this stage to identify costly information shortfalls, disconnects between departments, and disconnects between organizational systems and data that may not have been evident before the data architecture analysis.

Exploring the Characteristics of a Modern Data Architecture

Still waiting on a concrete definition of what a data architecture actually is? Start by looking at these characteristics a data architecture simply must include:

>> **A business orientation:** Rather than focus on the data or the technology during the definition phase, a modern data architecture starts with the business users and the overall business objective and flows backward. Customers can be internal or external to an organization, and their needs may vary by role, by department, and over time. A good data architecture therefore continuously evolves to meet new and changing business and customer data needs.

>> **Adaptability:** In a modern data architecture, data flows easily from source systems to business users. The purpose of the architecture is to manage that flow by creating a series of interconnected and bidirectional data pipelines that serve various constantly changing business needs.

>> **Automation:** To create an easily adaptable architecture in which data flows continuously and data integrity is protected, the architecture must be as automated as possible. The architecture must ensure the profiling and tagging of data at the point of data ingestion and map it to existing data sets and attributes — a key function of creating data catalogs as well, by the way. In the same manner, the data architecture must also enable the detection of changes in the data sources as well as quantify the impact of changes on any architectural component at any time. In a real-time production environment, it must be able to detect anomalies on the fly and either notify the appropriate instances (human and/or machine) or trigger alerts if needed.

>> **Intelligence:** The ideal data architecture has more going for it than just automation; it uses machine learning and artificial intelligence to actually build the data objects, tables, views, and models that keep data flowing. In other words, it uses intelligence not only for analyzing the data but also as part of managing and processing the data. Machine learning and artificial intelligence can be applied to identify data types, find common keys and join paths, identify and fix data quality errors, map tables, identify relationships, recommend related data sets and analytics, and so on. A modern data architecture uses intelligence to learn, adjust, alert, and recommend, making people who manage and use the environment more efficient and effective in their jobs.

>> **Flexibility:** A modern data architecture needs to be flexible enough to support a variety of business needs. That means it needs to support multiple types of business users, load operations and refresh rates (batch, mini-batch, and stream), query operations (create, read, update, delete), deployments (on-premise, public cloud, private cloud, hybrid), data processing engines (relational, OLAP, MapReduce, SQL, graphing, mapping, programmatic), and pipelines (data warehouse, data mart, OLAP cubes, visual discovery, real-time operational applications.) A modern data architecture has to be all things to all people in the company at any given time.

>> **A collaborative spirit:** Unlike in the past, where the IT department built everything, a modern data architecture usually splits the responsibility for acquiring and transforming data between IT and the business units. The IT department may still do the heavy lifting of ingesting data from internal operational systems and create generic reusable building blocks. However, data from external data sources like social media data, customer data, product performance data from live environments and so on, is usually collected by the business. The reason is that the business units already owns that interface, like IT owns the interface to the internal systems. Letting IT focus on the infrastructure backbone of data storage setup and management, as well as on data transfer, is usually a good split — once the data is acquired and ingested, data engineers in the business units are ready to apply data preparation and data catalog tools to create custom data sets to power the business units' analytical and machine learning activities run by data scientists

and business analysts. This collaboration between the data engineers and the data scientists means that IT doesn't have to be involved in business related details around the data.

» **Ease of governance:** A modern data architecture defines access points for each type of user to meet their data need. From the bird's-eye view, you generally have four types of business users — data consumers, data explorers, data analysts, and data scientists — and each type needs different access points to the data. Ensuring that access is what governance is all about, which means that the governance, surprisingly enough, is really the key to a good self-service environment.

» **Simplicity:** Your first assumption should always be that the simplest architecture is usually the best architecture. Ensuring such simplicity can be quite challenging, however, given the diversity of the data needs and the complexity of components in a present-day data architecture. To apply the simplicity rule, an organization with small data sets should seriously consider an out-of-the box analytics tool with a built-in data management environment. To reduce complexity in a big data context and avoid creating a rigid environment, organizations should strive to limit data movement and data duplication by promoting a unified data structure, a data integration framework, and a harmonized analytical and machine learning environment supporting innovation and experimentation, without adding infrastructure complexity. Exactly how to approach this is described later in this chapter.

» **Scalability:** In the age of big data and variable workloads, organizations need a scalable, elastic architecture that adapts to changing data processing requirements on demand. Many companies are now gathering around cloud platforms (both public and private) to obtain on-demand scalability at affordable prices. Elastic architectures free administrators from having to calibrate capacity exactly, control usage if necessary, and constantly overbuy hardware. Scalability also spawns many types of applications and use cases, such as on-demand development and test environments, analytical sandboxes, and prototyping playgrounds.

» **Security:** A modern data architecture must manage to be a collaborative and innovative workspace while at the same time being secure, reliable, and trustworthy. It must manage to provide authorized users ready access to data while keeping hackers and intruders at bay. It must do all that while still complying with privacy regulations, including governmental statutes like the Health Insurance Portability and Accountability Act (HIPPA) in the US as well as regulations like the EU's General Data Protection Regulation (GDPR). The data architecture shall encrypt data upon its ingestion into the data storage, masking personally identifiable information, and track all data elements in a data catalog, including their lineage, usage, and audit trail. Life cycle management ensures that each data object has an owner, a location, and a defined retention period.

>> **Resiliency:** A data architecture must also be resilient, with high availability, a robust disaster recovery capability, and a stable infrastructure for backup and restoring data. This is especially true in a modern data architecture that often runs on huge server farms in the cloud, where outages are common. The good news is that many cloud providers offer built-in redundancy and failover with good service level agreements (SLAs) and allow companies to set up mirror images for disaster recovery in geographically distributed data centers at low cost.

Explaining Data Architecture Layers

You need to be aware of various constraints and influences when deciding on a data architecture, because it might impact the architecture's design. These include aspects you'd expect, such as business requirements, key technology choices, financial considerations, different types of business policies, and data processing needs. But it's also important to understand the main architectural layers that make up the basis of any data architecture.

In the past, organizations built fairly static IT-driven data architectures, where systems were complex, difficult, time-consuming to design, and where damage to the database affected virtually all applications running in the environments. These were called *data warehouses*. Because of the underlying technology and design patterns, most data warehouses take an army of people to build and manage — so they provide a minimal return on your investment. Most are overvalued corporate data dumps, where an organization stores all data collected without a defined purpose and structure in the belief that just collecting and dumping the data in a data warehouse adds value in itself. However, there are some existing examples of well-designed and successful implementations that provide a well-functioning environment for data analysis.

REMEMBER

A modern data architecture may still act in part like a data warehouse, but ideally it should be a data warehouse that is flexible, scalable, and agile. Just remember that the storage aspects of a data warehouse comprise just one potential component of a modern data architecture. The new data environment should be approached like a living, breathing organism that detects and responds to changes, continuously learns and adapts, and provides governed, tailored access for every individual.

Figure 14-1 uses the data science flow I define in Chapter 1 to illustrate how you need to build up your data architecture in different layers. Each layer has a defined purpose in the data architecture, based on the specific business context of your company. This means that a data architectural realization setup and components you decide to use might look quite different, depending on whether you're focusing on internal business analytics or developing an architecture to support a commercial data product or service on a global scale.

Using data science ways of working to drive data architecture design is an excellent way of making sure you get a data architecture that supports the way your business needs to work. Once you defined this, you can then apply the needed systems and tools to realize your architecture in an end-to-end data science infrastructure, as exemplified in Chapter 18 of this book. But let's start by looking at each layer in more detail.

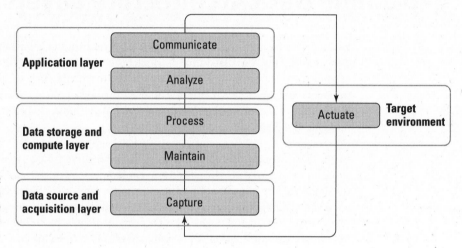

FIGURE 14-1: Using the data science flow to define your data architecture.

» **Data source and acquisition layer:** This layer is all about making sure you understand your data needs based on your business objective and what this means in terms of where the data resides, who owns it, how large it is, whether it's sensitive (and therefore needs to be anonymized), how you should collect it, collection frequency, and so on. It's also advisable to perform the first data processing activities already at the point of collection, because you don't want to spend time and money collecting and storing dirty data. Examples of early processing activities prior to storage include validating completeness of the data collected, identifying and removing duplicated data records, data aggregation to minimize transfer capacity impact, data anonymization for personal data, data encryption, and so on.

» **Data storage and compute layer:** In this layer of the data architecture, you need to consider aspects such as how you want to store the data (retention periods for different types of data, for example). You also need to consider the next level of data processing (data cleansing, mapping, labeling, and so on), and how this can be done with as little manual intervention as possible. (Automating data management tasks helps to protect data integrity by not unconsciously adding bias to the data.) In this layer, you also need to decide whether you want to store and process the data using an on-premises solution or a cloud solution. What you select could depend on the size of the data you're working with, but also on whether you expect the data to grow rapidly and unexpectedly, which would suggest that you need a cloud based solution for fast and easy scale-up of the environment. However, a public cloud solution — from Amazon, Azure, or Google for example — fits perfectly (even for small data environments) since it removes the upfront cost of investing in your own infrastructure as you only pay for capacity used. Another factor to consider is that, if you need to collect and compute data from many different countries in your environment, you might not be able to transfer the data out of all countries due to strict laws and regulations. To solve that problem, you should consider a distributed cloud setup, where data can be processed in a data center within country borders but where insights and models can be transferred to a central instance for reuse and sharing across the distributed setups.

>> **Application layer:** The application layer is straightforward. As its name implies, it's where you implement the applications and tools you want to run on top of your data. It can be a mix of different applications, like open source tools and frameworks such as TensorFlow, Scikit-learn, or Keras, but also out-of-the-box applications from established analytics vendors such as SAS, IBM, or Tableau. Here it's important to think through what type of users you will have in your environment as well as their level of competence and interest. Maybe all you have to do is ensure that insights are easily communicated through various predesigned dashboards and visualizations for decision support; but the best approach is usually to make sure you build the data architecture in such a way that you can swap applications in and out, depending on what becomes available in the industry, and also to support the changing expectations and needs in the organization. Users might start out by wanting things to be provided to them, but as maturity grows, users might want to do more themselves. This is especially true for companies investing in commercial data products and services.

REMEMBER

Flexibility in the application layer isn't the major cost in the architecture. If the bottom layers in the architecture are common to all, a lot is won in terms of keeping costs down and data integrity and reliability in the data up. Flexibility in the application layer ensures that users stay happy and that various needs are met. It also minimizes the risk of dissatisfied users branching off and building their own environment, in the process increasing total company cost as well as creating siloed data and insights.

>> **Target environment:** This refers to the environment where you intend to implement your insights and models. Again, what this really ends up being varies a lot from company to company. If the data architecture is built for internal analytics needs only, the target environment might be various internal systems, but it could also refer to how insights flow into, and are used in, various organizational structures and decision forums. In a live operational setting or for a commercial data product or service, the target environment could refer to the live production environment. The output from these target environments then feed new data back to the data source and acquisition layer, providing feedback data through the change it has implemented as part of the live production environment, and the data science cycle starts again.

Listing the Essential Technologies for a Modern Data Architecture

The drive today is to refactor the enterprise technology platform to enable faster, easier, more flexible access to large volumes of precious data. This refactoring is no small undertaking and is usually sparked by a shifting set of key business drivers. Simply put, the platforms that have dominated enterprise IT for nearly 30 years can no longer handle the workloads needed to drive data-driven businesses forward.

Organizations have long been constrained in their use of data by incompatible formats, limitations of traditional databases, and the inability to flexibly combine data from multiple sources. New technologies are now starting to deliver on the promise to change all that. Improving the deployment model of software is one major step to removing barriers to data usage. Greater data agility also requires more flexible databases and more scalable real-time streaming platforms. In fact, no fewer than seven foundational technologies are needed to deliver a flexible, real-time modern data architecture to the enterprise. These seven key technologies are described in the following sections.

NoSQL databases

The relational database management system (RDBMS) has dominated the database market for nearly 30 years, yet the traditional relational database has been shown to be less than adequate in handling the ever-growing data volumes and the accelerated pace at which data must be handled. NoSQL databases — "no SQL" because it's decidedly nonrelational — have been taking over because of their speed and ability to scale. They provide a mechanism for storage and retrieval of data that is modeled in means other than the tabular relations used in relational databases. Because of their speed, NoSQL databases are increasingly used in big data and real-time web applications.

NoSQL databases offer a simplicity of design, simpler horizontal scaling to clusters of machines (a real problem for relational databases), and finer control over availability. The data structures used by NoSQL databases (key-value, wide column, graph, or document, for example) are different from those used by default in relational databases, making some operations faster in NoSQL. The particular suitability of a given NoSQL database depends on the problem it must solve. Sometimes the data structures used by NoSQL databases are also viewed as more flexible than relational database tables.

Real-time streaming platforms

Responding to customers in real-time is critical to the customer experience. It's no mystery why consumer-facing industries —Business-to-Consumer (B2C) setups, in other words — have experienced massive disruption in the past ten years. It has everything to do with the ability of companies to react to the user in real-time. Telling a customer that you will have an offer ready in 24 hours is no good because they will have already executed the decision they made 23 hours ago. Moving to a real-time model requires event streaming.

Message-driven applications have been around for years, but today's streaming platforms scale far better and at far lower cost than their predecessors. The recent advancement in streaming technologies opens the door to many new ways to optimize a business. Reacting to a customer in real-time is one benefit. Another aspect to consider is the benefits to development. By providing a real-time feedback loop to the development teams, event streams can also help companies improve product quality and get new software out the door faster.

Docker and containers

Docker is a computer program that performs operating-system-level virtualization, also known as *containerization*. First released in 2013 by Docker, Inc., Docker is used to run software packages called *containers*, a method of virtualization that packages an application's code, configurations, and dependencies into building blocks for consistency, efficiency, productivity, and version control. Containers are isolated from each other and bundle their own application, tools, libraries, and configuration files and can communicate with each other by way of well-defined channels.

TECHNICAL STUFF

All containers are run by a single operating system kernel and are thus more lightweight than virtual machines. Containers are created from images that specify their precise content. A container image is a self-contained piece of software that includes everything that it needs in order to run, like code, tools, and resources.

Containers hold significant benefits for both developers and operators as well as for the organization itself. The traditional approach to infrastructure isolation was that of static partitioning, the allocation of a separate, fixed slice of resources, like a physical server or a virtual machine, to each workload. Static partitions made it easier to troubleshoot issues, but at the significant cost of delivering substantially underutilized hardware. Web servers, for example, would consume on average only about 10 percent of the total computational power available.

TIP

The great benefit of container technology is its ability to create a new type of isolation. Those who least understand containers might believe they can achieve the same benefits by using automation tools like Ansible, Puppet, or Chef, but in fact these technologies are missing vital capabilities. No matter how hard you try, those automation tools cannot create the isolation required to move workloads freely between different infrastructure and hardware setups. The same container can run on bare-metal hardware in an on-premises data center or in a virtual machine in the public cloud. No changes are necessary. That is what true workload mobility is all about.

Container repositories

A *container image repository* is a collection of related container images, usually providing different versions of the same application or service. It's critical to maintaining agility in your infrastructure. Without a DevOps process with continuous deliveries for building container images and a repository for storing them, each container would have to be built on every machine in which that container could run. With the repository, container images can be launched on any machine configured to read from that repository. Where this gets even more complicated is when dealing with multiple data centers. If a container image is built in one data center, how do you move the image to another data center? Ideally, by leveraging a converged data platform, you will have the ability to mirror the repository between data centers. A critical detail here is that mirroring capabilities between on-premises and the cloud might be vastly different than between your on-premises data centers. A converged data platform will solve this problem for you by offering those capabilities regardless of the physical or cloud infrastructure you use in your organization.

Container orchestration

Instead of static hardware partitions, each container appears to be entirely its own private operating system. Unlike virtual machines, containers don't require a static partition of data computation and memory. This enables administrators to launch large numbers of containers on servers without having to worry so much about exact amounts of memory. With container orchestration tools like Kubernetes, it becomes easy to launch containers, kill them, move them, and relaunch them elsewhere in an environment.

**TECHNICAL
STUFF**

Assuming that you have the new infrastructure components in place (a document database such as MapR-DB or MongoDB, for example) and an event streaming platform (maybe MapR-ES or Apache Kafka) with an orchestration tool (perhaps Kubernetes) in place, what is the next step? You'll certainly have to implement a DevOps process for coming up with continuous software builds that can then be deployed as Docker containers. The bigger question, however, is what you should actually deploy in those containers you've created. This brings us to microservices.

Microservices

Microservices are a software development technique that structures an application as a collection of services that

>> Are easy to maintain and test

>> Are loosely coupled

>> Are organized around business capabilities

>> Can be deployed independently

As such, microservices come together to form a microservice architecture, one that enables the continuous delivery/deployment of large, complex applications and also enables an organization to evolve its *technology stack* — the set of software that provides the infrastructure for a computer or a server. The benefit of breaking down an application into different, smaller services is that it improves modularity, which then makes the application easier to understand, develop, and test and to become more resilient to *architecture erosion* — the violations of a system's architecture that lead to significant problems in the system and contribute to its increasing fragility. With a microservices architecture, small autonomous teams can run in parallel to develop, deploy, and scale their respective services independently. It also allows the architecture of an individual service to emerge through continuous *refactoring* — a disciplined technique for restructuring an existing body of code, altering its internal structure without changing its external behavior (thus ensuring that it continues to fit within the architectural setting).

REMEMBER

The concept of microservices is nothing new. The difference today is that the enabling technologies like NoSQL databases, event streaming, and container orchestration can scale with the creation of thousands of microservices. Without these new approaches to data storage, event streaming, and infrastructure orchestration, large-scale microservices deployments would not be possible. The infrastructure needed to manage the vast quantities of data, events, and container instances would not be able to scale to the required levels.

TECHNICAL STUFF

Microservices are all about delivering agility. A service that is micro in nature generally consists of either a single function or a small group of related functions. The smaller and more focused the functional unit of the work, the easier it will be to create, test, and deploy the service. These services must be *decoupled*, meaning you can make changes to any one service without having an effect on any other service. If this is not the case, you lose the agility promised by the microservices concept. Admittedly, the decoupling must not be absolute — microservices can, of course, rely on other services — but the reliance should be based on either balanced REST APIs or event streams. (Using event streams allows you to leverage request-and-response topics so that you can easily keep track of the history of events; this approach is a major plus when it comes to troubleshooting, because the entire request flow and all the data in the requests can be replayed at any time.)

Function as a service

Just as the microservices idea has attracted a lot of interest in the software industry, so has the rise of server-less computing — perhaps more accurately referred to as Function as a Service (FaaS). Amazon Lambda is an example of a FaaS framework, where it lets you run code without provisioning or managing servers, and you pay only for the computing time you consume.

TECHNICAL STUFF

FaaS enables the creation of microservices in such a way that the code can be wrapped in a lightweight framework built into a container, executed on demand based on some trigger, and then automatically load-balanced, thanks to the aforementioned lightweight framework. The main benefit of FaaS is that it allows the developer to focus almost exclusively on the function itself, making FaaS the logical conclusion of the microservices approach.

The triggering event is a critical component of FaaS. Without it, there's no way for the functions to be invoked (and resources consumed) on demand. This ability to automatically request functions when needed is what makes FaaS truly valuable. Imagine, for a moment, that someone reading a user's profile triggers an audit event, a function that must run to notify a security team. More specifically, maybe it filters out only certain types of records that are to be marked as prompting a trigger. It can be selective, in other words, which plays up the fact that, as a business function, it is completely customizable. (I'd note that putting a workflow like this in place is tremendously simple with a deployment model such as FaaS.)

The magic behind a triggering service is really nothing more than working with events in an event stream. Certain types of events are used as triggers more often than others, but any event you want can be made into a trigger. The event could be a document update, or maybe running an OCR process over the new document and then adding the text from the OCR process to a NoSQL database. The possibilities here are endless.

FaaS is also an excellent area for creative uses of machine learning — perhaps machine learning as a service or, more specifically, "a machine learning function aaS." Consider that whenever an image is uploaded, it could be run through a machine learning framework for image identification and scoring. There's no fundamental limitation here. A trigger event is defined, something happens, the event triggers the function, and the function does its job.

FaaS is already an important part of microservices adoption, but you must consider one major factor when approaching FaaS: vendor lock-in. The idea behind FaaS is that it's designed to hide the specific storage mechanisms, the specific hardware infrastructure, and the software component orchestration — all great features, if you're a software developer. But because of this abstraction, a hosted FaaS offering is one of the greatest vendor lock-in opportunities the software industry has ever seen. Because the APIs aren't standardized, migrating from one FaaS offering in the public cloud to another is difficult without throwing away a substantial part of the work that has been performed. If FaaS is approached in a more methodical way — by leveraging events from a converged data platform, for example — it becomes easier to move between cloud providers.

Creating a Modern Data Architecture

In many larger companies, the IT function is usually tasked with defining and building data systems, especially for data generated by internal IT systems. It is many times the case, however, that data coming from external sources — customers, products, or suppliers —are stored and managed separately by the responsible business units. When that's the case, you're faced with the challenge of making sure that all share a common data architecture approach, one that enables all these different data types and user needs to come together by means of an efficient and enabling data pipeline. This data pipeline is all about ensuring an end-to-end flow of data, where applied data management and governance principles focus on a balance between user efficiency and ensuring compliance to relevant laws and regulations.

In smaller companies or modern data-driven enterprises, the IT function is usually highly integrated with the various business functions, which includes working closely with data engineers in the business units in order to minimize the gap between IT and the business functions. This approach has proven very efficient.

So, after you decide which function will set up and drive which part of the data architecture, it's time to get started. Using the step-by-step guide provided in this list, you'll be on your way in no time:

1. **Identify your use cases as well as the necessary data for those use cases.**

   The first step to take when starting to build your data architecture is to work with business users to identify the use cases and type of data that is either the most relevant or simply the most prioritized at that time. Remember that the purpose of a good data architecture is to bring together the business and technology sides of the company to ensure that they're working toward a common purpose. To find the most valuable data for your company, you should look for the data that could generate insights with high business impact. This data may reside within enterprise data environments and might have been there for some time, but perhaps the means and technologies to unearth such data and draw insights from it have been too expensive or insufficient. The availability of today's open source technologies and cloud offerings enable enterprises to pull out such data and work with it in a much more cost-effective and simplified way.

2. **Set up data governance.**

   It is of the utmost importance that you make data governance activities a priority. The process of identifying and ingesting data as well as building models for your data needs to ensure quality and relevance from a business perspective is important and should also include efficient control mechanisms as part of the system support. Responsibility for data must also be established, whether it concerns individual data owners or different data science functions. (For more on data governance, see Chapter 15.)

3. **Build for flexibility.**

   The rule here is that you should build data systems designed to change, not ones designed to last. A key rule for any data architecture these days is to not build in dependency to a particular technology or solution. If a new key solution or technology becomes available on the market, the architecture should be able to accommodate it. The types of data coming into enterprises can change, as do the tools and platforms that are put into place to handle them. The key is therefore to design a data environment that can accommodate such change.

4. **Decide on techniques for capturing data.**

   You need to consider your techniques for acquiring data, and you especially need to make sure that your data architecture can at some point handle real-time data streaming, even if it isn't an absolute requirement from the start. A modern data architecture needs to be built to support the movement and analysis of data to decision makers when and where it's needed.

REMEMBER

   Focus on real-time data uploads from two perspectives: the need to facilitate real-time access to data (data that could be historical) as well as the requirement to support data from events as they're occurring. For the first category, existing infrastructure such as data warehouses have a critical role to play. For the second, new approaches such as streaming analytics and machine learning are critical. Data may be coming from anywhere — transactional applications, devices and sensors across various connected devices, mobile devices and, telecommunications equipment, and who-knows-where-else. A modern data architecture needs to support data movement at all speeds, whether it's sub-second speeds or with 24-hour latency.

5. **Apply the appropriate data security measures.**

   Do not forget to build security into the architecture. A modern data architecture recognizes that threats to data security are continually emerging, both externally and internally. These threats are constantly evolving and may be coming through email one month and through flash drives the next. Data managers and data architects are usually the most knowledgeable when it comes to understanding what is required for data security in today's environments, so be sure to utilize their expertise.

6. **Integrate master data management.**

   Make sure that you address *master data management,* the method used to define and manage the critical data of an organization to provide, with the help of data integration, a single point of reference. With an agreed-on and built-in master data management (MDM) strategy, your enterprise is able to have a single version of the truth that synchronizes data to applications accessing that data. The need for an MDM-based architecture is critical because organizations are consistently going through changes, including growth, realignments, mergers, and acquisitions. Often, enterprises end up with data systems running in parallel, and often, critical records and information may be duplicated and overlap across these silos. MDM ensures that applications and systems across the enterprise have the same view of important data.

7. **Offer data as a service (aaS).**

This particular step is a relatively new approach, but it has turned out to be quite a successful component — make sure that your data architecture is able to position data as a service (aaS). Many enterprises have a range of databases and legacy environments, making it challenging to pull information from various sources. With the aaS approach, access is enabled through a virtualized data services layer that standardizes all data sources, regardless of device, applicator, or system. Data as a service is by definition a form of internal company cloud service, where data — along with different data management platforms, tools, and applications — are made available to the enterprise as reusable, standardized services. The potential advantage of data as a service is that processes and assets can be prepackaged based on corporate or compliance standards and made readily available within the enterprise cloud.

8. **Enable self-service capabilities.**

As the final step in building your data architecture, you should definitely invest in self-service environments. With self-service, business users can configure their own queries and get the data or analyses they want, or they can conduct their own data discovery without having to wait for their IT or data management departments to deliver the data. The route to self-service is providing front-end interfaces that are simply laid out and easy to use for your target audience. In the process, a logical service layer can be developed that can be reused across various projects, departments, and business units. IT could still have an important role to play in a self-service-enabled architecture, including aspects such as data pipeline operations (hardware, software, and cloud) and data governance control mechanisms, but it would have to spend less and less of its time and resources on fulfilling user requests that could be better formulated and addressed by the user themselves.

Chapter **15**

Focusing Data Governance on the Right Aspects

N ow more than ever, the ability to handle vast amounts of data in a way that manages to balance risks and business opportunities is critical to a company's success. Yet even with the emergence of data management functions and chief data officers (CDOs), most companies aren't performing at their best when it comes to managing and monetizing their data. Cross-industry studies show that, on average, less than half of an organization's structured data is actively used in making decisions and less than 1 percent of its unstructured data is analyzed or used at all. Many times, companies lock in the data, just to be on the safe side, and employees are forced to spend a lot of time explaining why they need a certain data set. At the same time, data breaches are more and more common, as data sets are spread in silos and their value is many times not understood or handled accordingly. On top of that, a common problem is that the company data infrastructure and applications don't live up to the expectations placed on them. In this chapter, I walk you through the key elements of data governance and guide you on the best way to approach the topic.

Sorting Out Data Governance

The concept of data governance refers to the people, processes, and system support required to establish a consistent and correct handling of an organization's data across the company. It supports data management with the necessary foundation, strategy, and structure needed to ensure that data is managed as an asset and transformed into meaningful and actionable insights.

Figure 15-1 shows that data governance is a capability that enables an organization to ensure the high data quality of your data throughout its complete life cycle. The key focus areas of data governance include ensuring availability, usability, consistency, integrity, and security of your data at all times and includes establishing processes to ensure effective data governance throughout the organization. The different areas managed through data governance can be explained according to this list:

>> **Data availability:** This term is used to describe to what extent a data element can be easily accessed at any level of performance. The level of data availability can be measured by factors like how easy the data is to manage and maintain, the ability to restore or recover any services or data in case of any error or failure, the ability to deliver a service, and the ability to understand problems with the data, diagnose their root cause, and repair them as soon as possible.

>> **Data usability:** This refers to the state of the data you currently have (in its raw format) and how it fits its purpose. How do you know whether your data is usable? Here are some questions you can ask: Is the raw data value correct or incorrect? How granular and precise are the data attributes? How integrated is the data with other data sources and data objects?

>> **Data consistency:** This term is used to describe how useful and reliable the data is from a trustworthiness perspective. Consistency is usually checked from three main perspectives: point-in-time consistency (that data stay consistent over time), transaction consistency (that data stays consistent during a transaction), and application consistency (that data stays consistent between different applications).

>> **Data integrity:** This refers to the maintenance and assurance of the accuracy and consistency of data over its entire life cycle. It's a critical aspect of the design, implementation, and usage of any system that stores, processes, or retrieves data. (Data integrity is the opposite of data corruption.)

>> **Data security:** This refers to protecting digital data, such as those in a database, from destructive forces and from the unwanted actions of unauthorized users — users who might initiate a cyberattack or a data breach, for example.

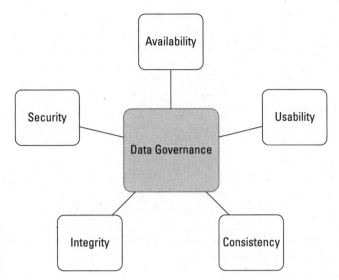

FIGURE 15-1:
The data aspects
managed by data
governance.

REMEMBER

As a starting point, understand and seek company agreement on what is expected from the data governance activities and frameworks. Is it something you engage in just to make sure you're toeing the line when it comes to laws and regulations, or is the ambition to leverage data governance as an enabler for a greater, much more reliable business? The starting point is important because it will help you determine your priorities and approach when establishing and implementing data governance.

Data governance for defense or offense

When it comes to data governance, you can play either defense or offense. Data defense is all about minimizing risk, and includes aspects such as ensuring compliance with regulations, using analytics or machine learning to detect and limit fraud, and building systems to prevent theft. Defensive efforts also include measures designed to ensure the integrity of data flowing through a company's internal systems. This happens by way of identifying, standardizing, and governing main data sources (customer, product, or sales data, for example) so that the company can rely on a single source of truth for its most important data.

Data offense, on the other hand, focuses on supporting business objectives such as increasing revenue, profitability, and customer satisfaction. It typically includes activities like data analysis and modeling that are designed to generate customer insights in order to support management decision-making. However, data offense also includes activities related to pursuing business opportunities with data products or services based on research or development work.

Every company needs both offense and defense to succeed, but getting the balance right is complicated and may differ a lot between different types of companies. These two approaches usually compete for limited resources, funding, and people. However, please note that while putting equal emphasis on the two is optimal for some companies, for others it might be a lot wiser to favor one or the other. This is highly impacted by the company context related to which industry it's part of and how competitive the environment is, as well as regulatory limitations.

Hospitals, for example, exist in a low competitive market with a highly regulated context where requirements on data quality and privacy protection are extremely high. They must therefore prioritize data defense over offense. Companies in the retail business, on the other hand, are much less regulated and are therefore able to work with sensitive personal data as part of a strategy for beating the competition and responding quickly to market changes. These types of companies typically prioritize offence over defense.

Objectives for data governance

You (or perhaps your bosses) might be asking why data governance is so important. Right off the bat I can tell you that ineffective data governance within a company inevitably leads to one thing: poor data. This poor data is visible through inconsistent definitions, duplicates, missing fields, and other classic data problems. These are clear issues that should be avoided.

Goals for data governance may be defined at all levels of the company, but by encouraging stakeholders to contribute to the goal setting, you may be able to ensure that they recognize the importance of data governance. In the following list, you can find some useful examples of data governance objectives, divided into the defensive and offensive camps:

Defensive:

» Increasing consistency and confidence in decision-making

» Decreasing the risk of regulatory fines

» Improving data security as well as defining and verifying the requirements for data distribution policies

» Designating accountability for data quality

» Enabling better planning by supervisory staff

» Reducing operational friction

» Protecting the needs of data stakeholders

» Training management and staff to adopt common approaches to data issues

Offensive:

>> Maximizing the income generation potential of commercial data products

>> Encouraging high degrees of sharing and reuse of data and insights

>> Using data derived insights to inform business investment decisions

>> Seeing that research and development activities are driven by data, analytics, and machine learning/artificial intelligence and are focused on exploring new business opportunities

>> Optimizing staff effectiveness

>> Minimizing or eliminating "re-work"

>> Establishing process performance baselines to enable improvement efforts

REMEMBER

You can realize any of these goals by implementing data governance programs or launching initiatives that use change management techniques.

Explaining Why Data Governance is Needed

Imagine that you've submitted a budget designed to beef up your data governance practices. You hear back that not a penny will be granted unless you can convince upper management that it's a good investment. What are the best arguments to use to save your initiatives as well as your budget? Read on to find out.

Data governance saves money

First and foremost, data governance increases efficiency in the organization. Duplicated accounts lead to duplicate efforts or, at the very least, to time wasted tracking down duplicate accounts in your marketing, sales, finance, development, or analytical efforts. Data governance reduces errors in the source data, giving your business a solid base to work from, and saves precious time that would otherwise be used correcting your existing data. Time saved is money saved.

TIP

Data governance forces your company to define its core data as well as the rules governing that core data. The initiation of a data governance project could be a golden opportunity to get everyone on the same page about core data definitions. The enforcement of these definitions ensures greater operational efficiency over time.

Bad data governance is dangerous

Lack of effective data governance is a security concern for two reasons:

» There are outside security risks associated with dirty, unstructured data.

» Bad data governance can result in regulatory compliance issues.

WARNING

Badly structured data poses a security risk for the simple reason that if you have dirty, unstructured data clogging your data pipeline, you can't quickly tell when something is about to go wrong and you can't efficiently monitor which data is at risk.

Regulatory compliance and data governance is becoming a hotter topic with each passing day. As people are becoming more aware of the importance of their personal data, governments are beginning to take extremely seriously how companies store, protect, and use their customers' data. With a messy, ungoverned data swamp, it may prove impossible for a company to guarantee that all data regarding a particular individual is deleted when requested. This opens up your company to great risk and potentially enormous fines.

Good data governance provides clarity

Effective data governance provides the peace of mind that your company's data is generally clean, standardized, and accurate. The effects of this reassurance resonate throughout a company and provide important benefits. An obvious but important benefit is assurance that the integrity in your data is kept over its life cycle, meaning that data is trusted and used as a base for important business decisions as well as for research and development of new insights or data products and services.

Establishing Data Stewardship to Enforce Data Governance Rules

Within an organization, a data steward is responsible for utilizing an organization's data governance processes to ensure the fitness of its various data elements. As such, data stewards carry out a specialist role that incorporates processes, policies, guidelines, and responsibilities for administering a company's entire data scope in compliance with policy and/or regulatory requirements.

Data stewardship is concerned with taking care of data assets that don't belong to the stewards themselves and may represent the needs of the entire organization. Others may be tasked with representing a smaller data scope related to a particular business unit or department or even a certain type of data. In some organizations, data stewards are senior representatives of appointed stakeholder groups — a structure designed to ensure sufficient engagement in — and decisions about — the treatment of certain data assets. However, in other organizations, data stewards operate independently, ensuring that the general rules and controls are applied to data appropriately throughout the organization.

REMEMBER

The overall objective of a data steward is ensuring data quality for the main data elements that have been decided on. This includes capturing metadata for each data element, such as definitions, related rules/governance, physical manifestations, and related data models. Data stewards begin the stewarding process with the identification of the elements that they will steward, with the ultimate result of standards, controls, and data entry.

TIP

The data steward needs to work closely with stakeholders involved with data standardization in order to drive alignment on data standards; with data architects in order to understand and secure adherence to data dependencies; and with system support experts in order to secure automated and built-in control mechanisms for data quality checks. Data controls can be preventive, detective, and corrective and be executed manually, aided by technology, or completely automated.

Implementing a Structured Approach to Data Governance

All organizations need to be able to make decisions about how to manage data, realize value from it, minimize cost and complexity, manage risk, and ensure compliance with ever-growing legal, regulatory, and other requirements. A company needs to create rules, ensure that the rules are being followed, and be able to deal with noncompliance, ambiguities, and any data-related issues that may arise.

REMEMBER

In short, a company needs to do more than just manage data. There's a need for a governance system that sets the rules of engagement for management activities across the organization. Small organizations or ones with simple data environments may be able to succeed in these goals through an informal system of governance. They may not even be aware of when they're switching between making management decisions and broader governance decisions. On the other hand, larger organizations or ones with more complex data or compliance environments generally find that they need to step back and agree on a more formal system of governance.

Defining and establishing a framework or a structured approach to data governance includes activities such as these:

>> **Define your objectives.** Ask yourself whether a defensive or offensive approach is most important for your line of business, market situation, and regulatory situation.

>> **Decide on the focus area.** You have to start somewhere, so ask yourself where your data governance project starts — full scope across the company or only for a selected unit or department?

>> **Set data definitions and rules.** What, exactly, do you need to govern? Avoid casting your net too widely, because it might hinder innovation and efficiency.

>> **Specify decision rights.** Who will be able to decide on the governance rules? What is the data governance framework needed for your company?

>> **Define and implement control mechanisms.** How will you ensure that rules are followed? Avoid manual (human) control as much as possible by building in control mechanisms to your data systems with as high a level of automation as possible.

>> **Identify data stakeholders.** Determine who'll be using the data and how. Take the time to really understand the business need and the stakeholders for the selected focus area.

>> **Set up a data governance board (DGB).** Data governors make up the DGB. They are ultimately accountable for business data use, data quality, and prioritization of data-related issues. They make decisions that impact data based on recommendations from the data stewards. The board has the authority to decide how the budget for data management improvements related to data governance shall be spent. This step is applicable mainly for larger companies or larger implementations when complexity and dependencies are significant.

>> **Assigning and training data stewards.** Who will be working with data governance on a daily basis? How will you capture the need across the organization and make sure that the framework stays relevant over time? Establishing the role of data stewards to manage data governance according to your line of business, is an important step.

>> **Designing and implementing needed processes**. The final step is to make sure you have processes in place that are sufficient yet clear and simple for your company to execute satisfactory data governance.

REMEMBER

One of the most important factors when it comes to data governance is ensuring that there's a common, agreed-on set of principles and best practices common to all teams and individuals in charge of collecting, governing, and consuming the data. Ensure that everyone is on board and that there are clear goals, clearly defined processes, and clear permission levels to make everything run smoothly.

TIP

The key to data governance is effective collaboration. The right data governance tools should go hand in hand with these principles. Make sure that whichever tools you're evaluating for adoption are easy to use for business and IT users alike, enable seamless collaboration across teams, and are flexible enough to evolve with your changing business needs.

Chapter **16**

Managing Models During Development and Production

Although managing data is essential in order to succeed with your data science investment, understanding why model management is a key part is equally important. In this chapter, I briefly explore what model management is all about, as well as list some of the important aspects to consider when it comes to model development and deployment.

Unfolding the Fundamentals of Model Management

An *algorithm* is a step-by-step method of solving a problem, commonly used for data processing, calculation, and other related computer and mathematical operations. An algorithm is also used to manipulate data in various ways, such as inserting a new data item, searching for a particular item, or sorting an item.

Technically, computers use algorithms to list the detailed instructions for carrying out a task. For example, to compute an employee's paycheck, the computer uses an algorithm. To accomplish this task, appropriate data must be entered into the system. In terms of efficiency, various algorithms are able to accomplish operations or problem solving easily and quickly.

So, an algorithm is the general approach you will take. The *model* is what you get when you run the algorithm over your training data and subsequently use to make predictions on new data. You can generate a new model with the same algorithm but with different data, or you can get a new model from the same data but with a different algorithm.

Working with many models

A common misunderstanding around machine learning models when compared to the software development space is the notion that the objective of a machine learning modeling session is to build one successful model, deploy it, and then walk away, patting yourself on the back for a job well done. That's a fantasy. In reality, working with machine learning models involves working with many models over an extended period, even after the model has been deployed in production. It's quite common to have several models in production at the same time and have new models ready to replace older models in production when conditions change. It's also important to be able to manage these model replacements in a smooth manner, without disturbing the ongoing service. In model development, you also work with more than one model as you experiment with multiple tools and compare model performance in order to find the best-performing model.

That's the general lay of the land, but it doesn't quite explain what model management is really all about. To get a better handle on that, consider a situation where an organization has hundreds of models embedded in various production systems to support decision-making in marketing, pricing, credit risk, operational risk, fraud, and finance functions. In this example, which is a common one across the software industry, data scientists across different business units are free to develop their models with no formalized or standardized processes for storing, deploying, and managing them. Some models don't have the necessary documentation describing the model's owner, business purpose, usage guidelines, or other information necessary for managing the model or explaining it to regulators, because the units were told to prioritize speed over proper documentation. Furthermore, after the model results are achieved in this imaginary scenario, they're subjected to limited controls and requirements as they make their way to decision-makers. Not surprisingly, because different data sets and variables were used to create the models, the results turn out to be inconsistent. There's little validation or back-testing for accuracy, and decisions are made on the model results as is — and then everyone just hopes for the best.

The scenario just described, with total modeling confusion, may look all too familiar to many organizations. In a diverse and loosely managed modeling environment, it can become quite difficult to answer critical questions about the predictive analytical or machine learning models that your organization relies on for not only the day-to-day business operations but also strategic decision-making. It's simply vital for your organization to build a solid foundation for managing models in a reliable, transparent, scalable, and reusable manner. But how should that be done?

A good starting point when reviewing your current model management situation or trying to determine how your architectural team conceives of it is to ask the following questions:

>> Are we tracking who created the models and why?

>> Do we know which input variables are used to make predictions or, in the machine learning case, which training data was used to train the model?

>> Are we keeping track of how the models are used?

>> Are we measuring model performance and do we know when these models were last updated?

>> Is there enough supporting documentation in place to enable model reuse by other data science teams?

>> Is it taking a long time to put new or updated models into production?

Faced with this list of questions, companies tend to respond in one of two ways: They're either able to answer these questions positively, but come to the conclusion that more could be done to increase efficiency and value from the models, or they're not able to answer any of these questions affirmatively. Why the latter? Because they haven't realized the importance of good model management in a company driven by data and machine learning/artificial intelligence. In a data- and model-driven enterprise, models are at the heart of critical business decisions. Models can identify new opportunities, help you forge new or better relationships with customers, and enable you to manage uncertainty and risks. For these reasons and many more, they should be created and treated as high-value organizational assets.

TIP

Model management isn't just about applying new guidelines or a new governance structure; you need to have software on hand that can wrangle your data into shape and quickly create many accurate models you can rely on. On top of that, it takes efficient and repeatable processes that are fully supported by a reliable infrastructure and your various architectural elements in order to manage and trace your models for optimal performance throughout their entire life cycle.

Making the case for efficient model management

The notion that efficient model management is crucial for the success of an organization is gaining more and more ground as the importance of data science is getting recognized in a broader sense. Some even say that, going forward, it will be a stronger competitive advantage to be model-driven, as opposed to being only data-driven. It also looks like the evidence is piling up that companies that are successful in getting value out of their data science investment are the ones that treat models as a new type of business asset.

Companies most successful in data science today treat models very differently from how they treat data and software. The way that they build models, develop models, deploy models, manage and have governance around models, as well as how they create the technology infrastructure systems to support models, are different from what they've done in the past when setting up systems for data or software. Why is that?

First of all, the raw materials data scientists use to create models are different from other business assets because models require computationally intensive algorithms. That requirement, of course, drives the growing need for elastic, scalable computational power as well as for specialized hardware, like graphics processing units (GPUs). Those are architectural components that software engineering teams don't normally need.

TIP

Another critical raw material for model development is the open source ecosystem. There are new tools, new packages, or updated packages coming out every day, especially around Python and R. If a company is trying to compete and have the best, most innovative models, they need ways to give data scientists quick access to the very rapidly evolving ecosystem without stifling their flexibility.

The third property that differentiates models from other types of software development is the process. Models by their very nature emerge from a research process, and such processes are inherently experimental, emergent, and exploratory. That's quite different from how software development works, and it's quite different from how systems acquire data. A data science team developing models might try hundreds of ideas before finding one that works; that's just fine, but it does create different requirements on the underlying infrastructure. Teams developing models need different capabilities to facilitate rapid experimentation and rapid exploration so that they can drive breakthroughs. In software, it's about de-risking and driving to clarity of requirements. In model development, it's about rapid experimentation where you try as many ideas as you can as fast as possible.

The fourth critical property of models to keep in mind is how they behave. In software engineering, there is typically a specification that developers aim for, and tests that can confirm whether the spec has been met. There's nothing of the sort when building predictive models. Instead, data science models are probabilistic. They don't have a correct answer. They just have better or worse answers when they're alive in the real world. What that means is that organizations need new ways for quality control, monitoring, governing, and reviewing models to ensure model reliability and anticipated behavior by the algorithm, meaning that it's performing as expected.

The unique requirements for succeeding with model management in data science suggests that model management should be treated as a dedicated discipline. Data infrastructures should not limit model management to a software application but should instead incorporate much more of a model driven approach, not only data driven.

Implementing Model Management

The next breakthrough in data science will probably not be new revolutionary algorithms (those will keep on coming, no matter what), but rather the ability to rapidly combine, deploy, and maintain existing algorithms in rapidly changing live environments.

Many corporations have now realized the need for a centralized repository for storing predictive models along with detailed metadata for efficient workgroup collaboration and version control of various models. Successful model management involves a collaborative team of modelers, architects, model scoring managers, model auditors, and validation testers. However, many companies are struggling with the process of signing off on the development, validation, deployment, and retirement life cycle management milestones for their models.

REMEMBER

You must readily know exactly where each model is in the life cycle, how old the model is, who developed the model, and who is using the model for what application. The ability to version-control the model over time is another critical business need that includes event logging and tracking changes to understand how the model form and usage is evolving over time.

Model degradation, where the model is no longer performing as expected and model accuracy is declining, is another serious challenge faced by many organizations. Standardizing the metrics used for measuring model performance is urgently needed. Currently, it's up to each company — or even each data scientist — to define and determine when a model needs to be retrained or replaced. On top of that, there's always a need for managing retired models because they need to be archived and not just thrown away. Finally, a more reliable process for managing your model scoring is a must because it's a key requirement to ensure that you can evaluate model performance and profitability over time.

Successful organizations recognize that models are essential corporate assets that produce and deliver answers to production systems for improved customer relationships, improved operations, increased revenues, and reduced risks. Few companies, however, are capable of fully managing all the complexities of the complete model life cycle, just because it's such a multifaceted task. So, if you can't do it all, what should you focus on? In other words, what does it take, from a model management perspective, to be able to make a lot of good, fast operational decisions that consistently reflect overall organizational strategy and at the same time keep your organization faster and better than anyone else's? Well, as in most cases, there's no silver bullet, but there are some main aspects to focus on:

>> **Data-driven systems:** The entire operational setup in the company *must* use data to produce answers for people or systems, depending on your level of automation, so that the right actions are initiated.

>> **Reliable and updated models:** Having relevant and up-to-date models that the business can rely on for optimal decisions and actions at the right time is key. These decisions can be made by machine intelligence driven systems that are using your models for automated decision-making in an operational setting.

>> **Integrated business rules:** The integration of business rules and a predictive analytical approach into operational decision flows has to occur if you want to provide the instructional insight needed for vetted, trusted decisions.

>> **Model monitoring:** Nothing will work for you in the long run if you don't find a way to manage and monitor your analytical models to ensure that they're performing well and continue to deliver the right answers.

>> A modern **data architecture:** Make sure you have a modern data architecture that addresses your needs and is supported by efficient and relevant processes that can grow to address new needs, like streaming data and building more detailed predictive models faster than ever.

Pinpointing implementation challenges

Although it might seem easy to move from a well-thought-out data science strategy into the implementation phase, it isn't always the case. There are still many problems that can arise during implementation. Being aware of these common challenges from a model management perspective helps you to navigate around them, or at least gives you some tips on how to handle them once they occur:

>> **Getting models into production too slowly:** Because processes are often manual and ad hoc, it can take months to get a model implemented into the production environment. And, because it can take so long to move models through the development and testing phases, they can be stale by the time they reach production — or they never get deployed at all. Internal and external compliance issues can make the process even more challenging, especially as the regulatory situation in data science is evolving at such a rapid pace.

>> **Difficulty interpreting model recommendations:** The step of translating model results into business actions for operational decisions requires clear, agreed-on business rules that need to become part of the governed environment because these are the rules that define how you'll use the model results. For example, a fraud detection model might return a fraud risk score as a number between 100 and 1,000 (similar to a FICO credit score). It's up to the business to decide what level of risk requires action. If the trigger for a fraud alert is set too high, fraud might go unnoticed. If the trigger for fraud is set too low, the alerts create too many false positives. Both outcomes will decrease the value these models create and also reduce trust in the results.

>> **Models not performing as expected:** Too often, poorly performing models remain in production even though they're producing inaccurate results that lead to bad business decisions. Model results change as the data changes, a reflection of new conditions and behaviors that the model might not be able to adapt to, even if it's a machine learning model. This would not be a problem if the inaccuracies were caught quickly enough, but that's often not the case. The main reasons for this situation are a lack of a central repository for models, no consistent metrics to monitor model performance, and insufficient guidance or control mechanisms to determine when a model needs to be retrained or replaced.

>> **Processes for model management not working in practice:** Organizations often find themselves in a reactive mode when put under pressure and are responding in a rush to meet deadlines. (This is especially true for data science teams in their early stages, when their processes are first being established and they feel they have much to prove to management.) It might cause situations where each group has a different approach for handling and validating a model, which can result in a wide array of reports with different levels of detail for review or models that are inconsistently described, making interpretation difficult. No one is sure how the highest scoring model (the champion model) was selected, how a particular model score was calculated, or what governs the business rules that trigger the model.

>> **Lack of transparency:** If you don't actively address transparency in model management, you're not going to gain much visibility into the different stages of model development or much knowledge of who touches the model as it goes through its life cycle. In a small company, that may be okay, but in a larger enterprise you'll soon find out that such a situation can be quite cumbersome. Conflicting assumptions may arise and cause additional confusion, and when, as a last resort, unbiased reviewers are called in to validate the models as they pass through each group, you're facing a big resource drain and an additional hit to the development lead-time.

>> **Loss of important model knowledge:** With inadequate documentation of models, important intellectual property will stay in the mind of the model creator, severely impacting the ability for model reuse. An approach that heavily depends on key individuals also increases the risk of losing vital information entirely — when that person leaves the company, the knowledge is gone.

>> **Insufficient skill sets:** Even with increasing numbers of data scientists entering the marketplace, the shortage of analytical skills needed for model creation and deployment is still a big challenge for many organizations. Without sufficient skillsets in the company, progress can be slow and results poor.

Managing model risk

A vital part of your approach for implementing model management should be focused on understanding and measuring the risk of using and trusting an artificial intelligence model for strategic decision-making and operational setups. Risk goes with the territory because machine learning/artificial intelligence models are *probabilistic:* — they give you the best answer possible, but that answer might still be wrong. It isn't an absolute truth.

Another important risk consideration stems from the fact that machine learning/artificial intelligence models are designed to learn dynamically, which means that, if they're deployed in a dynamic manner, they'll evolve in a live production environment. This also means that the decision framework for the model may change over time, moving away from the principles it was originally trained on in the lab environment when the model is exposed to new data which triggers the model to learn and respond to new behaviors. Therefore, it's important to implement sufficient policy constraints to make sure model learning stays under control.

A more obvious risk you need to manage when it comes to your machine learning/artificial intelligence models lies in the fact that poor training, bias, and bad or corrupt data can affect your model outcomes. (Garbage in, garbage out.) Securing diverse, and representative training data of sufficient quality is a good start when it comes to lowering this risk.

Measuring the risk level

The purpose of measuring the risk of a machine learning/artificial intelligence model is very much related to understanding and defining the risk profile for a certain model. Simply put, if you're considering using the findings and recommendations derived from a specific model for a very important (and costly) investment decision or for an important customer recommendation, wouldn't you like to know the risk involved with trusting the model for that?

So, what would such a risk assessment look like? You'd need to start by fully understanding the technical risks involved in trusting the model in relation to the impact such misplaced trust would have if the model failed. The technical risks associated with a model include aspects such as these:

>> The model's objectives

>> Its functional capabilities

>> The model's learning approach

>> The environmental conditions

>> The level of human oversight

The impact is first and foremost measured by the potential financial, emotional, and physical impact a model failure might have to external and internal users, but it also includes estimating the impact from a reputational, regulatory, and legal perspective.

TIP

Once you understand the technical risks and the impact of failure, you need to consider how to establish the right type of control mechanisms. They key here is finding the right balance in your data science infrastructure between a workspace which is innovative and productive while at the same time remaining accurate and reliable.

Identifying suitable control mechanisms

Understanding which control mechanisms to put in place for which risk isn't an easy task, but Table 16-1 shows a couple of examples of how this could be addressed.

TABLE 16-1   **Examples of Model Risks and Possible Control Mechanisms**

Model Risk	Control Mechanism
Insufficient model supervision	Procedures are in place to monitor the model performance and respond to deviations from the expected performance.
	Strict safety and control measures are employed to prevent uncontrolled evolution of the model.
Lack of model explainabiity	A data protection impact assessment has been performed and results have been communicated to relevant stakeholders.
Biased results	Collection of a diverse set of training data across all relevant classes to avoid latent bias
	Use of regularization techniques to penalize for imbalances in selection across targeted data types
	A diverse team is used to test the model outcomes for latent bias
Poor model performance	Procedures are in place to test the model under varied live conditions to help ensure required performance under deployment
	Cross-validation and assembling techniques (combining predictions from a few different models) are used to help prevent over-fitting of the model which occurs if the model performance is too tightly connected to a particular data set.

REMEMBER

Although risk awareness and control are definitely good things, data science by its very nature is all about using an experimental- and machine-driven approach to augment human behavior to reach beyond what is possible today. Controlling and constraining that approach too much from an infrastructure and process perspective will only hamper data science model innovation and productivity. The key is to find a balanced approach in terms of how to manage model risk and control versus model innovation and business creativity.

Chapter **17**

Exploring the Importance of Open Source

The biggest names in data science are open source, with many of them even part of the same (open source) Apache family: Spark, Hadoop, Kafka, and Cassandra. Though closed source databases are still incredibly popular, open source alternatives are growing at a rapid pace. It is clear that, if they keep growing, those closed source databases won't be that popular for much longer. This chapter focuses on explaining why open source is important in data science, as well as giving you an overview of popular tools and frameworks.

Exploring the Role of Open Source

The popularity of open source systems in data science is growing, for a number of reasons. First, open source principles are based on the sharing of assets, an approach that allows different people in different areas to effectively work together. When companies share their work and allow others to contribute, it allows for more people to find both new issues and new possibilities. Techniques like deep learning, for example, owe a lot to big players like Google and Facebook, which actively give their data and resources back to the community.

REMEMBER

It always looks as though technology is developing very quickly, but the process itself isn't a rapid one. If companies were to attempt to tackle big data software on their own, with no input or help from various open source software, it would be a painfully slow process. There is a serious need to keep up with the times, and data science is a rapidly growing field with a constant shortage of the right competence and skill sets. This not only affects small businesses looking to keep up but also major investors who could change the course of a business at large. Companies are looking to rapidly expand their data science departments and usages, but the talent pool and technology aren't yet there. Open sourcing that data and technology at least eases the burden and allows companies to move forward at an even pace.

TIP

The community approach also means that users have the chance to ask questions and get helpful answers. Rather than go into a tailspin whenever a problem arises, a user will likely find several others in the community who have the answer or, more likely, who know how to find it. Creative open source users also tend to look for ways to work economically and save money. They are likely to find or tweak inexpensive hardware, whereas a major software company with a monopoly may push users to buy very specific and expensive gear.

Understanding the importance of open source in smaller companies

Once companies decide to put their data to use, they often find themselves absorbed in activities focused on implementing a data lake. The overarching objective suddenly becomes gathering and storing data but without the proper resources or, for smaller companies, the funds to harness them, data is absolutely useless. If a small company were to pay for every bit of software and training required to use data, there would be a much smaller incentive to try to integrate big data into the workplace.

Open source, however, has that try-before-you-buy mentality. For companies that offer products based on open source software, potential customers are often familiar and comfortable with the open source aspects of products. New users can take a chance on data with little risk, and experts can move between different solutions with relative ease.

Understanding the trend

If current trends continue, the entire next-generation data platform will be open source, meaning gains for open source companies and those who build on them. In data science, open source is the norm. Even training in the area supports the open source community by often remaining free. Though university degrees will certainly prove useful in the future, many businesses and programmers are simply looking for further training on big data topics to add to their arsenal. Free online courses in data are plentiful, and programs from Udacity (`www.udacity.com`), IBM's Cognitive Class (`https://cognitiveclass.ai`, formerly Big Data University), and others are trying to fill the gap between data science wannabes and users. Even Google has held free courses on how to use data.

The incredible growth experienced by open source programs and communities is the real proof that it is the future of data. The companies that are taking great steps with data are the ones also pushing open source. This not only proves the effectiveness of open source but also shows where finances in data are headed and just where companies are placing their bets. SAS Institute, an American giant in data and analytics, is putting a lot of its investment in open source compatibility, understanding that the idea isn't meant to compete with open source but rather to figure out how to complement it. For example, in the new SAS cloud-based solution, a data scientist can continue to work in an open source environment using favorite open source tools or programming languages during development, but once it's time to put the algorithm into production, that person can deploy it into the virtualized SAS environment to ensure greater reliability, performance, and monitoring.

The past, present, and future of big data is strongly rooted in open source tech, and that will be one of its greatest strengths. With the shortage of data scientists and skilled workers, it will be paramount that companies and individuals have easy access to powerful and up-to-date solutions without fear of paying every last penny to stay in the game. Especially as companies like Google and Facebook share their knowledge, the future of data will only get better and more powerful.

Describing the Context of Data Science Programming Languages

The landscape of data science is evolving quickly, and tools used for extracting value from data science have also increased in number. To fully utilize the potential with open source tools and frameworks, it's important to strategically make sure that your company builds and acquires skills in open source programming languages in the data science space. Although there is no specific order to this list of popular languages for data science, Python and R are fighting for the top spot. However, having data scientists with more than one language skill gives your organization more flexibility.

How many open source programming languages are in the running? Let me count the ways:

>> **Python:** Python is an extremely popular, general purpose, dynamic, and widely used language within the data science community. It is commonly referred to as the easiest programming language to read and learn. Because it combines quick improvement with the capacity to interface with high performance algorithms written in Fortran or C, it has become the leading programming language for open source data science. With the advancement of technologies such as artificial intelligence, machine learning, and predictive analytics, the demand for experts with Python skills is rising significantly.

A weakness with Python is that it executes with the help of an interpreter instead of a compiler, which makes it slightly slower than for example C or C++. Python also has quite high memory consumption due to its flexibility in managing various data types.

>> **R:** R is an open source language and software environment for statistical computing and graphics, supported by the R Foundation for Statistical Computing. This skill set has high demand across recruiters in machine learning and data science.

R provides many statistical models, and numerous analysts have composed their applications in R. It's the favorite language for open statistical analysis, and there's a clear focus on statistical models that have been composed utilizing R. The public R package archive contains more than 8,000 contributed packages. In R, the unit of shareable code is the package. Microsoft, R Studio, and a number of other organizations give business support to R-based computing.

One disadvantage of R is that it's harder to maintain when the code grows bigger. Another issue is that because R is extremely flexible, you may find yourself in many situations when you can do something well in a hundred ways. For maintainability and for working in teams, this may not be what you want.

To support the usage of Python and R, you should also consider using Anaconda (applicable for both Python and R) or RStudio (only for R). Anaconda offers an easy way to perform Python and R machine learning on Linux, Windows, and Mac OS X and has over 11 million users worldwide, it is the industry standard for developing, testing, and training on a single machine, enabling individual data scientists to download Python and R data science packages, manage libraries, dependencies, and environments. It offers support for developing and training machine learning and deep learning models with Scikit-learn, TensorFlow, and Theano as well as analyze and visualize data using other specialized open source software.

» **Java:** Java is a popular, general purpose language that runs on the Java Virtual Machine (JVM). Many organizations, particularly multinational corporations, use this language to create back-end systems and desktop/mobile/web applications. It is an Oracle-supported computing system that empowers portability between platforms.

One big advantage of Java lies in its huge user base in enterprise software, which means there's quite a large community out there, with a lot of skilled developers available to you. It's been around for a long time, and most software engineers are packing Java skills. However, even Java has its drawbacks. For example, Java is comparatively slower and takes more memory space than the other native programming languages, like C and C++.

» **SQL:** SQL (Structured Query Language) is another popular programming language in the data science field that has been around for a while. It's great for querying and editing the information stored in a relational databases and has been used for decades for storing and retrieving data. It has proven to be especially useful for managing particularly large databases, reducing the turnaround time for online requests by its fast processing time. Having SQL skills can be an important asset for machine learning and data science professionals, as SQL is a preferred skill set for many organizations.

» **Julia:** Julia is a high-level dynamic programming language designed to address the needs of high-performance numerical analysis and scientific computing. As such, it is rapidly gaining popularity among data scientists. Because of its faster execution, Julia has become a perfect choice for dealing with complex projects containing high-volume data sets. For many basic benchmarks, it runs 30 times faster than Python and regularly runs somewhat faster than C code. If you like Python's syntax yet have to deal with a massive amount of data, Julia is the next programming language to learn.

» **Scala:** Scala (short for *sca*lable *la*nguage), is now the go-to language for functional programming. This general-purpose, open source programming language runs on the JVM. It's an ideal choice for those working with high -volume data sets and has full support for functional programming.

Because it was developed to run on the JVM, it allows interoperability with Java itself, making Scala a great general-purpose language while also being a perfect option for data science. (It just so happens that the cluster computing framework Apache Spark is written in Scala, so if you want to juggle your data in a thousand-processor cluster and have a pile of legacy Java code, Scala is a good open source solution.)

Most programming languages have drawbacks, and Scala is no exception. Scala is definitely hard to learn and therefore difficult to adopt. Moreover, it doesn't have much of community presence and is hampered by limited backward compatibility. If those minuses outweigh the pluses in your eyes, Scala isn't for you.

Unfolding Open Source Frameworks for AI/ML Models

A machine learning framework is an interface, library, or tool that allows developers to more easily and quickly build machine learning models without getting into the nitty-gritty of the underlying algorithms. It provides a clear, concise way of defining machine learning models using a collection of prebuilt, optimized components. Overall, an efficient machine learning framework reduces the complexity of machine learning, making it accessible to more developers.

Some of the key features of a good machine learning framework are that it

>> Is optimized for runtime performance

>> Is developer friendly and utilizes traditional ways of building models

>> Is easy to understand and code on

>> Provides parallelization to distribute the computation process, to make it faster

The dramatic rise of artificial intelligence in the past decade has spurred a huge demand for artificial intelligence and machine learning skills in today's job market. Machine-learning-based technology is now used in almost every industry, from finance to healthcare. In the following subsections I describe a selection of popular machine learning frameworks and libraries, pointing out their strengths and weaknesses when it comes to building machine learning models.

You're going to be making some weighty decisions when it comes to choosing a framework, but don't forget that open source allows you to try them out first. Just keep in mind that not all machine learning frameworks are optimized for all types of machine learning techniques. Though some are good for natural language processing (NLP), others have been built to focus on deep learning (DL), and though some are more suitable for different types of hardware, others are tailored for the cloud. It's important to consider what your focus area is and, because these frameworks are constantly evolving and also complement each other, allow for some freedom of choice for your users in the application layer.

TensorFlow

Developed by Google, TensorFlow is an open source software library built for deep learning or artificial neural networks. With TensorFlow, you can create neural networks and computation models using flow graphs. It is one of the most well-maintained and popular open source libraries available for deep learning. The TensorFlow framework is available in both C++ and Python formats. Other similar deep learning frameworks that are based on Python include Theano, Torch, Lasagne, Blocks, MXNet, PyTorch, and Caffe. You can use TensorBoard for easy visualization so that you can see the computation pipeline. Its flexible architecture allows you to deploy easily on different kinds of devices. On the negative side, TensorFlow doesn't have symbolic loops (symbolic-driven and dynamic programs for finding bugs) and doesn't support distributed learning, where machine learning algorithms are run in a distributed processing setup spread over several sites or target environments. Furthermore, it doesn't support Windows.

Theano

Theano is a Python library designed for deep learning. With the help of this tool, you can define and evaluate mathematical expressions, including multidimensional arrays. Optimized for GPU, the tool comes with a number of handy features, including integration with NumPy, dynamic C code generation, and symbolic differentiation. However, to get a higher-level, more intuitive view that make it easier to develop deep learning models regardless of the computational backend used, the tool will have to be used with other libraries such as Keras, Lasagne, and Blocks. The tool is great for cross-platform work because it's compatible with the Linux, Mac OS X, and Windows operating systems.

Torch

Torch is an easy-to-use open source computing framework for machine learning algorithms. The tool offers efficient GPU support, N-dimensional arrays, numeric optimization routines, linear algebra routines, and routines for indexing, slicing, and transposing. Based on a scripting language called Lua, the tool comes with an ample number of pretrained models. This flexible and efficient machine learning research tool supports a broad array of major platforms, including Linux, Android, Mac OS X, iOS, and Windows.

Caffe and Caffe2

Caffe is a popular deep learning tool designed for building apps, and it just so happens to have a good Matlab/C++/ Python interface. The tool allows you to quickly apply neural networks to the problem using text without writing code. The tool supports a variety of operating systems such as Ubuntu, Mac OS X, and Windows.

TIP

As new computation patterns have emerged — distributed computation, mobile computation, reduced precision computation, and more nonvision use cases, meaning when the use case has no image representation — the Caffe design has shown some limitations. The introduction of Caffe2 improves Caffe 1.0 in a number of ways, including first-class support for large-scale distributed training, mobile deployment, new hardware support (in addition to CPU and CUDA), and flexibility for future directions such as quantized computation.

The Microsoft Cognitive Toolkit (previously known as Microsoft CNTK)

Microsoft Cognitive Toolkit empowers developers to harness the intelligence within massive data sets through deep learning and by providing scaling, speed, and accuracy with commercial-grade quality and compatibility with a number of different programming languages and algorithms. It is one of the fastest deep learning frameworks with C#/C++/Python interface support. The open source framework comes with a powerful C++ API and is faster and more accurate than TensorFlow. The tool also supports distributed learning with built-in data readers providing a very efficient way to access data. It supports algorithms such as feed-forward, CNN, RNN, LSTM, and sequence-to-sequence. The tool's platform support is a tad limited because it works only with Windows and Linux.

Keras

Written in Python, Keras is an open source library designed to make the creation of new deep learning models easy. This high-level and intuitive neural network API makes it easier to develop deep learning models regardless of computational backend and can be run on top of deep learning frameworks like TensorFlow, Microsoft CNTK, and so on. Keras is known for its user-friendliness and modularity, making it the ideal tool for fast prototyping. The tool is optimized for both CPU and GPU.

Scikit-learn

Scikit-learn (formerly scikits.learn) is a free software machine learning library for the Python programming language. It features various classification, regression, and clustering algorithms, including support vector machines, random forests, gradient boosting, k-means, and DBSCAN, and it's designed to interoperate with the Python numerical and scientific libraries NumPy and SciPy. The tool supports operating systems like Windows and Linux. On the downside, it isn't very efficient with GPU.

Spark MLlib

Apache Spark MLlib is a scalable machine learning library that includes clustering, dimensionality, regressing, collaborative filtering, decision trees, and higher-level pipeline APIs. It is a distributed machine learning framework that can be used in Java, Scala, Python, and R. Designed for processing large-scale data, it has been developed on top of Apache Spark Core and is widely used and focused on making machine learning easy. The tool interoperates with NumPy in Python and R libraries.

Azure ML Studio

Azure ML Studio is a modern cloud platform that data scientists can use to develop machine learning models in the cloud. With a wide range of modeling options and algorithms, Azure is good for building larger machine learning models. The service provides a variety of storage space per account and applies a "pay-as-you-go" model and can be used with R and Python programs.

Amazon Machine Learning

Amazon Machine Learning (Amazon ML) is a robust, cloud based service that makes it easy for developers of all skill levels to use machine learning technology. Amazon ML provides visualization tools and wizards that guide you through the process of creating machine learning models without having to learn complex machine learning algorithms and technology, including other data science services like frameworks and data security services.

Choosing Open Source or Not?

Obviously, you have endless choices of tools and frameworks in the open source space in data science, and because it's the open source space that drives data science evolution, does that mean that open source is the only way to do successful data science? No, of course not.

However, it must be understood that open source is a powerful factor in the data science space. It isn't something to disregard or marginalize. Although your data science investment might seem like a small fish in the ocean, it is still part of the ocean, meaning that it needs to function within the vast data science ecosystem. Few data science investments made today can be seen as isolated environments not dependent on anything external, like data, regulatory demands, vendors, customers, and so on. Considering that, and the fact that most standardization today is also driven from a de facto standardization approach in open source communities, you need to understand and closely monitor what is happening in the open source space, even if you choose to invest in a fully commercial "ready-to-go" solution.

Chapter **18**

Realizing the Infrastructure

D ata plays a key role in every use case of data science, although the type of data used can vary. For example, innovation can be fueled by having machine learning models find insights in the large amounts of data being generated by businesses. In fact, it's possible for a business to cultivate an entirely new way of thinking inside the organization, based on data science alone, if management pushes in that direction. The key is understanding the role that data plays at every step in the data science workflow and how the infrastructure must be designed and operated to maximize utilization of the data as well as enable high data science productivity. In this chapter, I help you focus on how all the pieces need to come together to realize a productive data infrastructure supporting your data science setup.

Approaching Infrastructure Realization

A *data infrastructure* is a decidedly *digital* infrastructure promoting data sharing and consumption. As is the case with other infrastructures, it is the structure that is needed for a system to function. How to realize and set up the data infrastructure depends heavily on company objectives, the size of the company, its line of business, and other factors. But by using a reference model for your data infrastructure, you'll be able to get an overview of areas that need to be covered and what you need to consider in order to make strategic choices in each area.

A *reference model* for a data infrastructure is an abstract framework for understanding significant entities and relationships between them. The purpose is to facilitate understanding of existing data infrastructures when comparing them in terms of functionality, services, and boundary conditions related to the scope of what is included or not.

Figure 18-1 shows a bird's-eye view of a data infrastructure framework, without the included components for each layer and area. Each area covered in this framework needs to be analyzed thoroughly and components selected carefully in relation to the overall company strategy and ambition, as well as industry context, line of business, and legacy infrastructure setup.

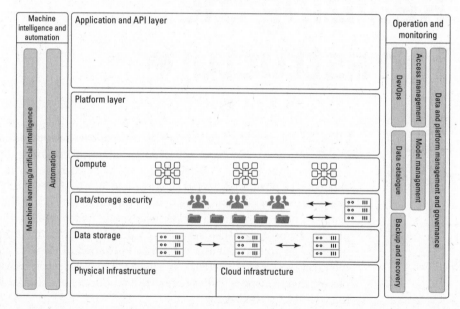

FIGURE 18-1: An example of a data infrastructure framework.

The different areas labeled in Figure 18-1 — physical infrastructure and data security, for example — represent the significant entities in a data infrastructure. The work on your data infrastructure realization should start from these important entities, where you need to determine how they'll serve the overall data science objective in terms of optimizing your data usage, and data science productivity. You know your data, customer, and market best, and by applying that knowledge and understanding of how the infrastructure needs to support your ways of achieving your targets, you'll be able to figure out how to realize that infrastructure in terms of which components should be placed in which layer.

Turning back to Figure 18-1, here's a quick look (starting at the bottom) at the entities and layers you'll need to work with in developing your data infrastructure:

>> **Physical infrastructure:** The hardware assets necessary for implementation, including the communication networks (cables) and data centers.

>> **Cloud infrastructure:** Hardware and software components — servers, storage, a network, and virtualization software — needed to support the computing requirements of a cloud computing model.

>> **Data storage:** Concerns archiving of data in various forms. However, different types of data storage play different roles in a computing environment. In addition to forms of hard data storage, there are remote data storage, such as cloud computing, significantly improving the ways that users access data.

>> **Data storage security:** A specialty area of security concerned with securing data storage systems and ecosystems and the data that resides on these systems.

>> **Compute:** Resources that are used to process data are called compute resources, and in cloud computing these are usually provided by central processing units (CPUs) working together in clusters. To enable fast and capable big data computation there are also other computational resources like accelerated processing units (APUs), and graphics processing units (GPUs).

>> **Platform:** The environment in which a piece of software is executed. It may be the hardware or the operating system (OS) or even a web browser and associated application programming interfaces or other underlying software, as long as the program code is executed with it. The platform layer is the stage on which computer programs can run.

>> **Applications and API's:** A layer that specifies the shared communications protocols and interface methods used by hosts in a communications network. It consists of protocols that focus on process-to-process communication across an IP network and provides a firm communication interface and end-user services. The application layer is used in both of the standard models of computer networking: the Internet Protocol Suite (TCP/IP) and the Open Systems Interconnection (OSI) model.

When realizing your data infrastructure, you'll also need to consider how automation and machine learning techniques will be used across different layers in the infrastructure, because using these techniques as part of the infrastructure processing activities is essential from a speed, cost, and data integrity perspective.

Another aspect is, of course, how you intend to operate the infrastructure and its data systems in practice. This includes aspects such as determining the principles for data management and governance, regulatory aspects, maintenance, and monitoring of the end-to-end infrastructure.

REMEMBER

It is one thing to define and set up your infrastructure, but in order to achieve a successful realization, you need to properly think through both operations and life cycle management of the end-to-end environment.

Listing Key Infrastructure Considerations for AI and ML Support

Historically, the infrastructure for artificial intelligence and machine learning projects have been set up and run by the data science teams themselves, but in larger companies these tasks are now slowly being transitioned to IT infrastructure professionals as these technologies start to move into the mainstream infrastructure. As this transition happens and artificial intelligence initiatives become more widespread, IT organizations need to start carefully considering what type of infrastructure best enables artificial intelligence productivity in this constantly evolving data science space.

TIP

Rather than purchase servers, network infrastructure, and other components for specific projects, the goal should be to think more broadly about the business's needs both today and tomorrow, similar to the way data centers are run today. How can the infrastructure be built in a way that it consists of both a stable foundation in the bottom layers for speed, cost efficiency, and reuse but with user flexibility and a self-service approach on top?

Location

Artificial intelligence and machine learning initiatives are not solely conducted in the cloud, nor are they handled only on premises. These initiatives should be executed in the location that makes the most sense, given the expected output. For example, a facial recognition system at an airport might be forced to conduct the analysis locally because of data privacy and security reasons, and in some cases perhaps depending on latency requirements (response time to and from the cloud). It's critical to ensure that the infrastructure can be deployed in various ways; in the cloud, in an on-premises data center, or at the edge (on a device) so that the performance of AI initiatives is optimized, depending on its requirements and context.

Location is also more than infrastructure location; it could also refer to geographical location. Whether your company is a global one or a local one will impact the geographical spread needed for your infrastructure setup.

One final location aspect to consider has to do with whether you're aiming for a data science environment for internal business efficiency gains or whether the infrastructure should also (or only) support a commercial business offering of data products and services. Location becomes a key component here if there is a data regulatory, system latency, or other need that forces you to be as close as possible to your customers.

Capacity

Artificial intelligence performance is highly dependent on the underlying infrastructure. For example, graphical processing units (GPUs) can accelerate deep learning by 100 times compared to traditional central processing units (CPUs). An underpowered server will cause delays in the process, whereas an overpowered server wastes money. Whether the strategy is end-to-end or best-of-breed, ensure that the computational hardware has the right mix of processing capabilities and high-speed storage. This requires choosing a vendor that has a broad portfolio that can address any phase in the artificial intelligence life cycle.

Data center setup

In terms of data centers, a data infrastructure doesn't live in isolation — it's always considered an extension of the current setup, by either expanding the number of data centers on hand or transforming parts of the current infrastructure to one driven by data science. Ideally, companies should look for a solution that can be managed with their existing tools (or at least as part of a configuration that complements what you already have) instead of scrapping everything and starting over. In some cases, however, this might not be possible, even as a stop-gap measure. If your current infrastructure is hopelessly outdated, with costly and low-performing legacy tools that cannot be virtualized or containerized, it isn't worth the effort to keep using it. If your company's ambition is to transform itself into a company fully driven by data and artificial intelligence, one that intends to build a virtualized business on a fully cloud-based infrastructure, the current setup just has to go.

End-to-end management

There's no single "AI in a box" that can be dropped in and turned on to kick off the AI process. It's composed of several moving parts, including servers, storage, networks, and software, with multiple choices at each position. The best solution is a holistic one that includes all (or at least most) of the components that could be managed through a single interface. Although this is complex, try to think "simplicity" in terms of how it needs to be managed.

REMEMBER

Utilize automation in as many aspects as possible in the management and operational aspects of your data environment.

Network infrastructure

When deploying artificial intelligence solutions, emphasize GPU-enabled servers, flash storage, and other computational infrastructure elements. This makes sense because artificial intelligence is heavily processor- and storage-intensive. Don't forget, however, that your data has to get to your storage systems and servers somehow, which means that you have to pay attention to your network capabilities. Think of infrastructure for artificial intelligence as a 3-legged stool, where one leg consists of the servers; another, of the storage system; and the third, the network. Each must be equally fast to keep up with each other and not cause an imbalance in the infrastructure, and it can never be stronger or faster than the weakest or slowest part. A lag in any one of these components can impair performance. The same level of due diligence given to servers and storage should be given to the network — checking link capacity for data transfer between point of collection to point of computing, for example. Remember that the network infrastructure setup could span over more than one country, at least for global companies or companies dependent on big data volumes from other countries.

Security and ethics

Artificial intelligence often involves extremely sensitive data, such as patient records, financial information, and personal data. Having this data breached could be disastrous for the organization. Also, the infusion of bad or biased data could cause the AI system to make incorrect inferences, leading to flawed decisions. The AI infrastructure must be secured from end to end with state-of-the-art technology, including both security aspects and control mechanisms for AI ethics. And although security aspects are seldom forgotten, ethical ones are. More details on control mechanisms for managing ethical aspects in AI models can be found in Chapter 16.

REMEMBER

As regulatory restrictions become stricter, they're starting to include ethical infrastructure principles — using representative and unbiased data, for example, or forming diverse and unbiased data science teams — that must be fulfilled in order to avoid situations where poorly handled data could cause AI systems to become discriminatory, intrusive, or even hazardous.

Advisory and supporting services

Although services like data science training and various consultancy assignments aren't technically considered part of the infrastructure, they need to be part of the infrastructure decision. Most organizations, particularly inexperienced ones, don't have the necessary skills in-house to make AI successful and productive. A services partner can deliver the necessary training, advisory, implementation, and optimization services across the data science life cycle and should be considered a core component of the deployment.

Ecosystem fit

Data ecosystems can be described as consisting of a number of actors that interact with each other to exchange, produce, and consume data. Such ecosystems provide various vital components for creating, managing, and sustaining data as part of a data infrastructure.

Some say that data science, especially with regards to machine learning and artificial intelligence, is at a maturity level comparable to where the software business was in the 70s or 80s. Therefore, staying ahead of the competition in terms of managing efficient machine intelligence ecosystems can become a major competitive advantage going forward.

REMEMBER

No single AI vendor can provide all technology everywhere. You must select vendors that provide broad ecosystem support and can bring together all, or a lot, of the components of AI to deliver a fully capable, end-to-end solution. Having to put together the components yourself usually leads to unnecessary delays and even failures. Choosing a vendor with a strong ecosystem might instead provide a fast path to success.

Automating Workflows in Your Data Infrastructure

In a data-driven organization, data drives every business process, but you can't fully accelerate and optimize its processes if you don't automate data management workloads every step of the way.

Manual touchpoints and workflows throughout the data management lifecycle impede many companies' ability to take in, aggregate, store, process, analyze, consume, and otherwise make the most of their data resources. Automating more data pipeline processes can help your company execute transactions, make decisions, rethink strategies, and seize competitive opportunities better and faster.

More and more data professionals are adopting an approach focused on creating an automation-driven architecture in which repeatable tasks, such as data integration scripts and machine learning models, can be deployed rapidly into production environments.

However, automating large parts of the data pipeline demands integration of DevOps practices into the working lives of all functions and roles dependent on the pipeline. This includes roles such as data scientists, data engineers, business analysts, and data administrators. Even IT operations and other stakeholders might be impacted, depending on your company setup and whether the pipeline is set up and operated by IT or not.

Automation also requires that DevOps practices span across your entire infrastructure, including your diverse data centers, mainframes, and private clouds, as well as any externally sourced "as-a-service" offering that is being used by the business. Ideally, from an operational perspective, you should have a single visual interface with which to develop repeatable scripts, run scheduled jobs, develop nuanced rules and orchestrations, and otherwise automate the scheduling, consumption, and administration of resources throughout your distributed data environment to fully utilize the time and cost efficiency gains of automated workflows.

Enabling an Efficient Workspace for Data Engineers and Data Scientists

Over the past five years, I've heard many stories from data science teams about their successes and challenges when building, deploying, and monitoring models. Unfortunately, I've also heard about the misconception that data science should be treated just like software development.

This misconception is completely understandable. Yes, data science does involve code and data, yet people leverage data science to discover answers to previously unsolvable questions. As a result, data science work is more experimental, iterative, and exploratory than software development. Data science work involves computationally intensive algorithms that benefit from scalable computational resources and sometimes requires specialized hardware like GPUs. Data science work also requires data — a lot more data than typical software products require. All these needs, and more, highlight how data science work differs from software development. These needs also highlight the vital importance of collaboration between data science and engineering for innovative, model driven companies seeking to maintain or grow their competitive advantage.

As the amount of data in an organization grows, so do the numbers of engineers, analysts, and data scientists needed to analyze this data. Today, IT teams constantly struggle to find a way to allocate big data infrastructure budgets among different users in order to optimize performance. Data users such as data scientists and analysts also spend enormous amounts of time tuning their big data infrastructure, which might not be their core expertise, or at least not what they are assigned to work on.

The importance of an efficient cross-team collaborative workspace shouldn't be underestimated. Such a collaborative workspace should be able to handle all analytical processes from end to end, across different systems and organizations, and ensure that productivity isn't lost along the way. As you might imagine, this isn't an easy task, but with a collaborative workspace approach for the entire data science team, you minimize the inevitable hand-offs between data engineers and data scientists, creating a seamless workflow from data capture to deployment of models into production.

The common, collaborative workspace should also have sufficient ecosystem support for the most popular languages and tools, which allows practitioners to use their preferred toolkit. A good cross-team collaborative workspace should also foster teamwork between data engineers and data scientists via interactive notebooks (which works as an interactive coding environment), APIs, or their favorite integrated development environments (IDEs), all backed with version control and change management support.

Practitioners must also be able to access all needed data in one place and automate the most complex data pipelines with job scheduling, monitoring, in predefined workflows. That access gives the data science teams full flexibility to run and maintain data pipelines at scale and at every part of the data science life cycle.

5
Data as a Business

IN THIS PART . . .

Exploring commercial opportunities in data science

Deciding on commercial approach

Using a data-driven approach to customer engagements

Working with data-driven business models

Considering new delivery models for data products and services

Chapter **19**

Investing in Data as a Business

The "data is an asset" idea is not new. However, despite the large number of people who have made the claim, there's still a huge difference between talking about making data an asset and actually *doing* it. And, when it comes to pushing the slightly more expanded message "data as a business," few are willing to take that ambitious step, even though (as I would argue) the possibilities are endless for those who dare to actually go on and do it.

So, yes, there's been a bit of a buzz out there about data for a while, but the interesting question right now is why an increasing amount of attention is being given to data as an asset and why does it seem as if some companies are discovering it for the first time? And, why do many businesses still undervalue data and information — or are unable to leverage it — although analysts, vendors, and others are repeating the message of the importance of data over and over again? This chapter tries to provide the answers to these questions.

Exploring How to Monetize Data

By now, almost everyone realizes that there's money to be made in data, but not everyone has a good grasp of *how* that money gets made. The following bullet list reveals the secrets by displaying examples of some of the different types of data monetization opportunities out there.

>> **Digital advertising:** Right content, right audience, right time

>> **Financial services:** Cross and upsell and detect fraud

>> **Managing traffic:** Alleviate congestion and optimize delivery routes

>> **Optimized billboard ads:** Understand the traffic and tailor the message

>> **Public transportation:** Passenger satisfaction, operational efficiency, revenue opportunities

>> **Retail:** Optimize store placements and staffing, monitor competitors

>> **Entertainment and Events:** Manage traffic, target promotions

>> **IoT (Internet of Things):** Add value through location data and more

REMEMBER

Data isn't only the main driver for connecting people — it is the lifeblood of so many company perspectives, like understanding and improving customer experience improvement and customer service. And it's not just about the data — it's also about getting access to it, whether the reason is to build new business models, do data-driven marketing, or simply gain access to the right data that enables better decision-making.

It isn't that companies fail to understand the importance of data, information, and actionable intelligence. (Well, some do.) It's mainly that many businesses often don't fully grasp how much of a business asset data really is or how the data is distinguished from the technology through which it flows. However, the emergence of a chief data officer (CDO) in many organizations and across industries indicates a growing recognition of data as a strategic business asset that stands on its own.

TIP

In most organizations with a CDO, that role will either participate in or effectively lead data monetization efforts as a way of demonstrating the CDO's own value. This leadership role can do much to enhance the growing influence of the CDO, but to truly realize true economic benefits of data, companies must champion a CDO's initiatives and start treating data as a real business asset.

Approaching data monetization is about treating data as an asset

Following the seven steps in this section will help your organization or company take a structured approach to monetizing data so that you can start treating data as an asset:

1. **Assign a data product manager.**

    Give your data the same product management attention that you give other valuable assets and competencies. Organizations typically have a defined approach for managing and marketing products. Likewise, if you're considering licensing data in any form, you need someone whose job is to define and develop the market for the data asset and to turn it into a real data product.

2. **Get to know your data and make an inventory of available data assets.**

    It is essential that you evaluate what data you have access to and what you need going forward. And, if you don't become fully data literate and truly understand the details of your data, you won't be able to leverage it as an asset. Make sure you identify all types of data — including operational, commercial, public, social media, and Internet content — that you can mine for new forms of value. Next, help business leaders understand the range of data available and use various data management and data mining techniques to refine the raw data into more consumable and communicable forms. (For more on such techniques, see Chapter 6.)

3. **Evaluate direct and indirect methods for monetizing data.**

    Indirect monetization requires using data internally to improve a process or product in a way that results in measurable outcomes, such as income growth or cost savings. Direct monetization involves a transaction of some sort, or incorporating data into a new data product or service. It can also mean actually selling the data itself (usually, by licensing it) in one form or another.

4. **Observe others.**

    Borrow ideas from other industries. Check out what other industries are doing in order to jump-start your own monetization efforts. It's becoming increasingly important to look beyond a certain industry, not just to find good ideas but also as an early warning sign about how other companies are evolving their information monetization initiatives that could intrude on your market in unexpected ways.

5. **Test ideas for feasibility.**

    Put ideas to the test by asking a series of feasibility questions regarding whether your ideas are practical, marketable, scalable, legal, ethical, economical, and so on.

6. **Prepare the data.**

   Think through how you're going to gather the data, and from which data sources. Then you need to work with the data to enhance its analytical and potential economic value. Again, think of how physical production processes use raw materials to eventually create finished goods.

7. **Decide on a marketing strategy.**

   Finally, for data products that you want to bring to a commercial market, you should focus on the marketing aspect. An important aspect to start with is to package the data product and determine how it will be positioned, priced, and sold. You also need to consider which terms and conditions will be applicable for the data product's specific usage. The appointed data product manager will play an important role in this process.

REMEMBER

Don't perceive monetizing data as an extraordinary task or one intended only for cutting-edge applications of digital business. Rather, you can view it as a core competency for every organization today — one, in other words, that has the potential to generate significant economic value from the varying range of data assets at each company's disposal.

TIP

ROI from data products will be achieved when data products are treated as real products and nothing else. An important step on this journey is to apply traditional product management methods to the data. You need to demystify the notion that a commercial data product is something different that needs to be treated with specific rules and methods.

Data monetization in a data economy

When treating your data products as any other product in your company's product portfolio, you need to continually remind yourself that data products are part of a global market phenomenon referred to as the *data economy.* Understanding the ecosystem of this global data economy is vital for you to succeed when it comes to introducing a new data product or service into that economy. Simply put, the data economy is an economy based on data, data technologies, and data products and services. It has its origin in the new global economy — the one based on the transition from a manufacturing based economy to a service and information based economy.

REMEMBER

The data economy is a digital ecosystem and a network of different players, such as data suppliers and data users. The term *data economy* refers to the ability of organizations and people to leverage data as an asset. Data is utilized to make strategic decisions, improve operational efficiencies, and drive sustainable growth, well-being, and innovations. The value and impact of data is increased by situational, contextual, historical, and time based factors.

WARNING

Integrating, refining, and sharing data increases its value and impact in a data economy. The effective use of data can lead to company growth, improvements in quality of life, and the creation of efficient societies. However, the effective use of data can be hindered by national or regional laws and regulations restricting data usage and the efficient exchange of data, which is explained in more detail in chapter 24.

Figure 19-1 shows the different technology areas enabled in the data economy and can be used to characterize companies and their roles, capabilities, and overall trends in how they currently act in the data economy as well as in the future market place. Companies grow their presence and potential value in the data economy in many ways and it is not necessary for a company to stay within one of these layers. Leading companies usually expand within a layer, or across multiple layers, or in the entire technology stack.

Architectural layers in the data economy	Examples of data enabled technology areas
Visualization provider	applications, user experience, user interface
Insight and execution generator	applications, methods/techniques, analytics and machine learning models and algorithms, open source, programming languages
Platform provider	sensors, devices, servers, cloud, lab, open source, networks
Aggregator	capture, transfer, transformation, quality, correlation, aggregation
Controller	API's, control, quality, anonymization, security
Enabler/Producer	sensors, applications, connectivity, cloud, social media, websites, open source, financial transactions, surveys, digitized hard copies, embedded chips, attached wearables, mobile phones

FIGURE 19-1: Different technology areas in the data economy.

The data economy can also be viewed in different ways in terms of how data is perceived in the perspective of the world's economy.

>> **The big data economy:** Can be defined as algorithm-based analysis of large-scale digital data for the purpose of predicting, measuring, and governing data assets.

>> **The human-driven data economy:** This is a fair and functioning data economy in which data is controlled and used fairly and ethically in a human-oriented manner. The human-driven data economy is linked to the MyData movement (see sidebar) and a human-centered approach to personal data management.

>> **The personal data economy:** This is enabled by individuals focused on using the personal data that all people generate and provide directly or indirectly. Consumers of personal data become the suppliers and controllers, like when Facebook uses our personal data to provide similar topics of interest to us in the application. Similarly, Uber declared recently that algorithms will analyze the personal data in real time and will charge customers what the algorithm predicts that you're willing to pay, rather than a flat rate.

>> **The algorithm economy:** This is where companies and individuals can buy, sell, trade, or donate individual algorithms or app components.

Looking to the Future of the Data Economy

The data-driven economy is increasing competitiveness, innovation, and business opportunities on a world-wide scale. Recent estimates report that rising global data flows have boosted world GDP by more than 10%. This can be compared to figures for Europe only, where the new policy regulations, legislative conditions, and investments in ICT are expected to increase the value of the European data economy to 739 billion euros by 2020, representing 4 % of the overall EU GDP. Key sectors in the data economy either are already data-driven or are on the way to becoming so in areas such as manufacturing, agriculture, automotive, telecommunications, and smart living environments. Healthcare and pharma are also at the core of the data economy.

The world is also moving toward a fairer data economy that benefits everyone. Managing personal information in a responsible manner makes everyday life easier and adds to the well-being of the many. A unified procedure opens up opportunities for user-oriented innovations and business activities.

Individuals are now starting to have more control over (and transparency into) the data concerning themselves. Individuals can actively define the conditions under which their personal information is used. Those service providers who are worthy of customer trust can also gain access to significantly more extensive and varied data e-services.

WARNING

All is not sweetness and light on the data economy horizon — some true challenges are definitely coming down the pike. It won't be easy to constantly come up with ever new approaches to dealing with data breaches as hacker techniques adapt to new security measures. The values to be gained through hacking also increase as the data economy grows. Other challenging issues include determining compensation to victims of data product malfunctions (accidents with self-driving cars, for example) and coming up with sufficient incentives for enterprises so that they take the necessary steps to invest in data security. Add to that the uncertainties for companies about data regulatory burdens and litigation risks and you can see that much work awaits companies and societies as we go forward.

REMEMBER

The regulation of the data economy is closely linked with data privacy. The present approach is flexibility, finding a balance between protecting privacy, and allowing citizens to decide for themselves. The European Union's GDPR regulation is one cornerstone of this new regulatory framework. A new paradigm for data governance is needed, with data ethics as a central component in all regulatory reforms.

Chapter **20**

Using Data for Insights or Commercial Opportunities

f you're planning to use data science mainly to enable data-driven operations and fact-based decisions and to drive internal efficiencies, you must understand your main strategic areas of concern from a business optimizer perspective. If, on the other hand, your main ambition is to underpin your commercial offerings using data science, there are some other strategic considerations to be aware of as a market innovator or disruptor. This chapter explains the strategic aspects you need to consider depending on what your business objectives are.

Focusing Your Data Science Investment

If you and your company have just recently embarked on the data science and machine intelligence journey, it isn't an easy task to strategically decide how you want to focus your investments going forward. Yet choosing the right starting point, is vital, knowing all along that such a decision matters tremendously! On top of that, the data science and machine intelligence areas are quite complex, extremely transformative, and continually evolving with new techniques and methodologies (including new technical solutions for faster and more efficient computation and analysis) coming seemingly every day.

Considering the level of investment needed in terms of money and the effort required to bring about change, how can you be sure that a choice you make today will still be valid a couple of years from now? The simple answer: You can't. That doesn't mean, however, that you should then wait until the data science field has stabilized and matured. If you do that, you can be sure that your competition has passed you by. Instead, focus your investment on the most flexible data architecture setup possible — one that will allow you to change direction if needed in terms of business focus and data scope. The idea here is that any setup you choose should allow you to swap out old applications and machine learning/artificial intelligence tools so that you can incorporate new ones.

REMEMBER

You should make one basic decision early on — whether to focus your data science efforts internally (on business effectiveness and efficiency) or externally (on commercial offerings). Just keep in mind that the main purpose of this (crucial) decision is to guide and focus your efforts rather than to decide the future direction of your business once and for all.

WARNING

If your strategy is to "go big" and spread your data science investment across both internal efficiencies and commercial opportunities from the start, that is of course an option, too. But be aware that focusing equally on both aspects as the first thing you do isn't an easy task — even when your company already has some basic understanding of data science. If your company is new to the data science area, I strongly recommend abandoning that approach: Start instead with an internal focus and then move outward. That will enable your company to leverage a stable data-driven foundation to underpin your commercial offering.

Determining the Drivers for Internal Business Insights

Data science and machine intelligence are having a fundamental impact on businesses and are rapidly becoming critical resources for market differentiation and sometimes even for company survival. It's all about ensuring that your company is focused on doing the right things (effectiveness) and doing them the right way (efficiency).

Recognizing data science categories for practical implementation

Although you might have the best intentions when it comes to your data science investment in terms of establishing a data-driven approach in your company, it isn't an easy task to manage a data-driven business on a day-to-day basis. Even if you have built up the best infrastructure support possible and have a great data science team driving your efforts, it is still hard work to get all aspects right from a practical perspective. There are so many aspects to consider and so many parts of the company that need to fundamentally change. At the same time, you're bedeviled by questions of not only where you should start but also how then to avoid getting lost in all the changes.

Well, being able to quickly categorize every potential impact into one of five categories and then being able to communicate the potential of each one is an efficient way to help leaders drive better results using data science. Luckily for you, I've done the spade work and can now describe these five categories for you:

» **Innovation:** This category is about fostering new thinking and identifying potential business and market disruptions based on data science.

Data scientists hold the ability to frame complex business problems as machine learning or operations research problems, which is the key to finding better, more optimized solutions to old problems. They may even reveal new problems and approaches that were previously unknown.

» **Exploration:** This category refers to how to explore unknown transformative patterns in data, thus identifying unknown business potential by thinking outside the box.

Data scientists should be encouraged to make data discovery expeditions, where there are no clear objectives other than to explore the data for previously undiscovered value. Being data driven is all about challenging old ways of addressing problems by getting rid of conscious or unconscious preconceptions of how things work and therefore must be handled. Data exploration enables you to let the data lead the way to new, more optimized solutions, based on facts.

» **Experimentation:** Let free experimentation and prototyping take place by challenging the status quo with radically new ideas and solutions, not just data insights. Experimentation usually happens in live settings, not in the lab.

With the availability of an ever increasing amount of data and constantly changing customer needs and expectations, human decision-making is becoming increasingly inadequate. Data science, and especially machine learning, excels in solving the kind of highly complex, data-rich problems that overwhelm even the smartest person.

The list of business or government challenges that data science can tackle is potentially endless. Taking just one example, imagine finding the most optimized engine for recommending items that a customer might be interested in based on previous behavior, purchases, preferences, and profile.

How would such a recommendation engine work? With experimentation, you'd use different machine learning algorithms in parallel in a live setting to generate recommendations. All the algorithms are given the same purpose and objective, which is to maximize *conversion* — in other words, maximizing the likelihood of customers buying something on the site.

Different potential buyers are exposed to different algorithms, and after either a predefined period has passed or a certain number of results have been achieved to secure the necessary statistical significance, the outcome is analyzed and one of the competing algorithms in the experimentation is appointed the winner.

» **Improvement:** This category is all about continuously improving existing business processes and current portfolio offerings.

Improvement is perhaps the most common application of data science since data scientists many times have established models for refining internal processes and methodologies related to the data their organization collects. Common examples are marketing firms using customer segmentation for marketing campaigns, retailers tweaking dynamic pricing models, and banks adjusting their financial risk models. In the product development dimension, improvement could include enhancing development and distribution efficiencies in terms of time and cost, but it could also mean enhancing a service offering with the support of machine intelligence capabilities and machine task automation.

» **Firefighting:** Firefighting regards how to identify the drivers of *reactive* behavior — the bad stuff that happens. (Clearly, you'd prefer to focus your efforts on predictive, proactive, and preventive behavior, but if you don't put out fires, your business may burn to the ground.)

Let's face it: Firefighting is sometimes a must. When something has gone wrong in your system — business profitability is decreasing, for example, or a customer has an urgent complaint — you need to react and respond as quickly and efficiently as possible. Data scientists can not only find the best solution to the problem fast but also help identify why this problem occurred in the first place and try to prevent it from ever happening again, by implementing algorithms to predict and prevent it going forward.

Applying data-science-driven internal business insights

Categorizing challenges is one thing, but how do you determine which data science activities are the most important? And how do you then apply those activities to gain real business value out of your data science investment? Last but not least, what role does the data scientist play in all this? I'll answer the last question first by showing how data scientists can apply practical internal business values in your company. So, here are the values you want to promote as well as advice on how data scientists can promote them:

» **Empower management to make better decisions**. If approached correctly, an experienced data scientist is likely to be seen as a trusted advisor and strategic partner to the organization's upper management. A data scientist can communicate and demonstrate the value of the company's data to facilitate improved decision-making processes across the entire organization, not only as stand-alone activities or predefined dashboards for management but also by integrating a need for data and insights into the operational model in the company. The data scientist has the ability to set up the model in such a way that the data truly becomes the fuel for the entire company operations, underpinning every decision, action, and evaluation.

» **Explore opportunities and how to apply insights**. The role of the data scientist is also to examine and explore the organization's data, after which recommendations can be made prescribing certain actions that will help improve company performance, better customer engagement, and ultimately increase profitability.

» **Introduce employees to the usefulness of the data science environment.** Another responsibility of a data scientist is to ensure that employees are familiar with (and informed about) the organization's data science development and production environment for analyzing and identifying value. Data scientists prepare the organization for success by demonstrating an effective use of the system to extract insights and drive action. Once employees understand the capabilities of the data science environment, their focus can shift to addressing key business challenges.

» **Identify new opportunities**. A vital part of that role is to question the existing processes and assumptions for the purpose of developing additional methods as well as analytical models and algorithms to continuously and constantly improve the value that is derived from the organization's data.

» **Promote decision-making based on quantifiable, data-driven evidence.** With the arrival of data scientists, the ability to gather and analyze data from various channels has ruled out the need to take high stake risks. Data scientists can now create models using existing data that simulate a variety of potential actions; in this way, an organization can determine which path enables the best possible business outcomes.

>> **Test decisions.** At the end of the day, it's all about making certain decisions (and not others) and then implementing the changes. But it doesn't end there. It's crucial to know the impact of the decisions made and deployed in terms of how they actually affect the organization. Data scientists can help the organization identify the key metrics related to important changes and quantify their success.

>> **Identify and refine the view of the customer.** Most companies have at least one source of customer data to work with, but if it isn't being used well, the data is pretty much worthless. One important aspect of data science is the ability to combine existing data that isn't necessarily useful on its own with other data points to generate insights an organization can use to learn more about its customers and other target audiences. A data scientist can help with the identification of the key groups with precision through an analysis of disparate sources of data. With this in-depth knowledge, organizations can tailor services and products to customer groups and help profit margins flourish.

>> **Recruit the right talent.** Reading through résumés all day is a daily, repetitive task for a recruiter, but that is now starting to change due to the possibility of using data science for these types of tasks as well. By mining the vast amount of data that is already available —in-house résumés and applications, for example, or even sophisticated data-driven skill tests and games — can help your recruitment team make faster and more accurate hiring decisions.

Using Data for Commercial Opportunities

When you want to make a strategic business move, you need to have proper reasoning and motivation behind your actions. Also, if you really want to seize opportunities, you can't afford to wait months for regular business evaluations. Data science gives business owners a way to make decisions quickly and efficiently while avoiding risks.

REMEMBER

To be clear, using data for identifying and seizing new commercial opportunities has little to do with making better business decisions regarding your company's current endeavors. Instead, it refers to how you can use data to identify, scope, and invest in new commercial business initiatives based on data and data-related products. In other words, it means investing in completely new products and services that can either complement your current line of business or disrupt your existing business model altogether. It really depends on the extent of your ambition and on which opportunities you find and are willing to invest in.

Defining a data product

Here's what seems like an easy question: What is a product based on data? A so-called data product, in other words? It turns out that the question isn't an easy one to answer. As in many areas of data science, there's no clear definition of *data product*, though — if forced to come up with a working definition — I'd say it's a product that facilitates an end goal through the use of data.

Perhaps this definition doesn't actually help your understanding of the concept because it might appear quite broad at first glance — referring to almost anything. Though it's definitely true that many different types of data products are available, you can nevertheless divide them into only two major categories:

» **Data *enabled:*** A functionally oriented product that needs data to fulfill its goal — it runs on data input to fulfill its functional objective, in other words. One example here is when data is used to derive a predictive insight about an automated system action that's needed in order to prevent a problem from occurring (automated decision-making). Without feeding the system with data, the system cannot analyze and act in advance to prevent the problem.

» ***Pure* data:** This type of product consists of data and has a data centered purpose (not a functionality-oriented one). In other words, it generates an insight as the end result, rather than any ability to perform a functional task. A pure data product can also refer to a situation where what you're selling is either the raw data or processed data itself or other related insights derived from data compiled into a report or set of recommendations.

REMEMBER

It pays to reflect a bit on the differences in definition between data products and other technology products. The different types are generally defined by diverse characteristics and should therefore be addressed differently from a strategic perspective. Though many of the standard product development rules applyto both technology products and data products — solving a customer need, learning from feedback, or prioritizing requirements, for example — there are still plenty of areas where the two types of products differ significantly.

This list uses popular products to spell out some of these differences:

» **Gmail:** Is Gmail a data product? No, Gmail is an email service with the primary objective of enabling written, digital communication between individuals. However, Gmail's sorting of our emails as Important or Not Important is a data product because the primary objective is to sort emails based on their data content and relevance, not on their functionality.

>> **Google Analytics**: Is Google Analytics a data product? Yes, it is. The main objective is to explain a quantitative understanding of online behavior to the user. Here, data is central to the interaction with the user and, unlike the other technology products focused on a functional outcome, its key objective is to derive insights from that data.

>> **Instagram**: Is Instagram a data product? No, but if you divide Instagram into different products, some parts (data tagging, search, and discovery, for example) can be considered data products.

Distinguishing between categories of data products

I talk about the distinction between data enabled products and pure data products earlier in this chapter, but there are other, more granular ways of dividing up the data product pie. One way is to sort the products into five main categories: raw data, processed data, algorithms/insights, decision support, and automated decision-making. Figure 20-1 gives a graphical representation of the range, and the following list describes some of the details for each product type:

>> **Raw data:** This term refers to collecting data and making it available just as it is (or perhaps with some small processing or cleansing steps). The user can then choose to use the data as appropriate, though most of the work will be done on the customer or user side.

>> **Processed data:** Processed data is one step up from raw data, meaning that some sort of data cleaning and transformation has occurred in converting the raw data into a format that can then be analyzed and visualized to provide insights to the user of the data product or the intended customer. In the case of customer data, additional attributes can be added for additional value — assigning a customer segment to each customer, for example, or calculating the likelihood of a customer clicking on an ad or buying a product from a certain category.

>> **Algorithms/insights:** Data products related to models and algorithms or algorithms-as-a-service are the newest types of digital data product offerings. Here, an algorithm acts on some data — sometimes in a machine learning context, sometimes not — and the result is new information or insights. An example is the algorithm used in Google Images. When the user uploads a picture, it receives a set of images that are the same or similar to the one that's uploaded. Behind the scenes, the product extracts an image's salient

features, classifies it, and matches it to stored images, returning the ones that are most similar. Insights are added to this same category because the data product can sometimes be the insight itself, not the algorithm that generated the insights. A typical buyer of an insight (via a report or an insight-as-a-service model) is nontechnical. A typical insight related to Google Images could be derived through using machine learning to compare hundreds of images of your product to detect certain patterns of customer preferences when using your products, for example. The insight into how customers prefer to use your product could then be used in future marketing campaigns or as input to model future product enhancements.

>> **Decision support system:** This category provides information to the user in order to support decision-making, though the final decisions are still made by the user. Analytics products such as Google Analytics, Flurry, and SAS Visual Analytics are examples that fall into this category. A lot of effort is needed in order to create a decision support system, and it's expected to do most of the job with the intention to give the user relevant information in an easy-to-digest format — dashboards to allow users to take better decisions, for example. When using these analytics tools, the insights gained could lead to changes in the editorial strategy, plans for addressing leaks in the conversion funnel, or a doubling down on a given product strategy. The important thing to remember with this type of data product is that, although the product has collected the data, compiled the data, and displayed the data, the user is still expected to interpret the data. Users are in control of the decision to act (or not act) on that data.

>> **Intelligent and automated decision support:** In this type of data product, all intelligence within a given domain is included, meaning that the product can stand on its own and both provide and act upon insights within the specific data product. One example is Netflix product recommendations, where data from previous user preferences on series and films are used by the algorithm to recommend new selections. Since the result of the decision on what to view is captured in the same environment (the Netflix application) the model can capture each choice and learn to give even more precise and intelligent recommendations in the future. Other examples of more complex data products in this category would include closed loop automation with examples such as self-driving cars and automated drones. This type of data product allows the algorithm to do the job, learn from data and actions, and then present the user with the final output. The outcome sometimes comes with an explanation of why the AI chose that option; at other times, the decision-making process is completely hidden.

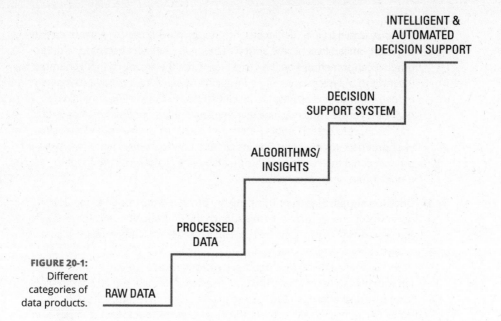

INTELLIGENT &
AUTOMATED
DECISION SUPPORT

DECISION
SUPPORT SYSTEM

ALGORITHMS/
INSIGHTS

PROCESSED
DATA

FIGURE 20-1:
Different
categories of
data products.

RAW DATA

REMEMBER

A main difference between these categories is the built-in level of complexity. More specifically, the categories in Figure 20-1 are classified in terms of their increasing internal complexity and (should have) less complexity on the user side. For example, though raw data has little built-in complexity to start with, it requires complex techniques and skills to develop a product that generates value out of the raw data. On the other hand, with a data product that is built on a complex machine learning algorithm, you get a simple user interface for the customer with less thinking required. The data product manages the complexity internally through the machine learning algorithm.

REMEMBER

Typically, (but not exclusively), raw data, processed data, and algorithms are focused on technical users. Insights, decision support, and automated decision-making products tend to have a more balanced mix of technical and nontechnical users.

Balancing Strategic Objectives

Suppose that you own a shoe company. Wouldn't it be useful if you found out that a segment of your target market prefers to buy running shoes in the month of June? Wouldn't it be more useful if you found out that the segment belongs to the 16–21 age group, that they prefer road running shoes to trail running shoes, that they can afford to spend $100 on a pair of shoes, and that they love the colors blue and red?

You don't always need to sell data to make money from it. Thanks to the ever increasing popularity of the Internet, affixing a small chip to every product (for example, shoes) and tracking the usage and other details is now simpler than ever. This doesn't mean that your company needs to listen to your customers' private conversations or keep track of everything your customers are up to. You only need to track the data that you think is beneficial for your business. That data may, however, range from nonsensitive to sensitive data (product usage, interests and preferences, or Internet activities, for example) to even your customers' friends' interests and SMS and call logs. Therefore, you must have a good strategy for handling data ethically and in a legally correct manner.

Hence, the applicability of data as input to or output from your business is an important strategic decision that needs some consideration. Spending time to understand the current trends in the market for your line of business is important, but so is making sure that your ambitions are feasible. If your line of business is more traditional and isn't yet digitalized and is remains far from being data driven, perhaps the best way to start is with an internal focus on turning things around, before you try disrupting the market with new data products.

Chapter **21**

Engaging Differently with Your Customers

Because humans everywhere now live in the age of the customer, it's time to clarify what the term customer experience management (CEM) really means. It may help, however, to first see what it is not. CEM is not about collecting feedback, responding to feedback, or tracking that tried–and–true metric of customer loyalty, your Net Promoter Score. None of these actions individually represents CEM. Instead, you could say that CEM refers to the complete philosophy and methodology that makes your business delightful to work with for your customers. In this chapter, I want to show you how an effective data strategy can guide you to a better and more insightful approach to your customers.

Understanding Your Customers

Optimizing the customer experience is a great way to attract new customers, but it's also one of the best ways to foster customer loyalty to retain the ones you already have.

Despite this benefit, marketers and other organizational leaders alike often neglect the customer before and after the sale. The biggest barrier to even beginning to turn around this counterproductive practice is usually the lack of a deep understanding of the customer in the first place.

REMEMBER

Having a comprehensive understanding of your customers is the key to achieving core business goals, whether you're trying to build (or optimize) the customer experience, create more engaging content, or increase sales.

To see how you can come to a better understanding of your customers, I recommend that you look at some key activities you need to perform in order to really get to know your customers. The next few sections show you the way.

Step 1: Engage your customers

An optimized customer experience is, of course, valuable for revenue and retention, but if you get it right, it can also be a great source of customer insight. Engaging with your customers in real-time has become more easily accessible, thanks to a variety of new tools. Messenger is becoming an ever more popular customer service channel, and tools like Drift allow you to talk with your customers as they browse your website. Drift is especially exciting because it acts as an entirely new way to approach the customer experience in real-time in a conversational format compared to traditional customer engagement. So, speed here is definitely a plus, but there are a number of other pluses, as Figure 21-1 makes clear.

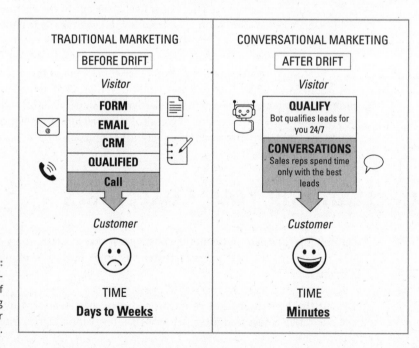

FIGURE 21-1: The old-versus-new ways of performing customer marketing.

Though channels like Messenger and Drift are clearly great ways to collect customer insight, they're not often used in the most effective manner. If your engagement is ad hoc or piecemeal, you're not putting the true power of these channels to use; such engagement needs to be part of a bigger plan. That means companies and organizations must have the foresight to invest the time and money it takes to understand the entire customer journey. It's not enough to take a single point along the way to survey and understand your customer; without a broader context, these spot-checks could be worse than useless. You wouldn't be able to answer basic questions, such as how did the customer get to this point or what were they looking for or where are they heading in the overall journey, because you don't have the information you need in order to come up with an informed answer.

If you invest the time needed in understanding the entire customer journey, you'll be able to flesh out how your customers experience your brand over the course of their relationship with that brand. That context will let you ask your customers the right questions at the right time, thereby building brand engagement as well as the kind of customer trust needed to help guide the journey to the point of purchase.

TIP

As you work to keep your customers engaged during the first stages of the customer journey, think of your relationship as a 2-way street. Encourage customers to share their thoughts and opinions by including a customer satisfaction survey on a regular basis in your ordinary emails.

Follow these three principles when designing a survey:

>> **Remove bias.** Ask customers for their opinions without projecting your own. Get their uninfluenced, impartial opinions. You want genuine insights, even if they're negative. An example might be something as simple as this: "What do you think we could do better?"

>> **Be concrete.** Use simple language that asks for feedback on a specific topic. For example, the question "How have you improved your marketing effectiveness using our machine learning algorithm?" will help to determine the value your customers are getting from you.

>> **Focus.** Your surveys should address just one area of the customer experience. The aim is to get insights that you can then act on.

Keep these principles in mind as you personalize your customer survey with questions relating to your brand and product or service.

Step 2: Identify what drives your customers

Many marketers make the mistake of using generic demographics — like age, profession, and location — to develop a sense of the range of their customer base.

These data points simply don't provide enough information to create messaging that resonates with your customers on an emotional level.

One way to dig deeper into customer preferences is to use the Acquisitions tab on Google Analytics to see which social media outlets, industry blogs, and professional forums your site traffic comes from. Then apply this information to your identities so that you can find out where and when to reach them more effectively.

TIP

Acquiring keyword data is another helpful way to discover the terms and descriptions that certain buyer identities use to describe your services. To segment customers based on keyword searches, for example, first use Google Webmaster Tools to create a list of common keywords that drive people to your site, group the keywords into overarching themes, and then assign them to different customer categories based on the data you have available. To put this effort into action, incorporate these keywords across your website and then map content marketing efforts and other online interactions towards these new customer categories based on what attracts different type of buyers. Being attentive to customer preferences and speaking the same language as your customers is a subtle way to make your current audience feel more welcomed.

Step 3: Apply analytics and machine learning to customer actions

From clicking on a link to reading a web page, every customer action offers valuable insight into customer behavior. To determine how customers interact with your website, you can try user behavior tracking tools such as Google Analytics and Inspectlet. They're great tools for gathering insights such as time-on-page and bounce rate. Inspectlet can even provide short videos of users on your page in real-time.

The behavioral data you collect should lead you to conclusions about what your audience doesn't understand, what they like and don't like, and how you can create a stronger website experience. If people had trouble navigating to a certain sales page, for example, you can adjust the interface to allow for a more user-friendly experience.

TIP

If people spend more time on one page than others, analyze that page's content to see what may be needing extra attention. For example, if people are spending too much time on the checkout page, perhaps it's time to improve the customer payment experience on your site. Most importantly, though, if you have a page with a high bounce rate, try to see what is making people leave.

Recommender systems first became popular in the retail industry, mainly in online retail or e-commerce for personalized product recommendations. One most common usage is for Amazon's section on "Customer who bought this item also bought . . .". Recommender systems could be seen as an intelligent and sophisticated salesman who knows the customer's taste and style and can thus make more intelligent decisions about what recommendations would benefit the customer. Though it started off in e-commerce, it is now gaining popularity in other sectors, especially in media. Some of the examples are YouTube "recommended videos" or Netflix "other movies you may enjoy". Other industries are now also realizing the value of using recommender systems. (The transportation industry is one example.)

Step 4: Predict and prepare for the next step

Creating a plan for future customer engagement is just as important as creating a plan for the present. This puts customer experience teams in the right frame of mind to respond to customers during stressful or challenging situations.

Predictive modeling software mines existing customer data to identify cyclical patterns and trends that can inform decision-making. Two great tools for these tasks are the custom analytics programs from RapidMiner and Angoss, both of which create realistic future models. To see how predictive modeling informs customer strategy, imagine that you work for a SaaS company that wants to adjust its product road map to anticipate customer needs. By looking at the historical behavioral data, you can see which features customers have found most valuable over time and which features they didn't use. Understanding your most popular and most visited pages can also influence your content strategy, focusing on topics and formats that will best solve your audience's challenges.

TIP

Identify similarities across the most commonly used features to determine why your customers liked them. Additionally, looking at market trends and analysis gives you a good idea of what other companies in your space have already accomplished so that you can devise new features that explore these areas.

REMEMBER

Many companies turn to market research firms only as a form of insurance — a means of reducing business risk related to investing in the wrong product or service, in other words. But market research can be used in product development not only as insurance but also as a tool to establish market needs and to obtain a better understanding of market potential. Continuous market research throughout the product road map naturally leads to more sales. The more you understand your market, the better product/market fit you have.

Step 5: Imagine your customer's future

The only way to understand the unique and dynamic customer buying journey is to put yourself in your customer's shoes. This is made possible by an advanced technique called *customer journey mapping,* a method where companies create a detailed, graphical representation of the customer journey based on critical touch points. These touch points are interactions between a customer and your brand before, during, or after purchase.

Modern-day customer interactions encompass a wide range of touch points: mobile, web, social, interactive voice response (IVR), in-store, chatbots, and more. This brings me to the concept of *omnichannel,* a cross-channel content strategy that organizations use to improve their customer experience. Customers today switch between many different channels frequently — say, in the middle of a purchase or even during discovery. Analyses of the trends in customer behavior across industries show that omnichannel is only going to get bigger with the growth and variety of channels; therefore, customer journey mapping has to include every touch point and channel where your customers have a presence.

Figure 21-2 illustrates the broad variety of possible touch points you can use to reach your customers as well as how these points vary depending on whether it's pre-purchase, during purchase, or post-purchase. Capturing data from all three phases enhances your overall understanding of what is driving your customer to buy — and, hopefully, buy again.

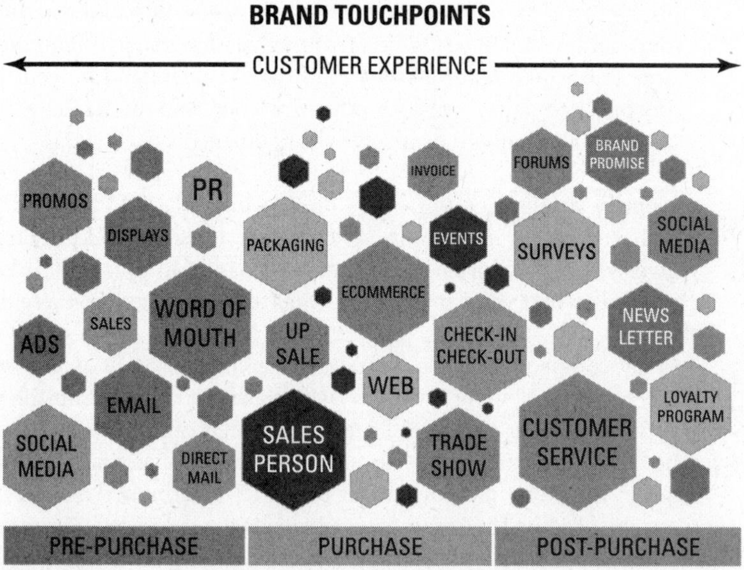

FIGURE 21-2: A word cloud for brand touch points.

The first condition to being omnichannel is that you need to be *multichannel:* You need to be available wherever your customers are. However, having these channels up and running is one thing; making them work together seamlessly as part of the overall journey is another.

Check out Uber as an example of how to define touch points and how to apply them to customer journey mapping. Minor touch points include activities like downloading the app or just following the app on social media. Major touch points include things like actually requesting a ride or completing driver training.

Once you define the touchpoints, you need to explore the circumstances affecting each of them. For example, a marketer at Uber might ask, "What influenced the rider to download the app for the first time? Was it related to Uber's customer referral program?" The internal team should be engaged with these issues to get a well-rounded perspective and promote collaborative problem solving.

When failed touch points are identified (when a customer fails to use the downloaded Uber app, for example), you need to establish a plan for contacting these customers. Creating milestones might be a good idea, such as when an app user hasn't logged in to the account in three months or when an avid customer suddenly stops using the product. It's best if the customer experience team can call, write, or meet with customers directly to understand why they're disengaged. If these resources aren't available, you could create an email marketing message specifically focused on reengaging your customers based on certain milestones.

Keeping Your Customers Happy

The first thing you need to address when aiming to keep your customers happy by improving customer satisfaction is to get a better understanding of what the current customer attrition rate actually is. In that way, you can focus your initial efforts on the group of customers most likely to leave or on their way to leave already.

To reduce customer attrition (also referred to as *churn*), you should use historical customer data to map snapshots of customers taken at a given point in time. Such snapshots would, for example, record who they are, what they bought, and how they interacted with the products and/or services sold to them. You should map that information to whether they later churned (ceased being a customer, in other words). You could then study each current customer you've determined is likely to churn and then rate how valuable that customer is. Finally, you could determine what action needs to be taken in order to prevent the most valuable customers from churning.

Here are some actions you can take to prevent your customers from churning:

>> **Enhance marketing campaigns by cross-selling products.** Make sure your marketing campaigns are really using the right message to target the right group of customers. There is nothing as annoying as being the subject of a marketing campaign that offers you something you have absolutely no interest in. It really gets you wondering whether the company knows its customers at all. Avoiding this embarrassment is best addressed by the cross-selling of products. Start by mapping customer/product pairs to purchase indicators as recorded in historical data. By doing so, you'll know whom to target when launching a new product or when promoting an existing one.

>> **Optimize products and pricing.** Even if you're able to offer the right product or service to the right customer, it's also important to offer it at the right price. To find out which price is right for a certain product, you need to map product characterizations and price to numbers of sales. Then you can change the price and other characteristics to see how they impact revenue (price × number of sales). This gives you a good understanding of the most optimized price level.

>> **Increase customer engagement.** Finally, it's important to know more about how you can increase your engagement with the customer. What is the customer really interested in? You can learn more about this by observing customer behavior when customers are presented with different products or services. This is needed in order to map customer/item pairs to indicators of customer interest. This enables you to predict needs and interests and take them into account when evaluating the service provided to the customer.

So, how do you know when a customer is served well? Simply put, serving customers well implies that you need to either offer your customers products that they are interested in and can afford or provide services they engage with.

TIP

To keep your customers happy and fully satisfied, it's vital that each and every part of your company collaborates with one another. Keeping your customers happy depends on not only the quality of your customer service crew but also other departments (those responsible for production, for example.) Only when all the gears in your company are well oiled and tightly connected can you expect the best results.

REMEMBER

Even if you implement all measures you can think of to make your company customer-centric, you can always do better. The same rule applies to customer service. Setting up some business goals, linked with customer service, as well as key performance indicators (KPIs), will help you stay on track with all your efforts to make customer satisfaction grow.

WARNING

If your customer comes with an issue in a communication channel that is less preferred — Facebook, for example — don't force the customer to use your chosen channel in its place. If the customer reached out to you on social media, it was because it was the most comfortable way for her to communicate. Instead, you should offer the customer some different choices, not only the one solution. Also remember to keep your customer informed about when the problem could be solved, instead of keeping the customer waiting. It's all about offering your customers the same services that you would demand from others.

Serving Customers More Efficiently

Serving customers more efficiently mainly refers to improving operations in order to reduce costs. But of course it also means serving customers well — as in anticipating issues before they occur or improving the handling of customer support requests when they arise.

TIP

Data science can increase efficiency through the use of supervised machine learning techniques. The idea is to map situations to outcomes so that you can predict outcomes in new situations. One example is when a customer has been exposed to a new product: The outcome here is defined by whether the customer will show interest in the new product. In such situations, machine learning techniques need examples to work with and train on. That means you need data on situations (characterized as finely as possible, along with any contextual information) and outcomes observed in these situations. An analysis of the sample data allows you to first find patterns and then the relationships between situations and outcomes. Predictions on outcomes are made automatically by using these relationships.

The following activities (presented in their business contexts) can help you improve efficiency in terms of your customer management through a predictive and preventive approach.

Predicting demand

Predicting demand is important to businesses that observe high variability in demand for their services and/or products — businesses that sell fresh goods and need to avoid having too much or not enough in stock, for instance. This enables benefits in terms of the ability to measure demand and the context in which it happened so you can map context to demand. You can also use the insights gained to determine how much staff to hire in anticipation of how busy the business is going to be.

Automating tasks

You can save time by having machines perform certain repetitive or intelligent tasks automatically. Sometimes you might already be performing these tasks with hand-crafted rules, but when you introduce machine learning abilities to run the activity instead, you can tap into a new potential of optimizing how the activity is done. Using machine learning to automate how the task is done means that the machine automatically learns rules from sample data, and, over time, it might optimize how the task is done, depending on which techniques you're using. In this context, one obvious example is the scoring of credit applications or insurance claims, where you're expected to either approve or reject something. Another example is automatically performing risk analyses from historical data using machine learning. This one gives you a better base for making decisions before investing time and money into new projects.

Making company applications predictive

You have much to gain by making applications used by employees related to customer relationship management, enterprise resource planning, human resources predictive. By adding predictiveness capabilities to these applications, people can do their jobs more efficiently. Here are some of the benefits of using predictive applications:

>> **You can prioritize things.** Predictive company applications enable you to direct user focus to what is most important. This can be email (such as Google Priority Inbox), customer support requests (so that you can reply more quickly to the most important ones), or other external requests toward your company that you need to reply to urgently, for example.

>> **You can better adapt the workflows.** A proactive approach enables you to use adaptive workflows based on predictions rather than on predefined manual rules. You could, for example, route customer support requests to those best equipped to handle them, in which case the outcome is a customer support team or person.

>> **You can adjust the user interface.** You can easily increase user efficiency by adapting the interface to show just what users need at the time they use the app. All you need to do is map a context to an action that will need to be performed to trigger the adjustment.

>> **You can automate user settings.** Predictive applications let you set configurations and preferences automatically by analyzing application usage data, and thereby speeding up user efficiency.

Chapter **22**

Introducing Data-driven Business Models

The increased use of data is transforming the way companies do business. With advanced analytics, machine learning, and access to new data sources, companies in one sector can play a role in the products and services of others — even those far removed from their traditional line of business. This blurs the boundaries between industries and changes competitive dynamics. Companies that embrace the full range of opportunities and transform their business models in parallel with these shifts will find new opportunities for revenue streams, customers, products, and services. In this chapter, I describe how you can approach the area of data-driven business models.

Defining Business Models

First you need a working definition of a business model. It's generally described as the foundation of how an organization creates, delivers, and captures value in economic, social, cultural, or other contexts. The process of business model construction and modification, also called *business model innovation*, forms a part of ordinary business strategy development.

The fact is, though, that the term *business model* is used for a broad range of informal and formal descriptions to explain core aspects of a business, including purpose, business process, target customers, offerings, strategies, infrastructure, organizational structures, sourcing, trading practices, and operational processes and policies including the company culture.

TIP

Given the wide use of the term "business model," I recommend defining it as broadly as possible. For me, that means defining business models simply as the design of organizational structures to endorse a commercial opportunity. Business models are used to describe and classify businesses, especially in an entrepreneurial setting, but they're also used by managers inside companies to explore possibilities for future development.

REMEMBER

Today, the type of business model that's needed for a certain company might actually depend on how the underlying technology is used. For example, entrepreneurs on the Internet have also created entirely new models that depend completely on existing or emergent technology. Using technology, businesses can reach a large number of customers with minimal costs. In addition, the rise of outsourcing and globalization has meant that business models must also account for strategic sourcing, complex supply chains, and moves to collaborative, relational contracting structures.

As you'd expect, business model design generally refers to activities that focus on designing a company's business model. It's part of the business development and business strategy process and involves design methods. However, there's a big difference between defining an entirely new business model when none is in place and changing an existing business model.

REMEMBER

In the case of designing a new business model, a common challenge is usually to understand and allocate needed resources in time. When changing an existing model to a new business model, however, the challenge is rather to manage resistance or lack of interest from employees as well as adapt organizational and product structures to new ways of developing and selling. And, depending on the size and distribution of employees, this can be a challenging task.

Technology-centric communities sometimes have specific frameworks for business modeling that attempt to define what can often be a difficult approach to defining business value streams. (At some point, tech start-ups have to start making money, right?) Business model frameworks represent the core aspect of any company, striving to represent the total picture of how a company selects its customers, but they also include how a company defines and differentiates its offerings, defines the tasks it will perform itself and those it will outsource, configures its resources, goes to market and creates usefulness for customers, and captures profits.

There's one final prism to use when looking at a business modeling framework: Is the focus on internal factors, such as market analysis, product/services promotion, development of trust, social influence, and knowledge sharing, or is the concentration more on external factors, like competitors and technological aspects?

It would seem as if we're asking business modeling frameworks to do too much, and it's true that the scope can be very broad — at times too broad. And yet, when used correctly, business modeling frameworks can be incredibly useful tools. In the context of data science, however, new frameworks for business modelling have emerged — data-driven business model frameworks. These will be explained and exemplified in more detail later in this chapter, but first I want to explain what a data-driven business model actually is.

Exploring Data-driven Business Models

The increased utilization of data in any modern business of today is challenging traditional ways of adding business value and present significant risks to companies that don't respond accordingly. And of course it offers opportunities to those that do. Companies that transform their business models in parallel with these shifts will find new doors opening for them.

For example, in the home thermostat market, which is a traditionally a relatively stable sector with a small, settled list of competitors, a start-up called Nest has been able to challenge the established companies by introducing a thermostat that uses analytics to learn customers' preferences by analyzing data patterns — patterns that are then used for building a model for how the thermostat should adjust itself accordingly. The example of how Nest's novel, data-driven business model enabled it to enter a market long closed to outsiders is a good example of how data-driven business models can totally disrupt any traditional market segment.

However, the payoff isn't just for new players. For established companies, new data-driven business models can help keep and expand their share in an existing market. One recent example in the automobile insurance sector is the Snapshot app offered by major player Progressive. With Snapshot, data is collected from a small device that customers plug into their car's diagnostic port to help calculate premiums based on actual driving habits. Among the data analyzed is when and how far the customer drives and the number of hard brakes he makes. Good drivers are rewarded with lower premiums. On average, it could mean a savings of 10 to 15 percent, which can be a compelling value proposition to many drivers.

Creating data-centric businesses

The large volume of data that companies generate and the insights that data generates may well have value to other companies and organizations, both within and outside the industry it belongs to. Social media sites, for example, often capture data related to users' preferences and opinions, which could be information of interest to manufacturers that want to better focus their product development efforts and marketing campaigns. Mobile network operators routinely collect subscriber location data, which could be of value to retailers that want to know where consumers are shopping. By making this information available (for a price, of course), companies can develop new revenue streams through data monetization.

TIP

Though the sale of personal information traceable to specific individuals can raise privacy concerns, companies can greatly reduce sensitivity by aggregating and ensuring the anonymity of data through segmentation, for example. This means that individuals are first put into a group or segment based on their consumption habits, neighborhood, age, and so on. When the grouping is done, all personal data (name, address, and phone number, for example) is then removed so that it becomes anonymized.

REMEMBER

Identifying relevant applications is just the first step in deriving value from big data. New capabilities, new organizational structures (and mindsets), and significant internal change will also be required. But you should not underestimate the importance of zooming in on the right opportunities. You need to think outside the box, embrace new models, and even reimagine how and where you want to do business. A culture that encourages innovation and experimentation — and even some radical thinking — will serve this undertaking well, but so will calling in outside help when needed to assess, prioritize, and develop the different routes to value.

Data and machine intelligence isn't just changing the competitive environment; it's fundamentally transforming it. And your business needs to change along with it. Seeing where the opportunities lie and creating strategies to seize them will help your company turn the data promise into a reality. And that new reality will enable you and your company to gain new customers, new revenue, and even new markets along the way.

Investigating different types of data-driven business models

An important first step in realizing the potential benefits of data in your business is deciding what the business model(s) will be. The data economy supports an entire ecosystem of businesses and other organizations. These are often dependent on each other's products and services, so the strength of the sector as a whole is crucial. For example, companies and organizations may share or sell data, models, algorithms, and insights, which is incorporated into new or enhanced solutions by other companies.

It's also worth considering that data products require a business model to determine how users will benefit from the service provided and how the value from data products and services will be generated. Many models are available for how to capitalize on the value of data and the services based on data. Which one you and your company should go for really depends on factors such as the type of service provided, whether it's related to a platform or a product, and how the customer will benefit from it. (One common monetization example is the free-mium model, where users are offered part of a service for free but are charged for upgrading to the full service or are charged a premium for additional data services with an existing product.)

Figure 22-1 shows different high-level categories of data-driven business models and examples of areas within each category. The next few sections look at the categories in greater detail.

Data-driven business model types	Examples of offerings
Differentiation through data	• Data-driven and predictive business • Business contextual relevance • Create new offerings
Data and insight brokering	• Sell data • Sell insights • Sell analytical models • Sell ML models • Provide benchmarking
Infrastructure brokering	• Analytics and statistics tools • Cloud and data center services (IaaS) • Platform services (PaaS) • Data and analytics consultancy services
Data delivery networks	• Cross-licensing • 2-sided business models • Targeted advertisements
ML/AI functionality enablement	• Intelligent automation • Technology evolution • Robotics • New intelligent systems

FIGURE 22-1: Different categories of data-driven business models.

Differentiation through data

The differentiation-through-data category of data-driven business models refers mainly to how you use data to *differentiate* your current business — taking steps to strengthen it and make it more competitive. This can be done by using data to better understand your market and your customers, using data to drive decisions throughout the company or becoming more predictive, proactive, and preventative in business operations and toward your customers.

This category can also include areas such as expanding your current business by developing new types of services based on data related to your current business. In this sense, differentiation also creates new experiences. For a decade or so now, the world has seen technology and data add new levels of personalization and relevance to advertisements and location-based services as two examples. Google's AdSense delivers advertising that is actually related to topics users are looking for. Online retailers are able to offer — via FedEx, UPS, and even the US Postal Service — up-to-the minute tracking of where your packages are. Map services from Google, Microsoft, Yahoo!, and now also Apple provide information linked to where you are.

Data and insight brokering

Another business model category relates to how you can become a broker of data and insights. This includes selling raw, aggregated, or processed data (cleansed, labeled, or even correlated data, for example) of which you are the owner. It could also include selling data of which you are not the original owner, but then you need to make sure you have the rights to sell the data to a third party.

Another business model in this category includes selling specific analytical models for stand-alone purposes or to integrate into another solution or other applicable usages. Data-driven business models offer opportunities for many more service offerings that will improve customer satisfaction and provide contextual relevance. Imagine a map-based service that links your fuel supply to the availability of fueling stations. If you were low on fuel and your car spoke to your maps app, it could not only provide you with routes to the nearest open gas stations within a 10-mile radius but also receive the price per gallon. Who wouldn't pay a few dollars a month for a contextual service that delivers the peace of mind of never running out of fuel on the road?

TIP

Here's another example. In this scenario, as part of a business, you manage to own millions of pictures of items, including descriptions of what these pictures depict. On top of using this data for enhancing your own business, you could sell access to this data set for the training of machine learning models, — Deep Learning models, for example — as an additional revenue source.

Data and insight brokering can also include selling generic or specific machine-learning-based models designed either to run as a stand-alone products or to be integrated into existing software for enhancing its output. An example of the latter is a web based application aimed at providing a meeting place or an online marketplace for people who want to sell and buy used goods — the Swedish company Blocket or the American counterpart eBay, for example. None of these firms had machine learning models enhancing the applications in the beginning; these kinds of functionality — the ones supporting search, recommendations, and automated classification of images when publishing a new ad — were added later on.

Finally, such brokering could also include benchmarking services, which in this context refers to using data from several companies in a certain market or business segment to compare aspects such as market penetration, customer rating, or adherence to a certain applicable standard.

Infrastructure brokering

Infrastructure brokering takes a slightly different tack from the previous two categories. It aims to sell products needed to enable the first two categories. For example, it could offer infrastructure solutions for acquiring and collecting data and/or storing and processing data offered via cloud services. It could also refer to various types of reporting or analytics tools, offered on-premise or in the cloud. The solutions could be used for many purposes, including data exploration, data visualization, deriving insights for internal usage, or even commercializing the outcome by selling the derived insights. Finally, this category could also include consultancy services connected to infrastructure setup and usage.

Data delivery networks

The data-delivery-networks category of business models refers to those areas where profit comes out of bringing different businesses together in various marketplaces for the sharing and selling of data products — in other words, a convenient place to meet and share, even for competitors. In such a scenario, retailers like Amazon could sell raw information on the hottest purchase categories, and additional data on weather patterns and payment volumes from other partners could help suppliers pinpoint demand signals even more closely. These new analysis and insight streams could be created and maintained by information brokers who could sort by age, location, interest, and other categories. With endless variations, brokers' business models would align by industry, geography, and user role.

Cross-licensing of data is one type of offering sometimes used among competitors. Here, both parties agree to give the other party a license to collect and use data owned and locked in by the other party. By using the model of cross-licensing, each party gains (or loses) equal insight into the competitors' data. You often see such cross-licensing used in the telecommunications equipment-vendor business.

That's because many telecom networks are serviced by multiple vendors that have delivered telecommunications equipment to an operator's network. Given this multivendor telecommunications environment, cross-licensing of data comes in handy when there's a need to know more about the installed base of a competitor's equipment — which hardware, software, or set of configurations are used, for example — or where there could be a need to gain access to performance data from a competitor's equipment in order to gain full insight into the performance of the entire network. The data and insights derived could then be used to sell insights or other types of data-related services.

The data delivery networks enable the monetization of data on a larger scale. To be truly valuable, all this data has to be delivered into the hands of those who can use it, when they can use it, through different types of marketplaces. The data delivery networks take the data and aggregate it, exchange it, and reconstitute it into newer and cleaner insight streams — kind of like what cable TV does in terms of content delivery. These data delivery networks will be the essential funnel through which information based offerings find their markets and are monetized. Although their primary function is to be a marketplace for making business, they also function as a hybrid between a new type of offering and a delivery model.

Few organizations have the capital to create end-to-end content delivery networks that can go from cloud to device. Today, only a few giants — such as Amazon, Apple, Bloomberg, Google, and Microsoft — show such potential, because they own the distribution chain from cloud to device.

Cross-licensing relies on an open marketplace that acts as a platform for data and model providers to meet the users. The 2-sided business model is similar in that it's built on the concept of bringing together the data and the different parties, but there's one significant difference — the 2-sided business model isn't open to everyone. It's a restricted setup, brought into being for only a specific purpose and outfitted with an active middleman that connects the different parties, securing both model delivery and monetization.

The basic concept of the 2-sided business model is that it has (at a minimum) three types of parties involved, although it could include many more. The main party acts as the middleman — the one offering a service to a client who is in need of insights from data but is unable to do that analysis by itself. There are many reasons why the client might not be able to do it — perhaps the company doesn't have access rights to the data or it lacks the right infrastructure for managing it or it lacks the domain expertise to analyze and draw conclusions from the data — but that doesn't hide the fact that the need is still there. Here's where the middle-man comes to the rescue, buying the needed data from other data vendors and then performing the analysis on behalf of the customer, which then in turn pays for the insights.

Here's an example: Imagine that a global coffee vendor wants to understand how well its marketing campaigns for coffee are working in a certain area in the United States. The vendor of this particular data delivery network service is a global telecommunications vendor, which has launched an entirely new service built on a disruptive business model. The way it works is that the vendor of the service buys data from two operators in the US and uses segmented location data for a group of people living in a certain area. (No individuals can be identified, because they're anonymized as part of a group living in a certain geographical area.) Patterns of movement to and from the closest coffee shops are then studied, using the data from the operators gathered from peoples' mobile phones. With that data, it would be possible to determine how well the marketing campaign has succeeded for people living in a certain area. And this can be analyzed without violating an individual's privacy.

Figure 22-2 extrapolates from my coffee vendor example, showing the 2-sided business model in action. I cover the steps in greater detail later in this chapter.

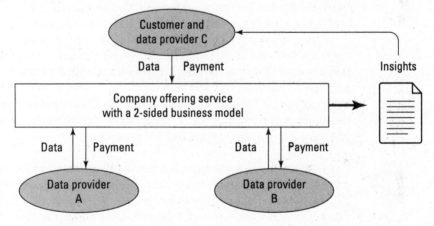

FIGURE 22-2:
The 2-sided business model (data driven).

Note that Figure 22-2 shows that the customer is also providing data (as Data provider C), including data such as geographical area, time range, and location of coffee shops, but lacks the needed data from data providers A and B (the operator data with location information of coffee customers). Without that data, the global coffee shop vendor can't carry out the analysis.

Data providers A and B are competitors in the same market and therefore would refuse to just hand over their data to a competitor, even if they were to be paid, because it could reveal sensitive information about their businesses.

This opens up a possible use of the 2-sided business model, where a third party offering both data and business understanding of the telecommunication business could act as a neutral player or middleman connecting the business of coffee shops with telecom operators.

Machine learning/artificial intelligence functionality enablement

All business models based on machine learning and artificial intelligence need data to exist and carry out their purpose (functional or other) and are therefore, per definition, data-driven business models. You can also use machine learning/artificial intelligence technologies to derive insights from the data, and those insights could be sold just as other insights can be sold. But despite the similarities with other models, business models based on machine learning and artificial intelligence are slightly different.

The main reason for investing in machine learning/artificial intelligence technology-based business models is usually to expand current business and technology with new and advanced techniques and functionality. This enhanced functionality can, for example, be used to evolve automation to a new level with intelligent automation, mainly focused on optimizing how to perform a certain automated task. For example, if the automation steps performed by any machine today are the same steps that were previously performed by a human in order to perform a certain service, with machine learning the machine can identify the best way to solve the task, regardless of which steps were previously performed. The machine isn't bound by a preconception of "the right way to do something," (assuming that the data, team, and algorithm are unbiased) but rather focuses on solving the task in the most optimized manner.

TECHNICAL STUFF

You could also use a machine learning/artificial-intelligence-focused business model to evolve the functionality of an already existing solution with the help of the dynamic and adjustable techniques that such a model offers. To see what I mean, here's an example of a telecommunications network where previously only nonmachine learning models were used in the software for thousands of base stations spread out across an entire country.

That's pretty much how things were until 2017, Now, however, you have a few machine language models being brought online inside the base stations, making it possible to dynamically adjust and better serve customers in real-time as the need for bandwidth changes with day-of-the-week, time-of-day, preferences for certain apps, geographical location, and so on. The machine learning models in the base stations are, of course, trained on real data before they're deployed, but they can then continue to learn the patterns for the different geographical areas they cover, which means they can then predict and prepare to serve customers as their needs arise. Instead of a one-model-serves-all (or nobody), the network dynamically adjusts proactively and in real-time to the constantly changing needs in the connected society.

Another way that machine learning/artificial intelligence can empower your various business models is to use it for completely new and disruptive business models, such as robotics. This is an expanding area that is now moving beyond the repetitive automation you find in factories, where the robots work alone, to scenarios where they become dynamic and intelligent assistants to humans in lab environments (co-bots), in our cars (self driving cars), in our gardens (robot lawn mowers), and even in our houses (robot vacuum cleaners).

REMEMBER

Many possible paths are open to you when it comes to monetizing the data revolution. What is crucial is to have an idea of which one you want to follow in your company. Only by understanding which business model (or models) best suits your organization can you make smart decisions on how to build, partner, or acquire your way onto the next evolutionary wave.

Using a Framework for Data-driven Business Models

As difficult as it seems to argue against the business value of data, leveraging the potential of data isn't as easy as it appears at first glance. The reasons are multilayered: Many companies lack expertise in the areas of data cleaning and storage, and data often only becomes valuable when aggregated with data from competitors or players in another industry, which might be either difficult or even impossible to achieve. This has given rise to several initiatives aimed at defining frameworks to support companies and organizations and offer a more structured approach to introducing data-driven business models.

REMEMBER

An important aspect to start with is to actively question your company's readiness and willingness to change and invest in data as a core part of the business, not just something that the company does on the side. Data-driven business models demand full dedication throughout the company, and it's dealing directly with your customers, so it's vital that you do it properly, once you decide to do it.

This short list of questions can be used as examples for how to approach your own company's self-assessment for readiness to introduce data-driven business models:

» Is my company ready to discuss data-driven business models?

» Which strategic business goals are my company pursuing? Are they strategically in line with a data-driven business model ambition — or in conflict with them?

» Is the ambition business-to-business (B2B) or business-to-customer (B2C) monetization?

» Is there organizational support (processes, governance, frameworks) for an idea to be evaluated in a structured way?

» Could the market potential be improved through cross-industry initiatives like an open source project or a standardization effort — and how would you approach that in that case?

After you have performed your company assessment and (hopefully) have decided to move ahead and introduce a data-driven business model, you have some key areas to consider:

» **Understand** what a data-driven business model means in your line of business.

» **Realize** the potential of a data-driven business model, and try to specify and quantify the relevance for your company's future.

» **Recognize** that data-driven business models are no mystery. They're already in use in various companies across different industry segments, even if most are still relatively new.

» **Use** a simple framework to guide the thinking and approach regarding data-driven business models.

» **Discover** existing and relevant patterns in the company, and get an overview of where you can get started and what to leverage early on.

Creating a data-driven business model using a framework

There's nothing simple about creating a data-driven business model for your company, so in order to offer you a practical approach to this task, I describe in this section the data-driven business model (DDBM) framework. DDBM can be used as a high-level innovation blueprint to identify benefits and challenges associated with leveraging data-driven thinking to construct data-driven business models.

The data-driven business model (DDBM) framework consists of six dimensions: key resources, key activities, value proposition, customer segment, revenue model, and cost structure. Figure 22-3 shows an overview of this model.

I describe the dimensions in the following sections.

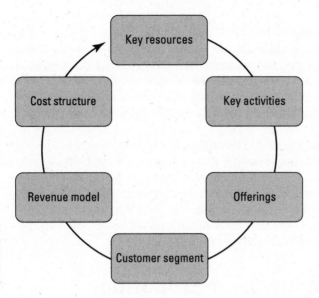

FIGURE 22-3:
Data-driven
business model
(DDBM)
dimensions.

Key resources

Companies need resources to develop their products or services as well as to create value. By definition, a DDBM has data as a key resource, but this does not imply that data is the only key resource of the respective business model. Your company might need other key resources to enable your business model — key competence and infrastructure, for example. But the main focus of the DDBM key resource is to explore and define what kind of data sources and data types are needed to fulfill the data-driven business model objective.

When identifying needed data sources, you should distinguish between external and internal ones:

» *External* data sources can refer to data types like customer or market preferences, open statistical data records, benchmarking data, or various social media data, like blogs.

» *Internal* data sources can refer to different databases with historical data, internal transactional system data, product and service data related to performance, quality, customer rating, as well as company financial data and so on.

Key activities

Like any other company, your company needs to perform different activities to develop, produce, and deliver its offering. In traditional product-centric business models, the key value-creating activities can be described using a traditional *value chain* — a high-level model used to describe the process by which businesses receive raw materials, add value to the raw materials through various processes to create a finished product, and then sell the finished product to customers. However, because the traditional value chain concept is primarily focused on the physical world and treats data as a supporting element rather than as a source of value itself, it's of limited use in the context of data-driven business models.

Instead, you need to identify all key activities related to your specific data-driven business idea, including all data science life-cycle-related activities you carry out on data — capturing it, maintaining it, processing it, analyzing it, communicating it, and actuating it. The data-science-related activities will be of varying degrees of importance, depending on what your business model looks like, but it's worth spending some time thinking through the needed steps and how to secure a stable data science foundation in your DDBM.

Offering/value proposition

A *value proposition* can be defined as an expression of the experience that a customer will receive from a supplier and that is measurable by its value creation. That means the value proposition is the value created for customers through the offering. However, because it's difficult to formalize and categorize the perceived value by a customer in any industry, the DDBM framework focuses on the offering instead.

What your company will offer as the core of the data-driven business model comes down to what is described earlier in this chapter as different types of business models: differentiation through data, data and insight brokering, infrastructure brokering, data delivery networks, and machine learning/artificial intelligence functionality enablement. It's important to have a solid business idea that you then take the time to specify properly and use the categories to define.

Customer segment

The customer segment dimension deals with the target group for the offering. Though there are several ways to segment customers, the most generic classification divides target customers into businesses or business-to-business (B2B) and individual consumers or business-to-customer (B2C).

B2B is a situation where one business makes a commercial transaction with another business. This typically occurs when a business is sourcing materials for its production process for output (a food manufacturer purchasing salt as a raw material to produce an enhanced output, for example). B2C, on the other hand, refers to a business that sells products or provides services to end-user consumers directly.

In many cases, companies can target businesses as well as individual consumers. In B2B trade, it's often the case that the parties to the relationship have comparable negotiating power and, even when they do not, each party typically involves professional staff and legal counsel in the negotiation of terms. B2C is instead shaped to a far greater degree by an unequal balance between the parties: the company offering the product or service and the end user or consumer. In that relationship, the company is in a superior position when it comes to the end user in terms of the economic implications and access to relevant information.

Revenue model

To survive long-term, every company has to have at least one revenue stream. Several different revenue models can be distinguished using classifications such as these:

>> **Asset sale:** Giving away the ownership rights of a product (a data product such as a data set, insights, or models/algorithms, for example) or a service in exchange for money

>> **Lending/Renting/Leasing:** Temporarily granting someone the exclusive rights to use an asset (a data set, for example) for a defined period

>> **Licensing:** Granting permission to use a protected intellectual property, like a patent (a model/algorithm, for example) or copyright, in exchange for a licensing fee

>> **Usage fee:** Charging a fee for the use of a particular service (a defined scope for Insights as a Service, for example)

>> **Subscription:** Charging for the use of a service or software product (machine learning enhanced software, for example) during a limited and agreed-on period

>> **Brokerage:** Charging for an intermediate service where the business model works as the middleman, connecting data and insights with other parties (sometimes by establishing new marketplaces for these parties to meet and make business)

>> **Advertising:** Providing advertisements on your site or in relation to a service. Doing so can supply an extra source of income or be your main income stream. For it to be effective for your advertisers, you need a good understanding of your target audience, in order to direct the right ads to the right target group, using the data at hand to explore and analyze the market and pricing potential.

TIP

Take the time to properly think through the type of revenue model or models your company is aiming for, both short-term and long-term. This will help you identify and drive other aspects in your data-driven business model when using this framework.

Cost structure

To be able to create and deliver value to customers, a company generates costs for labor, technology, purchased products, and so on. So, as part of this process, will the use of data enable a specific cost advantage? Well, typically a company would have a specific cost advantage if the data used in its product or service were created independently of the specific offering.

An example of this is a car manufacturer using data that is automatically created and stored by the electronics in the car. Then there are other companies, like Automatic, a start-up providing analytics for car owners like parking tracking, maintenance reminders, engine diagnostics, driving history and insights. To capture the same data, Automatic needs to install a specific hardware device connected to the car, which most likely would require a specific consent from each car owner as well.

Another example is Twitter, which could use its own data without additional costs to provide various analytical services like trends in opinions on a certain topic discussed in tweets, while companies like Gnip, a start-up company providing social media analytics, would have to pay Twitter for the same data, directly impacting its cost structure.

Putting it all together

After you have a proper understanding of your business idea and how you want to realize it through a data-driven business model, just go ahead and, using the DDBM framework outlined in this chapter, put together your six dimensions and the respective features per dimension. Sitting down and doing that work will help you define and develop a fully data-driven business model.

REMEMBER

For each dimension, at least one feature has to be selected; however, a company can have more than one feature for any dimension.

Chapter **23**

Handling New Delivery Models

Maybe you already have a pretty good idea about what data science means in your line of business, regarding both its challenges and potential. You might even have started to work through the different aspects of your own data science strategy, based on your business idea. Or, perhaps you're already constructing a full-scale data-driven business model and getting close to execution. No matter how far you have come, or if you have not even started, if you haven't thought through how you intend to deliver your new data products and services, you have left out a vital strategic aspect from your plans.

WARNING

Delivery models might seem like something that you can solve later, thinking that once you get started, you'll figure it out. But make no mistake, it's important to think through this aspect of your business model early on. How you intend to deliver — or might be forced to deliver, depending on customer demand or user expectations — can impose huge transformative changes on your company or organization.

Defining Delivery Models for Data Products and Services

A delivery model describes the way you intend to deliver the product or service offering you're planning to sell to a customer. For physical products, this means resolving how you plan to ship the product from the factory to a store where it will be made available for purchase by a customer. Depending on your business model, it could also be shipped directly from the factory to the end-customer — when it's been sold through online stores, for example. Things you need to consider in that context are mostly related to aspects like the number of factories and the location of factories (selecting countries for global enterprises), your need to have, depending on customer demand, expected delivery time, and frequency and desired ways to consume your products.

When it comes to data products and services, there are other considerations to take into account. For data products, it's mostly a case of digital and virtualized products and services, which require other types of delivery models and platforms, such as cloud-based services with different types of *as a Service* (aaS) models. Or, it could be unlicensed open source software or various types of data and machine learning/artificial intelligence marketplaces where some parts are open for everybody and other parts are locked unless you acquire a license.

WARNING

For data products and services, there are also legal, ethical, and security aspects to consider that differ from requirements on traditional hardware and software delivery models. Depending on legal restrictions in different countries, you might have to consider a delivery model where some countries in which you have a presence may have stricter legislation on data usage, especially related to using data containing personal information.

REMEMBER

If the data cannot legally leave the country, you cannot perform data processing, develop your models and insights, or deliver the outcome from another country than the one the data originated from.

Understanding and Adapting to New Delivery Models

In IT, the term *alternative delivery models* refers to replacing the traditional delivery models for software products and services with new kinds of strategies and processes that are intended to enhance the way technology is used. The rather broad term *delivery model* is often carefully applied to new service models that have been made possible by advances in technology, such as those that support web delivered services.

Some of the alternative delivery models that experts most commonly talk about involve cloud services and Software as a Service (SaaS) models. Here, instead of selling software in a box on a physical CD or another storage media, the software is delivered over the Internet or another type of network connection. With these new types of alternative delivery models, users can choose to purchase services with subscription fees or buy an entire package while still getting its implementation over the Internet. Thus, alternative delivery models have actually become an important term to talk about, representing a rapid shift in the business world and in the ways that people buy and use software applications.

REMEMBER

Delivering as-a-Service is also a suitable delivery model for data products. Data products as-a-Service means to provide them on demand — scalable and secure. A user interface is often implemented via an app or a web interface, and the whole service is often made available through a cloud based infrastructure, including various platforms and applications.

TIP

Organizations that are typically not in the software industry actually need to start acting like software companies when delivering data products. There's a lot to learn from software delivery models, but be aware that the traditional ones are also constantly changing. New technology advancements, cost efficiency requirements, and user demands are some driving factors behind the constant need to find better and more appealing ways to deliver software as well as data products and services.

From the point of view of a data science strategy, it's easy to forget or underestimate the importance for your business to choose the right delivery model. This task is very important in order to reach your customers in the way they expect and need and that suits your line of business. And because the customer expectation will change over time, your delivery model must be flexible, scalable, and built in a way that you can respond to shifting demands over time. Once you understand the way you need to deliver your offerings, you will discover that the selected delivery model will influence much more than you think. It usually impacts areas such as the product and service development lifecycle, geographical presence of development sites, competence strategies, organizational and support structures, and even the actual operationalization of the data products and services.

Introducing New Ways to Deliver Data Products

The area of recommending efficient delivery models for different types of data products and services is still being researched and discovered as this book is being written. However, in this section you'll find a high-level overview of some examples of different models being used for different data product and service categories. In Figure 23-1, a new column has been added to the table from Chapter 22 (Figure 22-1), where I map business models and offerings. (Note that Figure 23-1 adds just a few examples of the different possible delivery models to my previous list and should not be considered an exhaustive.

Data Driven Business Model types	Examples of offerings	Examples of delivery models
Differentiation through Data	• Data driven & Predictive Business • Business Contextual Relevance • Create new Offerings	☐ Self-Service Analytics environments ☐ Apps, websites, product/service interfaces ☐ Products & Services
Data & Insight Brokering	• Sell data • Sell insights • Sell analytical models • Sell ML models • Provide Benchmarking	☐ Downloadable files ☐ Websites ☐ API's ☐ Cloud-services ☐ Market places
Infrastructure Brokering	• Analytics & Statistics tools • Cloud and Data center services (IaaS) • Platform Services (PaaS) • Data & Analytics consultancy services	☐ Downloadable license ☐ API's ☐ Online services ☐ On-site services ☐ Cloud-services
Data Delivery Networks	• Cross-licensing • 2-sided Business models • Targeted advertisements	☐ Market places ☐ API's ☐ Cloud-services
ML/AI Functionality Enablement	• Intelligent Automation • Technology Evolution • Robotics • New Intelligent Systems	☐ Products & Services ☐ Online Services ☐ On-site Services ☐ API's

FIGURE 23-1: Examples of delivery models for different data-driven business models and data product and service offerings.

As you can see, there are many different types of delivery models, and sometimes the same delivery model can be used for different offerings and different data-driven business models. The following sections describe these different delivery models in more detail and include some contextual examples.

Self-service analytics environments as a delivery model

When investing in a data-driven business model aimed at differentiating through data, one example of a delivery model is to utilize a self-service analytics environment. Most of these ready-to-use analytics tools are easy to use and are usually available as both on-premise installations and cloud-based solutions.

By using an off-the-shelf product for exploring and generating business insights from your data to drive better decisions, you focus your efforts on the data preparation and data analysis rather than on investing in building your own tool or platform from scratch. This is especially suitable for companies that are new to data science (and thus with little or no analytics or machine learning/artificial intelligence competence in-house), but also for internal business analytics purposes in any type of company, regardless of their analytics maturity level.

REMEMBER

It's also possible to use the output from an off-the-shelf exploration or analysis tool to generate a suitable dashboard or another visualization that could be used externally as well — toward your customers, for example — thus saving you the time it would take to design your own. Another benefit of using ready-to-use analytics tools is that they come with interactive visualization views, which is seldom the case when you create a visualization in Python or R, the two most common programming languages for data scientists. *Interactive* visualizations means that you can easily click on different parts of a visualization to zoom in or out, select an area for further analysis, or even change the scope of what you're looking at and analyzing.

Figures 23-2, 23-3, and 23-4 show how easily you can use a single application for data exploration, analytics and visualizing insights. Start with one visualization for your data set, and then easily change to another when you want to expand the analysis. Or simply combine various visualizations in to one view (like the examples below) and connect the graphs so when you change the scope of one view, the other graphs adjust to that scope too. The case below shows how you can enhance your understanding by easily adding location data to the traditional data set you usually look at.

By adding geographical context to your analysis and visualizations by combining traditional data with location data, location analysis brings the "where" dimension to the forefront so that you can analyze data in new ways to get the full picture before making decisions, while identifying location-specific opportunities.

Figure 23-2 below shows how you can get an overview of your customer data using a set of variables like where they live, how old they are, and their level of customer satisfaction. These different data variables can then be used for further analysis and to search for possible dependencies. For example, the correlation matrix that has been automatically generated shows a strong correlation between "first order product quality" and "returning customer". Location data \ shown on the map indicates that the average customer loyalty probability across all the customers is 54 percent.

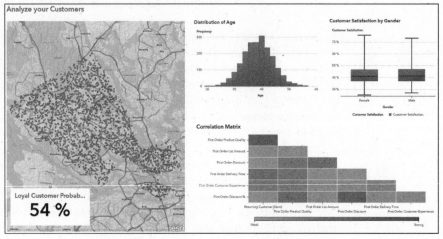

FIGURE 23-2:
Using an analytics tool to explore your customer data and possible correlations related to where they live, their age and their level of satisfaction.

Figure 23-2 is based on a screenshot generated using SAS® Visual Analytics software. Copyright © 2019 SAS Institute Inc., Cary, NC, USA. SAS and all other SAS Institute Inc. product or service names are registered trademarks or trademarks of SAS Institute Inc. All Rights Reserved. Used with permission.

The graph in Figure 23-3 zooms in on one specific geographical area of the customer base. You can see the round circle in the upper corner. The graph then automatically adjusts the other connected graphs (the bar chart showing the distribution of age, the box plot showing the gender distribution, and the correlation matrix). As you can see, the customer loyalty probability in this area is significantly higher than for the average customer — 82 percent.

The decision to use easy-to-consume interactive analytics tools, however, is not the right one for all companies. Analytics and machine intelligence mature companies tend to lean toward doing everything by themselves, especially when it comes to analysis as part of commercial data products and services interfacing the customers. For example, there is a common perception that without a unique design on the user interface visualizing the data and insights, it will not differentiate towards competition. But remember to think through what to focus your development work on; do you want to develop insights or develop a tool for visualizing your insights? Differentiating is important, but focus your company efforts on the right tasks.

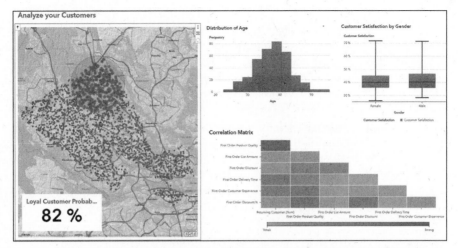

FIGURE 23-3:
Graph focused on a certain geographical area selected in the map using drag and drop.

Figure 23-3 is based on a screenshot generated using SAS® Visual Analytics software. Copyright © 2019 SAS Institute Inc., Cary, NC, USA. SAS and all other SAS Institute Inc. product or service names are registered trademarks or trademarks of SAS Institute Inc. All Rights Reserved. Used with permission.

REMEMBER

The analytics tool companies are investing a lot of money, competence, and time into making these tools user friendly and state of the art in most dimensions. That is what they are specialized to do. Most of the tools are also quite adaptable for different needs, so be sure to calculate the alternative cost and time before you embark on building your totally in-house solution.

TIP

For purely internal purposes, out-of-the-box tools for analytics tend to be more cost efficient and faster from idea to insight; offer a more stable production environment; and have the ability to make analytics accessible to more and different types of employees, supporting the implementation of a data-driven organization across different company segments.

Applications, websites, and product/service interfaces as delivery models

When your ambition is to use apps, websites, or existing product and service interfaces as delivery models for differentiating through data, it's all about sharing data and findings with your customers.

This can be done by making your users' own data available to them through either the communication channel they're using or the communication channel your company is offering. For example, a mobile operator can make data available to its subscribers about their own costs and usage, the best subscription offer based on usage pattern, location based services, and more.

This empowers subscribers and gives them contextual understanding of how they're actually using their mobile phones, which means that they can be more in control of their current and future usage, including their costs. At the same time, it empowers the company that shares the data, because it sends a signal of transparency to its customers and generates trust, which can strengthen brand perception.

Another example of how a company shares users' own data to empower their brand is the Nordic company Skistar, which has facilities for downhill skiing in the Nordic countries. The company has an app in which you can create an account and upload the ID number from your digital ski pass. The ski pass is reusable for as long as it does not break, and you just reactivate it by paying the applicable fee when you need it for a new period.

The ski pass automatically connects to the ski-system during your day on the slopes every time you use a ski lift. The app provides you with data on how many rides you have taken, distance you have traveled, vertical meters achieved, calories burned, and so on. All of it nicely is aggregated per day, week, month, or year. It also allows you to connect with your friends so that you can compare your results.

Figure 23-4 shows two views available to skiers using the Skistar ski resorts.

FIGURE 23-4: Tracking your day on the slopes.

A dummy example of how Skistar gives back the data to the skiers by connecting the digital ski pass with their app to generate simple, but fun, insights.

Another example is an online business that uses the data generated on its home page to offer its customers other recommended products or services based on previous purchase patterns through the website, or offering reduced prizes to users who show a particular interest in specific items.

Websites can also be useful as delivery models for data products such as insights that you sell. The insight result could be in the shape of a dashboard or some similar visualization. When you have published the dashboard, you can give the customer a secure link to their own website where they can consume the insights through an interactive view and also download a .pdf file with a static view.

TIP

For an existing product or service that you offer, you could use new or existing data that wasn't previously made available for customers. The data can then be added to the same system interface as before — a financial system, for example. The purpose here would be to enhance the experience by adding new data, which could improve the user perception of the same product or service without functionally improving it.

Existing products and services

By integrating data as input or a key resource into an existing product or service and making your offerings data driven, you'll be able to differentiate through data. Here, the original product or service wouldn't be a data product, but could be using different forms of data for contextual purposes rather than as its main driving force. This would be the case regardless of whether the products would be hardware, software, or other, and regardless of whether the products were on-premise or were virtualized and deployed through a cloud service. The delivery model involves enhancing existing products or services, or identifying new data product opportunities through data utilization.

One example of such an approach is when you start using a data-driven and predictive approach to an existing service offering. This is especially interesting for real-time operational types of service offerings, like the extensive and complex operations of a telecommunications network. Without a data-driven approach and without the help of techniques such as predictive analytics and machine learning/artificial intelligence, services tend to stay reactive to faults or different types of alarms. But when data and models are used proactively to identify patterns in the data, it helps to understand what is causing certain problems, allowing you to predict and prevent problems from ever happening in the future. This will in turn improve service performance and network quality, as well as satisfaction of service operations by the customer, the network operator, and even the mobile network end-users, like you and me.

Downloadable files

For offerings related to data and insight brokering, the delivery model of choice is often downloadable files. If you're offering a data set small enough to put into a file and download from a website, this is an excellent delivery model. This could, for example, be the case for a file with test data for model training. Downloadable files also work when you're selling stand-alone analytical or machine learning models.

Another example when this is applicable is when your offering is an Insight-as-a-Service or some sort of report meant to be delivered. Usually, the size of a compiled report with insights, recommendations, and different statistical visualizations suits the downloadable format quite well.

However, it's worth considering from where the customer downloads the files. Constructing an easy-to-use but secure website where they can access the files is a good idea. On this site, you can also take the opportunity to inform your customer about other current and coming products that you're offering, or even open up the site for other companies to buy spots for advertising for other related data products to your customer clientele. Just make sure you pick companies that you do not perceive as current or potential future competitors, and keep the website simple and clean, with the main focus on the files you're delivering. Make it simple to access what they're after.

APIs

API stands for application programming interface, a set of clearly defined methods of communication among various components such as web-based systems, operating systems, database systems, computer hardware, or software libraries. Using an API as a delivery method is useful when customers want direct access to the data product or service (data, model, or insight) in order to integrate the product or results directly into their system environment.

APIs can also be useful when you're selling a certain machine learning capability as a service and are including the infrastructure necessary to run the model. This means you're not selling the model itself, but only the ability to use the machine learning model. The delivery model approach is that the customer uploads the data to you, using the API, and then runs the model in your environment. This is machine learning as-a-Service as well as a form of infrastructure brokering.

A concrete example of this is Amazon, which is offering this type of service using its cloud environment and its machine learning algorithm for image recognition for various purposes, like facial recognition and analysis, object and activity detection, unsafe content detection, celebrity detection, and even analysis of text in images. Amazons image recognition offering enables you to search your image collection for similar faces by storing face metadata, using the `IndexFaces` API function. You can then use the `SearchFaces` function to return high confidence matches.

Cloud services

A *cloud* service is any service made available to users on demand via the Internet from a cloud provider's servers, as opposed to being provided from a company's own on-premises servers. Cloud services are designed to provide easy, scalable access to applications, resources, and services, and are fully managed by a cloud services provider. Examples of some well-known cloud providers are Amazon, Microsoft, and Google.

When you say you're using cloud services as a delivery platform, you could be offering a cloud service as an infrastructure or platform service for various services, like data storage, computation of data, or applications. But it could also refer to utilizing a cloud service as a delivery platform for data, insight, and model brokering, or a data delivery network for a marketplace, for example.

Because a cloud service can dynamically scale to meet the needs of its users, and because the service provider supplies the hardware and software necessary for the service, there's no need for a company to provision or deploy its own resources or to allocate IT staff to manage the service. This makes a cloud service an interesting delivery model for many different types of data products and services.

Online market places

Online marketplaces are sometimes also referred to as online e-commerce marketplaces. The marketplace is a type of e-commerce site where products or services are provided by multiple third parties and where transactions are processed by the marketplace operator.

REMEMBER

Online marketplaces are like platforms for multiple players and are well-suited fostering marketplaces for data products and data service offerings. They are already an important media and has the potential to become the main data delivery model in the future, driving deal-making in data, analytics, and artificial intelligence. It also enables advertising opportunities across multiple channels and industries.

A *data marketplace*, or *data market*, is an online store where people can buy data. Data marketplaces typically offer various types of data for different markets and from different sources. Common types of data sold include business intelligence, advertising, demographics, personal information, research, and market. Data types can be mixed and structured in a variety of ways. Data vendors may offer data in specific formats for individual clients.

Data sold in these marketplaces is used by businesses of all kinds, governments, business and market intelligence agencies, and many types of analysts. Data marketplaces have proliferated with the growth of big data, as the amount of data collected by governments, businesses, websites, and services has increased and all that data has become increasingly recognized as an asset. Data marketplaces are often integrated with cloud services. Figure 23-5 shows how the interaction between different marketplace actors may look.

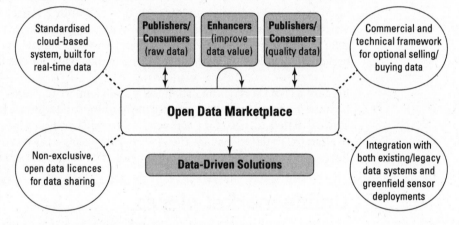

FIGURE 23-5: A model showing workflows on an open data marketplace.

Downloadable licenses

A software license is a kind of license that is used to set rules about how a piece of software can or cannot be used. After either downloading or buying the software, you need to agree with the license in order to use it.

For a business model like infrastructure brokering, downloadable licenses for different types of analytics software are common and useful. The downloadable software licenses are usually equipped with time constraints that make them impossible to use after the expiration date has occurred, unless the license is renewed.

Online services

An *online service* is a generic term that refers to any information and services provided over the Internet. These services not only allow subscribers to communicate with each other but also provide unlimited access to information. Online services can range from simple to complex. A basic online service may help subscribers gain needed data through a search engine, and a complex one might be an online mortgage application from a bank. Online services may be free or paid.

An online service is suitable for offerings like data and analytics consultancy services that don't need to be provided onsite. Many data scientists have found a lucrative business by selling their expertise online, delivering analytics and machine learning/artificial intelligence expertise in terms of data-driven recommendations and strategies, as well as machine learning/artificial intelligence models and solutions.

Onsite services

Onsite services is a delivery model that refers to services that take place on the same premises, or at the same location, as the customer. This type of service is usually needed when offsite services cannot be given or the customer is a complete novice. Compared to offsite services or online services, onsite support takes a longer time to set up and is usually more expensive.

6

The Part of Tens

IN THIS PART . . .

Grasping why you need a solid data science strategy

Learning about ten common mistakes to stay away from

Chapter **24**

Ten Reasons to Develop a Data Science Strategy

This book spells out many of the challenges you'll face when embarking on a data science journey within your company. It emphasizes what is fundamental and what not to forget, but it also points out areas of specific interest and choices of specific importance. One thing it hasn't done (yet) is make the argument for why it's vital for you to develop and document all your strategic ambitions into a data science strategy. That is what this chapter is all about. Enjoy!

Expanding Your View on Data Science

Taking the time to develop a data science strategy is crucial. It forces you to learn more about what data science really is before you start investing and making important choices. Having a strategy in place lowers the risk of missing vital steps and considerations along the way.

REMEMBER

Though data science is a blend of different disciplines — like mathematics, statistics, and computer science — do not be mistaken: It is a discipline of its own. Understanding the key concepts and considerations driving the area of data science is vital but often not even done.

My view is that when you truly understand what data science is all about, you'll look at your company in another light, from another perspective. It will be obvious to you what needs to be done differently, and you'll be able to explain why this is the case. Then you can motivate those around you to make the necessary changes, because in data science, it all starts and ends with data. Perhaps many companies that have been around for a while don't think of themselves as structured around data that way, but they need to be if they are to succeed in the new data and artificial intelligence age.

REMEMBER

Google uses data as the starting point for everything. By using artificial intelligence and machine learning techniques to detect patterns and deviations in the data, Google can decide in a truly data-driven manner which business to go for and which areas to prioritize and take action on. At Google, data drives organizational change, new innovation, and business priorities. And its overall leading slogan is, as you can imagine, *AI first*.

Aligning the Company View

If you drive your data science strategy the right way, you'll have an opportunity to bring people together around the business opportunities sure to result from your data science investment. It's important to formulate that vision and mission and capture it in a data science strategy that is agreed on by all stakeholders. By doing so, you ensure that everyone is committed to the stated objectives and that they're anchored in the organizational structure early on. That gives you a strong and solid foundation for the vast and challenging work ahead.

However, it's easier said than done to align an organization around data science. Why is that? Well, for starters, people's views about the insights into what data science is and how it will be transformative for different businesses are quite varied. That means you won't be starting at the same level of understanding of what it means to introduce data science into the company. If some enter into the undertaking assuming that data science can be added into a corner of the company as some kind of add-on and be expected to generate value, you'll have issues further down the line.

TIP

To get the full potential from your data science investment, you must treat it as the dominant discipline. If you are able to align your company around such a perception, and capture the details of how this will be approached as part of a data science strategy, you have positioned your company for success.

Creating a Solid Base for Execution

By actually writing down your data science approach and priorities, you're establishing the foundation for the plans needed to execute the strategy. It helps steer the business in the right direction and provides a baseline to rely on when challenges appear and new opportunities arise.

TIP

A vital component of such a solid base is an architectural drawing, in which your infrastructure can be realized and implemented. This requires quite a lot of detailed thinking in a cross-domain team setup, not only to detail the setup and execution approach in different domains but also to think through how this will be executed in a data- and machine-driven setup across the whole company in a fluid manner.

Of course, the strategy might need to change over time, due to changing needs or priorities in the company, or even to an evolving data science technology. But, regardless, it gives you a solid foundation to stand on and start with when considering a new direction or modifying plans regarding execution.

Realizing Priorities Early

To be honest, for a medium- to large-size company, making an end-to-end investment in data science is expensive. But because the improved business potential is much greater, companies are realizing the necessity of investing in a future driven by data science.

WARNING

In order not to get lost in all the unavoidable complexity on the way toward that future, it's crucial to understand and clearly set your priorities early and then try to stick with them when things get more difficult. Doing so will help guide you right during challenging periods.

What, then, are the typical priorities you need to consider early? Well, an important part of your work in coming up with a strategy should be to look at your current business setup. In doing so, some of the more important questions to consider early on are listed here:

>> What is it that you really want to change?

>> What is the data science potential in your line of business?

>> What are your true expectations?

>> How will you realize your expectations in practice?

Putting the Objective into Perspective

REMEMBER

Creating an end-to-end data science strategy forces you to not only set clear objectives but also consider them from many perspectives. It's not only about the business potential; it's also about the legal rights, privacy concerns, or other ethical considerations related to the data you're using.

When considering the context of the fundamental change that needs to occur in your business environment when introducing data science, you might need to consider to what extent your company depends on the following factors:

>> Data you might not own yourself, which could mean limitations on usage

>> The need to digitalize all parts of your business in order to become data driven from end to end

>> The necessity for new roles, competencies, and skill sets in data science among employees and managers

>> New laws and regulations that were previously not applicable

>> Working with new vendors and partners related to data and infrastructure support

>> Potentially addressing an entirely new customer base

Creating an Excellent Base for Communication

Yes, it's a lot of work to put a data science strategy in place, aligned and anchored with main stakeholders, but once it's in place, it will provide you with an excellent base of communication. You can easily use the written strategy and work its defined objectives and challenges into presentation material and company targets.

The strategy can be used to build up a communication plan for the different target groups identified, including the different priorities and considerations agreed on regarding the new mindset and culture you want to enforce.

TIP

You can turn the content from your data science strategy into more consumable formats, like an FAQ, and then turn selected parts into external material for communication with your customers, partners, and vendors.

Understanding Why Choices Matter

TIP

A strategy is all about making choices — choices for what is important to pursue and what is not worth going after. If your strategy is to try to do everything, you're lost. That is worse than a bad strategy; it's no strategy at all.

REMEMBER

Because the choices you make in the strategy will be the guiding star for coming choices and priorities during the challenge of fully introducing data science, you absolutely must make the right choices at the beginning. Making the wrong choices at that point is sure to have a severe impact on the overall success of your investment in data science.

So, what can you do to make sure you make the right choices? I recommend the following:

>> Take the time you need in order to get your strategy right, and be sure to iterate. Don't rush!

>> Provide your main stakeholders (and you yourself) with a basic level of understanding in data science.

>> Involve internal *and* external data science experts in the area to make sure you gain a broad and varied perspective on the market situation.

>> Take advice from your data scientists internally (if there are any), and let them contribute actively to the strategy.

>> Engage main stakeholders in decisions regarding cross-domain challenges and priorities, even if it's difficult and cumbersome.

>> Make tough choices, but be ready to adjust along the way depending on enhanced understanding or changing conditions.

Identifying the Risks Early

By actually taking the time to consider risks as part of your data science strategy, you can not only detect risks early but also potentially prevent them from ever becoming a reality.

TIP

Finding a good structure to use when identifying potential risks is the key, and it will help you through this not-so-fun exercise. I know it's much more appealing to think about all the new possibilities the future may bring rather than what can potentially go wrong with your investment. However, it is time well invested to do this.

Some main risk areas to consider include the ones described in this list:

- » **Data:** Are you in ownership control of all the data you will need in order to realize your internal efficiency ambitions or for realizing external business opportunities? If not, have you secured the necessary legal rights to the data for what you want to do today and potentially in the future?

- » **Competence:** Do you have the necessary skill set to execute on your strategy? If not, have you set the right business ambition in relation to the availability of such competence — considering the time it takes to internally build experience and/or attracting and retaining data scientists among the scarce number available on the market, for example?

- » **Infrastructure:** Have you thoroughly examined the risks related to your architectural ambitions? (Examples here include going open source or not, virtualized and cloud based environment or not, and distributed and local setups or centralized setup.) There are many risks associated with the infrastructure architectural choice as well as the implementation challenges (setups for global companies moving data and distributing computation and automation cross borders, for example.)

Thoroughly Considering Your Data Need

REMEMBER

Performing a thorough inventory of your data need is vital when it comes to your data strategy work. It provides a practical understanding of the business priorities, infrastructure need, legal and ethical considerations, data governance aspects, as well as business potential of that strategy. It all starts with the data. It's as simple as that.

The data inventory should include aspects such as these:

- » Classification of data in terms of type, format, degree of sensitivity, collection point(s), and ownership

- » Grouping of data types into data categories with similar attributes (lowering the number of individual types to handle)

- » Usage need in terms of needed level of data granularity, collection frequency, and data retention periods

TIP

Once you have the inventory in place, you can use it to create a data model to help your understanding of (and preparation for) data interoperability (which data needs to be combined with which, and how can it be analyzed together?); how the data need impacts the infrastructure setup (what requirements may be derived from the collective data need?); and what must be protected from a legal and security perspective (which laws and regulations are applicable for which data types, and what does that mean?).

Understanding the Change Impact

The data strategy is a good way to get a firm grip on the total scope of the change that is needed in order to achieve your objectives. That means you can start planning early for the necessary cultural shift in mindset and behaviors that is needed. It enables the transition to be well planned and proactive so that it isn't rushed but is introduced step by step. Allowing employees to mature in their perception of what data science is and what this will enable is the next step.

REMEMBER

One aspect of data science that is significant to acknowledge has to do with people's fear of how the introduction of automation will impact ordinary jobs. (This is closely linked to the further fear that machine learning algorithms will replace the need for humans in the workplace.) Such fears need to be taken seriously, and it's important to communicate clearly what the intent is with the change, how it will impact your employees' tasks and roles, what benefits it will bring, and what opportunities are opening up as a result of the change.

TIP

Becoming data driven and investing in data science also means that you should apply the same thinking when managing change. Approach the transformation program from a data-driven angle, and use analytics and machine learning techniques to measure and understand the change efficiency and impact. Using a method like sentiment analytics, for example, enables you to understand how the change is perceived among stakeholders. Other aspects you want to cover include to what degree the change is actually happening and whether there are specific change roles that are more efficient than others. What are they doing that others are not doing?

REMEMBER

By defining a data science strategy, you get an opportunity to secure a broader management understanding of what data science really is, the opportunities it enables, and the fundamental change impact that data science imposes.

Chapter **25**

Ten Mistakes to Avoid When Investing in Data Science

Although you must focus on your data science strategy objectives in order to succeed with them, it doesn't hurt to also learn from others' mistakes. This chapter gives you a list of ten challenges that many companies tackle in the wrong way. Each section not only describes what you should aim to avoid but also points you in the direction of the right approach to address the situation.

Don't Tolerate Top Management's Ignorance of Data Science

A fundamental misunderstanding occurs in the area of data science regarding the target group for data science training. The common view is that as long as the skill set for the data scientists themselves is improved, or for the software engineers who are training to become data scientists, you are spot-on. However, by adopting that approach, the company runs the significant risk of alienating the data science team from the rest of the organization. Managers and leaders are often forgotten.

REMEMBER

If managers don't understand or trust the work done by the data scientists, the outcome won't be utilized in the organization and insights won't be put into action. So, the main question to ask is how to secure full utilization of the data science investment if the results cannot be interpreted by management.

This is one of the most common mistakes committed by companies today, and the fact is that there's also little training and coaching available for line management and for leaders. But without some level of understanding of data science at the management level, how can the right strategy be put in place, and how can you expect management to dare to use the statistical results to make substantive decisions?

WARNING

Without management understanding of data science, it's not only difficult to capture the full business opportunity for the company, but it might also lead to further alienation of the data science team or to termination of the team altogether.

Don't Believe That AI Is Magic

Data science is all about data, statistics, and algorithms. There's nothing magic about it — the machine does what it's told to do. However, the notion that the machine can learn causes some to think that it has the full ability to learn by itself. To some extent, that is correct — the machine *can* learn — but it's correct only within the boundaries you set up for it. (No magic, in other words!) A machine cannot solve problems by itself, unless a machine is allowed to develop such a design. But that's advanced technology and not today's reality.

WARNING

Overestimating what artificial intelligence can do for your company can really set you off on the wrong track, building up expectations that can never be met. This could lead to severe consequences both within the company and externally, with impacts not just in terms of trust and reliability but also in terms of financial performance. As important as it is not to underestimate the potential in artificial intelligence, one should also avoid the opposite extreme, where its potential is overestimated. I repeat: Artificial intelligence isn't magic. Yes, it's called artificial intelligence, but a more correct definition is actually *algorithmic* intelligence. Why? Because at the end of the day, very advanced mathematics are applied to huge amounts of data, with the ability to dynamically interact with a defined environment in real-time.

Don't Approach Data Science as a Race to the Death between Man and Machine

Some people tend to believe that task automation, driven by machine learning predictions, truly means the end of humans in the workplace. That prediction isn't one that I believe in. However, it does mean a significant change in competence and skill sets as well as a change in which job roles will be relevant and which types of responsibilities will be the focus in the workplace.

Like the introduction of the Internet in the workplace, introducing artificial intelligence in a more mainstream format will change what jobs are and how they're performed. There will be a lot less "hands-on" work, even in the software business. And yes, machines will most probably do a lot of the basic software development going forward, which means that people in the hardware-related industry will not be the only ones replaced. At the end of the day, basically all humans will be impacted as machine learning/artificial intelligence and automation capabilities and capacity expand and evolve beyond what is possible to do today.

However, this also means that humans can move on to perform other tasks that are different from the ones we do today — managing and monitoring models and algorithms and their performance, for example, or setting priorities and acting as a human fallback solution in cooperation with the machine. Other typical human tasks might be managing legal concerns related to data, evaluating ethical aspects of algorithm-based decision-making, or driving standardization in data science. You could say that the new human tasks will be focused on managing the machines that manage the original tasks — tasks that were previously perceived to be either boring and repetitive or too complex to execute at all.

WARNING

This "putting man against machine" business isn't the way to approach your data science implementation. Allowing the narrative to be framed that way may scare your employees and even prompt them to leave the company, which isn't what you want. Your employees are valuable assets that you need in the next stages as well, but perhaps in new roles and with new acquired skill sets.

TIP

Embrace what the machine learning/artificial intelligence technology can do for a specific line of business. Company leaders who understand how to utilize these techniques in a balanced approach between man and machine to augment the total performance and let the company evolve beyond its current business are the leaders whose companies will succeed.

Don't Underestimate the Potential of AI

As strange as it may seem, some companies just don't understand how transformative artificial intelligence really is. They refuse to see the fundamental shift that is already starting to transform society, and cannot see artificial intelligence as anything other than just another software technique or a set of new programming languages.

TIP

The key here is to a) take the time to truly understand what data science is really all about and to b) not be afraid to accept help from experts to identify and explain the strategic potential for your specific business. Because the area of data science is complex, it requires domain expertise and experience in terms of both the development of a strategy and its implementation. It also requires the ability to read and interpret where the market is moving in this area.

WARNING

By underestimating the impact that artificial intelligence can have on your business, you run the risk of significantly limiting the future expansion of your company. Later, once the true potential is really understood, you will find yourself entering the game too late and being equipped with the wrong skill set. You may finally be put out of business by competitors that had seen the potential much earlier and therefore invested earlier and smarter in artificial intelligence.

Don't Underestimate the Needed Data Science Skill Set

A typical sign of companies underinvesting in data science is when you find small, isolated islands of data science competence spread out in different parts of a large company. In smaller companies, you see a similar symptom when a small-but-competent data science team is working on the most important project in the company but the only one outside the team that realizes its importance is an outsider like yourself.

Both of these examples are signs that top management in the company has not understood the potential of data science. They have simply realized that something is happening in this area in the market and are just following a trend to make sure that data science doesn't pass them by.

WARNING

If the awareness and competency level of management doesn't improve, the area will continue to be underinvested, distributed in a way that it cannot reach critical mass, and therefore rendered incapable of being scaled up at a later stage.

Don't Think That a Dashboard
Is the End Objective

It may sound strange for, someone knowledgeable in data science, to say that anyone can think that the main outcome of data science is a dashboard. I can assure you, however, that this is a common misunderstanding. This isn't only wrong — it's also one of the main reasons that many companies fail with their data science investment.

At many companies, management tends to think that the main purpose of analytics and artificial intelligence is to use all that big data that has been pumped into the expensive data lake, to automate tasks and report on progress. Given such a mindset, it should come as no surprise that the main focus of management would be to use these techniques to answer *their* questions with statistically proven methods that could produce results that could be visualized in a nice-looking dashboard. For someone new to the field of data science, that might actually seem like a good approach. Unfortunately, they would be wrong.

REMEMBER

To be absolutely clear, the main objective of analytics and machine learning/ artificial intelligence isn't simply to do what you've always done but using more machines. The idea is to be able to move beyond what you're able to do today and tackle new frontiers.

If the only end goal was to create a dashboard in order to answer some questions posed by a manager, there would be no need to create a data-driven organization. The idea here is that, in a data-driven organization, it all starts with the data and not with the manager and the dashboard. The starting point is what the data is indicating that you need to look at, analyze, understand, and act on. Analysis should be predictive, in order for the organization to be proactive and for its actions to be preventive.

The role of the dashboard should be to surprise you with new insights and make you discover new questions you should be asking — not to answer the questions you've already come up with. It should enable teams to monitor and learn from ongoing preventive actions. The dashboard should also support human or machine discovery of potential trends and forecasts in order to make long-term strategic decisions.

WARNING

In the real world, the steps needed to design a dashboard tend to end up being the most important tasks to discuss and focus on. Often, dashboards end up driving everything that is done in the data science implementation program, totally missing the point about keeping an open and exploratory approach to the data. This tends to happen because the dashboard is the simplest and most concrete deliverable to understand and hold on to in this new, complex, and constantly changing environment. In this sense, it acts like a crutch for those unwilling or unable to grasp the full potential of a data-driven business.

REMEMBER

You run the great risk of missing the whole point of being data driven when your starting point is all about designing the dashboard and laying down all the questions from the start. By doing so, you assume that you already know which questions are important. But how can you be sure of that? In a society and a market now undergoing huge transformations, if you don't look at the data first and let the algorithms do the work of finding the patterns and deviations hiding there, you might end up looking at the entirely wrong problem for your business.

Don't Forget about the Ethical Aspects of AI

What does artificial intelligence ethics actually refer to, and why do you think it's of the utmost importance? Well, there are many aspects surrounding the idea of ethics in AI, many of which can have a severe impact on the artificial intelligence results. One obvious but important ethical consideration is the need to avoid machine bias in the algorithms — biases where human preconceptions of race, gender, class, or other discriminatory aspects are unconsciously built into the models and algorithms.

Usually, people tend to believe that they don't have biased opinions, but the truth is that we all have them, more or less. People tend to lean in one direction, subconsciously or not. Modeling that tendency into self-learning algorithms can have severe consequences on the performance of the company's algorithms.

One example that comes to mind involves an innovative, online, and artificial-intelligence-driven beauty contest. The algorithm had learned to search for the ten most beautiful women in the US, using only digital photos of women. But when studying the result from the contest, it became clear that something must have gone wrong: All of the ten most beautiful women selected by the algorithm were white, blonde, and blue-eyed. So, when studying the algorithm again, it turned out that the training set used for the algorithm had a majority of white, blonde, and blue-eyed women in it, which taught the machine that this was the desired look.

Other aspects in addition to machine bias include areas such as the use of personal information, the reproducibility of results outside the lab environment, and the explainability of AI insights or decisions. It's also worth noting that this last aspect is now a law within the GDPR (General Data Protection Regulation) in the EU.

REMEMBER

Ethical considerations are for our own, human protection as machine intelligence evolves over time. You must think about such aspects early on. It's not only a fundamental aspect to consider as part of your data science investment, but it's actually also hugely important to consider already from the start, when designing your business models, architecture, infrastructure, ways of working, and the teams themselves. Not wanting to break the law is of course important, but securing a sustainable and trustworthy evolution of artificial intelligence in your business is far more important.

Don't Forget to Consider the Legal Rights to the Data

When becoming data driven, one of the most common mistakes is to forget to make a proper analysis of which data is needed. Even if your main ambition with your data science investment is focused on internal efficiency and data-driven operations, this is still a fundamental area to address.

Once the data need is analyzed, it's not unusual to discover that you need other types of data than you originally thought. It might be data other than just internally generated data, owned by you. An example might be faults found in your products or services, or perhaps performance related data. It could even be the more sensitive type of data, which falls under the category of privacy data, related to how your products or services are being used by your customers.

Data privacy is an area that's getting more and more attention, in society with consumers' enhanced awareness of how their data is being used and also in terms of new laws and regulations on data. One concrete example is the General Data Protection and Regulation law (GDPR), introduced in 2018 within the EU with significant penalties for violators.

Although you might not have any plans for monetizing your data or to build new products based on the data, the whole rights issue is still central — even when all you want to do is analyze the data in order to better understand your business, enhance and innovate the current portfolio, or just improve the efficiency of your operations.

WARNING

No matter what your reasons are for using the data, you still need legal rights in place in order to use it! It's absolutely vital to address this early on as part of the development of your data strategy. If you don't, you might end up either violating the law regulating data usage and ownership or being stuck in terms of not being able to sell your new fantastic product or service because it's using data you aren't entitled to use.

Don't Ignore the Scale of Change Needed

If you don't take the time to properly sketch out the different change scenarios for your business when introducing a data science strategy, you most likely will fail. The fundamental shift needed in the company to become truly data, analytics, and machine driven is significant and should not be underestimated.

The most common mistakes in data science related to managing change are listed here:

>> Underestimating the scope of the change and not taking seriously enough what has to happen

>> Failing to recognize that business models are sure to be impacted when introducing data science

>> Approaching customers with a value argumentation based on introducing data science techniques without explicitly explaining what the customer value is

>> Pricing models to stay the same or not reflect the increased value, only the lowered cost

>> Focusing single-mindedly on cost efficiency when it comes to business operational changes

>> Neither measuring nor understanding operational improvements

>> Carrying out organizational changes on so small a scale that everything stays the same in practice, ensuring that the actual change never occurs

>> Building the cost and dimensioning model on old and outdated criteria, therefore ensuring that the model won't capture the new values

>> Failing to see the change that data science imposes on the company and not understanding that change from an ecosystem perspective

>> Underestimating the need for communication related to the change

Don't Forget the Measurements Needed to Prove Value

REMEMBER

A common mistake is to forget to introduce baseline measurements before the data science investment is made and implemented. Most of the focus in these cases tends to be on the future measurements and the results targeted with the investment. This is usually because of a resistance toward investing in new measurements in the current situation, because it's being abandoned for the new strategy. Unfortunately, this means that the company will lack the ability to statistically prove the value of the investment in the next step. Don't fall into that trap! It could truly backfire on the entire strategic ambition, when top management or even the board of directors asks what the value was of this major investment.

WARNING

Financially, you could, of course, be able to motivate the investment on a high level; however, it would be difficult to prove individual parts. Efficiency gains such as speed, agility, automation level, and process reactiveness versus proactiveness are values that are more difficult to prove and put a number on if you haven't secured a measurement baseline before executing your data science strategy.

Index

Numbers

A

collaboration, 179, 201

commercial opportunities, 247, 248

commercial/business models, 30

communication, 16–17, 162, 300–301

companies, changing to data-driven view, 51–63

  approaching, 53–56

  getting started, 63

  obstacles, 56–59

  techniques for, 59–62

  understanding, 52–53

competence, 28–29, 167–171, 302

complexity of data science, 163

  as business potential, 33–34

  managing, 40

  overview, 32–33

  pitfalls, 34–39

    1-tool approach, 37

    being report-focused, 38–39

    focusing on AI, 36–37

    investing in data lakes, 35–36

    investing only in certain areas, 37–38

    overload of data, 34–35

    underestimating need for skilled data scientists, 39

compute resources, 225

Computer Associates Technologies, 56

computer science, 156

compute layer, 182

conceptual data architecture, 177

consistency, data, 194

container image repository, definition of, 185

container orchestration, 187

container repositories, 185–186

containers, Docker and, 185–186

control mechanisms

  identifying, 211–212

  implementing, 200

conversational platforms, 79–80

conversion, definition of, 246

core data, data governance and, 197

cost structure, 280

CPUs (central processing units), 225, 227

cross-functional skills, 166

cross-licensing, 271–272

cross-team collaborative workspace, 230–231

cross-training, 168

cryptography, blockchain and, 78

CSO (chief strategy officer), 146

CTO (chief technology officer), 146

cultural fit, 165

customer attrition. *See* churning

customer experience management (CEM), 255

customer journey mapping, 260–261

customer satisfaction surveys, 257

customer segment, 278–279

customer service channels, 256–257

customers

  anticipating issues, 263

  applying analytics and ML to actions of, 258–259

  engaging, 256–257

  improving satisfaction of, 261–263

  journey mapping for, 260–261

  motivators, identifying, 257–258

  overview, 255–256

  planning for future of, 259

  refining view of, 248

  satisfaction surveys, building for, 257

  serving efficiently, 263

D

dashboards, 309–310

  for descriptive analytics projects, 58

  for diagnostic analytics projects, 58

  insights to transformation investments on, 62

data

  access issues in teams, 126–127

  analyzing, 311

  as asset, 237–238

  availability of, 194

  big data, 69–71

    value, 71

    variety, 71

    velocity, 71

    veracity, 70, 71

    volume, 70

J

Java programming language, 217
Java Virtual Machine (JVM), 217
Julia programming language, 217

K

Keras, 220
key performance indicators (KPIs), 262
keyword data, 258
knowledge, 68
KPIs (key performance indicators), 262

L

latency requirements, 226
layers, of data architectures, 181–184, 239
leasing (revenue model classification), 279
LEDR Technologies, 62
legal issues
  data science strategy, 28
  international data transfers, 43
  management and, 106
  restrictions on delivery models, 282
  rights to data, 311–312
lending (revenue model classification), 279
licenses, downloadable, 292
licensing (revenue model classification), 279
location, as infrastructure consideration, 226–227
locking data
  CDO role in, 151
  defined, 36
  democratizing data versus, 109
logical data architecture, 177
loops, symbolic, 219
Lua scripting language, 219

M

machine learning edge, 75
machine learning (ML)
  advanced analytics and, 23
  applying to customers, 258–259
  automation and, 19
  center of excellence (CoE) and, 137
  definition of, 158
  development of, 49
  differences between programming and, 47–49
  digital twins and, 77
  ethics and, 28
  human involvement with, 117
  infrastructure considerations for supporting AI
    and, 226–229
  introducing to data-driven companies, 116–117
  models for, 136, 204
  overview, 22–25
machine learning (ML) engineers, 157–158
machine learning/artificial intelligence (ML/AI),
    164, 210–211, 274–275, 309
machine-driven companies
  automating workflows, 116
  defined, 113–114
  digitizing data, 114–115
  introducing AI/ML capabilities, 116–117
  transforming into, 115
maintenance stage, of data science strategy,
    12–13
management
  addressing, 168
  data science and, 305–306, 308
  of data-driven company, 105, 106
  processes, 159
management model
  efficiency in, 206–207
  implementing, 207–212
  multiple, handling, 204–205
  overview, 203–204
  transparency in, lack of, 210
market disruptor/innovator approach
  governance programs for, 109
  overview, 108
market research firms, 259
marketing campaigns, 262
master data management (MDM), 191
mathematics, 156
MDM (master data management), 191
measurements, 30
Messenger channel, 256–257

About the Author

Ulrika Jägare is an M.Sc. Director in Technology and Architecture at Ericsson AB. With a decade of experience in analytics and machine intelligence as well as 19 years in telecommunications, she has held numerous leadership positions in both R&D and product management. Ulrika was key to the launch of Ericsson's machine intelligence strategy and commercial approach as well as the recent Ericsson Operations Engine — a new data and AI driven operational model for network operations in telecommunications.

In addition to this book, she is the author of two highly referenced technical books by Wiley: *Unified Analytics For Dummies (Databricks Special Edition)* and *Embedded Machine Learning Design For Dummies (Arm Special Edition)*.

Dedication

I dedicate this book to my patient and supporting family — Emil, Rasmus, and Fredrik. I love you all very much!

Author's Acknowledgments

I would like to express my gratitude to everyone who has helped me write and produce this book. Firstly, I would like to thank Lillian Pearson, who put me in contact with Wiley and for also writing the foreword to this book.

Additionally, I give a deep thanks to my innovative and competent colleagues at Ericsson for sharing all the ups and downs in our joint data science journey.

Then I would like to extend a huge thanks my husband Fredrik, who is also working in the data science area, for all the great discussions and elaborations.

Furthermore, I would like to thank the supportive editorial team at Wiley for the relevant and sometimes humorous feedback and suggestions; Katie Mohr, Paul Levesque, Becky Whitney, and other editorial staff.

Publisher's Acknowledgments

Acquisitions Editor: Katie Mohr

Senior Project Editor: Paul Levesque

Copy Editor: Becky Whitney

Editorial Assistant: Matthew Lowe

Sr. Editorial Assistant: Cherie Case

Production Editor: Mohammed Zafar Ali

Cover Image: © gleitfrosch/Getty Images